THE NEW ENGLISH

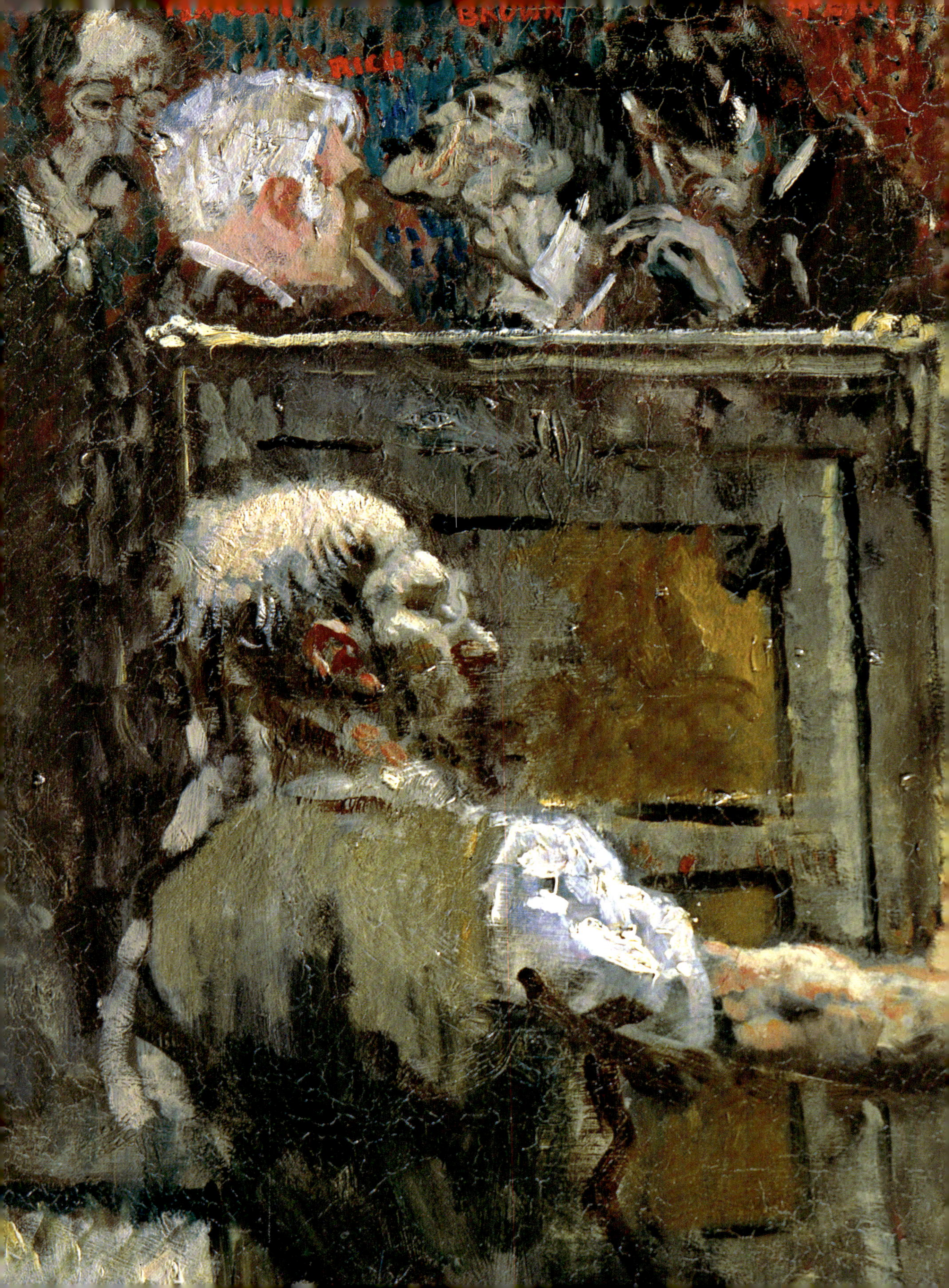
BROWN
RICH

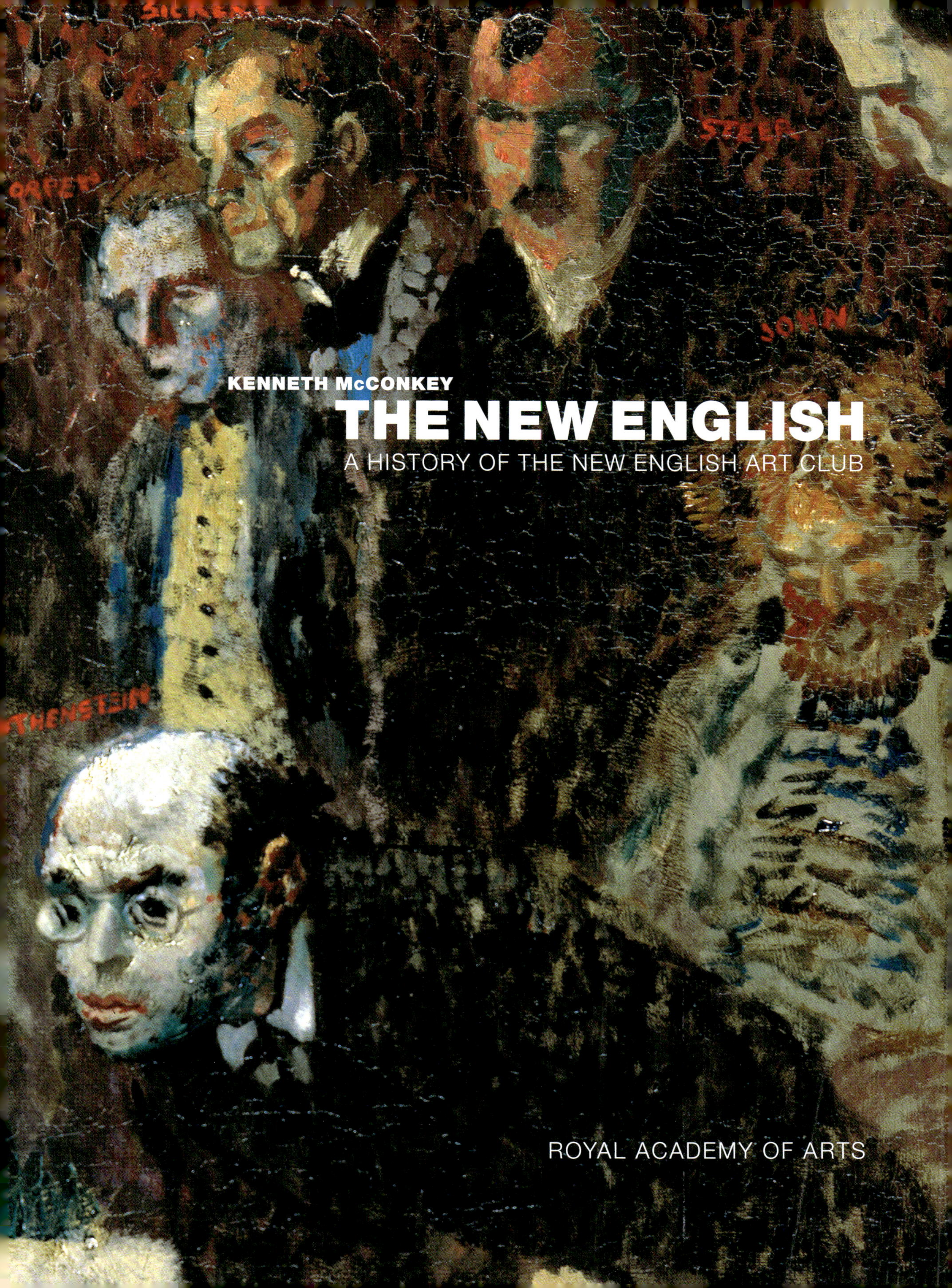

KENNETH McCONKEY

THE NEW ENGLISH

A HISTORY OF THE NEW ENGLISH ART CLUB

ROYAL ACADEMY OF ARTS

Frontispiece
William Orpen
The Selecting Jury of the New English Art Club, 1909 (detail)
Oil on canvas, 69.9 x 90.2 cm
National Portrait Gallery, London

Pages 6–7
Detail of fig. 21

British Library Cataloguing-in-Publication Data

A catalogue record for this book is available from the British Library

ISBN (hardback)
10: 1-903973-98-8
13: 978-1-903973-98-1
Distributed outside the United States and Canada by Thames & Hudson Ltd, London
Distributed in the United States and Canada by Harry N. Abrams, Inc., New York

EDITORIAL NOTE
Measurements are given in centimetres, height before width.

Dates of exhibition are used as dates of creation, except in cases where the latter are known.

Royal Academy Publications
David Breuer
Harry Burden
Claire Callow
Carola Krueger
Peter Sawbridge
Nick Tite

Copy-editing and proofreading: Rosalind Neely
Picture research: Sara Ayad
Design: Maggi Smith
Colour origination and printing by Conti Tipocolor SpA, Italy

Contents

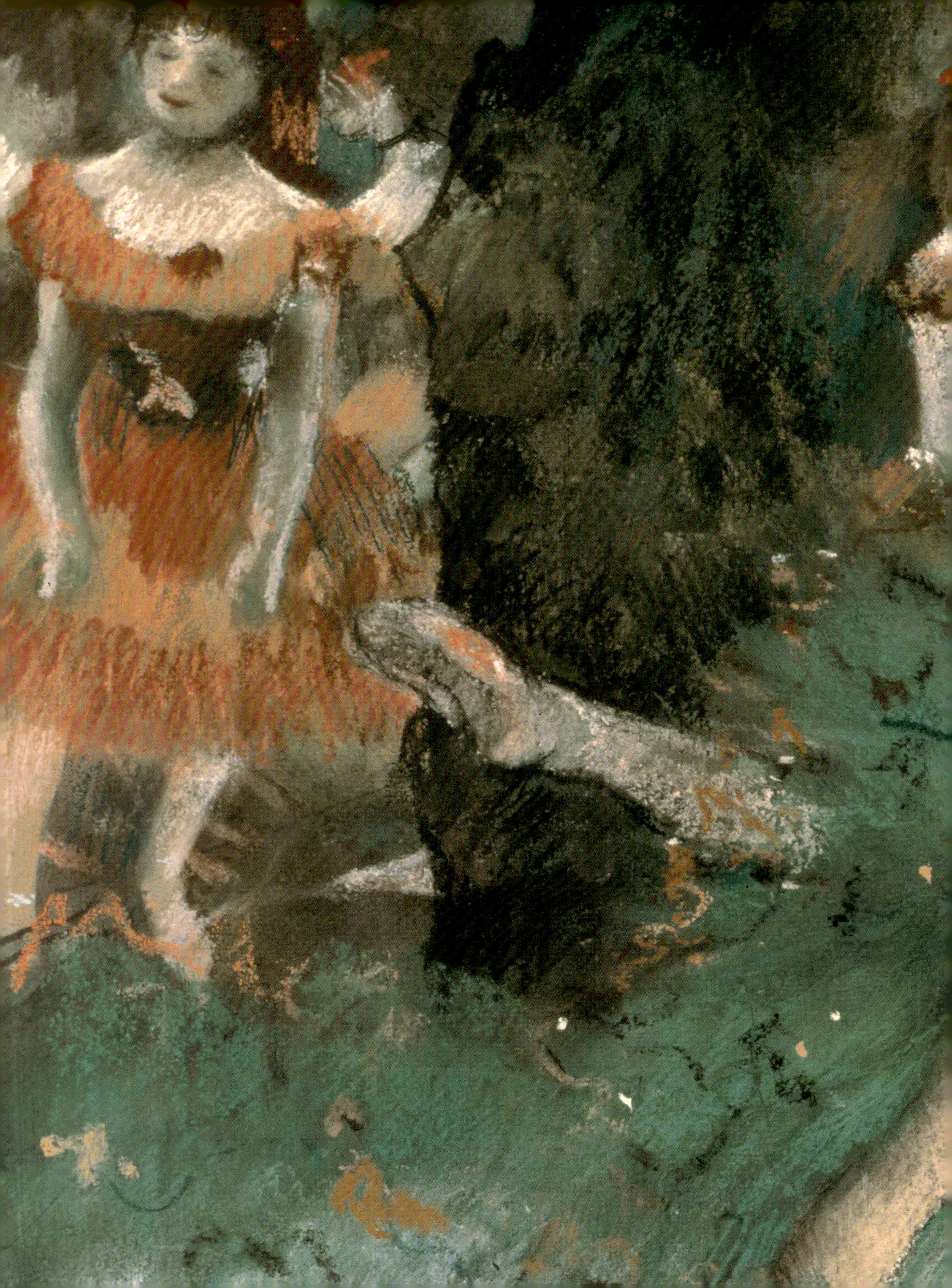

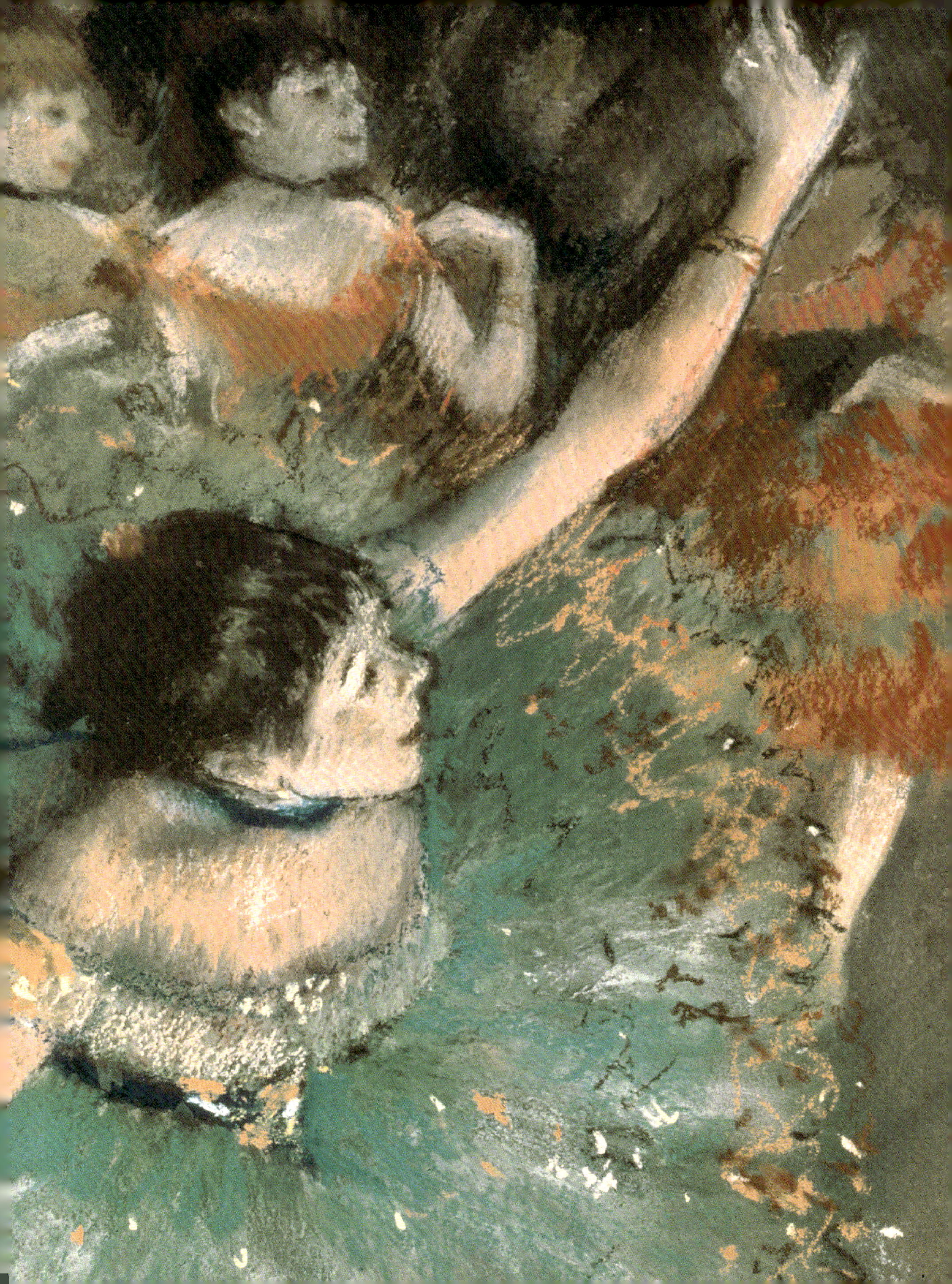

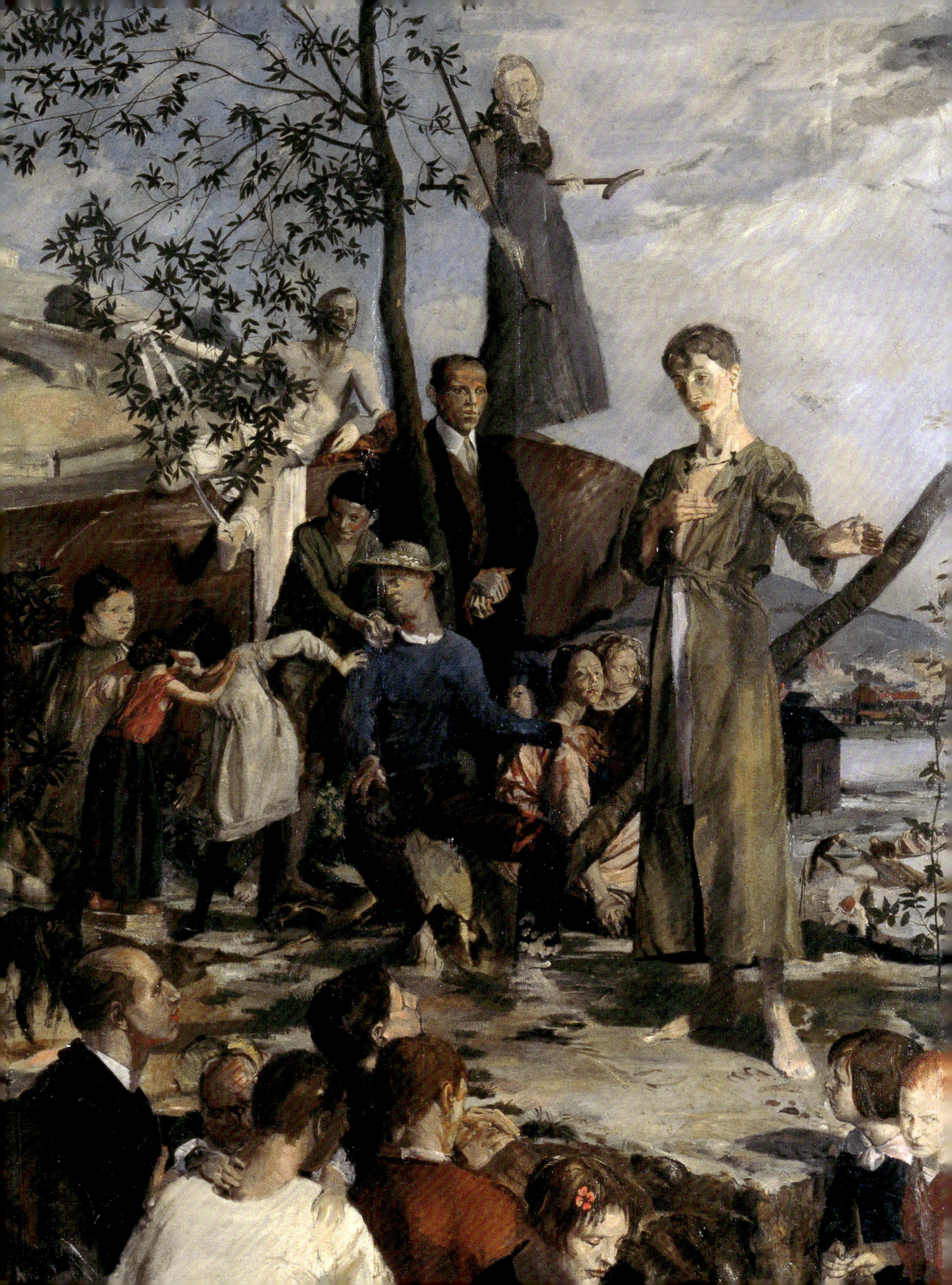

Foreword

To this day the New English Art Club is known only to cognoscenti – its aims unrecorded and its history untold.

In 2002 the members set out to rectify this situation and, with the help of Sotheby's, staged a highly successful sale of their work. This book was made possible by the generosity of those club members who donated works to that sale, and to Henry Wyndham, Sotheby's chairman and long-time club supporter, who conducted the proceedings.

At this point we had already approached Kenneth McConkey, a leading historian of British art, who had also been one of the club's regular advocates. He was keen to undertake the task and his rich and detailed account is provided in the pages that follow.

We also needed a publisher of equal dedication, and this we found in Royal Academy Publications. There is, for us all, a splendid irony in the fact that the club, initially an anti-Academy group, should be so elegantly displayed by the organisation it at first set out to reform.

Tom Coates
President, New English Art Club

Ken Howard
Past President, New English Art Club

Detail of fig. 123

Acknowledgements

About fifteen years ago William Bowyer, venerable former honorary secretary of the New English Art Club, aided by Patricia Lambert and Mary Jackson, first invited me to one of its press lunches – joyous events filled with animated conversation. In the gossip, as much as in its annual lectures and displays of distinguished past members' work, there were often flashes of an important history as yet untold. Ken Howard, Bowyer's successor, determined to address this situation, savouring the irony that the club's history would in the end be told courtesy of the Royal Academy of Arts. Charlotte Halliday, an honorary life member, made the archives of the club available to me, along with much sound advice, and, of the other honorary life members, Diana Armfield, Fred Dubery, Bernard Dunstan and Margaret Thomas gave me their first-hand accounts of the club in the post-war years. I am also grateful to Tom Coates and the executive committee members for their help and advice.

The present publication would not have been possible without the assistance of current club members – particularly those who generously contributed work to the sale in September 2002. Henry Wyndham and his colleagues at Sotheby's officiated at the event and its success was assured with donations from Charlotte Ardizzone, Diana Armfield, Barry Atherton, June Berry, Francis Bowyer, Jason Bowyer, William Bowyer, Bob Brown, Peter Brown, Diana Calvert, Tom Coates, Jane Corsellis, Patrick Cullen, Fred Cuming, Stuart Denyer, Fred Dubery, Bernard Dunstan, Harry Eccleston, Tom Espley, Michael Fairclough, Roy Freer, Denis Gilbert, David Gluck, Charlotte Halliday, Charles Hardaker, Karn Holly, Ken Howard, Mary Jackson, Pamela Kay, Peter Kuhfeld, Ann R. Le Bas, Andrew Macara, Jennifer McRae, Jack Millar, Anthony Morris, Arthur Neal, David Parfitt, Richard Pikesley, Edward Pullée, Michael Pullée, Salliann Putman, Jacqueline Rizvi, Sue Ryder, Maurice Sheppard, Dawn Sidoli, Richard Sorrell, Ruth Stage, Benjamin Sullivan, Margaret Thomas, Daphne Todd, Jonathan Trowell, John Ward, Jenny Wheatley, Michael Whittlesea, Charles Williams, Jacqueline Williams, Duncan Wood, Leslie Worth and Martin Yeoman.

Throughout its realisation, members of the art trade have enthusiastically supported the project. They include Claire Bailey-Coombs, Chris Beetles, Patrick Bourne, Frances Christie, Richard Green, Elizabeth Harvey-Lee, Rachel Hidderley, Alan and Mary Hobart, Jonathan Horwich, Susan Kent, Victoria Law, David Messum, Andrew McIntosh Patrick, James Rawlin and Peyton Skipwith. The staffs of national and municipal galleries have assisted me in locating works of art in their collections. In the first year of the project, Cecilia Holmes and Kim Pearson, research assistants at Northumbria University, catalogued the club's archive and assembled some of the review material on my behalf. Robert MacLean and his colleagues at the University of Glasgow and Lisa Cole and her colleagues at the Hyman Kreitman Research Centre at Tate Britain, London, assisted my search for particular information, as did the staffs of the Witt Library, the Courtauld Institute of Art, London, the National Art Library at the Victoria and Albert Museum, London, Newcastle, Newburn and other libraries. This volume was aided by grants to Northumbria University from the club and the Leverhulme Trust.

I am grateful to the staff of Royal Academy Publications, particularly to David Breuer, Nick Tite and their immediate colleagues, who took on the task of seeing this history into print. Sara Ayad has skilfully traced obscure illustrations and their copyright holders, while Rosalind Neely has provided excellent editorial support and Maggi Smith an elegant overall design. Finally, no text is produced these days without a struggle with new computer programmes. For this my daughter Sarah, herself a New English exhibitor, was invaluable.

Kenneth McConkey
July 2006

Detail of fig. 13

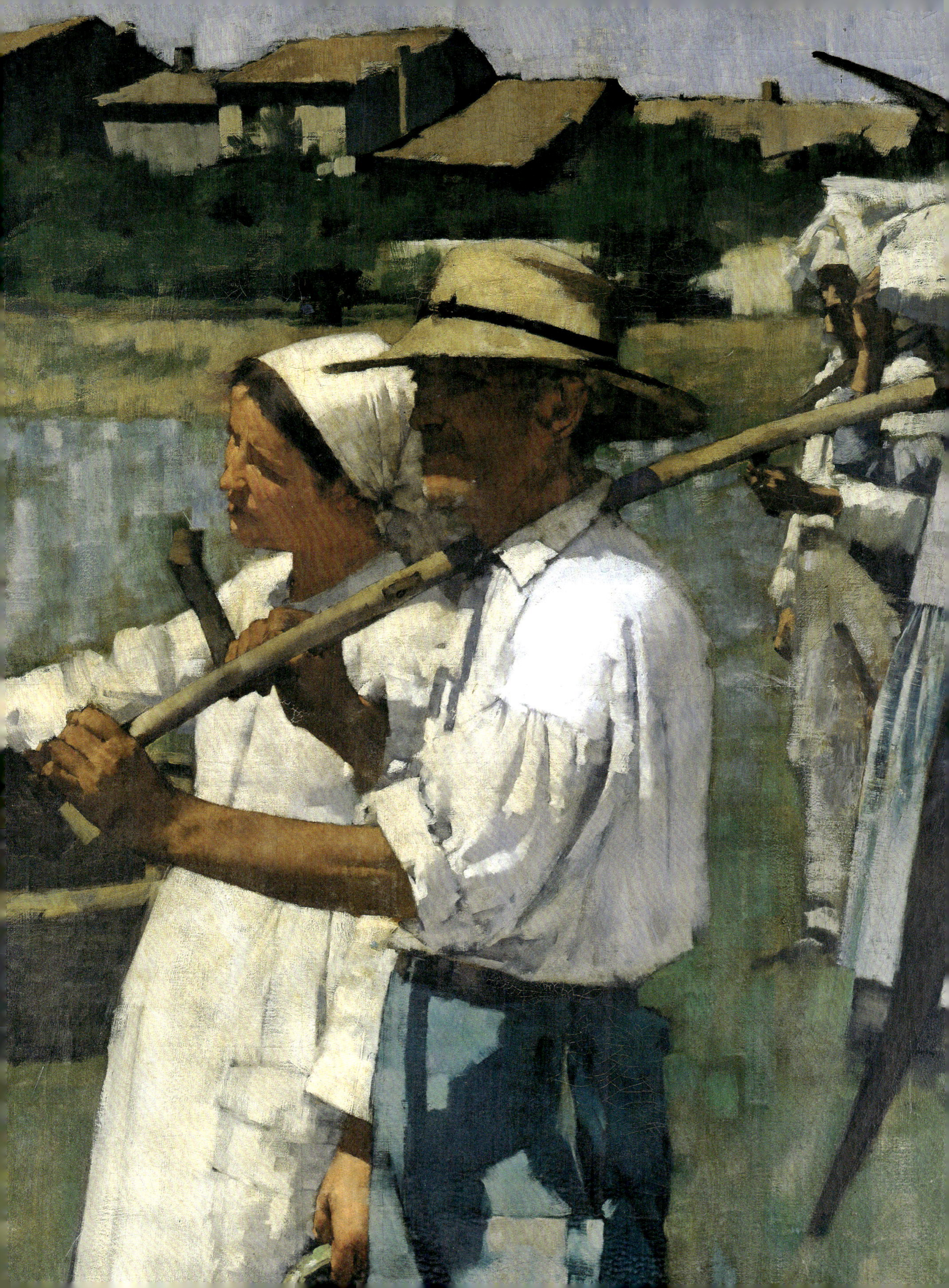

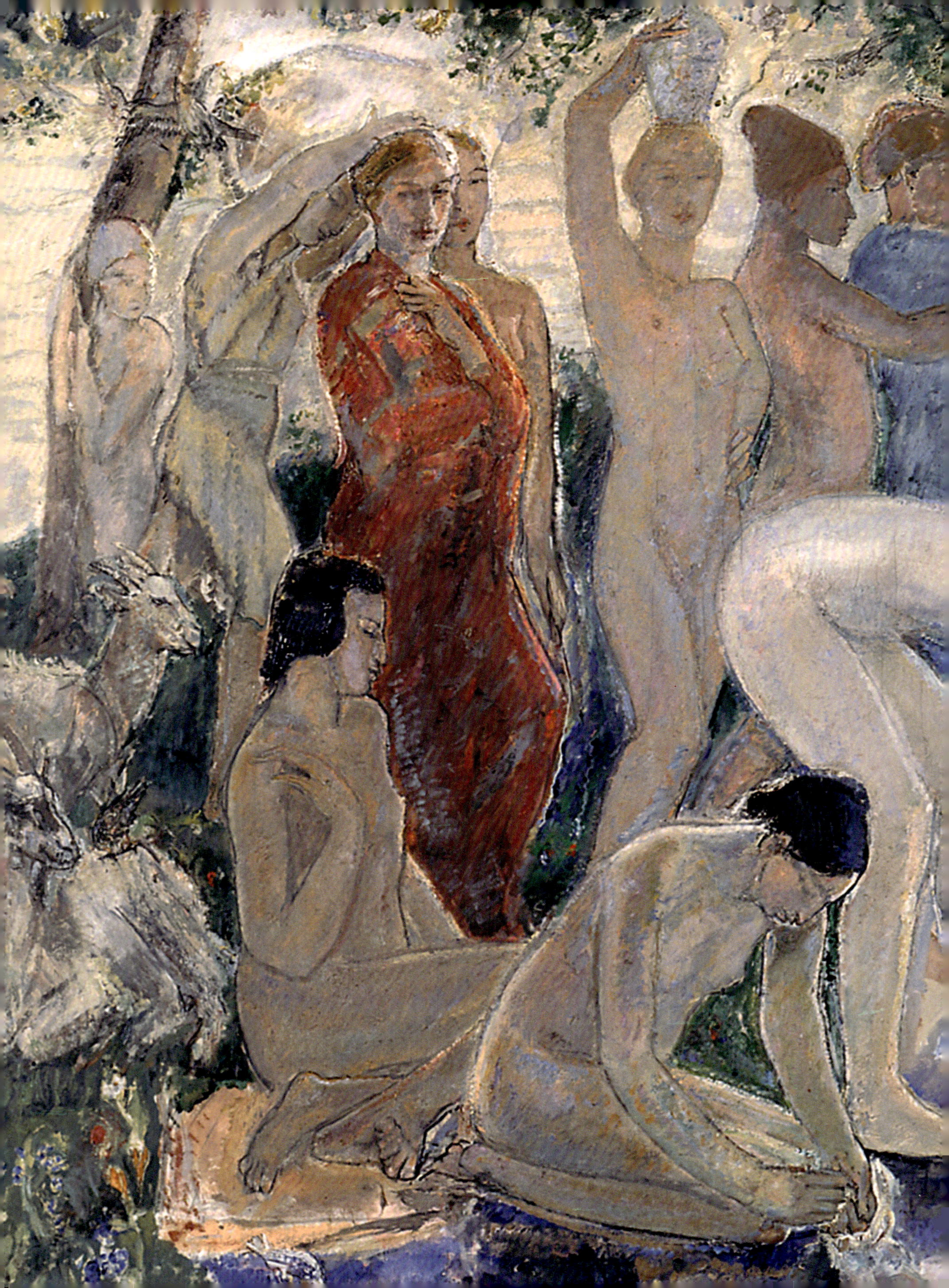

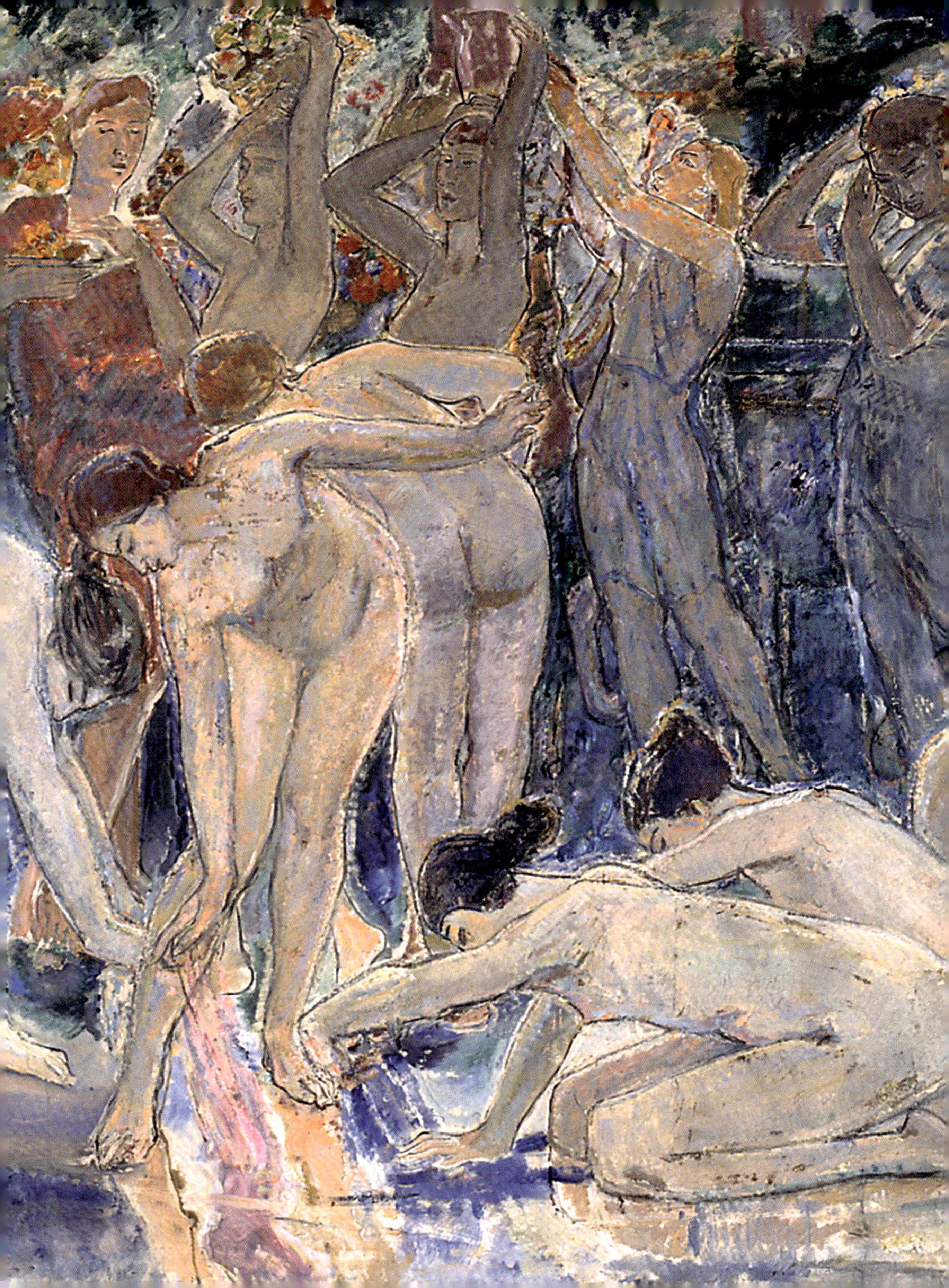

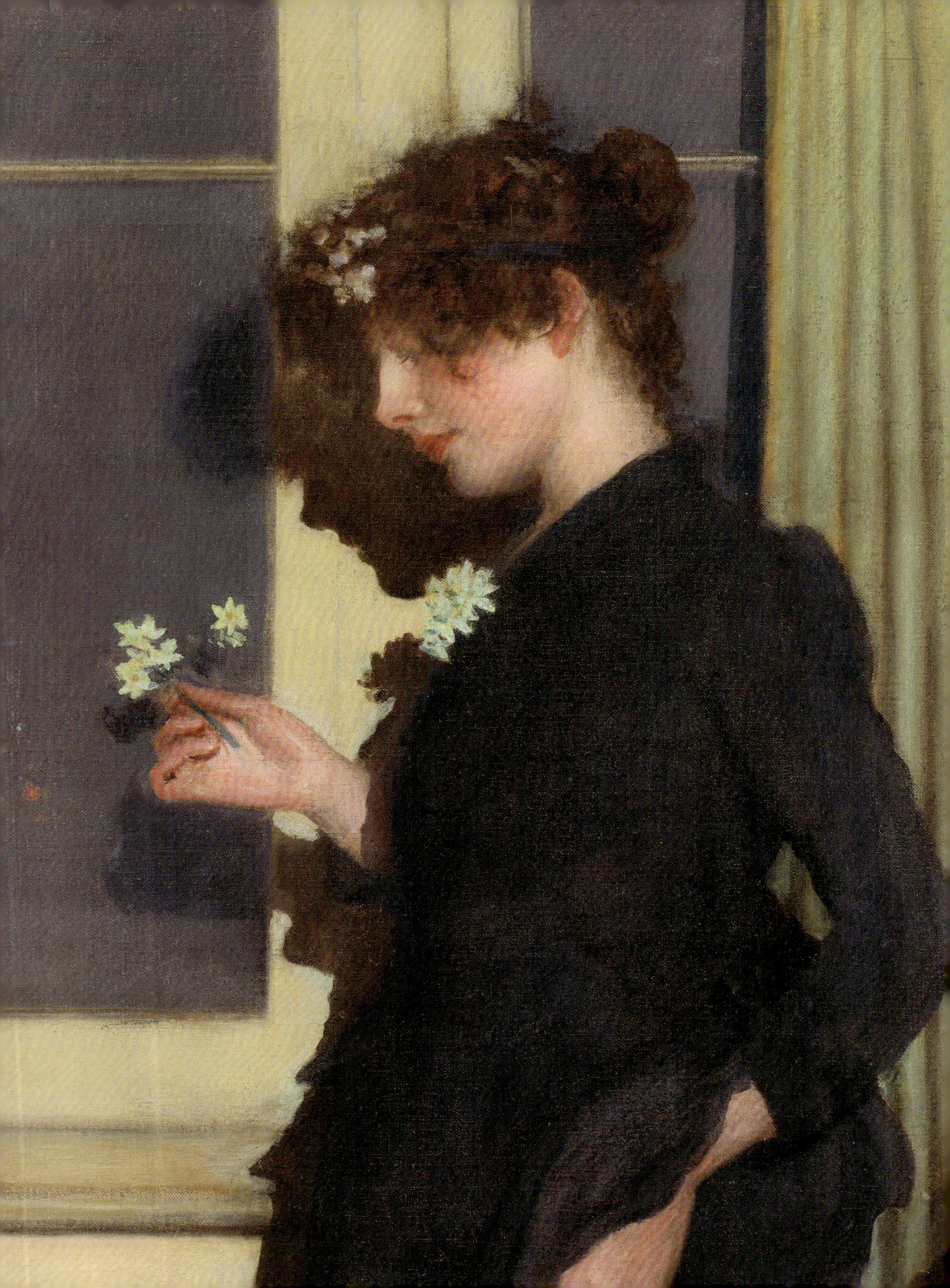

Introduction

In the years after its founding, journalists occasionally resorted to a cheap line on the New English Art Club. They would say that it was not new and not English. Once raised, the shibboleths of 'newness' and 'Englishness' would reverberate through several newspaper columns, the former implying an obligation to supply novelty or to be at the 'cutting edge', the latter a watchword for eccentricity or a repellent for imported ideas. The words were always used in a relative sense – applying to beliefs about the current state of art in Britain with specific works in mind. 'New' and 'English' were not absolute terms, although those who employed them often assumed they were. Being new and English in the 1890s was very different from what it would be 30 years later and the relative newness or Englishness of an exhibition was more often to do with relating its content to other concurrent exhibitions than with taking a longer view. Historical perspective was frequently limited to the previous spring or winter, or at best to a two- or three-year span. At its inception in 1886, the new organisation declared its presence in a spirit of rivalry, so such comparisons were to be positively encouraged.

The club was also not a club, in any accepted sense of the term. It had neither a clubhouse, a place for out-of-town members to stay, nor even a permanent staff. On fourteen occasions during its existence, its London exhibitions moved from one gallery to another, with consistent attempts to stage exhibitions in the provinces. At the beginning the club ran with a very simple constitution, reprinted in catalogues from 1888 up to the Great War. All matters to do with membership and the selection of exhibits would be decided on a majority vote. While the need for an executive committee was clear from the outset, rules of quorum appear not to have been discussed. This was a society run by artists for artists, so meetings were often informal and occasionally unconstitutional. Until very recently, there was no president or patron, the chair passing by election at each meeting. Honorary Secretary and Honorary Treasurer positions were re-elected annually, as were members of the executive committee and the selecting and hanging juries (fig. 1). Initial disputes revolved around loyalty and personal integrity, based upon financial surety, the nature of the organisation that had been brought into being and the types of art it would represent. There was always a membership fee with the expectation of prudence and probity in financial management on the part of the treasurer, but profit was never the *raison d'être*. Debates occasionally occurred on the application of surpluses to specific purposes. The club was also sometimes in deficit. By the early years of the new century, auditors had been appointed to assure members of the appropriate handling of receipts.

Previous page
Detail of fig. 108

Detail of fig. 31

Institutions regularly in the public eye create expectations and trail their histories. Exhibitions become recurring fixtures. Anniversaries, retirements and memorials occur at regular intervals. Age and experience at times weigh heavily upon younger up-and-coming members. An internal dynamic created by momentarily influential members at times imposed its convictions on others. By the 1925 retrospective exhibition, checks and balances militated against the formation of cliques. Those minutes of executive and annual general meetings that have survived record issues raised and resolved – but it is rarely possible to reconstruct the debates. The New English has never allowed itself, nor been allowed, to forget its past. This is a two-edged sword that, in the eyes of some, brought the new and the English into immediate conflict. The founders were not conscious of setting up an institution that would still exist 120 years later. Had they opted for the alternative title – 'The Society of Anglo-French Painters' – it is unlikely that the club would have survived much beyond the Great War.

The circumstances that brought the club into being would never be replicated. Within a few years its founders, all of the same generation, began to invite younger and older artists, whose interests the club was obliged to represent. While this was done purposefully, within fifteen years it was no longer possible to generalise on the basis that all exhibitors were of roughly the same age and had similar backgrounds. After forty years, reviewers had to be aware of beginnings, middles and ends of careers, as annual catalogues simply listed names and picture titles. It is only when the overall profile of a single exhibitor is constructed that the tensions between individual and group identity begin to

Fig. 1 The last jury of the club at the Dudley Gallery, 1904. (*Back row, from left to right*: Walter Russell, David Muirhead, Alfred Rich, Ambrose McEvoy, Henry Tonks, Augustus John, D. S. MacColl, P. W. Steer, Muirhead Bone, Francis Bate. *Front row, seated*: Fred Winter, Fred Brown, Roger Fry, William Rothenstein). Photograph. Unknown photographer NEAC Archive

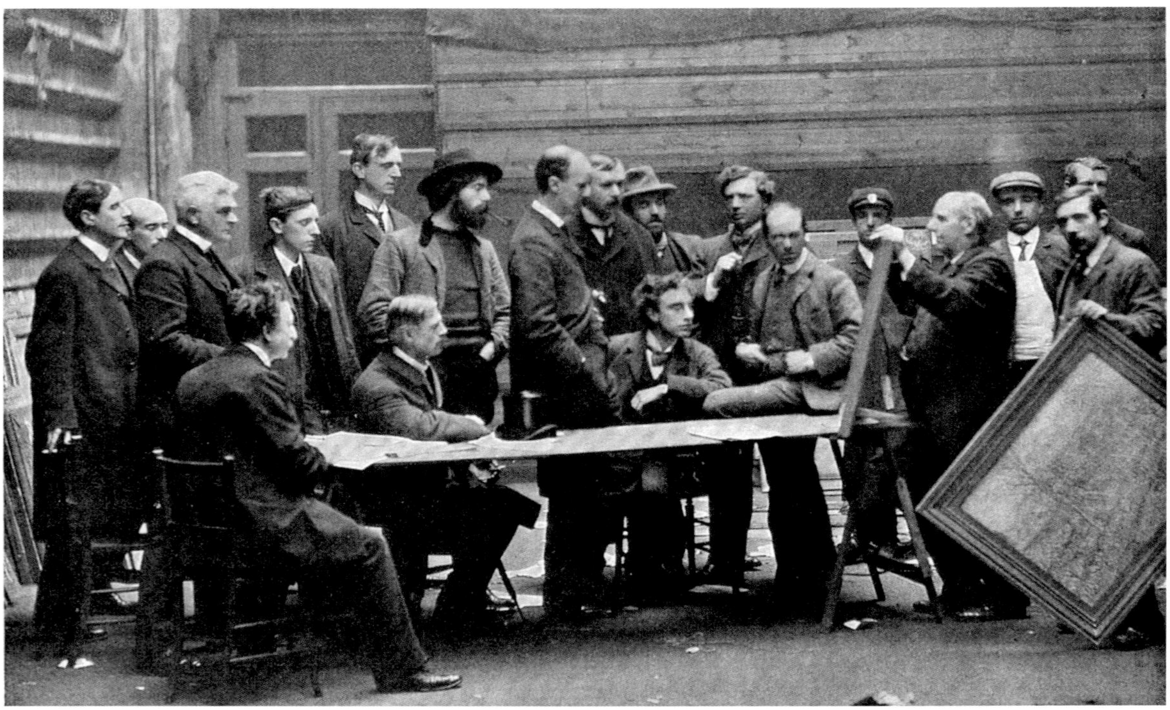

emerge.[1] The club contains life spans that interlock and disconnect, and having at any one time between 50 and 80 members, plus up to 100 other exhibitors, means that 'name-checking' is unavoidable. Nevertheless, this history cannot be a sequence of potted biographies such as may be found in a dictionary. In a study of this kind, while being ever mindful that organisations are composed of individuals, it may well be the case that long exhibiting careers are referenced in no more than a line or two.

The New English was a society born at a time when democracy, self-help and cooperative ideals were in the air. The final quarter of the reign of Queen Victoria was marked by civil strife, colonial wars and an increasing dismay at the scale of social change in the wake of industrialisation. Endless pressure groups for everything from women's suffrage to the preservation of churches were formed. Rival art societies came and went and members were at times acutely conscious of the need for new practices, but not always willing to embrace them. If anything, the pace of change accelerated with the approach of war and at that point, taking in muralists and tempera painters, alongside Impressionists and Post-Impressionists, Hispanic-inspired realists and cabinet painters, the club was more eclectic than it had ever been.

The art world in the early twentieth century has been difficult for writers to capture. Surveys of Victorian art tend to tail off in the 1880s just when the story begins to be interesting and those artists who created the possibilities for new approaches have often been neglected. Yet these changes were broadly similar to those occurring elsewhere in Western Europe and North America. The content of early exhibitions related more to international trends in Paris than to ongoing tendencies in the Royal Academy. 'Newness', as it apparently came from elsewhere, was immediately at variance with 'Englishness'. One could say that what was 'new' eventually became 'English' a generation later, but this would not be strictly true, and it only takes us a short way into a long history. Working lives with consistent commitment to club exhibitions over 50 years may see a painter in and out of the mainstream – however that is defined. He or she seeks approval from older artists at the beginning and confers it – sometimes ungraciously – upon the younger at the end. A painting of gypsies shown in the 1950s may have been produced by an artist who first tackled the subject when it was fashionable before the Great War. Disconcertingly, artists do not follow the script.

Forming a sequential narrative of the club's unfolding up to the present, writing an institutional or 'official' history, involves a critical consciousness of historical processes. The total time span is divided into phases, indicated for ease of recognition by labels borrowed from elsewhere, such as 'inter-war' or the '1950s'. They carry complex homogenising associations. At times particular individuals are singled out because they appear to typify the characteristics of the age. Terms like 'John's' or 'Spencer's generation' become an easy shorthand. It is worth pausing and asking what we might mean by such abbreviations. The artists who formed the club were all of the same generation – they were born around 1860, in the heyday of Pre-Raphaelitism. They went through processes involved with training and travel at roughly the same time, and although personalities occasionally clashed, a common set of characteristics distinguishes them from their predecessors. It is clear that they felt this distinction important – although for some it was undoubtedly more important than for others. Augustus John's and Stanley Spencer's generations, those born around 1875 and 1895, function within the same sets of social and economic parameters in which training and experience react with gender, class and nationality. John and Spencer provide access to art school contemporaries who, *en masse,* were directed towards the club. They might not all agree, but all experienced the world in broadly similar ways – being affected by the same news items, being aware of the same bestsellers and hearing about the same scientific discoveries. Spencer's generation was more profoundly affected by war than older first-generation exhibitors, even though both experienced loss.

Talking of a 'generation' contains pitfalls and self-delusions. It papers over differences, the most obvious of which is the distinction between men's and women's experiences. Even though from the 1880s onwards, art schools and exhibiting societies were more liberal than before, for a young woman studying in Paris it was still considered desirable to secure the services of a compliant mother or maiden aunt as a chaperone. Early exhibitions were dominated by men and when, by the 1930s, women's work was being shown in equal numbers, some older male exhibitors were dismayed. Class issues may also be significant, as can particular provincial backgrounds, within a common nationality. Being London-based, the club attracted more exhibitors from the Home Counties than from other parts of the British Isles. Art schools established to develop particular skills tended to be social levellers in that they prized innate abilities more than class background or conventional forms of intelligence. It is always necessary to attend to the visual. We need to avoid the trap of thinking that 'generations' are cocooned compartments and move as homogeneous collectives through time. This is not to imply that friendships formed in youth do not last, it merely recognises that artists come to prominence at different points in their careers and those considered of one generation may not all conveniently be 'born at the right moment'. In one sense, the history of the club was never simpler than at its inception. Spencer's generation includes Ben Nicholson and Graham Sutherland. Ken Howard's generation, which incorporates artists as diverse as Howard Hodgkin and Peter Blake, is so wide-ranging as to make generalisations problematic. Such difficulties increase with the 'baby-boom' generation emerging with the expansion of higher level art education from the late 1960s and the reduction in state funding in the 1980s. None of the demographics is watertight. Artists existed back there in their own time with none of the comforting distillations available to us. Studying the club's history enables preconceptions to be challenged, but only if we are prepared to accept that, back in 1900 or 1950, things might have happened differently. The historian's approach must be indeterminist. Only when he or she acknowledges that at any point in the past the possibilities were limitless can the full richness of a moment in time – any single show – be appreciated.[2]

Detail of fig. 124

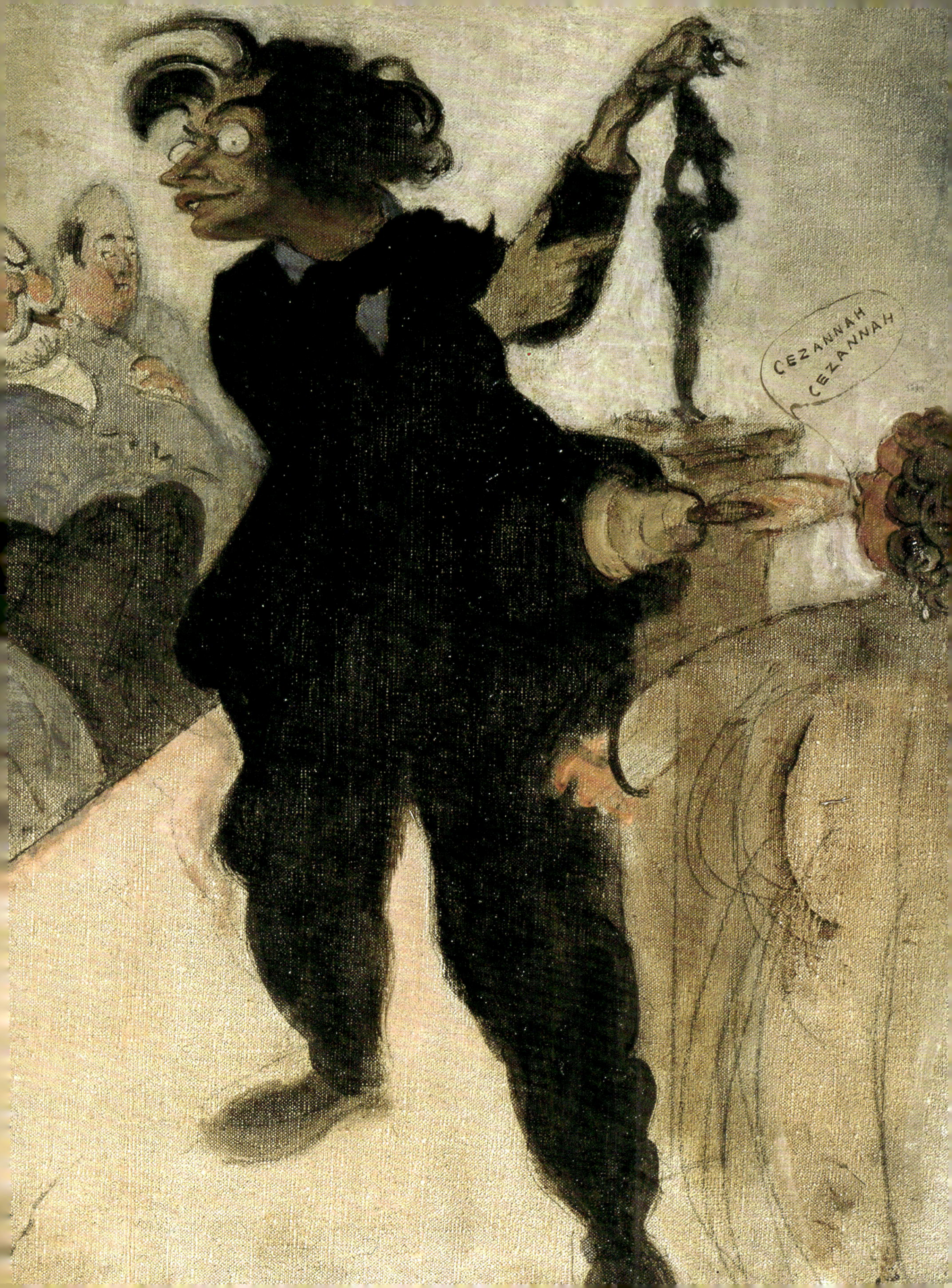

CEZANNAH CEZANNAH

Throughout its history, the New English has been an active agent in the distillation process – simply as a consequence of its annual selections that are the result of the continual recasting of shared values and beliefs. Measuring today's achievements against those of the past is part of this process, but there can be no gold standard. Reassessments, surveys and retrospectives were part of the club's creative ongoing development. By the 1920s its central role in British art was easily acknowledged. Frank Rutter observed that half of the current crop of Royal Academicians had been former club exhibitors, and that from its ranks were drawn the Director and Keeper of the National Gallery, the Keeper of the Tate Gallery, the Principal of the Royal College of Art and the professors at the Slade School of Fine Art.[3] For the first time in 1895, critics started looking back to the club's early days. Ten years later, with the demolition of its regular exhibition venue at the old Dudley Gallery, London, another watershed was reached. The club's retrospective was staged in 1925, and, in 1935, when Alfred Thornton published his short account of its first 50 years, some of the elderly exhibitors were again brought back. A full-scale retrospective was organised in Birmingham Art Gallery in 1952, a celebration of the 'early years' was held at the Fine Art Society in 1968, and a centenary exhibition was staged at Christie's in 1986. Even today, annual exhibitions make a special feature of the work of a distinguished forebear.

While the Academy dominated the Victorian period, the first half of the twentieth century was definitely 'New English'. By the end of the 1930s, public gallery curators were installing 'New English' rooms. The term did not imply a retreat into narrow nationalism so much as a willingness to celebrate the British moderns. There were, nevertheless, dissenting voices. Roger Fry regarded the British as a minor school, while R. H. Wilenski, reflecting on the early years of the club, observed the timidity of its members' acceptance of Impressionism.[4] This line was accepted more or less uncritically and it became the underlying assumption of much of the writing of Herbert Read, Eric Newton, Robin Ironside and Stephen Spender, finding its most potent and damning expression in the writings of Douglas Cooper. Self-deprecation became a national malaise – attitudes that remained in currency until a generation ago. Just when it became possible for younger researchers to reassess the early years of the club, the club itself was in danger of becoming an anachronism. Orthodox history up to 1950 becomes alternative history after it.

Back in the mid-1920s, when Fry and Wilenski were questioning the probity of British art, Englishness was identified with tradition and convention rather than 'experimentation'. This latter term had a specific resonance. It alerted readers to the racial and imperialist assumptions of much art criticism up to that time. 'Experimentation' was a byword for abstraction and the Latin races, particularly the French, were heavily committed to it. Impressionism, once absorbed, had been replaced by 'strange creeds', all directed at the rejection of picture-making. For Anglo-Saxons 'our habit of mind leads us instinctively towards naturalism'.[5] There was an assumption that, if experimentation did not work, a painter could return to a more traditional style, as André Derain and Pablo Picasso had done in the 1920s. Despite claims to the contrary, an explicitly figurative tradition did not break down in Britain after the war, even though its tenets were conspicuously rejected by some.[6] The belief that British painters would pull away from abstraction and revitalise representational painting persisted after the Second World War. Even as the Royal Academy timidly attempted to absorb artistic novelty in post-war Britain, a new modernist academy, coached by Arts Council 'experts', emerged. The club in reactive mode became the bastion of an Englishness construed as the sensitive recording of atmospherics in the urban scene or in landscape. In daring to deal with the contingent and the familiar, New English painters appealed to a middle-aged, middle England ostensibly more interested in techniques and effects than in ways of seeing. Many of its members were doing what they had always done, but they found themselves unjustly written out of history. During the last 40 years, the New English has come to represent an unseen, uncelebrated undercurrent, the persistence of which will continue to challenge the historian of the future.

To achieve a sense of the moving consensus within the club, the writer asks a series of questions. What did New English Art Club exhibitions look like? What did they contain? Who attended their shows? Who bought from them? Given its longevity, the answers to these questions can change year by year. The world moves on and the fluctuations within club exhibitions do not neatly conform to the accepted patterns of art history. We find no Cubism, Abstract Expressionism or Minimalism. Even with a restricted 'British' frame of reference, club exhibitions at times appear strange and uncomfortable – particularly in the post-war period. It would not have occurred to 'hard-edge' abstractionists of the 1960s or 'BritArtists' of the 1990s to exhibit there. The press cuttings are often no more than titbits from lowbrow journals. The club represented middle England – the world of the flower-piece, the interior, the south coast shoreline, the London river or the Tuscan hill towns. That these subjects continued to be admired was evidence both of the strength and the weakness of continuing fascinations with the art of the past. At the time of its inception, the club *was* the history of British art – now, apparently, it is no longer. An orthodox history becomes an alternative one. But who says so? Yet this in itself is just how we write about it. For painters who go into the studio every day and see the same things, it is a different story.

NOTES

1 Charles Baile de Laperriere, *The New English Art Club Exhibitors, 1886–2001*, 4 vols, with a Foreword by HRH The Prince of Wales, KG, KT, GCB, OM, Hilmarton Manor Press, Calne, 2002.

2 I paraphrase Johan Huizinga's 'The Idea of History' in Fritz Stern (ed.), *The Varieties of History from Voltaire to the Present*, Vintage Books, New York, 1956, p. 292.

3 Frank Rutter, *Some Contemporary Artists*, Leonard Parsons, London, 1922, pp. 16–18.

4 R. H. Wilenski, *The Modern Movement in Art*, Faber and Faber, London, 1928 (8th ed., 1946), pp. 113–5.

5 A. L. Baldry, *Contemporary Figure Painters*, Studio Publications, London, 1925, pp. 3–5.

6 John Rothenstein, *Time's Thievish Progress*, Cassell, London, 1970, pp. 224–5.

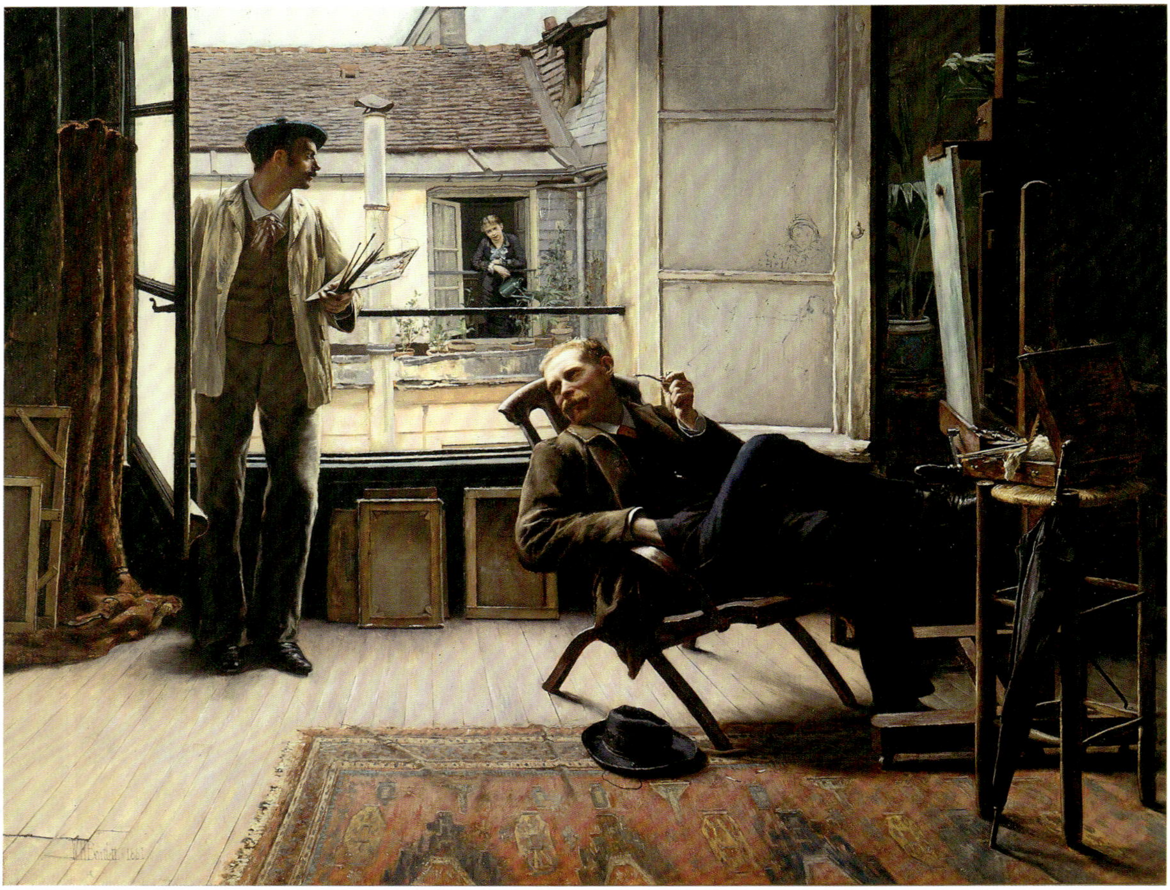

Fig. 2 William Henry Bartlett
The Neighbours, 1881
Oil on canvas, 99.1 x 128.3 cm
Private collection

CHAPTER 1

'A balm in Gilead' 1880–1887

In 1881 an artist in a garret studio in Paris, listening to his friend's deliberations, was momentarily diverted by the sudden appearance of a young woman at the window opposite. The canvas placed on an easel facing the light had claimed their attention up to this point when the painter suddenly looked away and his friend realised he was no longer listening. This is the scene depicted in *The Neighbours* (1881; fig. 2), a painting by William Henry Bartlett. A contemporary caption writer described the woman as an *ouvrière*, a cheerful working girl of the type portrayed in contemporary fiction, while the young men are 'rising geniuses' at work on their 'masterpieces for the coming Salon'.[1] Neither the young men nor their neighbour has been identified. The men, if friends of Bartlett, are likely to come from solid British middle-class backgrounds; they are ambitious, industrious and possess a modicum of talent. They are faces in the crowd in contemporary atelier photographs.[2] Paris in the final decades of the nineteenth century thronged with art students of all nationalities. They came like 'flights of birds ... to occupy their little hotels and lodgings' according to one writer. They also 'fade away' whence they came, to be replaced by others. Their youthful idealism for the most part went unrecorded.[3]

The Neighbours attests to the unwitnessed, unpublished moment when this history begins. Thoughts and ideas will be taken out and tested on others in studios and cafés; they will add to the sum of common experience and help to form the shared ideals of the peer group. According to reliable witnesses, the New English Art Club originated in such circumstances. Fred Brown (fig. 3), one of Bartlett's friends, who went to Paris in 1883, recalled that criticism was levelled at the British art establishment, its ruling élite and the huge conservative pressure to resist change in the art schools and annual exhibitions. The curriculum of the Government Art Training School in South Kensington, London, was, he felt, devised 'with the deliberate intention of preventing [students] from practising art'.[4] 'The management of exhibitions' in England and France was compared to the detriment of the former.[5] Things needed to change.

In broad cultural terms, the last two decades of the nineteenth century were ones in which the new middle classes enjoyed unparalleled confidence. All the secrets of science and medicine would, it was thought, be revealed through trained processes of observation. Interpretive looking would lead to greater knowledge and understanding of the firmament, the natural world, the origin of the species and the recesses of the human psyche. This was an age of positivism and empiricism. Photography, the latest tool, far from killing painting, underscored the primacy of vision. A painter's act of recording in this age of

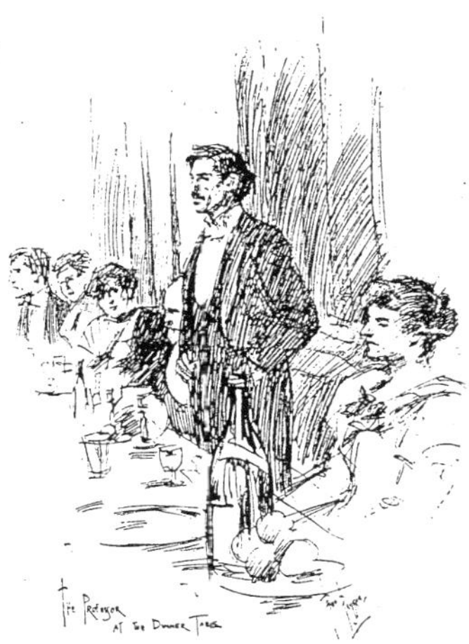

Fig. 3 Unknown artist
Fred Brown
Hyman Kreitman Research Centre, Tate Britain, London

photomechanical reproduction had a new urgency. Words such as 'Impressionist', with no settled definition, were loosely applied to novel ways of seeing, supported by new developments in the science of optics. There was no singular gaze. Glances, glimpses, long concentrated looking and the staccato activity of a painter referring constantly between a canvas and some selected motif were all acknowledged for their intrinsic quality and were, to some extent, built into the training that these young painters underwent.

Larger historical processes, in which rapid technological advances in engineering, transport and in print media, developing on the back of burgeoning empires and creating vast wealth for the mercantile and manufacturing classes, were less obvious but no less real. Brown and Bartlett's generation was programmed to believe in the relationship between progress, material wealth and racial superiority.[6] Increased visual and verbal literacy brought the makers of images to public consciousness as never before and there were more young painters and sculptors than ever. And for the students in the garret, Paris and not London had become the world centre for art production. New exhibiting protocols and international networks were emerging all the time and, in the moment of youthful idealism, conscious career-building is less likely to have been at issue than the shortcomings of the British training system that experience in Paris at the time exposed. State support for the visual arts in France, the greater liberality of French art education and the attraction of Paris itself, a modern, recently remodelled city, led to a large number of Channel crossings. The packet-boats and mail-coaches of Thackeray's day had been replaced by steam-driven craft, with connecting trains from Boulogne and Le Havre.[7] Paris was no longer so difficult to reach. French artists had apparently more direct control of the annual Salon, and the ateliers, even though the master seldom visited more than once a week, were somehow more serious places of instruction than their London equivalents.

Were they to admit to these conditions, established painters in Britain, members of the Royal Academy, could do no more than ruminate upon this drain of young talent and await the reflux to wreak revenge. Seen from the Latin Quarter, London's art establishment, to which the young artists in the upstairs room would eventually have to return, was self-serving and reactionary. Too many entrenched opinions, too much money chasing mediocre products, too much philistine criticism, in short, too much power lay in the hands of too many old men. New ways of doing things had to be found, and new opportunities provided, to support the new art. It was inevitable that the first salvo should be aimed at the Royal Academy. It was 'no longer a name to charm with', according to W. E. Henley, one of the sympathisers supporting the new school, who wrote:

> The time is passed of its authority in matters of art ... and though to be rejected [at its summer exhibition] is still a serious disappointment, it is no longer a disgrace ... as an educational institution it has little or nothing to teach; and its students, as soon as they have passed the curriculum it imposes on them, make hast to betake themselves to France, to learn not

only how to paint and draw, but to forget as much as they can of the theory and practice acquired in its schools.[8]

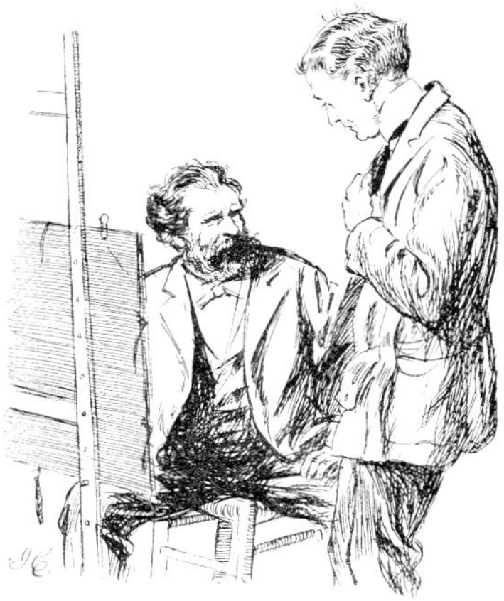

Fig. 4 John Cameron
'Bouguereau and the English Student'
Location unknown

The art student experience in France consisted of three essential ingredients. The first was related to atelier training – characterised by keen competition and scathing criticism (fig. 4).[9] The second concerned solidarity – expatriates shared lodgings, cheap restaurants and places of recreation, whose popularity changed with each succeeding wave. The third involved exhibiting and market structures in which the Salon outclassed the Royal Academy. Proactive dealer networks were seen to be extending taste by supporting new art. British painters fitted into the pattern of French life, decamping in the summer months to rural and coastal resorts that became popular as artist colonies in which atelier practices were applied *en plein air*. Why was it necessary or desirable in 1880 to be painting out in the open, when, for generations, artists had eschewed raw experience in favour of storytelling and the re-creation of history, in the studio? While working in such places was not unknown in Britain, their French equivalents became more popular as a result of state patronage for grand depictions of rural life in the early years of the Third Republic. Painting in Normandy or Brittany, or in the villages in Fontainebleau, like John Lavery's unidentified artist in *The Principal Street in Grez* (1884; fig. 5), one was part of a community that might include artists from all over Europe and North America, and, in some cases, even Japan. Common experience led to a sense of common purpose and similar ways of observing and recording.

In Paris, groups of artists staging their own exhibitions directly stimulated a lively trade in contemporary art and London felt the ripple effects. Bond Street entrepreneurs such as Agnew, Colnaghi, Deschamps and Tooth imported Salon paintings, often attempting to band painters together as groups and societies, even though they merely represented current stock. By the 1880s more pictures were being submitted to the Royal Academy but the number of acceptances did not increase *pro rata*.[10] Artists disgruntled with the Academy could present a business opportunity for the merchant in pictures. While the Grosvenor Gallery's success might have been an encouraging sign, the capacity to absorb increased production was a matter of constant debate. In London potential purchasers would, for instance, form an orderly queue for the opening day of the annual exhibition at the Institute of Painters in Watercolours.[11] Reitlinger has described the period as the 'golden age' of the living painter.[12] It was a seller's market.

New societies, such as the 'Painter-Etchers', began to appear.[13] Such was the growing confidence of the Institute of Painters in Watercolours that its president, Sir James Linton, took the risky step to commission new galleries in Piccadilly that opened in the presence of the Prince of Wales in 1883. Simultaneously Linton passed the watercolourists' old galleries to the dealer, Martin Colnaghi, and, faced with the task of securing financial viability for the new premises, he floated a sister society – the Institute of Painters in Oil Colours. This society would occupy the space in the winter and would not be in direct competition with the Royal Academy summer exhibitions. Formed initially

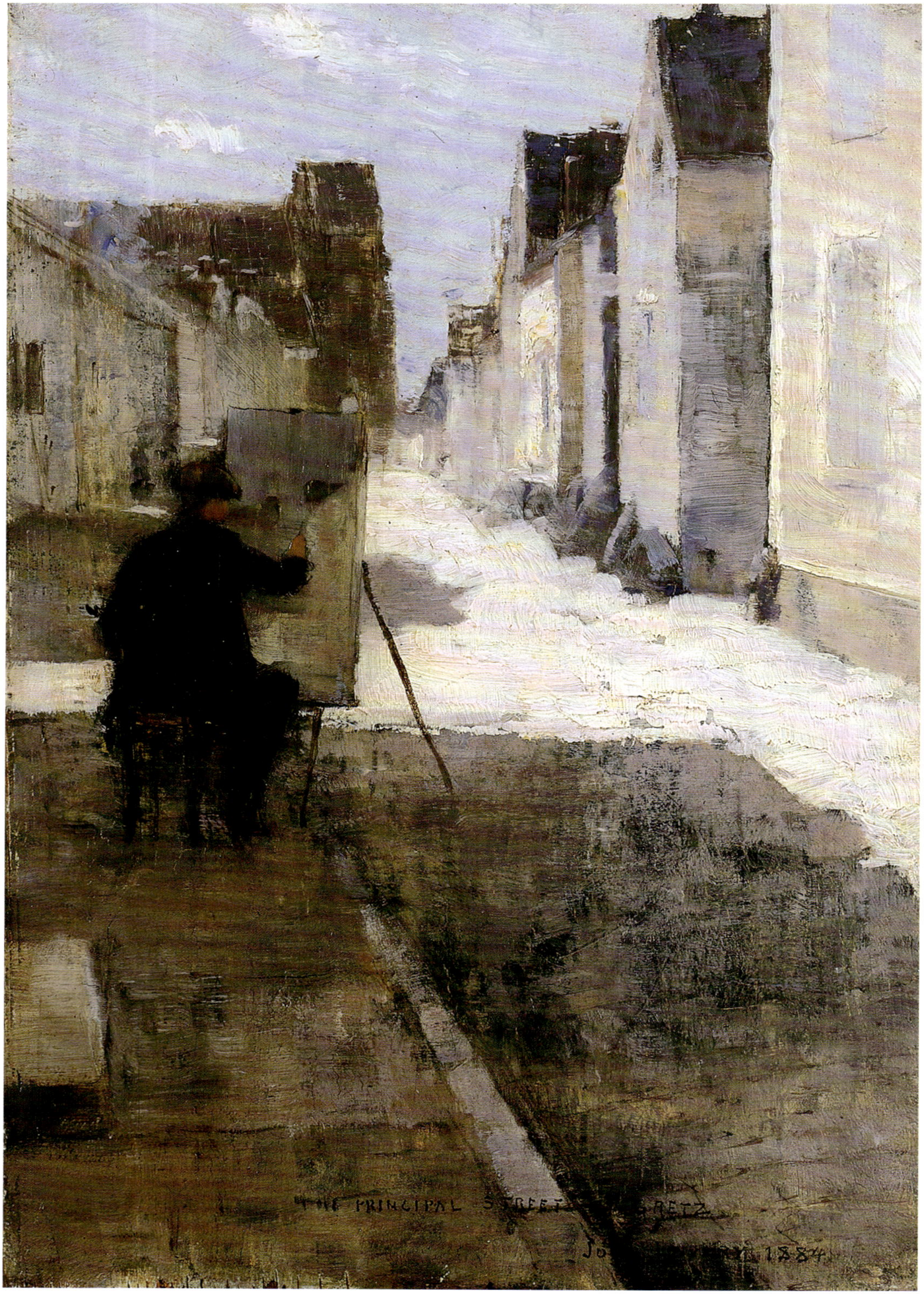

Opposite
Fig. 5 John Lavery
The Principal Street in Grez, 1884
Oil on canvas, 32.5 x 23 cm
Private collection

from the ranks of those watercolourists who also painted in oils, and, given the limited scale of the exhibiting space, the new institute could only accept, for the most part, small works. While its profile was essentially conservative from the outset, it nevertheless provided a much-needed addition to the art calendar.[14]

Although well supported, the 'Painters in Oil Colours' alone could not satisfy the demands of the expanding art economy. In a swelling market one had to rise with the tide – if not rise above it. The Society of British Artists, which, like the old watercolour societies, had been formed in the early years of the century, needed to look to its laurels. Such was its complacency – its galleries in Suffolk Street were quiet places for courting couples – that it would never have claimed the limelight, had it not been for diplomatic contacts with the notorious James McNeill Whistler in the second half of 1884. It is equally unlikely that his election to membership and rapid promotion to the presidency would have occurred had the society not realised that, as a polemicist and opponent of John Ruskin, he could potentially lead the younger generation.[15] For his part, he needed a platform and, assuming control of the society in June 1886, he became tantalised by the thought of wreaking his own revenge on an Academy that had made its dislike of his work obvious from the beginning. Although he was up for a fight, the society, 'the British' – as he later disparagingly dubbed its members – were not.[16] Suffolk Street, in the lively young painters' patois, became known as 'Suffocation Street'.

However, before Whistler's presidency began, the groundswell of young painters, provoked by critics like Henley, was such that a challenge to the Academy caucus became inevitable. The conformity of its annual exhibitions was assured by a rulebook that enabled academicians and associates to exhibit up to eight works annually. In addition, distinguished foreign exhibitors brought in because of reciprocal deals with other academies, and the best viewing places 'on the line', in the best rooms, were covered. Henley fearlessly named names. The likes of John Rogers Herbert, a devout painter of biblical scenes, Edwin

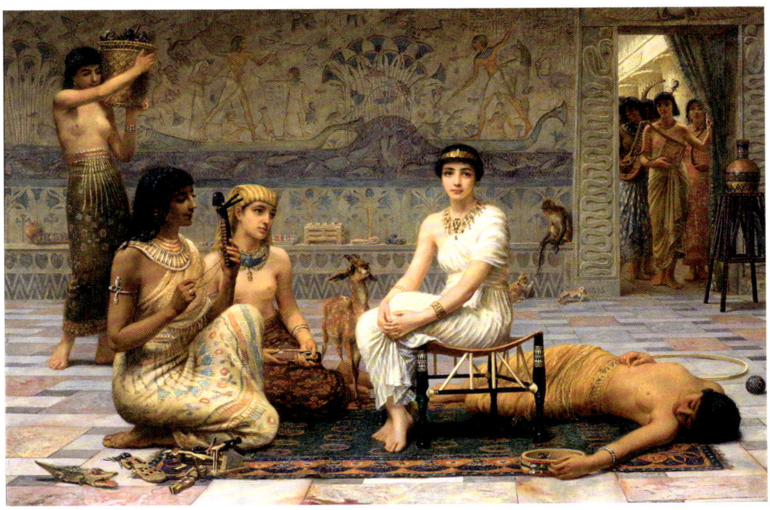

Right
Fig. 6 Edwin Lumsden Long
Love's Labours Lost, 1885
Oil on canvas, 127 x 191.1 cm
Dahesh Museum of Art, New York

Lumsden Long, painter of ancient history and Sidney Cooper, a tireless exponent of herds and flocks, were simply banal (fig. 6). The Academy would have 'looked all the better' had 'these gentlemen ... been less magnificently represented'. Thirty or forty freed-up spaces could, he estimated, be given to outsiders, presumably painters of his own generation.[17] Those who did manage to gain acceptance for their work, like Stanhope Forbes, might be applauded, but they were nonetheless swamped by inferior work.[18] The issue boiled down to whether it was desirable to seek reform from within or stand outside and attempt to bring the whole edifice down by introducing an entirely new exhibiting structure. At this juncture those who had begun to show at the Institute, and who would migrate to the club, comprised an important faction.

Had either of these possibilities been taken up what would the curious or acquisitive visitor have seen? In his reviews of the exhibitions held by the Institute of Painters in Oil Colours in 1883 and 1884, Henley gave significant space to younger painters, especially George Clausen. Although one could not speak of an 'Institute school', this was where he was to be found.[19] *The Day Dreams* (1883; fig. 7) and *A Field Hand*, also known as *A Woman of the Fields* (*c*. 1882), respectively drew praise and qualified censure, but their importance was self-evident. For the previous two years, Clausen had aggressively aligned himself with the strongest currents in contemporary French painting. He was the principal apologist for the rural naturalism led by Jules Bastien-Lepage, a painter whose work had outraged London critics when they saw it at the Grosvenor Gallery in 1880.[20] Bastien-Lepage confronted the viewer with peasants in the open fields who were so shockingly naturalistic that they could almost be mistaken for being real. He had, according to one critic, managed 'to rid himself of all personal feeling and turn himself into an artist's photographic apparatus'.[21] To obtain similar working conditions Clausen found it necessary to move from London to a hamlet near St Albans, where his Institute pictures were painted.

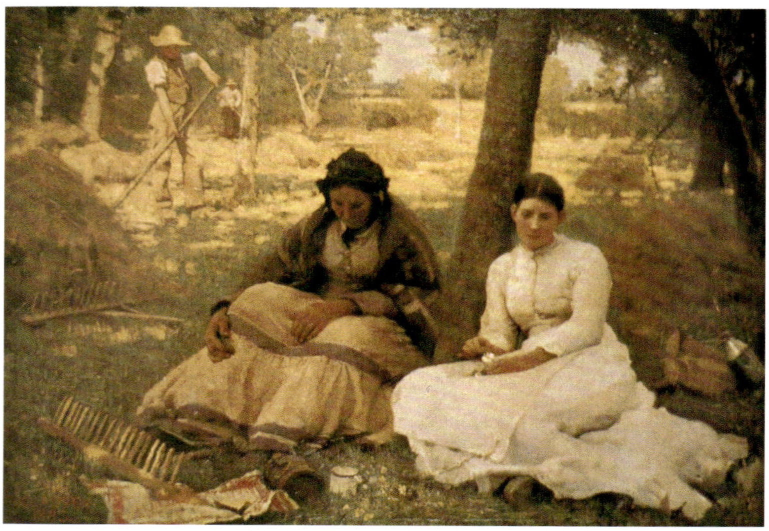

Fig. 7 George Clausen
The Day Dreams, 1883
Oil on canvas, 70 x 152.5 cm
Philadelphia Museum of Art, Philadelphia

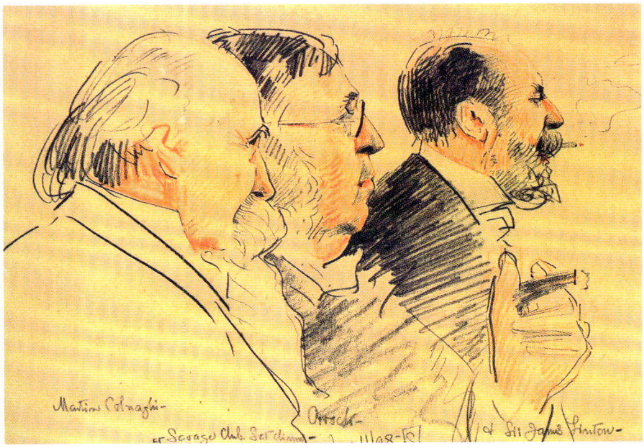

Fig. 8 Robert Ponsonby Staples
Martin Colnaghi, James Orrock and Sir James Linton at a Savage Club Saturday Dinner, 1898
Pencil and coloured crayon,
17.1 x 22.9 cm
Private collection

In doing so, he was not the only British painter profoundly affected by the rural naturalism of the Salon. Virtually all of those who had passed through the Ecole des Beaux-Arts or the Académie Julian in Paris, and who had worked in the artist colonies in France, were similarly smitten. Salon Naturalism spread across borders with the speed of a locomotive; it was the first truly international style, simultaneously practised with minor local variations across Europe, Scandinavia and North America. The Newlyn and Glasgow schools adopted Bastien-Lepage's ideals, as did such painters as Henry Herbert La Thangue, Fred Brown, Herbert Dalziel, Edward Stott and many others. Naturalism developed its own characteristic shorthand. Painting on the spot, an artist would adopt a recognisable series of mannerisms, blocking in the whole landscape, painting across forms to give a sense of breadth and solidity, and using thick, fluid 'fatty' pigment, applied without correction. Some of this sketching technique survived in the studio, in more finished pictures, where detail might be worked up from drawings, painted studies of fragments of the composition and with the aid of photographs of figures and other details. Surviving, uncorrected sketch techniques, typically deployed in landscape backgrounds, gave a sense of circumstantial authenticity.

At this point, the 'few words' dropped in the ateliers and London studios became 'more formal'.[22] John Bartlett, an art dealer, prompted by his son, William Henry Bartlett, the painter of *The Neighbours* (fig. 2), joined forces with Brown, who had a studio attached to their house.[23] Brown took the Bartletts to see Philip Wilson Steer and Mark Fisher, and with the assistance of William James Laidlay, they drew up a list of potential sympathisers.[24] The elder Bartlett, some time late in 1885, brought Martin Colnaghi (fig. 8), son of the West End dealer, into the discussions and he offered his new premises, the Marlborough Gallery, conveniently located opposite Marlborough House in Pall Mall for the first exhibition.[25] A meeting of interested parties in January 1886, staged at the gallery, ended in jubilation – the painters left this meeting in such good spirits that the 'drowsy precincts of Pall Mall' rang 'with the glad news that there is *a balm in Gilead*' – the words of a popular non-conformist hymn.[26] A committee was formed and the opening was provisionally booked for 5 April, a month before the Royal Academy's.[27] There was consensus on the title. Initially the 'Society of Anglo-French Painters' and several other variants had been proposed, but this was changed by common consent to 'The New English Art Club'.[28] From the start the club was to be managed by an elected committee served only by an honorary secretary and honorary treasurer.[29] To preserve the club's distinctiveness, there would be no president. Those attending would elect a chairman at each meeting, and there would be no more than 50 members.

Given the recent exposure of some key exhibitors, Colnaghi must have had some idea of the likely content of the show, as well as a certain self-interest in the promotion of new work. However, he began to have doubts about financial risk, especially if there was no certainty of kudos, and, in the end, saw no reason why he should support a miscellaneous group of young painters rent-free. After seeing Henry Scott Tuke's *The Bathers* (1886) three weeks before the opening, and sensing bad publicity and possible financial loss, he bowed out. Urgent discussions ensued. W. J. Laidlay, who was a pupil of Carolus-Duran in the late 1870s, and had shown at the Society of British Artists, came forward to stand as guarantor for the club, and the Marlborough, along with the services of Colnaghi's gallery assistant, Frank Willett, was retained. Laidlay's only conditions were that the exhibitors send their best works and remain loyal to him for a second exhibition the following year in order that he might recoup his outlay.[30] A turnstile was hired and sandwich-board men employed, enabling the inaugural exhibition to open on 12 April 1886, one week late (fig. 9).[31] There was no manifesto. A note in the catalogue simply informed visitors that:

> This Club consists of 50 Members, who are more or less united in their art sympathies. They have associated themselves together with the view of holding an Annual Exhibition, hoping that a collective display of their works, which has hitherto been impossible, will prove not only of interest to the public, but will better explain the aim and method of their art.[32]

The exhibition contained 58 works by painters who were mostly in their late twenties or early thirties. There were two pieces of sculpture, both by James

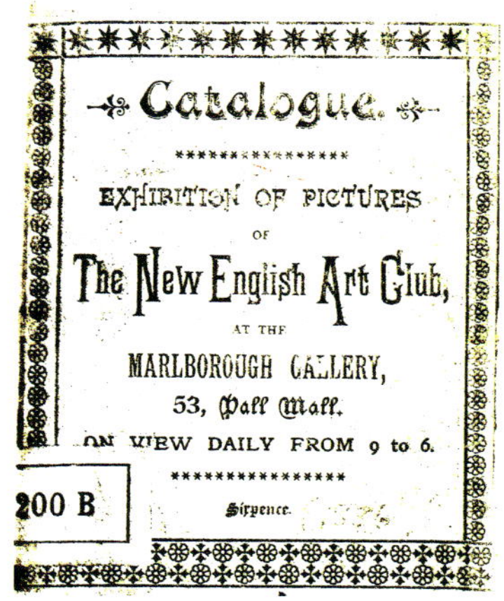
Catalogue.
EXHIBITION OF PICTURES
OF
The New English Art Club,
AT THE
MARLBOROUGH GALLERY,
53, Pall Mall.
ON VIEW DAILY FROM 9 to 6.
200 B
Sixpence.

Fig. 9 Catalogue of the first exhibition of the New English Art Club, 1886
National Art Library, Victoria and Albert Museum, London

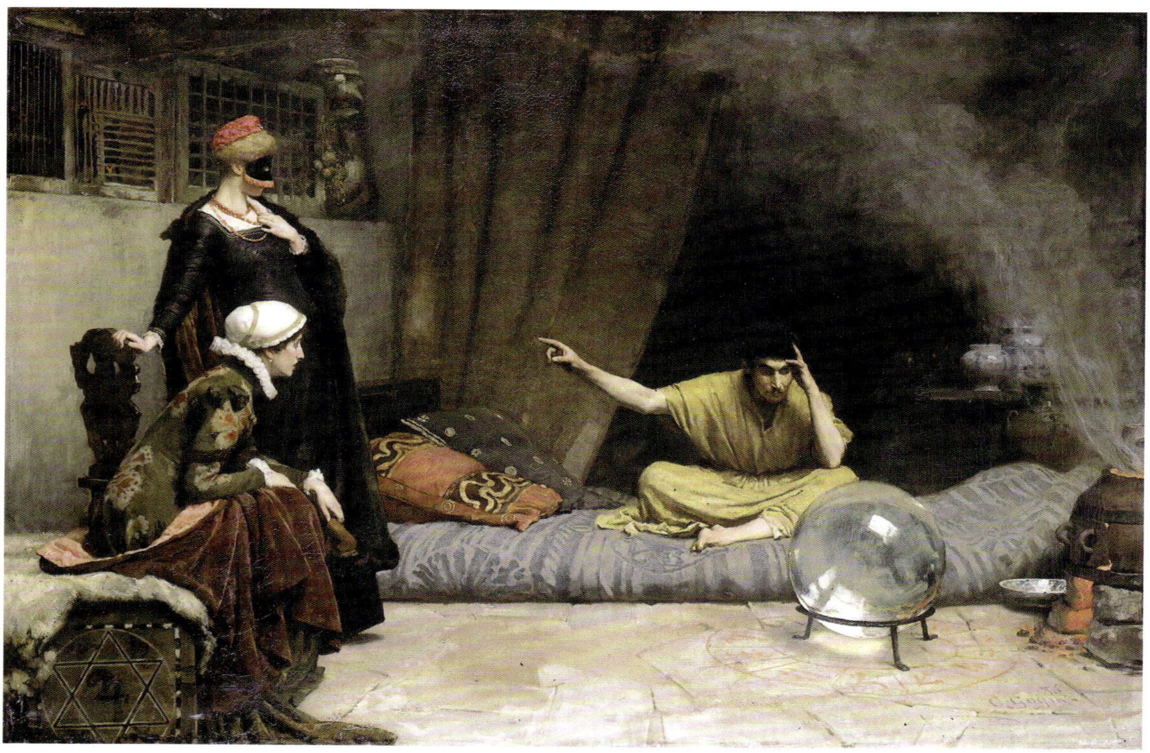

Fig. 10 Charles Gogin
The Soothsayer, 1886
Oil on canvas, 122 x 184.5 cm
Private collection

Fig. 11 Arthur Hacker
The Cradle Song, 1886
Oil on canvas, 57 x 48 cm
Collection Linda and Daniel Bader

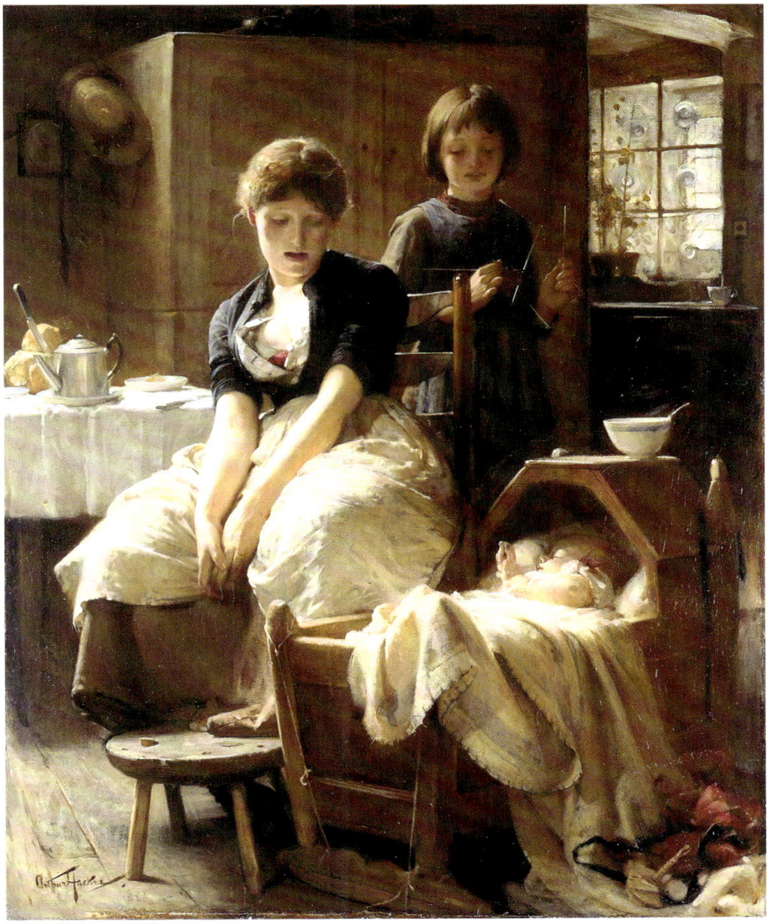

Havard Thomas.[33] Apart from two Venetian scenes by William and Marian Logsdail, a *Japanese Study* by Horace Fisher and Henry La Thangue's recently painted *In the Dauphiné*, most of the canvases represented palpably 'British' subjects. Head and full-length studies of fisherfolk, which could loosely be labelled 'Newlyn', accounted for about ten of the total number and there were portraits by Alexander Mann, John Singer Sargent and L. B. Hall. Costume pieces like Charles Gogin's *The Soothsayer* (1886; fig. 10) and Maurice Greiffenhagen's *Laertes and Ophelia* (1885) were instantly compared to the kind of medieval narratives painted by artists such as Jean-Paul Laurens in France and William John Waterhouse in England.[34] Gogin, who had served as an illustrator for Samuel Butler's travels in northern Italy, was, according to *The Saturday Review*, treating 'an attractive subject in an ordinary sort of handling that will frighten nobody'.[35] The same low-key acceptance awaited Arthur Hacker's *The Cradle Song* (1886; fig. 11), a work that *The Art Journal* found 'entirely pleasing and justifiable in motive'.[36] Despite the variety of subject matter, coherence was derived from the fact that all the exhibitors were young and were influenced to some degree by contemporary Salon painting. General approval, with one or two exceptions, greeted the 'modern aims and modern aspirations' of the club.

Exceptions were, however, important. Philip Wilson Steer's *Andante* (1886), which may have looked weak or unresolved to the hangers, was skied, and Fred Brown's *Hard Times* (1886; fig. 12), which ostensibly had much in common with *Cradle Song*, provided a more challenging piece of social observation.[37]

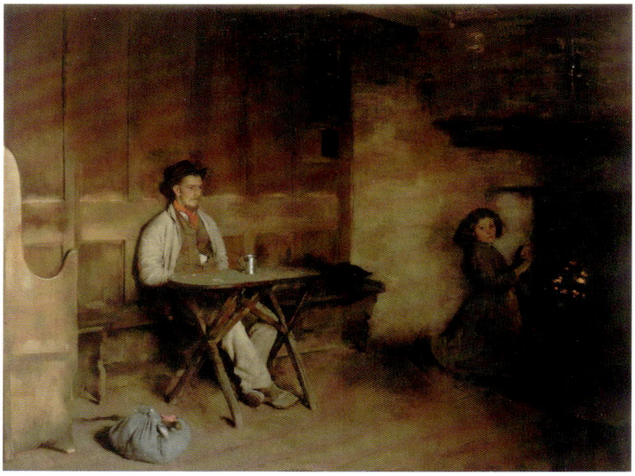

Fig. 12 Frederick Brown
Hard Times, 1886
Oil on canvas, 72 x 93 cm
Walker Art Gallery, Liverpool

If any single painting could be advanced to prove the more aggressive Francophile allegiances of the club, it was surely Henry Herbert La Thangue's *In the Dauphiné* (1886; fig. 13). William James Laidlay was spiteful about this picture, referring specifically to the fact that it was posted in the catalogue as an 'unfinished sketch'.[38] Critics recognised its closeness to Salon precedents and referred to it as:

> the largest, and – perhaps partly because it is unfinished – the most pronounced example of the distinguishing tendencies of the school. The touch is square, broad and systematised; and the colour high, bluish, and open-air-like, though it must be confessed, without sufficient delicacy.[39]

Two points are obvious. The first is to do with technique and finish and the second relates to the 'evident preoccupation about material', which the critic noted when comparing the big La Thangue with Tuke's *Bathers*. With La Thangue, the square brush style was at its most extreme. He was latterly credited with leading what became known as the 'Square Brush School', described as a:

> technical method which puts paint on canvas in a particular way with a square brush ... those who practice it in its simplest form leave the brush-marks and do not smooth away the evidence of method, thus sometimes insisting on the way the picture is painted, perhaps at the sacrifice of subtleties in the subject.[40]

Further debate ensued as to whether this method had actually originated in classes taught by the marine painter, James Clarke Hook, at the Royal Academy Schools and could thus be claimed as British, but this came after the event.[41] *In the Dauphiné* closely followed French methods of building up a composition in uniformly solid, opaque paint, applied self-confidently, and without subsequent alteration.[42] Brushmarks in the clothing of the harvester do not follow the fall of the fabric. Edges sometimes are blurred, giving the sense of arrested motion, and a single instantaneous perception of the whole.[43] While others applied this method, they selectively 'finished' their pictures to the extent that heads and hands, the focal points in a figure composition, were painted with great detail.

Fig. 13 Henry Herbert La Thangue
In the Dauphiné, 1886
Oil on canvas, 238.7 x 158.7 cm
Private collection

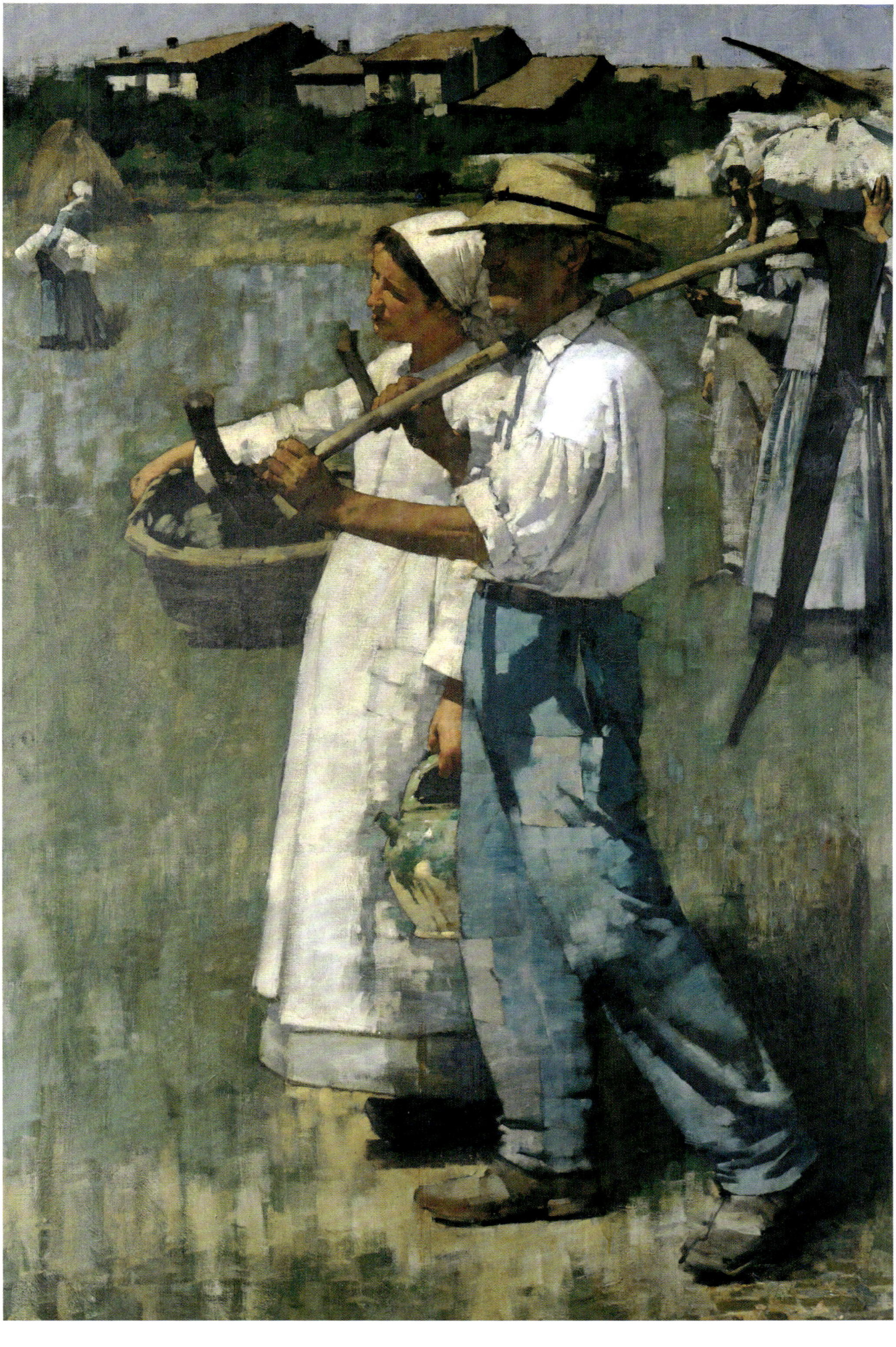

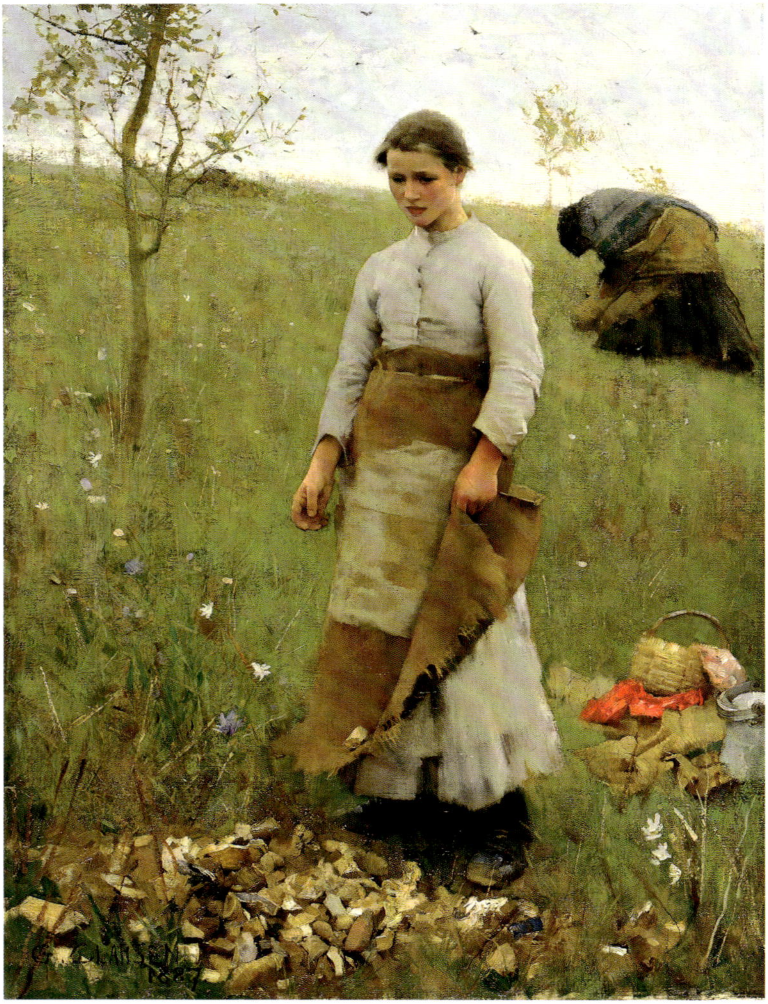

Fig. 14 George Clausen
The Stone Pickers, 1887
Oil on canvas, 106.5 x 79 cm
Laing Art Gallery, Newcastle upon Tyne

This method is apparent from Clausen's first two New English exhibits, *The Shepherdess* (1885; Walker Art Gallery, Liverpool), shown in 1886, and *The Stone Pickers* (1887; fig. 14), exhibited in the following year. For La Thangue, as for Stanhope Forbes, Frank Bramley, Albert Chevallier Tayler, Tuke and Clausen, a set of technical procedures had become a way of re-enforcing solidarity. Nowhere was this clearer than in the original illustrations of works in the show, commissioned by the *Pall Mall Gazette 'Extra'*. Tayler, in his *The Latest Novelty from London* (1886; fig. 15), for example, was so keen to demonstrate the application of systematic directional strokes that his drawing almost loses its coherence.

In the following weeks, some of the members may well have reflected upon the use of the phrase 'more or less united'.[44] Critics who alluded to the Pre-Raphaelites, and who saw the club as representative of the 'rising painters of the day', created expectations. However, confusion persisted as to the kind of

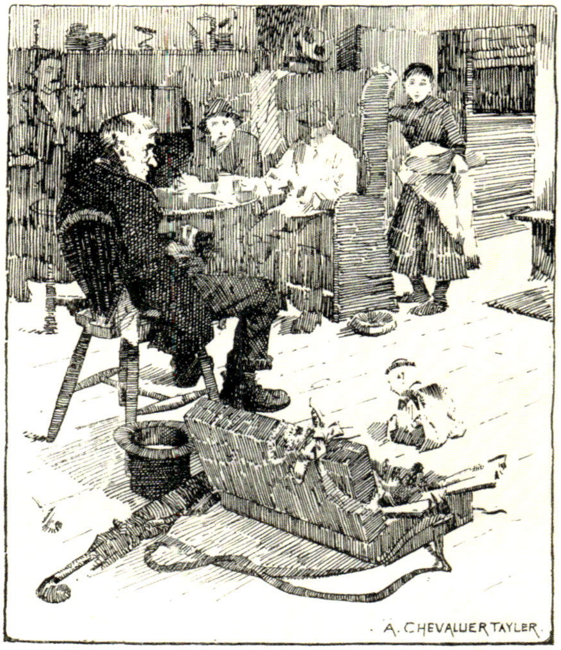

Fig. 15 Albert Chevallier Tayler
The Latest Novelty from London, 1886
Location unknown

exhibition this was. Laidlay had insisted upon the submission of only the best work, but there was a distinction to be made between 'best' and 'important'. Some painters, La Thangue for example, had submitted large canvases suitable for the Salon, while others like Forbes and his Newlyn colleagues saw the club's ambitions as more equivalent to those of the Institute of Painters in Oil Colours or the Society of British Artists and saved their greatest efforts for the Royal Academy. Generally, the first New English show was not a 'large miscellaneous exhibition' and its distinction from the Academy was obvious.[45] Indeed, a week after its opening, it was written off by the Academy's president, Frederic Leighton.[46] George Bernard Shaw, writing in *The World* a year later, essentially concurred. 'These gentlemen are painting short-sightedly in more senses than one,' he declared, 'the trick of drawing and colouring badly as if you did it on purpose is easily acquired; and the market will be swamped with "new English art", and the public tired of it, in a year or two'.[47] And if Gogin and Greiffenhagen supplied the main costume-pieces, the preponderance of what might be called 'peasant genre' confirmed the Gallic inspiration of the exhibitors. Association with Bastien-Lepage and Laurens made it obvious that many exhibits were 'an expression of the ideas and practice of a coterie trained in a certain view of nature'.[48] Although not fully representative of the tendencies of modern French art, the club allied itself to what in Paris were nationally approved tendencies, and this was potentially more offensive than had Impressionism, or some other minority style, held sway from the start.

Student solidarity was not enough to hold such a heterogeneous group together and it must have been obvious that some of the key exhibitors, who could not be present at the meetings, remained unsure or misinformed about what had happened. If La Thangue's extreme position as a would-be Salon painter attracted censure, the post-mortem on the first show, which he initiated, led to a root-and-branch debate amongst the committee members on the kind of organisation they had initiated. A significant sub-set felt that the club should be thrown open to a much wider constituency, along the lines of the newly reformed Paris Salon. Such a project would clearly have taken the club away from 'coterie' to consensus. On 18 May 1886 the 'committee-men' of the New English Art Club repaired to the Monico Restaurant in Chelsea. Ensuing discussions were self-critical. What they had recently achieved in their inaugural exhibition was, in the view of some of those present, severely limited. La Thangue 'unfolded a great scheme, nothing less than organizing a great exhibition in which every artist in the United Kingdom would be entitled to vote for the selecting and hanging juries'.[49] This was variously dubbed the 'Bigger' or 'National Movement', for which there was a great deal of enthusiasm. Envisaged as something much larger than an exhibition of 58 paintings by artists who all knew one another, it might conceivably be much bigger than the Academy. Taking such an idea into the public arena would be tantamount to raising a revolutionary flag. Artists of the New English would be spoiling for a fight.

The euphoria did not last long. Within a week there were voices of dissent within the ranks and the unity of the Monico group descended into petty misunderstandings and squabbles. By the time this was set to run, Laidlay, conscious of his personal financial commitment, had effectively reined in the club by reminding the members of their promise and threatening to resign. At a General Meeting on 12 June 1886, La Thangue was 'comprehensively sat on', the 'Bigger Movement' was rejected, Laidlay was reinstated as Hon. Treasurer and T. B. Kennington agreed to act as Hon. Secretary for the forthcoming year.[50] Bartlett senior was asked to look for an alternative venue for the second show and he eventually came up with the space occupied by the Dudley Gallery in Maskelyne and Cook's Egyptian Hall in Piccadilly.[51] It was, however, not quite the end for the 'Bigger Movement'. While its separation from the club was important, it did not stop the pursuit of what was termed a 'National Movement for Reform of the Royal Academy', based upon what La Thangue referred to as the 'universal suffrage' of all the artists in Britain.[52] Clausen mustered the support of long-time Academy outsiders like Walter Crane and William Holman Hunt and letters were written to *The Times*. Rattled reactionaries replied.[53] The whole protest was conducted in an atmosphere already charged by Ruskin's attack on the contemporary English School. So pervasive had the desire for naturalism become by 1884 that, when asked to pen the introduction to *The English School of Painting* by the French writer Ernest Chesneau, the aged John Ruskin inveighed against the younger generation, pronouncing that British painting was losing its national character.[54] Chesneau waded into the debate, declaring the English School to be 'in peril', Clausen replied and the issues were recycled over the next few years in polemical articles, letters to the papers and grumpy reviews, some of which were directed at the club.[55]

La Thangue had unleashed a torrent. 'Englishness' and 'Britishness' were bigger issues than picking a suitable name for the club. In the mid-1880s, engaged in the scramble for Africa, Britain was only too conscious of its importance in the world. Gladstone told readers of *The Fortnightly Review* that 'the sentiment of Empire' was 'innate in every Briton'.[56] Ruskin's polemic on the English School was unleashed as General Gordon fell before the spears of the Mahdi. Britain's authority in the world suffered a momentary loss of confidence and at that moment the need for national reinforcement was strong. Responsibility to strive for greatness in the British school of painting, if nothing else, meant finding a way that was emphatically not French. Even someone so thoroughly French as Chesneau, praising the glories of Hogarth and Turner could see this. While it was impractical to kick-start a huge project like that advocated by La Thangue, the debate did point to wider, representative ambitions that the club was loath to relinquish completely, even if the expression of such ideals at that point was inappropriate. Fred Brown, with the assistance of Thomas Cooper Gotch and Kennington, agreed to draft a rudimentary constitution with a set of exhibition rules that appeared in print in catalogues after 1888.[57] They simply indicated the method of introducing new members, the level of subscription and the category of 'honorary membership' for financial benefactors. Members could submit two works and they could invite other artists to do so. Members and non-member exhibitors from the previous year then voted for a selection jury of fifteen, plus a hanging committee of five.

The air was sufficiently clear for the second exhibition to be planned for the following April. If the club was tracking the Royal Academy, its principal rival lay elsewhere in the Society of British Artists. Under Whistler's presidency, the society was also taking on the Establishment, but in a different way. In his dealer shows with Charles William Dowdeswell, Whistler had pioneered the exhibition as aesthetic installation.[58] This approach was now rigorously applied to the society's show, in what *The Times* described as 'an elaborate arrangement of awning and decorations in yellow and gold.'[59] While club members sympathised with greater openness, opportunity and mutual support, Whistler and his followers were élitist and exclusive. Within the British Artists there was something of a cult.[60] Less, in their exhibition, was more. There had to be 'clean spaces' around the pictures and the effect of sunlight in the main gallery was reduced by a muslin awning suspended from the ceiling. The New English, while not competing on these terms, would accept the work of painters who were regarded as associates of Whistler, alongside the 'Institute' faction and more radical French-inspired canvases such as those of Philip Wilson Steer. In a less precious display, one observer noted several ladies who:

> essayed unbeknownst to the gentleman in charge, to test the durability of the works with their umbrellas, and resorted to other mean devices to attract public attention to themselves, and their dresses, and their friends' works, and eventually groaned under the weight of ecstasy opposite Mr Steer's two works, *The Pier Head* and *Chatterboxes*, managed to create so much muffled confusion.[61]

Fig. 16 Marianne Stokes
Polished Pans, 1887
Oil on canvas, 59 x 79.3 cm
Walker Art Gallery, Liverpool

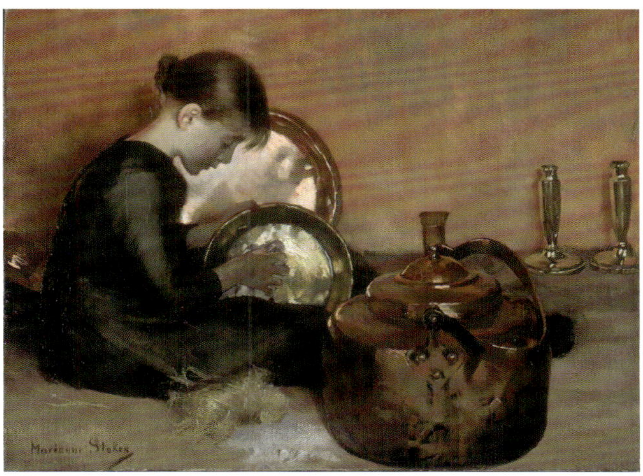

The club's membership was extended to 80 and the number of controversial or specially invited exhibits increased.[62] This more eclectic display was less dominated by the Newlyn School and its 'pronouncedly mechanical touch'.[63] Americans like Hiram Bloomer and Dewey Bates, and Glasgow-based painters such as Edward Arthur Walton, James Paterson and Lavery were included for the first time.[64] In the absence of Henry La Thangue, the standard bearer of rustic naturalism became George Clausen, whose *Stone Pickers* (fig. 14) was regarded as the leading example of the Bastien-Lepage tendency, and a rallying point for those who are 'anxious to take what is best out of the French

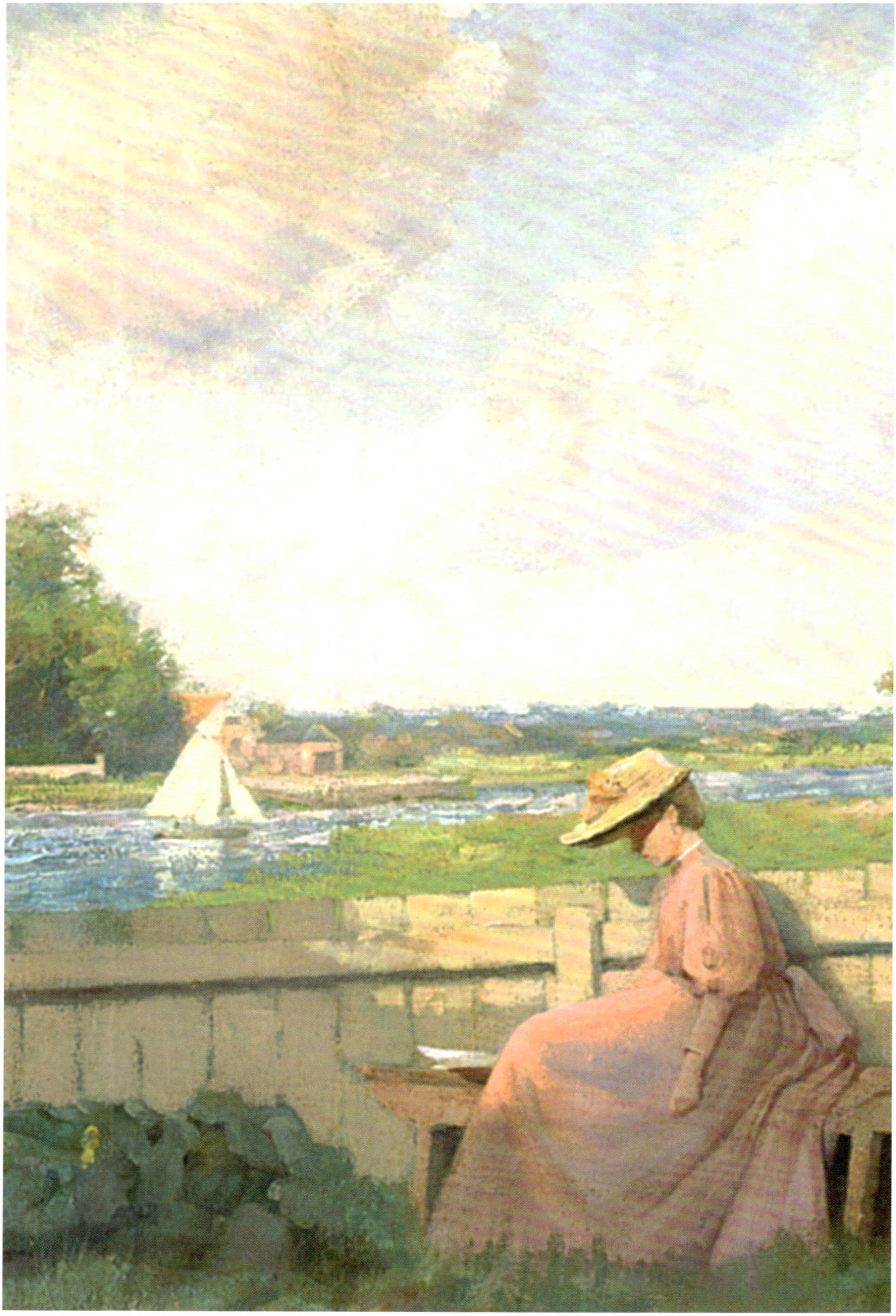

Opposite
Fig. 17 Francis Bate
A Girl Reading by a River, c. 1892
Oil on canvas, 96.5 x 62 cm
Private collection

masters'.[65] This category could include Marianne Stokes's *Polished Pans* (1887; fig. 16), Herbert Dalzeil's *Winter Work* (1886) and T. F. Goodall's *The Bow Net* (1886).[66] And if Newlyn seemed less obvious, it was because the likes of Frank Bramley, showing the vaguely aesthetic *Weaving a Chain of Grief* (1887), reserved his fish quay subject matter for the Academy.[67]

However, the most cogent defence of *plein-air* Naturalism came from Francis Bate, who entered the club in 1887, having written *The Naturalistic School of Painting*, published in the same year from the sympathetic offices of *The Artist*. Bate's view of the world was entirely positivistic. In a text that combined theory and practice, he advocated a rigorous objectivity in the observation of the natural world in outdoor light. Since the artist's palette could not replicate the full range of light and shade visible to the naked eye, there was justification for his own early Hampshire and Thames valley scenes painted in a high key (fig. 17). Even abstract ideas like 'Charity' were better tackled through Naturalism than through what he termed conventional symbolism.[68] As these views became unfashionable, Bate would easily have been sidestepped in future years had he not secured his position as secretary and treasurer of the club.[69] His political and organisational skills were formidable, and he became a prominent figure in Berkshire, where he lived.

Bate shied away from the social realistic tendencies of another early office-holder in the club, Thomas Benjamin Kennington. *The Battle of Life*, shown in 1887, addressed the very abstractions to which Bate was referring, by looking into the denizens of the East End, there to find 'poverty', 'maternal love' and the human spirit triumphing in adversity. Yet the harshness of life in the garrets and sweatshops described by contemporary writers such as Walter Besant, and reflecting the emerging ideas of the 'condition of England' novel, stood in sharp contrast to the flowering countryside painted by Bate and others. If Kennington's 'battle' exemplified the former, Clausen's *Stone Pickers* (fig. 14) expressed the latter. But where this remained within the bounds of everyday experience, Alexander Harrison's *In Arcady* (1885; fig. 18) went beyond them.

Right
Fig. 18 Alexander Harrison
In Arcady, 1885
Oil on canvas, 197 x 290 cm
Musée d'Orsay, Paris

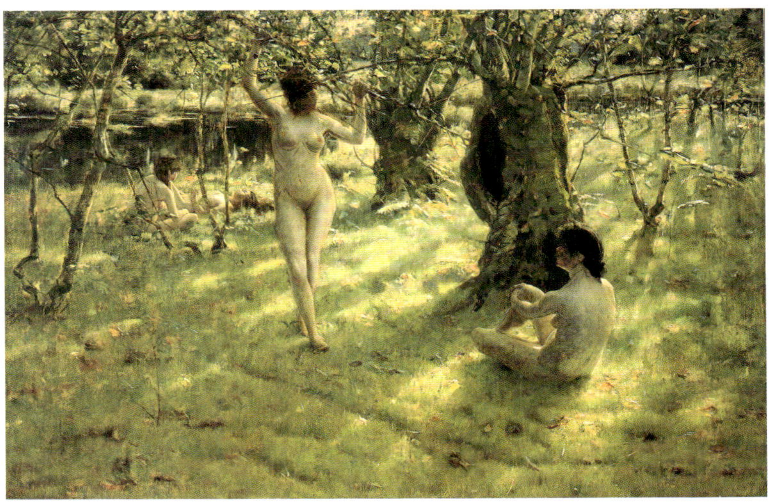

The American painter's sunshine, lush vegetation and healthy naked bodies alluded to a forbidden world of sensual delight – a world which was formerly imagined, but which now must be constructed with documentary accuracy. Harrison approached the task with Anglo-Saxon discipline and the absurdity of his practice was not immediately apparent to those who believed that naturalism was a panacea.[70] Conceptually it remained deeply problematic. For some British reviewers, nowhere save in France could one come upon such an improbable scene, yet as a Parisian import, *In Arcady* carried tremendous authority. There were tales of the notorious teacher, Horace Lecoq de Boisbaudran taking his models and students into secluded woodlands where students would be encouraged to memorise the effect of sunlight on naked flesh. Despite its risky subject matter, its formidable naturalism was described as 'a marvel of strong painting' and 'straightforward force'.[71] Yet there was nothing straightforward about *In Arcady*. As with most big *plein-air* pictures, it was likely to have been collaged together from small *plein-air* studies, drawings and photographs,

Fig. 19 Théodore Roussel
The Reading Girl, 1886–7
Oil on canvas, 152.4 x 161.3 cm
Presented by Mrs Walter Herriot and Miss R. Herriot in memory of the artist 1927. Tate, London

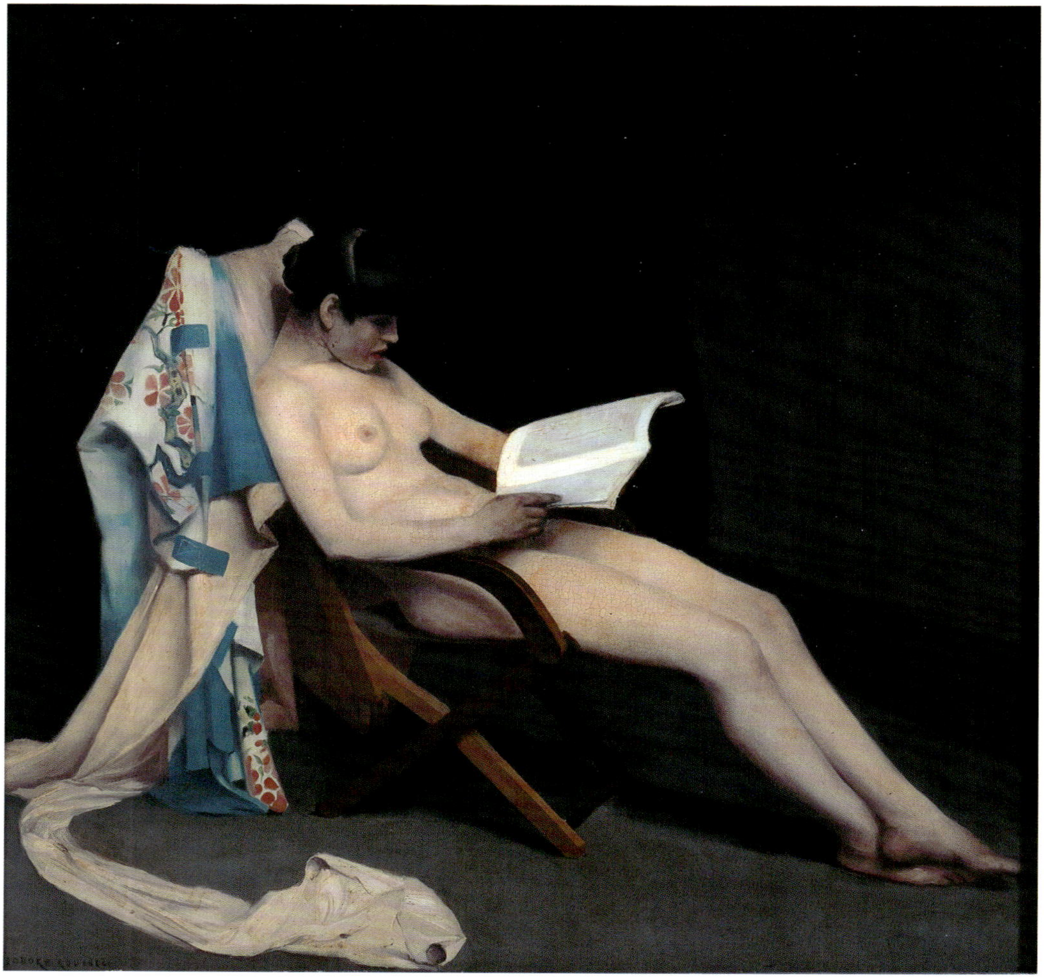

even though its author might wish us to believe that it was painted from start to finish in the open air.[72] But this is less important than the obvious *coup* in securing such a controversial Salon hit for the club and thus underwriting the box office. Laidlay could not complain. In constitution and content, the New English was nothing less than 'a miniature Salon',[73] and the press comments about the 'progress' of club members towards the 'French school of Impressionism' are to be taken in this context.[74]

If anything, the deep relationship with French art became more evident from Théodore Roussel's *Reading Girl* (1886–7; fig. 19), a work in which the educated eye could find obvious echoes of the world of Manet and Whistler, in both the subject and its treatment. The girl is portrayed with frontal frankness. Having removed her kimono, she sits on a campaign chair, ostensibly reading. Roussel gives no suggestion of the detail of the boudoir that might be usual for such scenes, and his figure is nude, not *déshabillée*. He too has deployed his skill in the service of reality, for the girl lacks the honeyed tones of Leighton's nudes, and her hands redden as she holds her journal. Neither classical goddess nor contemporary courtesan, she is a life model whose surface sensuality is in the eye of the beholder, to whom she is oblivious. She has been patiently studied, but to what end? Roussel at this point was engrossed in what he referred to as 'Positive Chromatic Analysis' and the 'rational perspective of colour' – the belief that perspective could be calculated mathematically by means of fixed colour and tone gradations.[75] The revolutionary nature of this was far from evident to those outside his immediate circle. The critic of *The Spectator* commented that 'our imagination fails to conceive of any adequate reason for a picture of this sort. It is realism of the worst kind ...'.[76] The mismatch between 'realism' and 'science', between public perception and artistic experiment may have led to the selection of the more independent club rather than the British Artists for its exhibition.

The contrast between this and Sargent's *Portrait of Robert Louis Stevenson and Mrs Stevenson – Sketch* (1885; fig. 20) could not have been more marked.[77] The canvas would have remained 'grotesque' and caricatural, had not *The Saturday Review* leapt to its defence, explaining that 'for the sake of those who may not understand the meaning of "a sketch", we may point to the walking figure which it would be impossible to render so instinct with life and gesture by closer and more explicit workmanship'.[78] Four years after the publication of *Treasure Island*, Stevenson was at the height of his celebrity, and this daring 'sketch' could almost be regarded as a careful piece of image management. The male genius paces the floor rehearsing his ideas, while his wife apparently ignores him. Animation, in a figure 'instinct with life', was a new quality found in one of the other notable canvases, Jacques-Emile Blanche's *Dieppe Casino, Evening*. According to *The Daily Telegraph*, this Whistlerian scene with its 'blue lady with two phantom children', one of whom was 'an all but invisible ghostling', also deployed sketch techniques to render an impression rather than hard facts.[79] Both pictures began with different premises and ended up being about similar challenges. There was a modern way of seeing which admitted the fragmentary and which caught movement either in the moving scene, or in the nervous flicker of the artist's eye.

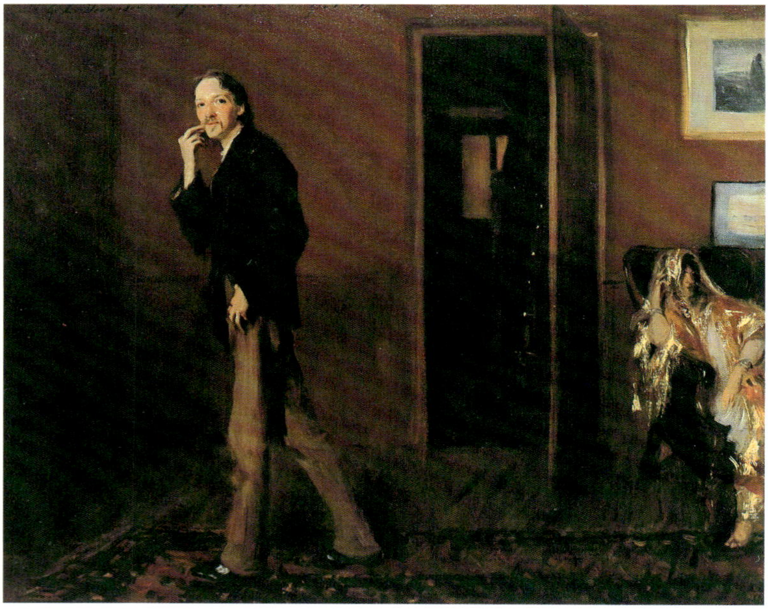

Fig. 20 John Singer Sargent
Portrait of Robert Louis Stevenson and Mrs Stevenson – Sketch, 1885
Oil on canvas, 52.1 x 62.2 cm
Private collection

Critics sensitised to the debate about national characteristics would have none of this. Not inclined to pick on patient study of still-life 'nature', in the open air or otherwise, their knives were out for 'systems which bear the names of realism, naturalism, impressionism'. In this the club appeared 'a good deal more revolutionary than its innocent looking title would imply' and a conservative Academician would think it 'much more new than English'.[80] While the 1887 exhibition attracted sufficient notice to dispel any immediate thoughts of a radical rethink of the club's scale and general philosophy, it could not be immune from external developments. Critical attention ensured that visitors would thread their way to the back of the Egyptian Hall, but on the whole it did not speculate upon the club's future direction. To show that he empathised with the new painters, two of Whistler's works had been included 'ex-catalogue' in 1887.[81] His presence indicated the importance that the club would have for his soon-to-be disenfranchised followers. Although his 'eccentric' decorations at Suffolk Street and draconian hanging policy must have seemed like a diversion to serious young painters with the Academy in their sights, his prompt ejection from the British Artists, after securing its 'Royal' status, was to have immediate and far-reaching consequences. Nevertheless, by the time their own exhibition closed, the members had lived up to their pledge to Laidlay. Honour was satisfied. At this point he suggested somewhat surprisingly that a committee be formed comprising Havard Thomas, Forbes, Tuke, Brown and La Thangue, to debate the future direction of the club. This proved unnecessary, with or without La Thangue, and so it was decided at the Annual General Meeting in 1887 that the club should continue. Nevertheless, behind the scenes the preparations were being made to change its direction.

NOTES

1 The picture was illustrated in *The Graphic*, 22 April 1882, p. 394, with an accompanying description, which identifies the woman as 'one of those light-hearted *ouvrières* on whose struggles and temptations so many *feuilleton* writers have loved to dwell'. The setting is a shared 'garret studio *au cinquième*' in one of the few streets not yet improved by Haussmann.

2 See Edward Morris and Amanda Kay, 'British Art Students in Paris', *Apollo*, vol. 135, 1992, pp.78–84; also Catherine Fehrer, 'New Light on the Académie Julian and its Founder (Rodolphe Julian)', *Gazette des Beaux-Arts*, vol. 126, nos 1384–5, 1984, pp. 207–16; also Barbara H. Weinberg, *The Lure of Paris, Nineteenth-Century American Painters and Their French Teachers*, Abbeville Press, New York, 1991, pp. 221–62; also *Overcoming All Obstacles: The Women of the Académie Julian*, Gabriel P. Weisberg and Jane R. Becker, exh. cat., Dahesh Museum, New York, 2000. Although the young woman is not an art student, women were admitted to the Académie Julian – albeit in segregated classes – in the 1880s.

3 Logan Pearsall Smith, *Unforgotten Years*, Constable, London, 1938, p. 184.

4 Fred Brown, 'Recollections', *Artwork*, vol. 6, no. 23, autumn 1930, p. 160.

5 Fred Brown, 'Recollections, II, The Early Years of the New English Art Club', *Artwork*, vol. 6, no. 24, winter 1930, p. 269.

6 See, for instance, William Ewart Gladstone, 'England's Mission', September 1878, quoted in Michael Goodwin (ed.), *Nineteenth-Century Opinion*, Penguin, Harmondsworth, 1951, pp. 268–72.

7 'Mr Titmarsh [W. M. Thackeray], *The Paris Sketch Book*, London, 1840. Thackeray makes much of the discomfort of travellers crossing the Channel.

8 W. E. Henley, 'Current Art IV', *The Magazine of Art*, 1885, p. 470.

9 Shirley Fox, *An Art Student's Reminiscences of Paris in the Eighties*, Mills and Boon, London, 1909, and Julius M. Price, *My Bohemian Days in Paris*, T. Werner Laurie, London, 1913, provide two of many reports of the treatment meted out to aspiring painters by the *maîtres*. For an account of Americans who had similar experiences in Paris during this period, see Barbara H. Weinberg, *The Lure of Paris, Nineteenth-Century American Painters and Their French Teachers*, Abbeville Press, New York, 1991.

10 In 1860, 2,612 works were submitted to the Academy. By 1884, this number had increased to 8,093, although only a quarter of these works were actually shown.

11 Norman Wilkinson OBE, PRI, 'The Royal Institute of Painters in Watercolours', *The Studio*, vol. 128, 1944, p. 7.

12 G. Reitlinger, *The Economics of Taste, The Rise and Fall of Picture Prices, 1760–1960*, Barrie and Rockcliff, London, 1961.

13 What later became known as the Royal Society of Painter-Etchers and Engravers (RE) was formed under the presidency of Sir Francis Seymour Haden in 1880. Its first exhibitions were held at the Fine Art Society in New Bond Street, London. For a general discussion of artists' societies at this time, see Julie F. Codell, 'Artists' Professional Societies: Production, Consumption and Aesthetics' in Brian Allen (ed.), *Towards a Modern Art World, Studies in British Art 1*, Yale University Press, London and New Haven, 1995, pp. 169–87. For more on the RE, see Martin Hopkinson, *No Day Without a Line: The History of the Royal Society of Painter-Printmakers, 1880–1999*, Ashmolean Museum, Oxford, 1999.

14 Gerald Moira, V-PROI, 'The Royal Institute of Oil Painters', *The Studio*, vol. 128, 1944, pp. 36–7. Under Linton's presidency, despite its initial composition, the Royal Institute of Painters in Oil Painters (ROI) soon established itself as an independent body and invited members who were not also watercolour painters. It included work by future luminaries of the early exhibitions of the New English Art Club, such as Clausen, La Thangue, Hacker and others, see Anon., 'The Institute', *The Magazine of Art*, 1884, pp. 160–3; Anon., 'The Royal Institute', *The Magazine of Art*, 1885, pp. 133–6. Writing about the recently formed Institute of Painters in Oil Colours in the late 1880s, Arthur Strong declared that it 'fairly represents the main tendencies in and the normal level of English Art. It stands, as it were, midway between the pedantry which still distinguishes the Academy, like an order of knighthood, and the second-hand French finery of the NEAC' (S. Arthur Strong, *Critical Studies and Fragments*, Duckworth, London, 1905 [1912 ed.], p. 155).

15 Whistler had common cause with the younger generation against the Academy since the bitter disputes over his submission of *Arrangement in Grey and Black, No. 1, Portrait of the Artist's Mother* (1871; Musée d'Orsay, Paris), in 1872. Controversy attended his exhibits at the first Grosvenor Gallery show in 1877 and he was famously accused of 'hurling a pot of paint in the public's face' by John Ruskin. Whistler sued Ruskin for libel the following year and was awarded damages of one farthing. He nevertheless continued to show at the Grosvenor until 1884, when his portrait of Théodore Duret was rejected and *Arrangement in Black: Portrait of Lady Archibald Campbell* caused embarrassment to the gallery owners, Sir Coutts and Lady Lindsay. The sitter's retreating pose and 'come-hither' look led to suggestions that she had been recast as a streetwalker. Whistler had to find a new exhibiting venue quickly. The move to the Society of British Artists in the winter exhibition of 1884 'startled' artistic society, according to *The Times*, 3 December 1884.

16 For further reference, see A. Ludovici, 'The Whistlerian Dynasty at Suffolk Street', *The Art Journal*, 1906, pp. 193–5 and 237–9. See also Ronald Anderson and Anne Koval, *James McNeill Whistler, Beyond the Myth*, John Murray, London, 1994, pp. 272–82.

17 W. E. Henley, 'Current Art IV', *The Magazine of Art*, 1885, p. 470.

18 See, for instance, reference to Forbes's *A Fish Sale on a Cornish Beach* (Plymouth Art Gallery), shown at the Royal Academy in 1885, in *Painting in Newlyn, 1880–1930*, Caroline Fox and Francis Greenacre, exh. cat., Barbican Art Gallery, London, 1985, pp. 54 and 108–9. The Academy never completely closed its doors on the younger generation.

19 Wilfrid Meynell (ed.), *The Modern School of Art*, Cassell, London, vol. 4, n.d. [*c.* 1887], p. 134.

20 Kenneth McConkey, 'Rustic Naturalism at the Grosvenor Gallery', in *The Grosvenor Gallery, A Palace of Art in Victorian England*, Susan Casteras and Colleen Denney (eds), exh. cat., Yale University Press, London and New Haven, 1996, pp. 129–45; see also Kenneth McConkey, 'The Bouguereau of the Naturalists – Bastien-Lepage and British Art', *Art History*, vol. 1, no. 3, 1978, pp. 371–82. See also *Sir George Clausen RA, 1852–1944*, Kenneth McConkey, exh. cat., Cartwright Hall, Bradford, Royal Academy of Arts, London; City Museum and Art Gallery, Bristol; Laing Art Gallery, Newcastle upon Tyne, 1980, pp. 29–33.

21 Harry Quilter, *Sententiae Artis*, William Isbister, London, 1886, p. 163.

22 William James Laidlay, *The Origin and First Two Years of the New English Art Club*, John Lane, London, 1907, pp. 7–8. See also Anna Gruetzner Robins, 'Feuds and Factions at the New English Art Club' in *The New English Art Club Centenary Exhibition*, Anna Gruetzner Robins and Francis Farmar, exh. cat., Christie's, London, 1986, pp. 5–13.

23 The younger Bartlett had begun to exhibit landscapes in 1874 while still a student. A pupil of Jean-Léon Gérôme, he also worked at the Académie Julian, showing an interior of one of its painting studios during a model's rest period at the Society of British Artists in the winter of 1881 (unlocated). Bartlett's father took a commercial interest in promoting the work of his son's generation.

24 Fred Brown, 'Recollections, II, The Early Years of the New English Art Club', *Artwork*, vol. 6, no. 24, winter 1930, p. 269.

25 Colnaghi had taken over the building formerly occupied by the Royal Institute of Painters in Watercolours, before its move in 1883.

26 The meeting took place on 4 January 1886, William James Laidlay, *The Origin and First Two Years of the New English Art Club*, John Lane, London, 1907, p. 20. The late 1880s was a period of Methodist revival. I am grateful to George McConkey and Patricia Duddy for their assistance in determining the origins of this hymn.

27 This comprised Bartlett, Gotch, Brown, Solomon J. Solomon, Hacker and Tuke, with Colnaghi in the chair. See William James Laidlay, *The Origin and First Two Years of the New English Art Club*, John Lane, London, 1907, p. 17.

28 William James Laidlay, *The Origin and First Two Years of the New English Art Club*, John Lane, London, 1907, p. 15, lists the options as: (1) The Pall Mall Gallery or Institute; (2) The English Renaissance; (3) The New English Art Institute; and (4) The Society of Anglo-French Painters. Obviously titles involving the word 'institute' were dismissed.

29 Initially the committee comprised six exhibitors (Bartlett, Gotch, Brown, Solomon, Hacker and Tuke), under Colnaghi's chairmanship. It was felt desirable that the committee members should be London-based. No exhibitor should show more than three works. A membership fee was set at 3 guineas.

30 Fred Brown, 'Recollections, II, The Early Years of the New English Art Club', *Artwork*, vol. 6, no. 24, winter 1930, p. 270, indicates that Laidlay's liability was £85.

31 William James Laidlay, *The Origin and First Two Years of the New English Art Club*, John Lane, London, 1907, p. 57; in the event, according to Laidlay, the 70–100 daily visitors to the exhibition failed to cover the cost of hiring the turnstile.

32 'Catalogue – Exhibition of Pictures of the New English Art Club at the Marlborough Gallery, 53 Pall Mall', 1886, unpaginated.

33 Although sculpture made occasional appearances at club exhibitions, it was, and has remained, essentially a painters' society.

34 Sold at Christie's, London, 9 November 2001, lot 49, *The Soothsayer* carried the caption, 'The Seeds of Time Grow, Blossom and Bear Fruit Within the Mystic Crystal of This Globe, and Lo! Thy Future Doth Unfold Itself in Such Sad Wise, That the Beholding of It Makes My Speech Halt'. This was to be Gogin's only New English exhibit.

35 *The Saturday Review*, 17 April 1886, p. 541.

36 *The Art Journal*, 1886, p. 252. Today we would not overlook the innocence of the daughter, the prettiness of the young mother and the fact that she has been breast-feeding her infant.

37 *Andante* is now known only in reproduction. A study for it was sold at Sotheby's on 8 November 1989, lot 48. For further reference to Brown's *Hard Times*, see *Impressionism in Britain*, Kenneth McConkey, exh. cat., Barbican Art Gallery, London, 1995, p. 105; see also *Hard Times: Social Realism in Victorian Art*, Julian Treuherz, exh. cat., Manchester City Art Gallery, 1987.

38 William James Laidlay, *The Origin and First Two Years of the New English Art Club*, John Lane, London, 1907, p. 55. It was in fact subtitled 'An Unfinished Study' in the catalogue. George Bernard Shaw, 'The Spring Exhibitions', *The World*, 28 April 1886, also commented sarcastically that this 'unfinished study' was a 'strange proceeding' and 'surely the public impatience to see the work could have been restrained pending its completion'. Quoted from Stanley Weintraub (ed.), *Bernard Shaw and the London Art Scene, 1885–1950*, London and Penn State University, University Park, 1989, p. 98.

39 *The Saturday Review*, 17 April 1886, p. 541.

40 Morley Roberts, 'A Colony of Artists', *The Scottish Art Review*, 1889, p. 72.

41 A. S. Hartrick, *A Painter's Pilgrimage through Fifty Years*, Cambridge University Press, Cambridge, 1939, p. 28, contends that the 'square brush act' started in 1883, when Bastien-Lepage gave painting lessons to a group of British and American followers. While this might have occurred, it is unlikely to be the 'origin' of the method.

42 Walter Sickert, recalling this debate in later years, credited La Thangue with having adopted and developed the methods of his day in the use of 'an opaque mosaic for recording objective sensations ... in personal manner' in *The New Age*, 7 May 1914, quoted from Osbert Sitwell (ed.), *A Free House, Being the Writings of Walter Richard Sickert*, Macmillan, London, 1947, p. 271. Other artists who had been to France in the early 1880s employed the 'opaque mosaic', but not to the same degree.

43 La Thangue understood these processes completely, and, in the much less ambitious *Return of the Reapers* (1886; Tate Britain, London), we see a higher level of finish than in the present work. In both, however, La Thangue's preoccupation with what we might refer to as 'materiality' is evident. Even the glazes of the rustic water-jug, to be held above the head for drinking, as in Manet's *The Water Drinker* (1862; Art Institute of Chicago), are treated in such a way as to accentuate the solidity of the object. Such effects, dependent upon the regularity of brushstrokes, as in a Cézanne, impress ideas of three-dimensionality upon the viewer, and make the experience of La Thangue's grand 'unfinished' peasants of the Dauphiné compelling.

44 Bartlett, one of the prime movers, for reasons that remain obscure, resigned between the first and second exhibitions.

45 *The Saturday Review*, 17 April 1886, p. 540, took up the comparison between this and the Academy in the following terms. While the club was not comprehensive, 'The Academy, indeed, is not intended to give a purely aesthetic pleasure to the connoisseur; it is a *resumé* of the whole endeavour of a country, a sort of official recognition of all the various aims of art rather than a place where they can be separately studied and really enjoyed'.

46 William James Laidlay, *The Origin and First Two Years of the New English Art Club*, John Lane, London, 1907, p. 57, records that about a week after the exhibition opened Leighton visited and 'I was in the gallery most of the time he was there, and although I did not of course speak to him, I can testify to the careful examination to which he subjected our work. Just before leaving he got into conversation with Mr Willett, and asked a good many questions with regard to our society and the work of "these impressionists", as he somewhat unfairly called us all, for we were anything but all from one school. Then, after a few complimentary words, our distinguished critic volunteered the remark, "The second year will try these men, and the third year will probably disband them." Willett asked Laidlay what he meant and Laidlay replied, "Heaven only knows, unless, indeed, some thirty years' experience of art and artists and a knowledge of the power of the Academy and the way it deals with competing societies can have suggested the happy thought, and led him to disbelieve in the possibility of any permanent combination of artists."'

47 George Bernard Shaw, 'Picture Shaws', *The World*, 20 April 1887; quoted in Stanley Weintraub, 'In the Picture Galleries', in Michael Holroyd (ed.), *The Genius of Shaw*, Hodder and Stoughton, London, 1979, p. 45.

48 Kenneth McConkey, 'The Bouguereau of the Naturalists – Bastien-Lepage and British Art', *Art History*, vol. 1, no. 3, 1978, pp. 371–82.

49 Fred Brown, 'Recollections, II, The Early Years of the New English Art Club', *Artwork*, vol. 6, no. 24, winter 1930, p. 270.

50 William James Laidlay, *The Origin and First Two Years of the New English Art Club*, John Lane, London, 1907, p. 125.

51 This was a sub-let room and vestibule area at the back of the building used by the Dudley Gallery. Its principal drawback was that visitors to club exhibitions rubbed shoulders with those who came to the Hall for its more popular entertainments.

52 Ironically, for all his present hostility to the idea, Laidlay was no supporter of the Academy, as his W. J. Laidlay, *The Royal Academy: Its Uses and Abuses*, Simpkin, Marshall, Hamilton, Kent, London, 1898,

makes clear. He remained in the club until 1892 and thereafter returned to the Royal Society of British Artists, standing unsuccessfully against Alfred East for its presidency in 1906.

53 *The Times*, 7 August 1886, 14 August 1886 and 21 August 1886.

54 Ernest Chesneau, *The English School of Painting*, Cassell, London, 1885, pp. iii–xliii. For a fuller account, see *Impressionism in Britain*, Kenneth McConkey, exh. cat., Barbican Art Gallery, London, 1995, pp. 30–42. The 'Bigger Movement' attracted widespread support, organised an Academy Reform Committee and presented Leighton with a petition containing over 700 signatures. La Thangue remained a driving force – see H. H. La Thangue, 'A National Art Exhibition', *The Magazine of Art*, vol. 10, 1887, pp. 30–2; also H. H. La Thangue, 'Politics in Art', *The Artist*, 1 April 1889, p. 97.

55 Ernest Chesneau, 'The English School in Peril', *The Magazine of Art*, 1887, p. 27; George Clausen, 'The English School in Peril: A Reply', *The Magazine of Art*, 1887, p. 224. See also Ernest Chesneau, *The Education of the Artist*, Cassell, London, 1886; Sir James Linton, 'The Practical Education of the Artist', *The Magazine of Art*, 1886, p. 158, and W. P. Frith, 'Art Education', *The Magazine of Art*, 1888, pp. 101–4.

56 William Ewart Gladstone, 'England's Mission', September 1878, quoted in Michael Goodwin (ed.), *Nineteenth-Century Opinion*, Penguin, Harmondsworth, 1951, p. 268.

57 Fred Brown, 'Recollections, II, The Early Years of the New English Art Club', *Artwork*, vol. 6, no. 24, winter 1930, p. 276.

58 *Mr Whistler's Gallery, Pictures at an 1884 Exhibition*, Kenneth John Myers, exh. cat., Freer Gallery of Art, Washington DC, 2003.

59 *The Times*, 5 April 1887, p. 4. For a fuller consideration of Whistler's exhibition strategies, see Deanna Marhon Bendix, *Diabolical Designs, Paintings, Interiors and Exhibitions of James McNeill Whistler*, Smithsonian Institution, Washington DC, 1995, pp. 205ff.

60 Whistler, for instance, insisted that his principal pupils describe themselves in public as *élèves de Whistler*. See, for instance, Frank Rutter, *Theodore Roussel*, London and New York, 1926, pp. 11–12. For further reference, see Anne Koval, 'The Artists Come Out and the British Remain: the Whistler Faction at the Society of British Artists' in Elizabeth Prettejohn (ed.), *After the Pre-Raphaelites: Art and Aestheticism in Victorian England*, Manchester University Press, Manchester, 1999, pp. 90–111.

61 *The Bohemian*, 23 April 1887.

62 The previous summer, in considering the financial outturn of the first exhibition, it was at first felt that 60 members would assure minimum viability. This was later raised to 80.

63 *The Art Journal*, 1887, pp. 158–9.

64 Bloomer showed *An Old Orchard* (10); Bates, *The Signalman* (13); Walton showed *Portrait* (28) and *Landscape* (36); Paterson, *Moniaive* (11); Lavery, *A White Rose* (16) and *Portrait of a Girl in White* (69); the exhibition also included works by Whitelaw Hamilton, Alexander Mann and James Cadenhead.

65 *The Scotsman*, 7 April 1887; see *Sir George Clausen, RA 1852–1944*, Kenneth McConkey, exh. cat., Cartwright Hall, Bradford; Royal Academy of Arts, London; City Museum and Art Gallery, Bristol; Laing Art Gallery, Newcastle upon Tyne, 1980, pp. 44–6.

66 Stokes, along with Elizabeth's Armstrong's *First Love*, was written up in the *Lady's Pictorial*, 16 April 1887, which, while noting that the Society of Lady Artists was exhibiting simultaneously, regretted the fact that there were so few women in the New English.

67 *The Bohemian*, 23 April 1887, complained that Bramley's young woman lacked obvious signs of grief and had a 'wooden face'.

68 Francis Bate, *The Naturalistic School of Painting*, Offices of 'the Artist', London, 1887, pp. 44–6.

69 D. S. MacColl, *The Life, Work and Setting of Philip Wilson Steer*, Faber and Faber, London, 1945, pp. 34–5. *Impressionism in Britain*, Kenneth McConkey, exh. cat., Barbican Art Gallery, London, 1995, pp. 100–1.

70 American painting at this point was considered as the bridge between the Gallic and Anglo-Saxon artistic worlds. See Walter Williams, 'The Academy and the Salon', *The National Review*, vol. 7, March–August 1886, p. 519. For Harrison, see Annette Blaugrund (ed.), *Paris 1889, American Artists at the Universal Exposition*, Pennsylvania Academy of Fine Arts and Harry N. Abrams, New York, 1989, pp. 160–4. Harrison showed two nude studies at the NEAC in 1888.

71 *The Magazine of Art*, 1887, pp. xxv–xxvi; *The Saturday Review*, 9 April 1887, pp. 515–6; *The Bohemian*, 23 April 1887, also remarked that 'if in Arcady such colours, figures and scenery are common. Save us from it'.

72 G. P. Weisberg in *Beyond Impressionism, The Naturalist Impulse*, Harry N. Abrams, New York, 1992, p. 151, illustrates a series of similar but not identical photographic poses. A small compositional study, dating from *c.* 1885, approximately 22 x 41 cm in size, exists in a private collection.

73 *The Scotsman*, 7 April 1887.

74 *Building News*, 8 April 1887.

75 Frank Rutter, *Théodore Roussel*, The Connoisseur, London and New York, 1926, pp. 14–15.

76 *The Spectator*, 16 April 1887, p. 527.

77 It was ironic that Sargent was showing his big *Carnation, Lily, Lily, Rose* (1885–6) at the Royal Academy simultaneously. It could, as an outdoor scene, have been compared with Harrison's canvas.

78 *The Art Journal*, 1887, pp. 158–9; *The Saturday Review*, 9 April 1887, pp. 515–6. See also *The Globe*, 6 April 1887; *Court and Society*, 13 April 1887; and *The Bohemian*, 23 April 1887.

79 *The Daily Telegraph*, 9 April 1887.

80 *The Times*, 5 April 1887, p. 4.

81 Several reviewers referred to them. *The Scotsman*, 7 April 1887, described them as 'a soft-toned etching' and 'a curious, rosette-like study' 'interesting only for its technique', but 'quite out of place in an exhibition of finished pictures'. Whistler would, of course, contend that his work was indeed finished. 'Finish', as we have seen from the debate around La Thangue's work of the previous year, was a contentious issue.

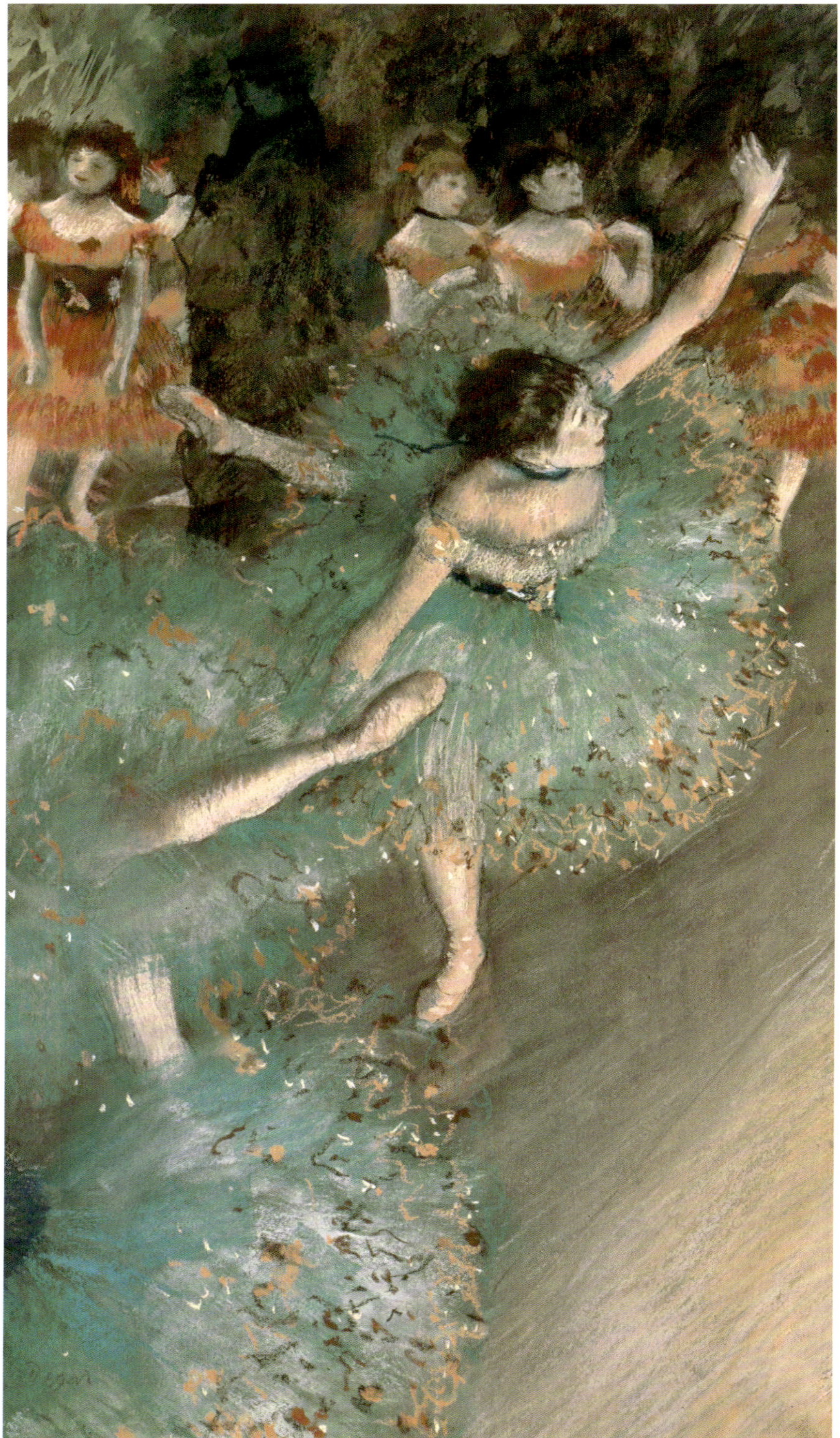

CHAPTER 2 **Successful Failures** 1888–1895

Walter Sickert exhibited at the club for the first time in 1888. A loyal member of the Whistler faction at the Royal Society of British Artists up to the end of the previous year, he now courted Fred Brown and threw open his studio in Broadhurst Gardens for meetings with him, Steer, Roussel, Bate and Sydney Starr.[1] Having exhibited at the Institute, and staged a solo exhibition at Dowdeswell's, he told Blanche, in an undated letter, that he planned to infiltrate the club with a sense of purpose, and that at the same time he had become conscious of the possible antagonism of some of its members.[2] Sickert realised that, once a member, Brown's constitution would enable him to propose other friends and supporters. He also knew the value of controversy, and, as Whistler had secured the presence of Monet in the previous winter's British Artists exhibition, he could immediately consolidate his position with the loan of Degas's *Danseuse Verte* (*c.* 1880; fig. 21), which had been recently purchased by his wife, Ellen.[3] This clearly took the club a step further than Harrison's Salon painting of the previous year and it was to be the first in a series of distinguished Impressionist loans to the early shows. Coupled with Sickert's own offerings, it was a step too far.[4]

Opposite
Fig. 21 Edgar Degas
Danseuse Verte (also known as *Swaying Dancer* or *Dancer in Green*), *c.* 1880
Pastel and gouache on paper, 64 x 36 cm
Museo Thyssen-Bornemisza, Madrid

Below
Fig. 22 Walter Richard Sickert
Gatti's Hungerford Palace of Varieties – Second Turn of Katie Lawrence, 1888
Oil on canvas, 84.4 x 99.3 cm
Art Gallery of New South Wales

Although the 1888 exhibition was larger than the previous two, the significant shift towards French Impressionism was obvious to critics, even if they were unclear about its meaning.[5] 'Public recognition' for the club began to be synonymous with the term.[6] To prove the point, *The Magazine of Art* cited three examples typifying different degrees of engagement – the first of which was an upright version of Sickert's *Gatti's Hungerford Palace of Varieties – Second Turn of Miss Katie Lawrence*. Although it is now presumed destroyed, we can obtain a sense of what it looked like from a closely related alternative version (1888; fig. 22).[7] This canvas revealed Sickert's current fascination for the café-concert interiors beloved by Degas, but hitherto largely unrecorded in Britain.[8] Newspapers tell us that his picture contained 'a strangely disproportionate female figure in the centre, ugly and stiff as a marionette, with gloomy surroundings, and a curious jumble of hats and fiddle-heads for a foreground'.[9] Others found it a 'rather disagreeable failure' and 'uncompromisingly ugly'.[10]

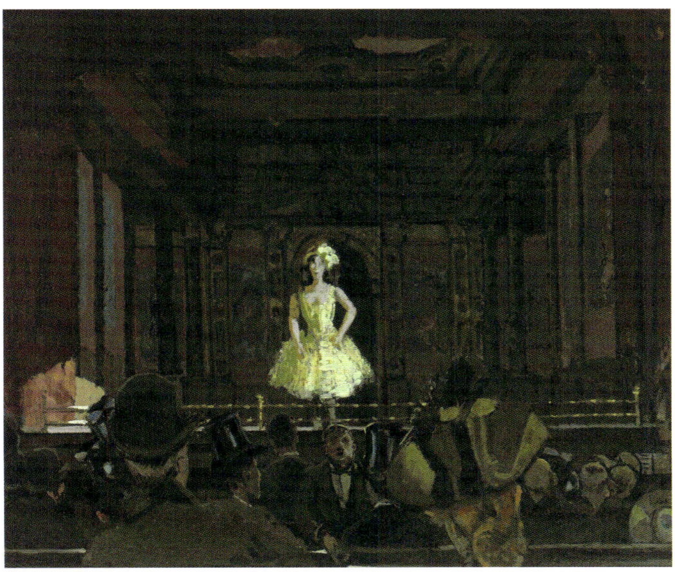

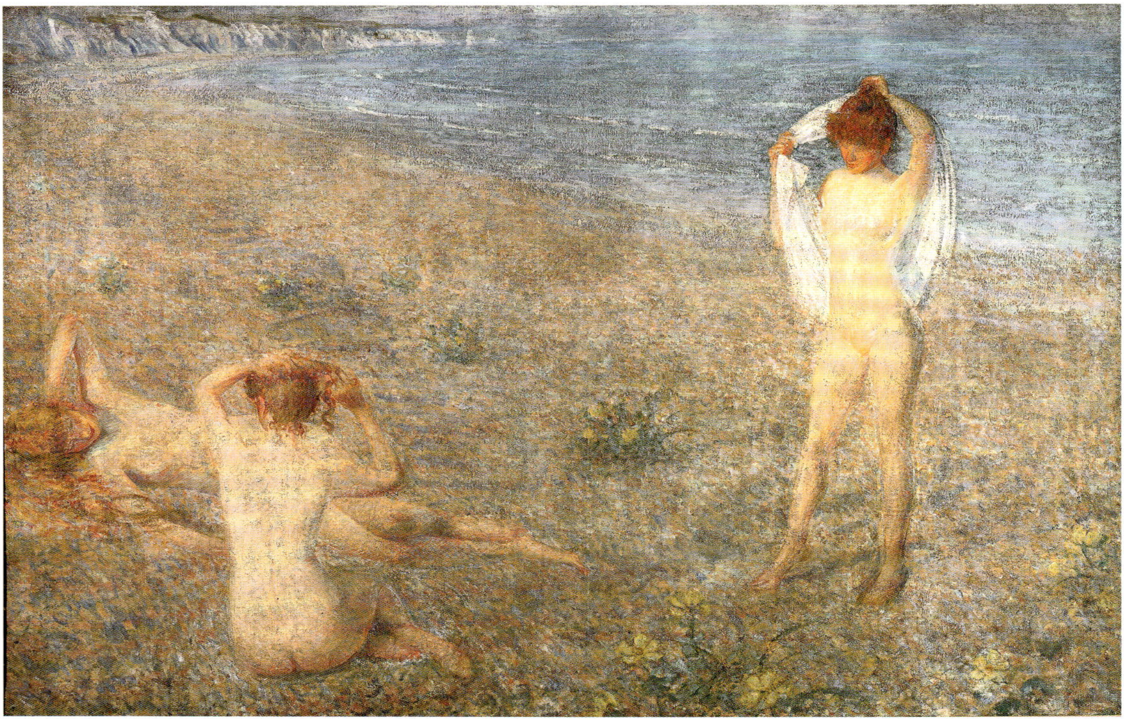

Fig. 23 Philip Wilson Steer
A Summer's Evening, 1888
Oil on canvas, 146 x 228.6 cm
Private collection

The contrast between the almost incandescent stage performer, built up in layered impasto, and the graphic notation of the audience in the stalls appeared too extreme to be believable. For all the variety of the 'hats and fiddle heads', the Katie Lawrence figure seemed wooden and the ensemble extraordinarily formal. A tension existed between full-length portrait conventions, where there was no discernible background (which Sickert admired), and the urgent need to convey a sense of place and time, associated with a fleeting experience.[11]

Having been allocated a central position on one wall, *Gatti's Hungerford Palace* ... was as unavoidable as Philip Wilson Steer's *A Summer's Evening* (1888; fig. 23), *The Magazine of Art's* second example. 'An ambitious work', it 'halted', according to the reviewer 'between a failure and a triumph'.[12] Others found the picture difficult to accept, for, although it could be compared stylistically with Monet's work, in its scale and its parade of nudity, it clearly sought to outstrip him. It was 'Impressionist', but it went beyond the impression. Where Harrison's and Roussel's nudes of the previous year had been safely naturalistic, and therefore believable, Steer's were flimsy. Rather than emerging clearly from their surroundings, they seemed to dissolve into them. He had quite deliberately heated his palette and the effect was summed up by *The Daily Telegraph*, in the following terms:

> Above all, the British Philistine will wonderingly inquire what manner of yellow maidens, with flame-coloured hair, are those whom Mr P. Wilson

Steer (74) has found undraped on a burning beach flowing with streams of molten lava. This is a picture you could warm your hands at, or boil eggs over, and it should be looked at – just once.[13]

Taking his directions to Arcadia from Harrison, and possibly from Seurat, and, like Sickert, measuring up to Salon scale, Steer slipped easily into a conceptual realm, placing him beyond the scope of most other New English exhibitors.[14] Where naturalism and Arcadia were inimical, Steer's heady mix of Impressionism and Divisionism blended his improbable nudes into the shingle, sand and chalk cliffs of the English coast.

The Magazine of Art's third example from the 1888 exhibition was William Llewellyn's *Eventide* (1888; fig. 24), a sentimental picture of an elderly couple sitting in their cottage garden at sunset. Unlike the Steer and Sickert canvases, this work was thoroughly acceptable. 'Just such a picture', the writer remarked, 'as one would be glad to live with'.[15] Llewellyn's path to conventional success was assured; already showing at the Royal Academy, he became an Associate in 1912, was knighted in 1918 and in 1928 became the Academy's president. It must have been obvious, even in 1888, that his future did not lie with the club – any more than Laidlay's, Hacker's, Gogin's or Forbes's.[16] Summing up its three examples, *The Magazine of Art* found the first 'bad in subject and treatment', the second, 'a successful failure', while the third was 'good, sound, healthy work'.[17] Female nudes were marginally less offensive than female music-hall performers.

Such remarks are likely to have enflamed the internal tensions in the club. The visual range of the New English, which had, twelve months earlier, been defined by Newlyn Naturalism, followers of Whistler and a few representatives of the Glasgow School, now had a new orientation. New stars were arriving in its solar system. On *The Magazine of Art's* gauge, somewhere between Steer and Llewellyn, lay Fred Brown's *When the Setting Sun is Low* (1888; fig. 25), one of the most discussed pictures of the year. An elegiac canvas, showing a group of figures by a riverbank, it could easily have lapsed into the poetic greys of Frank O'Meara and William Stott of Oldham. Instead, it placed the brick red and orange faces of country folk against dark greens and blues, creating a surface excitement previously unseen in Brown's work.[18] Brown's reputation, like Steer's, at this point soared. A respected teacher at the Westminster School of Art, he was beginning to supply new exhibitors to the club from classes that reflected the practices of the ateliers and were dubbed the 'Impressionist Academy'.[19]

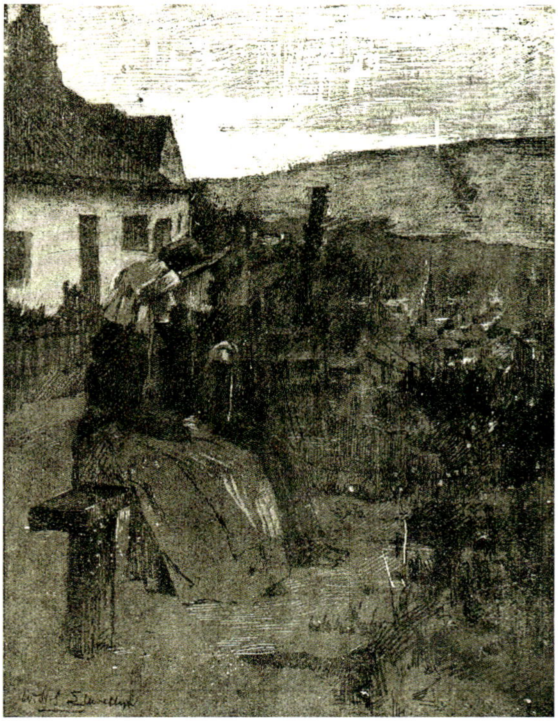

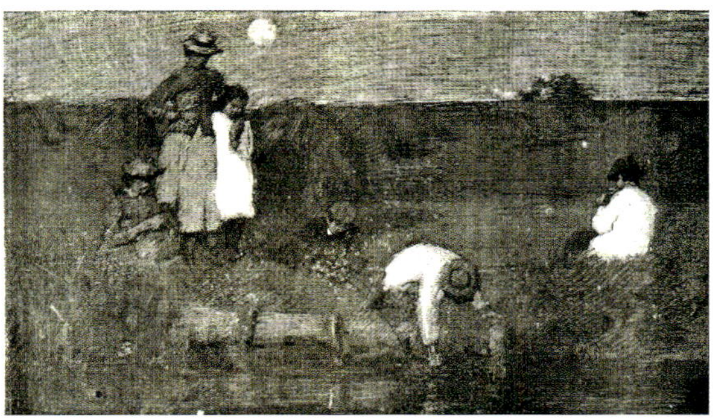

Top
Fig. 24 William Llewellyn
Eventide, 1888
Location unknown

Above
Fig. 25 Frederick Brown
When the Setting Sun is Low, 1888
Sketch, 50.8 x 60.96 cm
Location unknown

Sargent's work was absent from the 1888 exhibition and Whistler, still technically President of the Society of British Artists, was represented only by a small painting and an etching.[20] Solid naturalistic genre painting continued to make up the core and it became Sickert's declared objective to change this state of affairs. In the run up to the 1889 exhibition, clearly nervous about his standing in relation to the club's conservative members, he wrote to Blanche of his intention to maintain a low profile:

> Our friends i.e. the Impressionist nucleus of the NEAC have all advised that *my name must not this year appear* much in proposing and seconding people as my work is said to be most unpopular with the dull but powerful section of the NEAC the people whose touch is square and who all paint alike and take their genealogy I believe from J. P. Laurens.[21]

In practice, this situation could not be maintained for long. He was prepared to exploit a vague constitution to consolidate his position and that of his friends. From its inception, due to many exhibitors living in the country, a London-based caucus effectively managed the club's affairs. Although it had worked satisfactorily up to this point, Brown's constitution did not specifically allude to the composition of such a group. Now with the bureaucratic Bate as both treasurer and secretary and with no office holders other than annually elected selectors and hangers, it soon became necessary to formalise the executive committee.[22] The amended constitution first appeared in the 1889 catalogue and the Impressionist nucleus – Bate, Brown, Roussel, Steer, Sickert – was in charge, supported by Sargent, Alfred Lys Baldry, James Elder Christie and Moffat P. Lindner.[23] Few of the Bastien-Lepage followers had survived.

Simultaneously, Sickert was energetically committed to the progressive nucleus, later to emerge as 'London Impressionists'.[24] In the face of counter-arguments that it was more élitist than the Academy, he summarised the previous objectives of the club and concluded that they were being achieved. This action may have seemed presumptuous to some founder members whose stake in the club at this point was greater than his, had they known in advance about his plans. Nevertheless, the New English, Sickert claimed, was 'throwing open its competition for wall-space to all comers'.[25] There were members who would not refuse to support any new applicant and it would be 'difficult to formulate a fairer or more generous scheme'. This argument was to some extent disingenuous, because a rigorous selection process existed and, given the size of the venue and the number of members and their friends who were likely to be shown, the scope for broader representation was severely limited. As far as Sickert was concerned, this was a positive advantage. When it came to exhibitions, the club resembled 'a small and select private collection' in which each of the works had its own sense of purpose, in contrast to the 'depôts' of art such as the Royal Academy.[26] In securing this exclusivity, it had actually gone in the opposite direction to that suggested by La Thangue. The common purpose of the few now took precedence over the democracy of the many. Underlining the

Fig. 26 G. W. Thornley after Edgar Degas
The Song of the Dog, *c*. 1888
Lithograph issued by Boussod, Valadon & Co., 42.1 x 20 cm
Private collection

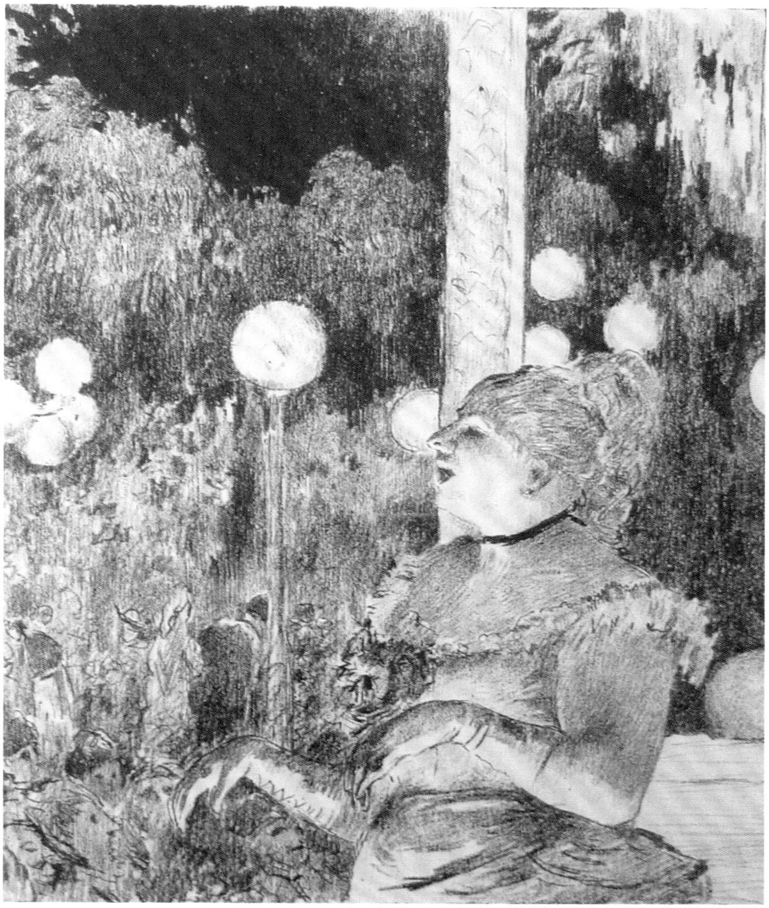

new sense of direction, visitors to the spring exhibition in 1889 walked past a frieze of four prints after Degas by G. W. Thornley (*c*. 1888; fig. 26), photographs of works by Manet and Degas, and prints and drawings by Charles Keene and Whistler.[27]

At the same time, Sickert's *Collins's Music Hall, Islington Green*,a less ambitious work than *Gatti's Hungerford Palace...* rekindled the virulent criticism of the previous year. Accused of aping 'certain painters in Paris [who] have painted music-halls', he felt compelled to defend himself. Stating fundamental beliefs later reprised in the 'London Impressionists' catalogue, he wrote:

> It is unnecessary to go so far afield as Paris to find an explanation of the fact that a Londoner should seek to render on canvas a familiar and striking scene in the midst of the town in which he lives ... I found myself one night in the little hall off Islington Green. At a given moment I was intensely impressed by the pictorial beauty of the scene, created by the coincidence of a number of fortuitous elements of form and colour.[28]

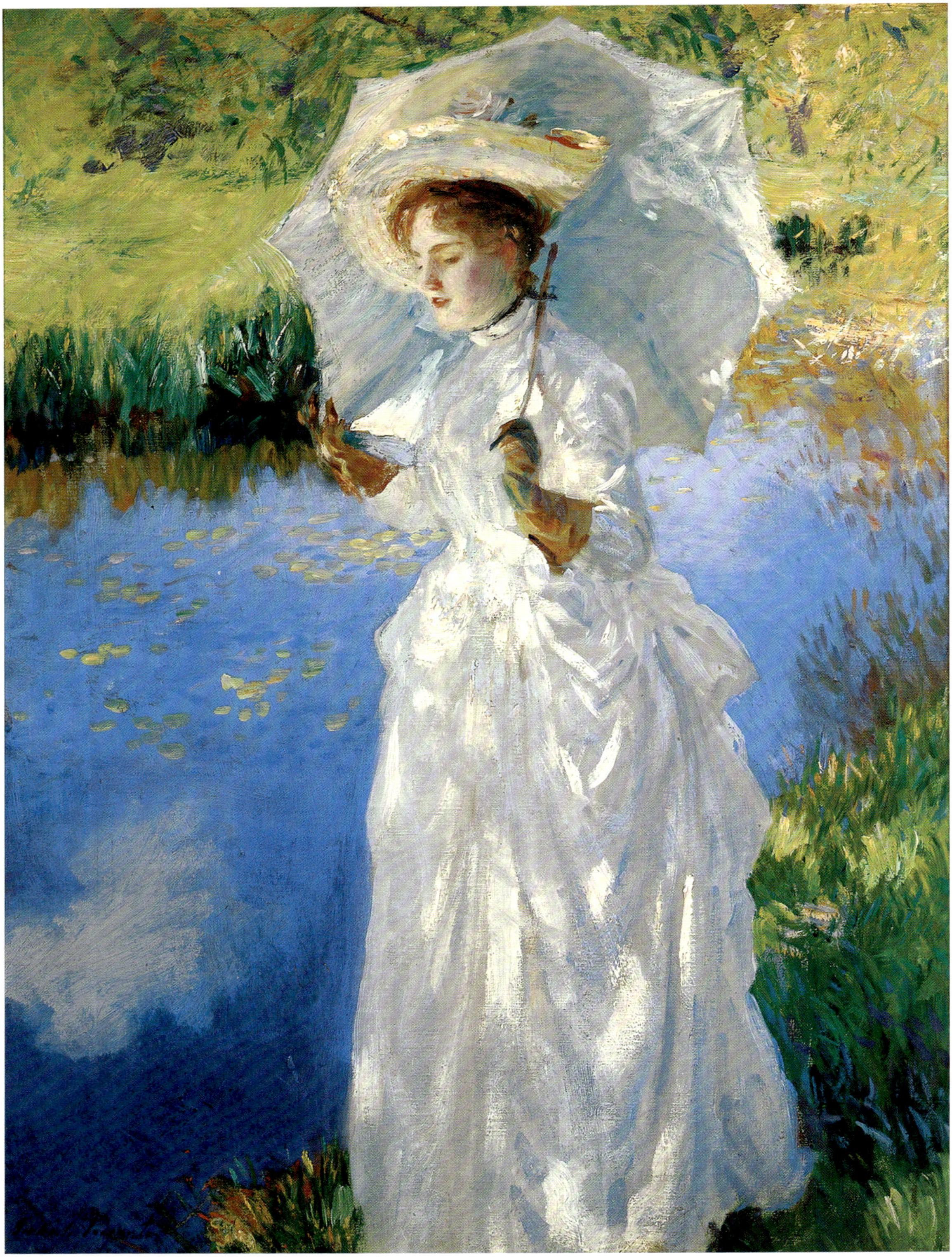

Opposite
Fig. 27 John Singer Sargent
A Morning Walk, 1887
Oil on canvas, 67.3 x 50.2 cm
Private collection

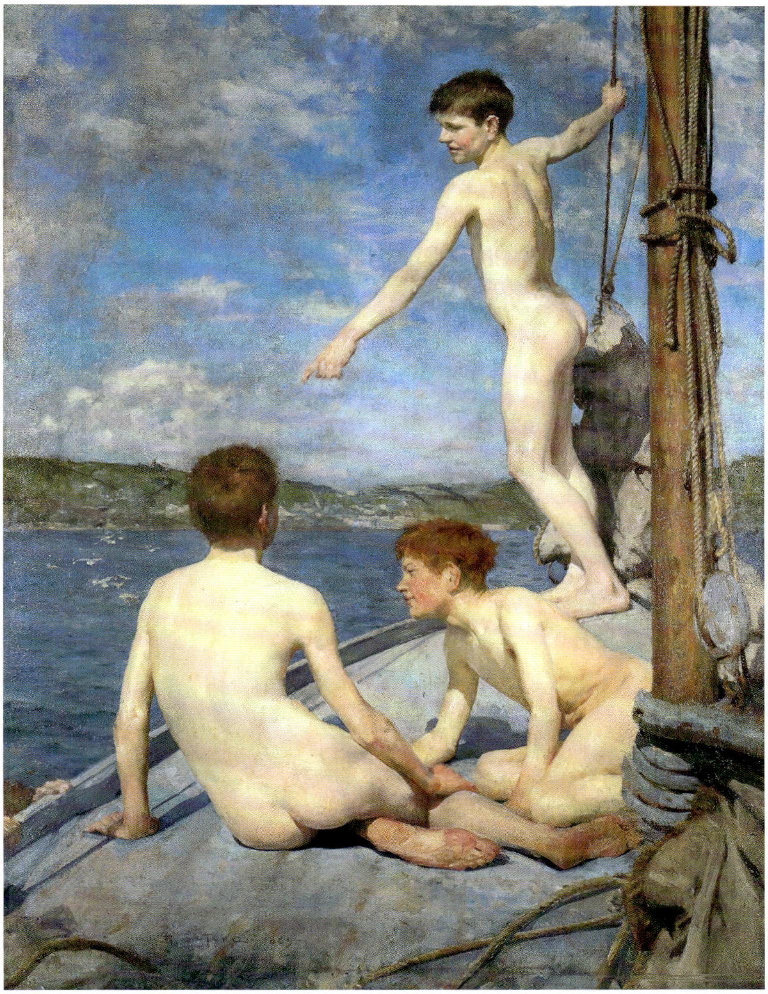

Right
Fig. 28 Henry Scott Tuke
The Bathers, 1889
Oil on canvas, 116.8 x 86.3 cm
Leeds City Art Gallery

This aside, Impressionist highlights of the exhibition were Sargent's *St Martin's Summer* and *A Morning Walk* (1887; fig. 27), two paintings that had obvious kinship with the work of Monet, who was staging a solo exhibition in Bond Street.[29] The coincidence of the two exhibitions made more informed comparisons possible. One reviewer even took the opportunity to describe the walk from one show to the other, ending up uncomfortably in the midst of a 'gang of mutual admirationists' at the New English. The men were 'harsh' and 'impolite' and the women's dresses were products of 'the suburban dressmaker, that supreme atrocity monger'.[30] The pictures were examples of the crazes of the moment, with Tuke's *Bathers* (1889; fig. 28) and Brown's *A Water Frolic* (1889) replaying Harrison, while Starr's *Raffalovich* (1889) demonstrated the continuing importance of Whistler.[31] The Impressionist takeover was not yet complete. In 1889 Forbes showed *The Bridge* (1886), and Elizabeth Armstrong, whom he later married, exhibited a large pastel of three little girls singing, *Three Blind Mice*

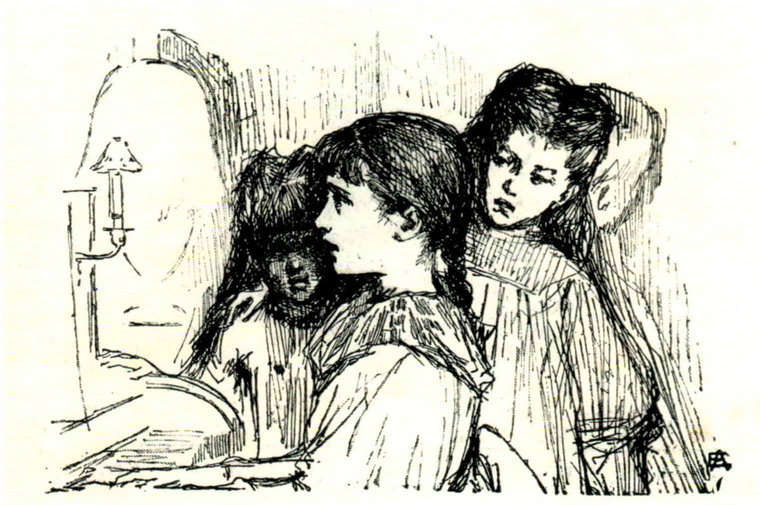

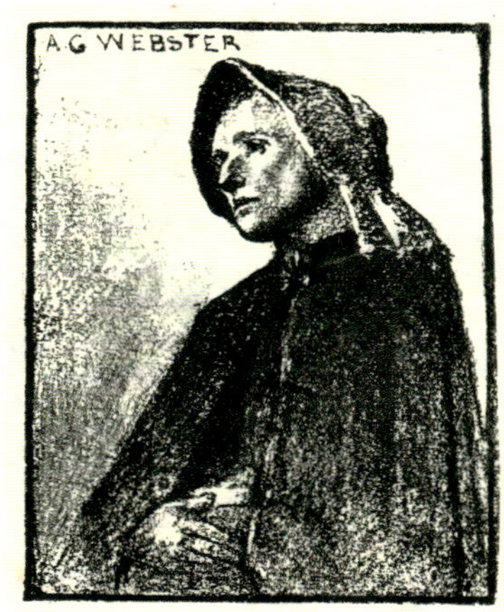

Above left
Fig. 29 Elizabeth Adela Armstrong
Three Blind Mice, 1889
Pastel on paper
Location unknown

Above right
Fig. 30 Alfred George Webster
During the Strike, *c*. 1889
Location unknown

(1889; fig. 29). Social realist subject matter and servile labour were evident in Alfred Webster's *During the Strike* (*c.* 1889; fig. 30) and James Guthrie's *In the Rope Walk* (1888), both of which avoided Kennington's clawing narrative of the previous year. Whistlerian London scenes were represented by Paul Maitland, Alan Wright and others and the year was also noteworthy for the showing of two flower-pieces by Francis James.[32]

However, the appearance of the exhibition as a whole is likely to have conditioned much that was written about it. There were not too many pictures and they were admirably arranged in a light 'most cleverly modified by something that looks like a thing for protecting meat from summer flies which hung under the skylight'.[33] This was a velarium, a muslin awning of the type Whistler had used in his brief reign at the Royal Society of British Artists. More than any single picture, it must have signalled to critics that there was a new regime. If the dominants were 'London' and 'Impressionist', the 1889 New English remained heterogeneous. What it lost in exclusivity and visual coherence, it gained in the catholicity of the work on show.[34] To underline the emergent tendencies, Sickert's group of ten close associates, labelled 'London Impressionists', occupied the Goupil Gallery in December of that year. Supported by David Croal Thomson, the manager at the Goupil, this spin-off show clarified the agenda, at least in so far as Sickert was concerned. In the catalogue he took a loyal Whistlerian line, insisting on the beauty of London and the moral obligation to paint modern city life.[35] Nothing was to be painted merely because it exists, and while its great fanfares were not necessarily beyond the range, the treatment of civic processions by young aspiring, ambitious would-be Academicians such as William Logsdail plumbed the depths of artistic vulgarity.[36] 'Impressionists' looked for different things – their 'great ungainly London' was one of 'nooks' and 'corners which escape the common eye'.[37] They selectively focused on qualities of light and atmosphere, on colour harmony, tonal nuance and discretion in handling. Yet even within the London Impressionists, in his emphatic allegiance to the city, Sickert occupied a minority position. In the end, Impressionism more fundamentally addressed the quality of perception and questions of *métier*. Shared understandings on these issues had an undeniable impact upon the selection criteria for the immediate future of the New English.

In 1890, the club temporarily forsook the Egyptian Hall for 'four sumptuous rooms' in the newly constructed Humphrey's Mansions in Knightsbridge – 'further west than any picture-show had before dared to tread'.[38] It had been noted that since the Egyptian Hall in Piccadilly was used for popular entertainments, as well as art exhibitions under the auspices of the Dudley Gallery, it proved sometimes difficult for gallery visitors to get in.[39] Yet this was not the main reason for the move. George Moore, in his essay on 'Art for the Villa', proclaimed his belief in the need to open up new markets beyond those associated with the Royal Academy. Previous ages had cathedrals and palaces to provide the setting for art, but 'the dominant influence of the nineteenth century is the Hampstead villa'.[40] Artists needed to face up to this demand. With lower ceilings and windows rather than skylights, the suite of rooms in Knightsbridge gave a more domestic scale and more intimate display. The drawbacks of uneven lighting meant that some pictures were easier to see than others, and, while the new space permitted a larger exhibition, not being in Mayfair proved an added inconvenience to would-be visitors.[41] The club was part of the social

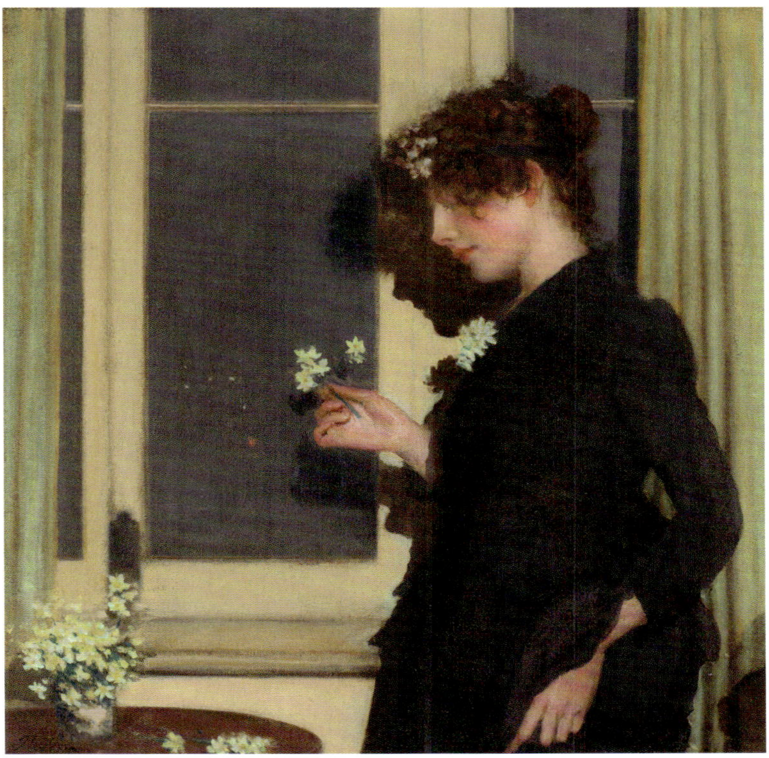

Fig. 31 Philip Wilson Steer
Jonquil, 1889
Oil on canvas, 91.4 x 91.4 cm
Richard Green, London

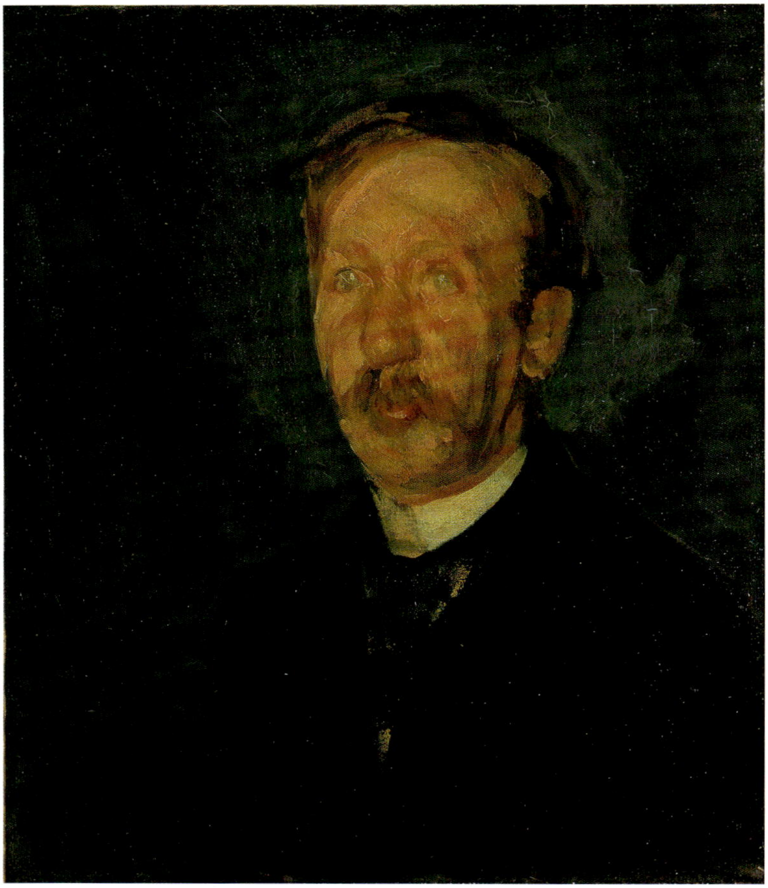

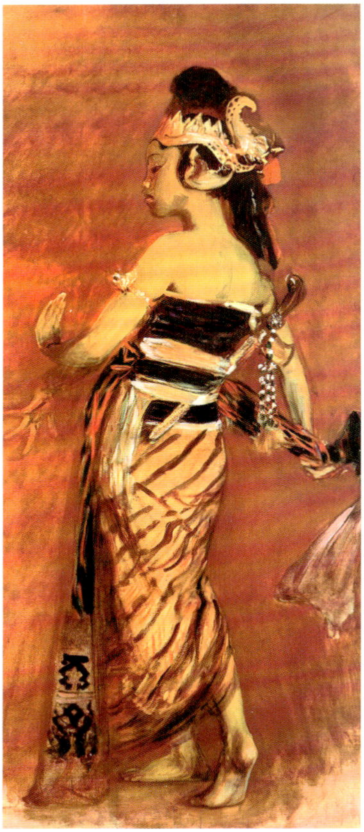

scene. In addition to free open evenings for working men, it provided free afternoon tea, gave smoking concerts and its private views attracted aesthete aristocrats and other London *glitterati*, such that *The Standard* noted:

> Today the crowd at the private view was beyond description. Parties of guests lingered in the corridor, waiting to see some of those already in possession coming to the door to struggle out, and, peradventure leave a foot or two of standing room.[42]

Amidst the excitement, it was evident that Steer and Sickert were continuing in the leading roles. Steer, who seemed to be wavering between a 'Monet' mode, a 'Rossetti' mode and something that was more characteristically his own, exhibited *Jonquil* (1889; fig. 31) and *Signorina Zozo in 'Dresdina'*.[43] Sickert's *George Moore* (1890–01; fig. 32), according to *The Standard*, showed 'the Impressionist in lawless mood' for, although the sitter 'may have sinned against good taste in his novels ... he never looked inane, with sightless blue eyes wanting in eyeballs'.[44] However, as may have been predicted, a perpetual 'moving stream'

Above left
Fig. 32 Walter Richard Sickert
George Moore, 1890–01
Oil on canvas, 60.3 x 50.2 cm
Presented by the Contemporary Art Society 1917. Tate, London

Above right
Fig. 33 John Singer Sargent
Javanese Dancer, 1889
Oil on canvas, 179 x 75 cm
Private collection

of visitors flowed past Sargent's ex-catalogue *Javanese Dancer* (1889; fig. 33) and *Javanese Girl* pictures drawn from a small body of work produced at the Exposition Universelle in Paris the previous year.[45]

Elsewhere there were Whistlerian echoes in Lindner's *Moonlight* (*c.* 1890; fig. 34) and William Stott of Oldham's *The Amethyst Cloud, Jungfrau* (1888). Jacques-Emile Blanche and Maurice Greiffenhagen were much in evidence as portraitists. The Glasgow School was present in Lavery, Guthrie and others, but Newlyn artists had all but disappeared.[46] Sickert, who did not cover the New English show, pursued his vendetta against the 'black monochromes' of Forbes and his coterie in his review of the Royal Academy.[47] Newlyn conservatism stood in bleak contrast to the radical thinking about Impressionism and its emergent markets in a club that walked a tightrope between catholicity and marginalisation. The shows were at once reactive and proactive. They had successfully absorbed the fallout from Whistler's days at the Society of British Artists and recognised the presence of 'out-of-town' groups such as the Glasgow Boys, who appeared in force in London in 1890 in the New English and in what was to be the final Grosvenor Gallery exhibition.[48]

Six months after the 1890 show, the time had come to take stock and Sickert, ever keen to appraise the current standing of a society that had weathered five stormy exhibitions, wrote to the editor of *Pall Mall Gazette*:

> ...the aim of the New English Art Club is to furnish a working model of an exhibition where every work has been submitted to a jury elected by the whole body of artists and exhibitors of the past year.... As a matter of history, the Impressionists have habitually supported the club by sending

Fig. 34 Moffat P. Lindner
Moonlight, *c.* 1890
Oil on canvas, 50.8 x 60.9 cm
Private collection

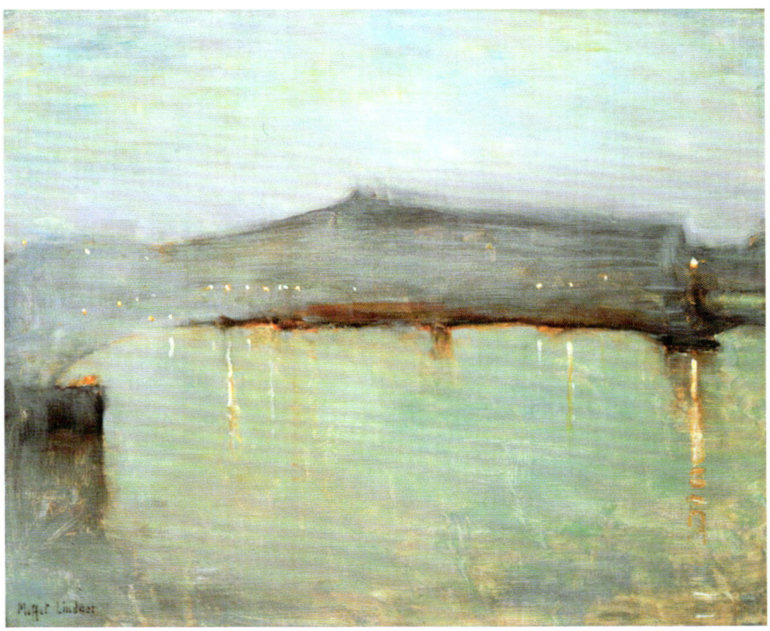

> their most important work ... and by regular attendance at general and committee meetings. The consequence is that year by year they have been more largely represented on the selecting and hanging juries.[49]

He was at pains, however, to point out that works were judged on their merits and not as a result of conformity to a style.[50] He held to a broad church – perhaps recognising the alienating effect his arrival had had two years earlier – but the tone had become more affirmative. The alternative exhibition models, open studios and small group shows were proposed in acknowledgement of the fact that solidarity might be temporary and that, with the club, a more stable institution had been created. The New English required direction, and, as he wrote in his article, he must have been confident of that direction, in the face of the persistent claim that it was dominated by a clique.

Although it had been inadequately housed in 1890, the club had secured its place as a regular fixture in the art calendar. The measures taken in the second year of its operation, with regard to subscriptions and the efficient marketing of the annual shows, created a climate of optimism that began to attract a coterie of private collectors. Alan Wright, an exhibitor who wrote occasional criticism, recalled that year by year the club had changed, 'until gradually [it] has come to be respected and acknowledged by the Press as a serious and earnest, if in their opinion a quixotic, enterprise for the advancement of art'.[51] While this statement may be going too far, there was sufficient confidence for the 1891 Annual General Meeting to approve the idea of spring and winter exhibitions each year. Now that the Royal Society of British Artists, which held winter shows, had reversed Whistler's policies, and the Royal Institute of Painters in Oil Colours remained essentially conservative, there was room for such a venture. Humphrey's Mansions were abandoned and the club returned to Piccadilly, to the Dudley Gallery in the Egyptian Hall.

At this time the New English obtained the services of supportive critics as Dugald Sutherland MacColl took up a post with *The Spectator* and the already sympathetic George Moore became art writer for *The Speaker*.[52] Henry Tonks later recalled that if 'it had not been for the articles signed "GM" and "DSM" we should have hardly survived'.[53] Although they did not always agree, these two formed a powerful alliance that focused upon, but was not exclusively applied to, the club's exhibitions. They were joined by Robert Allan Mowbray Stevenson, an equally lucid, though more conservative, supporter of the new painting.[54] All three had art student backgrounds. Moore and Stevenson travelled to France in the 1870s and both had turned to writing by the beginning of the following decade. Of the two, Moore's credentials were impeccable. A former pupil at the Académie Julian, he had gatecrashed the Impressionist circle and had been painted by Manet. While most of his British and Irish contemporaries spoke highly of the training schools in Paris, he alone was critical. He watched the exponential growth of Julian's in 1880s with a jaundiced eye, declaring that 'all the poor folk that go there for artistic education are devoured'.[55] Stevenson, the cousin of Robert Louis Stevenson, was first a pupil of Manet's rival, Carolus-

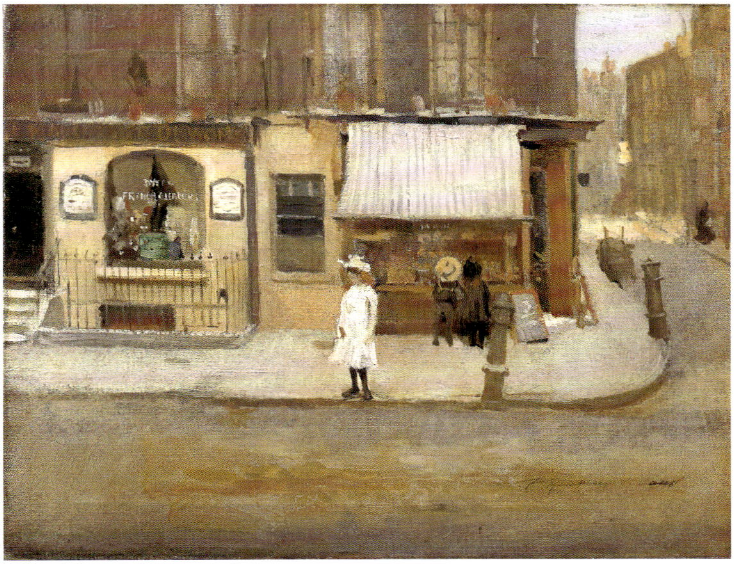

Fig. 35 Florence Humphrey-Holland (née Pash)
Over the Way, c. 1890
Oil on canvas, 40.7 x 50.8 cm
Private collection

Duran, before becoming an early chronicler of the artists' colony at Grez-sur-Loing, of which he had been a part.[56] MacColl's direct connections with the club were more recent and, if anything, more profound. He had studied under Brown at the Westminster School of Art and at this point had his own ambitions as a painter, exhibiting in the shows he also reviewed. Moore and he were not averse to acting in concert.[57]

Brown taught at Westminster after leaving the Government Art Training School, South Kensington, in 1877, and his last few years there furnished the New English with a select group of exhibitors, the most important of whom was Tonks. A former medical student who started with the club in its first winter exhibition, Tonks maintained a regular profile thereafter.[58] His first exhibits were landscapes and it took him a few years to attract critical attention. However, the event that was to have important consequences for Tonks, Steer and the club was Brown's appointment to the Slade School of Fine Art in 1892, to fill the professorship vacated by Alphonse Legros. Up to this point the regime at the Slade had been severe. Commencing with the study of the antique, students at first made line drawings in charcoal in order to achieve accuracy in the observation of contour. On this foundation, a graded process was developed that took the student through the use of monochrome to the notation of local colour. It was inevitable that some stages were given more attention, became ends in themselves and were trademarks of the school. Brown was commended to the Slade governors, not only for his thoroughness in the pursuit of fine draughtsmanship, but also for his 'delightful sympathy which enables him to place himself in the students' position and feel their difficulties'.[59] When he left for the Slade, his adoring Westminster students staged a celebratory dinner in his honour on 7 February 1893, at which 'the New English Art Club appeared in strong force' (see fig. 3).[60] In his after-dinner speech, Brown indicated that women painters were now doing better work than the men, amongst his current crop of hopefuls. Although they continued to be in the minority at the club, painters like Gertrude May and Florence Pash, whose *Over the Way* (c. 1890; fig. 35) was shown in 1891, entered as interesting substitutions for Marianne Stokes and Elizabeth Armstrong, who had decamped. Throughout the 1890s women members gained in strength with the arrival of the redoubtable Clare Atwood in 1893 and Ethel Walker in 1898.[61]

When they joined Brown on the staff, Tonks and Steer found ample opportunities to discuss the club's affairs and consciously mould it through a steady stream of compliant students. If they and their critical friends, Moore and

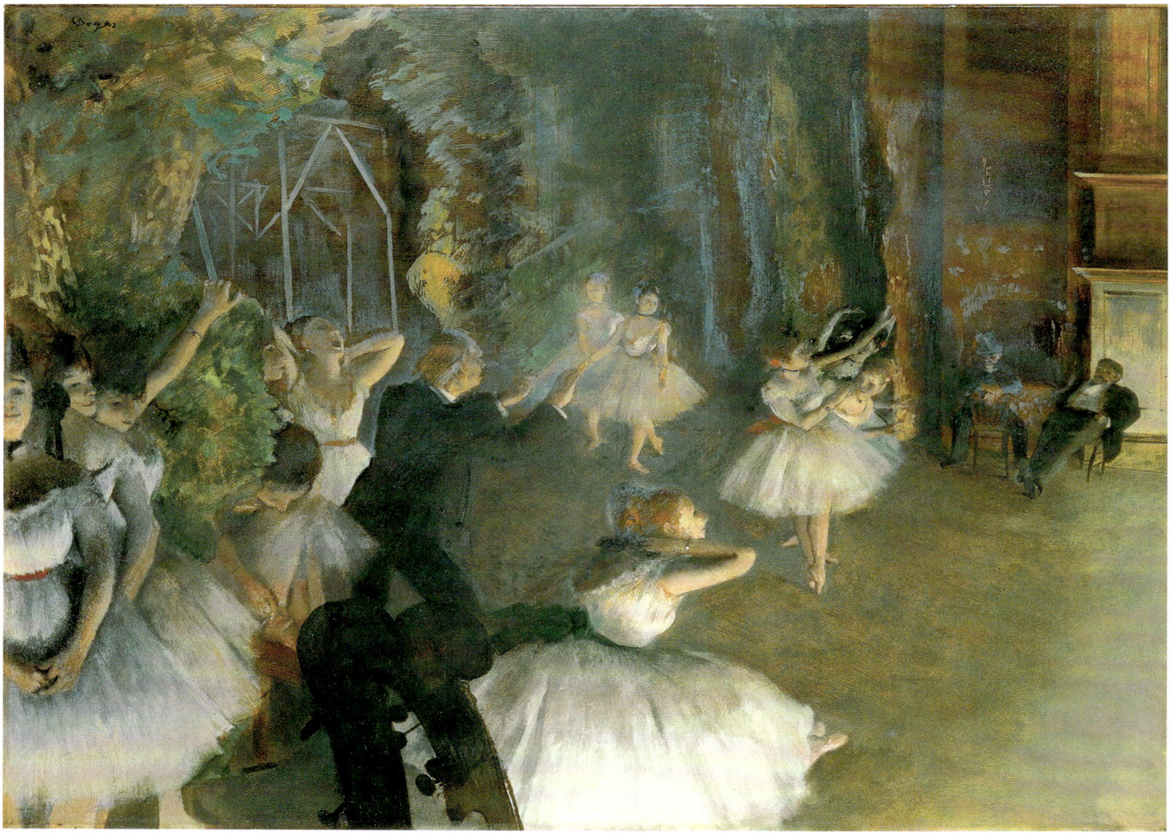

Fig. 36 Edgar Degas
The Rehearsal of the Ballet Onstage (also known as *Répétition*), c. 1874
Oil, watercolour and pastel over pen-and-ink on paper and board mounted on canvas, 54.3 x 73 cm
H. O. Havemeyer Collection. Gift of Horace Havemeyer, 1929. 29.160.26. Metropolitan Museum of Art, New York

MacColl, did not have a concerted programme with a single clear manifesto, they at least knew what they did not want. In his review of the 1891 exhibition, MacColl, with a year's experience, began in a forthright manner.[62] Newlyn had gone, save for a 'pleasing sketch' by Tuke and there was little of:

> Impressionism in the sense of Caran d'Ache's plein-airist who lays his landscape with a pale violet paint, and proceeds to paint what he sees, as he sees it, with such sincerity of temperament that a haystack becomes a three decker.[63]

Nervous about the emergence of an academic Impressionism derived from Monet, whose 'haystack' series had recently been shown in Paris, MacColl's favourites in the exhibition were the works of Steer and Sickert.[64] Both referred to Degas in their current work, indicating the broad agreement on his importance. While Steer proved to be an exception, there was general consensus at this stage on Degas.[65] Moore, as befitted his greater experience, was more critical of the show as a whole. He was anxious to obliterate the last traces of atelier 'plein-airisme' in a group of painters who, though they might have come from the ends of the earth, all travelled 'by way of Paris'. Finding little overall coherence, he declared 'everyone wears a garment of his fancy', while the ballerina's skirt in work by Steer looked like a piece of orange peel.[66] Other erstwhile London Impressionists were similarly treated to spicy approval.

After this exhibition closed, the executive committed itself to establishing the first winter venture, and, to do this, the works of the two most admired avant-garde foreign exhibitors – Monet and Degas – were included.[67] MacColl continued to feel uneasy about the former, but hailed the latter's *Répétition* (*c.* 1874; fig. 36) referred to as *Leçon de Dance*, 'a masterpiece'.[68] Moore hailed the show as simply 'the finest exhibition the club has ever held'. Comparing the Degas to Sargent's *Javanese Dancer* and *Nude Moorish Girl*, he came to the conclusion that the painter, in spite of his virtuosity, would remain a 'superb practitioner, but no more'. Steer, Starr and Greiffenhagen were all praised, while Paul Maitland was seen to be 'in full sympathy with the grey symbolic mournfulness of London' (*c.* 1890; fig. 38).[69] Moore's enthusiasm overflowed in front of the Degas, a picture he knew well. Dating from the mid-1870s, it had, he said, been done as a plate for *The Illustrated London News*, but the paper had rejected it, 'on account of its rectory circulation'. Degas, if Moore is to be believed, had been an early offender of British taste.[70]

Even at this point, the ambitions of the New English were restrained. The pre-Victorian past had to be carefully negotiated. The recent 'discovery' of the watercolours of Hercules Brabazon Brabazon led to his fast track to membership.[71] From the very start of the club, all the debates had centred on finding a British, rather than French, rationale for Impressionism. Brabazon, a watercolourist immediately applauded as the descendant of Turner, was worlds away from the timid products of an average exhibition at the Old Watercolour Society (see fig. 37). He was brought blushing into the daylight at the 1891 exhibition and encouraged, against his better judgement, to stage a solo show the following

Below
Fig. 37 Hercules Brabazon Brabazon
Santa Maria della Salute, *c.* 1890
Watercolour on paper, 15 x 23 cm
Courtesy of Chris Beetles, London

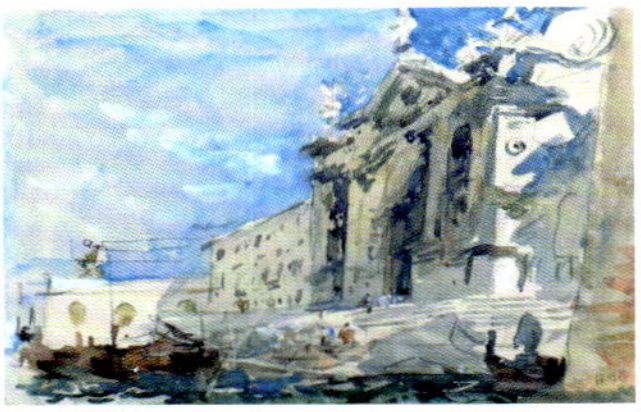

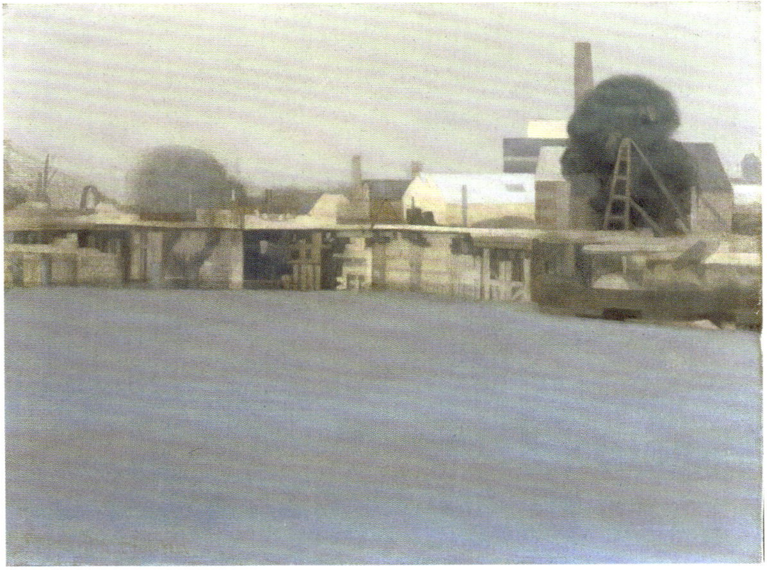

Right
Fig. 38 Paul Fordyce Maitland
Shrewsbury Dock, *c.* 1890
Oil on canvas, 33 x 40.5 cm
Private collection

year at the Goupil Gallery – but not before his exhibits at the New English were eulogised by Moore and MacColl.[72] The effect of Brabazon's inclusion was not momentary. A full re-interpretation of the native tradition had now been licensed.

Given the centrality of Monet and Degas, the insertion of Brabazon meant that the debate about Impressionism was hotting up in 1892. It came through in Moore's selections the following year. When he encountered Edward Stott's *On a Summer Afternoon* (1892; fig. 39) at the New English that spring, there could be no doubt in his mind that this was 'probably the most entirely satisfactory picture in the exhibition'. Stott had shown modestly at the club since its inception, had successfully broken away from the mechanical touch of Bastien-Lepage and had now come into his own. Moore particularly appreciated his observation of sunlight breaking through the branches and falling on the pale flesh of the boys sitting on the grass. A coloured patchwork of light picked out the figures and enveloped the entire scene in 'the silvery bloom of the atmosphere'. 'It would be difficult', he believed, 'to praise this part of the picture too highly' and:

Fig. 39 Edward Stott
On a Summer Afternoon, 1892
Oil on canvas, 56.2 x 71.6 cm
Private collection

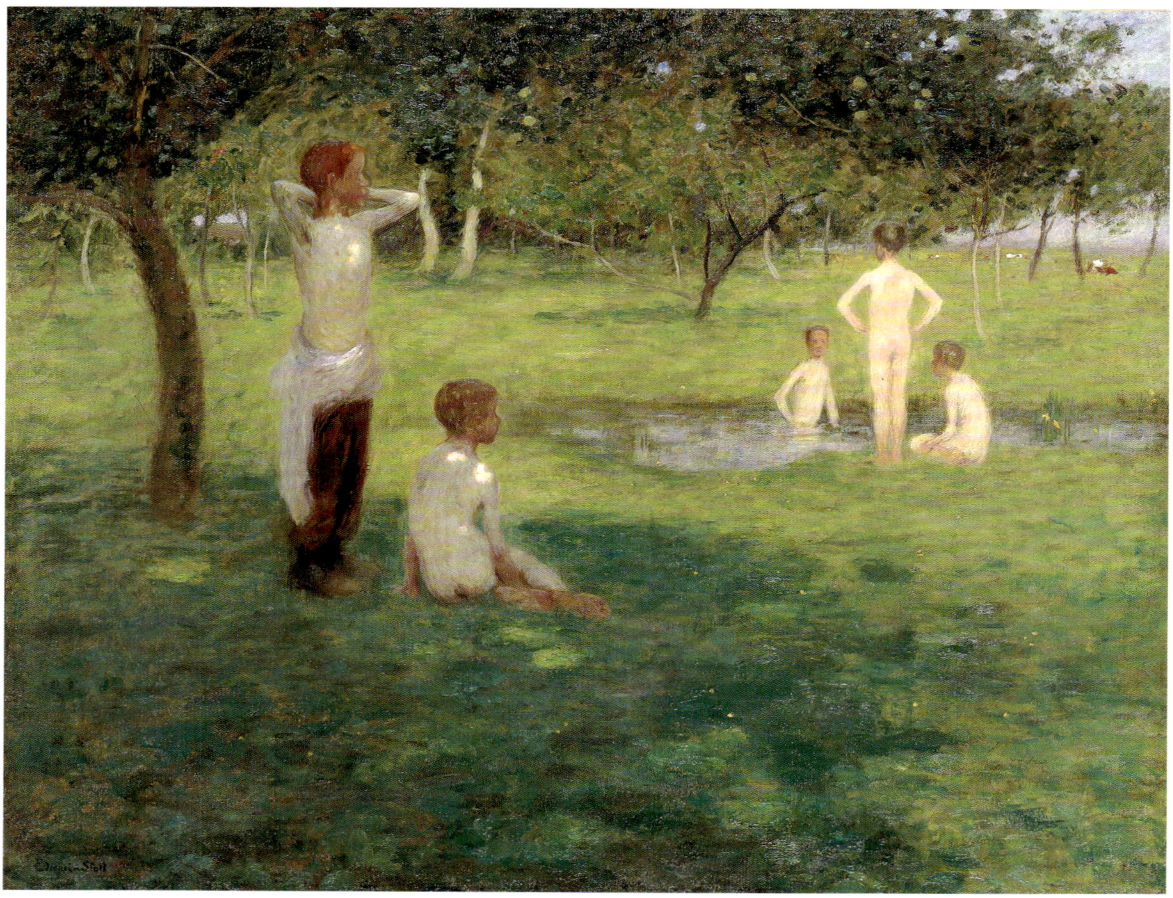

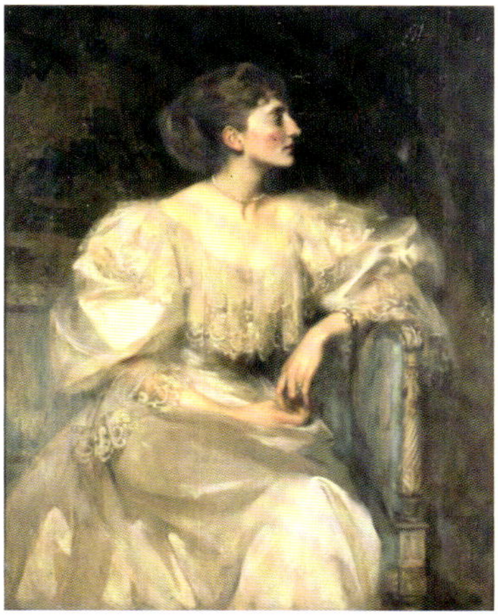

Fig. 40 James Jebusa Shannon
Diana MacDonald, 1894
Oil on canvas, 125 x 98 cm
Brighton Museum & Art Gallery

> The painting of the body is that fluid, limpid execution which we admire in the Dutch masters. The figure is in and not out of the atmosphere.... The painter has achieved something which I have often seen attempted, but hardly seen achieved before....[73]

Moore may have been casting his mind back to the naturalist Arcadias of Harrison and William Stott of Oldham several years earlier. Small, self-effacing, *On a Summer Afternoon* had all of the ingredients of what he was later to describe as visual 'enchantment'. Its action occurs in a spatial envelope which, for him was one of the defining characteristics of Impressionism. It created a total effect, in which there were no discordant parts. The painter had gone for colour harmony rather than the material or surface aspects of form and space. It was clear that, rather than borrowing theories and practices from elsewhere, Edward Stott had arrived at his own characteristic distillation.

When called upon to review the Royal Academy exhibition a few weeks later, Moore underlined his partisanship. Anyone who visited both exhibitions, he wrote, would be forced to conclude that 'whatever art there is at present in England is to be found at the New English Art Club rather than in the Academy'.[74] There could be no doubt that the ambience of the two exhibitions was radically different. That of the club was selective and aesthetic, while the Academy was bloated, brash and vulgar. Social columnists observed that the members of the club were 'good-looking and young' and that their wives, sisters and sweethearts were also 'decorative'. They noted with disappointment the absence of tea at the private view in the spring of 1892. A society reporter relayed this to members of the committee and 'adjourned to an adjacent confectioners with a party of festive souls, where we remained talking about Theosophy until, I am ashamed to say, the gallery was closed'. Someone was quoting from the *Lotus Eaters*, the reporter recalled, as he or she succumbed to the 'enervating effects of Tennyson and tea'.[75] This was nonetheless a new insertion in the exhibition calendar, recently reduced by the closure of the Grosvenor Gallery in 1890.[76] Despite the efforts of the committee, it was a magnet for eccentrics. One man, wearing 'a huge straw hat and brown boots', possibly R. B. Cunninghame Graham, who gave up his seat at the General Election of 1892, 'attracted great attention'.[77]

Such comments continued at the following winter and spring exhibitions, while concerted efforts to refine the content of exhibitions continued.[78] Having dispensed with 'Newlyn', 'New Glasgow' had also gone, and the club seemed to concentrate upon 'New Chelsea'.[79] There was now even a campaign against James Jebusa Shannon and his 'drawing-room following'. To Moore's regret, Shannon had become a painter of 'white satin duchesses', whose wistful looks should be celebrated elsewhere (fig. 40).[80] In the face of this undisguised hostility, the painter withdrew. The effect of these purges would have ensured a more distinctive profile for the club as it approached its tenth exhibition, had not events outside the members' control challenged the integrity of its most revered master.

When the Grafton Gallery opened with its first mixed exhibition in February 1893, it unleashed a tidal wave of antagonism that washed over the club. It contained a work illustrating the extreme effects of inebriation. Having recently acquired the title *L'Absinthe* (1876), Degas's painting caused a level of offence unrivalled by *Répétition*, or any other painting since Whistler's *Nocturne in Black and Gold: The Falling Rocket* (*c.* 1875) goaded Ruskin into libellous prose in 1877. Hissed at in a Christie's sale in 1892, it was now the butt of 'philistine' attacks by critics and by the distinguished Academician, Sir William Blake Richmond, before MacColl and Moore were mobilised in its defence.[81] If the depiction of a ballet rehearsal was possibly salacious, this celebration of the noxious green liquor of the Parisian cafés was a blatant assault upon taste and morals. Following this with a spring exhibition that contained two more works by Degas, as well as three by Monet (see fig. 41), was a risky strategy.[82] Critics other than Moore and MacColl approached the show with caution and some in the club felt that too much had been lost and that too many potential friends had been turned into enemies. More 'catholicity' was needed.[83]

The Studio, a new authoritative magazine, which might be expected to wave the flag for new art, typifies the caution. Under the pen of the aged Edwin J. Ellis, it summarised what the New English had set out to prove and asked where it might conceivably lead.[84] Ellis noted that Sargent 'proved' that 'a sketch of a man's head may be perceived to be a masterpiece when you almost shut your eyes to look at it, while under other conditions it is a wilderness of patches'. Monet 'proves' that he can 'make an afternoon sky look more tender in tone than he has really painted it, by forcing too much blue into the leaves of the trees that partly hide it, and also that a haystack, and nothing else, may be a picture, and a poetic picture, if painted in sunset colours with a free and bird's nest touch, while haze surrounds its russet pile, and pale cerulean hills are seen beyond'.[85] Jean-François Raffaelli, showing for the first and only time, 'proves ... that ugliness has beauty and scattering may well replace grouping, and that a dirty horse, a dirty woman and a dirty dog, all very small and squalid, may fascinate our eyes with delight, even when a cottage roof seems to grow out of the horse's tail, and the dog has only a hind leg and a half' (fig. 42).[86] Ellis and other critics set out to 'prove' that the allegiances of the club now lay firmly with French Impressionism of the most radical kind – citing Monet in particular. This placed MacColl and Moore in an awkward position. It was no longer sufficient simply to argue for tolerance, one had to be committed and discriminating. Monet's three canvases might dominate the spring exhibition of 1893 but they, as 'Degas-istes', had reservations. MacColl declared Monet 'more lopsided, less complete' and he wondered, fatally, what Turner would have done faced with a haystack – concluding that he would have been 'uneasy' about both the composition and the 'awkward' shape of the motif.[87] Moore was, if anything, more dismissive of Monet, regarding his pictures 'as brilliant as they are superficial, an externality and very little else'.[88] This contrasted with Degas's fuller statement and more considered result that, in countless ways, engaged ideas about modern life. Monet's matted surfaces, his preoccupation with colour and light, his 'externality' was avoiding those intriguing situations in the theatre or the café-concert that attracted novelists and social commentators. He was a landscapist;

Opposite
Fig. 41 Claude Monet
Poplars on the Epte, 1891
Oil on canvas, 100.3 x 64.8 cm
Private collection

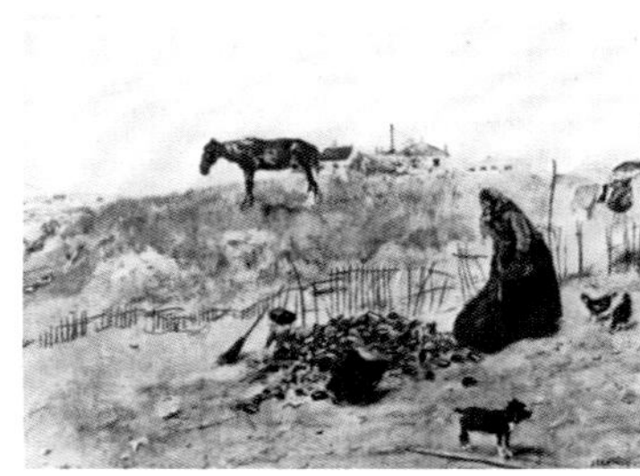

Fig. 42 Jean-François Raffaelli
La Butte des chiffonniers, *c.* 1889
Location unknown

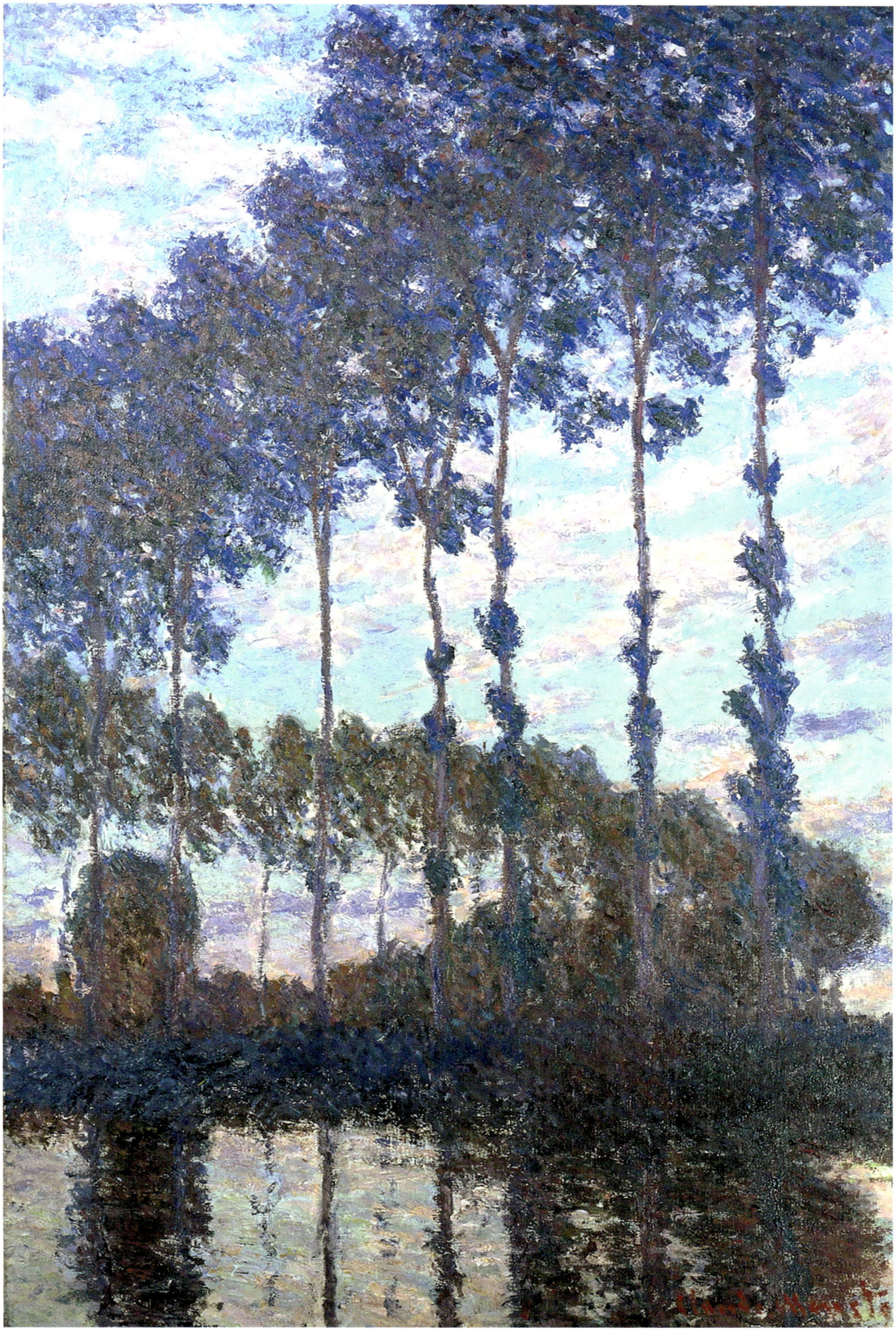

they were city-dwellers. Their opinions, though entrenched and predictable, pointed to one of the essential dilemmas of modern painting.

There were, nevertheless, other games to play. Apart from Steer and Sickert, there were new possibilities in the club that should be nurtured. Moore reported that 'members ... have been discovered reading Reynolds' Discourses on the Thames Embankment'.[89] While he probably recollected Steer's paper on Impressionism, delivered to the Art Workers' Guild, he is just as likely to have been referring to Charles Wellington Furse.[90] Furse's *Portrait of R. Allison Johnson Esq, Master of the North Hereford, on his Horse Bendigo, With his Hounds, 'Gaylass', 'Flourish', 'Spangle', etc.* (1893; fig. 43) represented 'a deliberate return to the pictorial conventions of the eighteenth century'.[91] Yet this young painter was trying to apply modern open-air techniques to what ordinarily would have been done in the studio. His thinking was influenced by Whistler, and, like many of his contemporaries, he looked for Impressionism in the work of Velázquez.[92] With Steer, Sickert and Moore, Furse regarded Newlyn naturalism as 'a journalist's catalogue of facts' and praised spontaneity, intuition and imagination, with little appreciation of chromatic theories of the later Impressionists.[93] When he weighed into the *Absinthe* debate, it was to reaffirm the 'traditions of the National Gallery'.[94]

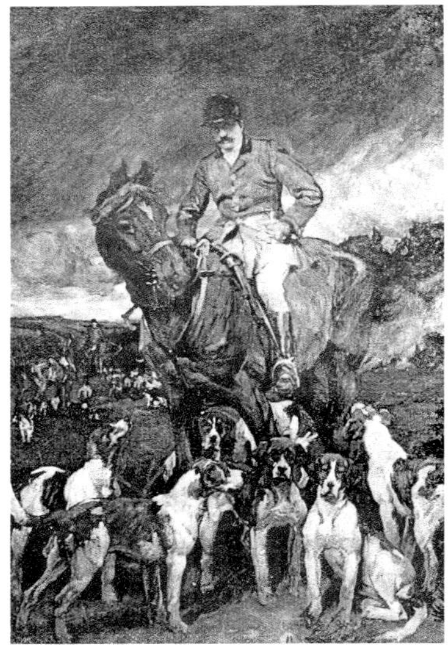

Fig. 43 Charles Wellington Furse
Portrait of R. Allison Johnson Esq., Master of the North Hereford, on his Horse Bendigo, With his Hounds, 'Gaylass', 'Flourish', 'Spangle', etc., 1893
Location unknown

While the result in the Master of Foxhounds portrait proved fascinating, it did not necessarily point the way forward, anymore than the fanfare for Brabazon had done in 1891. The response to the work merely indicated the readiness of critics to justify experiment in terms of what were regarded as the great traditions of British painting. Indeed, as the 1890s progressed, not only did this tendency increase, but also a reverse influence, manifest in Jacques-Emile Blanche's aping of English style, was taken as confirmation of the importance of these very traditions. Paul Helleu was courted for similar reasons.[95] Brabazon's importance more generally confirms the increasing commitment of the club to drawings and watercolours, and while painting moved unsteadily in the direction of Impressionism, there were fewer radical precedents in this area, beyond the legendary Degas exhibits, backed by aphorisms relayed by Moore. This made it possible for Aubrey Beardsley, one of Brown's most original Westminster students, to appear at the club's 1893 exhibition. Fêted by Joseph Pennell, he showed *Salomé* (1893; fig. 44) and *La Femme incomprise* (1893), examples of what MacColl referred to as his 'freakish talent'.[96]

These debates did not stop the development of the idea for the first non-London show of 74 pictures which, balanced with a collection of the work of local artists, was staged in Newcastle upon Tyne. Since the beginning, selections of work from the spring shows had toured to the Autumn Exhibition at the Walker Art Gallery in Liverpool. Unsold pictures might then continue on their way to shows in Dublin or Glasgow, before returning to their makers. The Newcastle venture was somewhat different in that the works were presented as those of the club – or as the *Newcastle Courant* described it, 'The Impressionist School of Art'.[97] Even though Steer and Sickert provoked serious reservations, the local reporter concluded that 'although we may disagree with this school ... there is

Opposite
Fig. 44 Aubrey Beardsley
Salomé, 'J'ai baisé ta bouche, Iokanaan', 1893
Ink on paper, 28 x 15 cm
Princeton University Library, Princeton, New Jersey

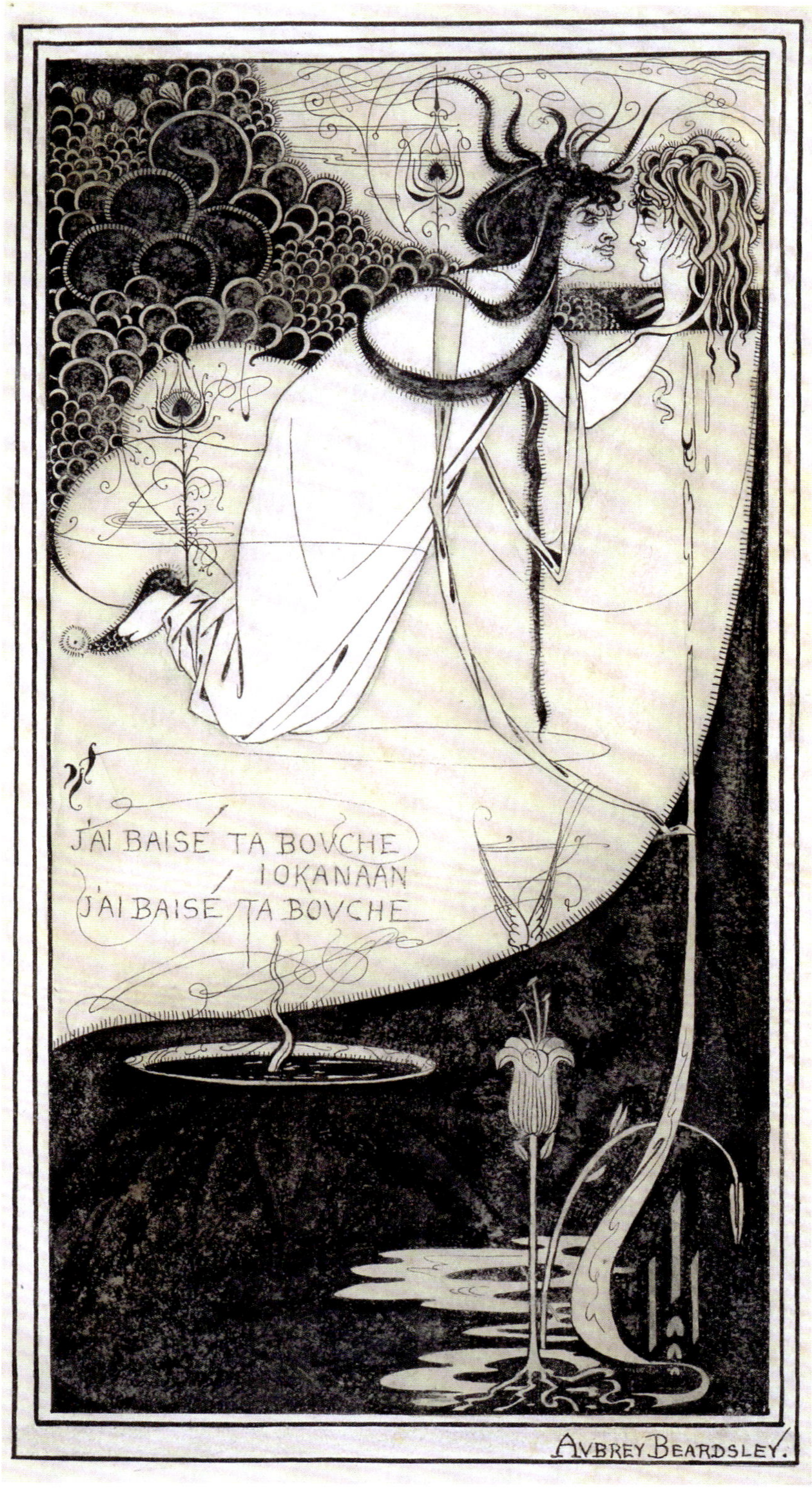
J'AI BAISÉ TA BOUCHE
IOKANAAN
J'AI BAISÉ TA BOUCHE
AUBREY BEARDSLEY

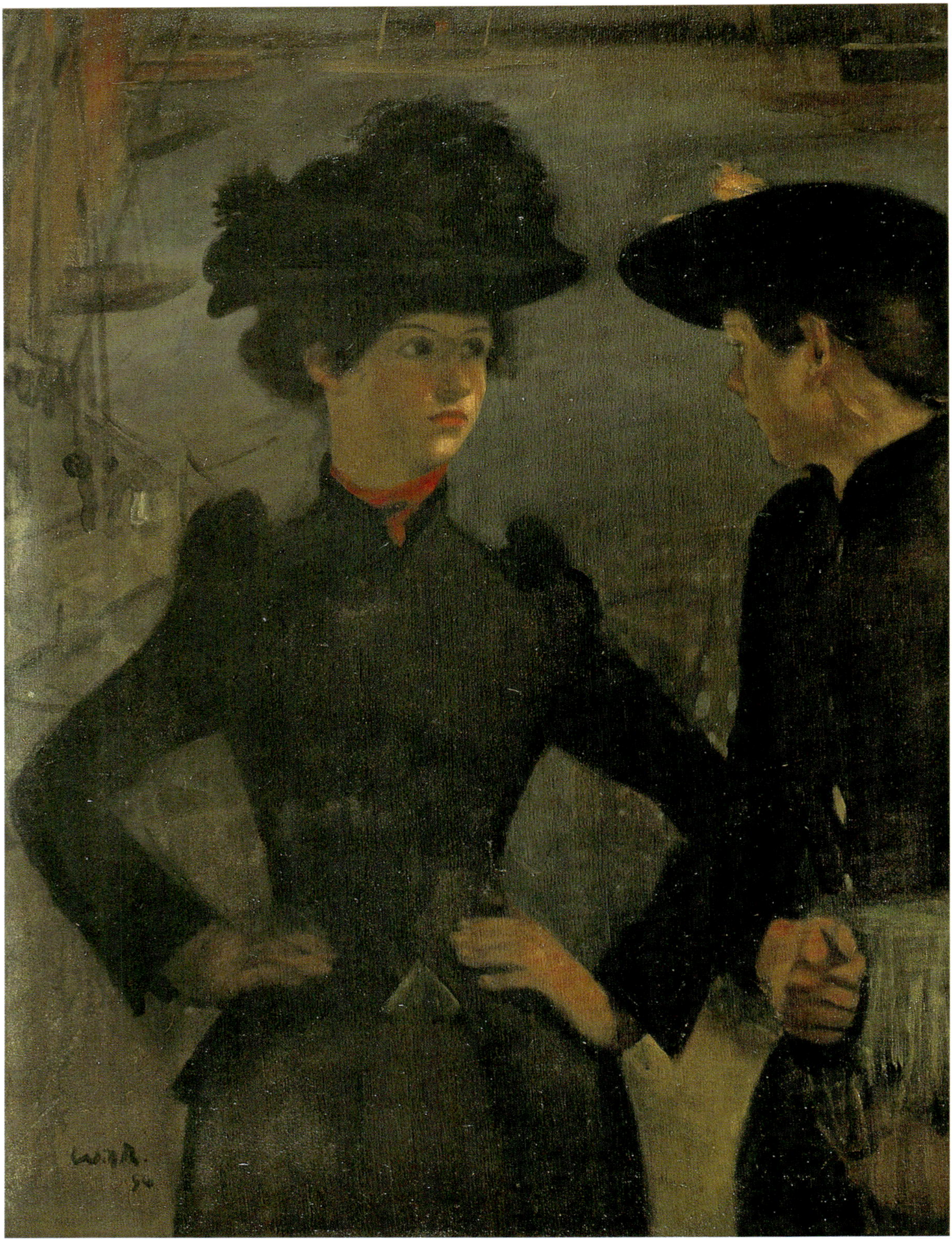

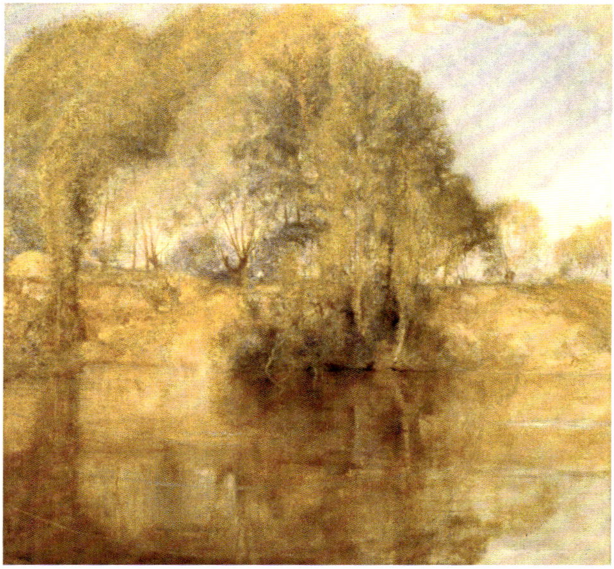

something in it'.[98] The precedent was set and repeated on other occasions as a way of affirming the wishes of members to be representative.

Alongside work by Stott and Mark Fisher, the landscapists, Henry Muhrman, J. L. Henry, Moffat P. Lindner, Buxton Knight and Charles E. Holloway provided much to commend in the club's conservative core. These shows also saw the arrival from Paris of Charles Conder and William Rothenstein. Moore was initially enraptured by Conder's decadence, hailing his exhibits in the winter of 1893 as 'the painting of chlorosis, of consumption, of Bright's disease, of every languid malady'.[99] His hyperbole can only be justified as a result of his having met the dissolute Conder – for Conder's work at this point consisted of pale landscapes produced in the Seine valley and on the French coast that would not immediately arouse suspicion (see fig. 45).[100] Rothenstein drew critical fire for his exhibits in 1894 – firstly with a portrait of Conder, shown in the spring, and secondly with a picture of *Coster Girls* (1894; fig. 46) in the winter exhibition.[101] They fulfilled all the criteria. The first was a Whistlerian full-length portrait, while the second was a slice of modern city life. According to Frederick Wedmore, it showed an innocent 'little doll' accompanied by an older woman with 'a Past'.[102] While such pictures assured the club's publicity, the solid landscapes, overlooked in critical dogfights, represented its core. These works, such as Lindner's *St Ives: Night Trawlers* (1894), Alfred Thornton's *Autumn Landscape* (1894) and Henry's *Boulogne Harbour – Twilight* (1894) were consistently praised, even though, matched against Monet, they would probably have been regarded as pre-Impressionist or Whistlerian.[103] Typically they were regarded as taking forward a distinctly conservative British tradition that had yet to come to terms with Steer, a painter whose Impressionist phase was fully set out in his solo exhibition in 1894.[104]

At times there was, to some outside the fold, a whiff of corruption about a club that seemed to have reduced itself to a mutual admiration society. It had lost what some regarded as its strongest members and its ruling 'clique' was no better or worse than that of Burlington House.[105] Furthermore, their work was symptomatic of decadence.[106] Viewed positively, the club had, by 1895, gone through a lengthy process of refinement. Unfazed by controversy, its regular exhibitors on which it could depend were supported by a reservoir of new talent supplied increasingly by the Slade – a pattern that would persist for the next thirty years.

Above
Fig. 45 Charles Conder
Vétheuil, 1892
Oil on canvas, 97.8 x 101.5 cm
Private collection

Opposite
Fig. 46 William Rothenstein
Coster Girls, 1894
Oil on canvas, 100.3 x 76.2 cm
Sheffield City Art Gallery

NOTES

1 Professor Fred Brown, 'Recollections, II, The Early Years of the New English Art Club', *Artwork*, vol. 6, no. 24, winter 1930, p. 277. These events are quoted extensively in the Sickert literature. See, for instance, Robert Emmons, *The Life and Opinions of Walter Richard Sickert*, Faber and Faber, London, 1941, p. 98; also Matthew Sturgis, *Walter Sickert: A Life*, HarperCollins, London, 2005, p. 152. At these meetings there was much talk of the newly established 'democratic' election processes for the selection and hanging committees, which had to be manipulated to consolidate Sickert's 'progressive' London-based painters.

2 The letter to Blanche indicates that he believed that the club would be 'the place I think for the young school of England'; quoted in Wendy Baron, *Sickert*, Phaidon, London, 1973, p. 22.

3 Sickert married Ellen Cobden in the summer of 1885. He also arranged for his wife's Whistler, *A White Note* (1861), to be shown at the club in 1888.

4 See, for instance, *The Birmingham Daily Post*, 9 April 1888; *The Daily Telegraph*, 19 April 1888; and, while *The Kensington News*, 14 April 1888, declared Degas's 'moral purpose – to show how naughty the ballet really is', *The Times*, 9 April 1888, commented favourably upon 'a marvellous performance in pastel by the French artist, Degas, who, since the death of Manet, stands almost at the head of the Impressionists'. For an account of the effects of French painting at this time, see Edward Morris, *French Art in Nineteenth-Century Britain*, Yale University Press, London and New Haven, 2005, pp. 271–6.

5 In 1888, 127 works were shown, as opposed to 107 in 1887, and 60 in 1886. There were changes in the club administration in 1888, as a result of the secretary and treasurer roles being taken by Francis Bate. Something of a local politician in his native Berkshire, Bate remained in the post at the New English for a further 31 years until his retirement in 1919 (Alfred Thornton, *Fifty Years of the New English Art Club, 1886–1935*, Curwen Press, London, 1935, p. 5). He had refused to take office in the early stages of the club's existence because of its association with a 'dealer' – presumably either Colnaghi or Bartlett senior.

6 For a discussion of what this term actually meant in 1888, see *Impressionism in Britain*, Kenneth McConkey, exh. cat., Barbican Art Gallery, London, 1995, pp. 42–52. The confidence in the direction of the club was reflected in Anon., 'The New English Art Club', *The Saturday Review*, 14 April 1888, pp. 442–3, which stated: 'It began as an exposition of the views of a clique; it now tends to express tolerably fully the revival of art in England amongst the younger men.... There are no bad pictures at the New English Art Club.'

7 For further reference, see Wendy Baron, *Sickert*, Phaidon, London, 1973, pp 28–9 and 302.

8 For a discussion of Sickert and music-hall performers of the period, see Anna Gruetzner Robins, 'Sickert, Painter-in-ordinary to the Music-Hall' in *Sickert*, Wendy Baron and Richard Shone (eds), exh. cat., Royal Academy of Arts, London, 1992, pp. 13–23. Robins points out that the picture was only accepted after considerable debate. Stanhope Forbes, in a letter to Elizabeth Armstrong (Tate Gallery Archive; variously quoted, see Edward Morris, *French Art in Nineteenth-Century Britain*, Yale University Press, London and New Haven, 2005, p. 273), described it as 'tawdry, vulgar and the sentiment of the lowest music hall', going on to forecast that 'unless the Whistler influence is stamped out the club will go to the bad'. I am grateful to Francis Greenacre for giving me access to the Forbes correspondence in 1980.

9 'Art Notes', *The Magazine of Art*, 1888, p. xxx.

10 *The Times*, 9 April 1888; *Birmingham Daily Post*, 9 April 1888. *The Daily News* described the figure as 'a kind of electrified marionette', while, for *The Table*, 21 April 1888, it was a 'hideous nightmare'. For a selection of other reviews, see Matthew Sturgis, *Walter Sickert: A Life*, HarperCollins, London, 2005, p. 153. Sturgis also describes Sickert's infatuation with such performers as Katie Lawrence.

11 The picture was around 1.25 metres high and wider than would be the normal proportions for a full-length portrait. Wendy Baron, *Sickert*, Phaidon, London, 1973, p. 302, notes that the version shown at the New English may be reflected in a drawing published in *The Idler* in March 1895. For further reference, see Gruetzner Robins in *Sickert*, Wendy Baron and Richard Shone (eds), exh. cat., Royal Academy of Arts, London, 1992, p. 15.

12 'Art Notes', *The Magazine of Art*, 1888, p. xxx.

13 *The Daily Telegraph*, 19 April 1888. For *Truth*, 3 May 1888, Steer 'kills everything in the gallery', while *Life*, 12 April 1888, considered that *A Summer's Evening* 'will serve as a terrible warning to all young ladies who bathe at sunset. Any process which is so desperately unbecoming they should certainly avoid'. Of all the works in the 1888, Steer's was the most extensively discussed. The Tate Gallery Archive cuttings volume (TGA 7310.2) lists over twenty references.

14 For a fuller discussion, see Bruce Laughton, *Philip Wilson Steer*, Clarendon Press, Oxford, 1971, pp. 14–15.

15 'Art Notes', *The Magazine of Art*, 1888, p. xxx, declared that W. H. S. Llewellyn's *Eventide* was 'moderate in size, quite and subdued in colour ... is nevertheless one of the gems of the exhibition. The subject is an old one, as old as the happiness of married life – just an aged couple, side by side, looking out together into the perfect peace of the sunset ... just such a picture as one would be glad to live with'.

16 Brown and Bate staged a dinner for Laidlay in 1889 in order to thank him for his support in the first two years of the club's existence. He remained a member until 1892.

17 'Art Notes', *The Magazine of Art*, 1888.

18 See *The Times*, 9 April 1888; *The Saturday Review*, 14 April 1888, pp. 442–3; *Essex County Chronicle*, 20 April 1888. The intense colour and frieze-like composition of *When the Setting Sun is Low* for many critics reshaped Fred Walker's well-known *Sunny Thames*, a mood piece with which it was frequently compared.

19 Brown had begun to teach at Westminster in 1877 in classes that were held in the old Architectural Museum at the corner of Tufton Street. In old age he remained highly critical of the teaching he had received in the Government Art Training system, and took the rigorous drawing methods he had imbibed in Paris with him to the Slade in 1892. See Professor Fred Brown, 'Recollections', *Artwork*, vol. 6, no. 23, autumn 1930, p. 153–4.

20 See note 3 above. Whistler also showed an etching entitled *Grand Place. Brussels* [*sic*].

21 Wendy Baron, *Sickert*, Phaidon, London, 1973, p. 23. Jean-Paul Laurens was professor at the Ecole des Beaux-Arts from 1886 and he also taught at the Académie Julian. For Sickert, uncritical acceptance of atelier practice was no longer axiomatic – if it ever was – and in his future writings he would deliberately praise certain Victorian classicists who would otherwise be regarded as anathema.

22 The early decision not to have a president was maintained. The chair at these committee meetings passed with the votes or consent of those present – as in general meetings.

23 Baldry, better known as a critic, was at this point a painter of sub-Whistler London scenes; Christie, a Scots genre painter, was based in London, as, at this time, was the St Ives school painter, Peter Moffat Lindner. Lindner's early work, like that of Baldry, was Whistlerian.

24 See Anna Gruetzner Robins, 'The London Impressionists at the Goupil Gallery, Modernist Strategies and Modern Life' in *Impressionism in Britain*, Kenneth McConkey, exh. cat., Barbican Art Gallery, London, 1995, pp. 87–96.

25 Following the Laidlay/La Thangue dispute, the wall space was already a contentious issue. In 1887 *Truth* attempted to show that a higher proportion of space was available to non-member exhibits in the Royal Academy and that, far from being democratic, the club was a closed shop. T. C. Gotch attempted to clarify the position in a letter to the editor stating that the selection jury treated members and non-members alike.

26 In the shows around 1890, five out of every six works were rejected. Sickert wrote: 'The New English Art Club is an experiment in the direction of radicalism in the management of picture exhibitions. Exhibitions are hung by juries elected by members and exhibitors of the past year. Any painter who can obtain a signed invitation from two members of the club may submit two works to be considered on precisely the same footing as those of members. I am told that nothing but the financial impossibility of the thing has till now prevented the New English Art Club from throwing open its competition for wall-space to all comers. Practically this is already done, as there are members of the club who consider it a point of duty to refuse their signature to no applicant.... It would be difficult to formulate a fairer or more generous scheme.... The gallery as at present hung presents the appearance rather of a small and select private collection, in which each work has its *raison d'être*, than of the fatiguing depôts which mostly do duty for art galleries in this country. It has, however, the added *cachet* that no private collector can command, since it is the result, worked out with as much correctness as the average human machine is capable of, of the concentrated judgement of a formidable section of the painters of this country.' *The New York Herald*, 14 April 1889; quoted in Anna Gruetzner Robins, *Walter Sickert: The Complete Writings on Art*, Oxford University Press, Oxford, 2000, pp. 34–5.

27 There were fifteen of them, approved by Degas, recently issued as sets by Boussod, Valadon & Co. Charles Keene was particularly admired by Sickert and Matthew Sturgis, *Walter Sickert: A Life*, HarperCollins, London, 2005, p. 167, makes the plausible suggestion that this prelude to the show was Sickert's doing.

28 Walter Sickert, 'New English Art Club Exhibition', *The Scotsman*, 24 April 1889; the adverse criticism of Sickert's work had appeared in *Echo*, 22 April 1889. Sickert did have some defenders, such as Frederick Wedmore ('The New English Art Club', *The Academy*, 27 April 1889, p. 294), who regarded the painter's *Collin's Music Hall, Islington Green*, as 'his last and most successful transcript of music-hall illumination and music-hall character'.

29 Anon, 'Art in May', *The Magazine of Art*, 1889, p. xxxiii; see also *The Sunday Times*, 14 April 1889; 'Real Art Workers – Our Artist Says a Word for the New English Art Club', *Star*, 15 April 1889; for further reference, see the Tate Gallery Archive cuttings volume TGA 7310.3.

30 *Land and Water*, 20 April 1889.

31 Frederick Wedmore, 'The New English Art Club', *The Academy*, 27 April 1889, p. 294.

32 Francis E. James, who first exhibited landscapes at the club in 1888, was fêted by the Impressionist clique at this time and Sickert wrote the preface for his exhibition at the Dudley Gallery in 1890 (see Anna Gruetzner Robins, *Walter Sickert: The Complete Writings on Art*, Oxford University Press, Oxford, 2000, pp. 81–2). He continued showing flower-pieces until 1920, the year before his death. He should be credited as the first committed exponent of a genre that gathered strength in the club with the arrival of Gerard Chowne, Ethel Walker and Clare Atwood in the late 1890s; see T. Martin Wood, 'Modern Flower Painting and its Character', *The Studio*, vol. 37, 1906, pp. 191–203.

33 *Land and Water*, 27 April 1889.

34 *Land and Water*, 27 April 1889: 'There is the same indefinable stamp about it [the exhibition] which marks the school.'

35 For Sickert's preface to the London Impressionists catalogue, see Anna Gruetzner Robins, *Walter Sickert: The Complete Writings on Art*, Oxford University Press, Oxford, 2000, pp. 60–1.

36 Logsdail and his sister had abandoned the club after its first show.

37 George Moore, 'The New English Art Club', *The Hawk*, 1 April 1890, p. 374. This phenomenon – recording London streets, particularly those of Chelsea, Maida Vale and Marylebone – is particularly clear in the work of Roussel and Starr – see, for instance, 'Diploma Gallery of Modern Pictures', *The Whirlwind*, vol. 1, 1890, pp. 72 and 120; vol. 2, p. 120.

38 Alan Wright, 'The New English Art Club', *Atalanta*, 1891, p. 565.

39 For instance, *Stock Exchange*, 27 April 1889, noted that: 'There is one drawback to this young and enterprising society's exhibition, and that is the entrance and exit at certain hours, when the box office of Messrs Maskelyne's entertainment is besieged by a struggling mass, through which it is well-nigh impossible to penetrate in or out.'

40 George Moore, 'Art for the Villa', *The Magazine of Art*, 1889, p. 300, reprinted in *Impressions and Opinions*, David Nutt, London, 1891, p. 297.

41 In 1890, 182 works were shown. *The Magazine of Art* (1890, 'Art in May', p. xxxiii), for instance, noted that 'the rooms are large and low and are lighted only from the side. The result is that only an insignificant percentage of the pictures hung there can be properly seen at all'. See also *The Saturday Review*, 5 April 1890, p. 408, and *The Speaker*, 12 April 1890, pp. 399–400.

42 *The Standard*, 31 March 1890. *The Sunday Times*, 30 March 1890, noted attendees, including Sir Edward and Lady Fry, Sir Hugh Adair, Lord and Lady Ribblesdale and others. The show was supplemented by other special events, such as a smoking concert.

43 *The Speaker*, 12 April 1890, pp. 399–400. Moore held the view that Steer's prices would rise as he became famous and it would be 'well for the first Art patron who takes him up' (*The Hawk*, 1 April 1890, p. 374).

44 *The Standard*, 31 March 1890. It did not escape the attention of one critic that, by painting portraits, Steer and Sickert were 'on the high road for admission to the Royal Academy' (*The Star*, 2 April 1890).

45 The Javanese village with its troupe of dancers and musicians was one of the highlights of the Exposition Universelle. It is difficult to identify which of his large dancer studies was shown. The *Javanese Girl* may be *Javanese Girl at her Toilet* (1889; private collection). See *Sargent's Women*, Warren Adelson et al., exh. cat., Adelson Galleries, New York, 2003, no. 19.

46 The Newlyn painters were preparing for their own London showing – 'An Exhibition of Pictures by Artists Residing in, or Painting at, Newlyn, St Ives, Falmouth etc., in Cornwall – a Collection Illustrating the Artistic Movement Associated with that Part of England', at Dowdeswell's Gallery. According to *The Saturday Review*, 13 December 1890, pp. 676–7, the show only 'gives a number of second-rate examples of the Cornish movement'.

47 Walter Sickert, 'The Royal Academy Exhibition', *Art Weekly*, 10 May 1890, quoted in Anna Gruetzner Robins, *Walter Sickert: The Complete Writings on Art*, Oxford University Press, Oxford, 2000, p. 62.

48 The club had William Kennedy's *Stirling Station* (1887) and Alexander Roche's *Good King Wenceslas* (1887), while the Grosvenor included John Lavery's *Dawn after the Battle of Langside* (1883–7), Guthrie's *In the Orchard* (1885), Arthur Melville's *Audrey and her Goats* (1884–9) and Edward Atkinson Henry and George Hornel's *The Druids Bringing Home the Mistletoe* (1890). George Moore, for whom these young painters were 'slack-baked boys', viewed the Glasgow phenomenon as a temporary return to the mannerisms of the Salon, and more or less indicated that such painting would not be tolerated in future.

49 Walter Sickert, 'The New English Art Club and its Aims', *Pall Mall Gazette*, 3 October 1890, quoted in Anna Gruetzner Robins, *Walter Sickert: The Complete Writings on Art*, Oxford University Press, Oxford, 2000, p. 80.

50 Sickert's actual words, quoted in Anna Gruetzner Robins, *Walter Sickert: The Complete Writings on Art*, Oxford University Press, Oxford, 2000,

p. 80, were: 'No, sir: in spite of much insinuation to the contrary, the Impressionists have neither the will nor the power to turn the New English Art Club into an exclusive Impressionist Exhibition. For such a purpose the formation of groups such as the Society of London Impressionists, or the method of opening their studios to the public for one day a week, is far more suitable and convenient.'

51 Alan Wright, 'The New English Art Club', *Atalanta*, 1891, p. 563.

52 MacColl's first NEAC review appeared in *The Spectator* on 5 April 1890. For MacColl, see Maureen Borland, *D. S. MacColl: Painter, Poet, Art Critic*, Lennard Publishing, Harpenden, 1995. For Moore, see Adrian Frazier, *George Moore, 1852–1933*, Yale University Press, London and New Haven, 2000.

53 Henry Tonks, 'The Vicissitudes of Art' in *Fifty Years, Memories and Contrasts: A Composite Picture of the Period 1882–1932, by Twenty-Seven Contributors to The Times, with a Foreword by G. M. Trevelyan OM*, Thornton Butterworth, London, 1932, p. 59.

54 For Stevenson, see W. E. Henley, 'A Critic of Art, I.M. RAMS, 1847–1900' in *Views and Reviews. Essays in Appreciation, II Art*, David Nutt, London, 1902, pp. 160–74. See also Denys Sutton, 'Biographical Study, R. A. M. Stevenson, Art Critic' in R. A. M. Stevenson, *Velasquez*, G. Bell and Sons, London, 1962.

55 George Moore, *Confessions of a Young Man*, Heinemann, London, 1886, p. 99; see also George Moore, 'Meissonier and the Salon Julian' in *Impressions and Opinions*, David Nutt, London, 1891, pp. 249–78. For Moore's own experiences of the Académie Julian, see also Adrian Frazier, *George Moore, 1852–1933*, Yale University Press, London and New Haven, 2000, pp. 28–9.

56 Kenneth McConkey, 'British Artists at Grez-sur-Loing' in Toru Arayashiki (ed.), *The Painters in Grez-sur-Loing*, Japan Association of Museums, Tokyo, 2000, pp. 48–78 and 255–262.

57 Moore, for instance, wrote to MacColl asking him to review his recent criticism when published in book form as *Modern Painting*, Walter Scott, London, 1893. His first letter notes: 'I suppose you are busy working for your exhibition' and the second, presumably when the review had not yet appeared, becomes more imperative. The review will be 'of great importance' and 'every copy of the book sold means the propagation of our ideas' (MacColl Papers, M632 and M633, 12 August 1893 and n.d., Glasgow University Library Special Collections).

58 D. S. MacColl, 'Professor Fred Brown: Teacher and Painter', *The Magazine of Art*, vol. 17, 1894, pp. 403ff. For Tonks, see Joseph Hone, *The Life of Henry Tonks*, Heinemann, London, 1939. See also Randolph Schwabe, 'Three Teachers: Brown, Tonks and Steer', *The Burlington Magazine*, vol. 82, 1943, pp. 141–6.

59 Burlington Fine Arts Club, *Illustrated Memoir of Charles Wellington Furse ARA*, Burlington Fine Arts Club, London, 1908, p. 53.

60 'Three Cheers for Professor Brown – Notes at a little Dinner', *The Westminster Budget*, 9 February 1893.

61 Pash, later Mrs Florence Humphrey-Holland, showed at the club until 1904, returning in 1945 and 1948. She was accompanied in 1891 and 1892 by Mrs Cyprian Williams and by Gertrude May – the latter a favourite of George Moore. Atwood's career with the club continued unbroken until 1956. Although the club remained male dominated until the early years of the twentieth century, notable painters like Alice Fanner, Mary Hogarth and Jean Inglis joined with Ethel Walker in the late 1890s.

62 While he wrote, MacColl also painted, and he started to exhibit at the club in spring of 1892.

63 Tuke's sketch was *Reefing the Mainsail, A Sketch at Sea* (1891; 54). D. S. MacColl, *The Spectator*, 10 April 1891, pp. 544–5.

64 D. S. MacColl, *The Spectator*, 10 April 1891, pp. 544–5. Steer's *Ballerina Absoluta* (1890–1) was, for instance, 'an eccentric specimen' and a 'very large joke', while Sickert's *Dieppe* (1890–1) was 'positively charming'.

65 Elie Halévy, who visited the key members of the group at MacColl's house in November 1890, noted that Degas, through Moore, 'ruled' over the group. See Adrian Frazier, *George Moore, 1852–1933*, Yale University Press, London and New Haven, 2000, p. 208.

66 G. M., 'The New English Art Club', *The Speaker*, 18 April 1891, pp. 460–1. Moore criticised the painters for chasing superficial Parisian tricks of the moment. 'In the New English Art Club we look in vain for national characteristics – for a guiding principle; instead of a well-ordered regiment, animated by a well-considered aestheticism, marching to a definite goal, we have a crowd of stragglers, running and leaping, loitering and larking, walking and sitting down to rest. Everyone wears a garment of his fancy, and a multi-coloured, ill-organised crowd they are. They might have come from the various ends of the earth, provided they had come by way of Paris, and sign of a sojourn in that city is the family likeness which runs through this group of painters.' Steer's work was a strange upright composition entitled *Ballerina Absoluta*.

67 Monet was represented by two works, courtesy of Sargent, *Early Spring* (53) and *Orange and Lemon Trees* (also known as *Gardener's House*; 1884; 65).

68 D. S. M., 'Impressionism and the New English Art Club', *The Spectator*, 5 December 1891, p. 809, refers specifically to works by Monet and Degas on display. Monet was an 'experimentalist', and analyst of 'the force and vibrating colour of sunlight'. One of his pictures would be 'more in place in some museum of painting research than in a gallery of pictures'. On Degas, however, he was much more positive, stating that: 'There might be a question, indeed, to those who can only feel on sure terms with things baptised beautiful by antiquity, or safe-conducted by an acceptable subject; but for those who take beauty wherever it is to be found, and with a keener pleasure when it is neighboured by the common, or dissembled in the seeming trivial, here is a pleasure indeed ... for incredible fineness of drawing and sense of relation, here a bit finished to the finger-nails, there a form lost and surmised in the dusty air and light of the stage; for keenness of vision and strength of memory the most momentary and elusive – for all these qualities, the picture is a triumph.' For reference to this particular work, see *Degas*, Jean Sutherland Boggs et al., exh. cat., Metropolitan Museum of Art, New York, 1988, pp. 227–9.

69 G. M., 'The New English Art Club', *The Speaker*, 5 December 1891, pp. 676–8.

70 This picture had come to Britain before April 1876 and was acquired by Captain Henry Hill of Brighton. It was purchased by Walter Sickert on his wife's behalf in May 1889, when it was entitled *Répétition*.

71 He was proposed by Steer and Francis James.

72 In reviewing his exhibition, Moore noted that 'the sketch he exhibits at the New English Art Club is a singularly beautiful tint of rose, spread with delicate grace over the paper.... It was his genius not to see things – to leave out the drawing is better than to fumble with it, and all his life he has done this'. Quoted from C. Lewis Hind, *Hercules Brabazon Brabazon, 1821–1906: His Art and Life*, George Allen and Co, London, 1912, pp. 99–100.

73 G. M., 'The New English Art Club', *The Speaker*, 16 April 1892, p. 467.

74 G. M., 'The New English Art Club and the Academy', *The Speaker*, 21 May 1892, pp. 616–7.

75 *Westminster Times*, 15 April 1892; see also *Black and White*, 16 April 1892.

76 Winter exhibitions of current art were not unusual at this point, although larger galleries reserved this period for loan exhibitions of old masters. The New Gallery, at the time of its formation in 1888, had taken some of the most important Grosvenor exhibitors for its spring shows. In the 1890s, like the Royal Academy, it staged important Old Master loan exhibitions. The Grafton Gallery, which opened in February 1893, had a similar profile.

77 *Westminster Times*, 15 April 1892.

78 See, for instance, the *Court Journal*, 26 November 1892, while, on the same day, *Land and Water*, noted: 'Composed as the club is almost exclusively of young men of some social standing, whose tailors live in or near Bond Street, and whose artistic tastes have found their highest manifestation in their selection of singularly beautiful women for wives, their privy peep is an exceedingly pleasant function. But the young gentlemen of the club are mostly wits and critics first, and artists and painters after, and the room rang with pleasant "chaff".'

79 See *Land and Water*: 'Newlyn and all that it contains were expelled years ago. New Glasgow, to my infinite regret, receives the next black ball. And now even the inner circle of New Chelsea is taught to recognize that the club is on the march.'

80 G. M., 'The New English Art Club', *The Speaker*, 26 November 1892, pp. 645–6, wrote, 'the rejection of Mr Shannon's portraits will probably cost the club four guineas a year, the amount of his subscription, and it will probably lose the club the visits of his numerous drawing room following.... Either way we may or we may not have a gallery from which popular painting is excluded. I think we should: but I know that Academicians and dealers are in favour of enforced prostitution in art. That men should practice painting for mere love of paint is wholly repugnant to every healthy-minded Philistine'.

81 When Alfred Thornton, a member of the MacColl circle at the time, serialised his 'Diary of an Art Student of the Nineties' in *The Artist*, 1934–5, he provoked a letter from Arthur Kay, the picture's owner in 1892–3 (vol. 9, no. 2, April 1935, p. 54). Both accounts were subsequently published; see Alfred Thornton, *Diary of an Art Student of the Nineties*, London, 1938, pp. 22–33; Arthur Kay, *Treasure Trove in Art*, Edinburgh and London, 1939, pp. 27–30. For a selection of hostile reviews and the responses of MacColl and Moore, see Kate Flint (ed.), *Impressionists in England, The Critical Reception*, London, 1984, pp. 279–296.

82 Monet showed examples from his *Poplars, Haystacks* and *Creuse Valley* series. Degas showed *Design for a Fan* (3) and *Au Café Concert* (31), priced at £150.

83 *The Pall Mall Budget*, 20 April 1893; see also *The Art Journal*, 1893, p. 158; *The Saturday Review*, 15 April 1893, p. 403.

84 Ellis, a painter of an earlier generation and regular exhibitor at the RBA since the late 1860s, was deputed to review the Dudley Gallery for *The Studio*, while Francis Bate, NEAC secretary, reviewed the New Gallery, the acknowledged descendant of the Grosvenor Gallery in the same issue.

85 *The Studio*, vol. 1, 1893, pp. 79–80.

86 This was *La Butte des chiffoniers* (untraced) from *Les Types de Paris*, 1889. A loosely related but not identical work is contained in the National Gallery of Canada, Ottawa.

87 D. S. M., 'The New English Art Club and the Meissonier Exhibition', *The Spectator*, 22 April 1893, pp. 523–4. 'In the poplar picture, it is true, he has conceived a very grand arrangement; but in detail the composition is marred by harshness. In the haystack picture, again, what he has succeeded in rendering with rare justice and beauty is the colour-value of the haystack against the distance, and the dead-blue distance against the dark primrose and flushed orange and rose of the sky. No one probably has ever done it so well. Turner, who perhaps set him on the track, is left behind; compared with the unity of effect, the *Téméraire* splits into arbitrary lights, false values and crude colour ... but Turner would have been uneasy over the composition of forms in the haystack picture. He would hardly have allowed so awkward a shape to call attention to itself ... it would be absurd to say that there is no drawing in Monet ... but delicacies of contour are not to be found in him; all his handling goes to build up colour with the utmost life and brilliancy in it.'

88 G. M., 'The New English Art Club', *The Speaker*, 15 April 1893, pp. 422–3.

89 Ibid.

90 D. S. MacColl, *The Life Work and Setting of Philip Wilson Steer*, Faber and Faber, London, 1945, p. 177.

91 G. M., 'The New English Art Club', *The Speaker*, 5 April 1893, pp. 422–3.

92 Kenneth McConkey, 'The Theology of Painting – The Cult of Velazquez and British Art at the Turn of the Twentieth Century', *Visual Culture in Britain*, vol. 6, no. 2, 2005, pp. 189–205.

93 C. W. Furse, 'Impressionism – What it Means', *Albemarle Magazine*, August 1892; quoted from Anon., [D. S. MacColl], *Illustrated Memoir of Charles Wellington Furse ARA*, Burlington Fine Arts Club, London, 1908, p. 48.

94 Charles W. Furse, 'The Grafton Gallery. A Summary', *The Studio*, vol. 1, 1893, p. 33.

95 Helleu showed two drypoints in 1892 and *La Fontaine de Latone, Versailles*, in 1894.

96 Joseph Pennell, 'A New Illustrator: Aubrey Beardsley', *The Studio*, vol. 1, no. 1, pp. 14–19; D. S. M., 'The New English Art Club and the Meissonier Exhibition', *The Spectator*, 22 April 1893, p. 524. MacColl praised Beardsley's 'fancy and designing power' and concluded: 'He is a prodigy of appreciation and manner, and, when he has digested Burne-Jones and the Japanese and Schwabe, ought to do good work.'

97 The Newcastle show was carefully timed for the months of July and August and it therefore did not clash with the more important provincial shows.

98 *Newcastle Courant*, 29 July 1893, p. 5. I am grateful to Laura Newton for tracing this review for me.

99 G. M., 'The New English Art Club', *The Speaker*, 25 November 1893, pp. 582–3.

100 Conder had shown for the first time in the previous spring. In addition to his manner, Moore may well have been impressed by his exploits in Paris and his recent trip to Algiers as the companion of the French aristocrat, Henry de Vallombreuse. See Ann Galbally, *Charles Conder: The Last Bohemian*, Meigunyah Press, Melbourne, 2002, pp. 89–95.

101 Like Conder, Rothenstein had started exhibiting in the spring exhibition of 1893. His exhibits mentioned here are *L'Homme qui sort*, dating from 1894 (91), and *Coster Girls*, from 1894 (89).

102 Frederick Wedmore, 'The New English Art Club', *The Studio*, vol. 4, 1894, pp. 71–5. Degas, whose work was not shown in 1894, was, nevertheless, there in spirit in Marcellin Desboutin's portrait etching of the painter, executed in 1895 (32).

103 G. M., 'The New English Art Club', *The Speaker*, 14 April 1894, p. 417. See also Frederick Wedmore, 'The New English Art Club', *The Studio*, vol. 4, 1894, pp. 71–5.

104 Steer's first solo exhibition was staged at the Goupil Gallery in February 1894. See Bruce Laughton, *Philip Wilson Steer*, Clarendon Press, Oxford, 1971, pp. 49–57.

105 Anon., 'The New English Art Club', *The Saturday Review*, 14 April 1895, pp. 505–6.

106 Hubert Crankanthorpe, 'Reticence in Literature, Some Roundabout Remarks', quoted from *The Yellow Book – A Selection*, London, n.d., p. 101. Crankanthorpe declares: 'The language of the coster and cadger resound in our midst, and, though Velasquez tried to paint like Whistler, Rudyard Kipling cannot write like Pope. And a weird word has been invented to explain the whole business. Decadence, decadence: you are all decadent nowadays. Ibsen, Degas, and the New English Art Club; Zola, Oscar Wilde and the Second Mrs Tanqueray.'

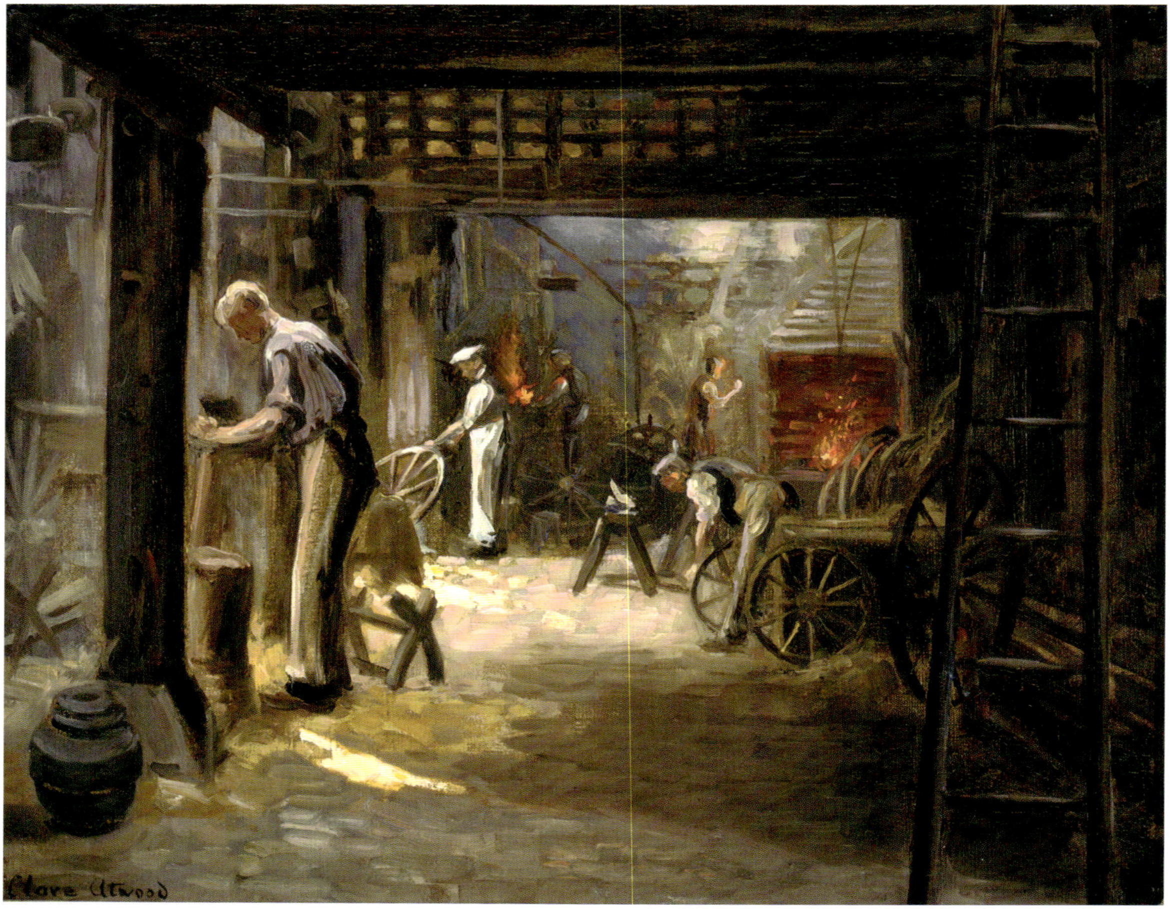

Fig. 47 Clare Atwood
Interior of the Coach-Wheelwright's Shop at 4 Marshall Street, Soho, c. 1897
Oil on canvas, 46.6 x 50 cm
Museum of London

CHAPTER 3

'The public no longer giggles' 1895–1905

In Brown, Steer and Tonks a powerful alliance was forged between the centre of innovative art teaching and the controlling group of the New English. The Slade curriculum placed great emphasis on Raphaelesque traditions of drawing, the painterly realism of Velázquez in portraiture and John Constable in landscape painting. The students Brown imported from Westminster were eclipsed by those of the late 1890s generation of painters, who included Clare Atwood (see fig. 47), Gwen John, Augustus John, William Orpen, Ambrose McEvoy, Albert Rutherston and Edna Clarke Hall.[1] In these years the young Roger Fry was also a keen exhibitor.

All saw their natural outlet in the twice-yearly New English exhibitions. In their early work these artists, prompted by Tonks, at first sought to revive narrative painting, before, in John's case, developing a new decorative approach to landscape. Before their arrival, anxieties about the future of the club were already being expressed. 'What is the clientele of the New English Art Club at the moment?' asked the art critic Frederick Wedmore in 1896. His answer was simple – a few worldly types, 'the professed adherents of two or three intelligent sects'.[2] The club's coterie of collectors, which, by 1900, included Hugh Hammersley, Augustus Daniel, Judge Evans and Geoffrey Blackwell, were lawyers, bankers and publishers who remained loyal to Steer and Tonks throughout the Edwardian years and purchased Muirheads, Chownes and Russells on their advice. From an artist's point of view, the speculative aspect of making a submission was reduced and, as with every recurring exhibition, the borders of acceptability were clearer the more confident an exhibitor became. This is not to say that juries operated according to a fixed formula, but, had a painter gone to the Slade, the understanding of New English Art Club requirements would have been implicit. With this basis of support, the club attained the 'dignity of an institution'. Critics who were fed and watered at the press days continued to offer a wide range of opinions, discoursing loudly as they took notes. Arnold Bennett, recently arrived in London, surveyed the scene at the winter exhibition of 1896, noting the array of:

> eccentric landscapes imitative of early Italian and Dutch work, a few soft hazy portraits, a few intelligent originalities, a few sterile meaningless absurdities, and one striking, shouting, insistent, dominant nude by Wilson Steer [fig. 48]. In the centre of the gallery a table with sandwiches, wines and cigarettes, which everyone carefully avoided in spite of whispered invitations from a middle-aged male attendant.[3]

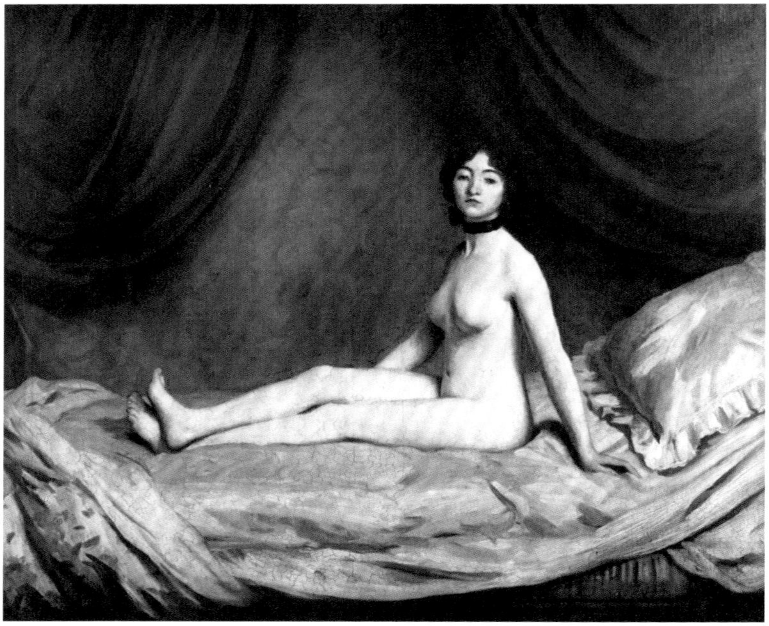

Fig. 48 Philip Wilson Steer
Nude Seated on a Bed, 1896
Oil on canvas, 94 x 109.2 cm
Private collection

The 'originalities' and 'absurdities' sometimes included works by featured artists and distinguished foreign exhibitors who came in for as much critical drubbing as any other exhibitors. Legros lacked 'sensational shock', when he was persuaded into the club for a one-off showing in the winter of 1896, and Monet's submissions in 1900 were not regarded as 'important'.[4] For a potential buyer, this implied that one should not waste money on an unimportant Monet, when the best British work was available. MacColl even claimed that:

> in France the great wells of inspiration are running dry ... our time, whose energy runs to science, to engineering, to exploration and commerce, produces only one or two real painter's talents in a generation ... [and] Steer is one of these.[5]

In the 1896 spring exhibition, Steer showed *Richmond Castle Through the Trees* (1895), a magisterial – but sadly destroyed – landscape framed in white, emulating the plain sections used by the Impressionists.[6] Something new and uplifting was at once in evidence. It was, according to *The Saturday Review*, 'quite apart from other landscapes'. Where we might expect a series of references to great traditions, to Gainsborough, Turner and Constable, the writer sought simply to separate this magisterial work from the others on display.

> The landscapes of his contemporaries are often charming; but if they are frankly painted from nature, they are liable to be slight; and if they are dignified, their dignity is, as often as not, bought at the price of pleasantly depressing sadness. Here is a landscape which is a frank piece of nature

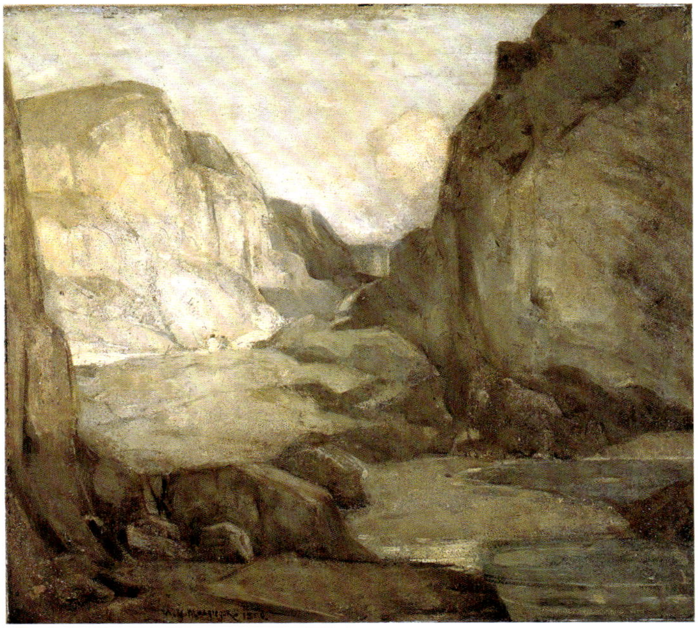

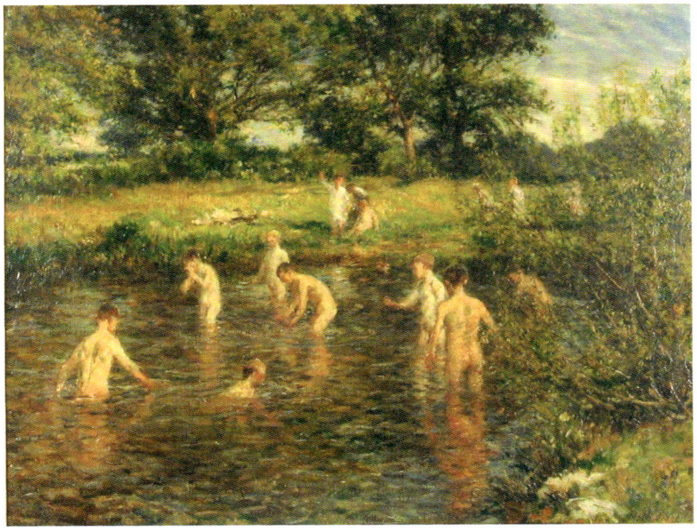

and yet it is not slight in feeling; it is full of weight and dignity, and yet it is not low-spirited.[7]

This set the tone for the criticism of Steer's work for the next ten years. British painting desperately needed a worthy successor to the great landscape tradition and others followed where he was leading. His distillation of experience threw up new possibilities. His noble ruins stood for national strength and steadfastness and caught the mood of Britain's isolation in a world of rival scheming empires. Anglo-Saxon chauvinism functioning through layers of memory and desire mystically informed Steer's later brushwork and provided much for his students to absorb. This extended beyond landscape into figure painting, interiors and nude studies.

A phalanx of maturing landscape painters was responsible for the bulk of New English exhibits in the late 1890s. Henry Muhrman, David Muirhead, James L. Henry, Mark Fisher, William Yorke MacGregor, Roger Fry and Henry Tonks were individually matched with earlier English and French masters, from whom, it was hoped, new practices would spring. Fry, for instance, in his painting of Lake Nemi, borrowed 'the spectacles of Richard Wilson', while MacGregor painted in 'a sombre key ... after the style of Legros'.[8] In the 1898 winter exhibition, MacGregor (see fig. 49) and Fisher (see fig. 50) were compared in order to explain the extremes of tolerance in the club. Fisher, 'the Impressionist', if not exactly 'Monetesque', had developed his own characteristic approach to strong sunlight, 'glittering on every leaf and grass blade', while MacGregor painted the shapes of nature in the reduced light of evening. MacColl proposed 'a magician in the form of Hegel' to reconcile these approaches.[9] Thus the belief that the British landscape school could be moulded and led by Steer was so powerful that it produced false claims and an uncomfortable 'catholicity'.

The search for viable Old Master traditions also affected figure painting in the late 1890s. *Hispagnoliste* conventions in the painting of full-length portraits remained strong, although the Whistler/Velázquez model was increasingly

Top
Fig. 49 William Yorke MacGregor
A Rocky Solitude, 1896
Oil on canvas, 62.9 x 67.7 cm
National Galleries of Scotland, Edinburgh

Above
Fig. 50 Mark Fisher
The Bathers, *c.* 1895
Oil on canvas, 61 x 75.5 cm
Dublin City Gallery The Hugh Lane, Dublin

challenged by new discoveries, one of which was Goya. During the winter of 1894, William Rothenstein travelled to Spain, and, with the help of his companion R. B. Cunninghame Graham, gained access to tawdry taverns away from the tourist routes. Here he witnessed true Spanish gypsy dancing – the subject of *Hablant Espagnol* (1894; fig. 53), a work that he sent to the New English 1895 spring exhibition.[10] It had marked him out henceforth as 'one of the ablest members of this confraternity'.[11] More Spanish-inspired portraits followed, but there was an internal struggle being waged between Goya's dark romanticism and the Whistlerian decorum typified by Rothenstein's fellow traveller, William James Yule (see fig. 51).[12]

Other models were being tested throughout these years. In the winter of 1897 Charles Haslewood Shannon returned to the club with *Souvenir of Van Dyck – Miss Kate Hargood in a Marmiton Dress* (*c.* 1896; fig. 52), a harmony in silvers, pinks and browns that brought elements of the Spanish masters, Whistler, Théodule Ribot and others under the aura of Anthony van Dyck.[13] In some senses 'Van Dyck' merely created a diversion. To the left, on the floor, lies a discarded mask – a reference to Watteau, the *commedia dell'arte,* and the fact that, in the eighteenth century, Van Dyck styles of dress were revived at masques. MacColl wondered if Shannon might not be 'in danger from his scholarship and critical interest'.[14] For all this, his work was neither a pastiche,

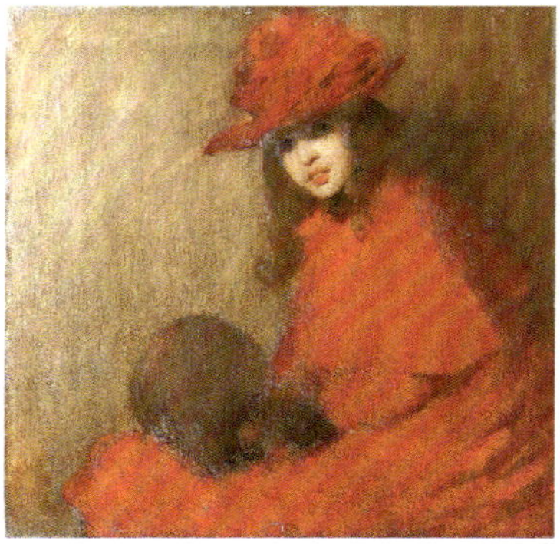

Fig. 51 William James Yule
Girl in Crimson, 1895
Oil on canvas, 77.5 x 77.5 cm
Private collection

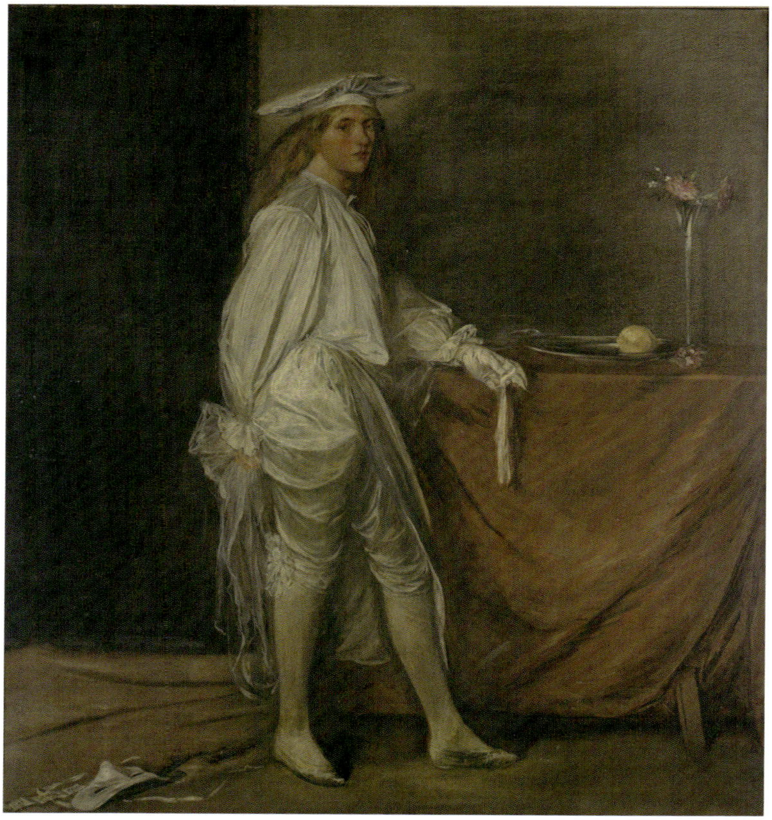

Fig. 52 Charles Haslewood Shannon
Souvenir of Van Dyck – Miss Kate Hargood in a Marmiton Dress, c. 1896
Oil on canvas, 103 x 95.3 cm
Felton Bequest, 1906. National Gallery of Victoria, Melbourne, Australia

Fig. 53 William Rothenstein
Hablant Espagnol, 1894
Oil on canvas,
81.3 x 45.7 cm
Private collection

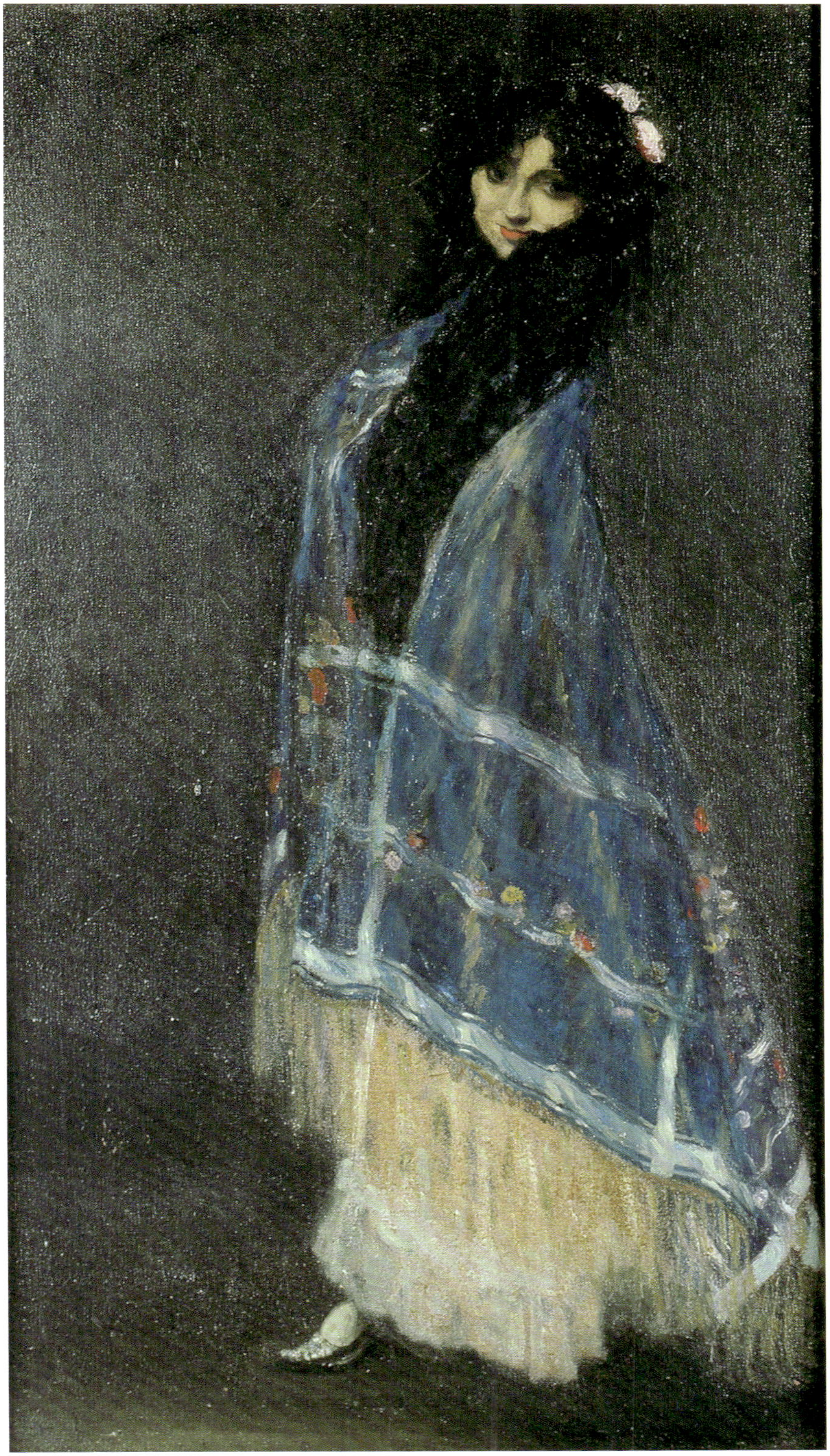

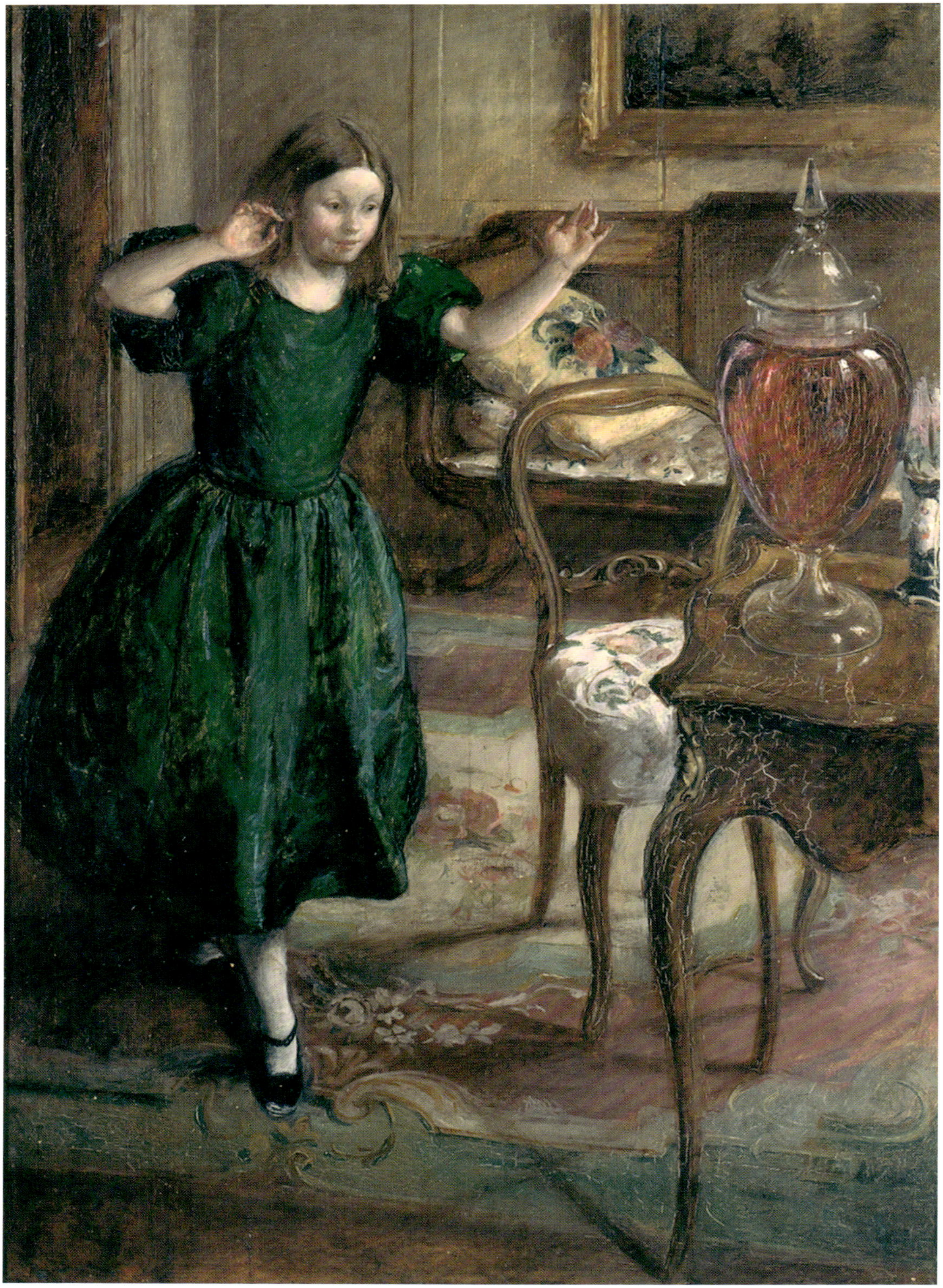

Fig. 54 Henry Tonks
Rosamund and the Purple Jar, 1900
Oil on wood, 52.7 x 37.5 cm
Purchased 1923. Tate, London

nor the sum of unresolved parts. *Miss Hargood* launched his career as a portraitist, whose subtle use of quotation greatly appealed to his actor and aesthete clientele.

There were yet other voices in this battle of styles. In the late 1890s, Tonks, faced with memorial exhibitions of work by recently deceased Pre-Raphaelites, had become fascinated by the art of the 1860s. He, 'of all the people in the world', wrote P. G. Konody in the spring of 1900, was 'imitating the Pre-Raphaelites of the second and third rank in the offensive ugliness of his *Rosamund* [in emerald green] *and the Purple Jar*' (fig. 54).[15] The idea behind the invitation to William Holman Hunt to show at the club was probably his, although it was greeted with open-mouthed incredulity, as Hunt's 'methods are in flagrant contradiction to all the theories advanced by [members of the club]'.[16] Hunt and Monet made odd bedfellows and, as the latter's works were regarded as lesser examples, the only conclusion to be drawn was that they were hung simply to reveal the very high standard of work by members. Whatever the reason, it was clear over these years that 'experimentalism', defined as continental styles, was 'out of fashion'.[17]

The reasons for this apparent retrenchment are more diverse than they at first appear. In 1898, a new London-based society began, specifically addressing the contemporary European and North American avant-garde. The International Society of Sculptors, Painters and Gravers appointed Whistler and Lavery as president and vice-president respectively. Its central caucus was supplied by members of the Glasgow School whose work had been shown in Munich, the Paris Salon, the Berlin Secession, the Venice Biennale and the Carnegie Institute in Pittsburgh. Glasgow painting was international; New English painting was English. Where the club showed isolated single examples from a select group of European painters, the International Society comprised Edouard Manet, Alfred Sisley and Henri de Toulouse-Lautrec, as well as Degas and Monet in a show that also included Rodin, Segantini, Thoma, Liebermann, Breitner, Knopff, Klimt and Puvis de Chavannes, with Cézanne, Redon and Denis in its large prints and drawings section. While it proved difficult for the International Society, with an ailing president, to maintain its standards in 1899 and 1901, its first exhibition thoroughly exposed the general banality of the Academy and the narrow specialisation of the club. Tonks, Steer, Sickert and Brown did not appear at the International. Sickert had by this stage squabbled with Whistler and was based in Dieppe. Blanche, Rothenstein, Conder and Furse did exhibit, but they were painters whose contacts with Paris had been maintained. Were it to succeed in spite of this proliferation of rivals, the New English required concentration of purpose, and this placed greater responsibility on its leaders to cultivate and retain the younger generation. Large state-sponsored 'Worlds Fairs' such as the Paris Exposition Universelle scheduled for 1900, which included representative displays of the British School, tended to operate on an invitation-only basis. New English artists, if they appeared in these places, were jockeying with Academicians and others. Such formations emphasised distinctions, categories and subsets within the homogenising whole of the national school.

Into this precious world of quote and counter-quote a new generation had emerged. Schooled for the most part at the Slade, it was nourished by regular study of the Old Masters in the National Gallery, London, to such a degree that, as Augustus John later recalled, 'a lifetime hardly provides time to sort out'.[18] Although this quotation suggests a lack of direction, the distinct preference for Dutch and Spanish, as opposed to Italian art, was clear, although it was later to change. Small, Spartan, perfectly painted interiors became the new distinguishing feature of club exhibitions. MacColl observed in 1901 that the club had gone through phases when theatre subjects, beach subjects and Arcadian subjects seemed to be on everyone's mind. 'Everyone' he recalled, would 'gossip a little about the new subject, and never talk it out'[19] and, while there had, of course, been interiors before at the New English, they had not been seen in such profusion. Rothenstein's *The Browning Readers* (1900; fig. 55), along with Orpen's *The Mirror,* exhibited at the New English 1900 exhibition, laid the blueprint.[20] We can imagine the 'gossip' in 1899, when Orpen, John, Conder, Herbert Everett and Albert Rutherston joined Rothenstein and Alice Knewstub on their honeymoon at Vattetot-sur-Mer near Dieppe. Preoccupied with Ibsen, Rothenstein was painting *A Doll's House.*[21] The dramatic lighting and tense, theatrical naturalism of this canvas contrasts with the calm formalism of *The Browning Readers* that followed. In one, literary subject matter was illustrated; in the other it was placed at one remove, as the 'readers', whose poses were drawn from Whistler and Puvis de Chavannes, were self-evidently not participating in a scene from Browning. The resulting work, hieratic in character, functions by association.[22]

It would be tempting to say that Orpen's *The Mirror* (1900; fig. 56) draws upon a similar repertoire, but it is essentially different. In one sense, a modernised version of Whistler's *Arrangement in Grey and Black, No. 1, The Artist's Mother* (1872; Musée d'Orsay), it carefully references an even more eclectic range of sources. Well-chosen pieces of classic English furniture are assembled, placed, observed and painted in a manner recalling the surface perfection of the work of seventeenth-century Dutch painters Gerard Terborch or Gabriel Metsu.[23] It was very much a 'thesis' picture. By the beginning of 1901, in *A Mere Fracture, In The Newcomes, Fitzroy Street* (1900; fig. 57), an even more confident and ambitious composer emerges.[24] In the statuesque decorum of its figure poses and the schematic arrangement of the room – its fireplace ranged parallel to the picture plane – it resembles, but is more complicated than, *The Browning Readers.*[25] The 'doctor' examines the

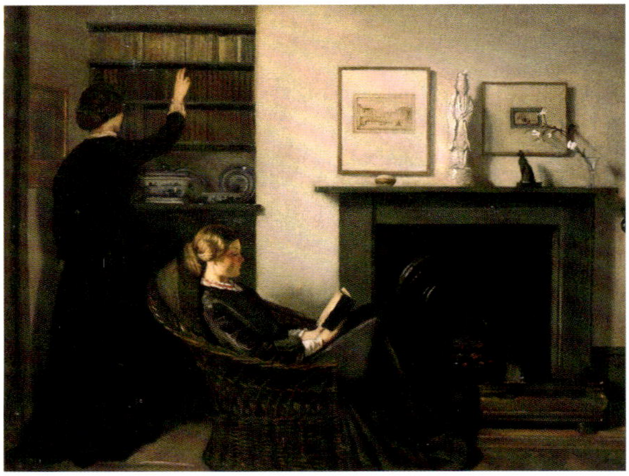

Fig. 55 William Rothenstein
The Browning Readers, 1900
Oil on canvas, 76 x 96.5 cm
Bradford City Gallery

Fig. 56 William Orpen
The Mirror, 1900
Oil on canvas, 50.8 x 40.6 cm
Presented by Mrs Coutts Michie through the National Art Collections Fund in memory of the George McCulloch Collection 1913. Tate, London

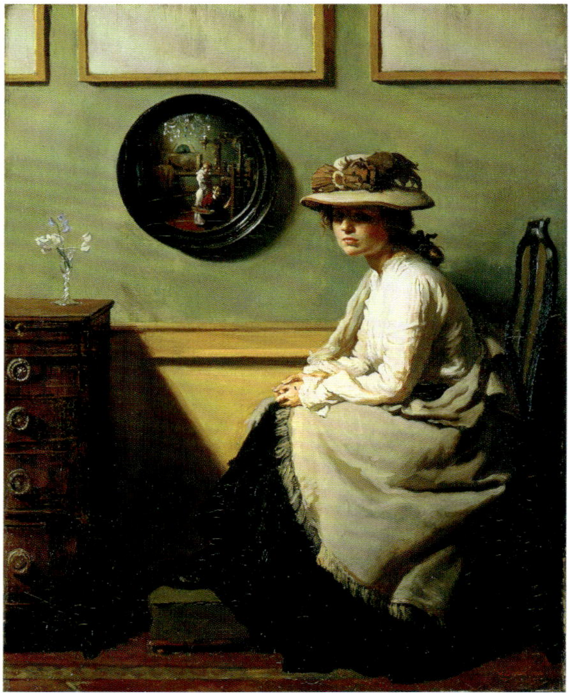

fractured limb with all the deliberation of Jesus washing Peter's feet. The action is framed by the positioning of the woman and man to left and right of the central figures, their poses echoing those of the nymphs who support the Empire clock on the mantelpiece. It may be a mere fracture, but the occasion is epiphanic. There is no before or after; what we see is akin to a *tableau vivant*. That this should all be associated with an incident in Thackeray's novel on art student life seems faintly bizarre – and yet, clearly, in its restored Regency fittings, this interior harked back to the social liberation of a unique, post-Napoleonic, pre-Victorian world, before the rise of the European bourgeoisie.[26] A new century, the end of the long reign, the arrival of the 'new' woman, the 'slum' novel, *psychologie nouvelle* and Bergsonian explorations of memory supply the lenses through which it could be viewed. Its appeal was obvious.

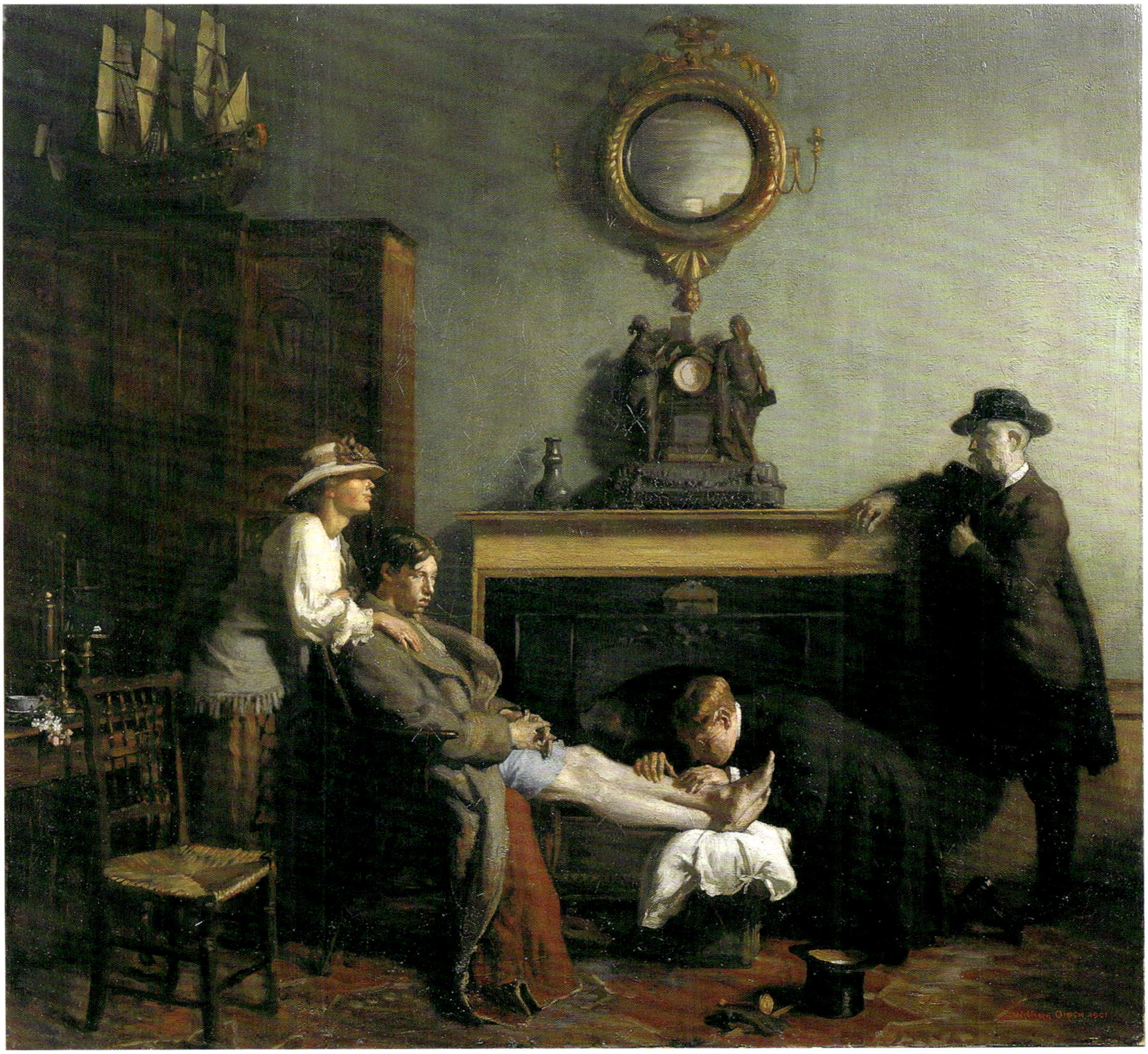

Fig. 57 William Orpen
A Mere Fracture, In the Newcomes, Fitzroy Street, 1900
Oil on canvas, 94 x 99 cm
Private collection

The process of redefinition of New English objectives was in full swing by 1902. Lewis Hind noted that: 'The public no longer giggles at the New English Art Club pictures'.

> The furniture of a room – flowers, books, vases, patterns of walls and papers – are no longer beautiful smudges that come together miraculously as you retire from the canvas. They are all painted punctiliously as in pre-Victorian days. They have become a novelty – *le dernier cri*.[27]

Gone are the seemingly radical bits of technique that characterised the club in its early days. Steer, Tonks and Walter Russell brought their loosely 'Impressionist' facture indoors at this period with some success. Steer's *Hydrangeas* (1901; fig. 58), a picture praised for its 'flickering play' of sunlight upon the 'pale stuffs' of a girl's dress and the sofa on which she rests, exemplifies the trend.[28] However, the 'beautiful smudge' style with which the older members of the club had been popularly associated was giving way to punctilious painting.[29] The plain walls on which were hung a few well-placed prints or traditional landscapes, complimented by single, simple pieces of classic English furniture,

Below and overleaf
Fig. 58 Philip Wilson Steer
Hydrangeas, 1901
Oil on canvas, 85.4 x 112.4 cm
Fitzwilliam Museum, Cambridge

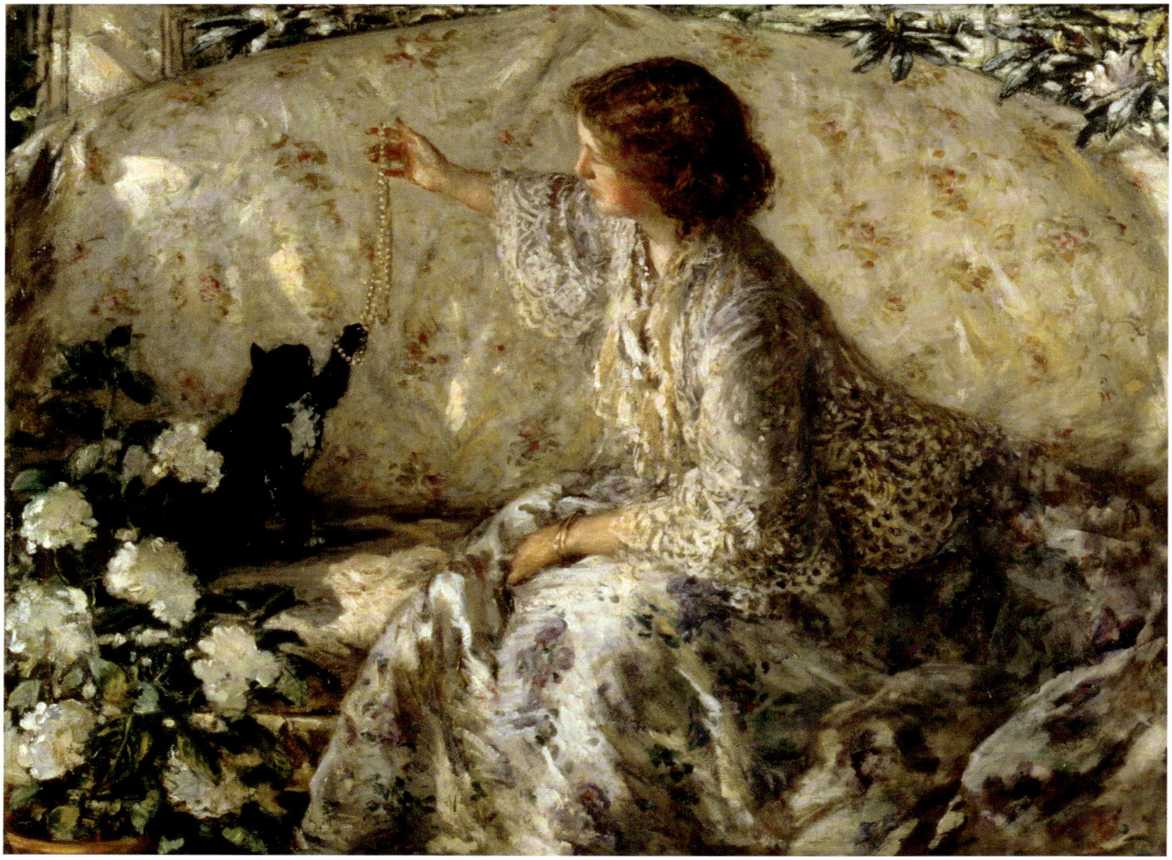

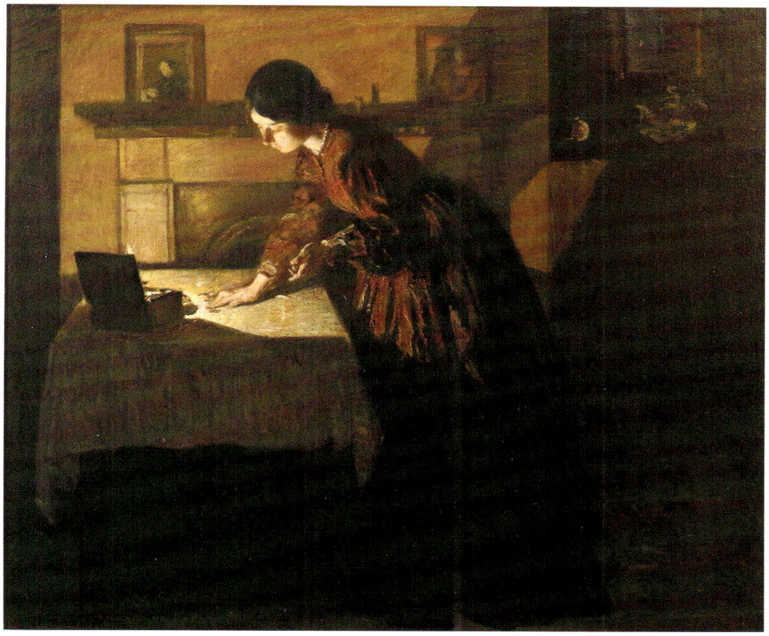

Fig. 59 David Muirhead
The Lost Piece of Silver, 1902
Oil on canvas, 91.5 x 106.7 cm
Private collection

soon became formulaic – inferring that these rooms were Spartan for reasons other than plain fact. Isolated objects, which in Vuillard lose their identity in palpitating surface, here take on a life of their own as they are passed from painter to painter.[30] *Blanc-de-chine* figures, single porcelain vases or framed prints become common features throughout.[31] MacColl, who observed this, proposed that it would take some latter-day Berenson to separate their works.[32]

The temporary nature of this inner city life is underscored by Orpen's *The Valuers*, in which a group of property agents debate the likely value of chattels.[33] They have discovered a picture in which ballet performers talk to their male admirers in the wings of a theatre. It was the sort of subject handled by Degas, and filtered into the British context by Conder. But here, in the back room of a house in Fitzrovia, its message is contained and it becomes an object of prurient interest. Such pictures had their supporters and imitators in a group of artists that included Gwen John, Edna Clarke Hall and Mary and Ambrose McEvoy, who worked new variations on the theme.[34] In reveries, such as David Muirhead's *The Lost Piece of Silver* (1902; fig. 59), Gwen John's *Interior with Figures* (1898–9), Mary McEvoy's *Interior: Girl Reading* (1901; fig. 60) and Ambrose McEvoy's *The Convalescent* (1903; fig. 61), there are equally bare settings, and the literary references are more vague, even though, in both, the subject matter is 'reading'. For T. Martin Wood:

> This art is wedded to literature – [it] comes from a page of a book as well as from life, and the artist's imagination passes from art to life and back again, finding no barrier to its dreams, embracing outer objects as part of

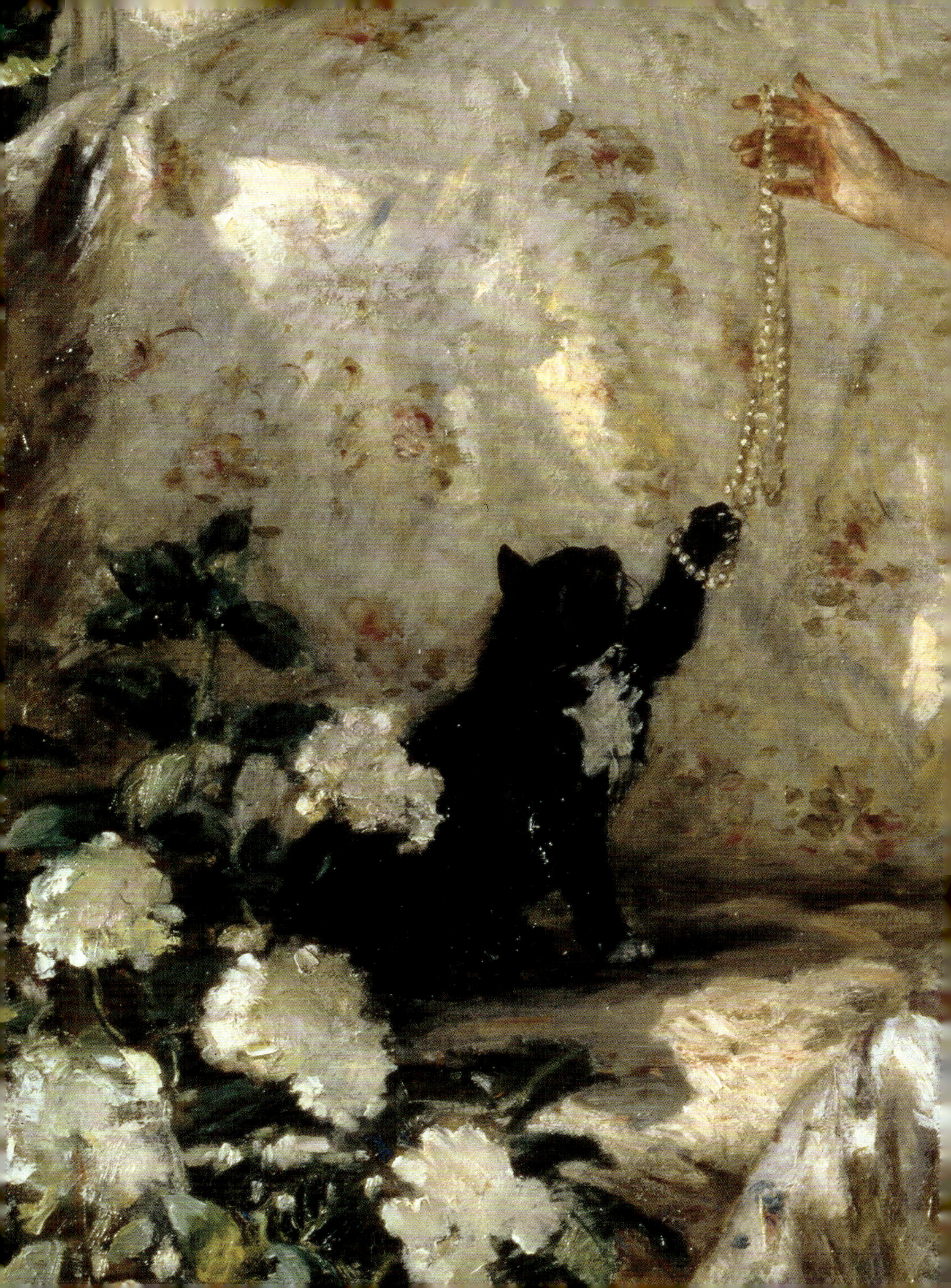

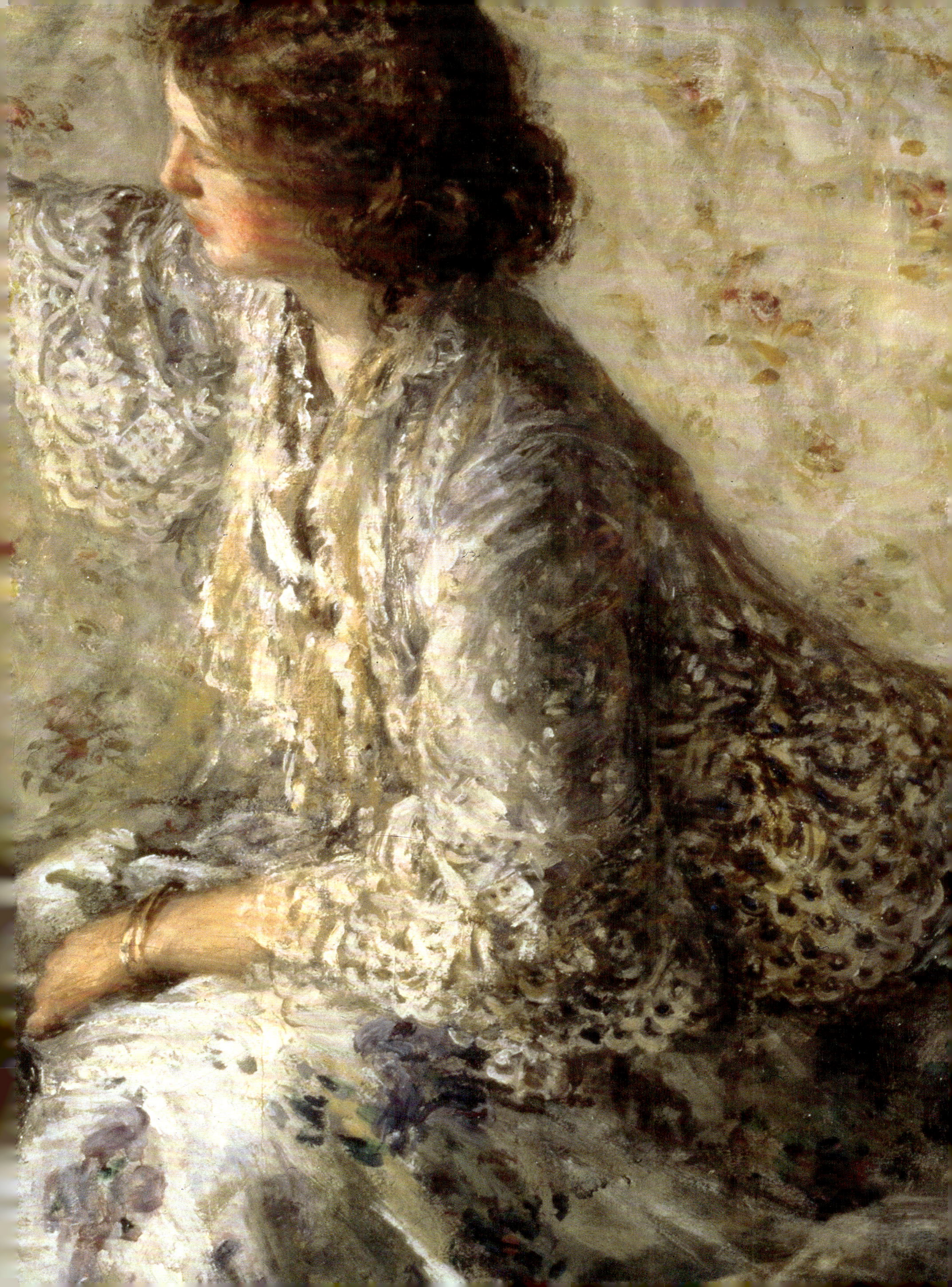

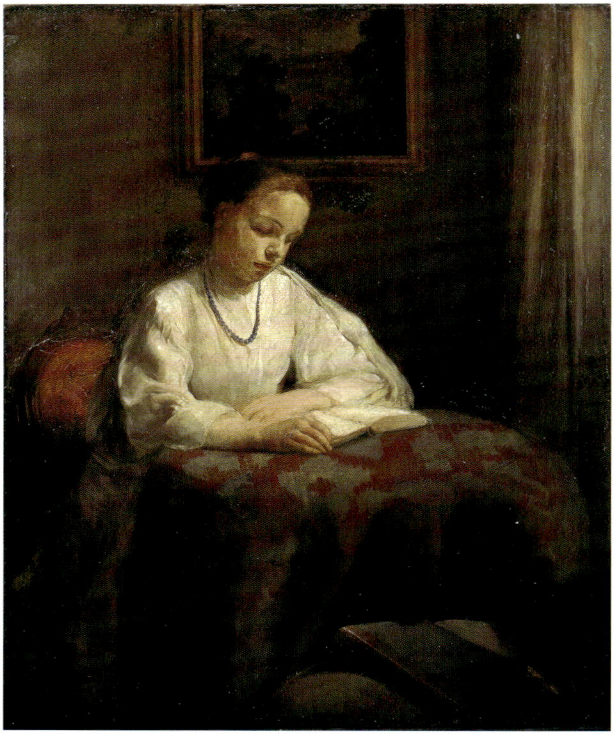

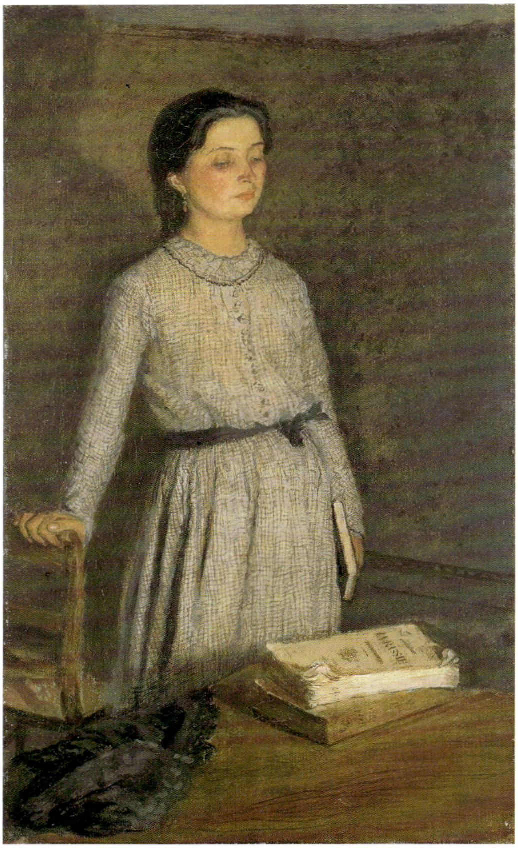

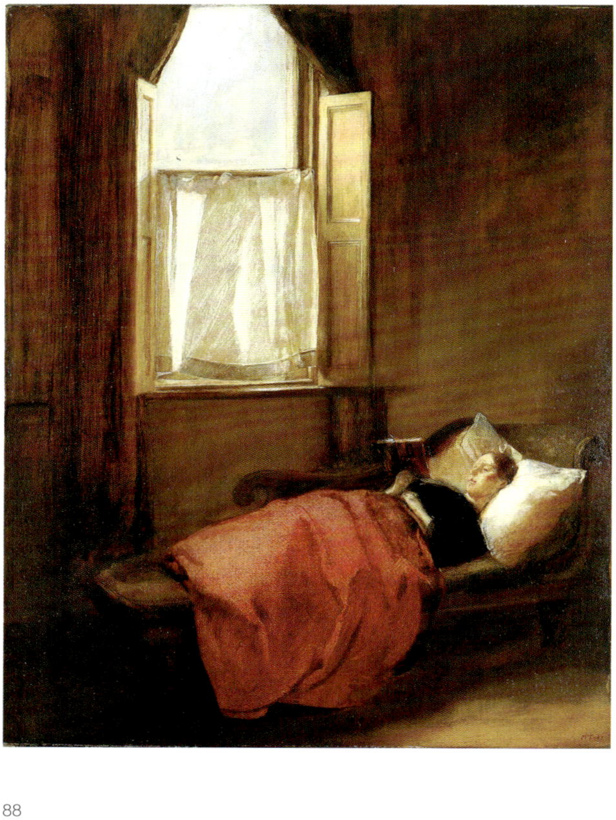

Top left
Fig. 60 Mary McEvoy
Interior: Girl Reading, 1901
Oil on canvas, 53.3 x 43.8 cm
Purchased 1927. Tate, London

Left
Fig. 61 Ambrose McEvoy
The Convalescent, 1903
Oil on canvas, 53 x 43 cm
Private collection

Top right
Fig. 62 Gwen John
The Student, 1903–04
Oil on canvas, 56 x 33 cm
Manchester City Art Gallery

them, meeting everyday people as if they, too, lived the interesting vivid life that is in books.... [35]

This ambience of literature fascinated the McEvoys. Aspiring and determined female students, who occasionally enriched their Spartan accommodation by the shrewd purchase of an early English landscape, also read serious books rather than the local paper or a 'shilling shocker'. This insistent imagery of female reverie, located in Pimlico interiors, rooms that 'a Thackeray character would live in', was that of the 'true intimist'.[36] As the phenomenon was dying, it achieved its zenith with the belated showing of Gwen John's *The Student* (1903–04; fig. 62) in the winter of 1909. Hailed by Laurence Binyon as 'the most memorable thing in the entire exhibition' it epitomised the virtues of reticence, tonal propriety and Slade draughtsmanship.[37]

Such attitudes to the interior were overhauled when Sickert reappeared in the club's spring exhibition in 1906 with *Noctes Ambrosianae* (1906; fig. 63) – a painting so striking that the phrase on everyone's lips, according to George

Fig. 63 Walter Richard Sickert
Noctes Ambrosianae, 1906
Oil on canvas, 63.5 x 76.2 cm
Castle Museum, Nottingham

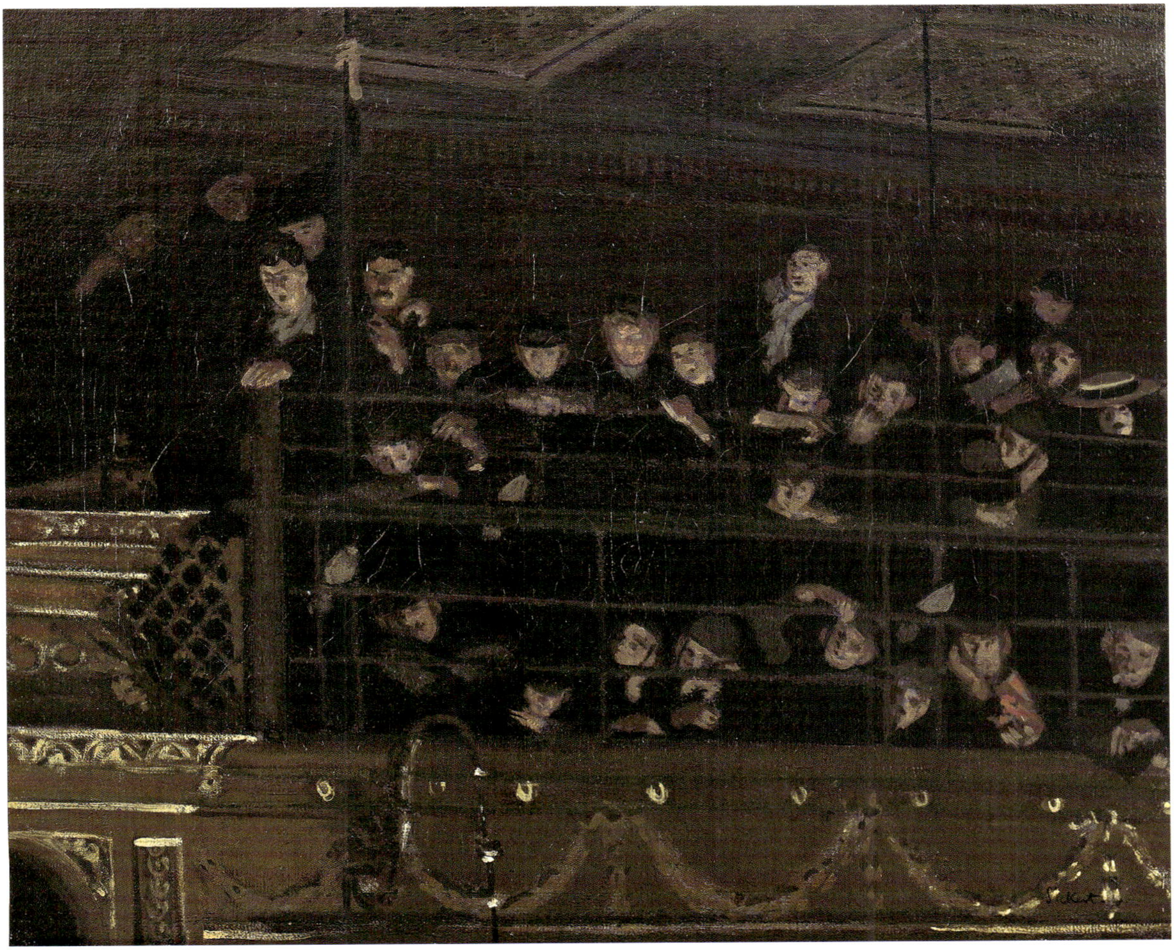

Moore, was 'Sickert has come back'.[38] Albert Rutherston, who had been exhibiting pictures of seamstresses and laundry girls at the club, claimed that he and Spencer Gore persuaded him to return.[39] Immediately impatient with the cosy world of his contemporaries on the jury of the New English, Sickert insisted upon reopening the window on the underclass maelstrom. In *The New Home* (1908), shown at the club in the same year, the impoverished coster woman, who has recently arrived in her lodgings, has yet to remove her hat. She is the new tenant of the New English room-set – a space which in itself has been dramatically changed.[40] Thinking perhaps of the painters of 'portrait interiors', he famously wrote that 'the more our art is serious, the more it will tend to avoid the drawing-room and stick to the kitchen'.[41] Elsewhere in his criticism, Sickert expanded upon the subject of wallpaper. When he entered the bed-sitting rooms that became *The New Home*, Sickert relished the 'wrong' wallpaper.[42] His denizens were dingy and the association with their inhabitants was accidental. The new home was not new or a home – it was a temporary abode.

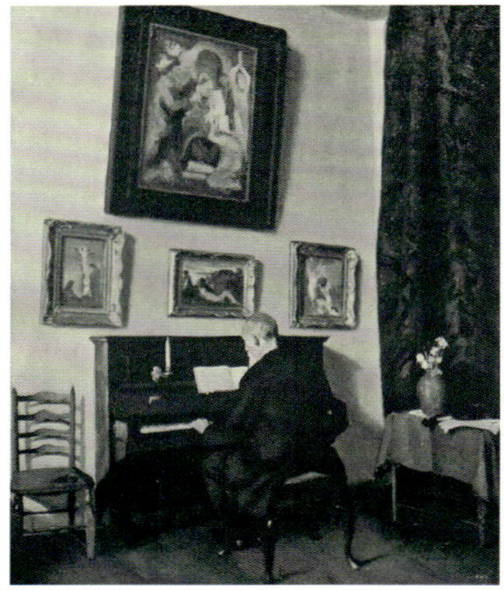

Fig. 64 F. H. S. Shepherd
Interior, 1909
Location unknown

Despite other fluctuations in fashion, interior painting, as Laurence Binyon noted in 1908, remained the trademark of the spring and winter shows. Speaking of Orpen, Tonks and Steer, he stated:

> Secluded from the unrestful emotions of our age, with its fever of ideas and its profound dissatisfactions, they remain serene. Collecting pieces of admirable furniture, choosing with fine judgement gaily harmonious patterns of fine chintz, their art dwells in charming interiors, where filtered sun caresses old silver and porcelain and bowls of flowers reflected in polished wood.[43]

This point was repeated a year later by T. Martin Wood when he observed that, with the majority of New English exhibitors, 'it is still the effects of nature that are pursued indoors'.[44] The club was firmly associated with the depiction of middle-class domesticity, in which a surrogate spectator might be found quietly reading a book or playing the piano, and this is what we see in the paintings by S. Noel Simmons (see fig. 65) and F. H. S. Shepherd (see fig. 64), which were chosen to illustrate the review.[45]

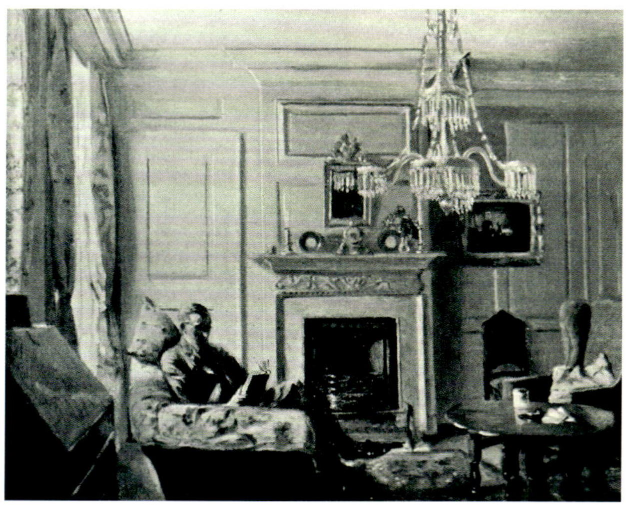

Fig. 65 S. Noel Simmons
The Cosy Corner, c. 1909
Location unknown

Repeating its point and reinforcing a stereotype gave the club a distinctive place in the concourse of clashing societies and conflicting artist groups. It remained in every sense different from the Academy to the extent that, in arguing 'the case for modern painting', it was the only significant opposition. In the words of 'a modern painter' it stood for 'democracy of the most uncompromising kind'. It tended to 'give prominence to artists who are making their reputations', although there were 'unshaken pillars'

Fig. 66 William Orpen
A Jury, 1905
Crayon on paper, 19 x 26 cm
Pyms Gallery, London

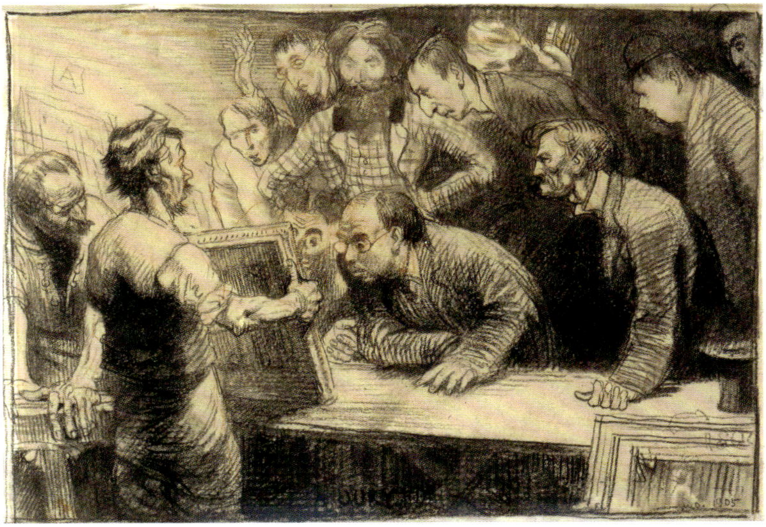

of the Establishment who remained devoted to it. While confirming what we know, the 'modern painter' reveals the club's real distinction in that:

> It anticipates movement after movement; but before time has been allowed for each movement to be accepted and made successful, it has passed on to some fresh innovation.[46]

For some of its adherents, however, the club had begun to signify resistance to change or was being led by the tastes of its refined constituency of supporters. While it had never courted the populism of the Academy, it also sought to place at the margins those painters who, although they came from the right stable, were judged to be out of step with the club's clientele. A rift emerged between the painters of these genteel interiors and those of Sickert, Spencer Gore, Harold Gilman and the members of the Fitzroy Street Group. In practice this divide expressed itself in hanging decisions rather than in edicts or policy statements.[47] Looking at the young middle-aged cronies in Orpen's *A Jury* (1905; fig. 66), it is clear why this should be so. The collective taste of Tonks, Brown, Steer, McEvoy, Rothenstein, Orpen and John tended to dominate successive exhibitions, so that, while looking at the work of Charles Stabb (see fig. 67), Simmons and Shepherd, their derivation was apparent.[48] Orpen's interiors remained influential beyond the confines of the New English Art Club. His *Night* series, for instance, unveiled in 1907 at the Goupil Gallery Salon (fig. 68), carries on a conversation with Sickert's Camden Town interiors while acting as the most powerful precedent for Clausen's *Twilight: Interior* (1909), shown at

Fig. 67 Charles Stabb
The Crumpled Dress, 1908
Oil on canvas, 71 x 76.5 cm
Walker Art Gallery, Liverpool

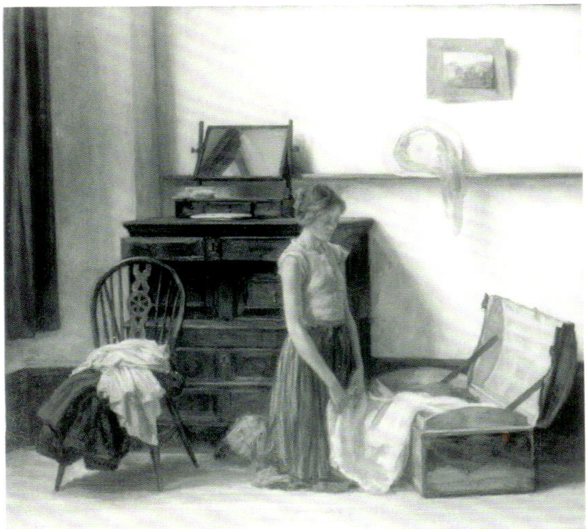

the Royal Academy in the same year.[49] There were bridges across both institutional and *genre* divides, as interiors sometimes became 'portrait interiors'. Objects, those special ceramics selected for a still-life by William Nicholson, expressed the personality of their owners.[50] His and Orpen's carefully crafted *petite maîtrise*, which typifies New English *intimisme* as much as anything, drove Sickert to the scullery in a fury. To judge by his advocacy of what became the Camden Town School, it is obvious that the retiring, bourgeois pursuits of the collector of Staffordshire are what he required his readers to reject. The devouring passion that Sickert sought in the 'murder' series, and which is coincidentally the subject of Orpen's extraordinary *Night No. 2,* is suppressed in favour of the lower-class lassitude of *Ennui* (fig. 98), shown at the club in 1914.[51]

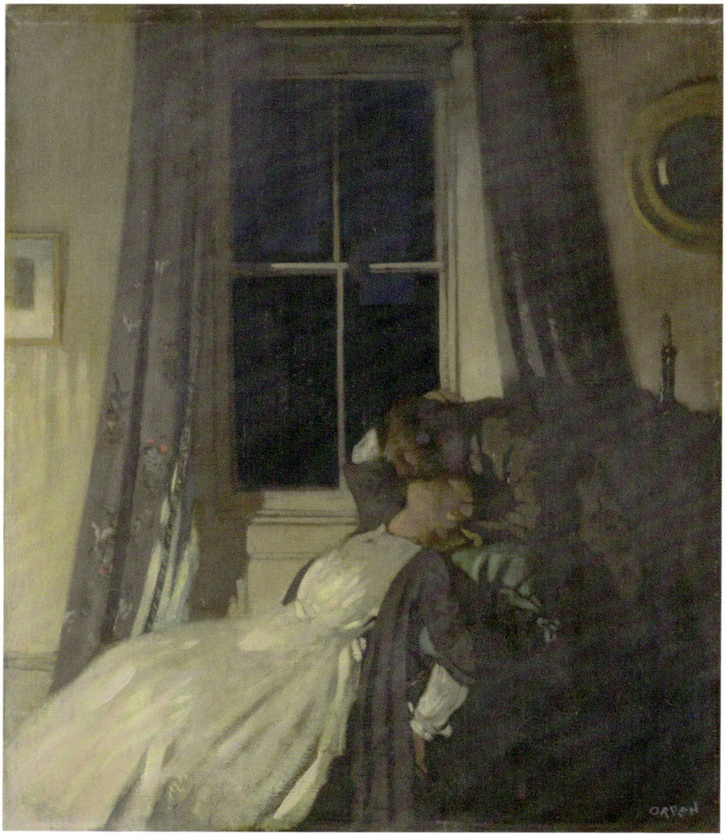

Fig. 68 William Orpen
Night No. 2, 1907
Oil on canvas, 76.5 x 64 cm
National Gallery of Victoria, Melbourne

The Edwardian New English exhibitions re-formed their visitors and clientele. Between 1901 and 1909, the shows discreetly directed purchasers towards the enclosed environment of reading, piano playing and quiet reflection, in the familiar surroundings of a consciously crafted space. The cabinet may be private, but it was not exclusive. We look into it to find the solitary inhabitant who elicits a more profound recognition in the viewer than in any other set of pictorial circumstances. Those who bought pictures might well go through the antics of *The Valuers* and identify objects, furniture or colour schemes, as, with easy intimacy, they slipped into the painting – for some indomitable New English collectors this became more than a temporary resting place of the mind.

NOTES

1 The 1890s cohort of new exhibitors included Alfred Lys Baldry, Walter Bayes, Hugh Bellingham-Smith, Henry Bishop, Gerard Chowne, Ronald Gray, Alfred Hayward, David Muirhead, Bertram Priestman, Alfred Rich, Walter Russell, William Shackleton and Alfred Thornton.
2 Frederick Wedmore, *The Studio*, vol. 6, 1896, pp. 213–4.
3 Flower Newman (ed.), *The Journals of Arnold Bennett, 1896–1910*, Cassell, London, 1932, pp. 23–4. Bennett's colourful description focuses upon a couple seated in front of the Steer, 'talking in loud Kensingtonian tones which outraged the prim silence of the gallery'. Nearby was an 'old and shabby art critic ... writing in a notebook, his red nose and small peering eyes bent down close to the page'. Dragged into the conversation, they concluded that the nude was 'not a masterpiece' – but, Bennett adds, 'the manner of this condemnation almost made me like it'. For further reference to the painting in question, *Nude Seated on a Bed* (1896), exhibited in the winter of 1896 (68), see Bruce Laughton, *Philip Wilson Steer*, Clarendon Press, Oxford, 1971, p. 67. The work was praised by Stevenson (*Pall Mall Gazette*, 20 November 1896) for its references to Manet and Velázquez.
4 *The Saturday Review*, 21 November 1896, p. 540; see also D. S. MacColl, 'The New English Art Club', *The Studio*, vol. 9, 1897, pp. 285–6. In 1897 the members of the club brought back Alphonse Legros as an honoured guest exhibitor. The retired Slade Professor, although he had been an authentic voice for French art in England since the 1860s, was now placed in a pantheon that included Puvis de Chavannes, Whistler, Degas, Watts and Burne-Jones. P. G. K. [Konody], 'The New English Art Club', *The Artist*, vol. 28, June 1900, p. 84, referred to Monet's *Effet de Neige* and *Vétheuil*, saying that neither could be 'counted among the master's important works'.
5 D. S. M., 'The New English Art Club', *The Saturday Review*, 21 November 1896, pp. 539–41.
6 Steer's *Richmond Castle* (1896) was acquired by Prince Matsukata and is presumed destroyed, see Bruce Laughton, *Philip Wilson Steer*, Clarendon Press, Oxford, 1971, p. 136; and *The Old Matsukata Collection*, Shoichi Ijiri et al., exh. cat., Kobe Shimbun, Kobe, 1989. *Vétheuil* was owned by Fred Brown and possibly shown at the spring 1897 exhibition.
7 Anon., 'At the New English Art Club', *The Saturday Review*, 18 April 1896, pp. 394–5.
8 D. S. M., 'The New English Art Club' *The Saturday Review*, 27 November 1897, pp. 587–8.
9 D. S. M., 'The New English Art Club', *The Saturday Review*, 19 November 1898, pp. 668–9, declared: 'If we can imagine a magician in the form of Hegel entering the gallery with a dialectic machine ready to apply to all the contraries he found there, these are two painters he would pounce upon to join in beautiful synthetic union.... In the morning we should see the Fisher-faculties with all their tackle ready at dawn, eager to go down to the pond and get to work, wondering what all the bother was about, but politely waiting for the MacGregor faculties to give the word. The MacGregor faculties are still in bed, reluctantly shaken from a dream in which the pond, the trees and the cows had assumed an almost Assyrian stateliness.'
10 William Rothenstein, *Men and Memories*, vol. 1, Faber and Faber, London, 1931, p. 223.
11 Anon., 'The New English Art Club', *The Saturday Review*, 24 April 1895, p. 506.
12 The portrait of *Ignazio Zuloaga* and *The Swordsman (R.B. Cunninghame Graham)* were shown in the winter of 1895 and the spring of 1896 respectively. Cunninghame Graham had accompanied Rothenstein to Spain and Zuloaga had been one of his fellow students at the Académie Julian.
13 Shannon had shown originally in 1888, but had not exhibited with the club during the high Impressionist years. For further reference, see E. B. G., *Charles Shannon*, Ernest Benn, London, 1924, p. 21; 'Tis', *Masters of Modern Art, Charles Shannon ARA*, Colour, London, n.d. (*c*. 1920). Shannon continued to paint *marmiton* subjects for a time before shifting his allegiances from Van Dyck to Titian and from the club to the International Society of Sculptors, Painters and Gravers.
14 D. S. M., 'The New English Art Club', *The Saturday Review*, 27 November 1897, pp. 587–8, discusses Shannon's *Souvenir of Van Dyck*, declaring that 'charm ... shines through in the portrait of a girl in fancy dress called *Souvenir of Van Dyck*. This deep-seated quality in an artist, not to be earned or learned, brought to him at his birth by the wind because it listed, coming out under his fingers beyond his knowing, without his helping, against his hindering, is clearer in Mr Shannon than in most of his gifted contemporaries. So many men are at war with their gist instead of being easily possessed by it and impelled. Manet would have given his fingers to paint woman with the elegance of Chaplin.... Even Mr Shannon is in danger from his scholarship and critical interest... Vandyck, Miss Hasgood [*sic*], a *marmiton*, a lemon, a flower glass, all beautifully arranged, but you see them being arranged, and the slim perpendicular of the glass holds its side of the space with a little anxiety'.
15 P. G. K. [Konody], 'The New English Art Club', *The Artist*, vol. 28, June 1900, p. 84.
16 Ibid.
17 C. L. H. [Lewis Hind], 'New Men and Old Manners', *The Academy*, 12 April 1902, pp. 391–2.
18 Augustus John, *Chiaroscuro: Fragments of an Autobiography*, Jonathan Cape, London, 1954, p. 25.
19 *The Saturday Review*, vol. 91, 20 April 1901, p. 498. For comparative material, see Tate Gallery Archive 7310.11. MacColl was of the view that the trend was initiated by Sargent's *Venetian Interior*. Works such as Philip Wilson Steer's *Mrs Cyprian Williams* (1891; Tate Britain, London) and Henry Tonks's *The Hat Shop* (1892; Birmingham Art Gallery), for instance, indicate the early interest in interior subjects among New English painters.
20 For reference to *The Mirror*, see Bruce Arnold, *Orpen: Mirror to an Age*, Jonathan Cape, London, 1981, pp. 78–80.
21 The scene in *A Doll's House* (1879) is derived from Act 3 of Ibsen's classic play, in which Mrs Linden and Kronstad, played by Alice Knewstub and Augustus John respectively, listen to the end of the dance taking place upstairs. The first substantial production of the play in England was staged at the Novelty Theatre, London, on 7 June 1889 by William Archer, although Rothenstein appears not to have seen it. He records that he first heard about Ibsen from Charles Conder, whom he met in Paris in the autumn of 1890, see *Men and Memories: Recollections of William Rothenstein*, Faber and Faber, London, 1931, vol. 1, p. 56. The play was extensively discussed in George Bernard Shaw's *The Quintessence of Ibsenism* (1891; 2nd ed., 1913), pp. 187–205. For further reference, see James McFarlane (ed.), *Henrik Ibsen*, Penguin, Harmondsworth, 1970, pp. 128–9. The setting appears to have been derived from the inn at Vattetot-sur-mer. Orpen would, therefore, have had the opportunity to see this picture emerge. At the same time both he and Rutherston painted bedroom scenes in the inn. Rothenstein submitted the picture to the British Section of the Exposition Universelle in 1900, where it won a silver medal. It was not exhibited at the New English until the spring of 1903.
22 The foreground figure, that of Alice Knewstub, is one of many variations on Whistler's *Arrangement in Grey and Black, No. 1, The Artist's Mother*, while the figure in the background taking a book from the shelves is derived from Puvis de Chavannes's *Le Ballon* and *Le Pigeon Voyageur* (both 1871; both Musée Carnavalet, Paris).

23 Orpen had recently engaged Whistler directly in his portraits of Augustus John and Herbert Everett. *The Mirror* (1900; Tate Britain, London) presents a female figure in surroundings that are not without their problems – her dress-style and confrontational stance, for instance, suggest a coster. One critic, for example, commenting upon the 'lowly' dress of the girl, stated that the picture was 'almost worthy to be classed with the worthiest of the old Dutch masters, whose imperishable gift for this type of subject is their strongest claim on posterity's admiration', see F. J. M., 'The New English Art Club', *The Speaker*, 24 November 1900, p. 201. In the patient attention to surface, Terborch and Metsu were seen as the primary sources, see P. G. Konody and S. Dark, *Sir William Orpen: Artist and Man*, Seeley Service and Co., London, 1932, p. 141.

24 Orpen added a portion of canvas to the left side of the picture in order to establish the setting with greater confidence. More elaborate than *The Browning Readers*, the picture nevertheless borrows significant aspects of its *mise-en-scène*, with strong light striking the fireplace from the right in both.

25 For further reference, see the Irish sale at Christie's on 22 May 1998, lot 21, entry by the Orpen Research Project (ORP). I am grateful to my colleague Christopher Pearson of the ORP for his collaboration on Orpen's work. The incident is taken from Chapter 22 of William Makepeace Thackeray's *The Newcomes* (1853–55), in which we learn that Mr Binnie, a friend of Clive Newcome, had fallen from a horse and 'wrenched' his ankle on the pavement. Newcome dispatched his friend, Arthur Pendennis, possibly the man on the right, to visit him and report back. This figure may, however, have been intended as 'a French consulting doctor', which William Crampton Gore reported as Orpen's own identification of this figure (quoted by Bruce Arnold, *Orpen: Mirror to an Age*, Jonathan Cape, London, 1981, p. 92). Gore himself played the attending English doctor, Pendennis, or the French doctor, the caretaker, Mr Hayard and Binnie was played by a fellow Slade student named Carr. Pendennis found Binnie being tended by his sister and her daughter, either of whom is being played by Emily Scobel.

26 Orpen was living in 21 Fitzroy Street, in close proximity to the house in Fitzroy Square reputed to be that in which Thackeray set his novel *The Newcomes*. Thackeray's reputation in the 1890s was rising, helped by the romanticisation of art student life in Paris, which found its principal expression in the publication of George du Maurier's *Trilby* (1894). Indeed, the re-issue of Thackeray's *Paris Sketchbook* (1840), as a pocket edition in 1885, may be said to have paved the way for Du Maurier in portraying an Englishman's view of the *vie de bohème*. Not long after *A Mere Fracture* was exhibited, Lewis Melville's 'Thackeray's London', *The English Illustrated Magazine*, 1901–2, pp. 329–41, was published.

27 C. L. H [Lewis Hind], 'New Men and Old Manners', *The Academy*, 12 April 1902, pp. 391–2, recognised that the club had been a launch pad for new talent, 'of those who were exhibitioners in the last decade in the last century, some are now in Burlington House, some have been "taken up" by dealers, some have tired, some have grown sad and civil in teaching, and a few have remained loyal to the club'.

28 *The Athenaeum*, 20 April 1901, p. 505.

29 While this was true up until 1905, in the second half of the decade 'Impressionist' interiors such as those by Steer and Russell once again captured attention. Steer's *The Music Room* (1906; Tate Britain, London), shown in 1906, for instance, was greeted with enthusiasm by critics in *The Speaker*, 23 June 1906, p. 270, and *The Studio*, vol. 38, 1906, p. 225, while George Moore in *The Saturday Review*, 23 June 1906, p. 785, declared Steer's objective to be no more than to produce 'a decorative scheme'.

30 F. J. M., 'The New English Art Club', *The Speaker*, vol. 6, new series, 12 April 1902, p. 106, noted: 'The genteel interior, always a feature of this club's exhibitions, is possibly more conspicuous this spring than it ever has been before. We are familiar with these interiors. They consist of dingy London rooms with plain walls, highly polished furniture, a green door or dado, one figure or more, and frequently a green-shaded lamp; and they suggest as they reappear, exhibition after exhibition, the presence somewhere of a property room which sundry enthusiastic and maybe promising art students take their turns at painting.'

31 It is the case that the Rothenstein and Orpen interiors occasionally contain some of the same props. The harpsichord noted in the background of Rothenstein's *An Interior* (1901) reappears in Orpen's *The Refugees* (1901–05). The Regency convex mirror, the ship model, the angle-bracket oil lamp and the circular inlaid tables also feature in Orpen's *A Window in London Street* (1901), Rothenstein's *An Interior* and other works. In Orpen and Nicholson's cases, these objects are extracted from the setting for special study in still-life paintings.

32 D. S. M., 'Picture Exhibitions of the Month', *The Saturday Review*, 7 December 1901, p. 711. MacColl declares: 'Now in the absence of documents the Berenson of the future, however acute, would probably hit on the facts that there were actually two ladies, two lamps, two houses and so forth. He would almost necessarily go off on the false scent of supposing that the same lady had been painted with variations in form owing to personal tricks of vision in the artist. But a critic as acute as Mr Berenson would notice a difference in the manner of drawing and putting on paint in these two pictures might connect the Orpen on the strength of this with other Orpens passing under other names (say Mr Legros for Verrochio, Mr Conder for Filippino) and thus finally surmise a "Friend of Billy" who, when he painted the "London Window", was attracted in his imitative days into the picture of another man.'

33 Shown in the spring exhibition of 1902 at the New English. F. M. J., 'The New English Art Club', *The Speaker*, vol. 6, (New Series), 12 April 1902, p. 106, noted that: 'The depth of the shadowy room [in *The Valuers*] is unmistakable, and the postures are easy and eloquent – particularly that of the self-satisfied, silk-hatted individual waving his left hand jauntily towards the suspended picture under discussion – while the pure painting of the whole calls for unstinted praise.'

34 Thus, for instance, a year later, C. L. H, in 'New Englishmen and Italy', *The Academy and Literature*, 11 April 1903, pp. 371–2, declared: 'The most devoted friend of the New English Art Club could hardly describe the present exhibition as new. The note is still, as it has been for the past two or three years, a room, beautifully painted, displaying the figure of a woman who seldom seems quite congruous of her surroundings. She is reclining on a couch, arranging prints or china, sewing or reading, or – singing while her husbands plays. Three years ago this return to early Victorian domesticity was a trifle novel: this year it is a trifle stale.... Many of the subjects are as anecdotic as the typical Royal Academy pictures that the New English Art Club was founded to exorcise.... The New English Art Club has become eclectic. The influence of certain personalities is obvious, and those who are not influenced by others pant up-hill trying to regain the heights they themselves once reached; but it is the same hill, not another.'

35 T. Martin Wood, 'The Pictures of Ambrose McEvoy', *The Studio*, vol. 42, 1908, p. 98.

36 *The Ambrose McEvoy Exhibition*, Christian Brinton, exh. cat., Duveen Brothers, New York City, 1920, unpaginated. T. Martin Wood, 'The Pictures of Ambrose McEvoy', *The Studio*, vol. 42, 1908, pp. 98–101. The reference to Thackeray is revelatory in this context, given Orpen's earlier work. Being essentially of the Regency and early Victorian era, he was seen as a writer who came from a period of innocence, uncontaminated by William Morris and the Arts and Crafts Movement.

37 Laurence Binyon, 'Our Young Painters and a Critic', *The Saturday Review*, 11 December 1909, continues: 'Here is that intensity, quiet and shy though it be, which counts for so much more than brilliancy, and which is so rare in contemporary art – it is a picture of singular delicacy

and beauty.' See also *The Outlook*, 11 December 1909, and *Westminster Gazette*, 30 November 1909, which describes the picture as one 'to be sought out'. *L'Etudiante*, a portrait of Dorelia McNeill, had actually been painted about six years earlier between 1903 and 1904. It was passed over in most reviews – see Tate Gallery Archive T.G.A. 7310.25. Having exhibited from the spring of 1900 to the winter of 1902, Gwen John returned to the New English in 1908. Her efforts to secure patronage through the club are recorded in her letters and notebooks. Thus, in September 1909, she wrote to Ursula Tyrwhitt that she hoped to do something specific for the club – 'a little picture to sell' – in order to cover outstanding dental bills. See Ceridwen Lloyd-Morgan (ed.), *Gwen John Letters and Notebooks*, Tate Publishing, London, in association with the National Library of Wales, 2004, p. 50.

38 George Moore, 'The Garret', *The Saturday Review*, 23 June 1906, p. 785.

39 Albert Rutherston, 'From Orpen and Gore to the Camden Town Group', *The Burlington Magazine*, vol. 83, p. 202.

40 See *Sickert Paintings*, Wendy Baron and Richard Shone (eds), exh. cat., Royal Academy of Arts, London, 1992, cat. 67, p. 204.

41 Osbert Sitwell (ed.), *A Free House, or the Artist as Craftsman, Being the Writings of Walter Richard Sickert*, Macmillan, London, 1947, p. 208 (extracted from *The Art News*, 12 May 1910).

42 Osbert Sitwell (ed.), *A Free House, or the Artist as Craftsman, Being the Writings of Walter Richard Sickert*, Macmillan, London, 1947, p. 92 (extracted from *The New Age*, 29 July 1910). Attacking the notion of 'refinement', the painter declared, 'with this goes, in the region of taste, an utter impossibility of living for twenty-four hours in a room with the "wrong" wallpaper, and as a corollary of the wallpaper, a mild liking for inoffensive and slight watercolours in the "*right*" mounts, framed in the "*right*" way'.

43 Laurence Binyon, 'Three Exhibitions', *The Saturday Review*, 6 June 1908, p. 720.

44 T. M. W., 'The New English Art Club's Summer Exhibition', *The Studio*, vol. 47, 1909, p. 178.

45 Simmons's *The Cosy Corner* (1904) and Shepherd's *The Bach Player* (1904), both unlocated, were 156 and 69 respectively in the NEAC spring exhibition in 1909. Simmons's panelled, painted interior, *The Cosy Corner*, replicates the setting of Rothenstein's *Mother and Child*, as does *In the Morning Room*, both painted in 1903, while Shepherd's *The Bach Player* relies heavily upon Orpen's *The Piano* (*c.* 1902). In both instances the rooms are austere and masculine. Both are purged of Victorian clutter.

46 Anon., 'The Case for Modern Painting, by a Modern Painter – IV The Royal Academy and the New English Art Club', *The Burlington Magazine*, vol. 11, April–September 1907, pp. 204–6.

47 Thus, for instance, by 1909 Spencer Gore began to observe that his, Henry Lamb's, Robert Bevan's, Harold Gilman's and Lucien Pissarro's paintings at the New English exhibitions were being rejected or 'gently pushed' into inner rooms.

48 Stabb's *The Crumpled Dress* (1908; National Museums on Merseyside), shown in the NEAC, repeats the *mise-en-scène* of Rutherston's *Confessions of Claude* (1901).

49 Orpen's *Night* (private collection), later known as *Solitude*, was exhibited at the Goupil Gallery Salon in the winter of 1907 (91); for further reference, see Bruce Arnold, *Orpen: Mirror to an Age*, Jonathan Cape, London, 1981, p. 214; see also *The Edwardians: Secrets and Desires*, Anna Gray, exh. cat., National Gallery of Australia, Canberra, 2004, p. 203. Clausen's *Twilight: Interior* was shown at the Royal Academy in 1909 (491).

50 William Nicholson, who showed at the club from the winter of 1908 to the spring of 1912, was more frequently associated with the International Society of Sculptors, Painters and Gravers. He exhibited two still-lifes at the club – entitled *The Canticelli Vase* in the winter of 1909 and an unidentified *Still-life* in the following spring. For further reference, see Lillian Browse, *William Nicholson*, Rupert Hart-Davis, London, 1956, p. 57 (142), in which it is dated *c.* 1913.

51 We may assume that *Night No. 2* was painted around the same time, or immediately after *Night*. A more complex work, it shows a male figure thought to be Orpen himself, embracing his wife, Grace, in one of the rooms of 13 Royal Hospital Road, Chelsea. See Bruce Arnold, *Orpen: Mirror to an Age*, Jonathan Cape, London, 1981, pp. 214–15. The picture makes an interesting play on Sickert's Camden Town murder series of 1908–09.

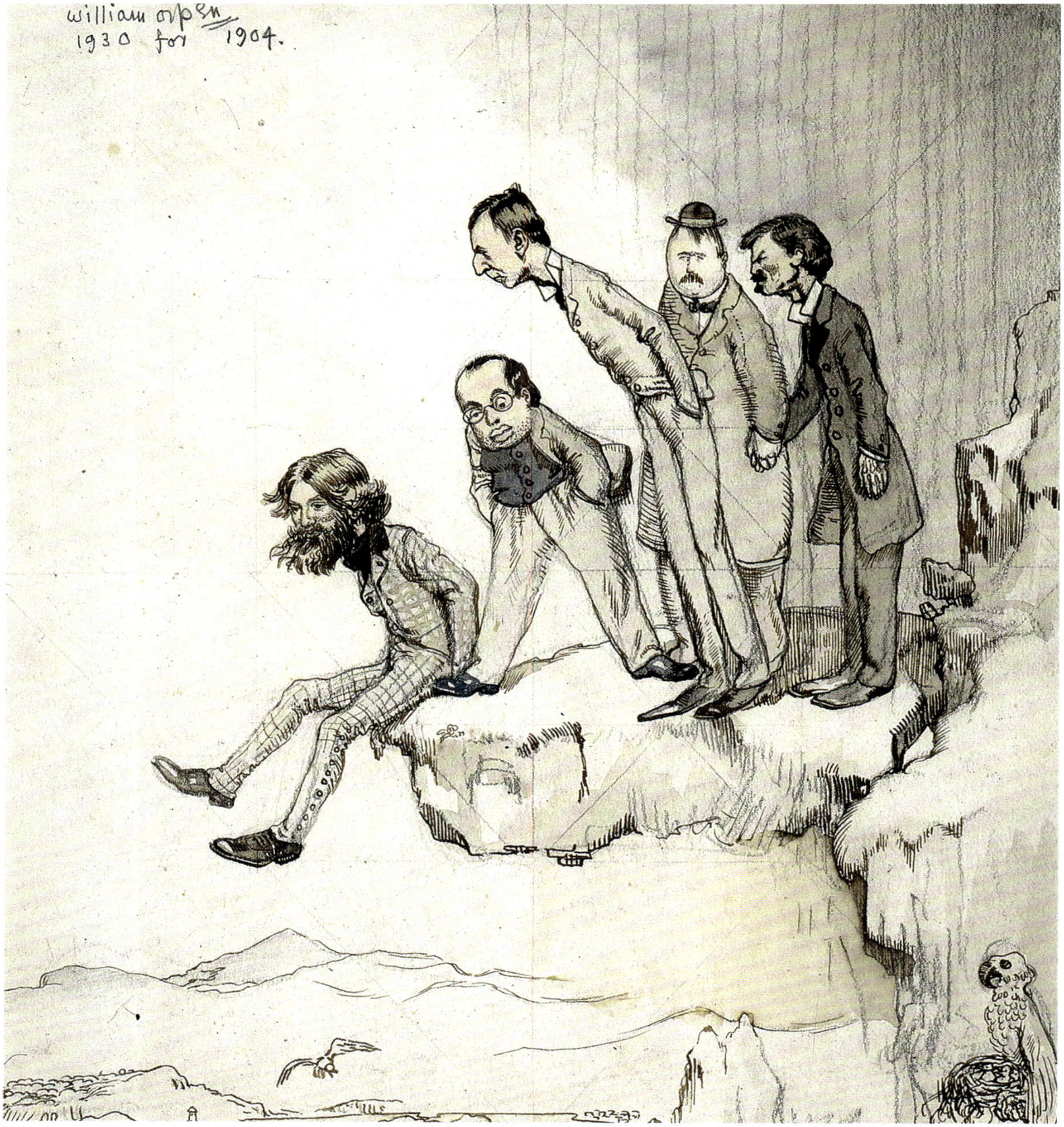

Fig. 69 William Orpen
Crisis at the NEAC, 1904
Pencil, ink and watercolour on paper,
24 x 21.5 cm
Shane Grant Esq.

CHAPTER 4 **'Its very name is a mockery'** 1905–1914

In the winter of 1904 the club's executive committee faced new problems. The Egyptian Hall, home of the Dudley Gallery, was sold and would soon be demolished. Muirhead Bone, the club's leading architectural draughtsman, recorded the event (fig. 70). Bone 'captured the attention of the larger public' at this time with his drawings of *The Demolition of St James's Hall* (1905) and *The Great Gantry, Charing Cross Station* (1905–06), shown at the club in the winter of 1905 and the winter of 1906 respectively, and he and MacColl should be recognised as founders of the New English topographical tradition (see fig. 71) that continues to the present day in the work of Charlotte Halliday.[1] Having been well housed since 1887, with the single exception of the Humphrey's Mansions experiment, the club was now homeless. In the circumstances it appears that Brown, who had taken a back seat recently, was persuaded to return to the election process and John lost out. It is he who perches dangerously at the edge of

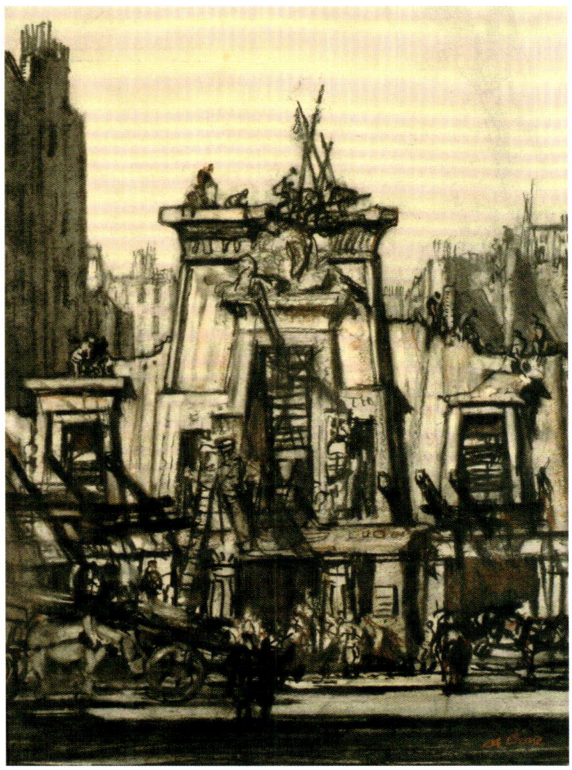

Fig. 70 Muirhead Bone
The Demolition of the Egyptian Hall, Piccadilly, 1904
Graphite on paper, 38 x 28 cm
Tullie House Museum & Art Gallery, Carlisle

the abyss in Orpen's humorous drawing, *Crisis at the NEAC* (1904; fig. 69). But were all of the club's principals vulnerable?

Following the success of the industrial exhibition at Wolverhampton in 1902, at which Steer, Tonks, Orpen, Nicholson, Rothenstein and Conder were shown as the leaders of British painting, and recognising that such out-of-town shows were important, the committee accepted the invitation to stage the following spring exhibition at the Royal Institution in Liverpool.[2] For that winter the galleries of the Alpine Club in Conduit Street were hired and thereafter, for the next four exhibitions, the club occupied a cramped gallery space at Dering Yard, off Bond Street. None of these places was a satisfactory solution and, in 1908, negotiations were conducted with the Royal Society of British Artists, now led by Alfred East, to place the club in their galleries in Suffolk Street.[3] To everyone's relief, this proved a satisfactory arrangement and the club remained in Suffolk Street on a renewable lease until the winter of 1920.

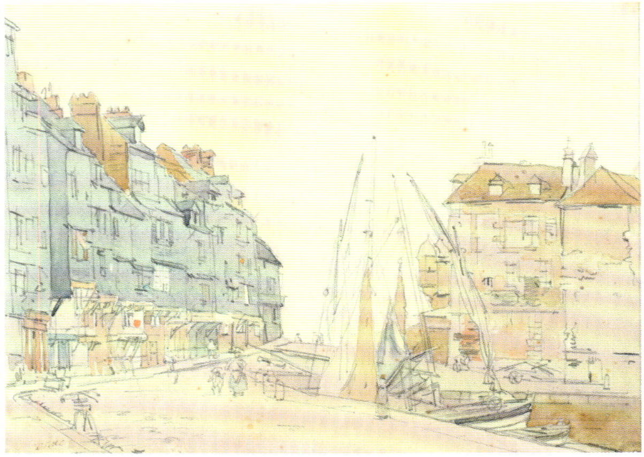

Fig. 71 Dugald Sutherland MacColl
St Catherine's Quay, Honfleur, *c.* 1906
Watercolour and drawing on paper, 22.9 x 30.5 cm
Purchased 1930. Tate, London

The club's reputation did not suffer as a result of the demise of the Dudley Gallery and, at the beginning of 1906, key members were selected for an important exhibition at Agnew's, badged as 'Independent British Art'. This filtered the important International Society of Sculptors, Painters and Gravers, the Scottish and Irish 'schools', and the New English, into a new configuration with the sole purpose of showing the best. David Croal Thomson, a consistent supporter of such artists as Steer, Lavery and Clausen when manager at Goupil's, moved to Agnew's in 1898 and was the guiding spirit behind the show. There was nothing revolutionary about it. It merely asserted that these artists, in mid-career and unrecognised by the Academy, had 'not received the appreciation they deserve'.[4] Brown's and Tonks's 'garden England' pastorals were prominent in the exhibition, while Orpen, Rothenstein and William Strang showed darker, working-class ghetto subjects.

'Safe' interiors were not the only paintings of interest to patrons of the New English in the years up to the Great War. If the interior mirrored an ideal space for contemplation, there remained a significant interest in the object, be it a still-life or figure subject. There were also new approaches to landscape painting that fully absorbed the innovation in Steer's most recent work. Landscape at the Academy had sunk to the depths and could no longer be regarded as representative.[5] Tonks, for instance, added anecdote to Steer's Arcadia, as such pictures as *The Lost Path* (*c.* 1906) indicate.[6] There was also a strong contingent of women landscape painters. By 1906 Ethel Walker, Clare Atwood, Beatrice Bland (fig. 72) and Edna Clarke Hall were joined by Fairlie Harmar (fig. 73) and Margaret Fisher Prout.[7] Bland, Harmar and later Prout took up residence in Cheyne Walk, alongside Ethel Walker – and such was their close relationship to their mentor that they were known as the 'Cheyne Walkers'. Was there a collective sensibility in the work of

Opposite top
Fig. 72 Beatrice Bland
Arundel Castle, indistinctly dated
Oil on canvas, 77 x 102 cm
Private collection

Opposite bottom
Fig. 73 Fairlie Harmar
Garden Gate, *c.* 1921
Oil on canvas, 63.5 x 76.2 cm
UCL Art Collections, University College London

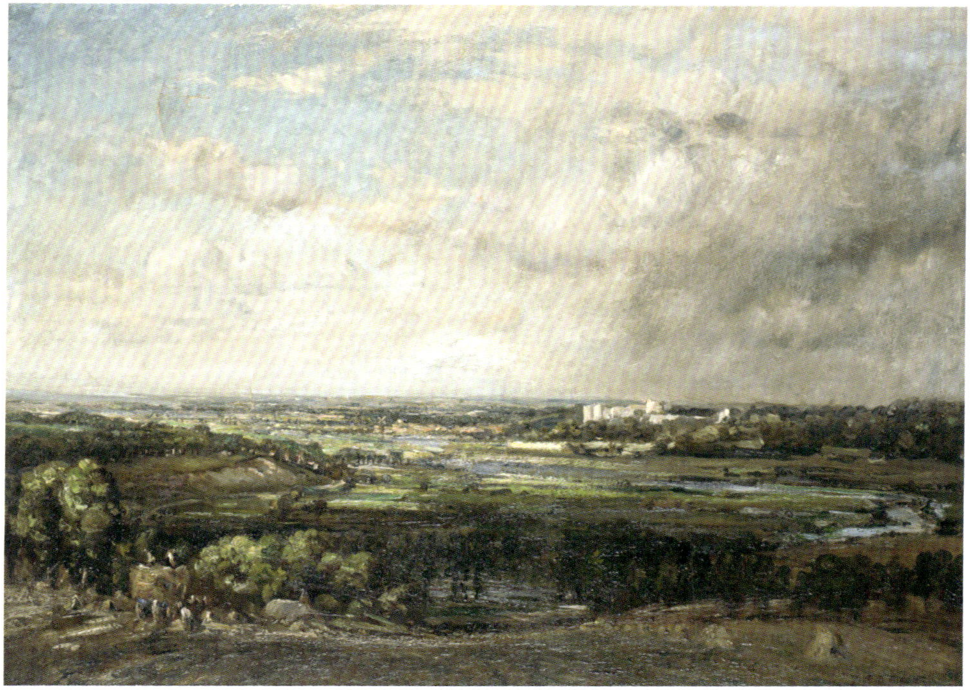

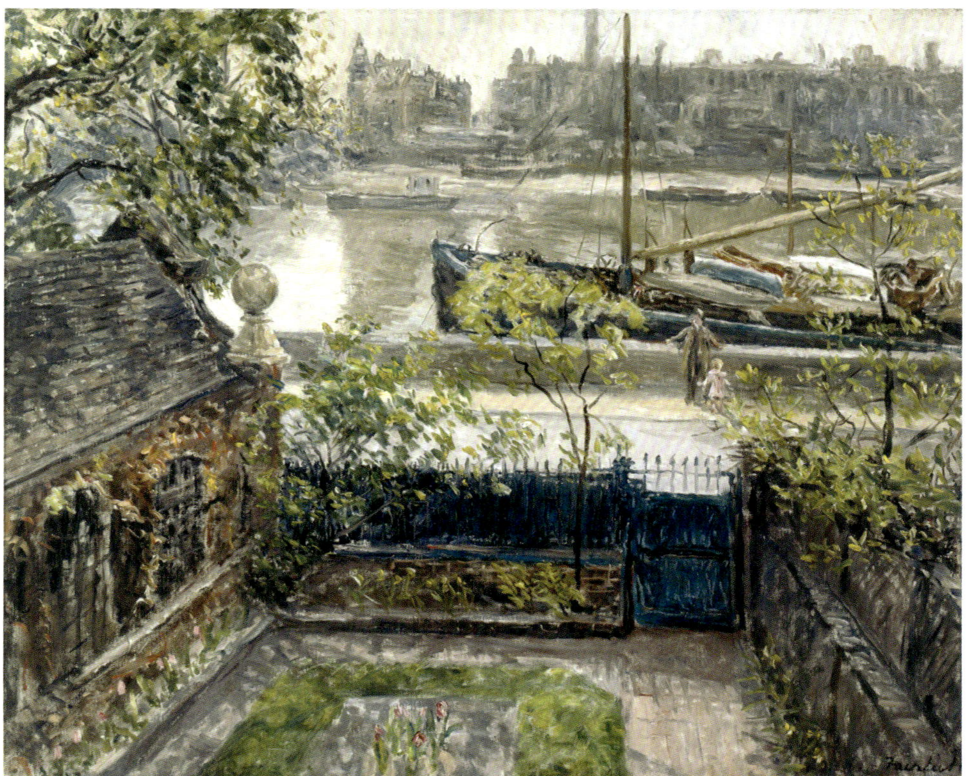

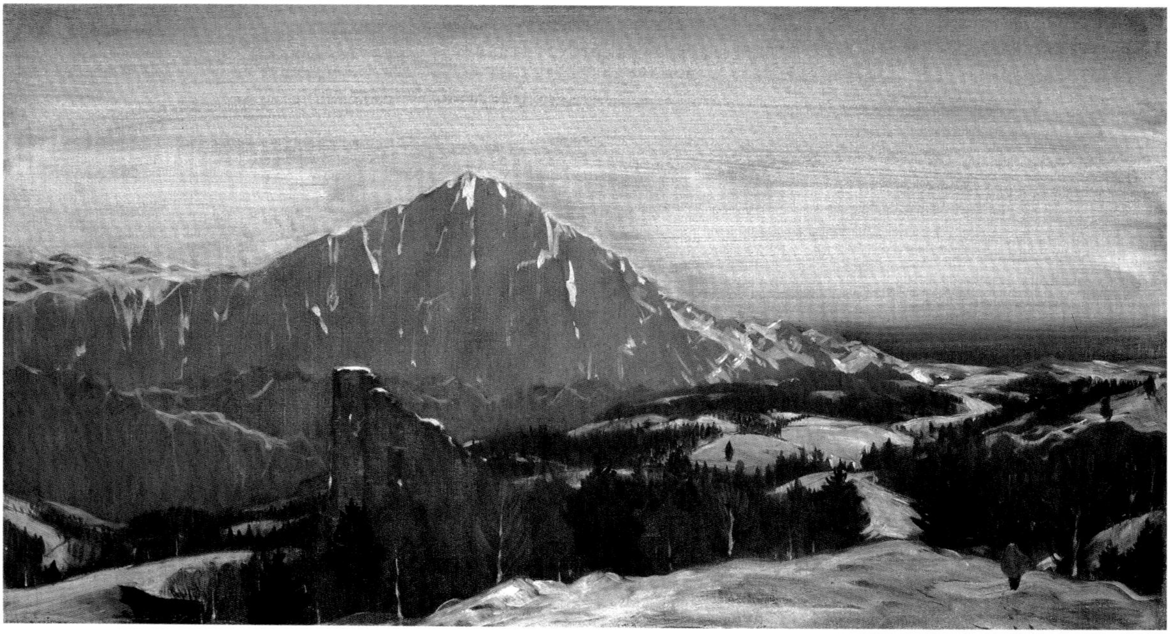

Fig. 74 Charles Holmes
Red Ruin, Lucerne, 1907
Oil on canvas, 45.7 x 81.2 cm
Presented by the Contemporary Art Society 1917. Tate, London

these 'Slade Ladies'? In most cases, as landscape and still-life painters, they were recognisably pupils of Brown and Tonks, but, in the case of Fisher Prout, daughter of Mark Fisher, a more cosmopolitan set of influences was apparent.[8]

None of these painters wished to be typecast. Like David Muirhead, they produced interiors, landscapes and the occasional portrait when circumstances permitted. The tranquil gardens and windswept ruins painted by Steer's immediate coterie – Tonks, Brown, Ronald Gray and Walter Russell had a critical edge on the Academy landscapes of David Murray, Alfred East and Alfred Parsons, but all were patently within an English tradition, the parameters of which had been set a century earlier. Charles Holmes, who from his earliest exhibits eschewed the 'Constable-esque', was increasingly drawn to remote and austere stretches of country, sometimes inspired by his travels in Europe. When he took *Red Ruin, Lucerne* (1907; fig. 74) to the New English in 1907, Steer reportedly commented that it made him shiver.[9] Its dark tonalities and simple segmenting of space were nevertheless admired by Robert Ross, who acquired it on behalf of the Contemporary Art Society, which, in turn, passed it to the Tate Gallery.[10] Industrial landscapes with their even simpler geometry lay in wait.

The affection for dark, unbroken planes was increasingly challenged after 1904 when Lucien Pissarro, having settled his father's estate, took on the mantle of the Impressionist tradition. As a critic of the New English brand of Impressionism, Pissarro was appalled at the regressive tendencies of recent exhibitions – 'our leading young artists have discovered that black paint is the last word in art', he wrote in 1899.[11] With the support of Sickert, and new exhibitors such as Spencer Gore, James B. Manson and James Brown, Pissarro wanted to see a return to the Impressionist colour application he understood.[12] *Grey Weather, June Afternoon, Finchingfield* (1905; fig. 75), likely to have been one of his 1905 winter exhibits, exemplifies the dense mosaic of tiny touches that was his father's legacy. Pissarro actively supported the club until his death in 1944 and his contributions soon became part of its defining character, to some extent blurring the active nature of the debate that he provoked. He consistently evaded the grand manner and the 'august site',[13] and, always an outsider, had no particular longing for the fine feeling of Gainsborough's or Constable's sketches. To this extent, Steer and he were poles apart. In equal measure, his muddy fields were no Cytherea, and, although they had their admirers, they jostled with the work of those for whom landscape was an invitation to fanciful escape, atmospheric bluster or blatant chauvinism.

Orpen, having set the hare running, had been among the first to escape the tyranny of the interior and, with one or two notable exceptions, his future roomsets would be more accurately described as 'portrait-interiors', giving equal status to an identified occupant and his or her possessions.[14] *Improvisation on a*

Fig. 75 Lucien Pissarro
Grey Weather, June Afternoon, Finchingfield, 1905
Oil on canvas, 53.5 x 64.8 cm
Southampton Art Gallery

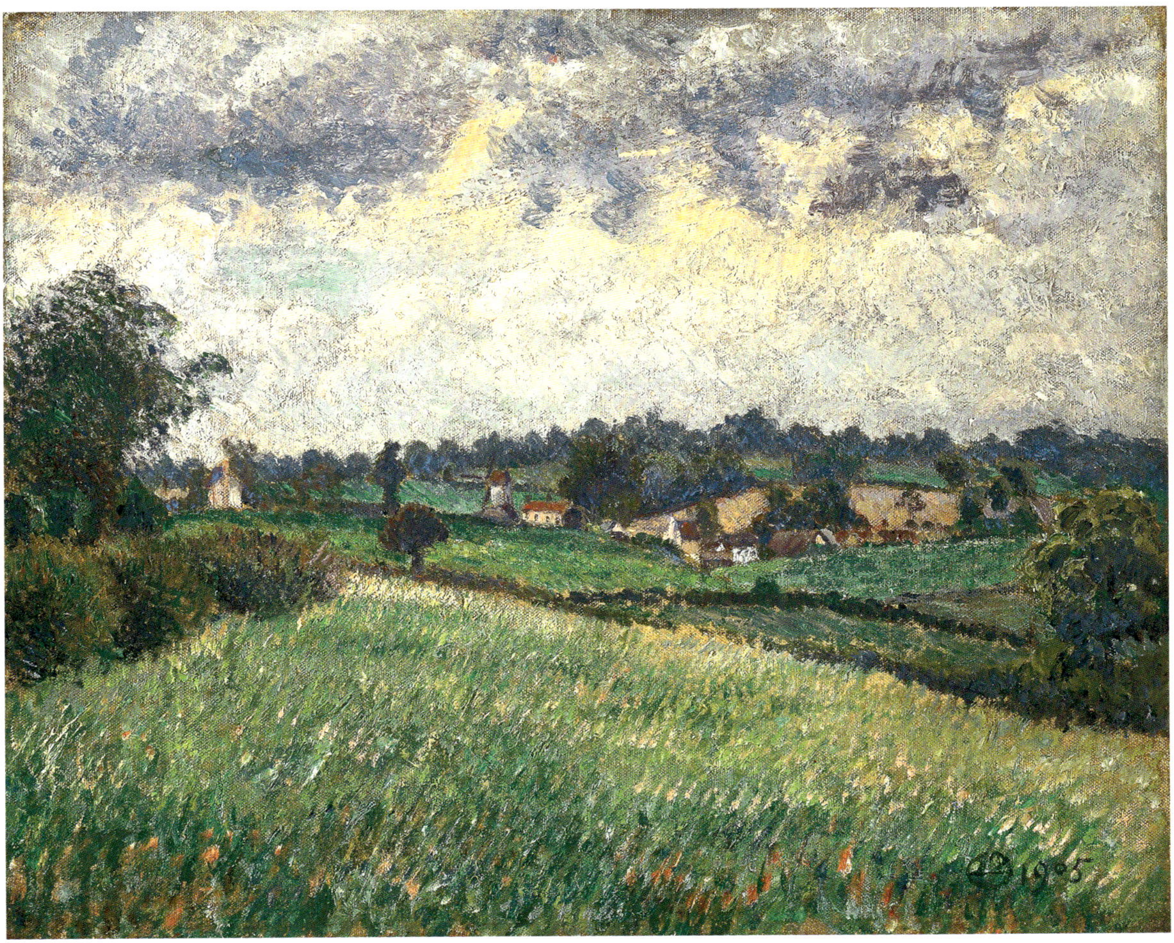

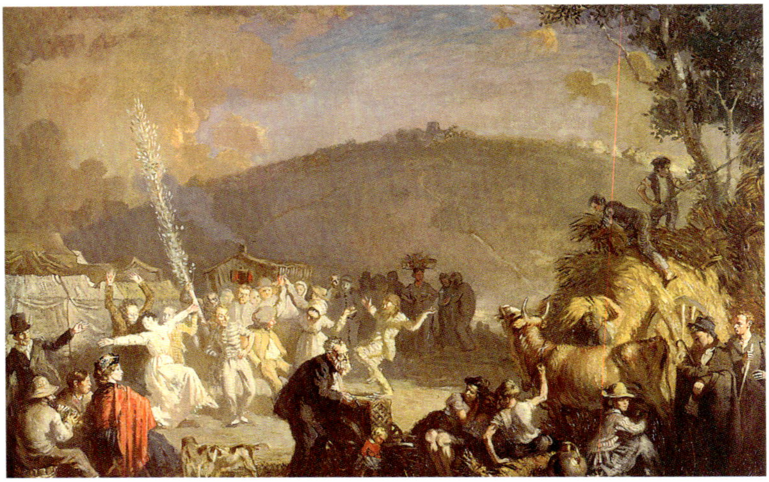

Fig. 76 William Orpen
Improvisation on a Barrel Organ, 1904
Oil on canvas, 110 x 153 cm
Walker Art Gallery, Liverpool

Barrel Organ (1904; fig. 76), shown in the same year, demonstrates the fundamental break with the past. A *kermesse,* night celebrations at a country fair, locked into the complete pictorial catalogue of rusticity. In the middle of a gypsy encampment, players perform a ritual dance, and, while field workers pitch hay, a cow is milked and peasants return from market, all to the strains of a barrel organ and a melodeon. Similar bawdy gatherings may be found in Rubens, but Orpen's 'droll company' was, in the words of Arthur Symons, 'swept together out of Goya, Watteau and other puppet shows, in an atmosphere obviously of no-man's land ... outside the severe window ... of his habitual pictures'.[15] Like Peter Pan, Orpen had taken flight, and his action served as an invitation to others. Conder's *Paysage fantastique* and De Glehn's *The Danaides* (both *c.* 1906 and shown in the spring of the same year) take us further outside the window. Having been out of fashion, Conder began to make a comeback and both he and De Glehn were producing paintings that could be described as 'decorative' – a critical term, which in practice meant a cluster of female nudes bathing in a forest pool or by the sea. Thus, his critics saw De Glehn as bringing Watteau 'up to date'.[16]

Yet this in itself was an oversimplification. Around the turn of the century, despite the ignominies of the Boer War and threats from France and Germany in the scramble for Africa, British national prestige was running high. The successful livery companies of the City of London, a number of semi-public institutions and a few private collectors of the 'Randlord' type commissioned murals from Frank Brangwyn and others.[17] De Glehn was not alone in wishing to use the New English as an opportunity to demonstrate his potential in this regard. Yet these painters, working in a recognised idiom, provided no more than the prelude for an extraordinary sequence of large canvases by Augustus John. Up to this point John, who had attracted the attention of critics in 1902 with the outstanding *Merikli* (1902), had not fulfilled his early promise. By 1906, he provoked considerable frustration. Moore, for instance, characterised him as the author of 'Chelsea' masterpieces – quick, accomplished drawings that were stylish but insubstantial. He nevertheless maintained the hope that John would one day have revealed to him 'the exact thing he came into the world to express'.[18] This did not happen for a further two years.[19] There were more, seemingly endless preparations until, in the spring of 1908, *The Young Pyramus* (1907; fig. 77) ushered in a new era, and the word 'decorative' was redefined. John followed this with an impressive series – *The Way Down to the Sea* (1909; fig. 78), *Forza e Amore* (1911) and *The Mumpers* (1912; fig. 85) – the last two of which were actually executed as commissioned decorations.[20]

From the start, these paintings aimed at public rhetoric rather than private reverie. Writing in *The Saturday Review,* Laurence Binyon explained the attraction of the first of these works. It was, he said, 'poignant and alive in its own imaginative world ... it possesses a spice of strangeness of beauty, which makes all its neighbours look tame and everyday'.[21] Others were more precise in their referencing. Puvis de Chavannes and 'portrait heads from the Greek cemetery at Alexandria, to be seen in the National Gallery' were his inspiration.[22] The sensual froth of the *Danaides* had been swept away. François Boucher was banned. In the painting of the same name, the young Pyramus takes his first steps in an austere landscape, in the presence of classical mothers (fig. 77). An everyday scene that John must have witnessed is treated with solemn, statuesque dignity. This was a miraculous moment that, for Binyon, called up the 'deep and central emotions' of life.

Thereafter John's work was eagerly awaited. During the following spring, the languid caryatids process to the water's edge, led by a naked boy in *The Way Down to the Sea* (1909; fig. 78). When *The Smiling Woman* (1908–09; fig. 79) was compared to the *Mona Lisa,* Leonardo seemed to provide the clue to John's

Below left
Fig. 77 Augustus John
The Young Pyramus, 1907
Oil on canvas, 120.6 x 150.5 cm
Johannesburg Art Gallery

Below right
Fig. 78 Augustus John
The Way Down to the Sea, 1909
Oil on canvas, 200.7 x 170.2 cm
Private collection

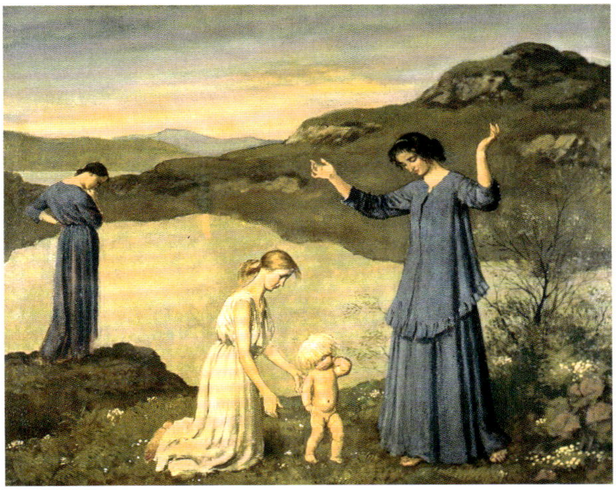

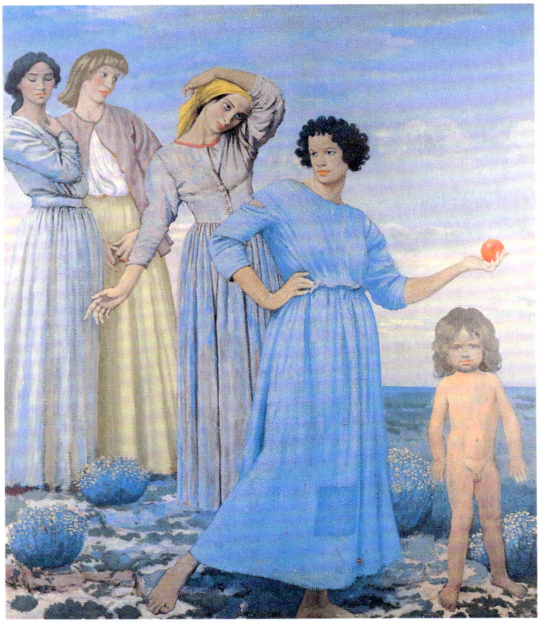

sources, and connections were made between his rugged setting and the Leonardesque landscape of rocks, rivers and sea. John's women ceremonially processing to the shore are at one with the elements. Nurturing and cultivation embodied the ageless virtues of Western civilisation. 'The time may come when the women ... will seem as beautiful as the Venus de Milo,' wrote *The Times* reviewer and, responding to his nervous approval, Binyon emphatically underlined John's efforts to break away from the world of appearances.[23]

> This process of building up a style to express that imaginative vision is bound to produce things that will inevitably seem ugly and awkward to the contemporary eye. What these large paintings attest beyond denial is character, life, and rhythmic power.... Like Puvis de Chavannes, he is happiest with a house-painter's materials and a blank wall.[24]

Pictures from club exhibitions at this time help to identify John's central preoccupations. One is Sargent's extraordinary *The Solitary* (1908; fig. 80), an attempt to fuse the natural lighting on a hillside near Purtud with a 'spiritual' subject. So powerful is the impression of dappled sunlight that the casual viewer might easily miss the figure. Orpen's Caravaggesque saints have been taken out into the daylight. Where John would simplify rocks, consign plants to the periphery and accentuate the statuesque in his figures, Sargent submerges his hermit in the palpitating surface of nature, downplaying biblical

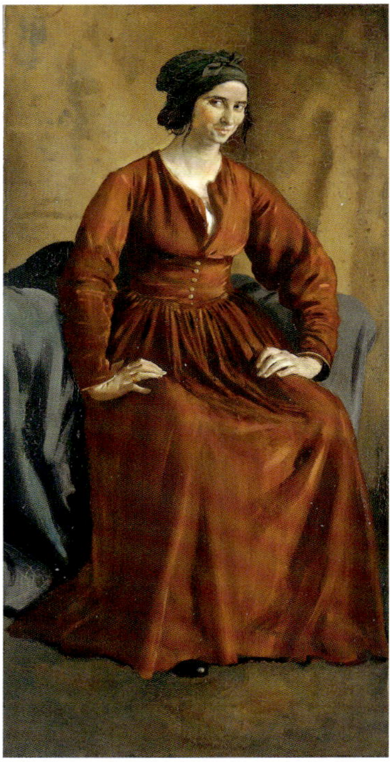

Above
Fig. 79 Augustus John
The Smiling Woman, 1908–09
Oil on canvas, 196 x 98.2 cm
Presented by the Contemporary Art Society 1917. Tate, London

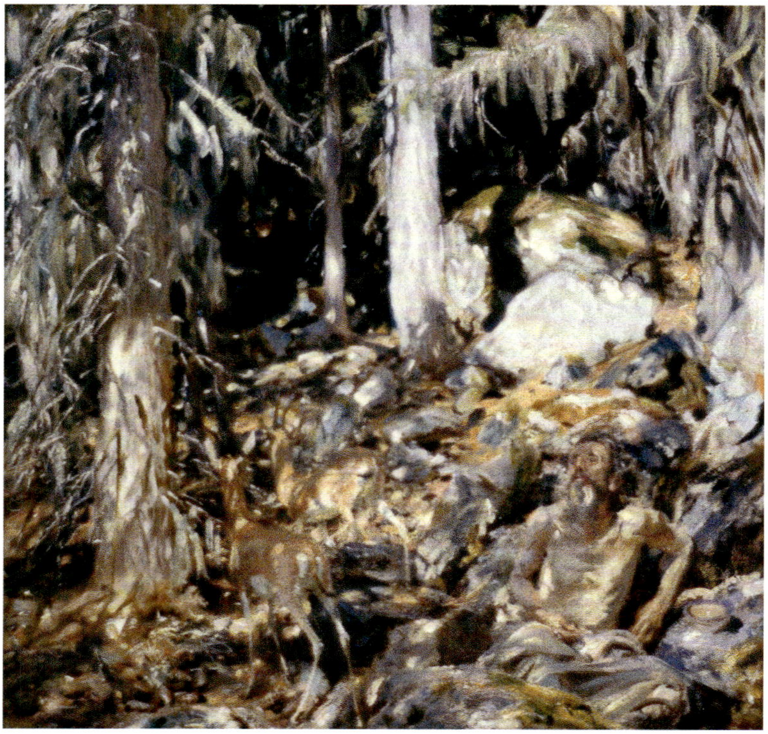

Left
Fig. 80 John Singer Sargent
The Solitary, 1908
Oil on canvas, 95.9 x 96.5 cm
Rogers Fund, 1911. The Metropolitan Museum of Art, New York

or mythological explanations.[25] His vagabond is no Job or exiled Ovid. For the present dazzled by the here-and-now, Sargent has revisited his early infatuation with Impressionism.

This path had closed for younger artists and John's message about 'the spirit of place' – in practice a rocky landscape uniformly lit and inhabited by solitary 'gypsy-esque' females – found receptive eyes and ears amongst his immediate following in works by James Dickson Innes, Derwent Lees, Henry Lamb and Ian Strang.[26] It breaks out in the brittle graphism of Albert Rutherston's *The Smart Visitor* (1911), in the early work of Paul Nash and in Gerald Leslie Brockhurst's *Seule* (1915; fig. 81).[27] At the same time the *Mona Lisa*-style half-length format enabled landscape and figure to come together in a mystic combination, provoked perhaps by familiar lines from Walter Pater. McEvoy's plaintiff *La Basquaise* (1913; fig. 82) was thus a figure described as coming from a race 'dominated more or less by the spirit of its environment'.[28] She was one of many representing race or class, and Brockhurst's *La Basquaise* (*c.* 1914), David Muirhead's *A Gypsy in Chelsea* (1910) and Francis Dodd's *Polly* (1911; fig. 83) are among her companions.

A further point of comparison is provided by Orpen's *Portrait Group (Homage to Manet)* (1909; fig. 84), a picture with a 'programme' of a very different

Below
Fig. 81 Gerald Leslie Brockhurst
Seule, 1915
Watercolour on paper,
19.6 x 24.4 cm
Albert H. Wiggin Collection,
Print Department,
Boston Public Library

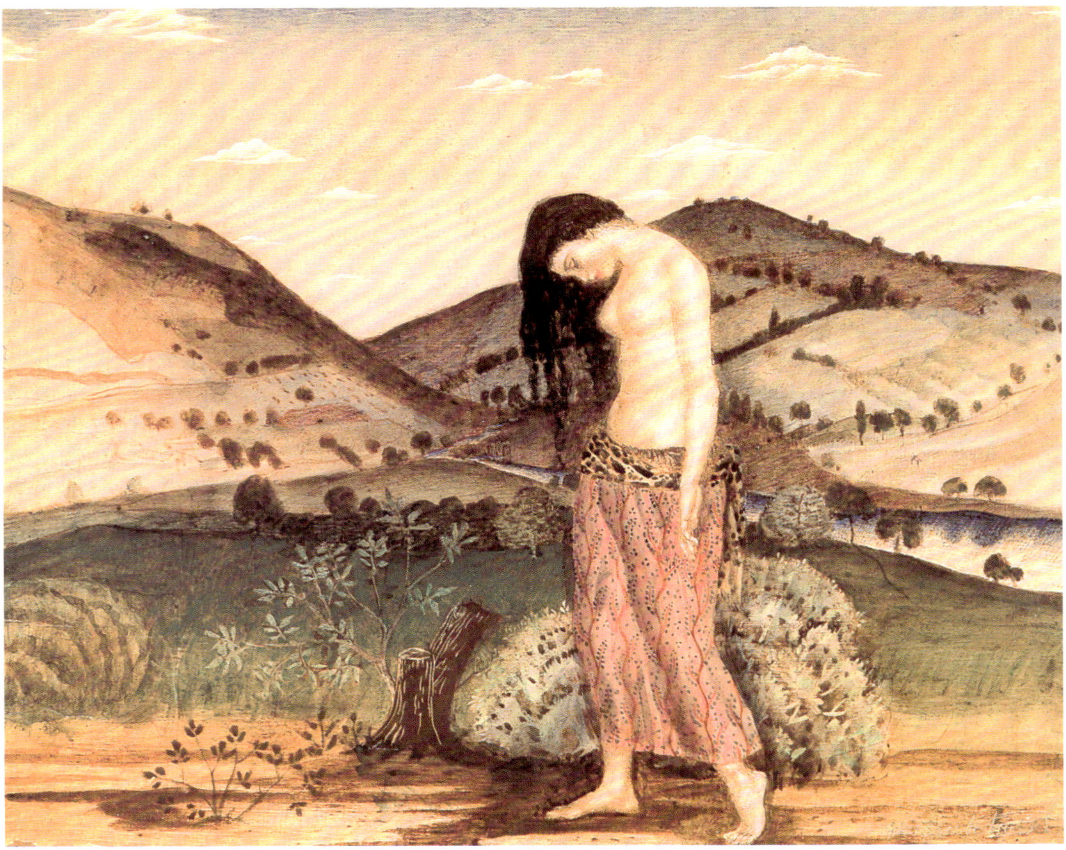

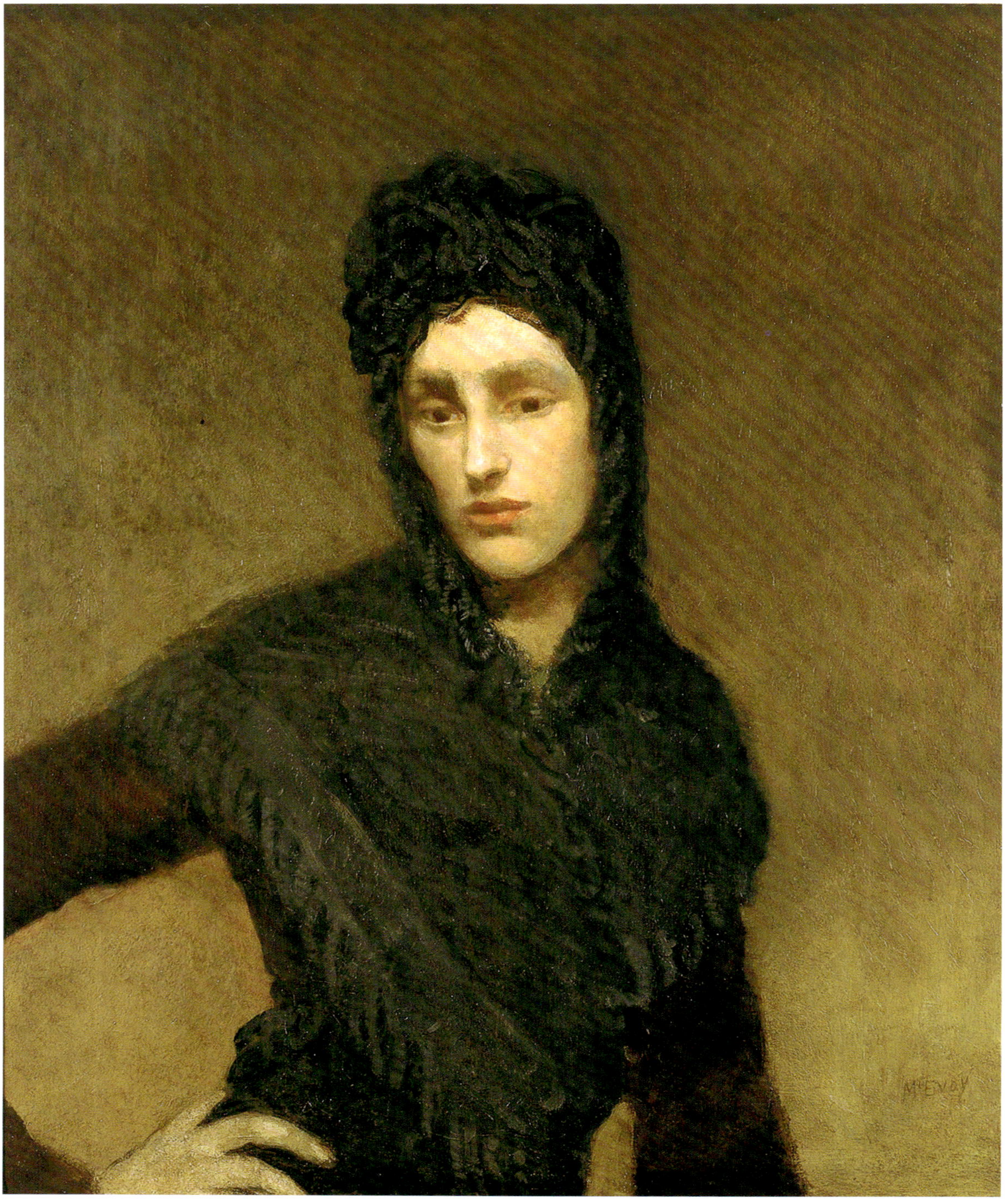

Fig. 82 Ambrose McEvoy
La Basquaise, 1913
Oil on canvas, 76 x 63.3 cm
Pyms Gallery, London

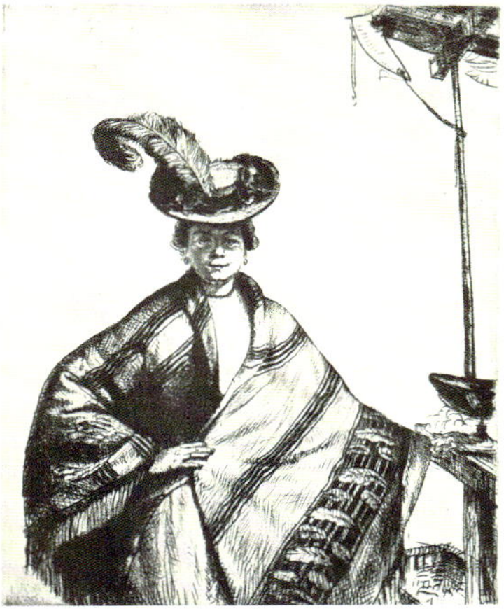

Fig. 83 Francis Dodd
Polly, 1911
Etching on paper
Private collection

kind. If more conservative viewers of *The Way Down to the Sea* (fig. 78) might prefer John's *Portrait of William Nicholson* (1909) in the same show, they might also refer to Orpen's orthodox reading of the New English caucus, and its common origins in the Slade and modern French art. Later retitled *Homage to Manet*, it portrays Sickert, Steer and Tonks, and their critic supporters, Moore and MacColl, as well as Hugh Lane, the collector of Impressionist and New English pictures. A balance was struck between tradition and the avant-garde of yesteryear, represented by the cast of Venus and Manet's *Eva Gonzalès* (1870).[29] The canvas celebrates Lane's acquisition of this work for the Municipal Gallery in Dublin, Moore's rambling reminiscences of the Impressionist painters and the general sense that a private, self-contained artistic coterie could now reveal itself. A contemporary observer noted that 'although the public does not go to the New English Art Club, the collectors do and it has the reputation ... of being one of the best galleries for selling in all London'.[30]

As John was seeking the timeless and universal derived from the Florentines and Puvis de Chavannes, Orpen was taking stock of the Caravaggesques

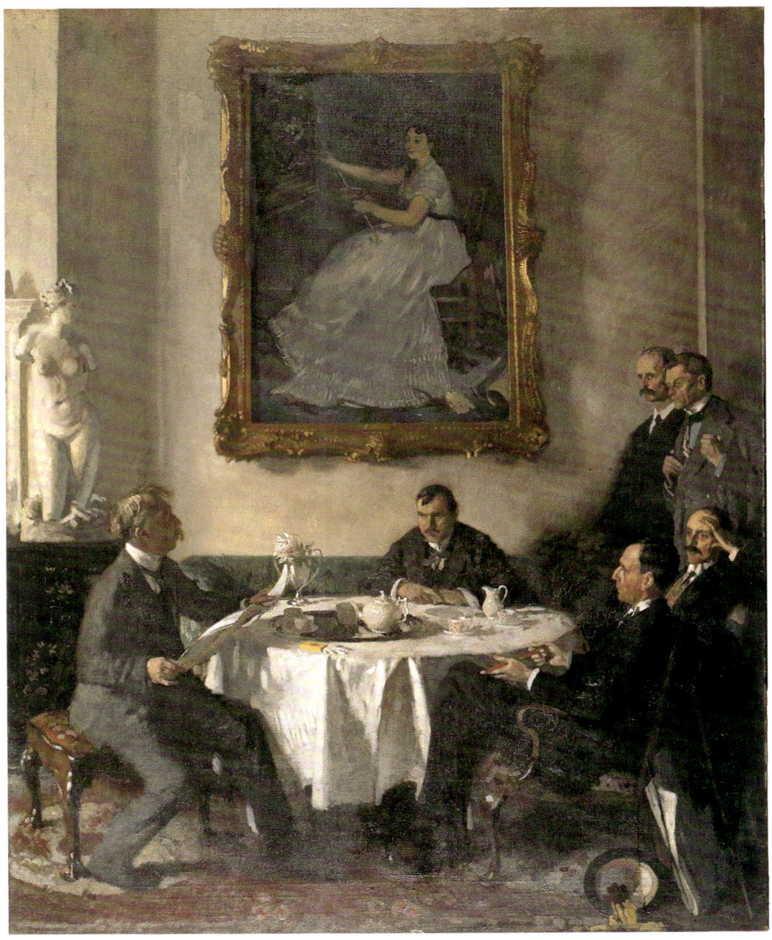

Fig. 84 William Orpen
Portrait Group (Homage to Manet), 1909
Oil on canvas, 163.8 x 130.2 cm
Manchester City Art Gallery

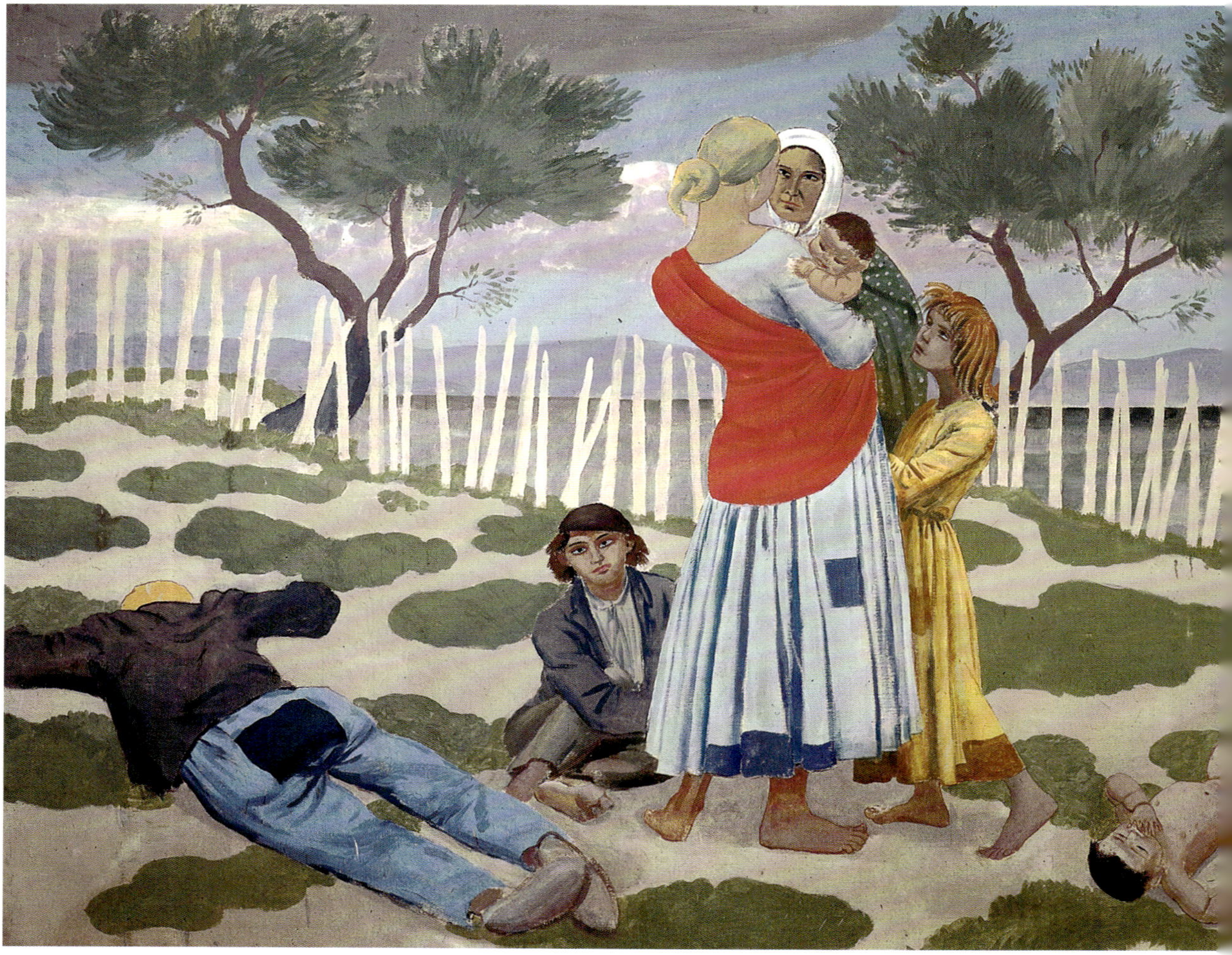

tradition in Manet. Lane was more interested in John than Orpen at this point. Living in the centre of what might be regarded as New English territory, he purchased *Forza e Amore* and *The Mumpers* (1912; fig. 85) as decorations for Lindsey House in Cheyne Walk.[31] Having been prepared by *The Young Pyramus* (fig. 77) and *The Way Down to the Sea* (fig. 78), critics regarded neither as unqualified successes, yet in the case of the first, it proved more successful than most of the works on show. Such was the belief in John that critics felt his new work must be in line with the most recent Parisian trends and if, in *The Way Down to the Sea*, he harked back to Florence, he had 'gone in heart and soul for Post-Impressionism' in *The Mumpers*. This massive canvas (254 x 619.8 cm), reputedly painted in four and a half days, presents a number of static groups of travellers by a campfire. Reviewers were divided, some finding it unattractive, while one wondered if it alone might give 'fresh life to a society that may serve again a useful purpose in the artistic economy'.[32]

Fig. 85 Augustus John
The Mumpers, 1912
Oil on canvas, 254 x 619.8 cm
City of Detroit Purchase.
Detroit Institute of Arts

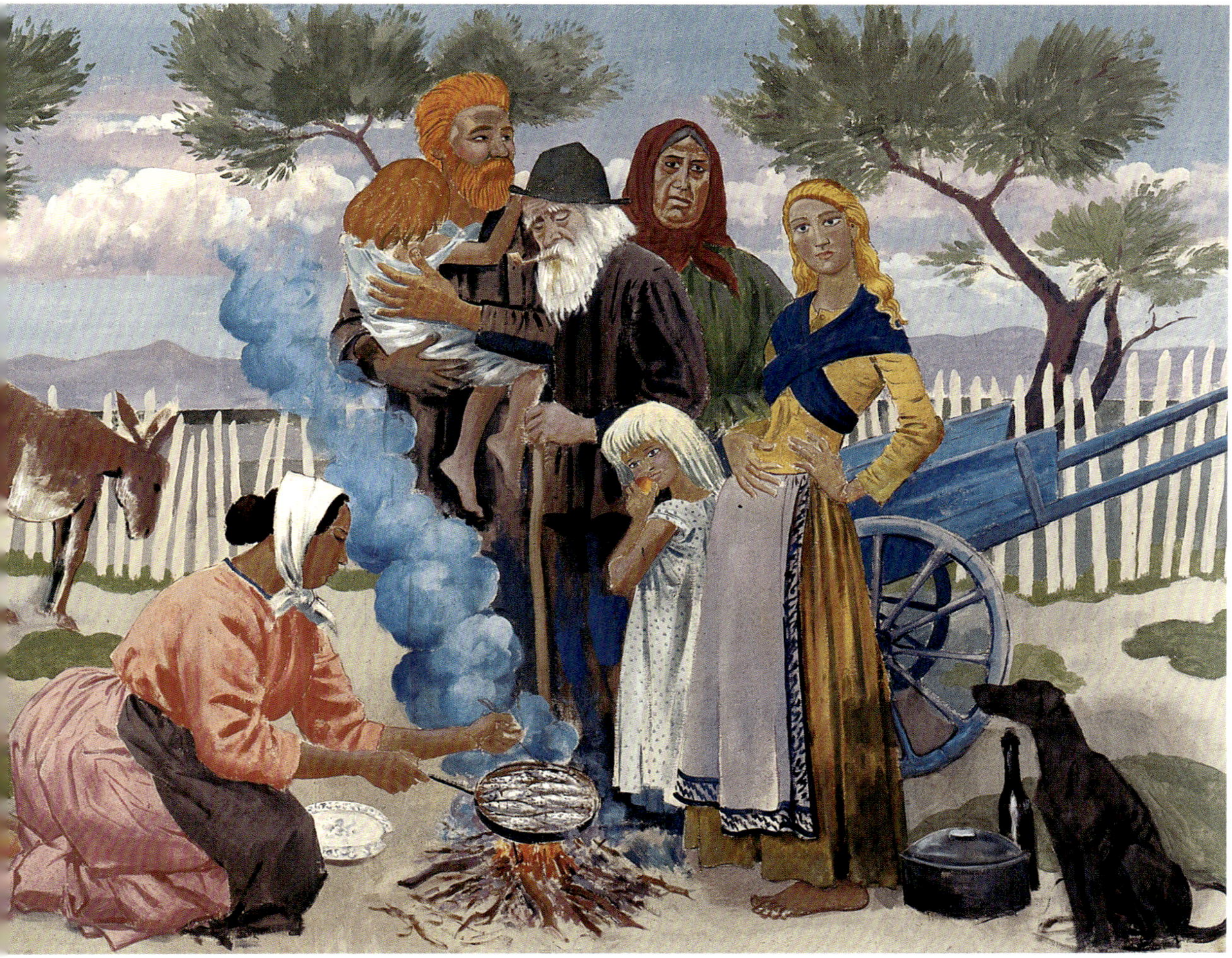

In essence, this 'purpose' could only be defined by the content of the shows. The majority of exhibits were non-controversial landscapes, portraits and interiors echoing the practices and precepts of Steer and Tonks. Typical examples such as De Glehn's *New England* (1911; fig. 86) and *The Picnic*, shown in the spring of 1912, took on Tonks's fascination with Victorian dress and Steer's mellow Impressionist palette. *The Academy* described the first of these canvases as:

> a really pleasant study of old America – America, that is to say, before it had been vulgarised by the war. It is a delightful picture of a girl in a full white dress with Victorian bonnet, knocking for admission at the door of a clean, white shingle house, with overhanging creepers, all bathed in brilliant sunshine'.[33]

That De Glehn should discover in the New World, this dream of mid-Victorian England – envisioned in authentic ruins and rustic bridges by Philip Connard and David Muirhead – provides a rich riposte to the 'modernity' that every other British artist-visitor saw.

Throughout the Edwardian years the club faced challenges from dealers who tempted such painters as John and Orpen into solo exhibitions – a relatively new phenomenon.[34] Having weathered the formation of the International Society in 1898, until the Allied Artists' Association (AAA) was formed by Frank Rutter ten years later, new societies had been much less of a threat.[35] In some senses the AAA could be regarded as the revival of La Thangue's 'bigger movement', a strand of – albeit suppressed – club idealism. In hiring the Albert Hall and with the inclusion of some of the leading Parisian radicals, the AAA appeared to be attacking the Royal Academy on a much broader front than either the Agnew's show or the International Society. Containing 3,061 catalogued items, it was certainly bigger than the Academy, and with Sickert, John and Spencer Gore, along with James Pryde and Walter Crane, as the hanging committee, club members played an active part in its affairs right from the start. Its character and content were so radically different from those of the New English, that fair comparisons could not be made.[36] It provided a *Salon des Refusés* for younger would-be New English exhibitors such as Robert Bevan, Harold Gilman and Charles Ginner, who sensed Tonks's hostility, and were looking for a supportive venue. They were painters who had more in common with Pissarro than with De Glehn and while the overall quality of AAA exhibitions may have been unpredictable, it fulfilled the important function of bringing them together in a liberal ambience. For a time it seemed that Spencer Gore, Lucien Pissarro, Gilman and the others who had been holding informal exhibitions in Sickert's studio at 19 Fitzroy Street for the previous two years would have an impact similar to that of the Impressionists at the end of the 1880s. Their increasing disaffection was evident by 1909 when Spencer Gore noted that his, Pissarro's and Henry Lamb's work was 'gently pushed' into the less prominent spaces in the New English and he was forced to conclude that 'they dislike our kind of painting'.[37]

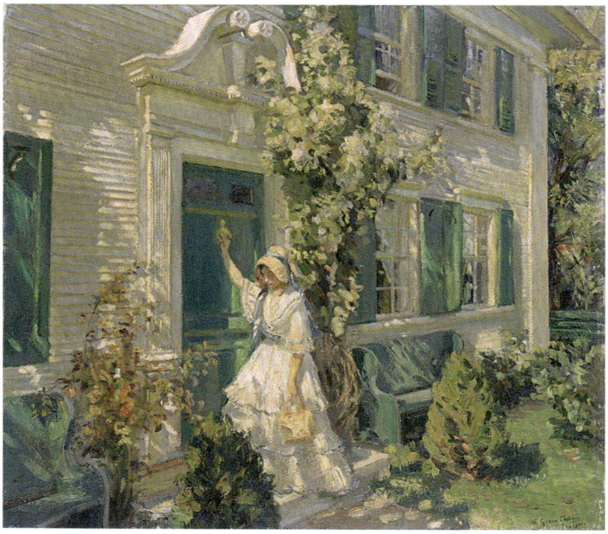

Fig. 86 Wilfrid de Glehn
New England, 1911
Oil on canvas, 71.1 x 77.5 cm
Felton Bequest, 1929. National Gallery of Victoria, Melbourne

Tensions of a different kind are likely to have been lurking under the surface. Gore and Gilman, for instance, had been teaching at the Westminster School of Art, which ought to have been in close alliance with the Slade. However, it had lately developed a unique range of drawing practices. Where the Slade taught flowing linearism, backed by careful shading, Westminster students used dots and broken lines to annotate the points of observation where a form changed direction or was thrown into shade. These differences were reflected in Gilman's paintings, which, when they arrived at the club, could not be classed as typical Slade products. Nevertheless, the forces represented in Orpen's *Portrait Group* in the shape of Tonks, MacColl and Steer were formidable. After Saturday viewings at Fitzroy Street, Pissarro, Sickert, John, Gore,

Fig. 87 Spencer Gore
Outbuildings, Hertingfordbury (The White Fence), c. 1910
Oil on canvas, 50.8 x 60.9 cm
Private collection

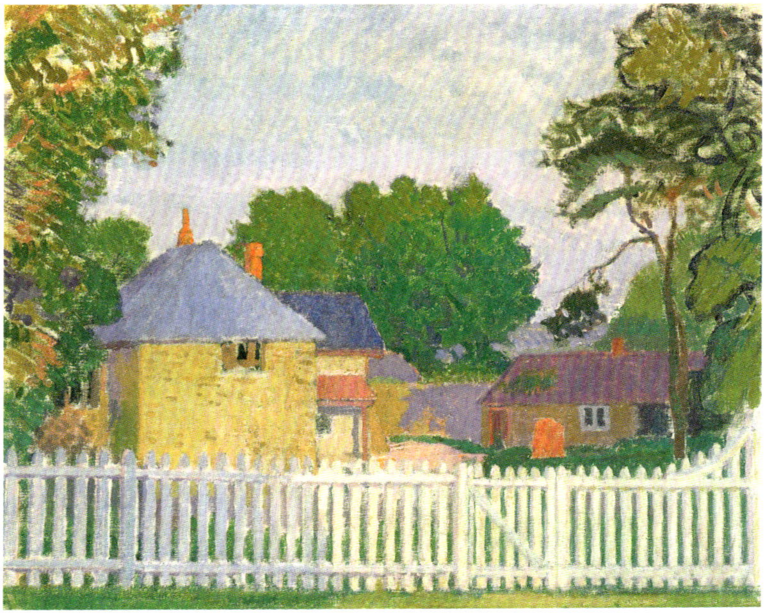

Gilman and Rutter, sometimes joined by Robert Bevan and his wife, Stanislawa de Karlowsa, dined together at a restaurant in Gordon Square, followed by drinks at the Café Royal. At these sessions the conversation would turn to the New English and 'the burning question' – 'should those present endeavour to capture and reform the club, or should they secede ... and start a rival society?'[38]

The arguments were suddenly overtaken and thrown into relief by the 'Manet and the Post-Impressionists' exhibition that Roger Fry curated at the Grafton Galleries in Bond Street. The show caused a critical furore – the combined meteoric force of Cézanne, Gauguin and Van Gogh, accompanied by examples of Matisse and Picasso, shook the art world.[39] Tonks is reported to have counselled his students not to go. The 44th club exhibition, in which Fry exhibited a large allegorical panel inspired by Guido Reni, for the ceiling of Ardkinglas House, coincided with the Grafton show.[40] Comparisons were not intended – but they were made – between 'the modernist movement among our painters' and 'the anarchistic absurdities of the Post-Impressionists'. The club was receiving muralists and tempera painters in the grand European tradition, and, while as an aesthete and critic Fry could appreciate the Post-Impressionists, when it came to executing a mural commission, he reverted to earlier conventions. He had exhibited regularly at the club since 1891, but his paintings of Florentine terraces and garden pools at the turn of the century indicated a growing scholarly interest in the working methods of the fresco painters of the Renaissance. It was an enthusiasm shared by the artists who formed the Society of Painters in Tempera in 1901.[41] In no sense a rival to the club, this small group came to prominence as a result of the growing number of mural commissions for public bodies in the Edwardian years, and, although its own exhibitions were

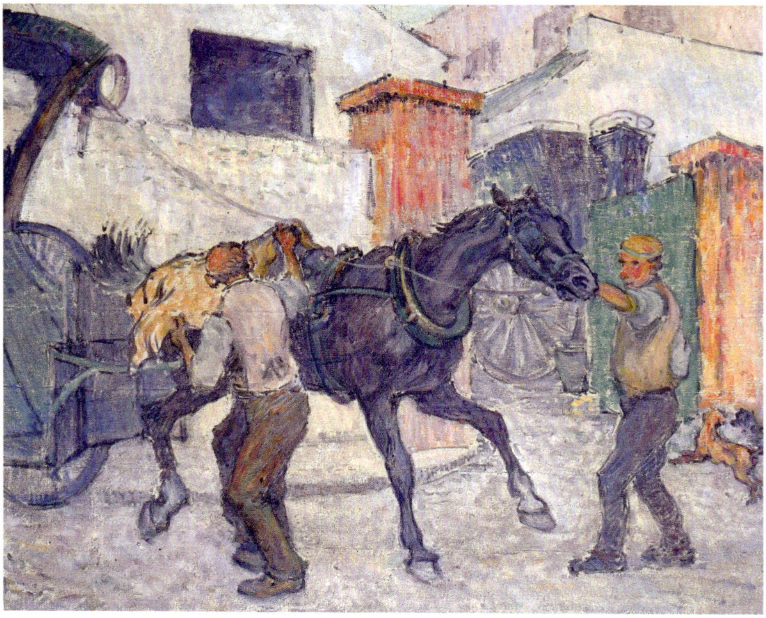

Fig. 88 Robert Bevan
The Cab Horse, exhibited 1910
Oil on canvas, 63.5 x 76.2 cm
Presented by the Trustees of the Duveen Paintings Fund 1949. Tate, London

infrequent, its members submitted regularly to New Gallery summers shows. With the closure of the New Gallery in 1909 they were homeless.

By 1910 distinct factions ranging from the antiquarian to the avant-garde had emerged in the club. The inclusion of Gore's *The Mantelpiece* (1910), *Taunton Vale* (1910) and *Outbuildings, Hertingfordbury (The White Fence)* (*c.* 1910; fig. 87), Lamb's *Breton Cowherd* (*c.* 1910), a work by Gilman, three by Maxwell Gordon Lightfoot and two cab yard pictures by Bevan (fig. 88), in the 1910 winter show, along with paintings by Steer, Sargent and Orpen, enabled finer discriminations to be made within the broad New English church. It did not escape attention that the club, with Sargent and Orpen, had 'one full-blown RA and one Associate'.[42] While its 'Englishness' was its 'undeniable' characteristic, one critic asked his readers to compare:

> the affectionate English beauty which Mr Wilson Steer has built up on the French Impressionist formulas with that of Cézanne and Van Gogh in the Continental Post-Impressionists at the Grafton Gallery and the racial difference is extraordinary.[43]

Although the club was praised, at this point, for not having spawned 'lots of little secessions', it was about to do so.[44] The Fitzroy Street Group artists were shortly to distance themselves from Steer's 'Englishness'.

In 1911, with Sickert as *éminence grise*, and Gore as president, they formed the Camden Town Group and staged their first exhibition. There were sixteen members.[45] Of these only Malcolm Drummond, Charles Ginner and J. Doman Turner had not yet shown at the New English by the time their exhibition opened.[46] The remaining thirteen, led by Gore and Gilman, withdrew from the club and saved their best work for the new group.[47] They might continue to submit to club exhibitions in the future, but they had their own platform, even though it was a relatively small one.[48] Not only did the Camden Town Group members take on Sickert's ideal of 'small pictures for small patrons', but their venue, the Carfax Gallery, was also so small that each painter had to be limited to a maximum of four exhibits. With such restrictions, could a painter afford the luxury of exclusive allegiance? Although it might attract attention, such a group did not carry the weight of the club, now firmly established in Suffolk Street. Its impact, its obvious alliance with broad Post-Impressionist practice and the critical attention it attracted weakened the club, and while comfort could be drawn from the knowledge that John and Orpen and their followers remained loyal, the club's more inclusive exhibitions were considered in the light of nascent rivalries. The interior painters (Stabb, Shepherd and Simmons), new recruits (such as Glynn Philpot, Alexander Jamieson and William Shackleton) and the women painters (Clare Atwood, Beatrice Bland, Fairlie Harmar and Margaret Fisher Prout) were too diverse to claim attention over the concerted Post-Impressionist observation of the Camden Town secessionists.

In the fevered world of pre-war art politics, however, history repeated itself. The third exhibition of the Camden Town Group coincided with Fry's even more radical 'Second Post-Impressionist' exhibition. Although the gap between the New English and the Post-Impressionists had widened by December 1912, differences also began to emerge in the group. Its internal factions were exposed and, although its members contributed to the 'Exhibition of the Camden Town Group and Others', held at the Public Art Galleries, Brighton, in 1913 and 'Twentieth-century Art – A Review of Modern Movements' at the Whitechapel Art Gallery, London, in 1914, the Carfax director, Arthur Clifton, did not consider further exhibitions commercially viable. While discussions on the Brighton show were taking place, the enlarged, re-formed Camden Towners re-emerged as the London Group, posing a more serious threat to the club, even though by the time of the opening of the Whitechapel exhibition Gore had died.[49]

Fig. 89 Mary Sargant-Florence
The Victory of Gareth, Working Cartoon for Oakham Old School Frescoes, 1908
Location unknown

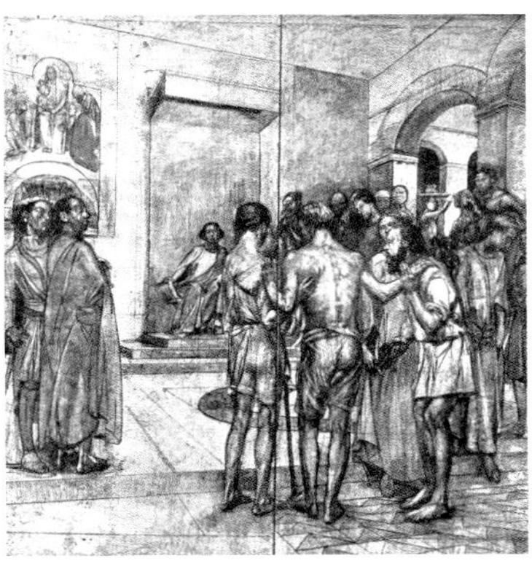

In retrospect it is impossible not to regard the London Group as the club's most serious rival. After the Great War, any balanced assessment of the relative status of art societies could no longer be reduced to the Academy and the club. More traditional New English members – this was how William Rothenstein was now perceived – found it difficult to get elected to the London Group. This was a society for the young in which even the likes of Sickert felt out of place. He and Lucien Pissarro had resigned from the new group before its first exhibition was held in March 1914.[50] Current perceptions are best left to Manson, who wrote to Pissarro in a valiant effort to retain his allegiance.

> You are quite content to be a member of the NEAC where you are practically all alone among a whole crowd of reactionaries: while as a member of the London Group you would have at least 11 followers, you would be among friends.... If we take that standpoint, what possible good service does one do

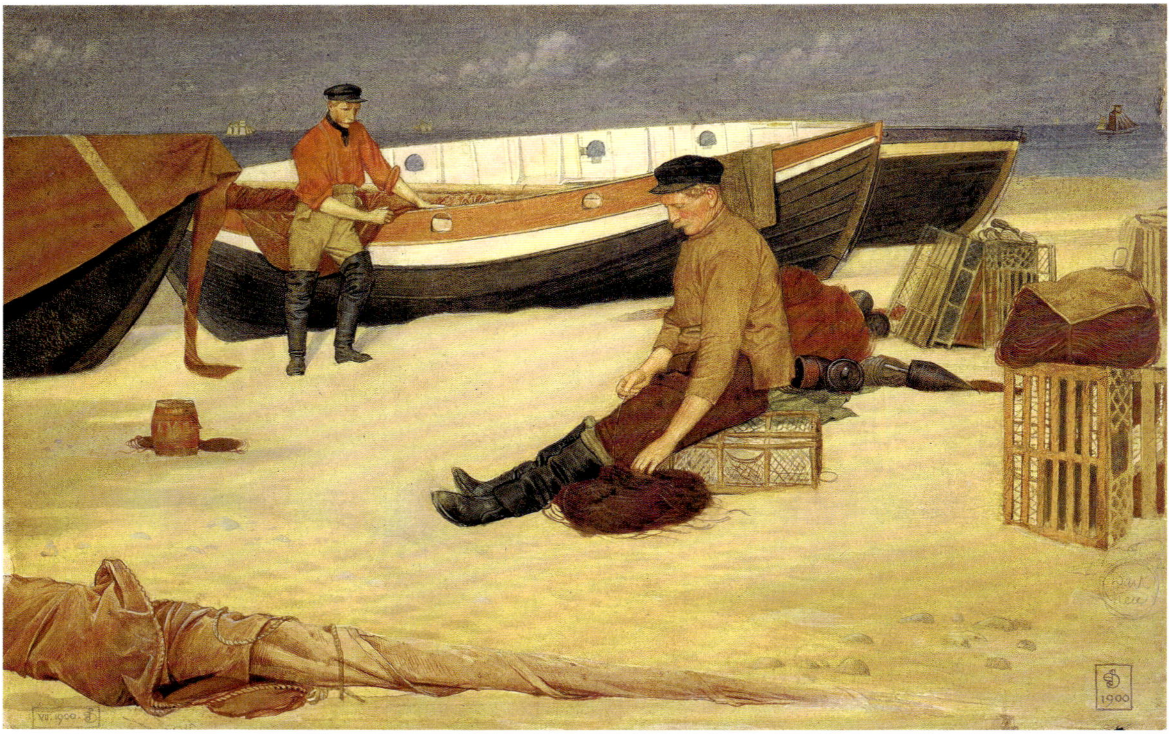

Fig. 90 Joseph Edward Southall
Cleaning the Lines, 1900
Watercolour on paper,
22.4 x 35.1 cm
Private collection

to Art by exhibiting at the New English? Its very name is a mockery. I cannot feel that I should be considering my ideal in art by exhibiting with them.[51]

Pissarro remained in the club, and Manson overcame his reservations the following year. Simultaneously Sickert renewed his allegiance to the club, sending what were his largest works to the club's spring and winter exhibitions in 1914. However, it was a very different place from that which the Camden Town School had left. In the midst of the soft and sunny arcadia, portrayed by Steer and De Glehn, there were new voices. In the winter of 1910, for instance, Mary Sargant-Florence returned to the club with cartoons for her murals on themes from Tennyson, at Oakham Old School (1908; fig. 89).[52] Joseph Southall began exhibiting in the spring of 1911 and other tempera painters of the Birmingham Group, refugees from the New Gallery, found their way into the club at this time.[53] In their adherence to William Morris ideals, and their belief in hand craft, these painters sought to revive the surface perfection of the Pre-Raphaelites. In such works as *Cleaning the Lines* (1900; fig. 90) and *On the Beach* (1911), Southall proposed a totally new approach to themes that had been the exclusive province of the British Impressionists.[54] When the selectors were tested in 1913 by Southall's and Margaret Gere's stiff renditions of biblical and mythological subject matter (fig. 91), a new direction was opening up, but it was one that must have seemed so far removed from the European avant-garde as to be characterised as anti-modernist.

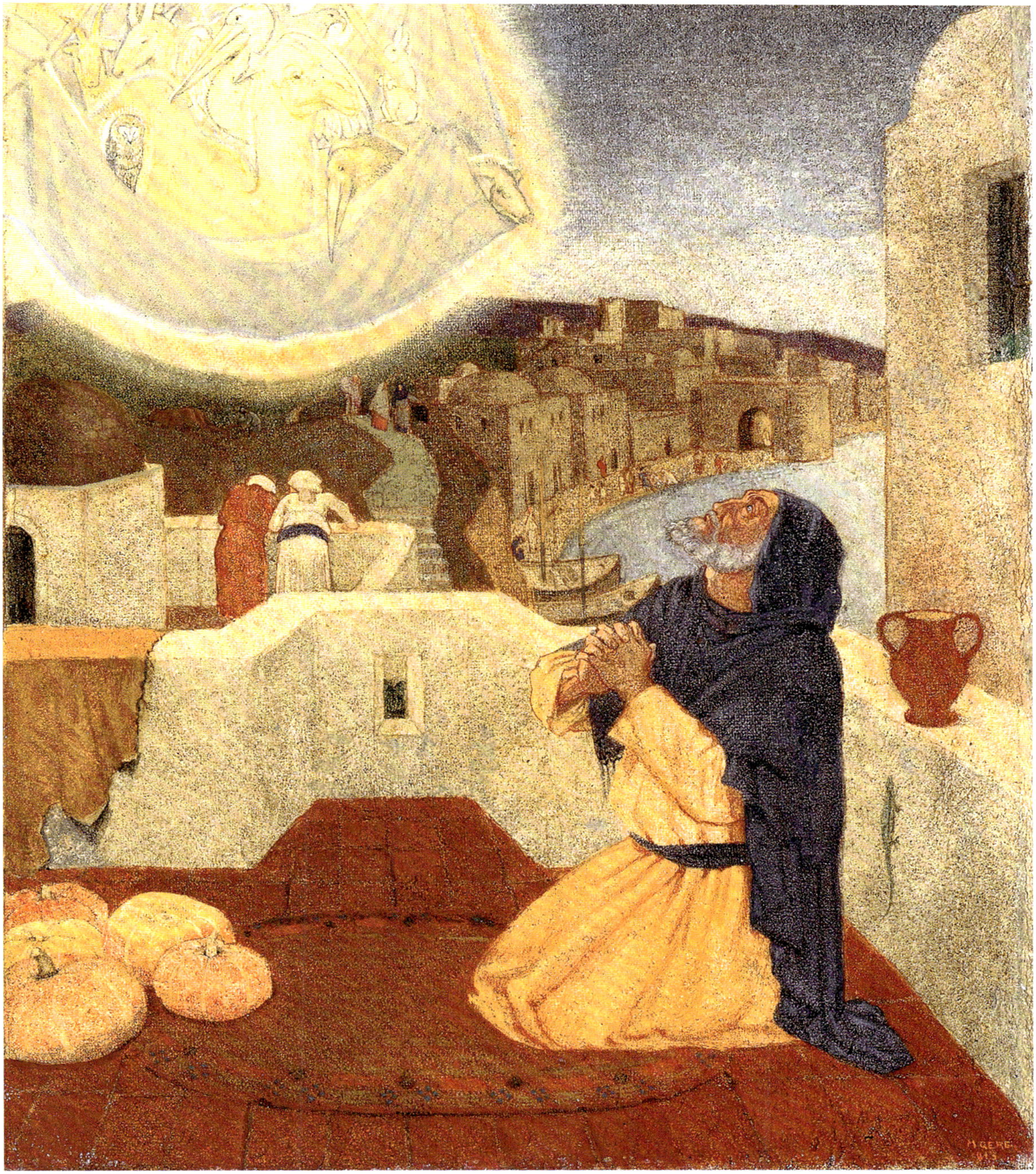

Fig. 91 Margaret Gere
The Visions of St Peter on the Housetop, 1913
Oil on canvas, 31.8 x 27.2 cm
Private collection

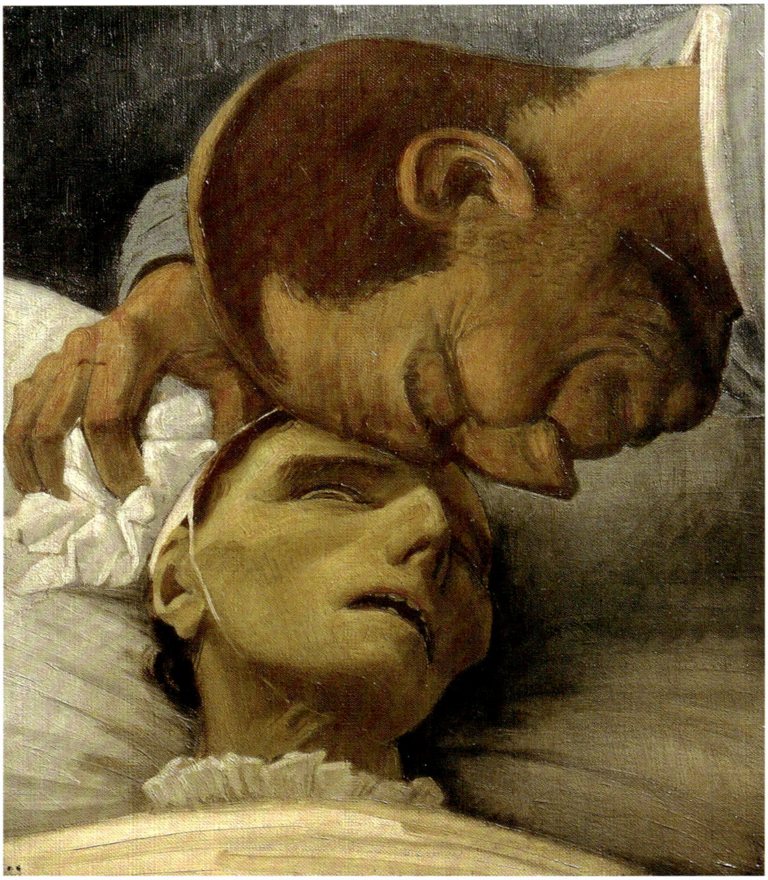

Fig. 92 Henry Lamb
Morte d'une paysanne (Death of a Peasant), 1911
Oil on canvas, 36.8 x 31.8 cm
Presented by the Trustees of the Chantrey Bequest 1944.
Tate, London

This same sequence of 'Georgian' club exhibitions contained inexplicable works like Henry Lamb's extraordinary *Morte d'une paysanne (Death of a Peasant)* (1911; fig. 92). The force, originality and concentration of purpose in this small canvas struck numerous New English visitors in the spring of 1911, *The Times* remarking on its 'primitive simplicity'.[55] And it remained vividly in the minds of later writers on British art, such as R. H. Wilenski, who described it as 'a very great picture in which distortion is used to suggest a rending emotion'.[56] Lamb had grown up with lugubrious engravings of late Victorian death-bed scenes and he would have seen the peasant burial vigils of the French *bande noire* painters, but all naturalistic theatre and religious observance was stripped away from this stark close-up study of two heads, dramatically posed at right angles to one another, defying all representational conventions in Western art.

Lamb's picture was incomparable, but he was not alone in presenting formidable studies of human heads. The ubiquitous gypsy and coster-girl prints of Francis Dodd and others continued. But more striking than those works in the 1912 exhibition was Mark Gertler's *Apple Woman and her Husband* (1911; fig.

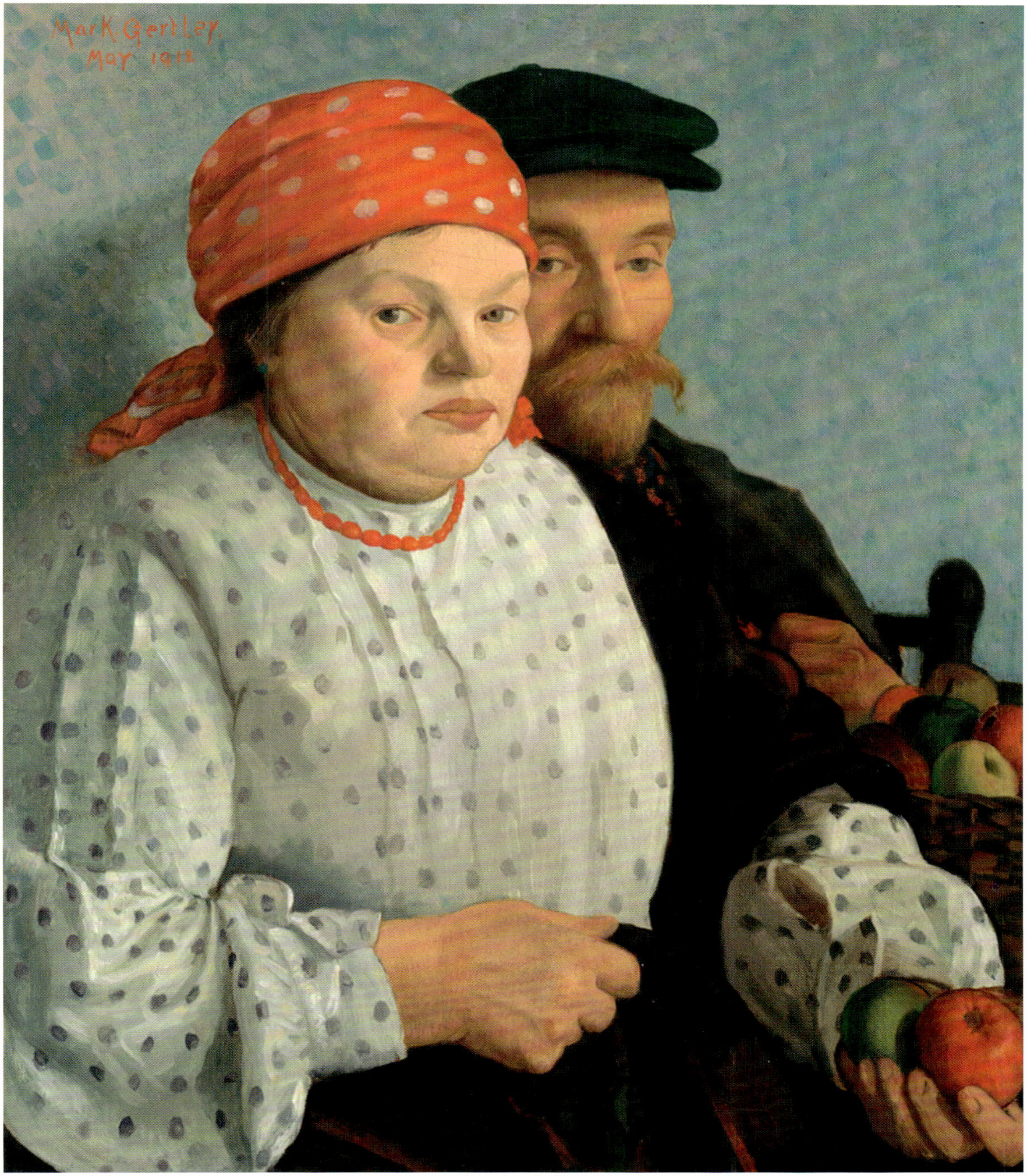

Fig. 93 Mark Gertler
The Apple Woman and her Husband, 1911
Oil on canvas, 66 x 56 cm
Purchased 1953. National Gallery of Victoria, Melbourne

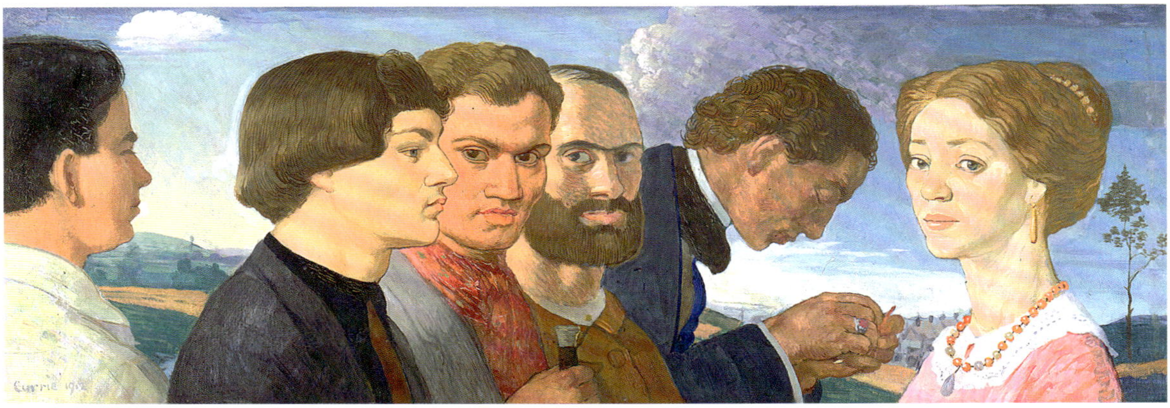

93), a double portrait of the painter's mother and father that reflected the enthusiasm for Cézanne at the time, mixed with that of the Italian Primitives.[57] Even if its coarse characterisations could be understood, there were other paintings in a similar vein, such as John Currie's *Some Later Primitives and Mme Tisceron* (1912; fig. 94).[58] Adopting the preferred medium of the Birmingham Group, Currie transformed his fellow artists, Mark Gertler, C. R. W. Nevinson, Edward Wadsworth and Adrian Allinson, into 'later' or Neo-Primitive *magi* paying homage to Mme Tisceron, the owner of the London café, 'Le Petit Savoyard', behind Shaftesbury Avenue. The disciplined use of tempera and the conceptual demands of mural painting seemed to be in tune with a world fast becoming uneasy with Edwardian hedonism.[59] The younger painters were pulling away and seeking a new direction. Obvious narrative had given way to obscurantist allegory, but Currie's leadership of the new tendency, after his disastrous love affair, was to be short-lived.[60]

Fig. 94 John Currie
Some Later Primitives and Mme Tisceron, 1912
Oil on canvas, 46.2 x 127.6 cm
Potteries Museum & Art Gallery, Stoke-on-Trent

Hugh Lane's mural commissions for his Dublin gallery provided one possible outcome for this new development. Initially admiring Currie's Irish subject matter, Lane rejected him in favour of John for his residence and Frederick Cayley Robinson for the new gallery in Dublin that bore his name. John and Orpen remained the club's strongest suit in these years when it was in danger of being upstaged by other radical groups, yet their adventure in grand mural painting was deeply flawed.[61] One obvious case of indecipherable allegory was Orpen's *Sowing the Seed* (1913; fig. 96), shown in the 1913 exhibition. This was the first of what became known as his 'Irish' Trilogy. It was a thinly veiled attack on the Board of Agriculture and Technical Instruction for Ireland, a body that had control over the Metropolitan School of Art in Dublin, where Orpen had been a visiting tutor since 1902. Over the years the board continually stressed the need for 'applied' and useful arts, over and above figure drawing and other skills associated with easel painting. Morris's ideals, which had taken root in some influential quarters in Ireland, were set up in opposition to those of Orpen's generation at the Slade. Although it was fairly obvious from the painting that the new seed was falling upon stony ground, the painter's attitude to the

Fig. 95 Mark Gertler
The Fruit Sorters, 1914
Oil on canvas, 75 x 62.5 cm
Leicester Museum and Art Gallery

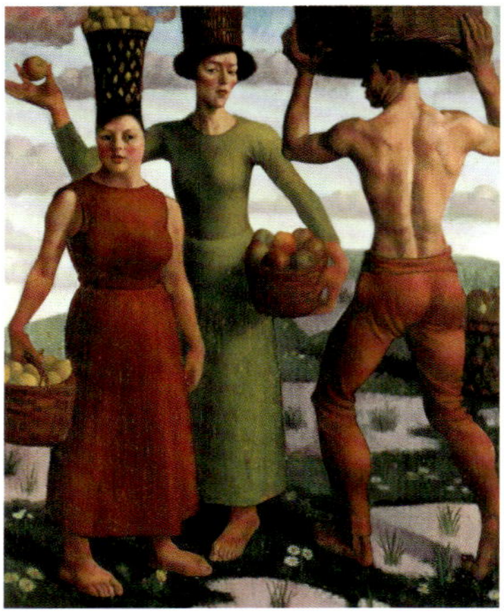

Fig. 96 William Orpen
Sowing New Seed in the Board of Agriculture and Technical Instruction for Ireland, 1913
Oil on canvas, 137 x 137 cm
Elliott Bequest, presented to the city of Mildura by Mrs Hilda Elliott in 1956.
Mildura Arts Centre, Victoria

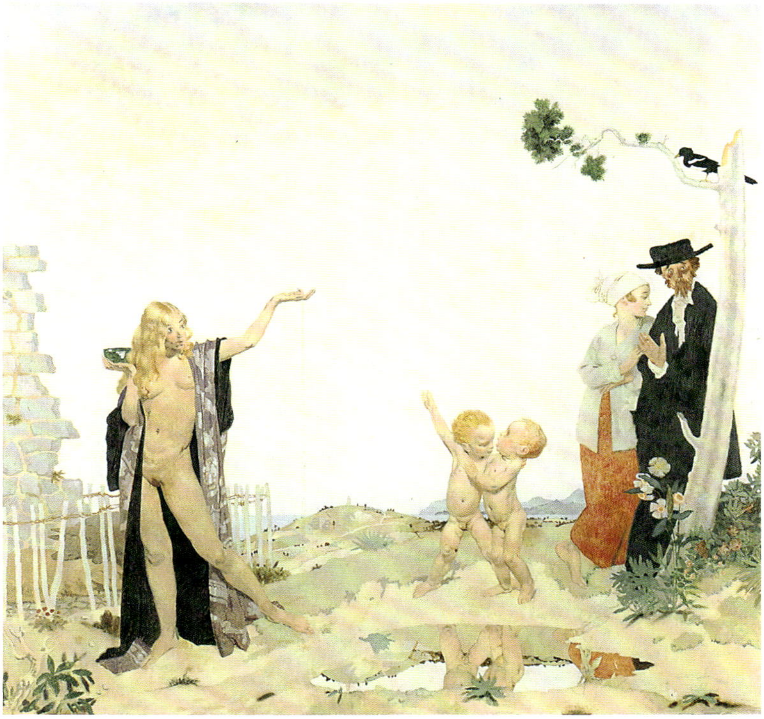

part played by the board was unclear even in the eyes of the Irish press.[62] He pressed on. The follow-on mural-style compositions, *The Western Wedding* (1914) and *Nude Pattern, The Holy Well* (1916) were regarded as a theatrical tableaux, scripted by Synge or Bernard Shaw and 'presented by Granville Barker'.[63] These 'Salon machines', including *The Mumpers* (fig. 85), pointed to the continuing need to find an appropriate visual language, a public rhetoric that would enable abstract ideas to be addressed. In *The Fruit Sorters* (1914; fig. 95), Gertler found a simpler and more dramatic solution to this problem and the statuesque severity of his figures with their basket/headdresses outstrips that of John's tinkers and Orpen's penitents.[64]

Whether consciously or not, Sickert presented in his submissions of 1914 his commentary on the recent preoccupations of his fellow exhibitors. The first was *Ennui* (*c.* 1914; fig. 98), an interior containing 'commonplace human types', which is essentially a critique of the earlier 'polite' portrait-interiors of Orpen's followers. A snobbish writer in *The Studio* noted that it conveyed 'a sinister insight into the emptiness of some people's lives ... with masterly directness of style'.[65] In one sense this was a summing up and a toning down, while in another it was a watershed.

Sickert followed it with a piece of generally approved opportunism. With his unerring eye for controversy, he seized the moment in *The Soldiers of King Albert the Ready* (1914; fig. 97), as Manet had done with *The Execution of Maximilian* (1867), and presented a large poster-like picture of Belgian infantrymen in

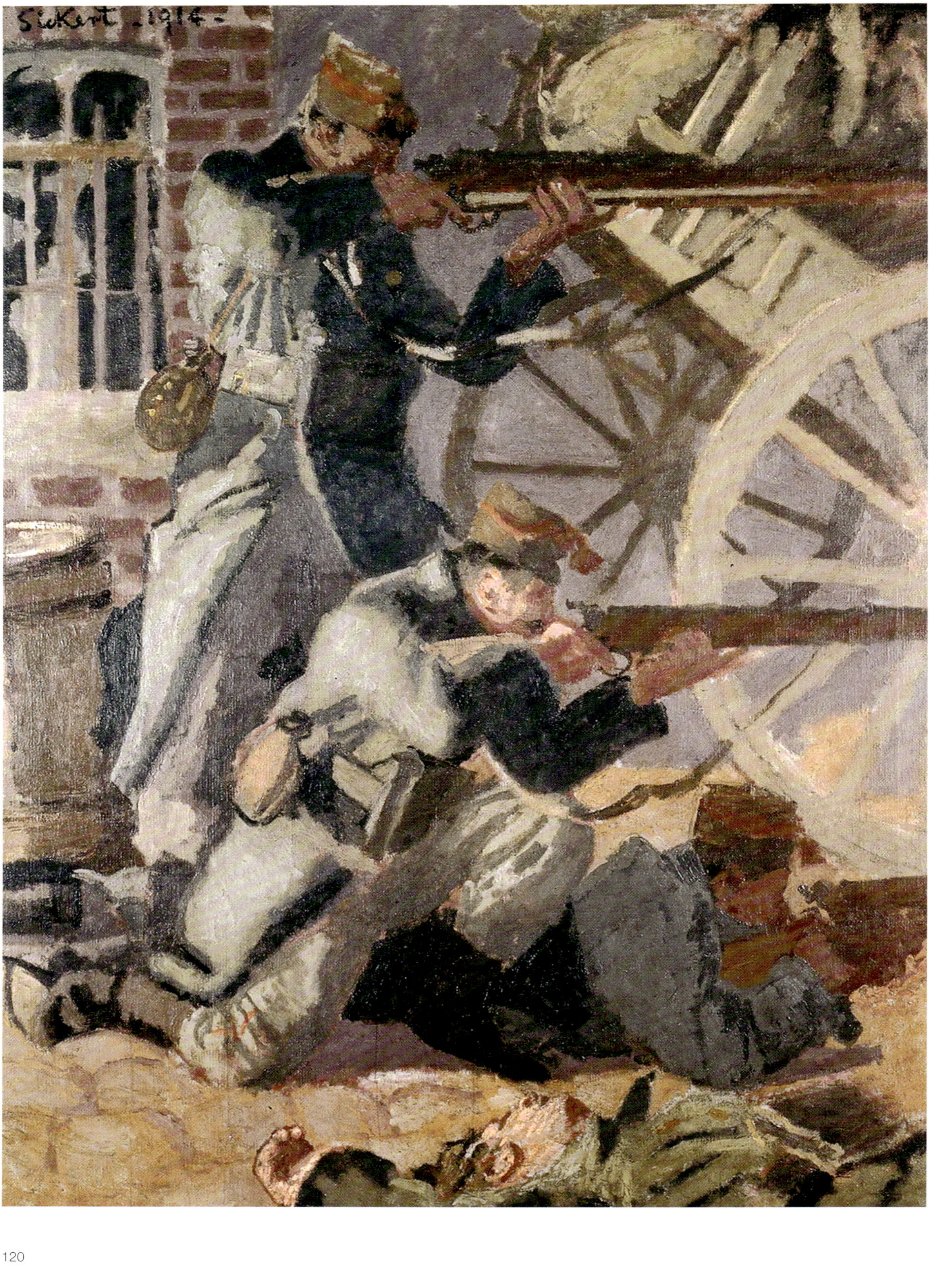
Sickert 1914

Opposite
Fig. 97 Walter Richard Sickert
The Soldiers of King Albert the Ready, 1914
Oil on canvas, 196.2 x 152.4 cm
Sheffield City Art Gallery

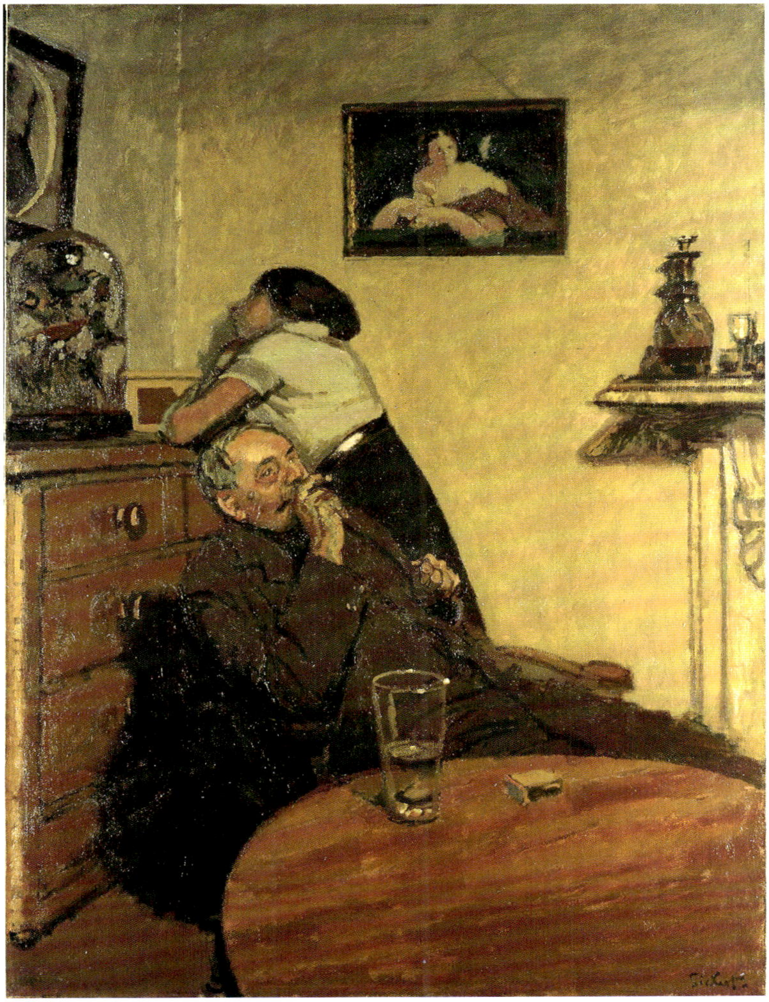

Right
Fig. 98 Walter Richard Sickert
Ennui, *c.* 1914
Oil on canvas, 152.4 x 112.4 cm
Presented by the Contemporary Art Society 1924. Tate, London

action, taken from a press photograph. *The Times* declared that 'while even the most idyllic poets are doing their best to sing about the war very few painters are trying to paint it'. While it lacked 'the surprises of observation' his 'war' picture had 'complete dramatic unity'.[66] This was an exceptional work. It came through the aesthetic filtering of photography and mass-reproduction. Sickert now returned to the very sources that he had disparaged in the work of the Newlyn Naturalists, twenty years earlier, but where they sought to deceive the eye, he was looking to refresh it. As such, *The Soldiers of King Albert the Ready*, painted with drab distemper on the crude hessian of a stage flat, had all the urgency of a one-off. It had something in common with John's and Orpen's mural experiments, but it was not a *machine du salon*.

One painting, Charles Maresco Pearce's *Summer in London* (1914; fig. 99), exhibited at the club in the spring of 1914, more graphically expresses the pre-war mood. It shows a busy London thoroughfare from an upstairs window overlooking the entrance to Meux's brewery. What we see is not Steer's atmospherics, but a marquetry of bright colours that recalls the work of the Camden Town painters – particularly in the reds of the motor-buses, the greens of the street-lamps and the touches of yellow in signs, hand-carts and the odd passer-by. But there is more than this. Grocers' delivery-boys racing a hansom cab, sandwich-board men and dray horses waiting for a space in the traffic tell us that London is open for business. Two fashionable ladies – one with a chow or a 'peke' – are followed by two nuns. It is the world into which the social recorder C. F. Masterman dropped in 1909, a world of 'little red houses in silent streets', from which the male population was 'sucked' at daybreak, while middle-class women engage in 'excursions to shopping centres in the West End' and indulge in 'pious sociabilities'.[67] In his commentary on the picture, T. Martin Wood stressed its Japanese effects – 'Japanese painters ... cultivated the habit of seeing the pattern that the colours and shapes in nature make ... without the modifications of shading'. A photograph could only give naturalistic monochrome – while Pearce 'refreshes our vision' by revealing 'forgotten aspects of nature to us'.[68] Pearce's document was as vivid as any scene in Arnold Bennett or H. G. Wells. Those who went to see it in the summer of 1914 shared in its innocent celebration, little realising that they stood on the edge of an abyss.

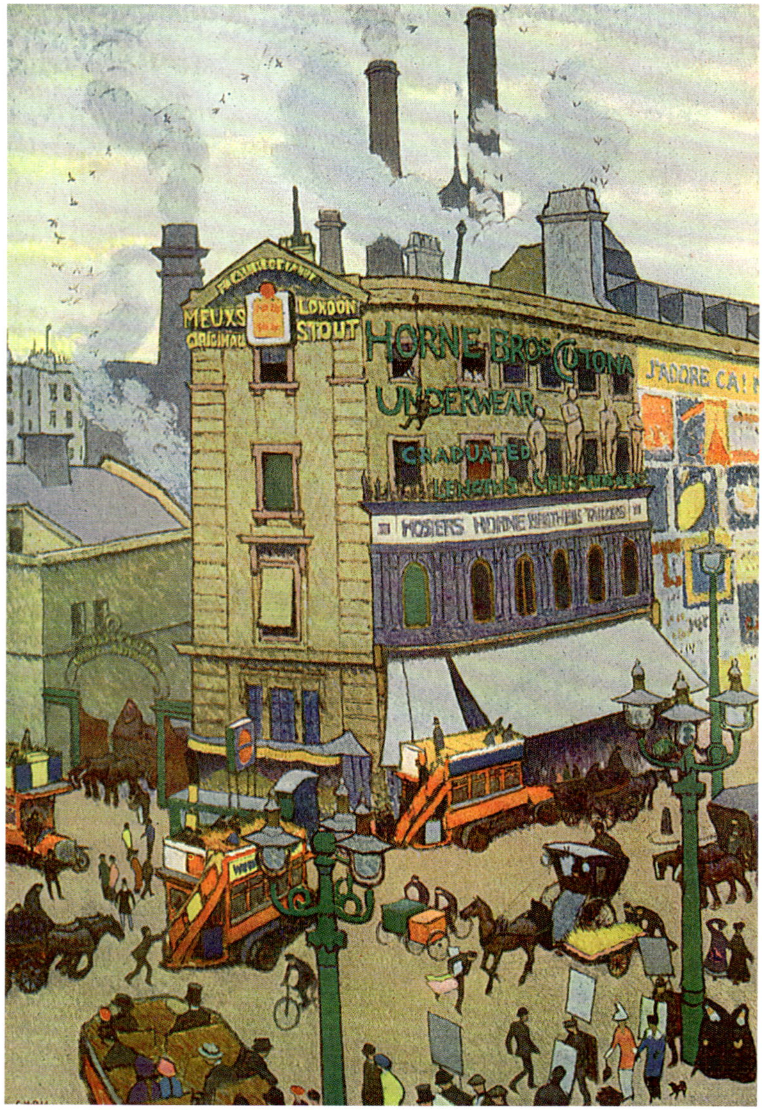

Fig. 99 Charles Maresco Pearce
Summer in London, 1914
Location unknown

NOTES

1 Frank Rutter, *Art in My Time*, Rich and Cowan, London, 1933, p. 94. Bone's *The Great Gantry, Charing Cross Station* was one of the first purchases of the National Art Collections Fund for the British Museum. For Bone, see *Muirhead Bone: Portrait of the Artist*, Peter Trowles, exh. cat., Crawford Centre for the Arts, University of St Andrews, 1987; also Introduction in *Muirhead Bone, 1876–1953*, Richard Ingleby, exh. cat., Fine Art Society, Edinburgh, 1990.

2 Frank Rutter, *Art in My Time*, Rich and Cowan, London, 1933, pp. 77–84, discusses the Wolverhampton exhibition and the work of the 'outsiders'.

3 East had shown in the club's second exhibition in 1887.

4 E. G. Halton, 'Independent British Art at Messrs Agnew's', *The Studio*, vol. 37, February 1906, p. 22. Sickert was also included, but hung on the stairs, 'as if', according to Frank Rutter (*Art in My Time*, Rich and Cowan, London, 1933, p. 125), 'to break modern painting gently to Messrs Agnew's eminently respectable clientele'.

5 Alexander J. Finberg, 'The Blight on Landscape Painting', *The National Review*, vol. 41, 1903, pp. 805–16, castigates the older generation of Academy landscapists, and critically examines Sir Edward Poynter's claim at the Academy dinner of that year that it was 'the principal exponent of the art of the nation', concluding that at 'the International, the New English Art Club, the New Gallery and the British Artists, there are artists ... who have a much better right to represent this phase of the national life than the whole body of exhibitors at Burlington House'.

6 This work remains untraced. Exhibited at Agnew's, it takes Steer's *Ludlow Walks* (*c.* 1898–9) and adds a country boy pointing the way to two women and a man who have lost their way.

7 Painters who started exhibiting at the club around this time included Maxwell Armfield, Else Atkins, Charles Cheston, Evelyn Cheston, Philip Connard, Sydney Lee, Mary McCrossan, Joseph Mason, Randolph Schwabe, F. H. S. Shepherd, Wyndham Tyron and Ursula Tyrwhitt.

8 Vincent Lines VPRWS, *Mark Fisher and Margaret Fisher Prout, Father and Daughter: A Record of a Hundred Years of Painting*, privately printed, distributed by Charles Skilton, London, 1966, pp. 28–37. A student at the Slade from 1894 to 1897, under Brown, Margaret Fisher Prout benefited from many of her father's contacts, being taken, for instance, to Whistler's studio in Paris in the mid-1890s.

9 Charles Holmes, *Self and Partners (Mostly Self), Being the Reminiscences of C. L. Holmes*, Constable, London, 1936, p. 250.

10 Mary Chamot, Dennis Farr and Martin Butlin, *Tate Gallery Catalogues: The Modern British Paintings, Drawings and Sculpture*, vol. 1, Oldbourne Press, London, 1964, pp. 295–6. The picture entered the Tate Collection in 1917.

11 Anne Thorold (ed.), *The Letters of Lucien to Camille Pissarro, 1893–1903*, Cambridge University Press, Cambridge, 1993, p. 602. See also W. S. Meadmore, *Lucien Pissarro*, Alfred A. Knopf, New York, 1962, p. 92, wherein this statement is dated 1900. It is likely that Pissarro was referring to the work of the French *bande noire* painters – principally Charles Cottet and Lucien Simon – who were enjoying temporary fame.

12 Gore started exhibiting at the club in the spring of 1906, Manson in the winter of 1909 and James Brown (as Prior Conway) in 1913. See Malcolm Easton, 'Lucien Pissarro and his Friends at Rye' in *Three on Holiday at Rye, 1913, A Group of Post-Impressionists, Lucien Pissarro, James Bolivar Manson, James Brown*, Malcolm Easton and Michael Parkin, exh. cat., Parkin Gallery, London, 1980.

13 Walter Sickert, 'The New English and After', *The New Age*, 2 June 1910, quoted from Osbert Sitwell (ed.), *A Free House! Or the Artist as Craftsman, Being the Writings of Walter Richard Sickert*, Macmillan, London, 1947, p. 59.

14 Orpen showed portraits and 'mother and baby' subjects in 1903 alongside his still-life, *Reflections, China and Japan* (1903; Hugh Lane Gallery, Dublin).

15 Arthur Symons, 'The New English Art Club', *The Saturday Review*, 19 November 1904, pp. 640–1.

16 T. Martin Wood, 'The Paintings of Wilfrid G. von Glehn', *The Studio*, vol. 56, June 1912, p. 7.

17 A. L. Baldry, *Modern Mural Decoration*, George Newnes, London, 1902; Clare Willesdon, *Mural Painting in Britain, 1840–1940: Image and Meaning*, Oxford University Press, Oxford, 2000.

18 George Moore, 'The Garret', *The Saturday Review*, 23 June 1906, p. 785.

19 Although John showed the regulation six works at the spring and winter exhibitions of 1907, they were all studies and small paintings.

20 *The Family Group*, shown at the 'Twenty Years of British Art' at the Whitechapel Art Gallery, London, in 1910, may also be taken as part of this group. See *Gwen John and Augustus John*, David Fraser Jenkins and Chris Stephens (eds), exh. cat., Tate Britain, London, 2004, p. 129.

21 Laurence Binyon, 'Three Exhibitions', *The Saturday Review*, 6 June 1908, pp. 720–1.

22 H. S., 'Art: The New English Art Club', *The Spectator*, 30 May 1908, p. 865. See also Tate Gallery Archive TGA 7310.23.

23 Anon., 'The New English Art Club', *The Times*, 22 May 1909, p. 10. For further reference to this work, see *Gwen John and Augustus John*, David Fraser Jenkins and Chris Stephens (eds), exh. cat., Tate Britain, London, 2004, p. 129.

24 Laurence Binyon, 'The New English Art Club', *The Saturday Review*, 29 May 1909, p. 684. See also Tate Gallery Archive TGA 7310.24. For a fuller discussion of this sequence of works, see Ysanne Holt, *British Artists and the Modernist Landscape*, Ashgate, Aldershot, 2003, pp. 49–79; see also Lisa Tickner, *Modern Life and Modern Subjects, British Art in the Early Twentieth Century*, Yale University Press, London and New Haven, 2000, pp. 49–77.

25 For further reference to this work, see *John Singer Sargent*, Elaine Kilmurray and Richard Ormond (eds), exh. cat., Tate Gallery, London, 1998, p. 251. A comparison could made between this picture and Orpen's *Job* (1905) or *The Saint of Poverty* (1905).

26 Innes showed at the club from the spring of 1907 to the winter of 1913. His early exhibits adopt the manner of Steer, his revered master at the Slade. While Innes's effect on John's work was reciprocated, Lees was considered subservient to both. Schwabe noted that 'when John sent one of his large charcoal cartoons to the New English Art Club, Lees followed it up in the club's next exhibition by a cartoon similar in size and handling'. See Randolph Schwabe, 'Reminiscences of Fellow Students', *The Burlington Magazine*, vol. 82, 1943, p. 9. Lees showed at the club from 1907 to 1917. For further reference, see John Fothergill, *James Dickson Innes*, Faber and Faber, London, 1946; Preface in *J. D. Innes*, Augustus John, exh. cat., Graves Art Gallery, Sheffield, 1961; David Fraser Jenkins, *J. D. Innes*, National Museum of Wales, Cardiff, 1975; for Lees, see Henry R. Lew, *In Search of Derwent Lees*, privately printed, Victoria, Australia, 1996. Ian Strang, son of William Strang, preceded Innes and Lees at the Slade but did not exhibit at the club until 1909. A noted etcher, and printer of etchings, he continued at the club until the winter of 1948.

27 R. M. Y. Gleadowe, *Albert Rutherston*, Ernest Benn, London, 1925, portrays Rutherston as 'the good boy of the New English school' (p. 13) and describes his move away from the *hispagnoliste* style of Orpen, to the more Blakeian manner of *The Smart Visitor* as having been led in part by Edna Clarke Hall. See also *Albert Rutherston, 1881–1953*, Max Rutherston, exh. cat., 180 New Bond Street, London, 1988, p. 7. For Brockhurst, see *A Dream of Fair Women, Gerald Leslie Brockhurst, RA, 1890–1978*, Anne

Goodchild, exh. cat., Graves Art Gallery, Sheffield, 1987, p. 47; see also *The Art of Gerald Leslie Brockhurst*, Thomas B. Brumbaugh, Andrew Ladis and Patricia Phagan, exh. cat., Georgia Museum of Art, University of Georgia, 1993, p. 74.

28 *Morning Post*, 4 December 1913.

29 For further reference, see Kenneth McConkey, *Memory and Desire, Painting in Britain and Ireland at the Turn of the Twentieth Century*, Ashgate, Aldershot, 2002, pp. 203–25.

30 Anon., 'The Case for Modern Painting, by a Modern Painter – IV The Royal Academy and the New English Art Club', *The Burlington Magazine*, vol. 11, April–September 1907, p. 206.

31 Robert O'Byrne, *Hugh Lane, 1875–1915*, Lilliput Press, Dublin, 2000, pp. 120–3.

32 Anon., 'Picture Exhibitions', *The Builder*, 13 December 1912, p. 706. See also C. H. Collins Baker, 'Norman Shaw and the New English Art Club', *The Saturday Review*, 7 December 1912, pp. 704–5; J. B., 'Art: The New English Art Club', *The Spectator*, 30 November 1902, p. 902; Anon., 'Current Art Notes: The New English Art Club', *The Connoisseur*, vol. 35, January–April 1913, pp. 49–50. See Tate Gallery Archive TGA 7310.27.

33 Anon.,'Two Exhibitions', *The Academy*, 29 June 1912, pp. 822–3.

34 There had been solo exhibitions since before the mid-nineteenth century. The purpose of these shows was often public entertainment as opposed to private gratification for individual clients, as the tours of celebrated works by Holman Hunt, Gustave Doré and Mihály Munhácsy indicate. This distinction began to be blurred in the 1860s and the arrival of cinema effectively killed the 'famous painting' exhibition.

35 Rutter's own account of the formation of the AAA is contained in Frank Rutter, *Since I was Twenty-five*, Constable, London, 1927, pp. 180–99. He notes that, on one occasion, soliciting support from a member of the New English, 'I put my foot into it badly'. Mentioning that a fellow member of the club had agreed to show with the AAA, he was told: 'That's just it, it's bad enough having to exhibit with the swine at the New English, but I'm not going to exhibit with him anywhere else if I can help it' (p. 184). During this ten-year period, the only new initiative that could be regarded as a threat to the New English was the formation of the Friday Club in 1905. It lasted until 1922 and, apart from the Bloomsbury painters, it attracted Atwood, Gertler, Innes and Lees, with Bomberg, Wadsworth and the Nashes joining just before the Great War – see Richard Shone, 'The Friday Club', *The Burlington Magazine*, vol. 117, May 1975, pp. 279–84.

36 The Allied Artists' Association was a completely open exhibition in which all fee-payers were entitled to show their work. There was no jury. The first show attracted over 3,000 exhibits and the Fitzroy Street painters (soon-to-be formed as the Camden Town Group) were its leading members. There were eight annual AAA exhibitions in all. For further reference, see Frank Rutter, *Art in My Time*, Rich and Cowan, London, 1933, pp. 134–7.

37 Kenneth McConkey, *Edwardian Portraits: Images of an Age of Opulence*, Antique Collectors' Club, Woodbridge, 1987, p. 46.

38 Frank Rutter, *Since I was Twenty-five*, Constable, London, 1927, p. 192; Rutter also notes that the Fitzroy Street Group would, during these years, visit Sickert at his house at Neuville. See also Wendy Baron, *Perfect Moderns: A History of the Camden Town Group*, Ashgate, Aldershot, 2000, pp. 43–5. There were differences of view in the members of this exclusive dining club – Gilman was in favour of a new society, John remaining loyal to the club, Pissarro favoured reform, Gore was undecided, and Sickert argued one week for, and the next against, a new society.

39 The Post-Impressionist exhibitions have generated a substantial volume of critical and historical writing. See, for instance, Charles Holmes, *Notes on the Post-Impressionist Painters, Grafton Galleries, 1910–11*, Philip Lee Warner, London, 1910; C. Lewis Hind, *The Post-Impressionists*, Methuen, London, 1911. For further reference, see J. B. Bullen (ed.), *Post-Impressionists in England, The Critical Reception*, Routledge, London, 1988; also *Modern Art in Britain, 1910–1914*, Anna Gruetzner Robins, exh. cat., Barbican Art Gallery, London, 1997.

40 Winter of 1910, no. 1; Frances Spalding, *Roger Fry: Art and Life*, University of California Press, Berkeley and Los Angeles, 1980, pp. 129–30. Despite his radicalism, as Spalding points out, this work, in its unmistakable echoes of Puvis de Chavannes and Guido Reni, is more likely to have been influenced by John than any of the French painters he was introducing to his British audience.

41 For further reference, see Mary Lago, *Christiana Herringham and the Edwardian Art Scene*, Lund Humphries, Aldershot, 1996, pp. 50–6. See also Abbie N. Sprague, 'The British Tempera Revival' in *Sixty Works by Joseph Southall 1864–1944, from the Fortunoff Collection*, George Breeze, Peyton Skipwith and Abbie N. Sprague, exh. cat., Fine Art Society, London, 2005, pp. 22–34.

42 Anon., 'Art Exhibitions: The New English Art Club', *The Times*, 26 November 1910, p. 6.

43 J. B., 'The New English Art Club', *The Spectator*, 26 November 1910, pp. 906–7.

44 Ibid.

45 Wendy Baron, *Perfect Moderns: A History of the Camden Town Group*, Ashgate, Aldershot, 2000, pp. 46–8. The original sixteen members were: Walter Bayes, Robert Bevan, Malcolm Drummond, Harold Gilman, Charles Ginner, Spencer Gore, J. D. Innes, Augustus John, Henry Lamb, Wyndham Lewis, Maxwell Gordon Lightfoot, J. B. Manson, Lucien Pissarro, William Radcliffe, Walter Sickert and J. Doman Turner. See also Wendy Baron and Malcolm Cormack, *The Camden Town Group*, Yale Centre for British Art, New Haven, 1980; *The Painters of Camden Town, 1905–1920*, Francis Farmar, exh. cat., Christie's, London, 1988.

46 All three subsequently exhibited with the club.

47 Gore and Gilman, for instance, withdrew from the club after 1911 and did not return until 1913 and 1914 respectively.

48 Malcolm Easton, 'Camden Town into London: Some Intimate Glimpses of the Transition and its Artists, 1911–1914' in *Art in Britain 1890–1940, An Exhibition of Paintings, Sculpture, Drawings and Documents from the Collection of the University of Hull*, exh. cat., University of Hull, 1967, pp. 60–75.

49 The group's name change and enlargement came at the insistence of the dealer, William Marchant, who offered the premises of the Goupil Gallery for the exhibition. See Wendy Baron, *The Camden Town Group*, Scolar Press, London, 1979, and Wendy Baron, *Perfect Moderns: A History of the Camden Town Group*, Ashgate, Aldershot, 2000; see also Denys J. Wilcox, *The London Group, 1913–1939: The Artists and their Works*, Scolar Press, London, 1995, pp. 1–8; see also *London Group 1914–1964, Jubilee Exhibition, Fifty Years of British Art*, Dennis Farr and Alan Bowness, exh. cat., Tate Gallery, London, 1964. Having fallen ill while painting in Richmond Park in winter weather, Gore died suddenly in March 1914, see *Spencer Frederick Gore, 1878–1914*, Frederick Gore and Richard Shone, exh. cat., Anthony d'Offay, London, 1983; Frederick Gore, 'Foreword' in *Spencer Gore in Richmond*, Frederick Gore, exh. cat., Museum of Richmond, 1996. The Whitechapel exhibition, which opened in May, divided the work of contemporary British artists into four groups: those led by Sickert and Pissarro, i.e. the Camden Town Group; those influenced by Puvis de Chavannes, Legros and John; those influenced by Cézanne, i.e. Fry, Vanessa Bell, Duncan Grant and W. B. Adeney; and those who 'have recently established a Rebel Art Centre', i.e. the Vorticists, see Introduction in *Twentieth-century Art: A Review of Modern Movements*, exh. cat., Whitechapel Art Gallery, London, 1914.

50 Sickert greatly objected to the work of British Cubo-Futurists such as Wyndham Lewis. Nothwithstanding Rothenstein's difficulties, the

group accepted younger, but more conservative New English exhibitors (for example, Randolph Schwabe in 1916 and Alfred Thornton in 1920).

51 Quoted in Wendy Baron, *Perfect Moderns: A History of the Camden Town Group*, Ashgate, Aldershot, 2000, p. 65. Pissarro objected to the young 'mathematical' painters in the group.

52 Sargant-Florence had not shown at the club since her first exhibit in the winter of 1894. Thereafter she exhibited regularly until her death in 1941.

53 Southall, like Sargant-Florence, was associated with the Arts and Crafts exhibitions. Maxwell Armfield, who first showed in the spring of 1907, returned to regular exhibiting in 1910, Charles and Margaret Gere began showing in 1910 and Arthur Gaskin in the winter of 1912.

54 For further reference, see *Joseph Southall, 1861–1944, Artist-Craftsman*, Charlotte Gere, exh. cat., Birmingham City Art Gallery, 1980, pp. 66–7. See also *Sixty Works by Joseph Southall 1864–1944 from the Fortunoff Collection*, exh. cat., George Breeze, Peyton Skipwith and Abbie N. Sprague, Fine Art Society, London, 2005.

55 'The New English Art Club', *The Times*, 22 May 1911; quoted in Keith Clements, *Henry Lamb: The Artist and his Friends*, Redcliffe, Bristol, 1985, p. 96.

56 R. H. Wilenski, *An Outline of English Painting*, Faber and Faber, London, 1946, p. 69. Wilenski and Keith Clements (*Henry Lamb: The Artist and his Friends*, Redcliffe, Bristol, 1985) both refer to Lamb's interest in the work of Mantegna.

57 For further reference, see *The Edwardians, Secrets and Desires*, Anne Gray, exh. cat., National Gallery of Australia, Parkes, Canberra, 2004, p. 168.

58 For reference to Currie, see *John Currie: Paintings and Drawings, 1905–1914*, Sarah Griffiths, exh. cat., Stoke-on-Trent Museum and Art Gallery, 1980, unpaginated, no. 16.

59 *The Observer*, 31 May 1914, announced 'the Neo-Primitives rule supreme'.

60 Currie committed suicide in October 1914, after murdering his mistress, Dolly Henry. At this time, Sargant-Florence was doing tempera demonstrations at the Slade.

61 Frank Rutter, *Art in My Time*, Rich and Cowan, London, 1933, p. 88, refers to Steer as the 'king' of the NEAC and John as its 'Prince of Wales'.

62 The picture was later re-titled *Sowing New Seed in the Board of Agriculture and Technical Instruction for Ireland*, see Kenneth McConkey, 'Politics and that Girl: A Study of William Orpen's *Sowing New Seed*' in K. Jeffrey and N. Garnham (eds), *Culture, Place and Identity*, University College, Dublin Press, Dublin, 2005, pp. 53–65. For a selection of reviews, see Tate Gallery Archive TGA 7310.28.

63 Anon., *The Times*, 1 December 1914, p. 9.

64 Sarah MacDougall, *Mark Gertler*, John Murray, London, 2002, pp 95–8. The tall, stylised baskets are reminiscent of the headdresses worn by the Pharisees in the background of Piero della Francesca's *Baptism of Christ* (1450s) in the National Gallery, London.

65 Anon., 'Studio-Talk', *The Studio*, vol. 63, 1914–15, p. 294.

66 Anon., 'The New English Art Club Exhibition', *The Times*, 1 December 1914, p. 9; see also Anon., 'Palette and Chisel', *Colour*, vol. 1, no. 6, January 1915, p. 202 (1914); Anon., 'Fine Arts – The New English Art Club', *The Athenaeum*, 5 December 1914, p. 594.

67 C. F. Masterman, *The Condition of England*, Methuen, London, 1909 (rev. ed., J. T. Boulton, London, 1960), p. 70; see also *Daily Chronicle*, 4 June 1914.

68 T. Martin Wood, 'Our Illustrations', *Colour Magazine*, vol. 1, no. 2, 1914, p. 42. See also *Bazaar*, 10 June 1914.

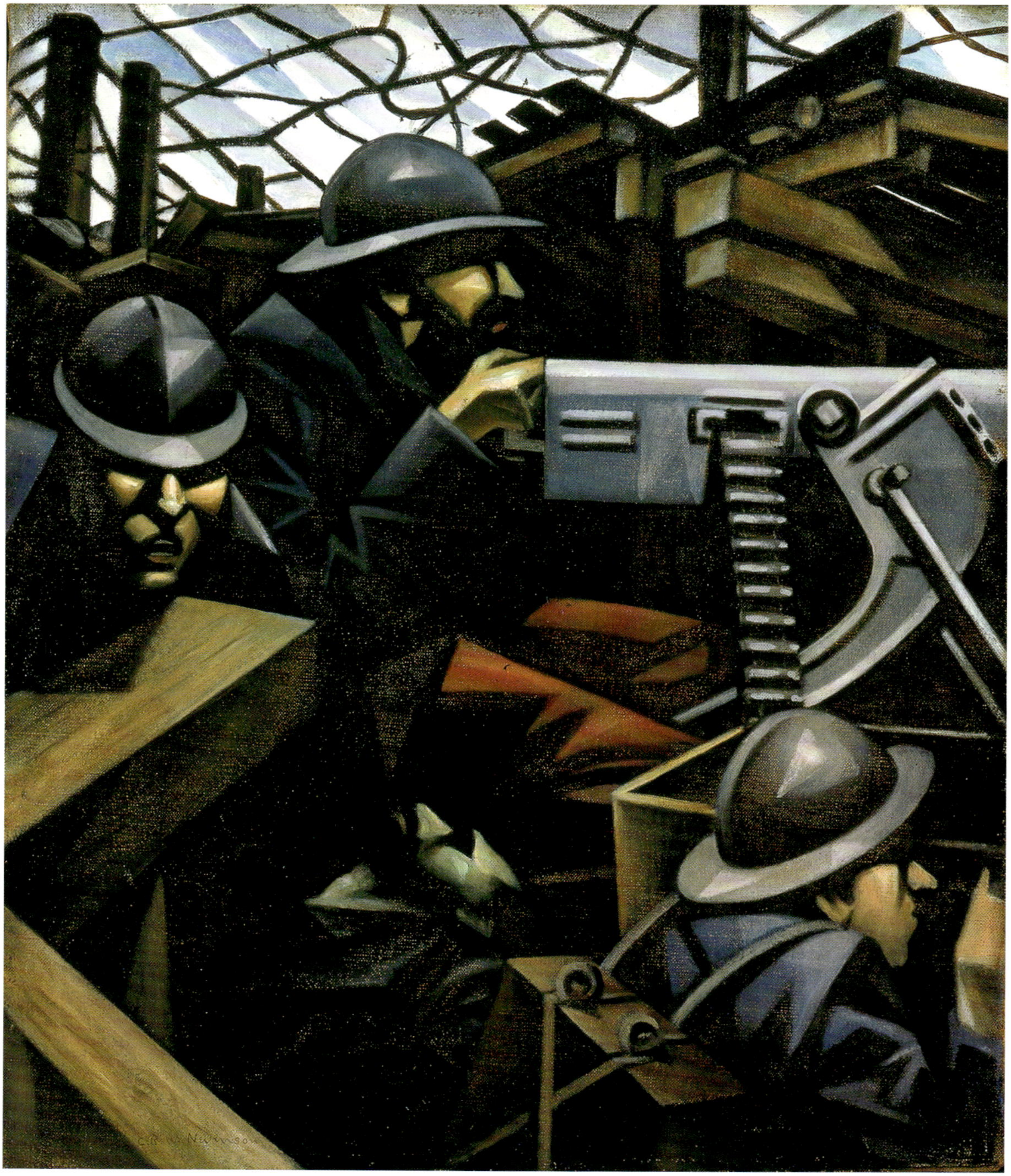

CHAPTER 5 **'Slade School Mecca'** 1914–1929

Newspaper cartoons that accompanied Fry's Post-Impressionist exhibitions expressed the popular mood of amusement, consternation and xenophobia that hardened into outright hostility when it became obvious that some British acolytes were following the Pied Piper of Cubo-Futurism, Filippo Marinetti. Fry's exhibitions, those in Brighton and at the Whitechapel Art Gallery, London, were a series of rain checks, a rapid and selective updating in which the recent advances of the avant-garde in Paris were presented with little consistency or coherence. Having abandoned their fascination with tribal artefacts, Purists and Futurists were drawing inspiration from mechanised factory production, the rhythmic repetitions of dance and sport and the rich visual possibilities of flight. C. F. Masterman had not predicted the 'machine aesthetic', but the condition of 'modernity', urban capitalist production and consumption was well attested. The Benin mask-maker, admired in Paris in the early days of Cubism, had become an automaton, and the tribal talisman had already been replaced by the machine, by the time the news reached London. In any case, for readers of Wilhelm Worringer filtered through the writings of T. E. Hulme and Ezra Pound, there was no contradiction between this particular primitivism and the geometric abstraction of a modern engineer's drawing. 'The tendency towards abstraction', according to Hulme, 'will culminate not so much in the simple geometrical forms found in archaic art, but more in the ones associated in our minds with the idea of machinery'.[1]

Much of the critical hostility was directed at the work of Wyndham Lewis and the Vorticists, artists who were regarded as even more of a foreign-inspired proselytising sect than the Impressionists had been.[2] After the outbreak of war, their work might even be judged as unpatriotic. British artists were permitted 'originality', but they could not be zealots. Despite the fact that the New English had generated important secessionist groups by 1914, it continued to attract important pictures such as those of David Bomberg and William Roberts. These painters and their new objectionable modernism were in evidence in the club as well as the London Group, even though their work must have occasioned the resentment of older members.[3] Shows of the group and the club that contained Tonks's and Walker's figure-pieces, Steer landscapes and harbour scenes, and large, important Orpens and Johns also displayed what were among the most avant-garde paintings being produced in Britain at that time.[4] William Roberts's *Ulysses* (1913; fig. 101) and *The Boxers* (1914) and David Bomberg's *Vision of Ezekiel* (1912) and *In the Hold* (1913–14) reveal figure groups translated into robot forms in a clearly delineated yet non-naturalistic spatial setting.[5]

Fig. 100 Christopher Richard Wynne Nevinson
La Mitrailleuse, 1915
Oil on canvas, 61 x 50.8 cm
Presented by the Contemporary Art Society 1917. Tate, London

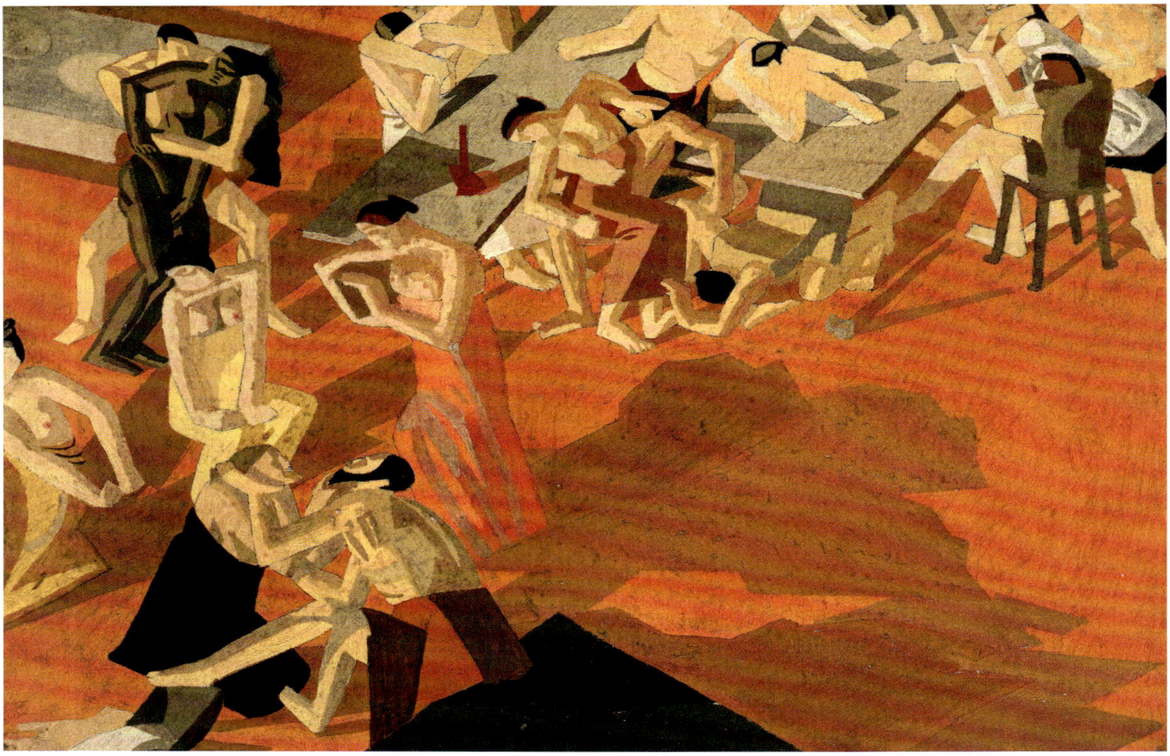

Above and overleaf
Fig. 101 William Roberts
Ulysses, 1913
Oil on canvas, 30.5 x 45.7 cm
Castle Museum, Nottingham

Structure derived from multiple viewpoints was rejected in favour of the elaborately interlocking movements of the production line. As in Fernand Léger, fractured figures are reconstituted as the anonymous cogs of modernity. Vorticists, whose manifesto Roberts was to sign, were keen to distinguish themselves from both Cubism and Futurism, and canvases such as *Ulysses* were the new blueprint, functioning also as 'machines' in that earlier Salon sense of being worked up from elaborate studies.

However, the appearance of a statement in *The Observer* in June 1914 on 'Vital English Art' effectively exposed Bomberg and Roberts and the activities at 38 Great Ormond Street as the Rebel Art Centre. C. R. W. Nevinson and Marinetti, the notorious Italian Futurist, had incorporated Roberts, Wadsworth, Wyndham Lewis and others as signatories to the article without their permission.[6] The declaration could so easily have put paid to any notion that they, as individuals, might submit their work to future exhibitions of the club. Bomberg, one of those whose name had been taken in vain, insisted that his address should not even be that of the Centre, and thus, as an independent and having distanced himself from Marinetti, felt he could return to the New English in the spring of 1915. He did so with *Billet* (fig. 102), an exceptional modernist war work painted before he

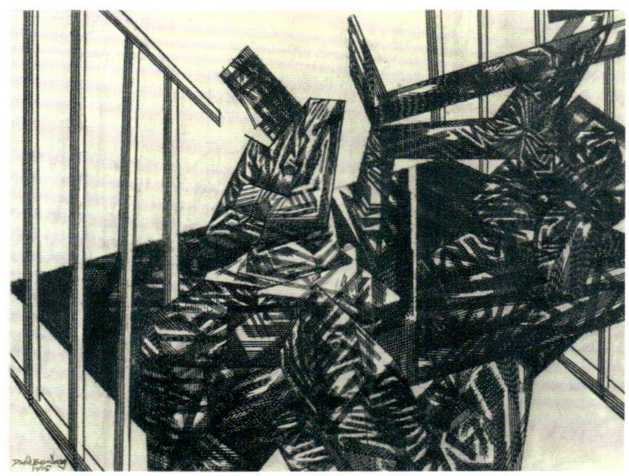

Below
Fig. 102 David Bomberg
Billet, 1915
Black ink on paper, 39.5 x 51 cm
Victoria and Albert Museum, London

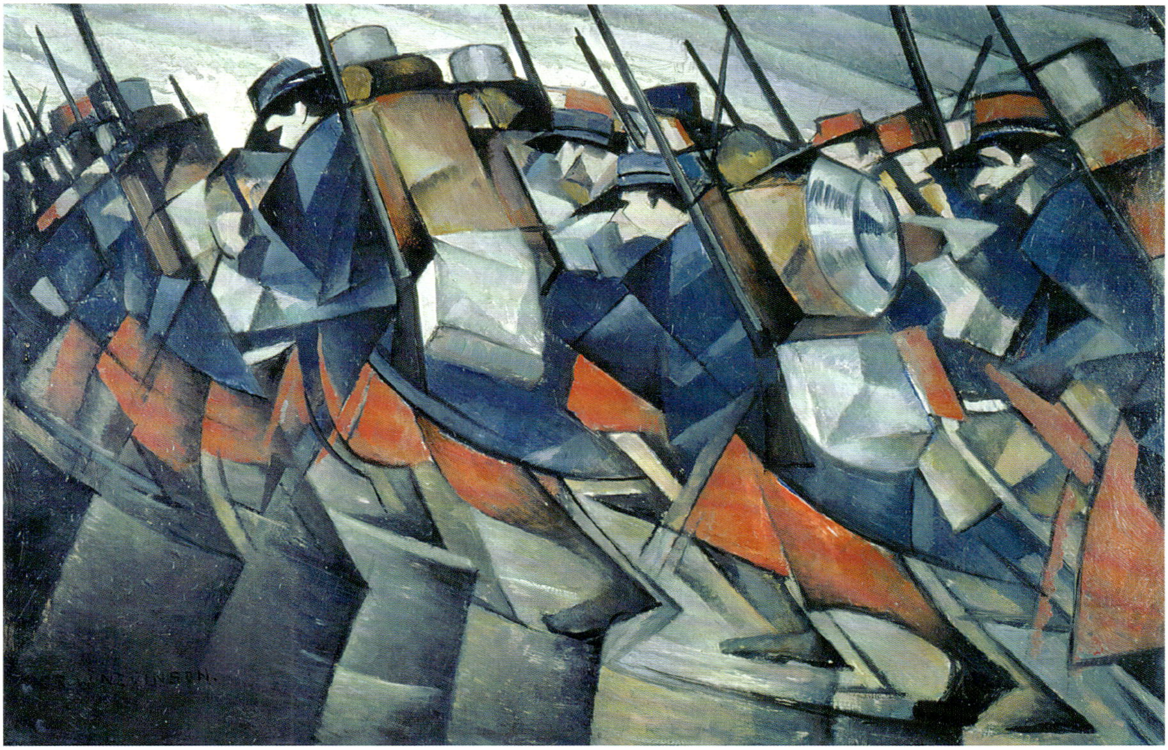

Fig. 103 Christopher Richard Wynne Nevinson
Returning to the Trenches, 1914–15
Oil on canvas, 51.2 x 76.8 cm
Gift of the Massey Collection of English Painting 1946. National Gallery of Canada, Ottawa

enlisted in the Royal Engineers. It was, however, soon upstaged by four works shown by Nevinson at the London Group.

As these paintings appeared, *The Times* critic conducted a dawn raid on Wadsworth, Roberts and Lewis, who were showing alongside Nevinson, for what he termed 'Junkerism'. Lewis mounted a robust defence, stating that the methodical and mechanised circumstances of the modern warfare demanded the search for imaginative solutions that did not play to popular jingoism.[7] What separated Nevinson was that, true to his Futurist ideals, he was one of the very few British painters who at this point had experienced the Western Front. Rutter declared that for him 'the realities of war proved a healthy corrective to the extravagances of artistic theories'. His 'peculiar triumph' was to be able to apply the staccato of Futurist 'lines of force' to the wholly new conditions of war. *Returning to the Trenches* (1914–15; fig. 103), his most extreme London Group exhibit, demonstrated resoundingly that this was 'not an affair of individuals but the creaking progress of a complicated machine'.[8] This comment echoed Alan Clutton Brock's measured critique on the dehumanisation of the great new industry of destruction – 'in war man behaves like a machine or part of a machine ... he ceases to be a person and is lost in a process'.[9] No one could doubt Nevinson's patriotism: there was nothing 'Junkerist' about his discovery of the foundation of a new realism and, although we might assume, along with Rutter, that the war precipitated a return to realistic painting, it was not an

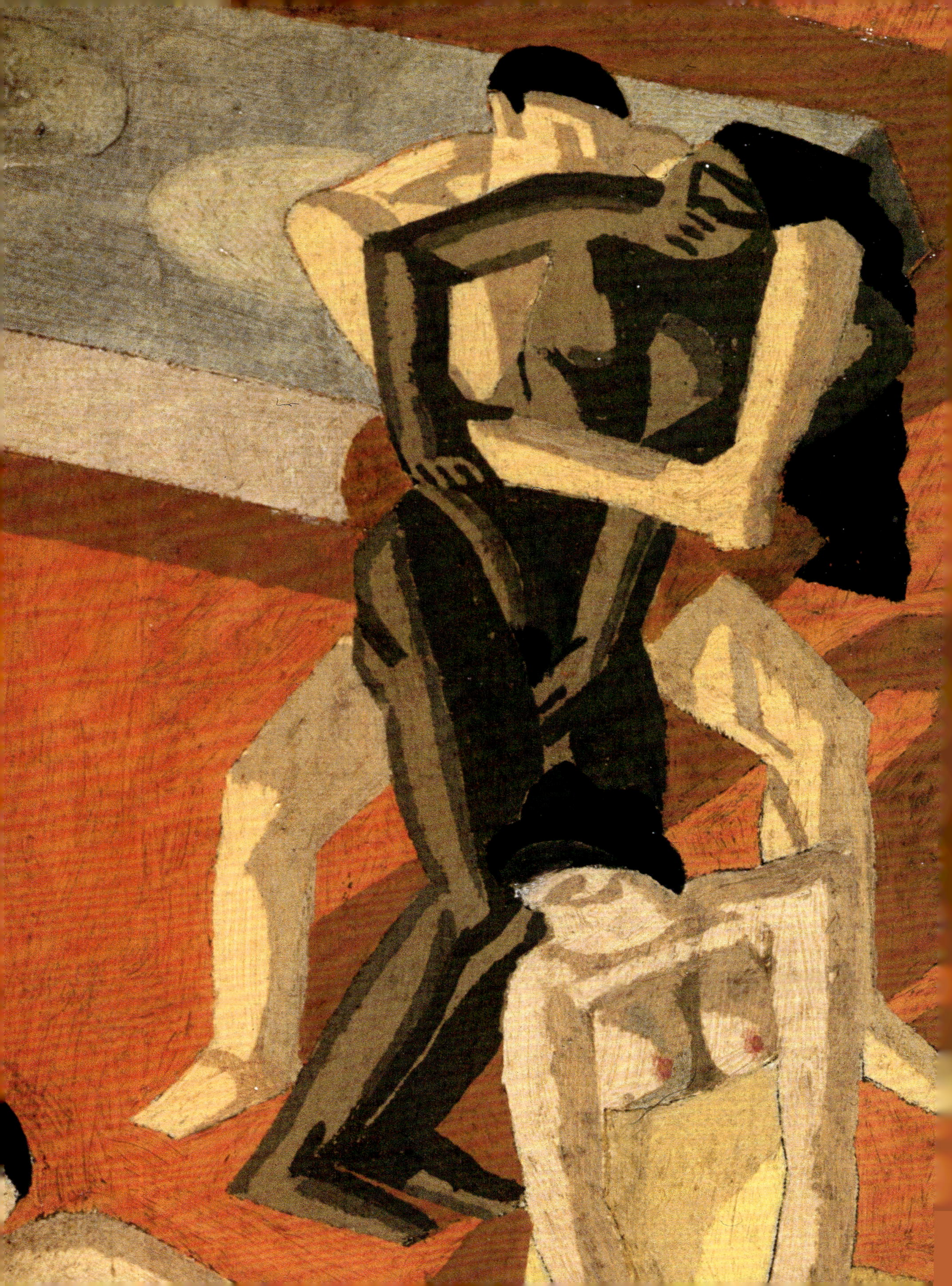

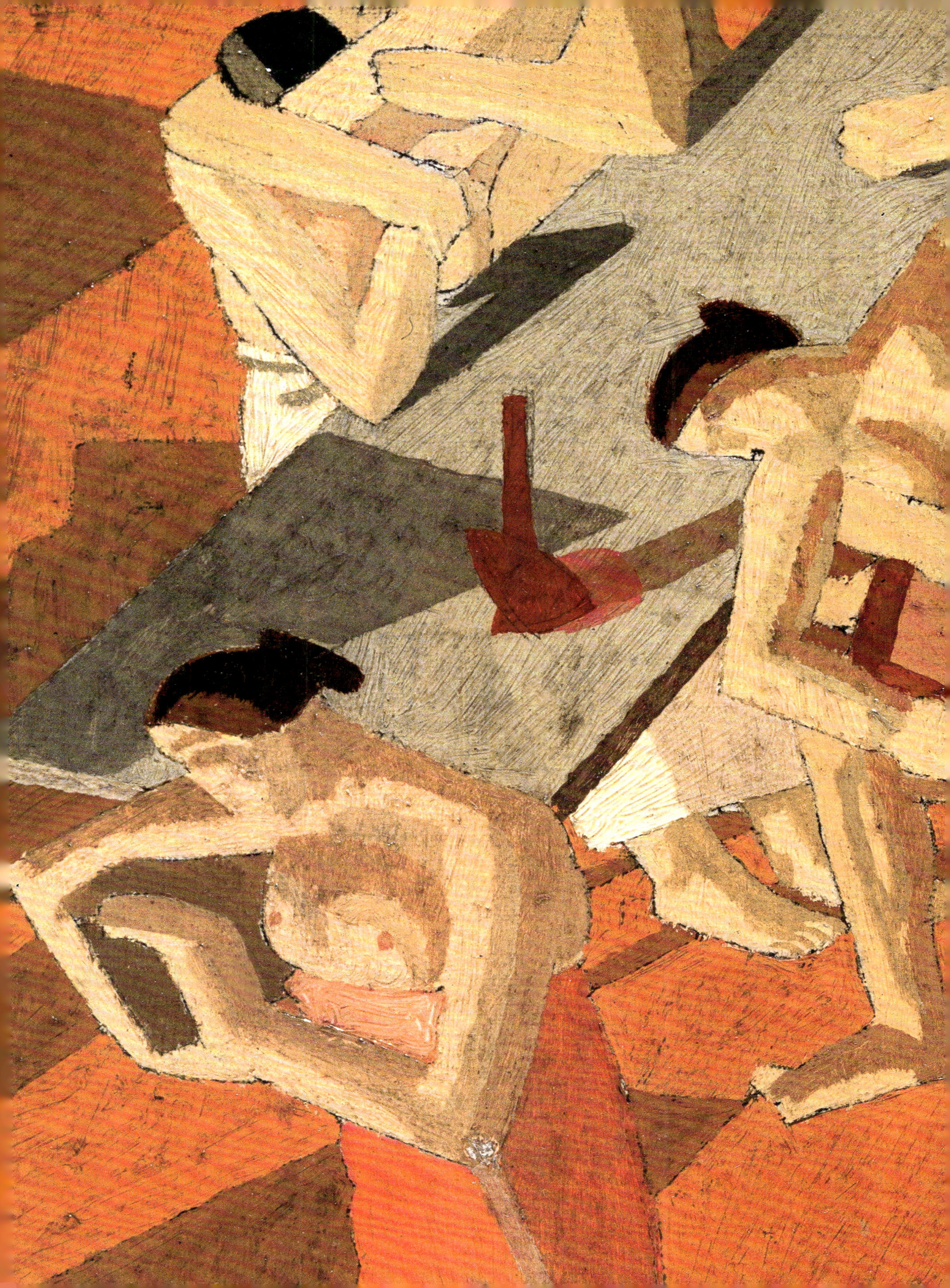

undifferentiated or consensually coherent concept. It merely recognised that a painter such as Nevinson, in *La Mitrailleuse* (1915; fig. 100), modified his style in such a way as to acknowledge the connection between 'person' and 'process'. The single purpose of the gunner and his 'machine' gun is to fire.[10] *La Mitrailleuse* was shown at the New English 1916 spring exhibition, along with two other Nevinson war works.[11] It had already been aired in the Allied Artists' Association exhibition earlier in the year. Looking back eighteen months to Sickert's *Soldiers of King Albert the Ready* (fig. 97) would emphasise the irrevocable force of Nevinson's vision. Sickert doffed his cap and stated that this was 'the most authoritative and concentrated utterance on the war in the history of painting'.[12] Like his riflemen, Nevinson's iconic 'Poilu' is seen in profile taking aim, but it is the indiscriminate aim of the automaton. Used as the frontispiece for Charles Mariott's *Modern Movements in Painting* (1920), it combined 'discreetly modified Cubism' with the 'force-lines' of the Futurists. *La Mitrailleuse* was a classic.[13]

In the Academy, the war had already descended into hackneyed heroism and 'home-front' anecdote, while, in the club, Fairlie Harmar's *Wounded Belgians Knitting Socks in Crosby Hall*, Maud Ireland Button's *A Belgian Refugee* and Dorothy Coke's *Allotments* (1917; fig. 104) in the winter shows of 1916 and 1917 strikingly contrasted with the dominant Home Counties landscapes. More typical club exhibits of these first years of the war were Atwood's *Children*

Fig. 104 Dorothy Josephine Coke
War Allotments in a London Suburb
(also known as *Allotments*), 1917
Watercolour on paper, 35.5 x 50.8 cm
Imperial War Museum, London

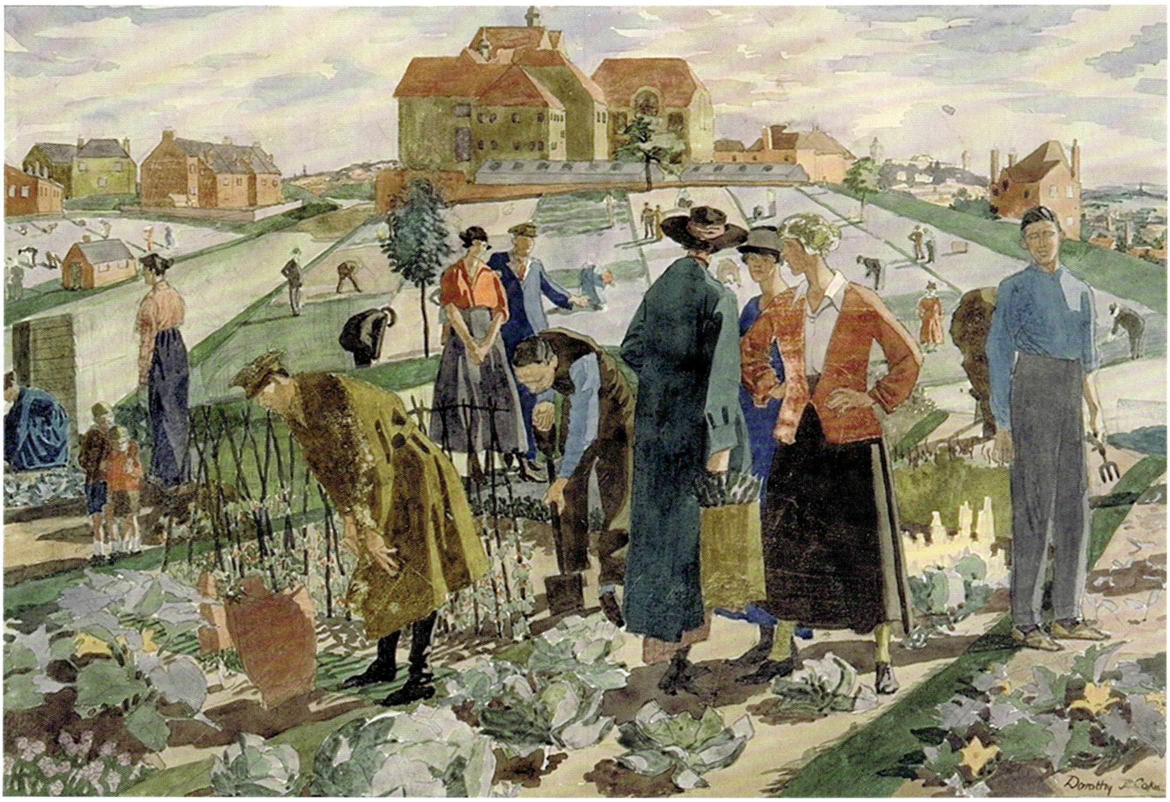

Playing (spring of 1915), Pearce's *The Locust Tree* (spring of 1916) and Alice Fanner's *The Palace, Hampton Court* (spring of 1916; fig. 105) – all of which refer to continuing traditions that would outlast the war.[14] In Fanner's case, Impressionism filtered through the work of Jacques-Emile Blanche proceeded at the leisurely pace of a sunny summer afternoon, while Atwood could easily have fitted into a Camden Town exhibition and Pearce, also a Post-Impressionist, relied heavily on the graphic intensity of Van Gogh.[15] Nevertheless, as the war dragged on, a mood of glumness prevailed between the lines of Holmes's account of his New English exhibit from the winter of 1917, *Whernside*, which, 'yielding to the general indifference', he used as a drawing-board when it was returned to his studio unsold.[16] New English exhibits suggest that artists were slow to react to the war until the arrival of Francis Dodd's portraits of British generals and Muirhead Bone's drawings of the Western Front and the Grand Fleet, in the summer exhibition of 1917. Moreover, such painters as Atwood and Colin Gill elected not to show war works in the club exhibitions, reserving them exclusively for the new Imperial War Museum, London, and the big Academy 'War Pictures' exhibition of 1919, which New English exhibitors dominated.[17] In all these examples the excesses of jingoism and sentimental patriotism that led to Frank Salisbury's popular hit, *Boy First Class, John Travers Cornwell VC*, at the Royal Academy in 1917, was avoided.

Fig. 105 Alice Fanner
The Palace, Hampton Court, 1916
Location unknown

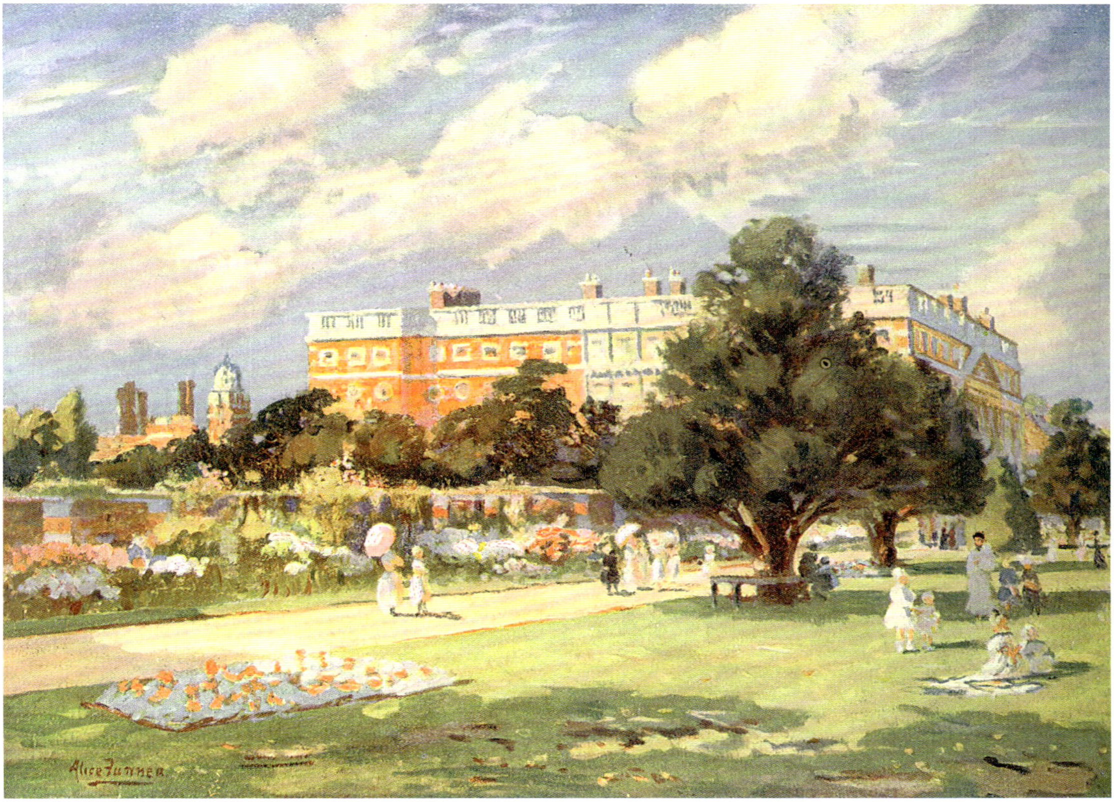

Looking back in 1922, Rutter recalled new developments in watercolour in the pre-war exhibitions. They emanated neither in the 'school of inspired blobs' of Brabazon, nor were they 'careful' tinted architectural studies in the manner of MacColl. By contrast, they had a 'naïve almost child-like outlook that annoyed some and proved irresistible to others': they were the watercolours and pen drawings of Paul and John Nash.[18] Their visionary character had been evident from the start to Gordon Bottomley, who advised Paul Nash that 'the world will want to make you paint its subjects before it will let you be successful, and there will be plenty of people ready to tell you that such accidental and skilful realism as that of the New English Art Club is what you want to aim at: but in truth you must never forget the visions which launched you into art'.[19] He need not have worried, for the club accepted the early work of both Nashes on its own terms.[20] The innocence, if it was ever truly present, did not survive the war, although much continued to be made of the fact that the self-taught John Nash had 'avoided' art schools.[21] By the early 1920s, and with exhibiting profiles at the club and the London Group, both Nashes, along with Ethelbert White, were spearheading a new approach to landscape that sidestepped the overt Cézannism of Fry and Bernard Adeney in the search for a topography of simple shapes and cool colour sparingly applied. It did not take long for the claims of national identity to be lodged – indeed in Rutter's and Wilenski's cases there was a conflation between phrases like 'very English', 'new English' and 'wholly English'.[22] And behind this lurked the pantheism of the first English watercolourists. At this moment of regrouping, not only had the Academy begun to look like the pre-war New English, but even the London Group had spawned more radical breakaways in the Seven and Five Society and a brief flowering of Vorticist members as 'Group X'.

Reaffirmations of belief in one form or another were a consequence of the war. Religion, orthodox or occult, was back in favour. The Old and New Testaments had been the inspiration for Stanley Spencer's earliest exhibits in the winters of 1912 and 1913.[23] In his case, the complimentary review in *The Times* of *The Centurion's Servant* exhibited in the winter of 1915 (1914; fig. 106) had a sustaining effect throughout the war.[24] It opened with the statement that this was 'the most interesting picture in the present exhibition' and was taken as proof that Spencer was 'keenly interested in the character of people and things ... not trying to be artistic after any fashion ... [and] the mere design of his picture, so simple, so unusual, appeals to the eye at once, as an original melody appeals to the ear'. The critic concluded that 'Mr Spencer is naturally primitive in his art'.[25] These were brave words on behalf of a picture that was not readily readable. 'Primitive' was one of the common epithets of approval for a work at the New English by this stage. Although it commonly referred to the pre- and early Renaissance Italian painters – in Spencer's case, it was Giotto – it tended, as in the case of the Nashes, to be deployed for work that was deliberately gauche. The opposite of the Mannerist and Caravaggesque sophistication of Sargent, now lingering in debased forms at the Royal Academy, it could simultaneously allude to both the Pre-Raphaelites and to the roots of European modernism. An 'absence of swagger and paraded facility' pervaded the early Spencer and

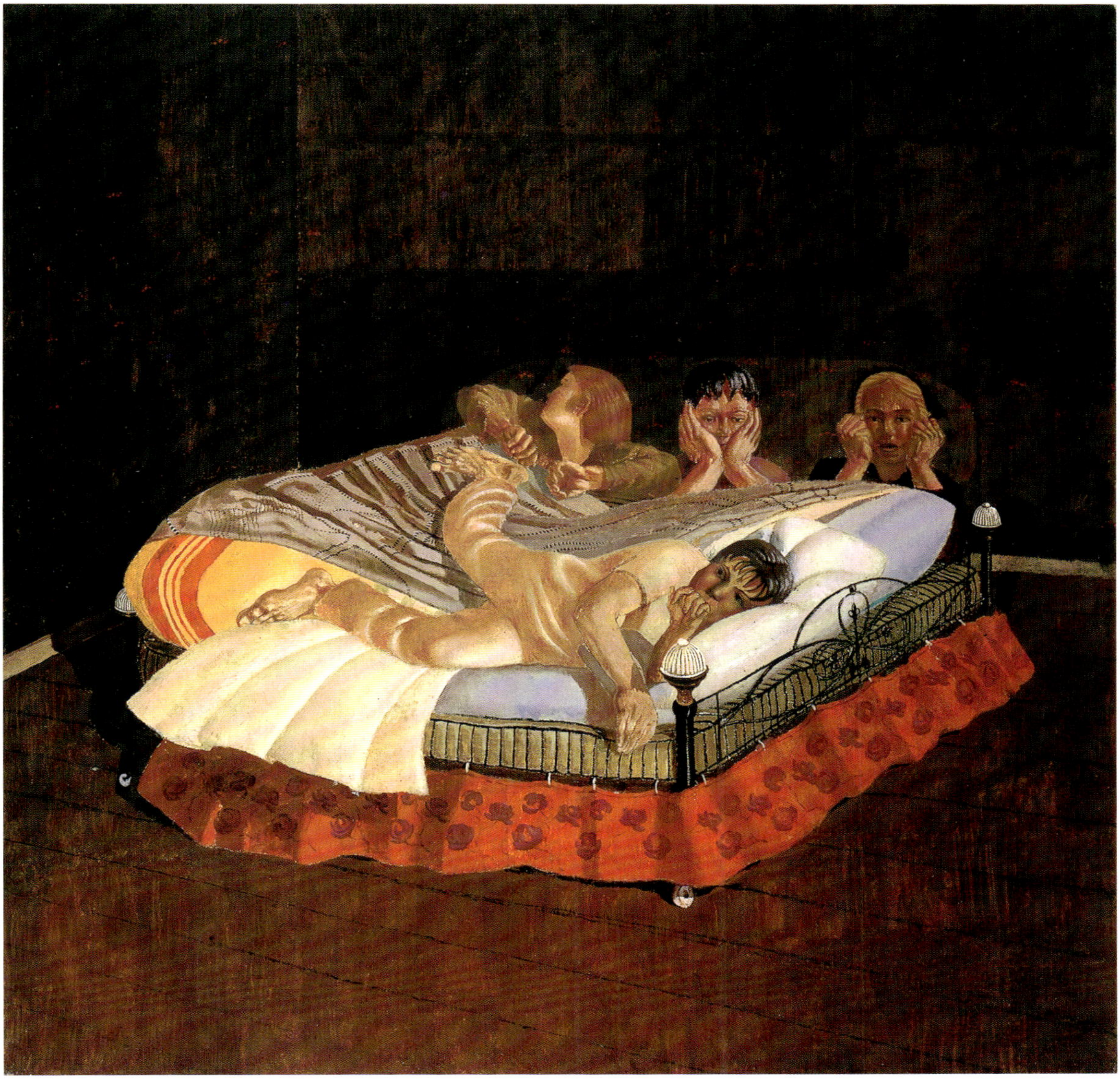

Fig. 106 Sir Stanley Spencer
The Centurion's Servant, 1914
Oil on canvas, 114.3 x 114.3 cm
Presented by the Trustees of the Chantrey Bequest 1960. Tate, London

his high seriousness justified the belief in some quarters that the differences between the New English and the London Group bereft of the Vorticists should be reconciled.[26] This merger did not happen, even though both societies collaborated in the 1920s.

Mural painting in the tradition of Piero della Francesca and Puvis de Chavannes, redeveloped by Sargant-Florence, was strengthened in these years by Frederick Cayley Robinson, an artist who returned to the New English in 1915.[27] He had been commissioned to paint decorations for the Entrance Hall of Middlesex Hospital.[28] These 'Acts of Mercy' were so sanitised that *The Times* found them unpalatable. Robinson was too worthy. Its critic professed a

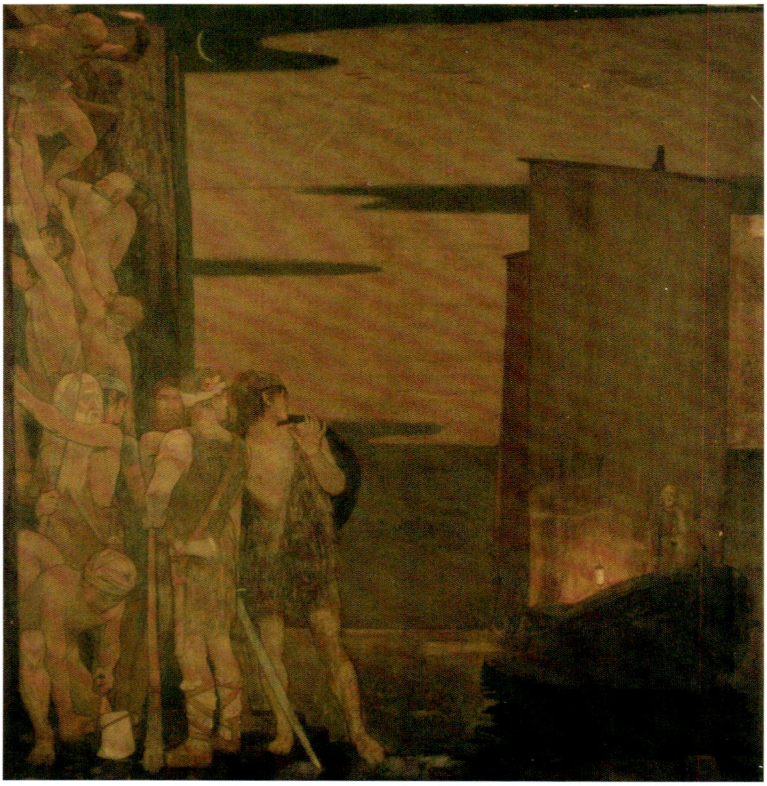

Fig. 107 Frederick Cayley Robinson
The Landing of St Patrick in Ireland, c. 1912–13
Oil on canvas, 201 x 191 cm
Dublin City Gallery The Hugh Lane, Dublin

preference for 'the wicked world ... even with the Germans in it'.[29] He followed them in 1917 with *The Landing of St Patrick in Ireland* (fig. 107), a mural mainly completed between 1912 and 1913 for Hugh Lane's Gallery of Modern Art in Dublin.[30] In the circumstances, with war raging, Lane's death on the Lusitania and the suppression of the Easter Rising the previous year, this could have been controversial, but it was not. Where Orpen, Lamb and Augustus John, using Puvis as a springboard, touched the contemporary Ireland, Robinson resorted to history and polished and perfected the syntax of cool delineation and muted colours.

At this point both John and Orpen had taken their turn at being 'primitive'. Their repertoires were fully formed – to the extent that a recognised set of clichés and conventions spun out to student followers. Models wore a certain style of clothes and assumed certain types of pose in John's work, in such a way that the use of 'stock' figures was being reported.[31] Orpen's sitters affected tousled hair, fresh complexions and gypsy shawls. At the other extreme, Walker, in the winter exhibition of 1920 re-stated her ambitions as a muralist with the much-admired *Decoration: The Excursion of Nausicaa* (1920; fig. 108), a work that T.W. Earp later described as 'exquisitely evocative of a classic Golden Age and the myths of the East'.[32] New directions, beyond the Post-Impressionist colour mosaic of the Camden Town painters, had developed in Walker's work around 1910 and her flowering as a painter of decorative schemes coincided with a fascination for theosophy.[33] The first fruits of this experimentation appeared in *The Bathers,* exhibited in the winter of 1910, *In the Garden of Images,* shown in the winter of 1912, and *Decoration for Spring, One of the Four Seasons,* winter of 1912. While many of these experiments have been reworked, disappeared, or been re-titled, her preoccupations can be deduced from friezes such as *Decoration in Oils, The Zone of Hate,* shown spring of 1917. The New English catalogue lists the five forces contained in *The Zone of Hate* as 'Hate, Life, Death, Destiny and the World Sorrow', flanked by figures representing the 'Mother of the Race' and 'The Earth covering the Dead'. At first sight it might seem that the mantle of G. F. Watts had fallen upon Walker. However, like many of her contemporaries, she reached for a symbolic language to explain a world in which politics, materialism and grating imperialist competition, culminating in the horror of the Western Front, could only be dispelled by supernatural forces. But it was not clear in 1920 whether *Nausicaa* was powerful enough to carry the new millennialist messages to a world that had experienced Armageddon.

In the immediate aftermath of the war, Francis Bate, who had served the club for nearly thirty years, retired from the honorary secretaryship and his place was taken by Francis Dodd.[34] The summer exhibition for that year was restricted to drawings and watercolours, including works by Henry Rushbury, Paul and John Nash, Charles Maresco Pearce, Evelyn Cheston, Allan Gwynne-Jones and Randolph Schwabe, while Dodd, Bone and Orpen showed war works, some of which had been borrowed from the newly formed Imperial War Museum. Amongst the far-flung landscapes, Katharine F. Clausen showed *From my Tent, Crete* (*c.* 1917) and Thomas Cantrell Dugdale, who had served with the Middlesex Yeomanry in Palestine, exhibited *Kustul on the Jerusalem Road* (*c.* 1918). At this point the finances of the club were in a ruinous state and it was decided to leave the security of the Royal Society of British Artists

Fig. 108 Ethel Walker
Decoration: The Excursion of Nausicaa, 1920
Oil on canvas, 183.5 x 367 cm
Purchased 1924. Tate, London

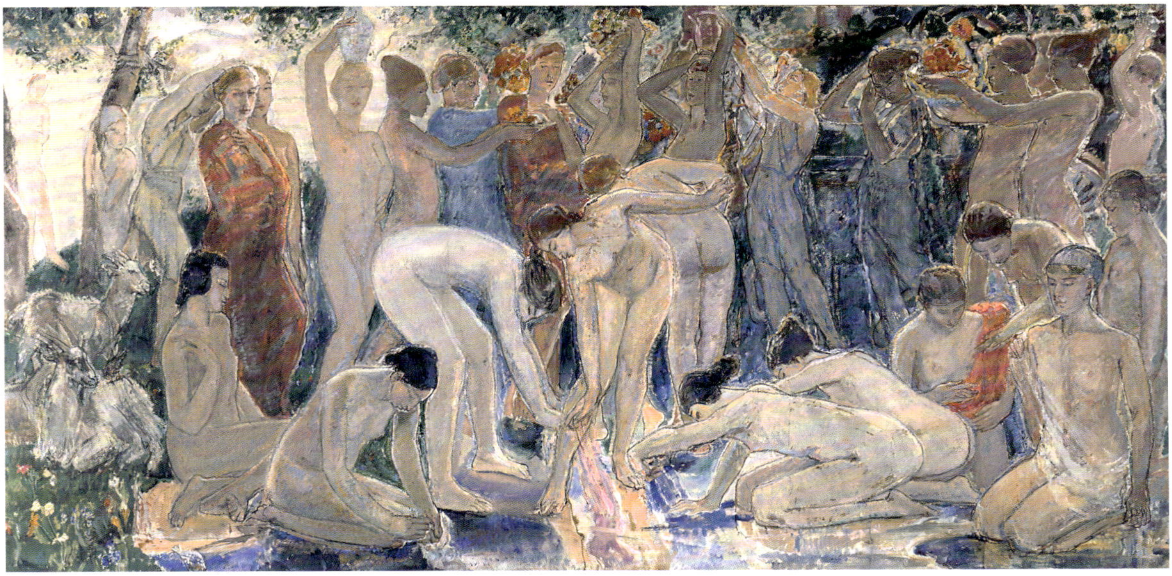

galleries for those of the Royal Watercolour Society in Pall Mall East.[35] After some debate, the offices of the honorary secretary and honorary treasurer were separated, the latter going to a non-exhibitor, the solicitor, Loughborough Ball.[36] Frederick Winter, who, throughout the war, had assisted in the post of exhibitions secretary, retired in 1920. The following year, Charles H. Collins Baker, painter, art historian and keeper at the National Gallery, London, with Holmes's approval, was drafted in to assist Dodd in the newly created role of deputy honorary secretary.[37] Throughout the war years, the club's losses hovered around £120. Members' subscriptions no longer provided sufficient revenue and it was reluctantly decided that submission and hanging fees of five and ten shillings respectively should be charged to non-member exhibitors.[38] With a fixed commission of 15% on sales, the deficit was cleared and a surplus of £50 created.[39] At the same time, to avoid Entertainment Tax, the club was registered as a Friendly Society.[40] Despite the brevity of Dodd's term of office, the club was in an optimistic frame of mind when he resigned in favour of Collins Baker.

A new purposeful academicism emerged in a series of strong exhibitions in the early 1920s that had a 'modish air'.[41] The general character of these shows was predetermined in Gower Street, to such an extent that *The Athenaeum* hailed the winter exhibition of 1919 in the following terms:

> The New English Art Club is the Mecca of the Slade School students, who habitually make their bow to the public at its exhibitions.... [The club] stands for something more tremendous to them – it stands for ART. When a Slade student applies the term 'good' to Piero della Francesca's *Baptism*, he means that it reminds him of things he has seen at the New English Art Club ... when he calls a modern picture 'good' he means that it is good enough for the New English Art Club.[42]

Heterogeneity in the club included Vorticist dogma, in small amounts, as well as the loose *facture* of Steer and Brown, with references to Gainsborough and Constable. What lay at the centre is revealed in the reference to Piero, the consistently influential Renaissance master for Spencer's generation.[43] Piero's *Baptism of Christ* (1449), freely available in the National Gallery, with its simple flat 'hand-coloured' marquetry of shapes, was constantly imitated. This Slade orthodoxy caused concern in some quarters, where it seemed that the 'possibilities of paint' were not being recognised. Too many members of the 'new school' thought of the medium 'too exclusively' as a 'device for the enlargement or reproduction of drawings'. Indeed, it was generally felt that Slade students, engrossed in careful shading, had no use for painting. Although their strengths were applauded, Paul Nash, Bernard Meninsky, Elliott Seabrooke, Neville Lewis and Allan Gwynne-Jones were not regarded as colourists.[44] With Rothenstein's appointment to the principalship of the Royal College of Art in 1920, some observers expected Slade dominance to be challenged, and, although painters like Charles Mahoney joined in 1927, and brought in students like Evelyn Dunbar in the mid-1930s, their emphasis was firmly on draughtsmanship.[45]

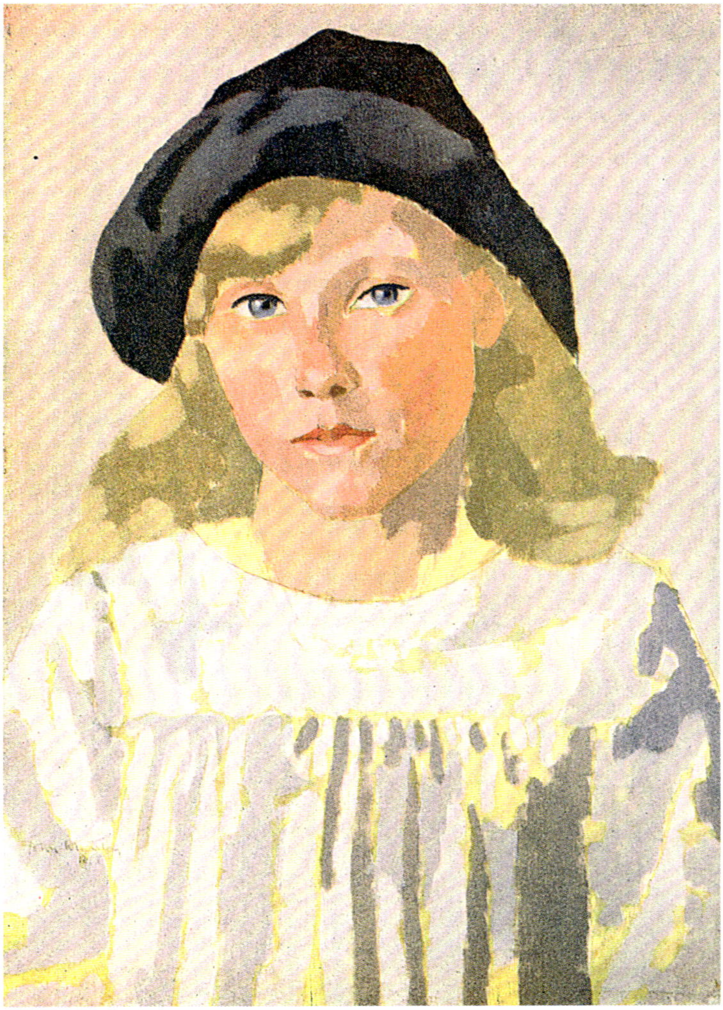

Fig. 109 John Wheatley
Alice, the Milkmaid, 1918
Location unknown

As ever, the New English was looking to introduce new talent, while the painters of the 1890s still held a controlling interest. Blake's febrile visions remained in vogue while John in Hispanic portraits maintained the great tradition and attempted spirituality through the eyes of El Greco. The repertoire of costers and gypsies was also revived in club exhibitions in the work of John Wheatley. *The Two Friends*, one of Wheatley's exhibits in the winter of 1921 recalling Dodd's *Polly* (fig. 83), shown in the winter of 1911, could have been produced at any point in the previous ten years. In such paintings as *Alice, the Milkmaid* (1918; fig. 109), Wheatley had also demonstrated an intelligent grasp of provincial Post-Impressionism. Not only do these works demonstrate the degree to which the human subject remained central, but they also point to the large number of watercolours, prints and drawings now being submitted. The millennialist sensibility, which elsewhere in Europe was expressed in Mondrian's 'Neo-plasticism', was nowhere to be found.[46]

One painter trained at the Slade who seemed to offer new hope was the exotic Alvaro 'Chile' Guevara, who emerged in the New English in the winter of 1915.[47] Guevara moved from Piero-like studies of figures in public baths and music halls to allegorical paintings, with *Medusa's Trial* – a strange courtroom scene, of 'no literary significance', shown at the New English in the summer of 1920. In the eyes of one critic, it resembled 'a fragment of a primitive fresco in rather bad condition'.[48] The winter show contained *The Signs of the Zodiac*, a picture of nudes in a 'primeval' landscape, 'comporting themselves' with equally 'primeval vivacity'.[49] The failure to find 'important' subjects, which were then not treated in a wholly satisfactory way, drove Guevara down the predictable path of Society portraiture and unfulfilled promise. He had been taken up by Edith Sitwell, and her portrait as *The Editor of 'Wheels'*, shown at the International Society in 1919, brought him great success. *Ronald Firbank Esq.*, *The Fur Coat*, *Mrs Lewis of the Cavendish*, all shown at the club between 1920 and 1922, reveal that he had found a modern way to do Sargent.[50] For a brief moment, in his rakish portrait of *Nancy Cunard* (1919; fig. 110), he had solved the problem of modernity with 'modishness'.[51]

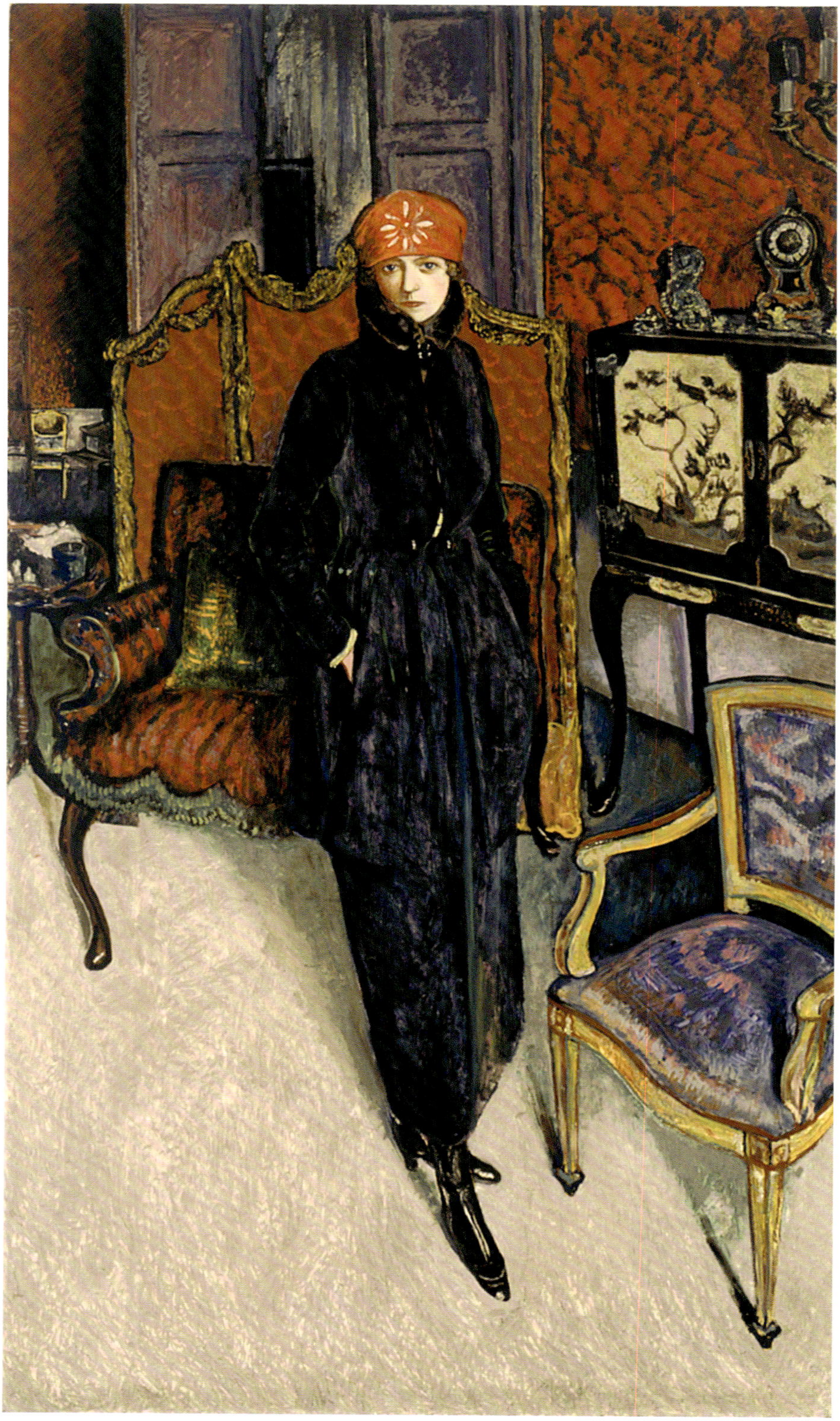

Fig. 110 Alvaro Guevara
Nancy Cunard, 1919
Oil on canvas, 213.7 x 122.2 cm
Felton Bequest 1954. National Gallery of Victoria, Melbourne

The routes to modernism through abstraction were at this point discredited and contact with the European avant-garde was severely limited.[52] The compass points provided by Purism and Futurism were gone, along with the scholastic dogmatism of the Vorticists, and the pointer was swinging wildly.[53] Young English painters did not rush to join André Lhote and Jean Metzinger, and the fortunes of Montmartre and Montparnasse were slow to revive. More than this, amid bumptious reports of the Peace conference, critics paraded public disillusionment. The Great War had not been 'a thunderbolt from the blue launched at an unoffending mankind: it was ... the natural result of a crude competitive system pursued almost to its limits ... individual, political and national rivalries which have been speeding to this end since the Middle Ages'.[54]

There was now no clear direction in life and art. Each of the club's landscapists retreated to his or her private Arcadia and, when their work was submitted, a number of tendencies were apparent.[55] A broadly based pre-war Impressionist faction, for instance, retained a rich palette and delighted in summer days. In 1921, for example, James Bolivar Manson complemented Lucien Pissarro's 'little blossom picture at the Unmentionable English', declaring that 'it was wonderful to come across it in that extraordinary *mélange*'.[56] Manson and Pissarro, having returned from a visit to Monet's studio at Giverny in 1919, were keen to extract from the London Group and the New English those artists who remained loyal to the French Impressionists. Pissarro wrote to Monet that meeting him had renewed his belief in the 'sensation as the foundation of everything'. Monet was a 'beacon' to such artists as Manson and himself, painters who were 'trying hard to react against the substitution of intellectualism for sensation'.[57] These former luminaries of the Camden Town and London groups now formed their own society. The Monarro Group – so titled as a conflation of the names 'Monet' and 'Pissarro' – held its first exhibition at the Goupil Gallery in February 1920 to good reviews. However, difficulties in organising the second exhibition the following year led to the dilution of the aims of the group and a loss of heart on Manson's part. Surveying this belated Impressionism, he felt that they were 'twenty years out of date'.[58]

At this point it was more important to catch up with Cézanne than Monet, as Alfred Thornton's acceptance by the London Group proves.[59] Fry's previously published essays, which now appeared as *Vision and Design* (1920), followed in 1922 by Clive Bell's *Since Cézanne*, underlined the French artist's importance. Young landscape painters of the Nashes generation, for whom the destructive power of mechanised war had obliterated the hedonism of sensation, were nevertheless filled with an urgent desire to portray the land renewing itself and Cézanne's detection of basic geometric solids in nature seemed to provide the best way to convey it. While painters such as William Lionel Clause and Elliott Seabrooke held to a modified form of divisionism and Hubert Lindsay Wellington represented a Gauguin- inspired faction, others analysed Cézanne's patient build up of *petites sensations* and brought them into a landscape where new meanings could be applied. Scenes of cultivation, the turning of the seasons and the relentless forces of nature came to the fore. The strength of landscape painting ranged across the Wittenham copses, proud elms and austere Dymchurch breakwaters drawn with measured deliberation by Paul Nash (see fig. 111), the rolling hills of Gilbert Spencer's *Cotswold Meadows* (*c.* 1920; fig. 112) to the downland pastures of Charles Cundall's *St Martha's Mount, Surrey* (1921; fig. 113) and the Welsh mountains of Walter Bayes's *The Ford, Railway Bridge, Arthog, North Wales* (*c.* 1917–20; fig. 114).[60] There was a fascination with the lines drawn on the surface of the terrain by field and furrow patterns that were ancient and everlasting – something that reverberates in the Post-Impressionist marquetry of Wellington (see fig. 115), as much as in the Holmes-inspired mountain ranges of Collins Baker. At the same time a mournful vapidity and eternal stillness infects the landscapes of John Nash and Ethelbert White (see fig. 116). For these painters, the blossom was yet to come.

It is obvious from this survey that the club hosted an extraordinary flowering of landscape painting around 1920. It would be easy to say that this arose as a result of liberation from the obligations imposed by the war, and the profound sense of release felt by soldiers like the Nashes, when they returned to the countryside. Britain's uplands and meadows contained a secret consolation. In a sense it was no different from that experienced by Edwardian landscapists who fled the ravages of industrialisation, but it was more intense. England's trees and lanes contained new lines and colours, springing from a consciousness of all those exciting pre-war exhibitions, but putting their mixed messages to work on an old subject in a serious and mature way. History was deeper than the Post-Impressionists and Cubists. The clues to this new landscape lay as much in the linearism of Francis Towne and the painters of the Norwich School as it

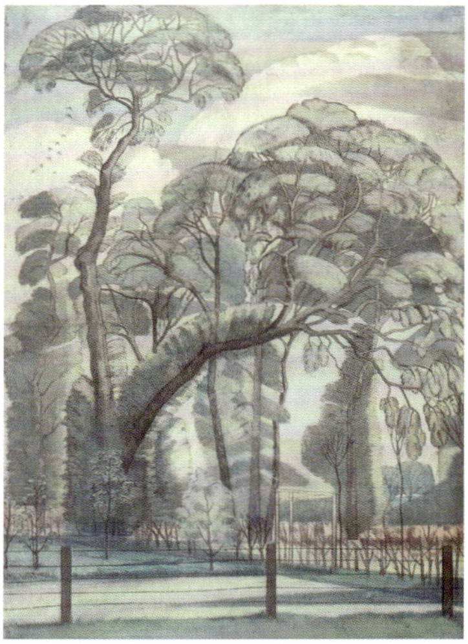

Above
Fig. 111 Paul Nash
The Elms, 1914
Watercolour on paper, 67 x 47.5 cm
Walker Art Gallery, Liverpool

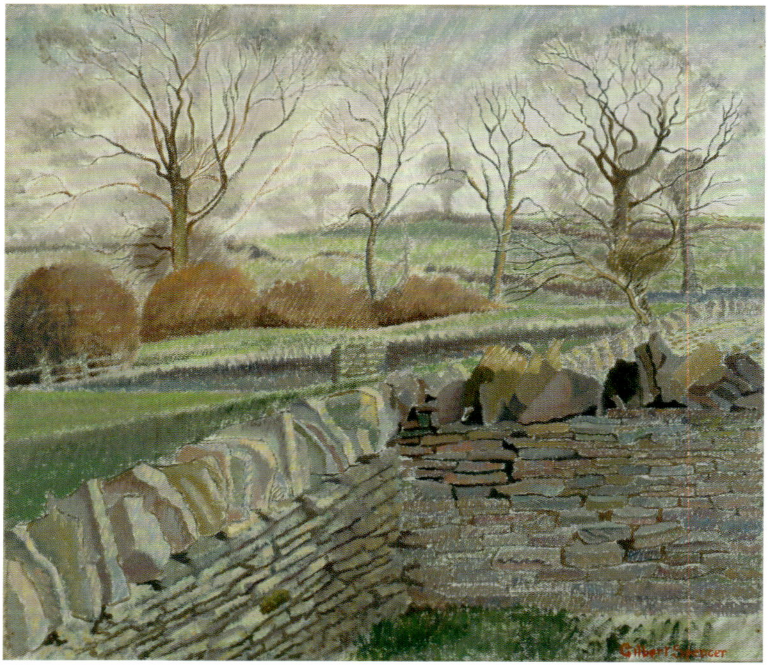

Left
Fig. 112 Gilbert Spencer
Cotswold Meadows, *c.* 1920
Oil on canvas, 39.6 x 45.1 cm
Tullie House Museum & Art Gallery, Carlisle

Opposite top
Fig. 113 Charles Ernest Cundall
St Martha's Mount, Surrey, 1921
Oil on canvas, 30.5 x 40.7 cm
Private collection

Opposite bottom
Fig. 114 Walter Bayes
The Ford, Railway Bridge, Arthog, North Wales, *c.* 1917–20
Oil on canvas, 103 x 144.5 cm
Tate, London

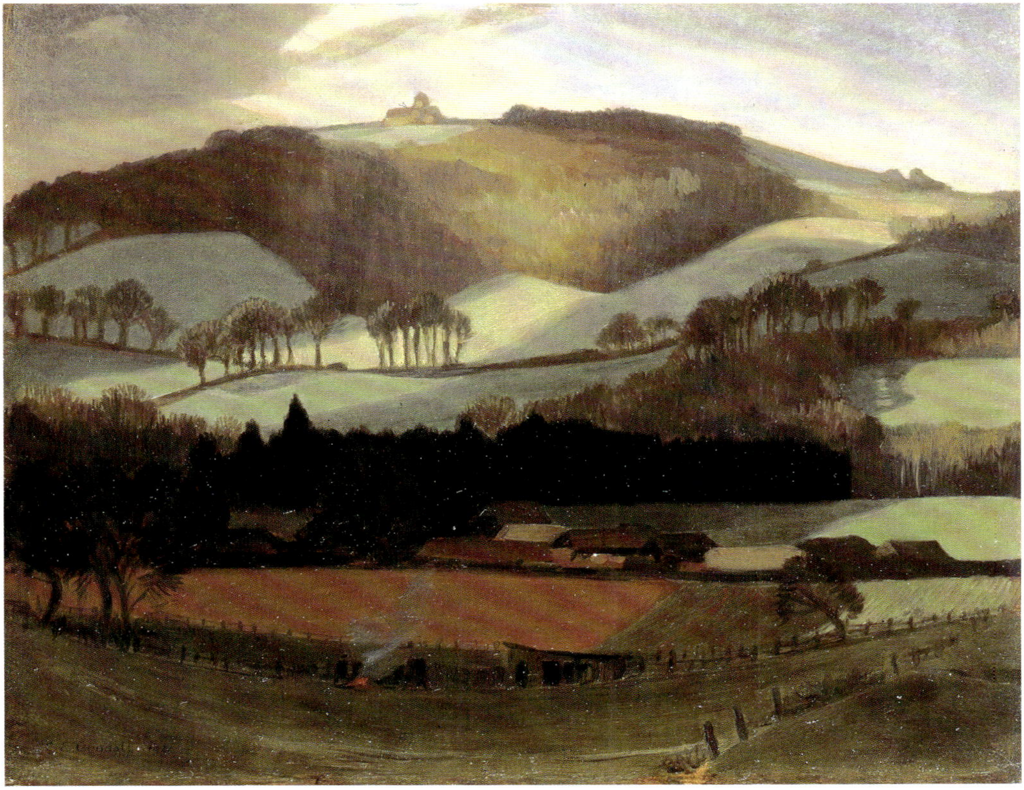

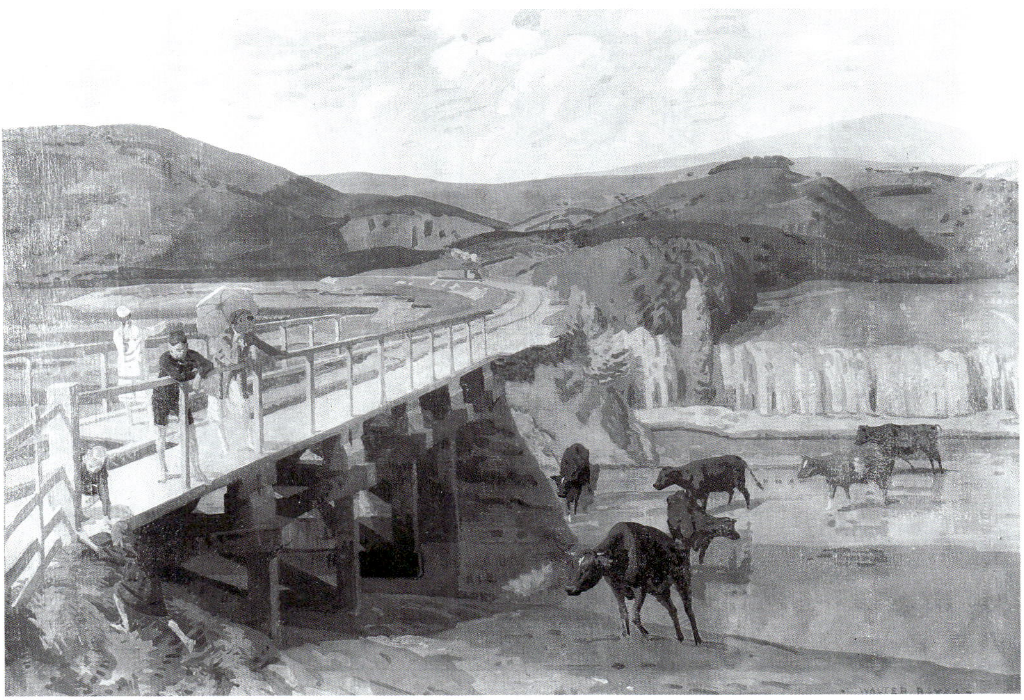

did in Matisse and the Post-Impressionists. Not that Fry's roster was neglected, but it was somehow tamed in unpretentious shows at the Leicester Galleries.[61] These gloomy willows, elms and beeches, these tapered hedgerows and rolling downs would spring to life – but what else? The time of innocent fairy fun, which many envisaged, had passed.

Whimsical, personal and 'primitive' pictures excited curiosity, only to be dismissed for lack of seriousness. Critics commented upon Thomas Lowinsky, who was 'playing at being a Florentine', while Ralph Chubb in *A Well* (*c.* 1920; fig. 119), was indulging a 'kind of modishness' that was 'already outmoded'.[62] Chubb resembled Blake in his belief in 'spiritual delight, mental pleasures, such as music and contemplation, serene physical health and beauty and activity, nakedness in perfect scenery beneath the sun, with freedom'.[63] His statuesque figures, uneasily placed in nature, drawing water, emphasise a contemplative calm that breaks into life in Stephen Bone's *Evening* (1930; fig. 117) and William

Fig. 115 Hubert Lindsay Wellington
Landscape, *c.* 1917
Location unknown

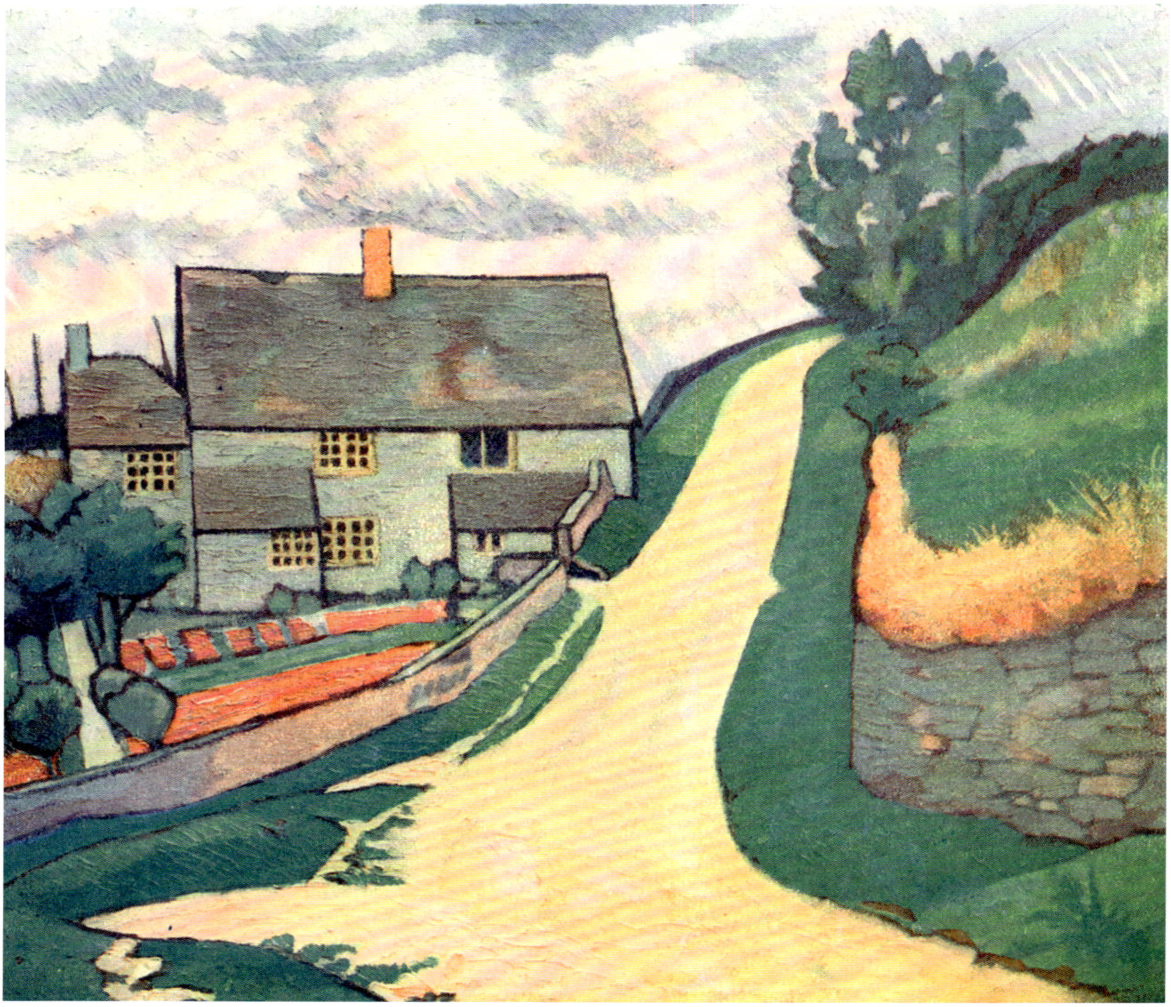

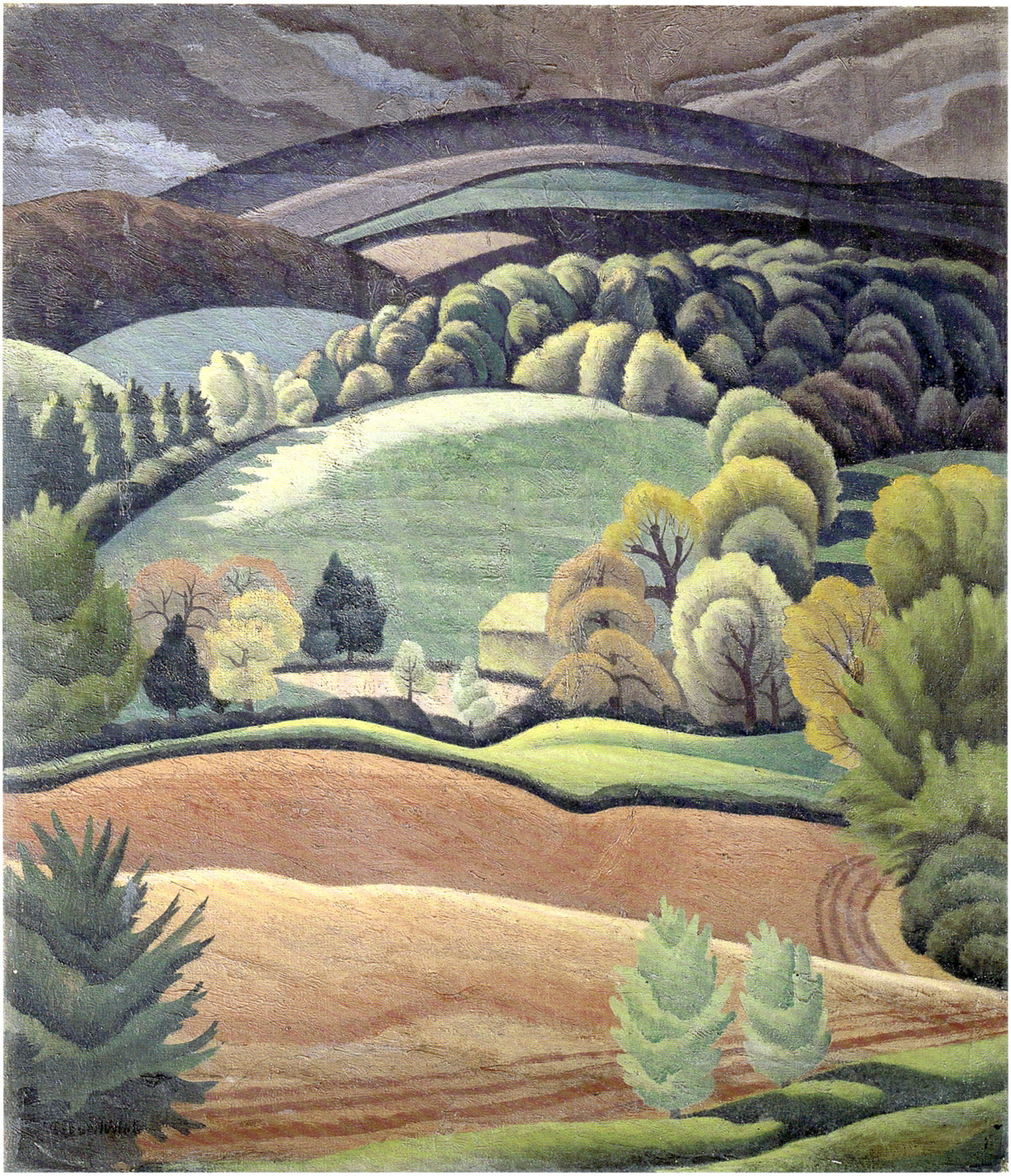

Fig. 116 Ethelbert White
Somerset Landscape, c. 1922
Oil on canvas, 61 x 50.8 cm
Private collection

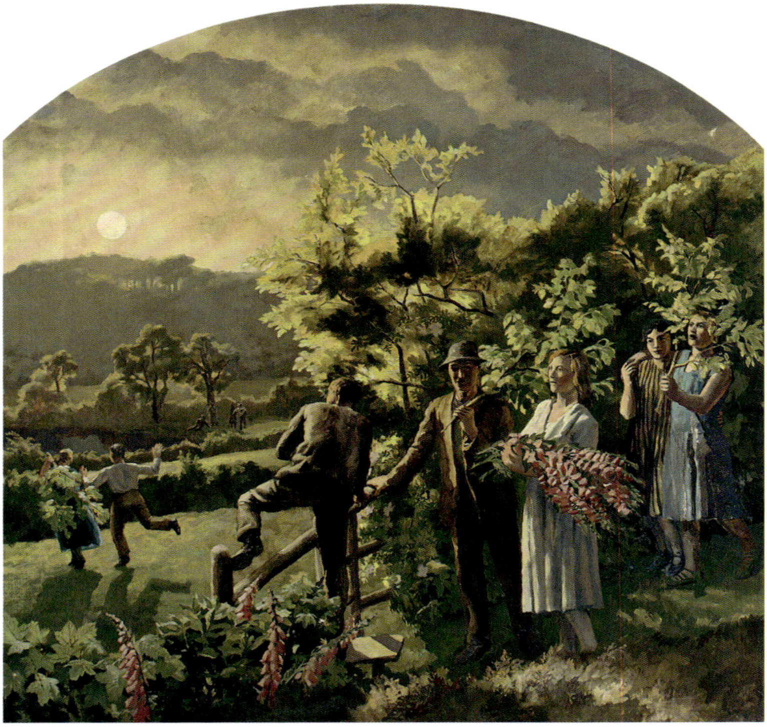

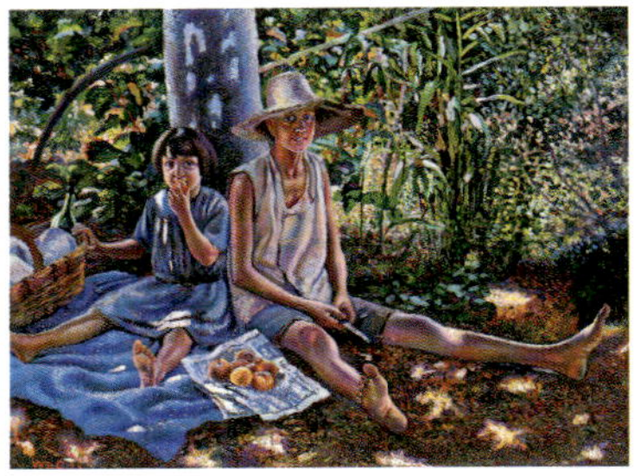

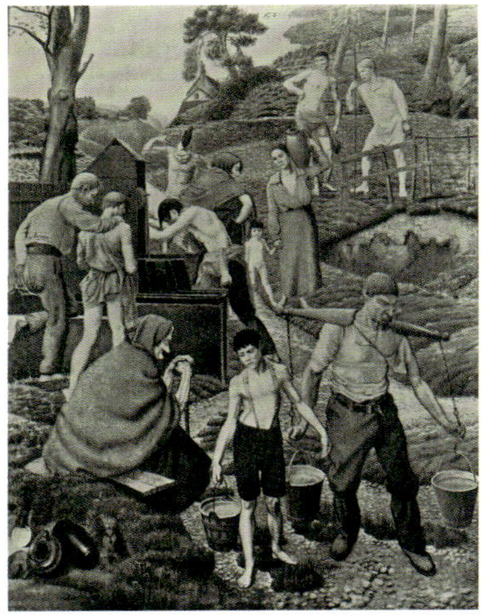

Lionel Clause's *Marcel and his Sister* (1923; fig. 118). These qualities, regarded as 'Giotto-esque', informed the biblical scenes of Dorothy Coke, Robin Guthrie, Stanley Spencer and Gilbert Spencer. Of this group, Lowinsky was the most consistently challenging. Emerging from the war with *The End of the World* and *The Annunciation* in the winter of 1920 and the spring of 1921 respectively, he had missed the modernist mainstream.[64] Preoccupied with Neo-Platonist symbolism, he returned to its roots in Botticelli, Pollaiuolo and Fra Lippo Lippi for later exhibits such as *The Dawn of Venus* and *Sappho* (fig. 120), painted in 1922 and 1923, but not shown until the winter of 1926 and the spring of 1927 respectively. They illustrate, in the first instance, the awakening of Venus from her shell in the depths of the ocean, before being swept ashore by Zephyrs, while, in the second, the diminutive Sappho casts her lyre aside before hurling herself to death. Neither painting gives any hint of drama. Improbable landscapes and weird rock formations, fabricated from memory and imagination, dominate both canvases.[65] These exceptional pictures came within three years of the publication of Fry's *Vision and Design*, one of the most influential art books of the early twentieth century, and they contain not a whisper of Cézanne or the French 'modernist' tradition. It would be tempting to describe them as Dali-esque, if that term were not anachronistic and did not diminish their power and originality.

In the winter of 1921–2, when some of these works were current, *The Saturday Review* invited MacColl, after an absence of over fifteen years, to return to its

Above left
Fig. 117 Stephen Bone
Evening, 1930
Oil on canvas, 122 x 122 cm
Private collection

Top
Fig. 118 William Lionel Clause
Marcel and his Sister, 1923
Oil on canvas, 50.6 x 65.3 cm
Manchester City Art Gallery

Above
Fig. 119 Ralph Chubb
A Well, *c.* 1920
Location unknown

offices to write on the New English.[66] Having paid his respects to the household gods, Brown, Steer and Tonks, who 'kept house for the homeless when houses were few', MacColl described the club as a 'nursery from which plants were extensively transferred and bedded out', a place for 'grafting and cross- fertilization'. However, after the blight of war, everyone looked for new ideas, for a 'rehandling of ancient myths, ironic or prophetic, as in the scriptures of our profoundest artist, Blake'. Not for the first time was William Blake held up as an exemplar. Collected covertly in the 1890s by Graham Robertson, he had been quoted frequently in the writings of Laurence Binyon and his work was celebrated in a major exhibition at the Tate Gallery, London, in 1913. After Armageddon, Blake's visionary utterances seemed more relevant than ever. Beyond this, MacColl had no recipe. His essay came at a time when he laid into the London Group, in a controversial attack on 'Fryism', and, for him as a committed exhibitor, the club continued to represent the progressive heart of British painting.[67] He saw the future in Spencer, Neville Lewis and Guevara, but two aspects of the club's current configuration were especially noteworthy. They were the New English 'school of drawing' led by Bone, Francis Unwin and Henry Rushbury and the women 'colourists', Walker, Bland, Atwood, Fisher Prout, Harmar, Evelyn Cheston, Ursula Tyrwhitt, Louise Pickard, Ethel Sands, Nan Hudson and Sylvia Gosse – all of whom had sustained the club throughout the war.[68] If the New English threatened to become a staid school of austere draughtsmen, it only had to look to the growing pool of women painters for life and colour. With this, MacColl put down his pen.

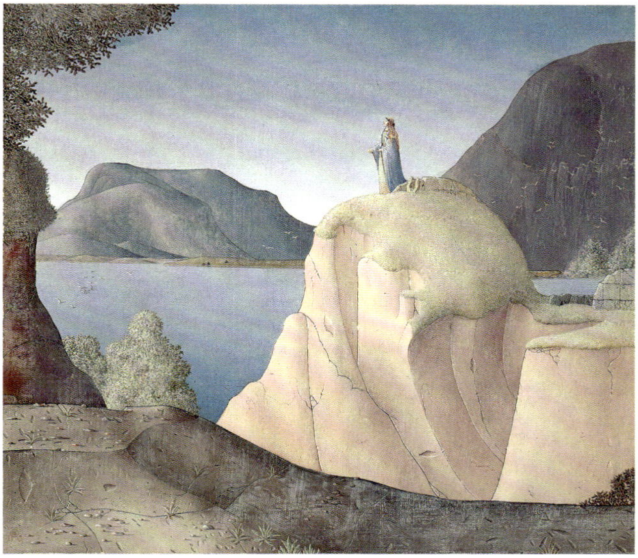

Fig. 120 Thomas Esmond Lowinsky
Sappho, 1923
Oil on canvas, 46.2 x 51 cm
Ferens Art Gallery, Hull

Was MacColl out of step with current feeling? The short-lived triumphalism of Lloyd George's Peace Conference sound bite – 'Hang the Kaiser and make Germany pay' – subsided, leaving a vacuum. Like Alfred de Musset's post-Napoleonic 'nervous and fevered' generation, the 'bright' young people who survived the war did so by papering over a profound sense of loss. Bottle parties on Tagg's Island, depicted by Alfred Munnings, caught the passing mood of dissipation that ended with the dissolution of the Liberal-Labour partnership and the General Election of 1924.[69] There had already been strikes and protest rallies in Trafalgar Square – depicted in Stephen Bone's *Demonstration of the Church Socialist League* (1922; fig. 121), exhibited in the winter of the same year.[70] Sunny scenes painted by Fisher Prout and Louise Pickard at Battersea Park (fig.122) or Richmond Bridge concealed polite dissenters. There was no more interest in 'Monarro' impressionism than in 'intellectual' abstraction.

Faced with mounting dissatisfaction at the condition of the Royal Watercolour Society's Galleries and the impending lease renewal in July 1923, the issue

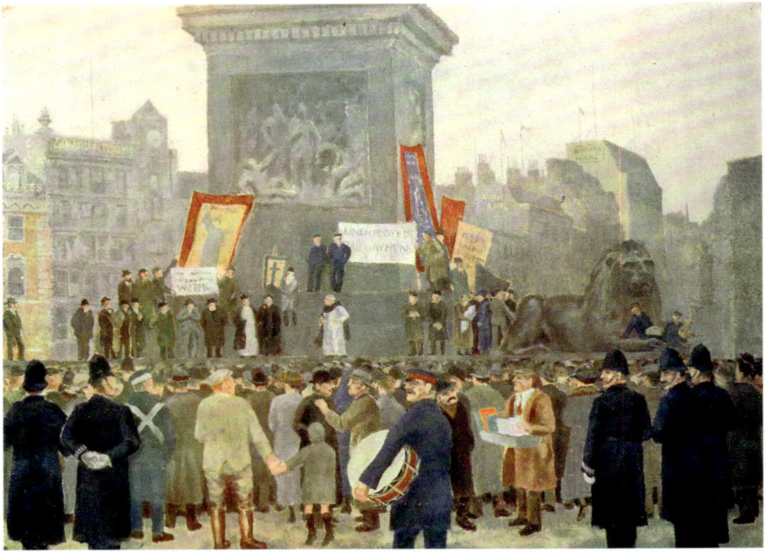

Fig. 121 Stephen Bone
Demonstration of the Church Socialist League, 1922
Location unknown

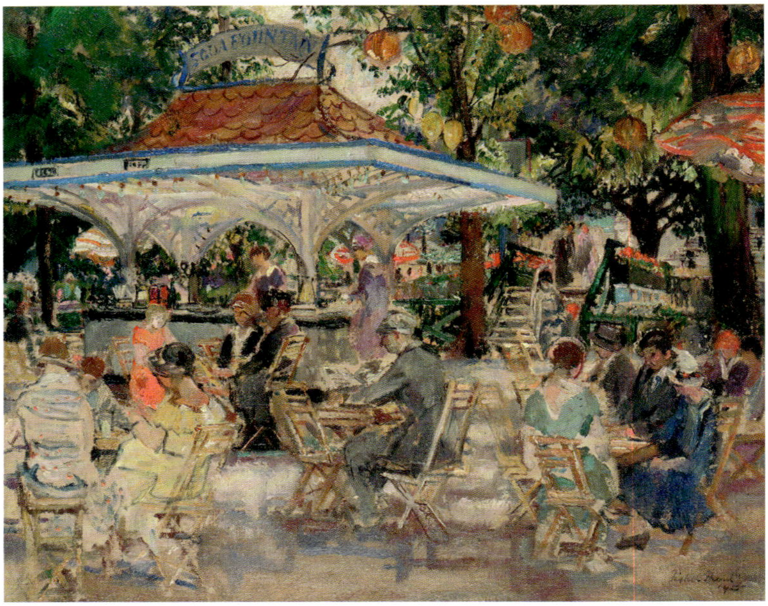

Fig. 122 Margaret Fisher Prout
Soda Fountain, Battersea Park, 1925
Oil on canvas, 47.5 x 58 cm
Private collection

of the lack of permanent exhibiting space for the club was reopened. For some time there had been growing dismay at the closure of larger commercial galleries in central London. The old New Gallery in Regent Street had been a cinema since before the war and the International Society of Sculptors, Painters and Gravers and the National Portrait Society, formerly under the wing of the Grosvenor Galleries, had relocated to the Grafton Gallery in Bond Street, which in turn had been sold for conversion into a cabaret. Large public exhibitions, popular entertainment in Victorian times, were now competing with nightclubs and picture houses. Facing high rents, the RWS in Pall Mall and the British Artists in Suffolk Street were also coming to the end of long leases, with no certainty of renewal, and at this point there was much discussion of the need for new space.[71] The winter General Meeting in January 1922 instituted a special reserve fund for the purpose of establishing permanent quarters and, although it received general support, time ran out before anything could be done and twelve months later a five-year lease was reluctantly renewed.[72] But the matter did not end there. In 1924, having just negotiated its lease on the RWS Galleries, F. G. Plummer approached the club with a rent-free space for a Retrospective Exhibition at the new Spring Gardens Gallery.[73] In the general malaise, Plummer's offer seemed hugely attractive, and a sub-let to the London Group of the RWS space was swiftly arranged.

By the winter 1923 exhibition, however, when Tancred Borenius stepped briefly into MacColl's shoes, the Symbolist tendencies evident in the previous half dozen shows seemed to have run out of steam. Robin Guthrie's *The Sermon on*

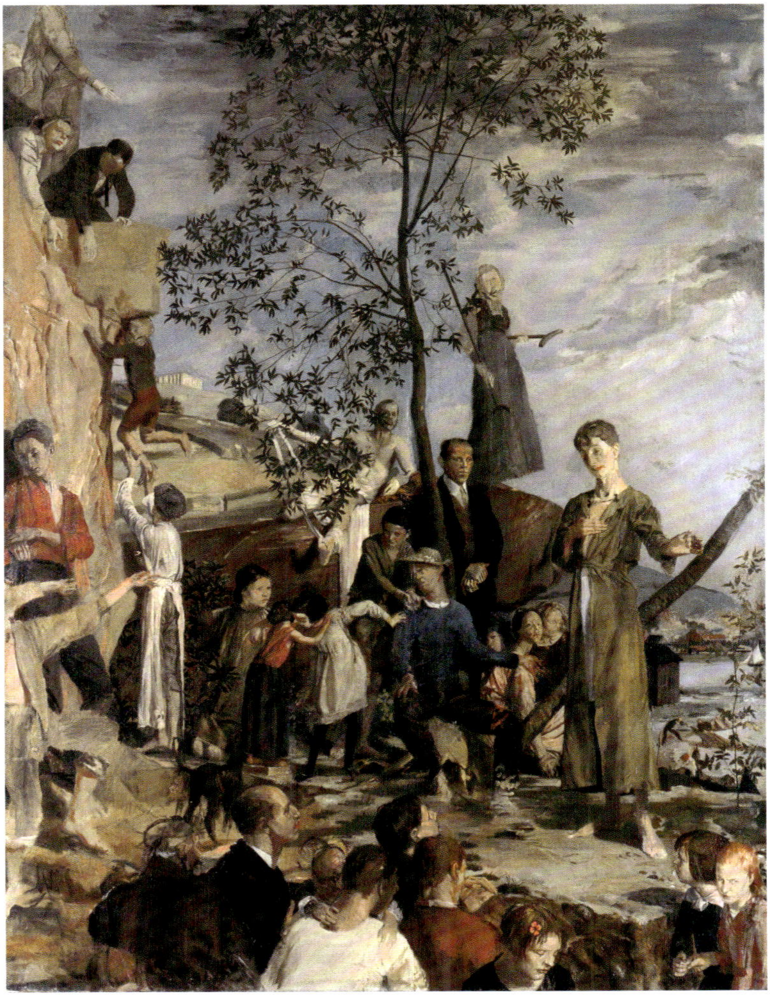

Fig. 123 Robin Guthrie
The Sermon on the Mount, c. 1922–3
Oil on canvas, 245 x 184 cm
Presented by the Trustees of the Duveen Paintings Fund 1949 and accessioned 1993. Tate, London

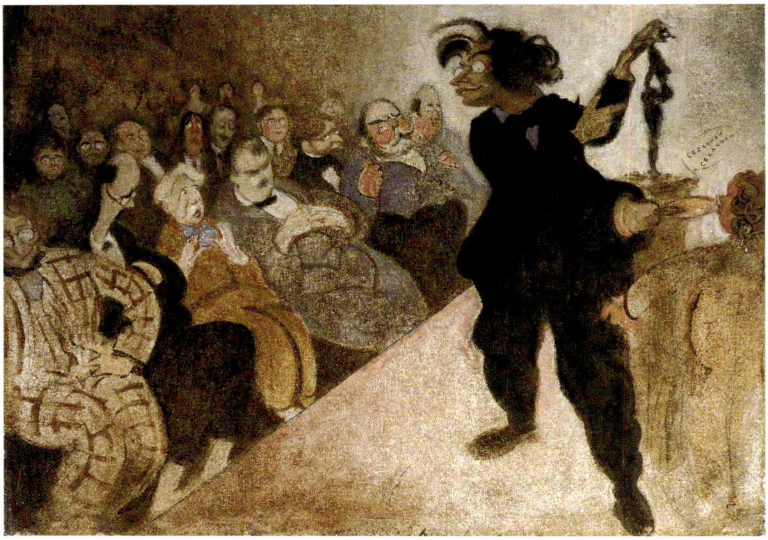

Fig. 124 Henry Tonks
The Unknown God (Roger Fry Preaching the New Faith, Clive Bell Ringing the Bell), 1922
Oil on canvas, 40.3 x 56 cm
Private collection

the Mount (*c.* 1922–3; fig. 123), was a notable exception. A recent Slade student, Borenius dubbed him '*alumno di Tonks*', and, while his stylised figures sometimes recall Epstein, the dry chalky pigment and blond tonalities of his work were 'after the manner which used to be Cazin's'.[74] However, the 'great popular draw' in the winter show of 1922–3 was an irreverent picture that recycled the recent past in an amusing way.[75] Henry Tonks's *The Unknown God* (1922; fig. 124) presented a caricature of Fry, the flamboyant magician, revealing to the chant of 'Cezannah, Cezannah', a modernist sculpture that looked suspiciously like a dead cat. The front row of the stalls was dominated by New English notables; sundry members of the Bloomsbury Group were consigned to the back.[76] Fry ceased exhibiting at the club back in 1910, along with Duncan Grant and, although Grant and Vanessa Bell obtained recognition in the 1920s for their decorative schemes, they and the Post-Impressionism for which they stood had slipped from critical favour. *The Unknown God*, for all its biting satire, was ruminative. The factions, publicly held in tension, would not resolve their differences, but, with a bloated Steer nodding in the front row and Sickert loud as ever in a music-hall suit, it was clear that they would have to learn to live with one another.

The exhibitions of the early 1920s continued to be dominated by large numbers of southern counties and West Country landscapes. For critics, they equated the club's 'Englishness' with the land, ruralism and the virtues of home fields. Only Charles Holmes remained consistently in touch with northern moors and fells. Northern France and northern Italy were, if anything, closer to home and more in evidence in club shows than the north of England. The reassurance supplied by Gwynne-Jones's *Fields near Ruan Minor* (1919; fig. 125) shown in the spring of 1920, lay in an ordered pantheistic landscape, untouched by war. In *Poltesco Farm, Ruan Minor* (1920–1), exhibited in the winter of 1921, cows are returning to a busy yard at dusk – a muddy utopia in which all the ills

Fig. 125 Allan Gwynne-Jones
Fields near Ruan Minor, 1919
Oil on panel, 25.1 x 35.5 cm
Manchester City Art Gallery

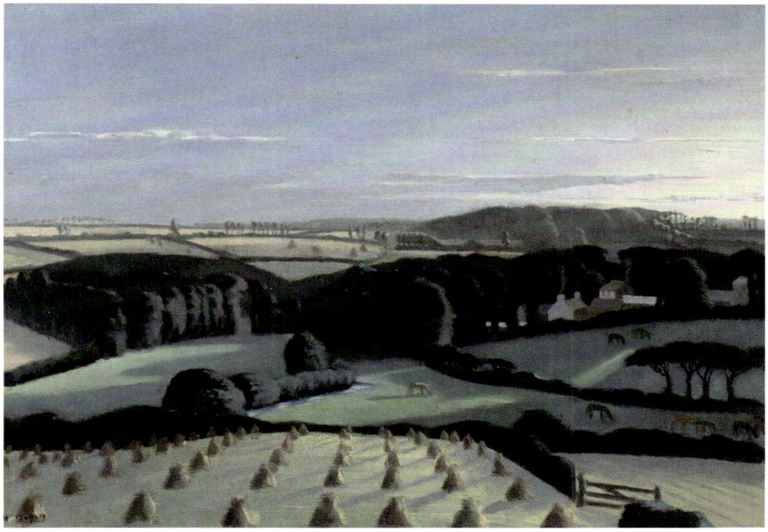

of the recent past would be assuaged by the simple rhythms of daily life in the depths of the countryside.[77] This became Stanley Baldwin's England – that of country smithy, the plough team and 'the last load ... of hay being drawn down a lane as the twilight comes on'.[78] It had changed since the days of Gladstone's imperialist sermonising. In the wake of the Irish Treaty, inward-looking Englishness, not greater Britishness, coupled with laissez-faire politics, dominated public consciousness and seemed to be reflected in club exhibitions. Even the Palmer-esque prints exhibited by Graham Sutherland at the end of the decade gave no hint of labour troubles in the north, the beginnings of unrest in the dominions and continuing economic depression. It would be simple to dismiss this retreat into ruralism, in favour of the dead cat of Cézanne-ist abstraction, were it not so clear that in Gwynne-Jones, as in Clausen's work of the 1920s, ruralism and landscape provided a secure and fertile soil for the imagination. In this uncovering of the taproot of romanticism, Englishness, as some commentators dimly realised, could be a way to newness.

Where formerly the club was an end in itself, it was becoming merely a stepping stone to official recognition at the Academy and a career managed by a fashionable dealer. The club's retrospective was seen as an opportunity to restate the strength of its position, and, although it was constantly talent-spotting and thus rejuvenating itself, there was a persistent leakage to dealers, who, after the fallow period of the war, were once again staging solo exhibitions. Barbizon House, established by David Croal Thomson in Henrietta Street, began in 1919 to publish an annual 'Record' of its most important sales that indicated the growing secondary market for New English pictures, especially those of Steer and Tonks. The Goupil Gallery, where Thomson had worked for eleven years up to 1897, continued its 'Salons' and tended to cream off the best of the Academy, the New English and the London Group. In these surveys,

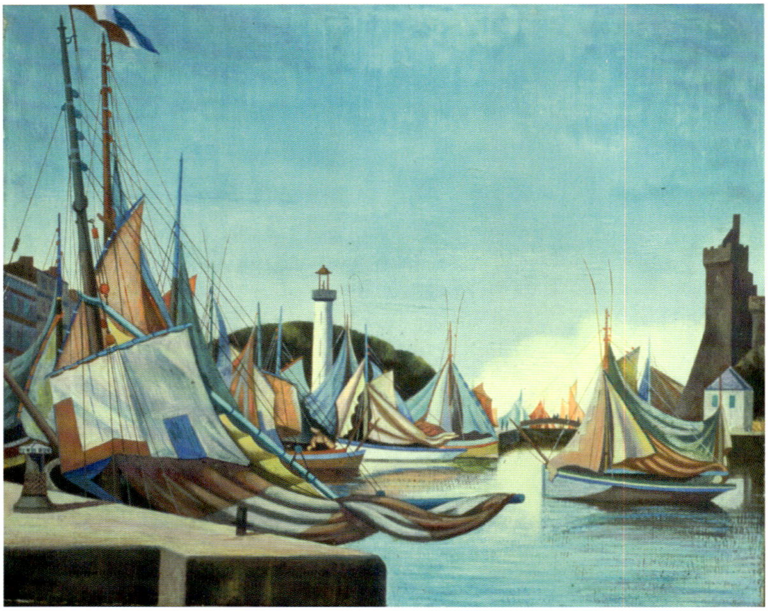

Fig. 126 Edward Wadsworth
La Rochelle, 1923
Tempera on canvas laid on panel, 49.5 x 58.5 cm
Purchased with the help of the MLA/V&A Purchase Grant Fund. Portsmouth City Museum

critics perceived the club as the centre ground of British painting. As in politics, the position was difficult to hold and old practices resumed, with radical members such as Nash and Wadsworth slipping away to the London Group and mature exhibitors such as Walter Russell joining the ranks of the Academy. Indeed, it was clear as never before that the club was becoming a testing ground for reputations that would then be taken elsewhere. Noting its forthcoming retrospective in 1925, *The Times* recast MacColl's 'nursery' metaphor and declared that, 'the present relation of the club to the Academy is not unlike that of a reservoir of pure scholarship and research feeding and improving the market where men buy pictures'.[79] This art economy only worked if the reservoir produced painters of quality and originality and, in 1923, when these attributes were in such short supply, people asked 'why stage an exhibition at all?' There was some excitement in the club the following spring when Edward Wadsworth returned to the ranks with *La Rochelle* (1923; fig. 126), an important canvas over which he had laboured throughout the winter.[80] No longer a 'Cubist', Wadsworth had, in the eyes of contemporary critics, broken through into a style that was characteristically his own.[81] In an institutionalised system ruled by the calendar, exceptional cases such as Wadsworth, working in the slow and difficult medium of tempera, tended to stand out and regular exhibitors correspondingly appeared routine. Those who did not augment their income with teaching, or were financially secure, were increasingly drawn away from the extraordinary *mélange* to dealers who could present a body of work. It was inevitably to their detriment that one year's exhibitions would be compared with those of the previous year and, although critics prophesied gloomily, their words are not to be taken at more than face value as the club remained the principal locus for new talent.

With the retrospective opening in January 1925, this was clear once again and there was a chance to demonstrate the continual development of British painting from Whistler to the generation at the time. The committee took the opportunity to underscore 'two fundamental rules' in the Preface to the catalogue:

> From the first, invited exhibitors found a place beside subscribing members, and to the latter no vested rights of exhibition were given. The works of members, equally with those of outsiders, had to pass the jury. In second place the jury itself was elected not from members only, but from the whole body of artists included in the previous exhibition. So far did the fear of official petrifaction extend that no President has ever been appointed.[82]

Differences of opinion were 'reduced to a friendly murmur'.[83] The burden of organising the exhibition in a matter of weeks fell to Collins Baker and, as with most retrospectives, there was an attempt to retrieve past losses. Fry was not included, nor were Bomberg and Wadsworth, but Grant, Roberts and Gwen John were. From the early years, Forbes, with *A Street in Brittany* (1881), borrowed

Fig. 127 Rudolph Ihlee
Sunset at Collioure, 1922
Oil on canvas, 63.5 x 76 cm
Private collection

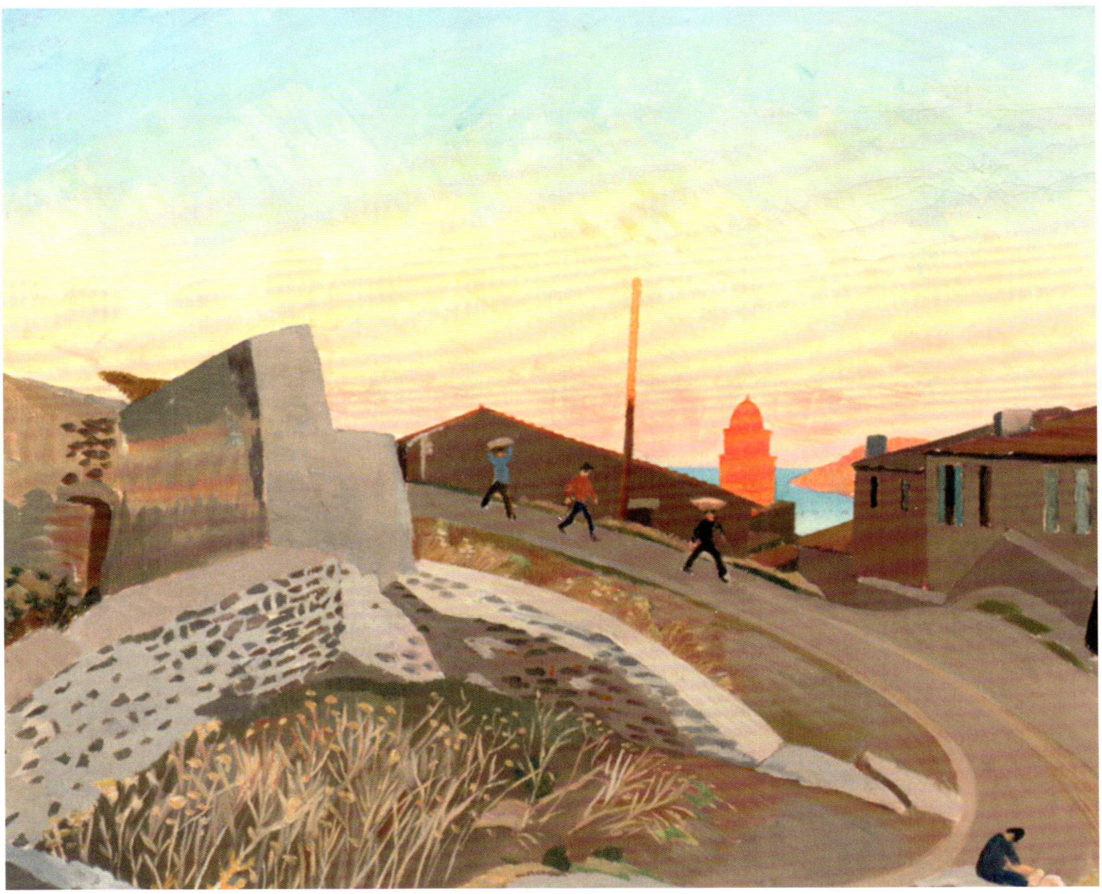

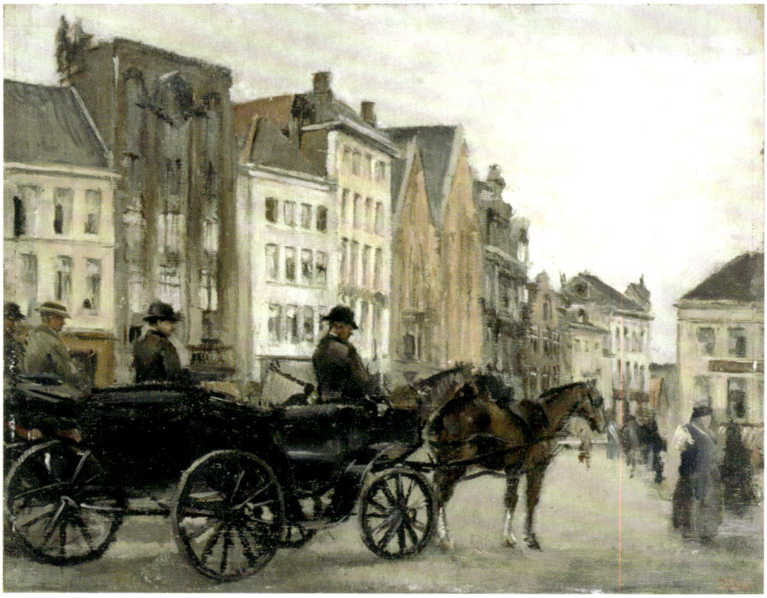

Fig. 128 Jesse Dale Cast
La Grande Place, Bruges, 1929
Oil on wood, 24 x 29 cm
UCL Art Collections,
University College London

from the Walker Art Gallery, Liverpool, was the sole representative of Newlyn, while Roche, MacGregor and Cameron were the only Scots. Clausen, now painting misty Essex landscapes, was, with *The Day Dreams* (see fig. 7), originally shown in the first Institute of Painters in Oil Colours exhibition of 1883, 'hardly recognizable'.[84] Steer and John, with sixteen and fourteen works respectively, were given most space. Landmark pictures such as Orpen's *Homage to Manet* (fig. 84) were brought back. In obtaining his selection, Collins Baker relied heavily on the collections of Sir Cyril Butler, Edward Marsh, Augustus Daniel and Geoffrey Blackwell, thus ensuring that the show was a success.[85] Queen Mary, who attended, bought a picture, and the Chantrey Bequest bought two.[86] Manchester City Art Gallery expressed interest in staging the exhibition and the Royal Birmingham Society of Artists requested a representative selection of members' works for their forthcoming show.[87] Such was the confidence in the future that the immediate plans for property acquisition were abandoned and the works donated for the special fund were returned.

The retrospective was followed by a series of strong exhibitions dominated by 'designed' landscapes and 'decorative' painting. At first, the work of Holmes and Nash took pride of place. Both consciously accentuated contours in order to reveal the elemental forces that bent and shaped their natural forms, but Nash's resignation in 1926, followed by that of his brother in 1927, were serious blows to the club. Their reductive landscapes were contrasted with the sweeping atmospheric panorama of Steer's *The Thames at Chelsea* (*c.* 1924) in the spring 1925 exhibition, full of 'brooding tenderness' and framed in a finely carved eighteenth-century section that complemented its mood. Steer's atmospherics rippled out in Alfred Hayward's *Sunset on the Lagoon, Venice* (1926) – the work of a painter whose exhibiting career lasted until 1973.

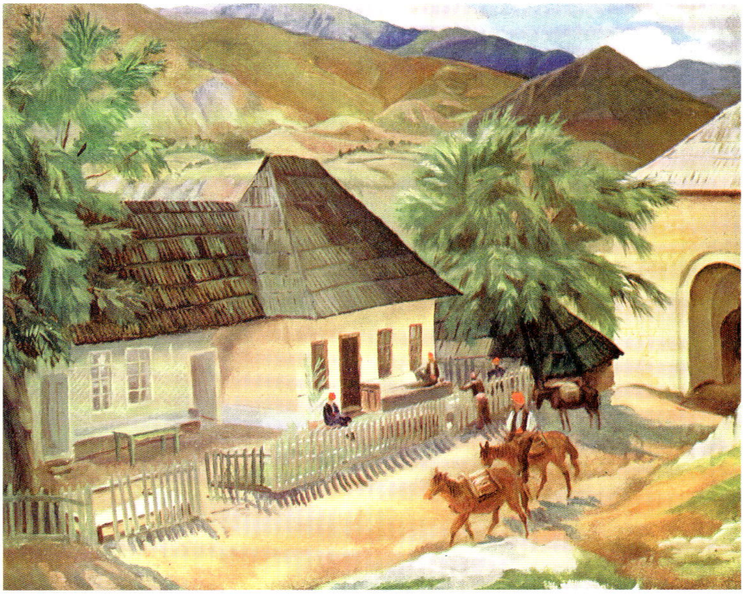

Fig. 129 Sidney Carline
A Bosnian Café, 1923
Location unknown

If there was a middle way in landscape painting, it was often discovered on wanderings on the Mediterranean coasts. Young painters Bernard Meninsky, Rudolph Ihlee, Jesse Dale Cast, Sidney Carline and Cundall, for instance, went to the South of France (fig. 127), Belgium (fig. 128), Majorca, the Balkans (fig. 129) and to Italy on painting forays, taking with them peculiarly English attitudes to colour, composition and motif.[88]

At this point, William L. Clause and Robin Guthrie were the strongest of the up-and-coming painters. 'Thorough, but rather stolid' painting characterised Clause's *The Two Friends*, shown in 1926, by an artist who, in his landscapes, consistently attempted to marry a Post-Impressionist touch with a rigorous approach to structure. Guthrie showed landscapes of Sussex suburbia, interspersed with portraits and decorative schemes, while other 'decorators', such as Mary Adshead and Philip Connard (see fig. 130), resorted to a fashionable repertoire of urns, semi-classical figures and sylvan glades. Adshead's Pompeian *Spring* (*c.* 1925) was hailed as 'a brilliant exercise, calling up in imagination, a room to go with it', while Connard was emphatically 'late Renaissance affected by China'.[89] Indeed, in his pale, lyrical sun-filled watercolours Connard takes the viewer to the edge of the world of chinoiserie. Although there were high-

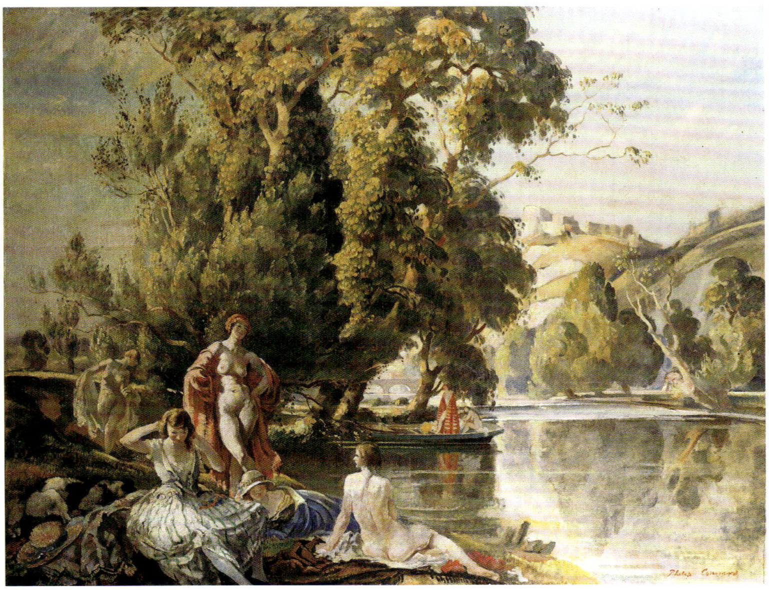

Fig. 130 Philip Connard
A River in France, 1924
Oil on canvas, 112 x 142.5 cm
Private collection

profile mural series being executed for great public buildings, for example, those for St Stephen's Hall in the Palace of Westminster, they were the last throw of bombastic imperialism, and the New English examples, when not designed for the modern villa, were aimed at theatres, restaurants, places of popular chic entertainment and ocean-going liners. The range was nonetheless too great to be captured in a few statements. That Adshead should take 'the lead' was indicative of a fecundity that defied simple messages and single Messiahs.[90]

For some critics this 'baroque' flip-side of cool modernism represented a retreat, but it was a long way from the nadir to which the Royal Academy had sunk following the death of Sargent and the wanton destruction of Charles Sims's *King George V* (1924). In the late 1920s the Academy's need for further infusions of talent from the New English and the London Group was frequently recommended.[91] Openness to new talents continued with the arrival of Archibald Hattermore, an English 'Douanier Rousseau', who, though he only showed five times between 1926 and 1928, got the club into difficulties.[92] Of more lasting significance was the arrival of Charles Mahoney in 1927. An assistant at the Royal College, he encouraged his students to challenge Slade hegemony by submitting to the club. The New English now represented the mainstream, with the Academy to the right and the London Group to the left, its position consolidated by the Rutherston Gift to Manchester in 1926.[93] Some painters who had abandoned the club – Nevinson for instance – were returning (see fig. 131). Such was its dominance that, when Duveen sponsored the third of his British and colonial exhibitions at the art gallery in the Imperial Institute in 1929, 31 New English painters were shown, alongside only 15 Academicians and 6 London Group members.[94] Yet, for all its failings, the London Group had by this stage diverted the flow of some Slade students into its ranks. Young painters such as William Coldstream and Claude Rogers, for instance, showed a few times at the club while still students, but, on leaving the Slade, went straight into the London Group.[95] The 'hobnailed enthusiasm' of the group's 'intellectual proletariat' was seen to have invaded the New English cloister.[96] There was a sense of foreboding, recession loomed and a feeling in some quarters that in its over-tolerance of eccentricity the club faced an uncertain future.[97]

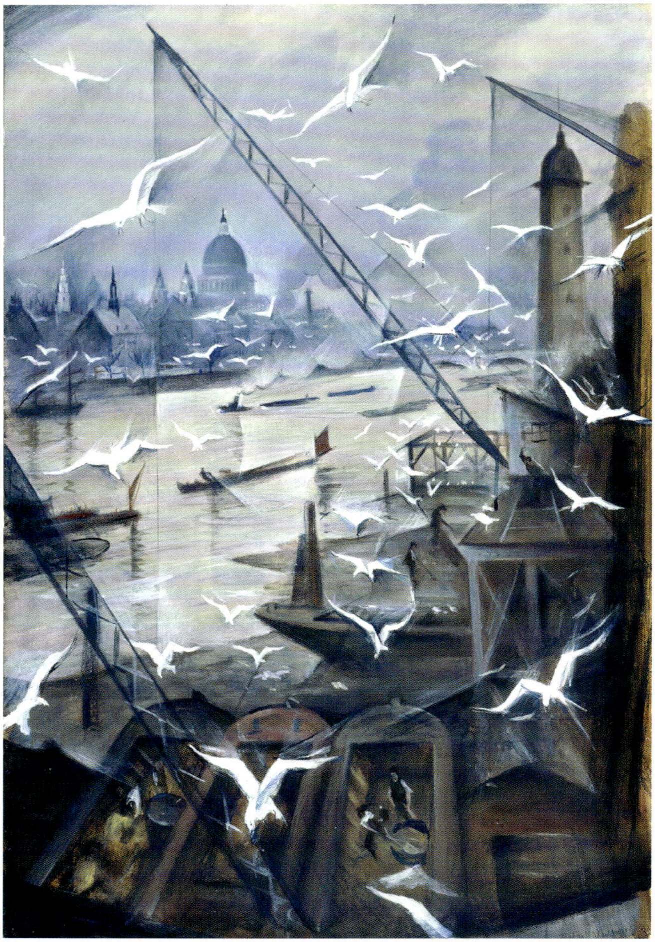

Fig. 131 Christopher Richard Wynne Nevinson
London Winter, 1929
Oil on board, 77.5 x 51.5 cm
Museum of London

NOTES

1 T. E. Hulme, *Speculations: Essays on Humanism and the Philosophy of Art*, ed. Herbert Read, Kegan Paul, London, 1924, p. 104, quoted in Richard Cork, *Vorticism and Abstract Art in the First Machine Age*, Gordon Fraser, London, 1976, vol. 1, p. 140; see also Richard Humphreys, 'Demon Pantechnicon Driver: Pound in the London Vortex, 1908–1920' in *Pound's Artists: Ezra Pound and the Visual Arts in London, Paris and Italy*, Richard Humphreys et al., exh. cat., Tate Gallery, London, 1985, p. 41.

2 For a full discussion of these and related works, see *Vorticism and its Allies*, Richard Cork, exh. cat., Hayward Gallery, London, 1974; for a comparative study of the European, Russian and American avant-gardes, see Introduction in *Abstraction: Towards a New Art, Painting 1910–1920*, Peter Vergo, exh. cat., Tate Gallery, London, 1980.

3 David Bomberg showed *Winter's Afternoon* in the spring of 1913, and *Plague*, *The Nurse Euryclea* and *Interval* in the winter of 1913 and William Roberts, *Ulysses* in the winter of 1913 (Castle Museum, Nottingham) and *The Boxers* in the spring of 1914. Fred Brown, who approved the Post-Impressionists, particularly Van Gogh, in 1912 declared himself 'dead against the admission of Cubism, which would be the ruin of the society', unpublished MS, 27 January 1921, MacColl Papers, Glasgow University Library, GB 0247 MS MacColl B621 and B627.

4 Tonks did not exhibit between the winter of 1910 and the spring of 1913.

5 *In the Hold* was exhibited at the London Group in the spring of 1914. For reference to *Ulysses*, see *Vorticism and its Allies*, Richard Cork, exh. cat., Hayward Gallery, London, 1974, p. 40. The work is now known as *The Return of Ulysses*.

6 Lewis had shown once at the club in pre-Vorticists days in the spring of 1904 and Wadsworth, who began exhibiting in 1911, did not resume until the winter of 1921.

7 *The Times*, 10 March 1915, p. 8; mentioned in Denys J. Wilcox, *The London Group, 1913–1939: The Artists and their Works*, Scolar Press, London, 1995, p. 8.

8 Frank Rutter, *Some Contemporary Artists*, Leonard Parsons, London, 1922, pp. 195–7. For further reference, see *C. R. W. Nevinson: The Twentieth Century*, Richard Ingleby et al., exh. cat., Imperial War Museum, London, 1999; *The Edwardians: Secrets and Desires*, Anne Gray, exh. cat., National Gallery of Australia, Canberra, 2004, pp. 197–8.

9 Quoted in William Orpen, *The Outline of Art*, George Newnes, London, n.d. [*c*. 1925], p. 373.

10 Before it was shown at the club, *La Mitrailleuse* was exhibited at the Allied Artists' Association, 'Eighth London Salon' at the Grafton Galleries.

11 Nevinson also showed *A Dawn, 1914* (120) and *On the Road to Ypres* (1916; 295).

12 Meirion and Susie Harries, *The War Artists*, Michael Joseph, London, 1983, p. 3. For a more detailed consideration of these developments, see Sue Malvern, *Modern Art, Britain and the Great War*, Yale University Press, London and New Haven, 2004.

13 Charles Mariott, *Modern Movements in Painting*, Chapman and Hall, London, 1920, pp. 158–9.

14 During these years Thomas T. Baxter, Eleanor Best, George Charlton, Karl Hagedorn, Dorothy Hutton, Percy Jowett, William Lancaster, A. Neville Lewis, Malcolm Milne, Orovida Pissarro and Henry Rushbury began to exhibit at the club. For Fanner, see C. Lewis Hind, 'Alice Fanner's Lyrical Painting', *The Studio*, vol. 66, 1916.

15 Van Gogh had been extensively represented with over twenty works in the Grafton Gallery in 1910. A selection of the artist's letters – Anthony M. Ludovici, *The Letters of a Post-Impressionist, Being the Familiar Correspondence of Vincent Van Gogh*, Constable, London, 1912, was published in translation.

16 C. J. Holmes, *Self and Partners (Mostly Self), Being the Reminiscences of C. L. Holmes*, Constable, London, 1936, p. 331. The picture was rescued by Collins Baker, purchased by Evan Charteris and presented to the Tate Gallery, London.

17 See *War Pictures, Exhibition at the Royal Academy, Issued by the Authority of the Imperial War Museum*, Walter Judd, London, 1919.

18 Frank Rutter, *Some Contemporary Artists*, Leonard Parsons, London, 1922, p. 207; Frank Rutter, *Evolution in Modern Art*, George G. Harrap, London, 1926, pp. 133–4. Despite the fact that Rutter placed the first exhibits of the Nashes from 1911 to 1912, Paul Nash first showed in the spring of 1913 and John in the winter of 1913. Both were selected for the Whitechapel 'Twentieth-Century Art' exhibition in 1914, and both were immediately appropriated by the London Group – John in 1914 and Paul in 1915.

19 Dr Andrew Causey, Introduction in *Poet and Painter: Letters between Gordon Bottomley and Paul Nash, 1910–1946*, 1955 (rev. ed., Redcliffe, Bristol, 1990), p. 23 (letter dated 3 September 1911).

20 Paul Nash exhibited for the first time in the spring of 1913 and John Nash in the winter of 1913.

21 Sidney Schiff, 'Preface', *John Nash*, The Fleuron, London, 1925, unpaginated. Schiff was an early collector of Nash, a literary critic, friend of James Joyce and early translator of Proust.

22 Frank Rutter, *Evolution in Modern Art*, George G. Harrap, London, 1926, pp. 132–4, in the context of a discussion of the club refers to the 'new English movement', describing White and the Nashes as 'wholly English'. See also R.H. Wilenski, *An Outline of English Painting*, Faber and Faber, London, 1946, p. 70.

23 In the winter of 1912 Spencer showed *Joachim among the Sheepcotes* and *David*, and *Zacharius* the following year.

24 *Stanley Spencer*, Richard Carline, Andrew Causey and Keith Bell, exh. cat., Royal Academy of Arts, London, 1980, p. 51; *Stanley Spencer*, Timothy Hyman and Patrick Wright (eds), exh. cat., Tate Britain, London, 2001, p. 94 (entry by Robert Upstone). Spencer had first shown at the club in the winter of 1912 and up to this point had exhibited biblical subjects exclusively.

25 *The Times*, 30 November 1915, p. 11, noted that, while the meaning in Spencer may be obscure, his painting had 'great technical beauty'.

26 Anon., 'Exhibitions', *The Athenaeum*, 4 December 1915, p. 424.

27 Robinson who, while a pupil of Royal Academy Schools, had shown once only at the club in 1889, was at that point influenced by the Cornish painters. Like Gotch and Elizabeth Forbes, he abandoned fisherfolk in favour of 'new' Pre-Raphaelite subject matter and an association with the tempera painters of the Birmingham Group. See C. Lewis Hind, 'Ethical Art and Mr F. Cayley Robinson', *The Studio*, vol. 31, 1904, pp. 235–41; see also Charlotte Gere Introduction in *The Earthly Paradise: F. Cayley Robinson and the Painters of the Birmingham Group*, exh. cat., Fine Art Society, London, 1975.

28 Clare Willesdon, *Mural Painting in Britain, 1840 – 1940: Image and Meaning*, Oxford University Press, Oxford, 2000, pp. 290–1.

29 Anon., 'Exhibitions', *The Athenaeum*, 4 December 1915, p. 424.

30 See Philip McEvansoneya, 'Hugh Lane and Mural Painting: Designs for the Gallery of Modern Art, Dublin', *Irish Architectural and Decorative Studies, Journal of the Irish Georgian Society*, vol. 6, 2004, pp. 163–81.

31 Anon., 'The Sophistication of Mr John, A Portrait Attitude', *The Times*, 27 May 1916, p. 9.

32 *Ethel Walker, Frances Hodgkins, Gwen John*, T. W. Earp, exh. cat., Tate Gallery, London, 1952, p. 2.

33 Obituary, *The Times*, 3 March 1951, p. 8. See also John Rothenstein, *Modern English Painters*, Eyre and Spottiswoode, London, 1952, vol. 1, pp. 75–84. Walker exhibited *The Bathers*, a study for which is contained in Tate Britain, London, at the 1910 winter exhibition. This reworking of a Conder motif pointed to the general direction of her allegorical painting over the following decade.

34 AGM Election, 8 May 1919. Bate had ceased exhibiting in 1906. A celebratory dinner was held in his honour in 1913, at which he was presented with a portfolio of members' drawings.
35 The club remained in the RWS Galleries until the winter of 1924.
36 Ball remained in the post until 1933.
37 Holmes was Director of the National Gallery and therefore Collins Baker's manager.
38 The watercolour hanging fee was fixed at half that for oils, i.e. five shillings.
39 AGM Minutes, 25 January 1921; Alfred Thornton, *Fifty Years of the New English Art Club, 1886–1935*, Curwen Press, London, 1935, pp. 12–13, credited Dodd and Ball with this turnabout in the club's finances.
40 There was much discussion in 1921 on this new Government levy on exhibitions that charged for admission. Exemptions were made for societies that, like the Royal Academy, could claim charitable educational purposes. Those like the New English, which did not run schools, were to be taxed even though they did not seek to make a profit. Serious objections to this legislation led to much legal wrangling, until the status of 'Friendly Society' was invoked. See 'Current Art Notes', *The Connoisseur*, vol. 61, October 1921, p. 121.
41 Anon., 'New English Art Club – The Test of Good Faith', *The Times*, 7 June 1920, p. 17.
42 Anon., 'Exhibitions of the Week', *The Athenaeum*, 9 January 1920, pp. 52–3, winter of 1919 exhibition. See also Alfred Thornton, *The Diary of an Art Student of the Nineties*, Sir Isaac Pitman and Sons, London, 1938, p. 51: 'At the end of the second decade of the twentieth century, critics of the club began to say that a Slade student's career was a safe one to the Tate Gallery via the New English. This was libellous, but there existed a *scintilla veritatis*.'
43 Although it would not necessarily be apparent to contemporaries, Spencer was closer to Giotto than Piero.
44 Anon., 'The New English Art Club', *The Saturday Review*, 15 January 1921, pp. 45–7, winter of 1920.
45 Rothenstein, besides being an Official War Artist, was already Professor of Civic Art at the University of Sheffield, a post he held until 1926. He consistently advocated opening up the club to a wider constituency and warned against the rejection of such painters as Duncan Grant, in the teeth of objections from Tonks.
46 Even with the emergence of the 'Seven and Five Society' in 1920, a spin-off from the London Group, which hosted the early work of Sidney Hunt and Ben Nicholson, there was no coherent commitment to abstraction in Britain.
47 Guevara came to Britain at the age of sixteen in 1910. He enrolled at the Slade in 1913 and won a sequence of awards, culminating in the Melville Nettleship Prize in 1915. For further reference, see Diana Holman Hunt, *Latin among Lions: Alvaro Guevara*, Michael Joseph, London, 1974; see also John Rothenstein Introduction in *Alvaro Guevara, 1894–1951*, exh. cat., P.& D. Colnaghi, London, 1974.
48 Anon., 'Exhibitions of the Week', *The Athenaeum*, 18 June 1920, p. 806; Anon., 'New English Art Club – The Test of Good Faith', *The Times*, 7 June 1920, p. 17.
49 Anon., 'The New English Art Club', *The Saturday Review*, 15 January 1921, pp. 45–7 (winter of 1920). *Medusa's Trial* and *Signs of the Zodiac* are untraced. Some of Guevara's work was believed to have been destroyed when the Bourlet warehouse was struck by a German bomb in December 1940.
50 While wishing to present his sitters full length, Guevara tended to stand close to them. The floor in the immediate foreground of his painting thus appears to fall away, as it does to a lesser extent in Sargent's naturalistic, and much reproduced, *Mrs Carl Meyer and her Children* (1898). However, as is clear from fig. 110, Guevara flattened perspectives and reduced the effect of light and shade in order to accentuate colour and expressive handling. There were obvious echoes of Matisse.
51 He ceased to exhibit when he returned to Chile in 1923, and, although he came back to Britain, it was to dealer's exhibitions and, after his marriage to Meraud Guinness, private commissions.
52 The Sitwells had organised an exhibition of modern art at Heal's in 1919 and there were small Matisse and Picasso shows at the Leicester Galleries in 1919 and 1921 respectively.
53 *Wheels*, edited by Edith Sitwell, continued to promote such painters as Lewis and Roberts. In 1920, Lewis launched Group X at Heal's in an attempt to rekindle the pre-war excitement of the Vorticists.
54 John Galsworthy, 'Where we Stand' (1920), quoted from *Castles in Spain and other Screeds*, William Heinemann, London, 1927, p. 19. The most vivid expression of this mood is, of course, William Orpen, *An Onlooker in France*, Williams and Northgate, London, 1921. For a magisterial account of the perceptions of the Great War, see Samuel Hynes, *A War Imagined: The First World War and English Culture*, Bodley Head, London, 1990 (rev. ed., Pimlico, London, 1992).
55 John Kinnersley Kirby, Job Nixon, Vernon Wethered and James Wilkie began exhibiting at the club during these years.
56 W. S. Meadmore, *Lucien Pissarro*, Alfred A. Knopf, New York, 1962, p. 174.
57 *James Bolivar Manson, 1879–1945: An English Impressionist*, David Buckman, exh. cat., Maltzahn Gallery, London, 1973, p. 24. Manson had begun to exhibit at the club in the winter of 1909. He was a founder member and secretary of the Camden Town Group, and a founder member of the London Group before his appointment to the staff of the National Gallery of British Art in 1917.
58 Ibid, pp. 26–9; by this stage Manson was Keeper at the National Gallery of British Art, Millbank, and there were heavy demands on his time.
59 Although he thought of himself as part of the younger generation, Thornton had actually begun showing at the New English at the same time as MacColl. When MacColl, who was returning to journalism at this point, attacked the London Group for repeating Paris fashions 'in sedulous if dowdy imitation', Thornton defended it, see Alfred Thornton, *Diary of an Art Student of the Nineties*, Sir Isaac Pitman and Sons, London, 1938, pp. 62–7.
60 Gilbert Spencer had begun to exhibit at the club in the spring of 1915 and Cundall in the spring of 1921. Spencer recalls Hilda Carline's early affection for him and his vain hope that if he was elected to the New English she might choose him rather than his brother. For Spencer, see Gilbert Spencer, *Memoirs of a Painter*, Chatto & Windus, London, 1974. For Cundall, see The Editor, 'Artists of Note: Charles Cundall ARA', *The Artist*, vol. 19, no. 61, March 1940, pp. 16–19.
61 Kenneth Clark, *Another Part of the Wood: A Self-Portrait*, John Murray, London, 1974 (rev. ed., Hamish Hamilton, London, 1985), p. 78, notes that these exhibitions were staged in 'small and modest' surroundings, with 'no attempt at deliberate showmanship, no expensive catalogues, no outpouring of champagne'.
62 Anon., 'New English Art Club – Exhibition at the RWS Galleries', *The Times*, 29 December 1920, p. 10.
63 Anon., 'The Goupil Gallery', *The Times*, 4 October 1929, p. 12; reviewing a show of the work of Ralph N. Chubb and William L. Clause.
64 *Thomas Lowinsky*, Monica Bohm-Duchin, exh. cat., Tate Gallery, London, 1990, p. 36.
65 Ibid, pp. 38–9.
66 D. S. MacColl, 'The "New English" Revisted', *The Saturday Review*, 7 January 1922, pp. 8–10 (winter of 1921).
67 Maureen Borland, *D. S. MacColl: Painter, Poet, Art Critic*, Lennard Publishing, Harpenden, 1995, pp. 248–52.
68 MacColl tactfully omitted himself from the first group. His watercolours were sold at club exhibitions in 1920 and 1923; see MacColl Papers, N81 and N88, Glasgow University Library Special Collections.

69 Stanley Booth, *Sir Alfred Munnings 1878–1959 – A Centenary Tribute*, Sotheby Parke Bernet Publications, London, 1978, pp. 120–1.

70 Bone, the son of Muirhead Bone and currently a Slade student, had begun to exhibit in the winter of 1920.

71 It was suggested at this point that the centre of London's art activity should move from the West End to Chelsea, where many artists lived and where there was an art school and arts club. In November 1923, *Colour Magazine*, vol. 19, nos 4–5, gave the inside of its front cover to an open letter from the secretary of the New Chenil Galleries to this end.

72 AGM Minutes, 27 January 1922, 30 June 1922 and 26 January 1923. The Fund would be established from the sale of one work to be donated by each member. By June 1922, seventeen works had been received, although thirty-nine members indicated that they approved of the plan and would comply.

73 Special General Meeting Minutes, 15 November 1924. After the initial free show, the club would stage its future exhibitions in Spring Gardens at a rent of £50 per week. In breaking its lease with the RWS, the club was able to sub-let its future time-slots to the London Group.

74 Tancred Borenius, 'The New English Art Club', *The Saturday Review*, 13 January 1923, p. 44 (a review of the winter 1922 exhibition).

75 Ibid.

76 Tonks wrote to Mary Hutchinson on 19 August 1922 that he was 'amusing' himself very much with scenes from the life of 'St Roger'. There were four in all. In her introduction to Joseph Hone, *The Life of Henry Tonks*, Heinemann, London, 1939, she referred to the panache with which Tonks 'could look at his adversary Fry and turn him into the most magnificent Dr. Nostradamus that ever was' (p. xxii). Borenius may have given so much space to the picture because he appears in it. He is thought to be one of the two unidentified figures in the background, seated beside William Rothenstein. The other is possibly the collector Geoffrey Blackwell, into whose collection the picture passed. Those in the front row are Sickert, MacColl, Moore, Steer, Eric MacLagan, Sargent and St John Hutchinson. Clive Bell, the magician's assistant on the extreme right, rings the bell. Fry's recognition of the importance of Cézanne dates back to his visit to the Pellerin collection in the Edwardian years, and to his celebrated article in *The Burlington Magazine* in 1909. Tonks shared Sickert's scepticism on the subject. For further reference, see Denys Sutton, 'A Shock for the Troops', *Apollo*, vol. 80, no. 32, 1964, p. 262 (fig. 2); see also Linda Morris (ed.), *Henry Tonks and the 'Art of Pure Drawing'*, exh. cat., Norwich Gallery, Norwich School of Art and Design, 1985, pp. 46–8.

77 For further reference, see David Brown, *Allan Gwynne-Jones*, exh. cat., National Museum of Wales, Cardiff, 1982, pp. 21–2. See also Ian Jeffrey, *The British Landscape, 1920–1950*, Thames and Hudson, London, 1984.

78 Stanley Baldwin, *On England and Other Addresses*, Philip Allan, London, 1926 (rev. ed., Penguin, Harmondsworth, 1937), p. 16.

79 'Forty Years of Art. Important Forthcoming Exhibition', *The Times*, 19 December 1924, p. 12. The exhibition actually opened on 5 January 1925.

80 Wadsworth had first exhibited in the spring of 1911, but not thereafter. For further reference to his sojourn in La Rochelle in June 1923, see Barbara Wadsworth, *Edward Wadsworth: A Painter's Life*, Michael Russell, Salisbury, 1989, pp. 124 and 126–7.

81 Frank Rutter, *Theodore Roussel*, Connoisseur, London, 1926, p. 129 (indicating, mistakenly, that the picture was shown in 1923); R. H. Wilenski, 'Modern Still-Life, the Paintings of Edward Wadsworth', *The Studio*, vol. 97, 1929, pp. 413–17.

82 Anon., Preface, 'Catalogue of the Special Retrospective Exhibition (1885– 1924) and of the Seventy-first Exhibition', London, 1925, unpaginated.

83 Anon., 'New English Art Club – A Retrospective Exhibition', *The Times*, 3 January 1925, pp. 8 and 14, selected works by John, McEvoy, Tonks, Dodd, Sargent and Steer for illustration.

84 Ibid. Fry, Bell and Grant were showing regularly with the London Group; Clausen was an Academician.

85 Butler led with seventeen loans, Marsh followed with eleven.

86 They were Ronald Gray's *My Mother* (1908) and Walter Wesley Russell's *The Blue Dress* (1908).

87 General Meeting Minutes, 11 February and 20 May 1925.

88 Meninsky's Provencal landscapes first appeared at the spring 1923 exhibition. For further reference, see John Russell Taylor, *Bernard Meninsky*, Redcliffe Press, Bristol, 1990; see also *Bernard Meninsky*, John Russell Taylor et al., exh. cat., Museum of Modern Art, Oxford, 1981. For Cast, see *Jesse Dale Cast, 1900–1976*, P. E. H., exh. cat., South London Art Gallery, 1980; see also *Jesse Dale Cast: Art and Life*, David Cast, exh. cat., The Strang Print Room, University College, London, 1994. Hilda, Richard and Sydney Carline all showed with the club during the 1920s. Hilda returning for the winter exhibitions in 1936, 1937 and 1938. See *The Spencers and the Carlines*, exh. cat., Morley Gallery, London, 1980, and *The Art of Hilda Carline, Mrs Stanley Spencer*, Alison Thomas, exh. cat., Usher Gallery, Lincoln, 1999. Cundall's work had by 1925 become too 'apocalyptic' for contemporary tastes, due to his excessive use of black, see J. B., 'The New English Art Club', *The Manchester Guardian*, April 1925. By the following year, under the Italian sun, this was modified.

89 *The Times*, 13 April 1926, p. 7. For Adshead's career as a muralist, see *Earthly Delights, Mary Adshead, 1904–1995*, Matthew H. Clough and Ann Compton (eds), exh. cat., University of Liverpool Art Gallery, 2005.

90 For a short, stimulating survey of landscape painting at this period, see Ian Jeffrey, *The British Landscape, 1920–1950*, Thames and Hudson, London, 1984; see also *Landscape in Britain, 1850–1950*, Frances Spalding and Ian Jeffrey, exh. cat., Hayward Gallery, London, 1983.

91 Anon., 'The Royal Academy Exhibition – The Oil Paintings – Some Successes and a Limitation', *The Times*, 3 May 1926, p. 8, talks about the Academy's inability to fill the third gallery of the summer exhibition with more than an incomplete portrait of the King by Richard Jack, and concludes that 'if they want the room they should call upon the young lions of the New English Art Club and the London Group to splash about in it'.

92 Hattermore was a full-time employee of the London Water Board and thus was classed as an amateur. As such he compromised the club's exemption from Entertainment Tax under its status as a Friendly Society.

93 Albert Rutherston had given 70 paintings, 400 drawings, 100 prints and 20 pieces of sculpture to Manchester City Art Gallery. They represented the recent tendencies in the club. Inaugurating the collection, Charles Holmes noted the predominance of the New English, stating that it had 'included in the space of its existence almost every considerable artist who ever made his reputation in England'; see Our Art Critic, 'Art in Manchester – The Rutherston Gift', *The Times*, 15 July 1926, p. 19. See also S. D. Cleveland, Foreword in *A Selection of Paintings and Drawings from the Rutherston Collection*, exh. cat., Arts Council, 1955.

94 Anon., 'Art Exhibition – The Imperial Art Gallery', *The Times*, 5 April 1929, p. 12.

95 For further reference, see Bruce Laughton, *The Euston Road School: A Study in Objective Painting*, Scolar Press, London, 1986, pp. 29–38. See also Jenny Pery, *The Affectionate Eye: The Life of Claude Rogers*, Sansom & Co., London, 1995, pp. 23–38.

96 Anon., 'Art Exhibitions, The London Group', *The Times*, 6 June 1925, p. 10.

97 Tis, 'Art Notes', *Colour*, vol. 1 (new series), no. 2, 1928, p. 26, noted that: 'This year's New English confirms one's impression, gained by all their recent exhibitions, that the club no longer stands for any principle. One has the very decided feeling that the advent of post-impressionism has wrought havoc in their judgement. In almost any other society's show that would not matter so much as it does here, because one had come to regard the New English as representing, if not an "ism", certainly a definite standard of achievement.'

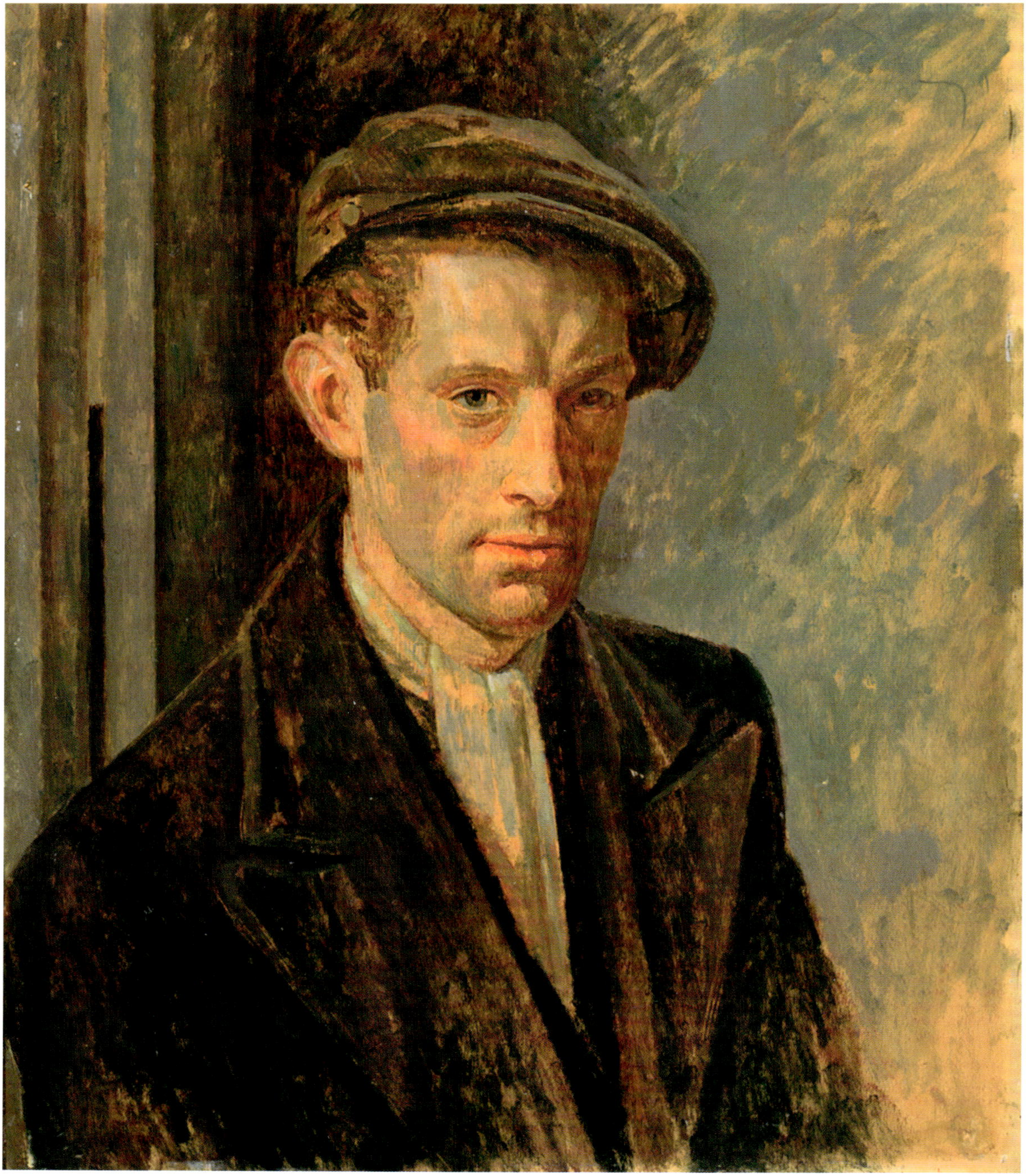

Fig. 132 Percy Frederick Horton
Unemployed Man, 1936
Oil on canvas, 44.5 x 38.2 cm
Sheffield Art Gallery

CHAPTER 6

'Spinsterish Integrity' 1930–1945

Misgivings about the club's direction at the end of the 1920s continued into the early 1930s. 'Modishness' seemed momentarily to have given way to the 'pleasantly old-fashioned'.[1] The new decade was marked by Tonks's *Sodales* (1930), a splendid conversation-piece showing two old boys by the fire – the snoozing Steer and zany Sickert. At this time Tonks and Brown were publishing their memoirs.[2] A reviewer from north of the border confirmed in 1930 that the New English remained nothing more than a 'super sketch club' for the Slade. What had changed since virtually the same observation was made ten years earlier? There was a continuing corporate interest in contemporary society in the urban crowd scenes of George Charlton and Barnett Freedman. Charlton, for instance, rivalled Rowlandson, while Freedman presented 'proletarians' who 'posture quaintly as though affected by the Russian ballet'.[3] Given the frieze-like format, the static poses taken from studies, the mounting social pressure from unemployment and the calls in some quarters for revolution, his *London Street Scene* (*c.* 1930) can be easily understood.[4] The deliberate gaucheness of Freedman's working-class heroes differs greatly from the suave rural bourgeoisie in Dorothy Coke's *Garden Party* (1929; fig. 133). The phrasing of Connard and Rex Whistler lingers in Coke's world, but not its paraphernalia. Harmless playful bunting links drooping trees that could have been extracted from a watercolour

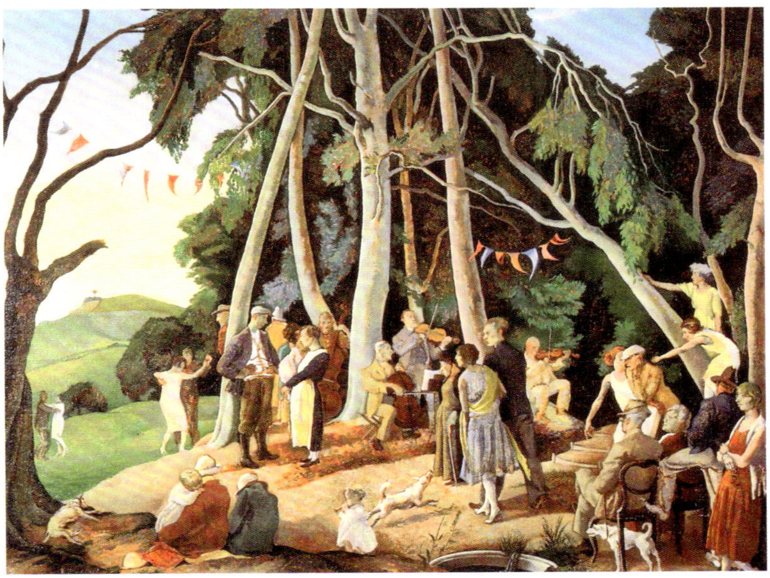

Fig. 133 Dorothy Josephine Coke
The Garden Party, 1929
Oil on canvas, 71.1 x 91.5 cm
Private collection

by one of the Nashes. Freedman and Coke open the new decade. They recall continuing concerns about health and vigour in a world that extolled the virtues of physical training, hiking and nudism.[5] The conditions that precipitated this social stratification had been clear for some time. Following the General Strike of 1926, Britain slid towards an economic slump. A moderate Labour government with a modest majority was returned in 1929, just a few months before the Wall Street Crash. With hunger marches and calls for a national government, the scene was set for the 'threadbare thirties'.

If Freedman, Coke and other exhibitors held a mirror up to contemporary Britain, the club itself entered a period when new societies were formed and old ones struggled for a role. The old International Society of Sculptors, Painters and Gravers re-launched as the short-lived National Society of Painters, Sculptors, Engravers and Potters in 1930, in the process attracting William Lionel Clause, Ethel Gabain, R.O. Dunlop, Bomberg, Bone and Walker. Most of these prolific painters remained committed to the club. By 1932, however, when the National Society contained such works as Bomberg's *Sunset, Toledo*, Gabain's *The Striped Shawl* and A. K. Browning's *Snowlight in Chelsea* (all *c.* 1931), the contrast with the staid New English was marked.[6] Many regular exhibitors found their way into the pages of *The Artist*, a magazine straddling the 'professional' and 'amateur' markets, which was cashing in on the potential popularity of New English painting in the face of difficult continental modernism. This publication carried clear, yet unspoken, inferences that *métier* was all-important and the discussion of *facture* became a matter of simple tools, well-tried recipes and an ambient temperature.

For the ageing Frank Rutter this was less of an issue, as he launched into a paean of praise for Steer's *Recumbent* (1933), a picture that he considered the best painting of 1933.[7] For others, this painting dominated the show and was, in the words of one writer, 'the only work destined to become an old master'.[8] But an Old Master delighting in the sensuality of a bygone age was out of tune with the times. Freedman's and Charlton's crowds were more portentous. There was a return to painterliness, led by women exhibitors whose confidence and maturity in landscape and still-life painting was the 'prevailing attraction' of the exhibitions of 1932 and 1933, and was summarised as 'colour, quality of paint, and atmospheric effect'.[9] Steer's *Recumbent* appeared at a moment when many artists were as equally apprehensive about abstract 'experimentalism', as about an Old Master's reverie.[10]

The debates about 'fine' and 'commercial' art sharpened as a number of painters looked to Moscow rather than Paris for leadership. In 1933 a new caucus led by Clifford Rowe and Misha Black, including Edward Ardizzone, James Fitton and Percy Horton, formed the Artists' International Association (AIA).[11] The objectives of the AIA were to do with agitation and propaganda against the state's evident incapacity to deal with widespread unemployment. The horrors of National Socialism in Germany and Communism in Soviet Russia were not yet apparent, and the AIA opposed the former and argued forcibly on behalf of the latter. While not directly opposed to the club, it soon provided a home for all those painters who regarded themselves as revolutionary and were attracted to the type of Socialist Realism emerging in Moscow. Huge conceptual problems dogged the very idea of art production in a revolutionary context. 'A work of art', as Stephen Spender remarked, 'cannot reach out into everyday life and tell us whom to vote for and what kind of factories to build'.[12] Fevered argument about first principles was both necessary and futile at the same time. The artist could not break free from a bourgeois system of commodity exchange.[13] Critics who, like Herbert Read, commented upon the poor quality of work in the first AIA exhibition in September 1934 brought bourgeois standards to the task.[14] Horton, who exhibited consistently at the club throughout the 1930s, typified the 'international' artists. As a teacher, he firmly held the view that art as a leisure activity for workers was a sop promoted by 'big industrial concerns'.[15] Works such as *The Unemployed Man* (1936; fig. 132), along with *The Postman* (1928) and *The Ironing Board* (1931), shown in spring of 1928 and winter of 1931, all convey his seriousness as a 'painter of the people' and his rejection of the so-called 'progressive' painting of the Ecole de Paris.[16]

The problematics of modernism impinged elsewhere. At the same time as the emergence of the AIA, Paul Nash, who no longer showed at the club, sought out members for a new group to be christened 'Unit One' that was to be inaugurated at the Mayor Gallery in Cork Street, London.[17] Ably supported by Herbert Read and Douglas Cooper, the seven painters, two sculptors and two architects who made up the group had little in common, other than that their work related to different, in some senses opposing, strands in the European avant-garde.[18] They, according to *The Times*, were linked to 'such arbitrary political methods as Hitlerism, Fascism and Bolshevism', while, at the same time, the young painters of the New English were seen as rejecting the 'general aim of modern art'. The 'good or "goodish"' works of 1933 were those that illustrated the

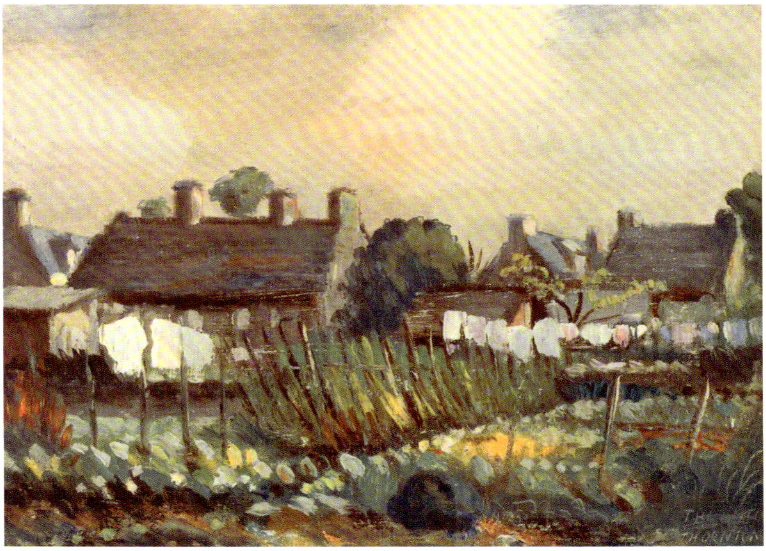

Fig. 134 Alfred Thornton
Washing Day
Oil on canvas (?), 22 x 32 cm
Location unknown

'pleasures of painting' rather than 'fundamental brainwork'.[19] Some club members must have felt that this definition sold them short. Alfred Thornton, the honorary secretary at the time, had taken in September 1933 to the columns of *The Artist* to explain 'Unity in Painting' (see fig. 134).[20] While many of his assumptions were those of an artist who had been exhibiting for forty years, they were nonetheless conditioned by an active interest in 'Gestalt' psychology and current philosophy. Drawing on R. G. Collingwood, Thornton aimed to explain that the making and receiving of art was 'a fundamental activity of the mind'.[21] 'Unity' was a collusion of painter and spectator, as an image passes into and out of the brain in the process of realisation. He illustrated this view in a number of ways, referring to Titian, Turner and Cézanne, but, as a child of his generation, he could not – could not be expected to – escape from the pictorial.[22] For all Thornton's mental rigour, 'nice quality of paint' and 'fine quality of pigment' were the phrases that littered the reviews when reference is made to the work of older artists, Fred Brown, Holmes, Walker and Pissarro. A covert message to do with handling, consistency and loyalty to reporting on the material world in this roll-call prevailed. It was framed by the 'national character' debates that greeted the Royal Academy winter exhibition of 1933–4 devoted to 'British Art *c.* 1000–1860', which provided the opportunity for a reassertion of Baldwin values.[23]

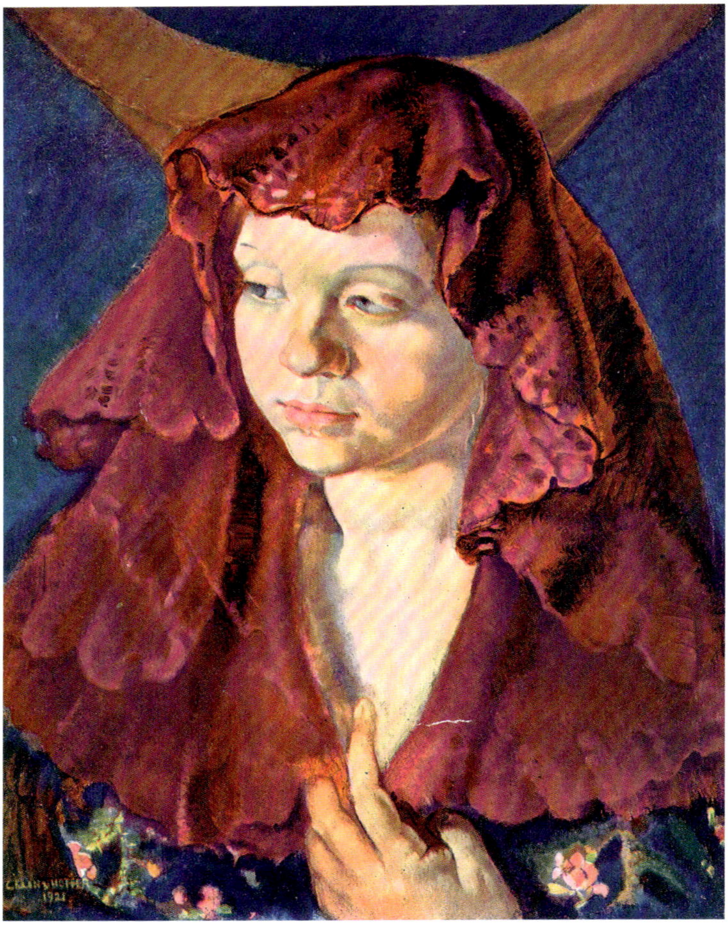

Fig. 135 Clara Klinghoffer
Portrait [of the artist's sister], 1921
Location unknown

The splintering of the art community continued. Elsewhere in London, two former Slade students, Rodrigo Moynihan and William Coldstream, along with Geoffrey Tibble and Graham Bell, persuaded the proprietors of the Zwemmer Gallery to show their 'Objective Abstractions' in 1934 – a further questioning of traditional practice.[24] Yet again, young painters were taking a critical stance on the increasingly discredited processes of observing and recording. Irrespective of the positions they assumed, these developments also indicated that a Salon, selected by a jury, would never be able to supply the profile young painters sought. A broad church like the New English could never risk the ridicule that greeted the Zwemmer show[25] – especially as it pondered the renewal terms of its lease on the Spring Gardens Gallery.[26]

Clara Klinghoffer (see fig. 135) and Gilbert Spencer were elected to membership in 1933, both having been regular exhibitors since the war. The former, living in Holland, was showing portrait studies of Dutch and Polish types, while the latter was rooted in English rural life – in a country accessible to the Austin Seven. Both artists' work had recently been purchased by the Trustees of the Chantrey Bequest, and both exemplified important strands within the club. Klinghoffer represented a group of artists who delighted in single studies of regional characters dressed in everyday garb. The expressive character of her work echoed Flemish and German realism.[27] To her side were less exotic New English painters such as Thomas Cantrell Dugdale and Percy Horton – both of whom were preoccupied with English class types. Spencer's Chantrey picture, *A Cotswold Farm* (1930–1), which appeared in the Goupil Gallery and the Royal Academy, went further in this direction, soon becoming the archetype of 1930s rurality, and the ultimate expression of the very qualities that those exploring the national character sought. When all industrialisation and imperial mercantilism was stripped away, Englishness came down to a yeoman and his team of shire horses. Gwynne-Jones's and Sutherland's arcadianism was reinvented.

In that year women painters took the lead in the club's exhibition. The formidable triumvirate of Beatrice Bland, Fairlie Harmar and Margaret Fisher Prout was praised for 'sparkling' effects that brought 'a ripple of feminine gaiety' to the show.[28] Vibrant flower-pieces and colourful landscapes revealed that painterly impressionism still blossomed in the hands of the 'Cheyne Walkers', and these women held their dominant position while the older male exhibitors had, for the most part, according to one reviewer, 'retired to the watercolour rooms'.[29]

The most significant exhibit of 1934 was *Pleasure Cruise* (1934; fig. 136) by Mary Adshead. Restless young sunbathers are camped on the deck of a ship in

Right and overleaf
Fig. 136 Mary Adshead
Pleasure Cruise, 1934
Oil on canvas, 142 x 182.2 cm
Purchased 1977. Tate, London

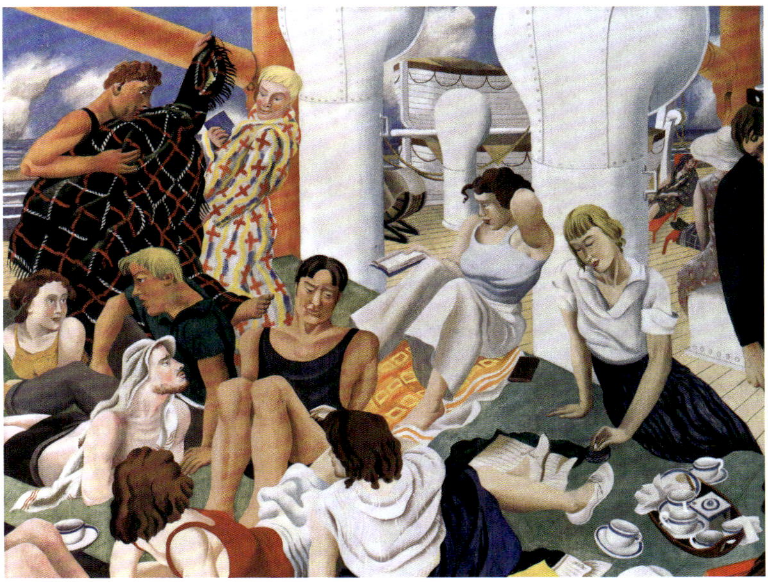

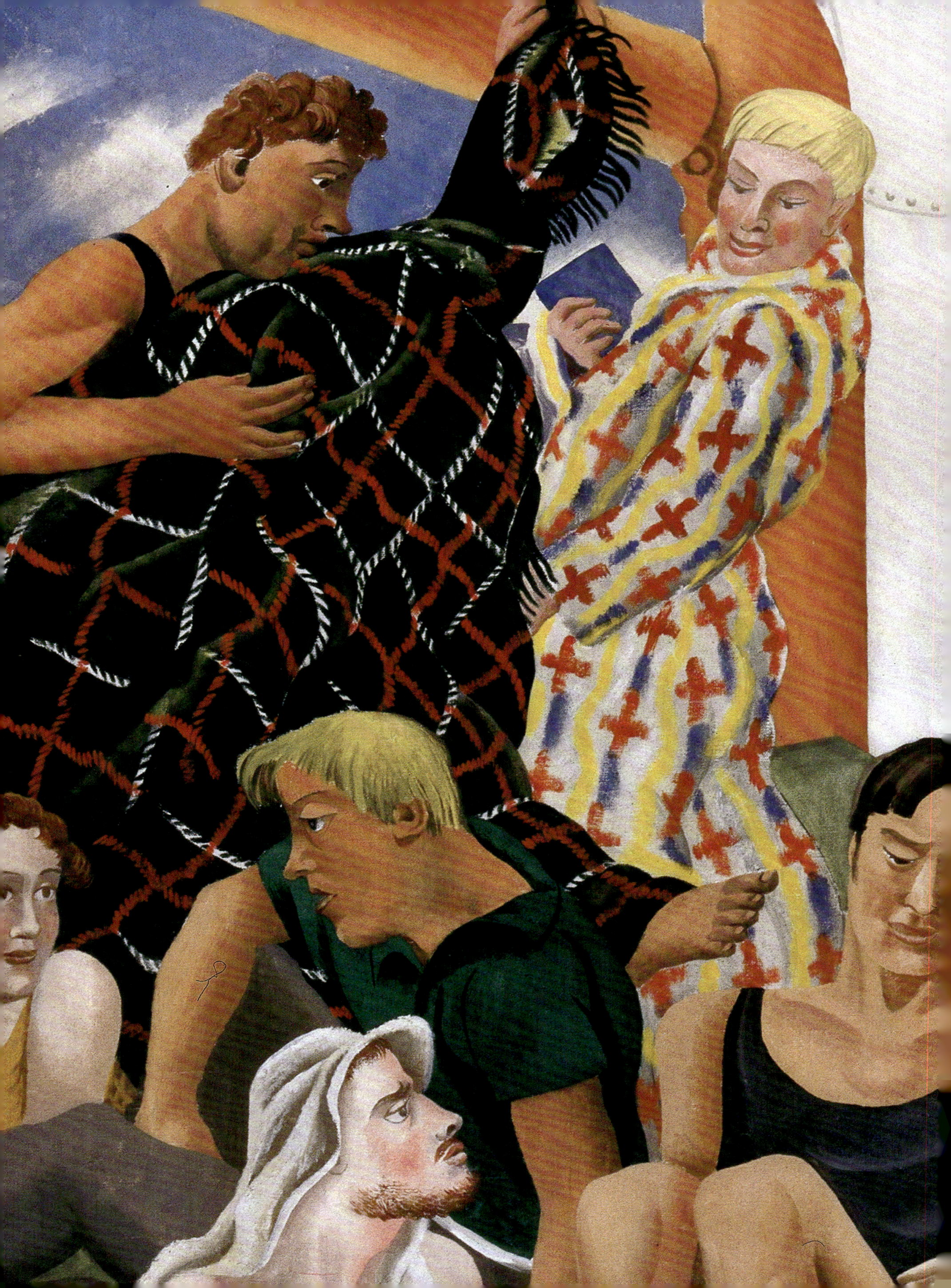

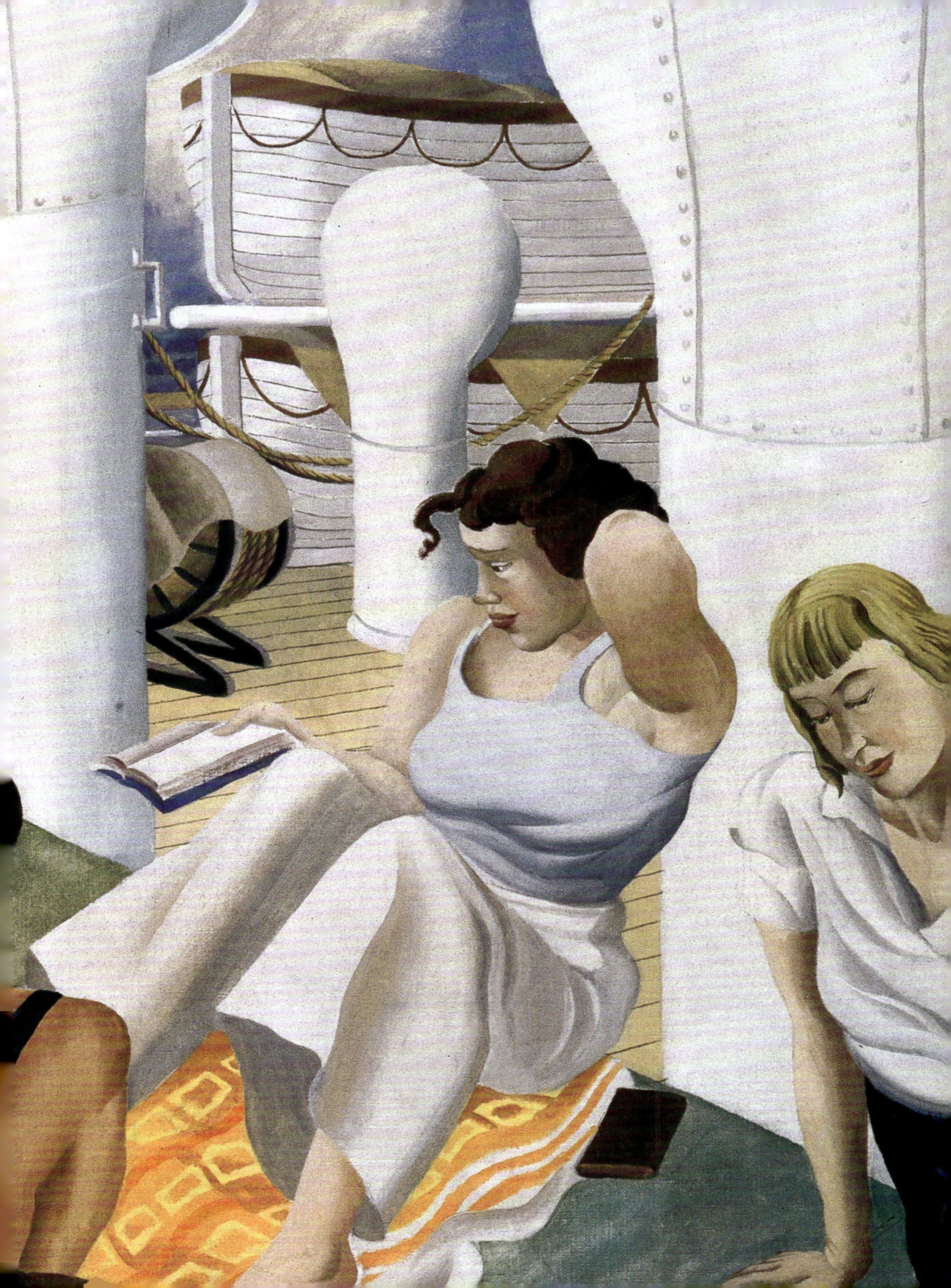

such a disarray of redundant arms and legs that a steward with a tray is obliged to pick his way between their 'vile bodies'. Throughout these closing years of George V's reign, heedless of hunger marches and Mr Hitler, these middle-class pleasure seekers lived only for today. They are a less sinister English equivalent to the young, mindless, muscular Berliners admired by Stephen Spender, but they have no yesterday and no tomorrow. The animated conversation of the moment occupies their full attention. Male exhibition reporters who were remorselessly condescending about women's painting made sarcastic quips like that in *The Times*, 'evidently Miss Mary Adshead went on her *Pleasure Cruise* with Mr Stanley Spencer, in spirit if not in fact', because Spencer's mannerisms are deployed to such a persuasive effect.[30]

Despite the dip in sales in 1934, the club initially remained poised for an outstanding jubilee exhibition.[31] By this stage plans were already in place for a show of strength to rival that of 1925 and remind everyone of the club's position as the senior radical group. The editor of the *The Artist*, Harold Sawkins, with an eye for an opportunity, approached the club with the proposal that his staff writer, Herbert Furst, should be commissioned to write the club's history. Not everyone approved of Furst and after some debate Thornton was given the task.[32] In character with its author, the history was devoid of triumphalism, yet he could boast that, while the club initially blew fresh air into British painting, 'it has given England a school of drawing and ... has done much to reform the Royal Academy'. Recent events, to which he made oblique reference, proved that club members within the Academy were still capable of challenging its preconceptions.[33] The tone, unlike Laidlay's elaborate self-justification for his role in the first two years, is measured and objective. Thornton had been a solid exhibitor without an axe to grind and, when he died four years later, he was remembered as 'a man of wide culture and an interesting writer, with a philosophical bent of mind'.[34] In his view, far from being 'unEnglish', the club stood for tolerance and liberalism in the best sense. Young talent would come in and pass on. Brown's, Steer's and Tonks's open house had provided the first important testing ground for succeeding generations and the club was 'still new and still English'.[35]

The jubilee exhibition was held shortly after the publication of *Fifty Years of the New English Art Club* and special efforts were made to demonstrate the liberalism Thornton described.[36] This was achieved in one leap by the acceptance of Spencer's *The Lovers (The Dustman)* (1935; fig. 137), a work that had been rejected by the Academy in May. Known more usually as *The Dustman*, this 'last day' narrative was of great personal significance in that it revisited the artist's earlier preoccupations with resurrection. In this case the dustman has leapt into his wife's arms in a passionate embrace, while his children kneel before him with votive offerings – a teapot, a jam pot and a cabbage or cauliflower.[37] Critics who guardedly supported Spencer in the Academy now had licence to turn against him. According to *The Times* this work was 'a thoroughly ugly picture'.[38]

The Spencer rejection had other implications for the club and the Academy. Sickert, whose attitude to the institution alternated between benevolence and

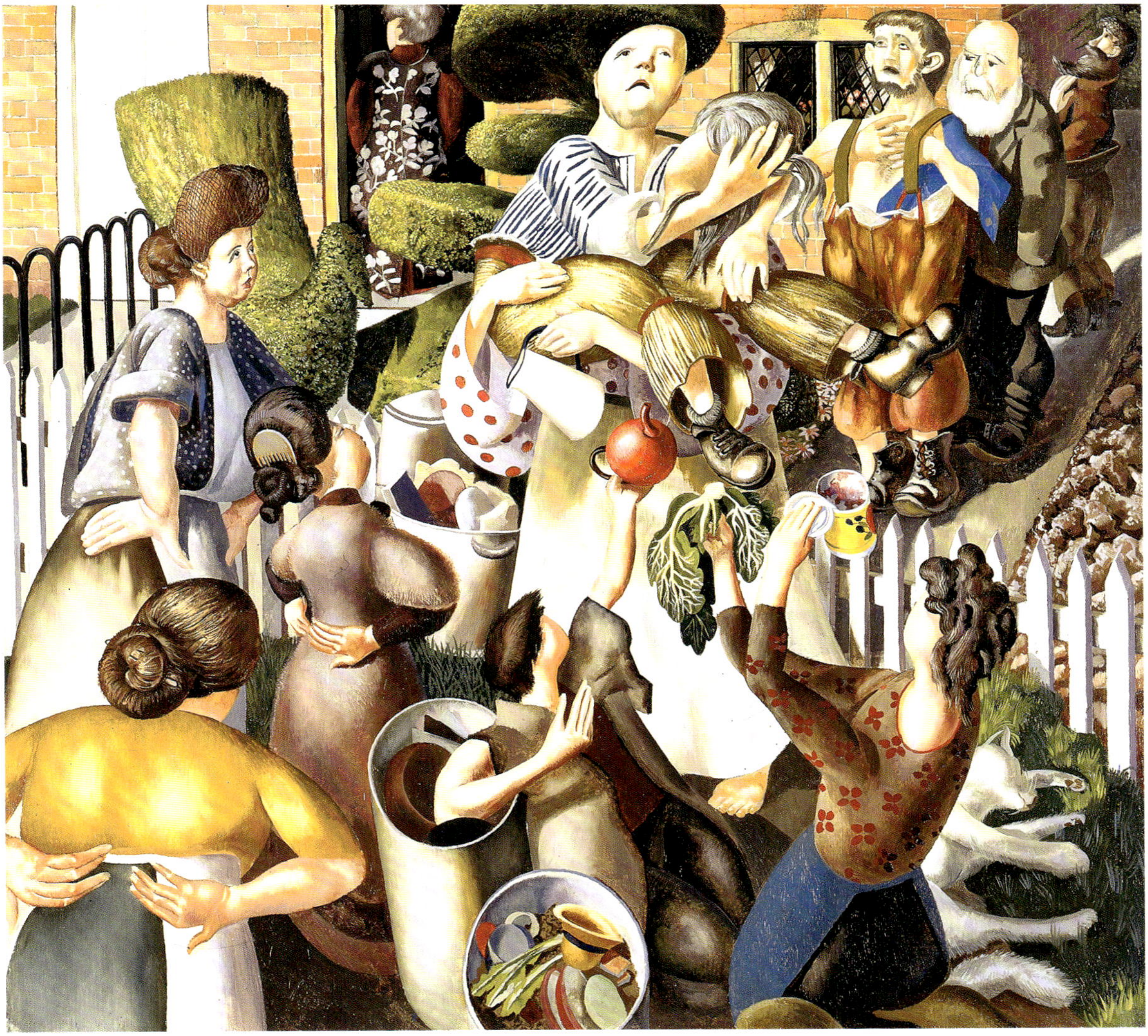

Fig. 137 Stanley Spencer
The Lovers (*The Dustman*), 1935
Oil on canvas, 114.9 x 122.5 cm
Laing Art Gallery, Newcastle upon Tyne

disdain, wrote to *The Sunday Times* in protest and, after a twenty-year absence, returned to the club with *The New Bedford* (1915–16), 'one of the solidest pieces of painting', already in the collection of Edward Marsh.[39] But it was a one-off, and not a recent work. Other 'retrospective' exhibits by older and former members were confined to a single wall – an 'unobtrusive Royal Enclosure', according to Eric Newton. In what was to be a rare early moment of generosity towards the club, Newton praised its recognition of its own strengths – 'light ... atmosphere and ... colour values' to which 'each member of the school contributes some slight addition' – and dubbed it 'the best of pre-Cubist British art'.[40] He could almost have been referring to George Charlton's *King George V's Silver Jubilee* (1935; fig. 138), a picture of crowds on the Embankment, waving as the royal parade passes. The show's core, 'the feminine contingent', Walker, Bland, Fisher

Prout and Harmar, continued to be much in evidence. In contrast to what else was happening in the art world of the mid-1930s, exemplified in its most extreme form in Ben Nicholson's *White Relief* constructions, this was an 'eminently conventional' exhibition, 'far from disturbing in its effect'.[41]

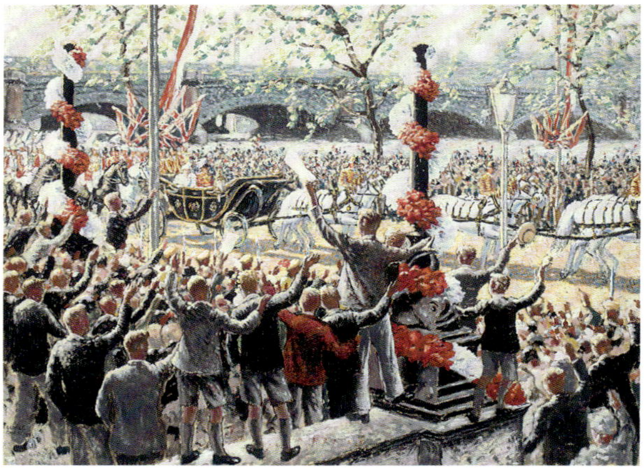

Fig. 138 George Charlton
King George V's Silver Jubilee, 1935
Oil on canvas, 76.2 x 104.1 cm
Private collection

With a published 'history', rooms in public galleries were devoted to telling the New English story. J. B. Manson, who had been Keeper at the Tate Gallery in the 1920s, had been adding New English works to the collection and, in the 1925 re-hang, a good portion of the space in Gallery XXI was allotted to club members. At that time Manson wrote that the founding of the club had been an 'act of liberation' in British Art and 'its influence has been immeasurable'.[42] In the 1938 re-hanging, the whole of Gallery XXI was given over to the club.[43] Its significance was further underlined in invitations to stage shows in Paris and Canada in 1938 and 1939. However, they were as much to do with the past and present rather than looking to the future, and, although the question of new directions was firmly on the agenda, it remained unanswered. Reviews, when they occurred, began to shrink to one or two paragraphs, placing the club, along with the London Group, in a critical box.

> The typical New Englander and the typical London Grouper would each be likely to accuse the other of caring nothing about colour; the simple explanation being that, with a common eye to decorative possibilities, one is thinking of colour in its atmospheric and the other in its constructive values.[44]

Young painters, when not showing with smaller radical, abstract or Surrealist groups, went straight to dealers for solo exhibitions. By the mid-1930s they had become the principal means of attracting critical attention. When they staged survey shows, dealers tended to follow the Duveen model and play safe. The need to be 'representative' – that is, to demonstrate established trends and reputations – far outweighed risk-taking. Increasingly after the outbreak of the Spanish Civil War and annexation of the Rhineland, tolerance was not enough and the ferment in British art was exposed in public squabbles – in the debate between Kenneth Clark and Herbert Read. In the columns of *The Listener*, Clark reflected upon the future of painting. While recognising that the Academy and the senior societies were failing, he attacked obscurantist abstract art. Read penned a churlish response, Clark counter-attacked and the matter descended into the 'Letters' columns, in which Roland Penrose called for an exhibition of 'super-realist' painting.[45] The debate amply demonstrated how confused and nervous the art world had become. These wrangles continued with Read and Anthony Blunt locked in battle over the touring of Picasso's *Guernica* (1937) in 1937, and between Blunt and Coldstream on the question of realism and social responsibility in 1938.[46] Solidarity only emerged over such issues as the war in Spain and members like Stephen Bone, son of Muirhead Bone, and Ethelbert White gave their support to AIA fund-raising and to the First British Artists' Congress and Exhibition held under its auspices in 1937.[47]

In the midst of such outside uncertainty, the club seemed to remain a haven of sanity. Indeed, there was a sense that no distant call to arms would disturb its equanimity. *The Times* wrote in 1936 that:

> the inclination is to wander about as at a pleasant, but rather vague, party of which nobody knows exactly the point. One murmurs to oneself or to a companion, 'so-and-so is here and looking very well, but what is the matter with…'.[48]

Within twelve months the party began to draw to a close. Two senior members, Tonks and Holmes, had died and the winter exhibition of 1937 contained memorial groups of their work.[49] It was clear that, while some young exhibitors were trying to engage with the contemporary scene, 'the status of art as a luxury trade for the benefit of the best people [was] more or less unquestionably accepted' at the club and 'women set the tone of the conversation'.[50] Although Bland continued to 'sparkle', and Nadia Benois flourished with rococo flower-pieces (see fig. 139), it was Winifred Nicholson who 'caught a momentary glimpse of reality' (see fig. 140).[51] But what reality? The instinct at this point would surely have been to sound a bugle and raise the red flag. Even in their quietly radical way, neither Nicholson, Dunlop, Walker, Rothenstein, Pissarro, A. K. Browning nor Cathleen Mann could stem the tide.

Fig. 139 Nadia Benois
Mimosa, 1930
Oil on canvas, 63.5 x 76.6 cm
Private collection

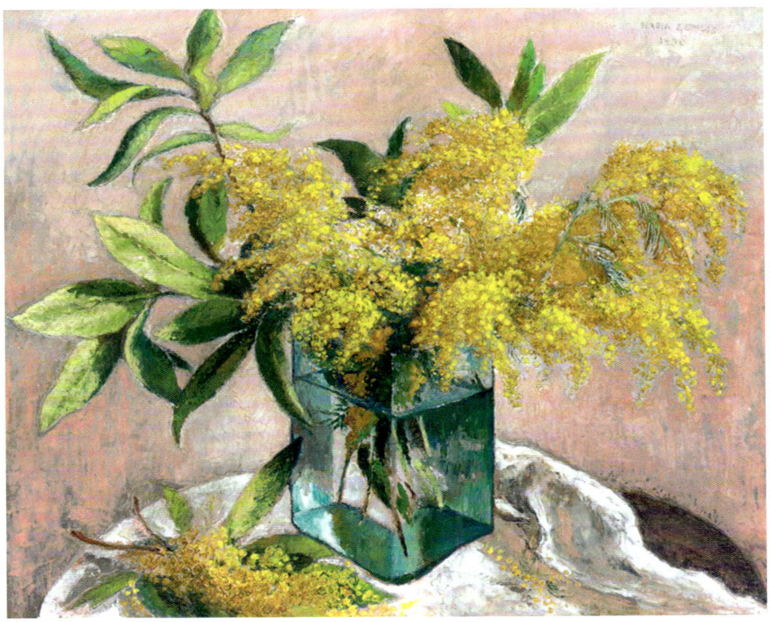

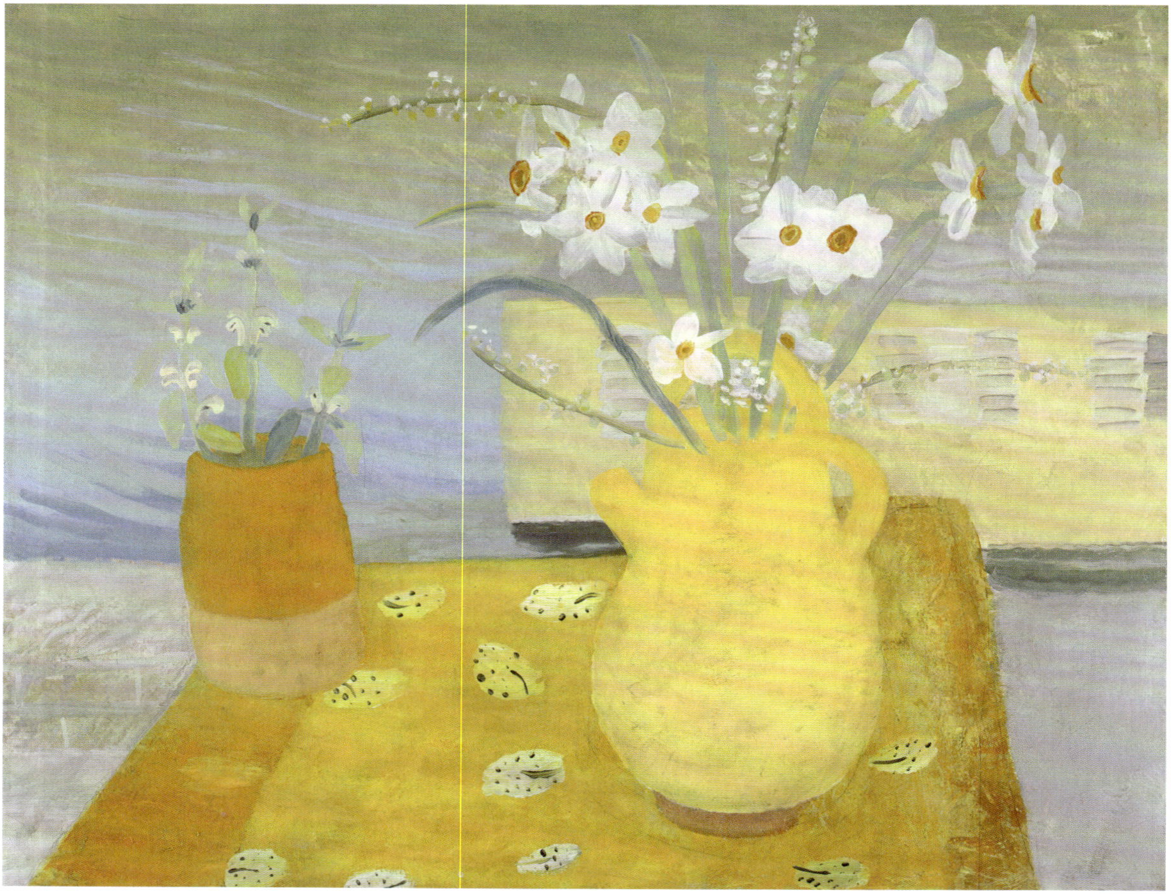

Fig. 140 Winifred Nicholson
Kate's Flowers, 1929–36
Oil on board, 60.7 x 76 cm
Purchased 1946. Art Gallery of New South Wales, Sydney

Indeed, clinging to 'the clink of teacups' was the only thing to do at that moment – as Spender noted when he visited Virginia Woolf. The AIA, having expanded to take in Ben Nicholson and Barbara Hepworth, was also supporting the Surrealists while simultaneously issuing anti-Fascist propaganda. It had lost its political edge to woolly intellectuals. Despite ideological justifications provided by Blunt and Francis D. Klingender, the Socialist Realist project lacked the moral authority of a popular front. Although in one sense it was no more than a reformed branch of the Slade church, an opportunity presented itself in October 1937 when the Euston Road School opened. Its 'socialist' mission placed it firmly outside the Establishment, but its revolutionary message – to wait patiently in the Life Room – was not in one sense at odds with the club's insistence on empirical observation. In a world waylaid by Freud, Jung and a plethora of creeds and manifestos, both represented the pictorial equivalent of 'common sense' philosophy. But should the school offer more? Looking at Wildenstein's show of the work of Coldstream, Graham Bell and Victor Pasmore in 1938, Horton cast a cold eye on its capacity to change the world and he recalled Sickert's dictum, 'There is more to a feast than the tiles and chimney pots of Fitzroy Street'.[52]

Serious reservations about the capacity of art to serve the revolution led to renewed public debate about the values associated with Englishness. Homeliness expressed in decorative domesticity and cultivated 'Constable' landscape remained central tropes. They stressed a form of private life impossible under Hitler and Stalin. Still-life paintings, mostly flower-pieces, exhibited in significantly high numbers in annual club exhibitions, were an affront to Social Realists and Surrealists alike. Ten years earlier T. W. Earp had observed that the 'general conditions of life in this country are to some extent accountable' for the popularity of still-life. He noted that:

> The English are essentially nature-lovers but the growth of the city and the scarring of the countryside by intensive industrialism which is so pronounced a characteristic of our day has removed from many city-dwellers their accustomed opportunity of enjoying country delights. For them the flower-piece is a symbol of holiday release.[53]

At once hedonistic and decorative, they sprang from a long western tradition originating with the Dutch masters, revived by Chardin and resumed by Manet and Fantin-Latour. But these English flower-pieces exhibited by Bland, Walker, Harmar, Fisher Prout, Gabain, Manson and many others constituted an essentially new phenomenon that remains unsung.[54] Even Augustus John in the 1930s would show vibrant studies of cinerarias or rhododendrons (see fig. 141) at the club. Easily dismissed as escapism, as well as being the ultimate expression of suburban 'Priestley' values, with the added frisson of a 'modern' touch, the flower-piece provided the ultimate evidence of retreat from the world outside. The blooms have been selected and, like those sunny days in the studio on which they were painted, will fade – but not before being 'memorialised'. And tomorrow, in dreary Metroland, hanging above the mantelpiece, they will draw sunlight back into the drawing room. Similar points would be true about landscape painting, a genre that, in the hands of Ronald O. Dunlop (see fig. 142), enabled the development of Expressionist handling, while, for White, it remained locked in the marquetry of flat interlocking shapes.[55] Both called out to Earp's English 'nature-lover' at a time when Germany appeared like a rabid fox in the middle of the map of Europe. They, and their colleagues in the club – Vincent Lines, Henry Bishop, Charles Cundall, Henry Rushbury and Rodney Burn – represented a gentility that remained as one of the earliest memories of Bernard Dunstan.[56]

No one expected more than this 'Englishness'. It was fully exposed in the spring of 1938, when the members were required to mobilise for an exhibition at the newly reopened Georges Petit Gallery in Paris.[57] For this occasion, some distinguished former members were invited back into the fold. Charles Cundall and W. L. Clause went to Paris to hang the 125 paintings, drawings and watercolours, five of which were purchased by the French Government.[58] MacColl

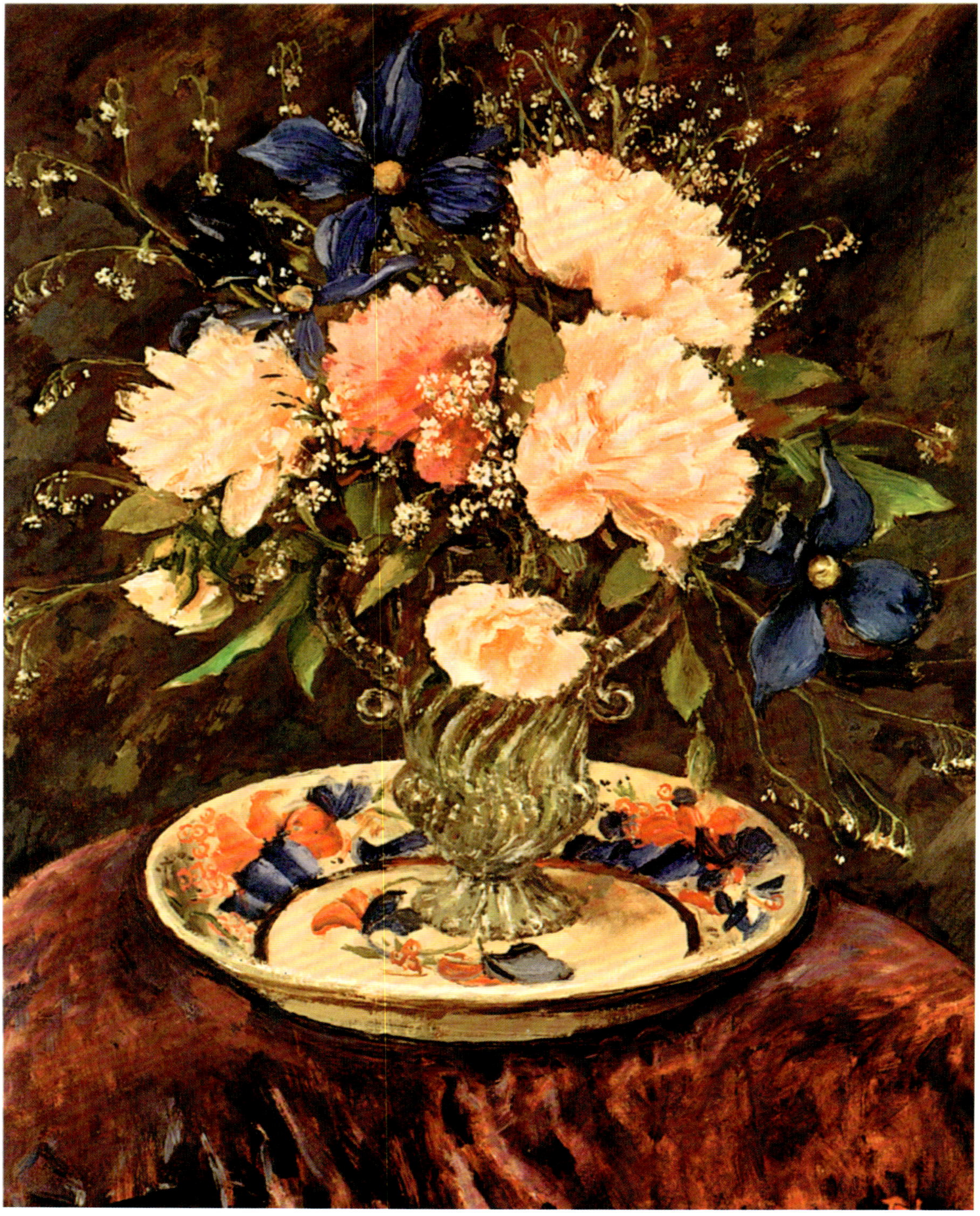

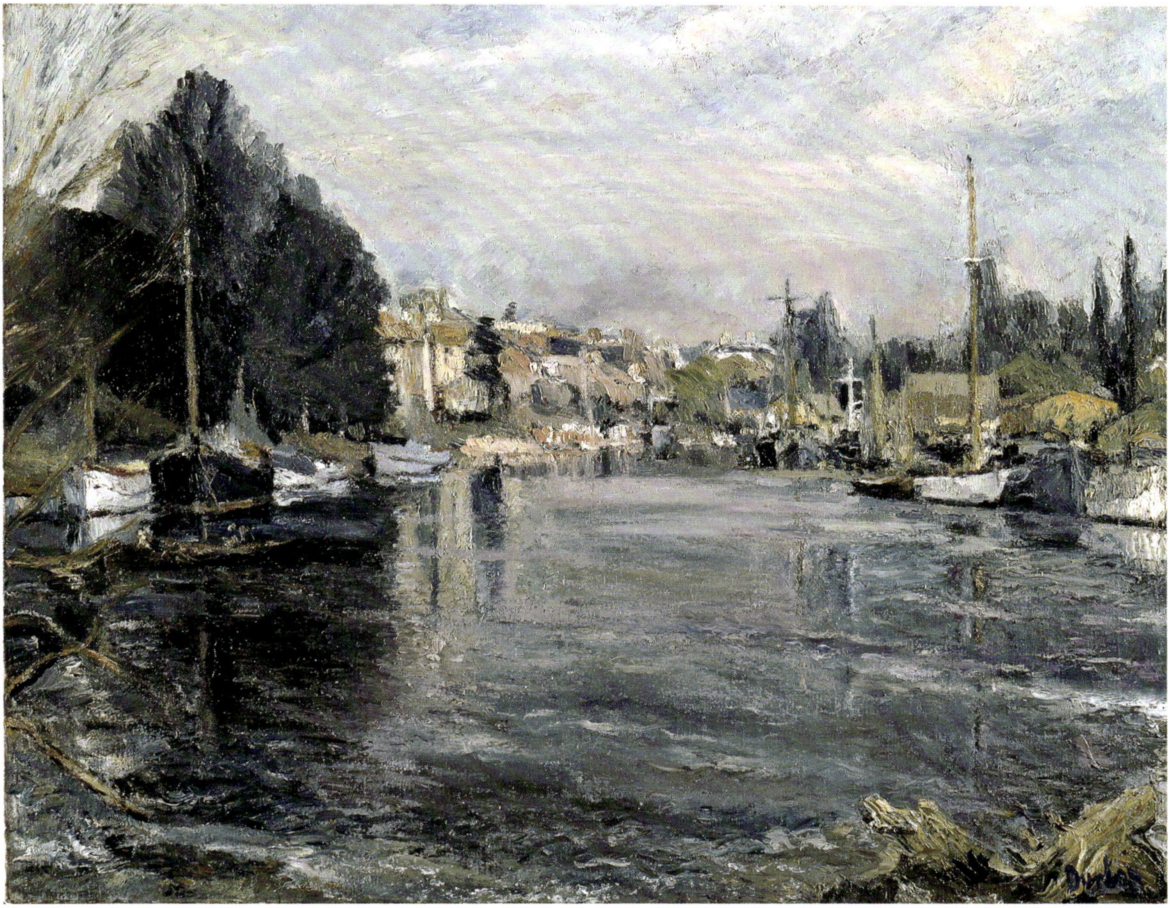

Above
Fig. 142 Ronald Ossary Dunlop
The Thames at Sunbury, c. 1943
Oil on canvas, 101.6 x 127 cm
Purchased from the artist 1943.
Royal Academy of Arts, London

Opposite
Fig. 141 Augustus John
Mixed Flowers in a Glass Jar, c. 1938
Oil on canvas, 78.5 x 63.5 cm
Private collection

produced an essay in French charting the history of the club for the exhibition catalogue. The official opening on 30 June was sponsored by the British Ambassador and was attended by André Dezarrois, Conservateur of the Musée du Jeu de Paume, and various diplomats, as well as the creaking relics of the age of Blanche and Proust, the Comtesse Greffulhe, the Princesse de Chimay and Baron Robert de Rothschild. The show, which included Spencer's 'eccentric' *Lovers* (fig. 137), was extensively reviewed in the French press and the works admired for their *qualité intime* – the only adverse comment being made in connection with Edward Wadsworth's *The Departure* (1938).[59]

Otherwise the exhibition was a great success precisely because it confirmed the continuing traditions of Constable and Turner in the eyes of the Parisian public. At home, the club's Establishment position was too central for some and there was a sharp exchange of letters between Charlton and MacColl, in which the former pointed out that 'young artists (not necessarily Bolshies) say "the New English – it's as bad as the Academy now"'. For him, its principal role was as the 'only hope' of the excellent students at the Slade, where he

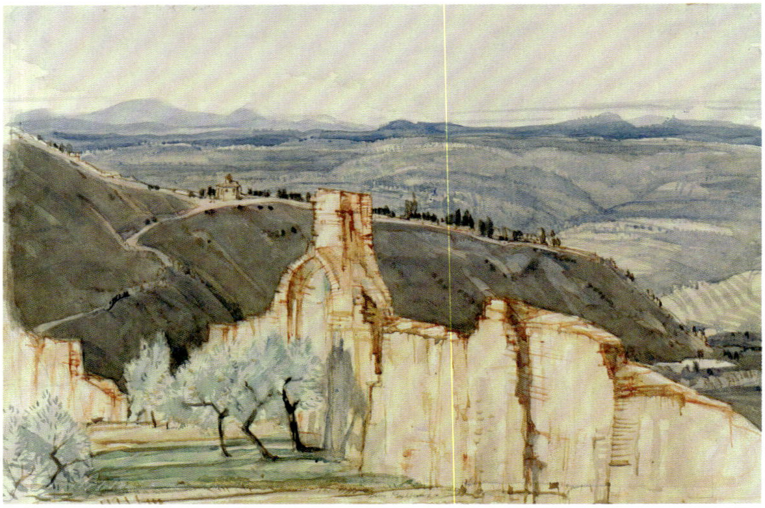

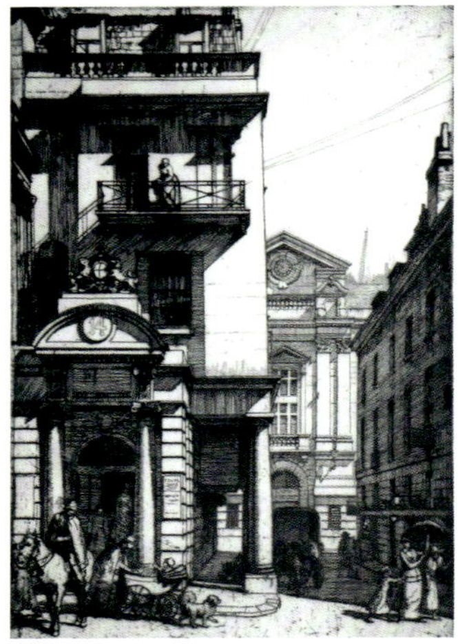

taught.[60] The club's obligation to the principal London art schools, the Royal Academy Schools, the Royal College of Art and the Slade was an important *raison d'être,* implicit in the regular showing of work by Randolph Schwabe and Henry Rushbury, artists who were working in the tradition of Bone and MacColl (see figs 143 and 144).

Above left
Fig. 143 Henry Rushbury
Siena, undated
Watercolour on paper, 31.2 x 47.2 cm
Temple Newsam House, Leeds

Above right
Fig. 144 Randolph Schwabe
London Street Scene (Untitled), 1910–14
Etching on paper, 34.2 x 22.7 cm
Collection Elizabeth Harvey-Lee

Paris, however, led to other proposals. Provincial galleries wanted to take New English work and, consequently, shows were arranged for Southport, Birkenhead, Bath and Worthing. At the same time the Art Exhibitions Bureau proposed a Canadian tour incorporating the National Gallery of Canada.[61] In anticipation of war, a scheme for 'recording the changing face of Britain' was launched by the Pilgrim Trust, sending such New English landscapists as Bayes, Hartrick, Vincent Lines and the young Kenneth Rowntree off around the English counties.[62] These and further exhibition plans were overtaken, but not arrested by external events. To paraphrase W. H. Auden, 'all the dogs of Europe' were barking in 1939. And, when the New English appeared to be carrying on business as usual, it was issued with a stern corrective by *The Times,* which noted that many of its artists have 'complete disregard of what we are getting from the newspapers and wireless'.[63] Nowhere was this more evident than in Leila Faithfull's *In the Luxembourg Gardens* (1939; fig. 145). Here was a park parade of mothers, matrons and children, in what could be any city in Western Europe or North America. The artist had found a place where the wireless did not reach.

The wake-up call came in the form of an incendiary bomb crashing through the skylight of the RBA Galleries during the winter exhibition of 1940. Only the glass on one picture was damaged and, after a quick clean up, the show remained open for business.[64] By this time the efforts of the club, the Academy and all of the major groups were curtailed by the war. The National Gallery collections were consigned to the caves of North Wales; the Royal College of Art staff and students, captained by Horton and Gilbert Spencer, decamped to the Lake

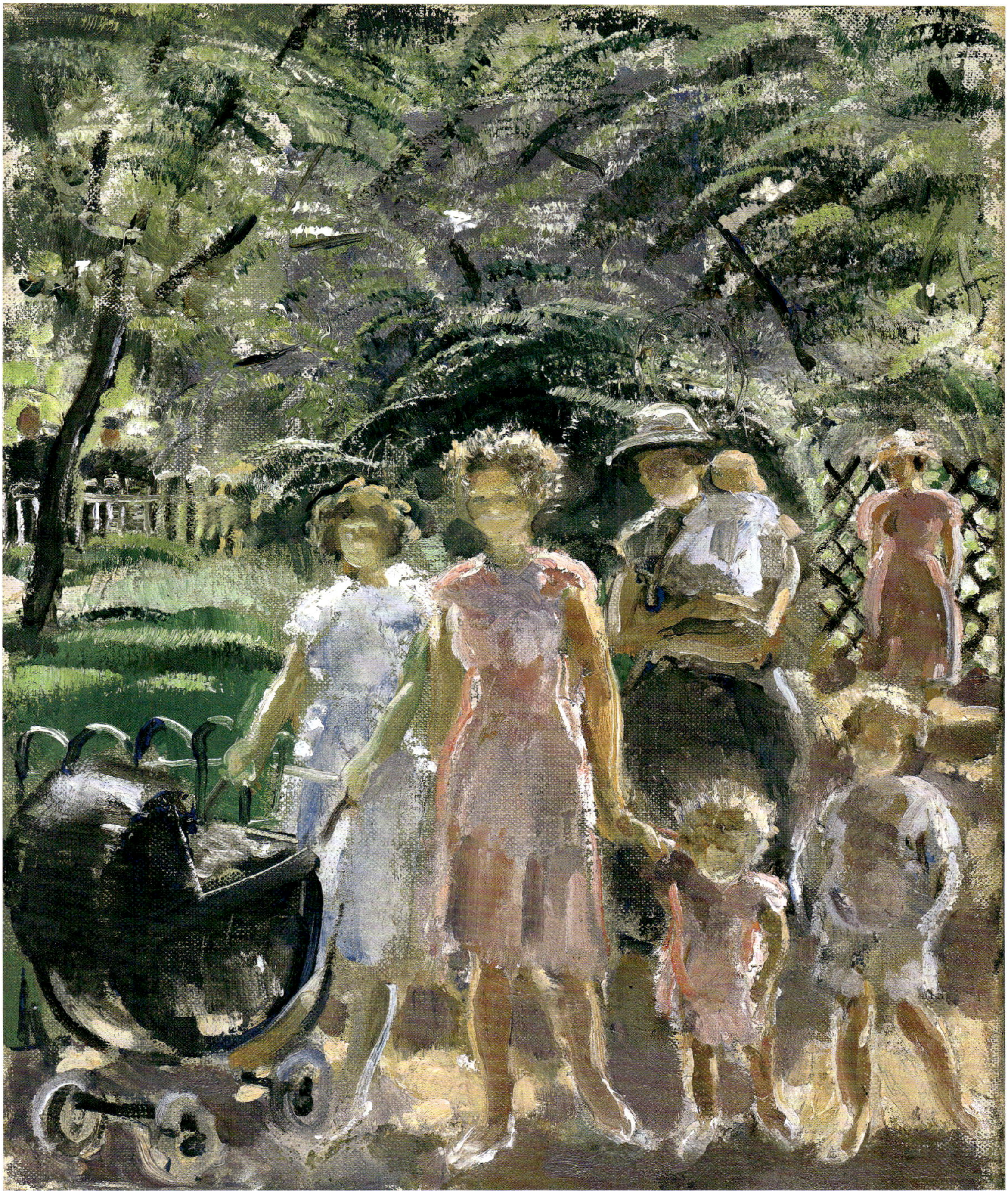

Fig. 145 Leila Faithfull
In the Luxembourg Gardens, 1939
Oil on canvas, 27.1 x 22.1 cm
Manchester City Art Gallery

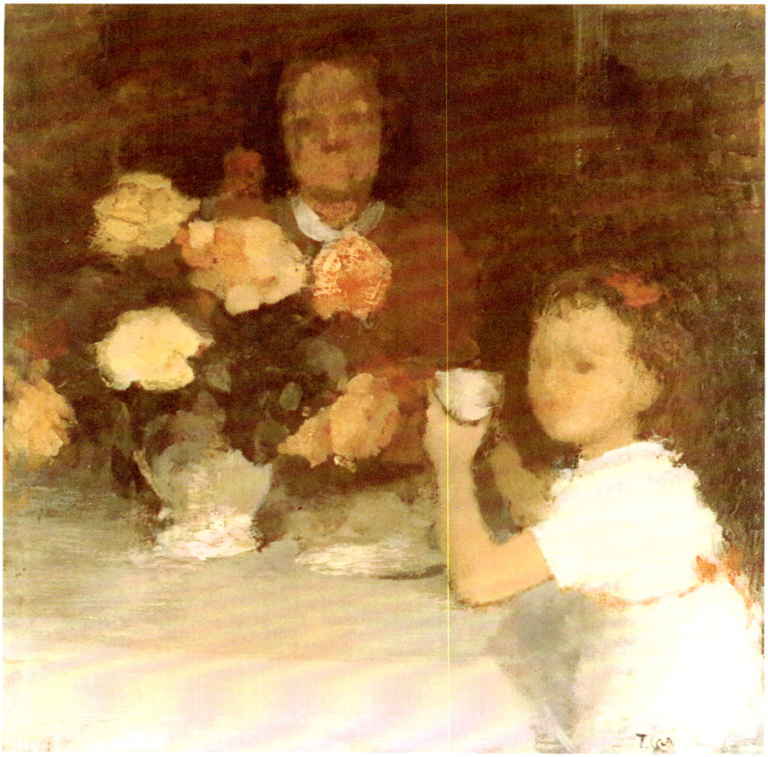

Fig. 146 Thomas Carr
Tea Table, 1940–41
Oil on board, 40.7 x 40.7 cm
Private collection

District; the Slade under Schwabe relocated to Oxford; and the Royal Academy Schools closed.[65] With the Euston Road School also shut and artists fleeing the capital, it was important to be seen to be carrying on, but those who remained did so in a state of siege. Looking back, with the images of Sutherland and John Piper in mind, Spender wrote: 'A little island of civilisation surrounded by burning churches – that was how the arts seemed in England during the war.'[66]

Although sales were few, the appetite for provincial tours increased and the members rallied in support of bookings that were made on behalf of Darlington, Sunderland, Middlesborough, Manchester, Bradford and Rochdale, between 1941 and the early months of 1943.[67] There was, nevertheless, unfinished business in the pre-war return to realism. The club at this time began to attract Euston Road-trained painters, who were left high and dry by its closure. 'Aims and ideals' were, as Bernard Denvir noted in 1946, shared between the club and the school.[68] Robin Darwin, Anthony Devas, Robert Buhler, Tom Carr and others were brought into the Establishment during the war years, with Carr's gentle kitchen 'teatable' studies of 1943 and 1945 typifying their retiring provincial *intimisme* (see fig. 146).[69] The war effectively exploded this group and spread its influence 'like a prairie fire' throughout landscape painting in England.[70] Political ambitions were radically simplified with the outbreak of war and avant-garde groups scattered. Using the example of the Official War

Artists' Scheme during the Great War, the War Artists' Advisory Committee established itself under the chairmanship of Kenneth Clark, on behalf of the Ministry of Information.[71] Exhibitors such as Stephen Bone, Cundall, Evelyn Dunbar, Richard Eurich and Thomas Hennell saw service in naval and airforce bases, although there was little evidence of this experience in their wartime submissions.

It could be argued that Steer's death at the end of March 1942 imposed a more fundamental change upon the New English than the outbreak of war. He was the remaining, continuously exhibiting founder member of the club whose loyalty had been unflinching, and his work was consistently admired over fifty years of exhibiting. *Autumn, Greenhithe*, painted in 1932, was regarded 'best of all' the watercolours and drawings in the winter show of 1940. A note in the 1942 catalogue indicates that it had not been possible, as intended, to display a representative selection of his work because of the war.[72] In any event, the Tate Gallery, London, had decided to stage a memorial exhibition in June the following year – for which MacColl penned a brief appreciation.[73] Alas, Steer did not rest peacefully. His reputation after his death suffered because of Robin Ironside and Douglas Cooper. The former, an assistant keeper at the Tate Gallery, was commissioned by Phaidon Press to produce a short monograph, in the same series as those on Spencer and John. For Ironside, there was a 'progressive Toryism about his art which effectively shielded him from the dangers ... of experimentalism'.[74] The author, in the opinion of those who knew the painter and had no time for modernism, had underestimated Steer's influence by failing to mention his long service at the Slade and his impact generally on British painting.[75] If this showed less than full respect for household gods, Cooper's attack was malicious. 'The problem of Wilson Steer', for Cooper, was, by extension, that of the club, and, ultimately, British painting in its entirety.

> The history of British painting from the refounding of the Slade School and that other gathering of amateurs the New English Art Club – of which Steer was an early member – is primarily the story of the natural and sensitive perception of British painters drowned by an unnatural obsession with, and misunderstanding of, the European contemporaries.

The world of art had gained nothing, he contended, from artists like 'Reynolds, Gainsborough, Romney, and Lawrence, Blake and the Pre-Raphaelites'. British painters were 'second-rate' and could be classed as either 'pretentious commercial bores' or 'modest distinguished amateurs'.[76] If Cooper revealed anything, it was that Britain, in his view, lacked confidence and pride in the quality of its art production. MacColl and Collins Baker were outraged. The former was already, with the assistance of the latter, collecting information from Steer's colleagues, collectors, pupils and sitters to produce a biography.[77] *The Burlington Magazine* printed a series of letters ranging from disdain for Cooper's 'slick' and prejudicial comments to mild approval for 'general truthfulness of his judgement' from his old ally, Herbert Read.[78] Others, such as

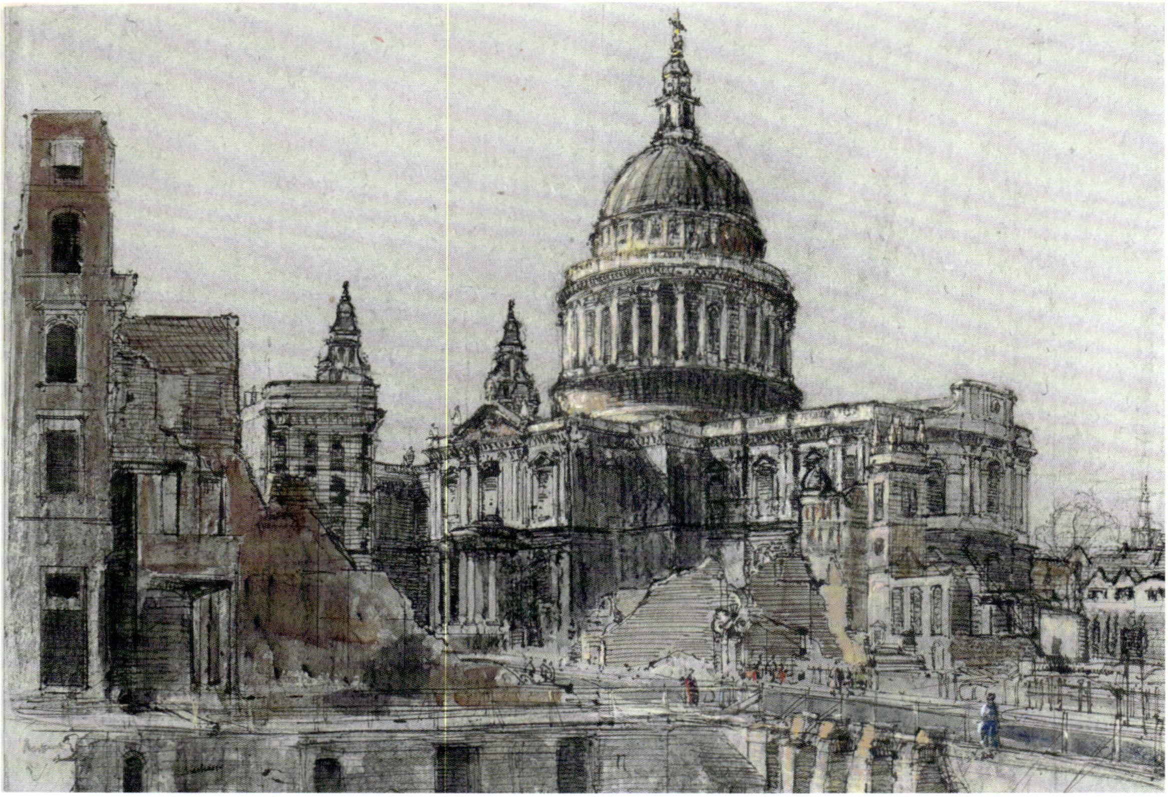

Fig. 147 Paul Ayshford (Lord Methuen)
St Paul's, 1942
Pen and ink, pastel and wash on paper, 51.4 x 62.2 cm
Victoria and Albert Museum, London

John Russell, were faintly bemused and found Cooper's invective difficult to understand. It was a point of view that 'only ignorance could excuse, or vulgar incredulity explain'.[79] But by this stage, according to Denvir, Impressionism in its 'more elementary and obvious forms' had migrated to the Academy, while, at the club, 'the criterion of excellence' tended 'to be the degree to which it was possible to approximate the work of the late Wilson Steer'.[80] The viability of this mainstream needed to be questioned, given that Sickert had also recently died and, although he had not shown since the winter of 1915, apart from inter-war retrospectives and the Paris and Canadian exhibitions, his impact on the club, while being less profound, was at crucial moments more decisive. His legacy lay in part in the work of Lord Methuen, who, taking his light sable drawing and restricted palette from Sickert's 'Echoes',[81] had been elected to membership in 1943.[82]

This legacy in landscape painting was not unchallenged. Stephen Bone, for instance, while acknowledging the importance of the club and paying his respects to Steer and Sickert, looked to Holmes and his father Muirhead Bone, as topographers who were blunt and objective.[83] In Muirhead Bone's case, there was an obvious legacy in the work of Rushbury and Schwabe, while Holmes was the unsung forebear of the more austere, 'abstract' landscapists of the inter-war period. Writing in the aftermath of the war, Stephen Bone was forced to conclude that there had been a decline in scenic beauty since the early nineteenth century – but then 'the strikingly picturesque scenery has interested artists less than the ordinary agricultural scenes of East Anglia or the Midlands'.[84]

However, during the Battle of Britain, this contest for the soul of the British landscape still had to be fought and only Nevinson in *The Return* (1940), a picture of aeroplanes casting shadows across fields, alluded to the events that everyone was hearing about on the wireless.[85] The following year, the exhibition contained a further crop of good landscapes, and, although Adrian Hill's large portrait of Winston Churchill was regarded as a disappointment, blitzed London was already taking on mythic majesty. Norman Hepple's *St Paul's and Queen Victoria Street after the Great Fires of May 1941* (1941) conveys something of the regal dignity of classic Picture Post photographs. His drawings and those of Methuen stand out as the most potent records of the devastation (figs 147 and 148).[86]

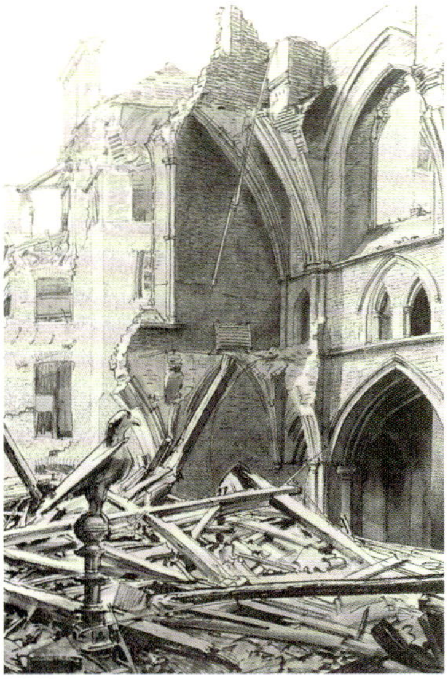

Fig. 148 Robert Norman Hepple
St George's, Fisher Street, W1, 1941
Graphite on paper
Location unknown

In spite of its 'business as usual' approach, there appeared to be little support for the activities of the club and the other artists' societies from the young mandarins of the art Establishment. Such was the scale of the problem that Hesketh Hubbard, vice-president of the Royal Society of British Artists, wrote to *The Times* asking why the keepers of the Tate Gallery preferred to shop with dealers rather than with the 'Royal or diplomad' societies. He received a predictable riposte from Sidney Pavière, the painter-curator of Preston Art Gallery, who considered the societies 'so doddering' that they would not admit younger, progressive artists. This view was essentially upheld by Jan Gordon writing the 'London Commentary' in *The Studio*. Looking at the current shows of 'imaginative' art at the Leicester, Redfern and Lefevre galleries one could only conclude that art at this point was still attempting to free itself from the 'boa constrictor of realism' and, 'now, to the dismay of the art master, the student is turning surrealistic before he has learned to draw'.[87]

A month or two later, Herbert Read, yet again, waded into the argument, defending modern art in all its manifestations against the narrowly national art favoured by the Nazis and the 'collaborationists'. History, he declared, will 'take as *representative,* not the tame and conformist products of the academies, but post-impressionism, cubism, constructivism and surrealism'.[88] The problem for the painter lay in Read's unselective catholicity. Buying into one body of precedent meant rejecting others. History included the products of the academies and, in little over a generation, with the revival of interest in the High Victorians, it began to be argued that they were in fact more 'representative'. Back in 1942, it appeared that the break with the past came not so much with Cézanne as with Cubism and abstraction, and the challenge facing Ben Nicholson and the late 1930s Constructivists lay in moving forward from there. At the same time the club was assimilating those painters who, having engaged European modernism, had returned to its roots via Euston Road. These artists wanted to find a different way, but faced entrapment in what could be the 'conformist' academicism to which Read alluded.

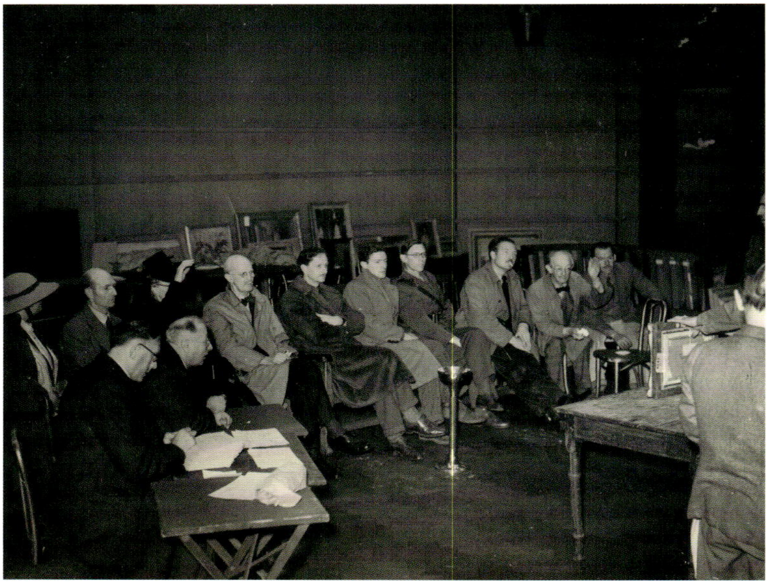

Fig. 149 The selecting jury of the New English Art Club, 1944. Photograph. Unknown photographer NEAC Archive

The dangers in this thesis only became apparent in 1944, when the Airborne Forces' charity exhibition was staged at Wildenstein's in Bond Street. It set out to demonstrate that 'the tradition of landscape painting', having moved to France after Constable, remained there with the Impressionists and Post-Impressionists, and then 'it returned to England with the New English Art Club and has since remained here'. Piper vigorously challenged this familiar line of argument on behalf of those who had not dropped out of European modernism after Gauguin, Cézanne and Seurat.[89] The rich fusion of Surrealism with the English landscape had already produced a significant group of 'neo-romantic' painters, who, while not much in evidence in either the club or the London Group, produced some of the best work for the War Artists' Advisory Committee. By implication, the timid products of the ex-Euston Road students now gravitating towards the club had little to offer.

In the winter of 1944 the Royal Academy revealed that it had invited the club (see fig. 149), the Royal Institute of Painters in Oil Colours, the London Group and three other societies to stage their forthcoming annual shows in its galleries, reacting at one level to Hubbard's attack on the young mandarins of the Council for the Encouragement of Music and the Arts (CEMA) and the Tate Gallery, and recognising that many younger members were already summer show regulars at Burlington House. It would have been difficult for the club to take up such an invitation while Steer and Tonks were alive. Comparisons could now be made and, while the institute contained craftsmen regarded as 'slick', and the London Group was 'adventurous' but slightly chaotic, the club displayed a 'patient but spinsterish integrity'.[90] 'Integrity' in post-war Britain was to become a byword for reactionary realism.

NOTES

1 'The New English', *The Times*, 11 November 1932, p. 12.
2 Professor Fred Brown, 'Recollections', *Artwork*, vol. 6, no. 23, autumn 1930, pp. 144–160, 249–79; Henry Tonks, 'Notes from Wander Years', *Artwork*, vol. 15, winter 1929, pp 213–35.
3 Our London Art Critic, 'The New English Art Club – Best Show for Several Years – Slade School Influence', *The Scotsman*, 12 November 1930.
4 See *The Studio*, vol. 104, 1935, p. 90; Arts Council, *Barnett Freedman, Memorial Exhibition*, exh. cat., Arts Council, London, 1958, nos 26, 39 and 52.
5 Robert Graves and Alan Hodge, *The Long Weekend: A Social History of Great Britain*, Faber and Faber, London, 1941, pp. 265–80.
6 'The National Society', *The Times*, 11 February 1932, p. 8.
7 Frank Rutter, 'New English Art Club – Steer's Magic – Best Painting of 1933', *The Sunday Times*, 22 October 1933.
8 Spectator, 'Art Exhibitions of the Year', *Art Review – A Survey of British Art in all its Branches – During the Year 1934*, The Artist Publishing Company, London, 1934, pp. 19–20.
9 'The New English', *The Times*, 11 November 1932, p. 12.
10 The term 'experimentalism' had been coined by the aged critic and sometime NEAC exhibitor, Alfred Lys Baldry in *Contemporary Figure Painting*, Studio Publications, London, 1925, to cover all modernist figure painting and give the implication that its excesses were no more than experiments.
11 Ardizzone showed from 1927 to 1928; Fitton from 1930 to 1934; and Horton from 1926 to 1950. Misha Black, Pearl Binder and Clifford Rowe, who were not club exhibitors, led in the formation of the AIA. For further reference, see *AIA: The Story of the Artists International Association*, Lynda Morris and Robert Radford (eds), exh. cat., Museum of Modern Art, Oxford, 1983.
12 Stephen Spender, 'Poetry and Revolution', *New Country*, March 1933, quoted in *The Thirties and After: Poetry, Politics, People, 1933–1975*, Fontana, London, 1978, p. 48.
13 Ibid. Spender arrives at extreme conclusions that were widely shared, stating that 'the artist today feels himself totally submerged by bourgeois tradition, he feels that nothing he can write could possibly appeal to a proletarian audience, and therefore he finds himself becoming simply the bourgeois artist in revolt, in short, the individualist.... For these reasons he is tempted to feel that the artist should go into active politics now as the revolution has no need for art' (pp. 50–1).
14 *AIA: The Story of the Artists International Association*, Lynda Morris and Robert Radford (eds), exh. cat., Museum of Modern Art, Oxford, 1983, pp. 13–14.
15 *Percy Horton, 1897–1970: Artist and Absolutist*, Janet Barnes, exh. cat., Sheffield City Art Galleries, 1982, p. 18.
16 *The Postman* may well relate to *The London Postman*, shown in the first AIA exhibition, where it was regarded by the recently founded *Left Review* as 'honest and skilful'. See *AIA: The Story of the Artists International Association*, Lynda Morris and Robert Radford (eds), exh. cat., Museum of Modern Art, Oxford, 1983, p. 14.
17 Nash had ceased regular exhibiting with the club in the spring of 1927, although he returned for the 1935 exhibition and was included in the Paris and Canadian shows.
18 Within Nash's seven, for instance, John Bigge was painting biomorphic abstractions, Edward Burra was producing Neue Sachlichkeit-inspired watercolours, Nicholson, Paris-derived abstraction, while John Armstrong and Tristram Hillier were regarded as English Surrealists. In addition to Nash and Wadsworth, the group included Barbara Hepworth, Henry Moore, Wells Coats and Colin Lucas. Cooper acted as its secretary. Mayor was keen to promote Read's *Art Now*, published by Faber and Faber in October 1933, which relied upon many of the Unit One artists. In 1933, Mayor showed the work of Georges Braque, Fernand Léger and Max Ernst. Nash had attempted a similar configuration at Tooth's two years earlier.
19 Anon., 'Art Exhibition – The New English', *The Times*, 20 October 1933, p. 10.
20 Alfred Thornton NEAC, 'Unity in Painting', *The Artist*, vol. 6, nos 1–3, September–November 1933, pp. 13–14, 46–7 and 79–80.
21 Thornton refers to R. G. Collingwood, *Outlines of a Philosophy of Art*, Clarendon Press, Oxford, 1924, a volume later rewritten as *Principles of Art*, Clarendon Press, Oxford, 1938 (rev. ed., Oxford University Press, Oxford, 1978).
22 Unjustly neglected, Thornton, an intellectual, continued to publish with *The Artist*, demonstrating eclectic tastes. His articles in the following spring on 'Drawing in Black and White', for instance, illustrated works by Picasso and Ben Nicholson (vol. 7, no. 1, March 1934, pp. 13–14; vol. 7, no. 2, April 1934, pp. 47–8). Material related to his term of office, including letters from Muirhead Bone, Charles Cundall and others is contained in the club archive. For a brief survey of Thornton's career, see 'Artists of Note: No. 15, Alfred Thornton NEAC', *The Artist*, vol. 11, no. 3, May 1936, pp. 90–3.
23 Andrew Causey, 'English Art and "The National Character" 1933–4', in David Peters Corbett, Ysanne Holt and Fiona Russell (eds), *The Geographies of Englishness: Landscape and the National Past, 1880–1940*, Yale University Press, London and New Haven, 2002, pp. 275–302. Causey's notes 1–4 give a thorough survey of the contemporary literature. For Baldwin, Englishness and the club, see Chapter 5. For a general account of British ambivalence on the question of industrialisation, see Martin J. Weiner, *English Culture and the Decline of the Industrial Spirit 1850–1980*, Cambridge University Press, Cambridge, 1981 (rev. ed., Penguin, Harmondsworth, 1985).
24 Both Coldstream and Moynihan had recently become fathers and would take their infants to the park together. On these occasions the idea of the Zwemmer show was formed. Despite Coldstream's diffidence, the works in the show were regarded as more anarchic than those in Unit One. For further reference, see Bruce Laughton, *The Euston Road School: A Study in Objective Painting*, Scolar Press, London, 1986, pp. 95–106; see also Bruce Laughton, *William Coldstream*, Yale University Press, London and New Haven, 2004, p. 28. For Moynihan, see *Rodrigo Moynihan, A Retrospective Exhibition*, exh. cat., Lawrence Gowing, Royal Academy of Arts, London, 1978, p. 8.
25 Newsreel interviews with the 'Objective Abstraction' painters were set to the tune of Laurel and Hardy.
26 By 1933 artists such as William S. Causer, R. O. Dunlop, Vincent Lines, L. S. Lowry, Patricia Ramsay and Rupert Shephard had begun to exhibit at the club.
27 Klinghoffer's Chantrey purchase, *The Old Troubadour* (1926), portrayed an old Savoyard, who serenaded the artist as she painted him in the autumn of 1926. For further reference, see J. B. Manson, 'Clara Klinghoffer', *The Studio*, vol. 94, 1927, p. 413; see also Ronald Alley, Dennis Farr and Martin Butlin, *Modern British Paintings, Drawings and Sculptures*, vol. 1, Oldbourne Press, London, 1964, p. 361.
28 Anon., 'Art Exhibitions – The New English Art Club', *The Times*, 17 October 1934, p. 12.
29 Ibid. Steer, Holmes, White, Schwabe and Maresco Pearce fell into this category, 'reminding one', according to *The Times*, 'of the man who gave up smoking because it was such a feminine habit'.
30 Ibid.
31 In 1932, for instance, sales accounted for £675 3s. 6d., while two years later they dropped to £323 9s. 6d. (Executive Minutes, 13 December

1934). In the early 1930s the additional costs of advertising on 'Tube Railways' was more than covered by increased sales and admissions – to some extent a tribute to the efficient and experienced secretarial support the club obtained in C. R. Chisman, the former secretary of Sir John Lavery. The club also benefited under the terms of a Deed of Trust, dedicating its surplus to the promotion of fine art, and thus avoiding Corporation Tax (AGM Minutes, 4 December 1931 and 16 June 1933).

32 Alfred Thornton, *Fifty Years of the New English Art Club*, Curwen Press, London, 1935; 14 pages with two appendices. This account, produced in a matter of weeks, needs to be read in conjunction with Thornton's *Diary* of 1938.

33 Ibid, 'A youthful septuagenarian, an ancient of our earlier days, gave his President trouble not many months ago, shortly after an *enfant terrible* of undoubted genius, who made his fame when a member of the Club, had added to the administrative difficulties of Mr Lamb'. Lamb was the secretary of the Royal Academy, and the two club members were Sickert and Spencer respectively.

34 Anon., 'Redfern Gallery – Oil Paintings and Wash Drawings', *The Times*, 21 April 1939, p. 29.

35 Anon., 'The New English Art Club', *The Times*, 21 October 1935, p. 15.

36 *The Times*, 23 October 1935, p. 18, illustrated works by John, Holmes, Pearce, Lilian Lancaster and Juan Stoll from the current exhibition.

37 See *Stanley Spencer*, Richard Carline, Andrew Causey and Keith Bell, exh. cat., Royal Academy of Arts, London, 1980, pp. 133–4; *Stanley Spencer*, Timothy Hyman and Patrick Wright (eds), Tate Britain, London, 2001, p. 183. Spencer exhibited *By the River* (University College, London), alongside *The Lovers*.

38 Pierre Jeannerat, 'Spencer's "Lovers" in London Exhibition – Brilliant Women Artists', 24 October 1935 (unidentified press cutting).

39 *The Sunday Times*, 5 May 1935, quoted in Anna Gruetzner Robins, *Walter Sickert: The Complete Writings on Art*, Oxford University Press, Oxford, 2000, pp. 676–7. Sickert also exhibited *The Divine Peggy* (*c.* 1930), a more recent painting lent by Sylvia Gosse. He had been represented with seven works at the 1925 retrospective, all of which came from private collections. Of the older generation, Clausen also returned to the club for its jubilee show, not for the same reasons, with a portrait of one of its distinguished early members, *The Late Mark Fisher RA.*, and a more recent *Still-Life*, see Anon., 'New English Art Club – Jubilee Show', *The Times*, 24 October 1935. Marsh was in many respects an ideal New English collector, describing himself as a 'consistent and brazen upholder of "representational" art'; see Edward Marsh, 'Patronage in Art Today' in R. S. Lambert, *Art in England*, Penguin, Harmondsworth, 1938, p. 81. See also Harold Nicholson, Introduction in *Paintings and Drawings from the Sir Edward Marsh Collection*, exh. cat., Arts Council, London, 1953.

40 Eric Newton, 'The New English Celebrates its Jubilee' in R. S. Lambert, *Art in England*, Penguin, Harmondsworth, 1938, pp. 54–8.

41 Spectator, 'Art Exhibitions of the Year', *Art Review – A Survey of British Art in all its Branches – during the year 1935*, The Artist Publishing Company, London, 1935, p. 22. The years from 1933 to 1939 saw ferment in the art world. See Andrew Causey, 'English Art and "The National Character" 1933–4', in David Peters Corbett, Ysanne Holt and Fiona Russell (eds), *The Geographies of Englishness: Landscape and the National Past, 1880–1940*, Yale University Press, London and New Haven, 2002 (note 23); *Art in One Year: 1935*, Richard Morphet, exh. cat., Tate Gallery, London, 1977; Charles Harrison, 'England's Climate' in Brian Allen (ed.), *Towards a Modern Art World, Studies in British Art 1*, Yale University Press, London and New Haven, 1995, pp. 207–25. For a general survey of the period, see William Feaver, 'Art at the Time' in A. J. P. Taylor and Ian Jeffrey introductions in *The Thirties*, exh. cat., Hayward Gallery, London, 1979.

42 J. B. Manson, *Hours in the Tate Gallery*, Duckworth, London, 1926, p. 120; see also *National Gallery, Millbank: Illustrated Guide, British School*, Robert Maclehose & Co at the University Press, Glasgow, 1925, pp. 100–20.

43 *The Times*, 15 October 1938, p. 10. See also W. S. Meadmore, *Lucien Pissarro*, Alfred A. Knopf, New York, 1962, p. 132. Southampton followed suit with its new gallery in 1939, see *The Times*, 27 April 1939, p. 14.

44 Spectator, 'Art Exhibitions of the Year', *Art Review – A Survey of British Art in all its Branches – during the year 1935*, The Artist Publishing Company, London, 1935, p. 22.

45 William Feaver: 'Art at the Time' in A. J. P. Taylor and Ian Jeffrey introductions in *The Thirties*, exh. cat., Hayward Gallery, London, 1979, pp. 32–3.

46 For Blunt, see Miranda Carter, *Anthony Blunt: His Lives*, Macmillan, London, 2001, pp. 205–8 and 221–5; see also Bruce Laughton, *William Coldstream*, Yale University Press, London and New Haven, 2004, pp. 55–60.

47 Not all activity was politically motivated. Chelsea remained the centre of London's 'Bohemia' and parties were frequently held in prominent studios. One favourite was Whistler's former studio in Tite Street, now occupied by Colin Gill, where in soirées one might find Mrs Ethelbert White performing flamenco songs to the strains of her husband's guitar. See *Picture Post*, no. 5, 1938, pp. 29–33.

48 Anon., 'The New English Art Club – Eighty-Seventh Show', *The Times*, 22 October 1936, p. 14.

49 Thornton, in his report to the club (AGM Minutes, 19 October 1937), paid tribute to Tonks's 'fine attitude towards painting' which 'he encouraged in his pupils', and to his humour expressed in a 'fine type of caricature'. Holmes, who had been working on behalf of the club until two weeks before his death, was a 'good artist' and 'a man of resource in unexpected difficulties'.

50 Anon., 'The Status of Art – The New English Exhibition', *The Times*, 21 October 1937, p. 12.

51 Ibid. 'It is of course, partly an accident of high key, but *Moss Roses and White Campanulas at Burwash*, by Miss Winifred Nicholson, has the oddest effect on this wall. So, across the clink of teacups and the muffled conversation of cultivated but rather dim people in a chintzy interior, you may meet the startled eyes of a girl who, whether at something said or something suddenly remembered, has caught a momentary glimpse of reality'. For Nicholson, see Alexander Watt, 'Artists of Note, no. 31: Winifred Nicholson', *The Artist*, vol. 14, no. 1, September 1937, pp. 26–9.

52 *Percy Horton, 1897–1970: Artist and Absolutist*, Janet Barnes, exh. cat., Sheffield City Art Galleries, 1982, p. 19. See also Bruce Laughton, *The Euston Road School: A Study in Objective Painting*, Scolar Press, London, 1986, p. 188. The Wildenstein exhibition was entitled 'A Cross-section of English Painting'.

53 T. W. Earp Introduction in Geoffrey Holme (ed.), *Flower and Still-Life Painting*, Studio, London, 1928, p. 19. Earp continues, 'the size of the average modern dwelling also makes the admission of the large picture impossible, and the still-life or flower-piece is a genre particularly appropriate to a small canvas'. The genre permitted the opportunity 'of investigating the various new problems opened up by modern painting'.

54 See *The Flower Show: An Exhibition on the Theme of Flowers in Twentieth Century British Art*, Norbert Lynton, exh. cat., Stoke-on-Trent City Art Gallery and Museum, 1986, for an exhibition that focused upon painting of the moment.

55 Dunlop, one of the most popular and saleable artists of the 1930s, exhibited every year with the club from 1930 to 1960. For his work at this period, see Herbert B. Grimsditch, 'Artists of Note, No. 22: R.O. Dunlop', *The Artist*, vol. 12, no. 4, December 1936, pp. 118–121. A practical theorist, he wrote books on still-life (1938) and landscape painting (1954), based upon articles first published in *The Artist*. For White at this time, see 'Famous Artists: No. 35, Ethelbert White, *The Artist*, vol. 8, no. 3, November 1934, pp. 88–9.

56 Bernard Dunstan, *The Paintings of Bernard Dunstan*, David and Charles, Newton Abbot, 1993, p. 17, notes that this generation of landscapists was 'admirable for its integrity and lack of pretension or competitiveness. They needed little in the way of worldly possessions; they lived simply; and they sold their pictures to a circle of faithful collectors'.

57 In 1938, the Louvre was staging a survey of British painting, to which this exhibition was a contemporary complement.

58 They were: John, *Cinerarias*, Rothenstein, *John and Elizabeth Rothenstein*, Steer, *The Parish Church at St Mary Magdalene, Bridgenorth*, Thornton, *The Thaw* and Paul Nash, *The Skeleton*.

59 *Beaux-Arts*, 1 July 1938, noted: 'J'ai trouvé à son exposition un tableau de Wadsworth qui passe en Grande-Bretagne pour un surréaliste, mais qui n'est qu'un très bel artisan du pinceau' ('At its exhibition I found a picture by Wadsworth who passes for a Surrealist in Great Britain, but who is really only a nice technician with a brush.')

60 MacColl Papers, C112 (20 March 1938), Glasgow University Library Special Collections.

61 Interim Report distributed in lieu of an AGM, October 1939.

62 The 'Recording Britain', administered by Kenneth Clark, Percy Jowett and Russell Flint, continued into the war and involved 97 artists who produced over 1,500 works, from which four volumes of reproductions were published by Oxford University Press between 1946 and 1949.

63 Anon., 'The New English – Women's Work in Oils', *The Times*, 25 October 1939, p. 6.

64 Notice, 28 October 1940. The club's administration was temporarily removed to the Royal Academy.

65 *The Artist as Evacuee: The Royal College of Art in the Lake District, 1940–1945*, Robert Woof, exh. cat., The Wordsworth Trust, Grasmere, 1987

66 Stephen Spender, *The Thirties and After: Poetry, Politics, People, 1933–1975*, Fontana, London, 1978, p. 91.

67 Notice, June 1942.

68 Bernard Denvir, 'Contemporary British Landscape Painting', in John Singer (ed.), *The Holiday Book*, William MacLellan, Glasgow, 1946, p. 69.

69 For Devas, see Anne Goodchild, *Anthony Devas 1911–1958*, Sheffield City Art Galleries, 1991, illustrating the portrait of Tom Carr by Devas. Carr was briefly a member of the club, exhibiting from 1943 to 1949. For further reference, see T. P. Flanagan Introduction in *Tom Carr: A Retrospective*, exh. cat., Ulster Museum, Belfast, and Douglas Hyde Gallery, Trinity College, Dublin, 1983.

70 R. O. Dunlop RA, *Landscape Painting: Ma Yüan to Picasso*, Seeley Service, London, 1954, p.159.

71 See, for instance, Robert Hewison, *Under Siege: Literary Life in London, 1939–1945*, Weidenfeld and Nicolson, London, 1977, pp. 141–54; see also, Colin Coote Introduction in *British Artists and the Second World War*, exh. cat., The Minories, Colchester; Royal Albert Memorial Museum, Exeter; Towner Art Gallery and Museum, Eastbourne; City Museum and Art Gallery; Plymouth, Art Gallery, Stafford; Art Gallery and Museum, Cheltenham; Keighley Art Gallery and Museum; Museum and Art Gallery, King's Lynn, Arts Council Gallery, Cambridge; Huddersfield Art Gallery, 1965; *War Artists*, exh. cat., Tyne and Wear Museums, n.d. [*c*. 1985].

72 *The New English Art Club, Catalogue of the Ninety-Third Exhibition, October 23rd to November 14th, 1942*, 1942, p. 7. Ironside and John Rothenstein organised a Steer memorial exhibition in the following year at the Tate Gallery, and a selection of works from this show was taken on tour by the Council for Encouragement of Music and the Arts.

73 Eric Newton, *In My View*, Longman's Green and Co., London, 1950, pp. 136–7.

74 Robin Ironside, *Wilson Steer*, Phaidon Press, London, 1943, p. 15.

75 John Rothenstein, appointed editor of the Phaidon series in which the *Steer* monograph was published, had suggested Ironside – 'a person who was remote from [Steer's] circle and inclined to be critical of the New English Art Club'. Steer had never heard of him, but accepted that he was 'the man for the job' on Rothenstein's recommendation; see John Rothenstein, 'Two Visits to Steer', *The Burlington Magazine*, vol. 85, 1944, pp. 203–5. This text is repeated in John Rothenstein, *Brave Day, Hideous Night*, Hamish Hamilton, London, 1967, pp. 101–4. For Rothenstein's edgy relationship with MacColl and Steer's friends and former pupils, see pp. 104–6. See also Dr John Rothenstein, 'Great British Masters – 22, Wilson Steer', *Picture Post*, no. 25, 1939, pp. 39–42. For the correspondence between Ironside and MacColl, see MacColl Papers, Glasgow University Library Special Collections, especially I13 (18 August 1943).

76 Douglas Cooper, 'The Problem of Wilson Steer: A Study in British Painting', *The Burlington Magazine*, vol. 84, 1944, pp. 66–71.

77 Collins Baker wrote to MacColl (see MacColl Papers, Glasgow University Library Special Collections, B50, 4 May 1944) that he could 'barely recall a sillier article but what puzzled me was its publication'.

78 'Letters – The Problem of Wilson Steer', *The Burlington Magazine*, vol. 84, 1944, pp. 128–9.

79 John Russell, *From Sickert to 1948, The Achievement of the Contemporary Art Society*, Lund Humphries, London, 1948, p. 93.

80 Bernard Denvir, 'Contemporary British Landscape Painting', in John Singer (ed.), *The Holiday Book*, William MacLellan, Glasgow, 1946, p. 68. Steer's work remained in currency, see, for instance, The Editor, 'Wilson Steer, OM, Paints a Watercolour', *The Artist*, vol. 19, April 1940, pp. 35–6. His effect upon older painters such as Connard, Russell and Vernon Wethered remained obvious at the time of his death. Denvir praises Bernard Dunstan for his attempts 'to restate' this tradition 'in a more contemporary idiom'.

81 Sickert's 'English Echoes' were a series of paintings based on the work of the Victorian illustrators, 'Georgie Bowers', Alfred Bryan, Adelaide Claxton, John Gilbert, Kenney Meadows and Francesco Sargent. They were first exhibited at the Leicester Galleries in May 1931.

82 Paul Ayshford Methuen had been a pupil of Sickert in 1927. In 1941 he wrote the brief introduction to the catalogue of Sickert's retrospective at the National Gallery, London.

83 Stephen Bone, 'Britain as seen by the Artists' in John Pennington Introduction in *The British Heritage: The People, their Crafts and Achievements as Recorded in their Buildings and on the Face of the Countryside*, Odhams Press, London, 1948, pp. 154–79.

84 Ibid., p. 179. Bone was writing at the same time as the publication of *Recording Britain*.

85 Anon., 'The New English Art Club', *The Times*, 25 October 1940, p. 6.

86 Edward Bishop, Mary K. Harrison, Charles Mahoney, William Narraway and Walter Woodington, all solid figurative painters, became New English regulars in these years.

87 Jan Gordon, 'London Commentary', *The Studio*, vol. 124, 1942, pp. 26–8. Gordon wrote, 'today ... the "diplomad" societies are leaning strongly backwards, while on the whole the *effective* buying elements in Great Britain, stimulated by the example of the Contemporary Art Society, are leaning forwards ... the Royal Societies as a whole are out of touch with this advancing element of the public ... the "diploma" is not of real value to the young artist (except in the teaching profession)'.

88 Herbert Read, 'Modern Art and French Decadence', *The Studio*, vol. 124, 1942, pp. 188.

89 Anon., 'From a Painter's Notebook – 1' in John Lehmann (ed.), *Penguin New Writing*, no. 24, Penguin, Harmondsworth, 1945, p. 169.

90 Eric Newton, *In My View*, Longman's Green and Co., London, 1950, p. 163. Newton had earlier commented upon the eclecticism of the London Group (p. 94). It was clear to Dennis Farr and Alan Bowness in 1964 that, true to its Camden Town roots, the London Group had difficulty with Surrealism and Neo-Romanticism.

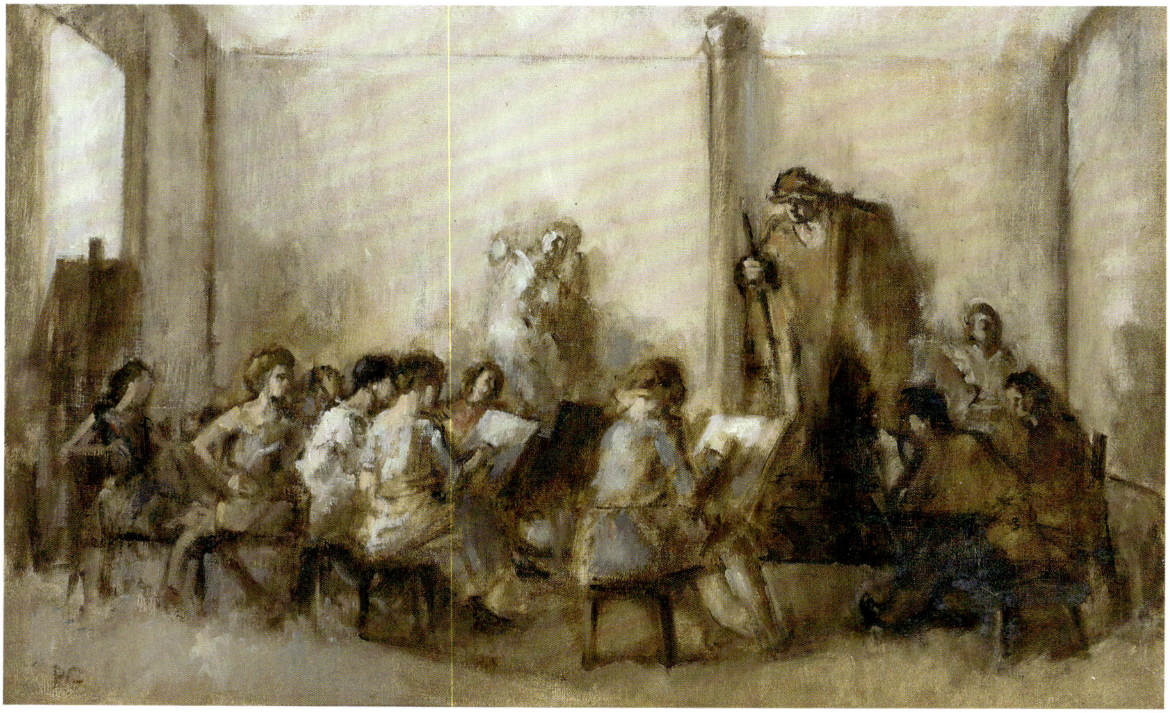

Fig. 150 Peter Greenham
The Art School, 1948
Oil on canvas, 40.6 x 61 cm
Private collection

CHAPTER 7 **'New Look' New English** 1946–1965

Britain emerged from the war to Herbert Morrison's plan for the rebuilding of London, R. A. Butler's education reforms and the inauguration of the Welfare State. The war spirit that had mystically transformed class struggle into class cohesion would take tangible form under a Labour administration, and the ideals envisioned in the Beveridge Report of 1942 could now be implemented. While suspicion of 'big business' and the pervasiveness of a 'kitsch' culture in formulaic Hollywood movies and imported popular forms of entertainment persisted, writers such as Herbert Read and Alex Comfort called for a more measured sense of social responsibility that accorded freedom of expression to the artist.[1] Socialist Realism, from which Read had always instinctively recoiled, was merely the illustration of an idea. As if to prove the possibility of a new contract between artist and society, at the end of 1945 the Victoria and Albert Museum took the important step of initiating a touring exhibition of the work of Picasso and Matisse. John Rothenstein, who became director of the Tate Gallery after Manson's departure, besotted by Picasso, was one of his first visitors after the war and immediately looked for ways to bring his work into the gallery's permanent collection.[2] Some young artists such as Robert Colquhoun and Robert MacBride were, despite the isolation of the war, deeply influenced and the adventurous few, like William Gear, took the opportunity to move to Montmartre and await the rebirth of modernism.

Peace brought young would-be artists in 'demob' suits to the doors of the Slade and the other London art schools. In the grey world of British art-school politics, Euston Road had captured the key constituencies – the Slade and Camberwell adopted Coldstream's and William Townsend's rigorous approach to drawing, while Moynihan and Kenneth Rowntree were appointed to the teaching staff of the Royal College of Art.[3] Burn at various times taught life classes part time at Camberwell and the Royal College, as well as undertaking his appointment as painting master at City and Guilds Art School in 1947, while Allan Gwynne-Jones and George Charlton continued at the Slade and Mahoney at the Royal College.[4] The dour, dusty seriousness of this world is well captured in Peter Greenham's *The Art School* (1948; fig. 150).[5] A new academicism was born, the effects of which are still evident in British painting today.[6] Prominent 1930s fellow-travellers Victor Pasmore and Kenneth Martin moved on, rejecting realism and embracing 'Constructionism', while immediate efforts were made by Robin Ironside and others to weave contemporary British 'Neo-Romantic' painting into a master modernist narrative.[7]

The club's place in the Academy undercroft was officially recognised, but this brought no favours. Its winter 1945 and spring 1946 exhibitions were, by special arrangement, held at Burlington House. A seminal survey carried out in part justification for the formation of the Arts Council declared the purpose of the New English as a recruiting ground 'for RA Associates'. The implication was that, if an academy exhibitor could also survive the rigours of the New English jury, he or she, after an apprentice period, was good enough to be elected associate of the Academy.[8]

The new Arts Council, not openly hostile to the club, nevertheless pursued its own separate agenda.[9] Thus, in post-war London, the club emerged to a world in which its very existence was relentlessly challenged. The attacks were levelled in a number of ways and they were often repeated year on year in the same newspaper columns. The hostile Eric Newton questioned the principles underpinning the kind of painting to which it was committed. Reviewing the winter 1946 show, and in the light of the Picasso/Matisse tour, he asked 'if the art of painting pictures consists in skillfully translating into paint a set of objects honestly and sensitively seen' – concluding that 'it is not a bad exhibition.... But of passion ... there is hardly a sign'. The clear message was always that 'honest seeing' and 'skilful translation' were not enough and that the 'rot' had set in with Impressionism.[10] A high level of competence was evident in New English shows, but competence was deep code for 'anti-modernist', 'reactionary' or even 'uninspired'. There was, of course, a double bind in this, as painters who took risks might be regarded as incompetent and end up being ridiculed or ignored. Carrying the heavy suitcase of European modernism, most art critics had by now accepted Fry's premise that British painting was 'a minor school'.[11] Criticism of club exhibitions, where it could be found, was not markedly different from that of the Academy and, as Newton pointed out on one later occasion, the club was five years younger than Picasso, and yet it behaved as if he did not exist.[12] For him, the era of annual Salons was over.

In any case, the pre-eminent annual Salon remained in Burlington House and it was obvious that 'the best note' within its summer exhibitions was that struck by the 'Post-New-English' – recently elected associates whose submissions were of 'extremely high quality'.[13] Such judgements were still possible because the Academy accepted a wide range of work, some of which could be regarded as a failed experiment. To underline its commitment to standards, the club became more exclusive and, in 1948, restricted the number of exhibits to those that could be hung 'on the line'. Since the late 1930s, the practice had always been to show two rows of pictures, those on the line and those below the line.[14] Judging from visitors' reactions this 'hyperselection' had little success, the show was not considered one of the best and the 'giant' was thought to be 'taking a doze'.[15] By contrast, the Royal Academy Summer Exhibition performed a 'social duty' – it was 'a necessity for dinner and cocktail conversations' – and its visitors spent most of their time in front of the pictures 'they hate most'.[16]

The noise of this rejection of abstraction, officially sanctioned by the Tate Gallery, boiled over in Alfred Munnings's speech at the Academy dinner of 1949, when he berated Picasso and those who had succumbed to modernism.[17] While older New English painters may have had some sympathy for Munnings's

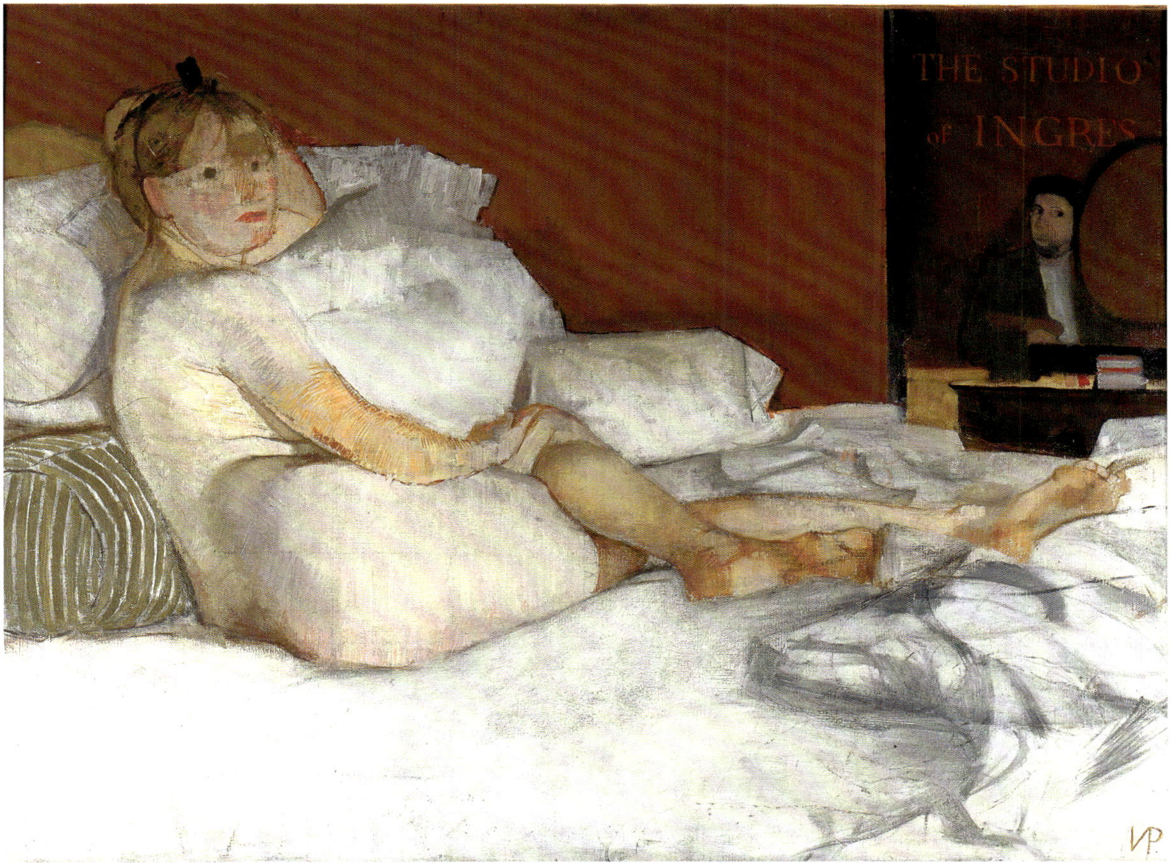

Fig. 151 Victor Pasmore
The Studio of Ingres, 1945–7
Oil on canvas, 76.5 x 101.5 cm
Private collection

view, agreeing that the museum and gallery Establishment was set against them, they kept a low profile and a quiet determination to support that which was self-evidently English. But what did this signify? Baldwin's Cotswold Arcadia would never come back in a socialist Britain that was investing heavily in low-cost concrete modernity. In the art politics of the period it meant agitating for better representation of artists' societies on the Arts Council's art panel and lobbying the Treasury for the provision of a new central London gallery for temporary exhibitions. Both tactics failed.[18]

In terms of new art, the unresolved position of English realism, undermined by Munnings's intemperance, had left some critics at the end of the war asking why Pasmore had not set up camp in the New English exhibitions. The reason became obvious after the completion of *The Studio of Ingres* (1945–7; fig. 151). The comparison between this work and Arthur Middleton Todd's *Model Drying Her Hair* (*c.* 1940; fig. 152) lay in the former's belief that the Euston Road painters had emerged from the impasses of modernism, rather than in a wholesale rejection of it. His work could not sit comfortably alongside that in the New English because its painters 'descend directly from the Impressionists'.[19] With

The Studio of Ingres, Pasmore reached his own 'abstract' turning point. There is nonetheless no disputing the immense influence his Hammersmith gardens canvases exerted upon future generations of New English adherents, and the comparison between his and White's garden and woodland paintings of the late 1940s is instructive. Those numerous students who collected the Penguin Modern Painters series could clearly see that from the soft greys of the London riverside crisp graphic structures were emerging.[20]

Of the other senior Euston Road figures, Coldstream became even more doggedly analytical in the observation of appearances – neglecting the sensuality of paint and submitting to the contingencies of the visual field by refusing to leave out things that happen to be there. Gowing at that moment also clung to Euston Road realism, reaffirming the 'strength of the insular position' that had begun with Constable, but recognising that 'the matter of painting is inarticulate and intuitive. In part at least it is immune from rationalisation'.[21] 'Matter' in this sense was material that goes into the making of a painting. Neither showed at the club, but their followers, students and colleagues did.

This underlining of individualism came at a time when leadership was required both in the art world and in the club. Rodney Burn, a supremely sensitive observer of the English scene, was elected honorary secretary in 1947 amid feverish debates about the role and purpose of the club.[22] A retiring and soft-spoken personality, he remained at the helm until 1963, bringing forward an interesting crop of new exhibitors. It was nevertheless obvious, but unstated, that one of the priorities for these young post-war painters was to secure a relationship with a reputable dealer. Bernard Dunstan recalls the legendary tolerance of the elderly Oliver Brown of the Leicester Galleries, when an art student would appear with a portfolio.[23] In such one to one encounters the judge and jury might be open to verbal persuasion. Dealers were keen to re-establish markets and mixed shows of the 'artists of fame and promise' type enabled them to do so. To help establish a foothold, a few outings at the club or the London Group might do some good, but when the work was laid out for Mr Brown, this was only a bargaining counter.

The solo exhibition – the one-person show – was the new objective and it was more important than sending work to the club or the Academy.[24] When they first appeared at the end of the nineteenth century, single-artist exhibitions were often a means of disposing of the mass of small pictures, studies and sketches that were carried out in preparation for a large Academy or club exhibit. By the 1930s this scenario had changed and dealers often had a say in what was submitted to a jury, in support of their market strategies, and the prices they could achieve.[25] In times of plenty, this could work to the advantage of the New English, and when strong personalities from the second generation of club members, such as Nevinson, Clause, Schwabe, Dodd, Bland and Walker were dying, it was necessary to find new talent.[26] Ringing changes sounded most clearly in 1948 when the club sustained its most serious loss in D. S. MacColl, an exhibitor since 1892 and the single most influential New English advocate in print.[27] In an elegant memorial address, Sir Eric MacLagan, recently retired Director of the Victoria and Albert Museum, praised his 'no small part' in the club's creation.[28]

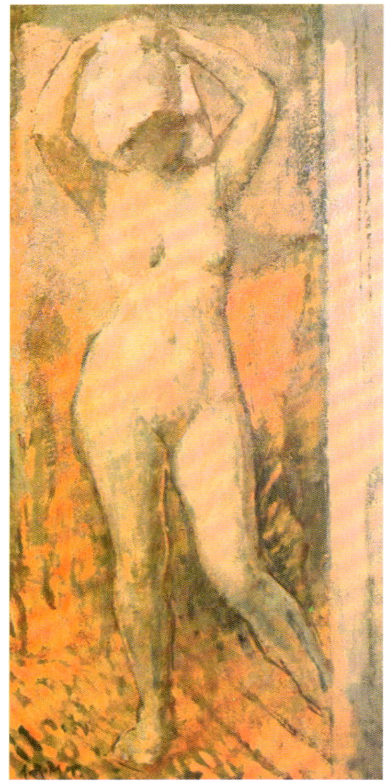

Fig. 152 Arthur Ralph Middleton Todd
Model Drying Her Hair, c. 1940
Oil on board, 50.8 x 24.7 cm
Private collection

However, with due respect to household gods, it was necessary to move on. In the late 1940s, Burn's jury was frequently damned for playing safe one moment and for taking risks the next. Some members lobbied hard for 'members-only' exhibitions; some believed that membership should confer the right to exhibit, as it did at the Royal Academy. How else could the loyalty of new members be assured, they argued? Private views were regarded as 'sedate affairs' and 'there were no drinks and certainly few sales'. Indeed, as Bernard Dunstan recalled, the younger painters did not expect to sell and 'the odd sale for 25 or 30 guineas from the New English was greeted with amazed pleasure, as a sort of gift from the gods'.[29]

In 1947 an attempt was made to inject new blood into the club by awarding exhibition space to ten London art schools, for student work.[30] On the face of it, given the senior positions many club regulars held in art schools, this seemed like a sensible suggestion. However, the Slade, formerly so loyal to the club, and its rival, the Royal Academy Schools, did not participate, raising legitimate objections on behalf of those students who had gone successfully through the normal jury process without being pre-selected by their tutors.[31] The integrity of the elected jury had always been one of the central tenets of the club and the defence of its role was paramount. The scheme was soon abandoned, but the need to nurture young talent remained one of the club's essential purposes and constant debating points.[32]

The more successful strategy was to continue taking the club to the regions. The unsold residue of the Canadian tour was finally returned in 1946 and the following year new selections from recent shows went on display at the City Art Gallery, Bristol, and the Ferens Art Gallery, Hull – a further selection being arranged for Sunderland Art Gallery in June 1949.[33] Thereafter club exhibitions were more regularly noticed in regional papers, if only to praise those local artists who had gained admission. Its side effect was to highlight the inadequacies of the London shows – pointing to the low profile of the Suffolk Street galleries and prompting a move to Royal Watercolour Society galleries at 195 Piccadilly, in the hope of boosting spring exhibitions by attracting Academy visitors on their way to or from the Tube.[34] The club was no longer opposed to the Academy, nor was it simply a way-stage for those who would go on to greater things, but it needed more recognition for the core values that lay with 'the more sensitive and scholarly painters of the time', such as White, Burn (see fig. 153), Todd, Lines, Lord Methuen and Anthony Devas.[35]

Fig. 153 Rodney Burn
Thames Road, Chiswick, *c.* 1963
Oil on canvas, 62.2 x 75.2 cm
Tullie House Museum & Art Gallery, Carlisle

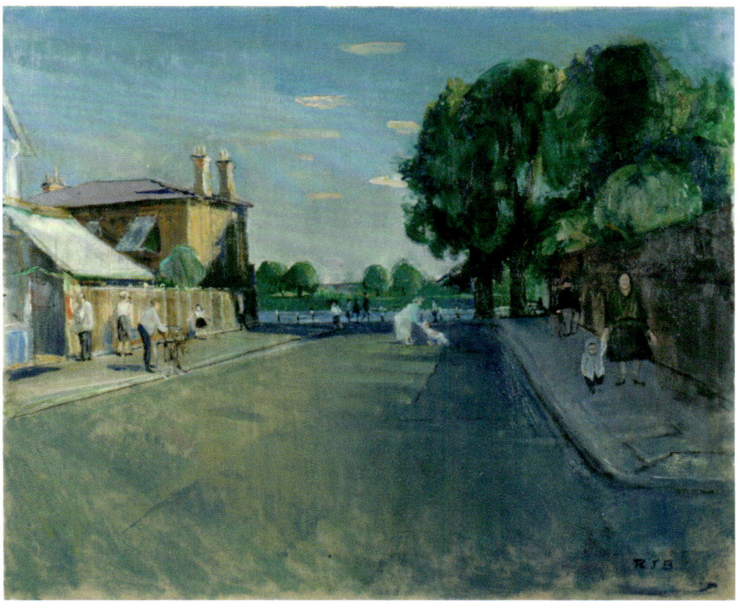

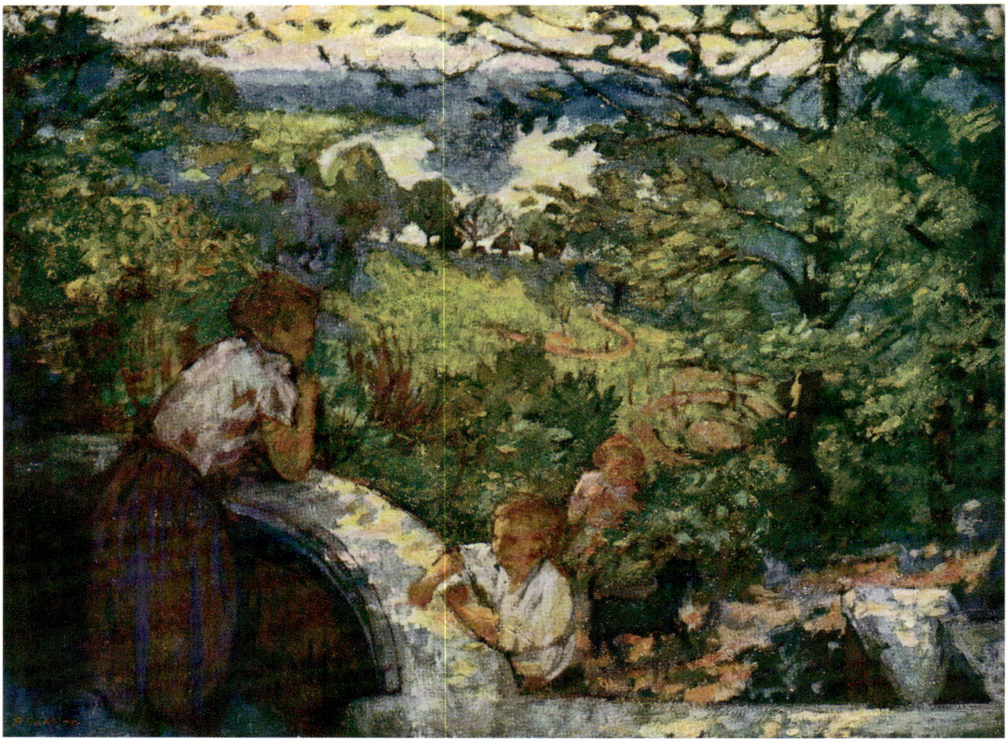

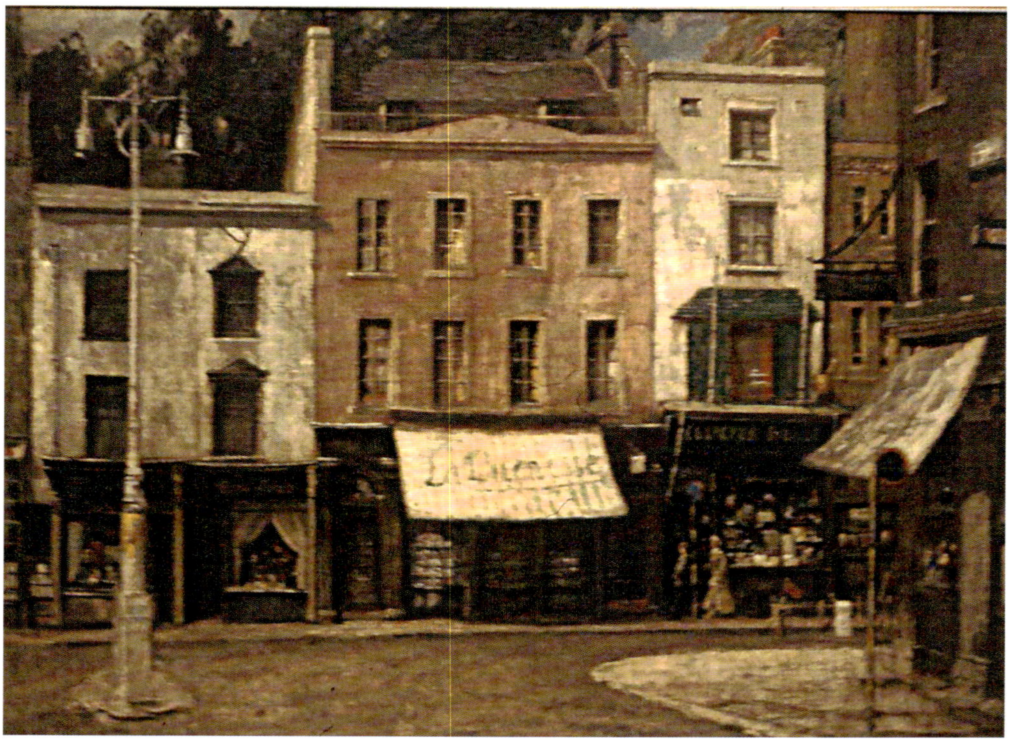

Opposite top
Fig. 154 Bernard Dunstan
Richmond Terrace, 1948
Oil on canvas, 81 x 61 cm
Private collection

Opposite bottom
Fig. 155 John Cole
Three Shops, Kensington, Church Street, 1945
Oil on canvas, 69.5 x 90.5 cm
Private collection

Breaking with the past and re-forming were issues that nevertheless dogged the club for the next twenty years. The words 'new' and 'English' were seen as contradictory – just as, in Whistler's day, the reactionary and avant-garde factions in the Royal Society of British Artists were regarded as 'British' and 'artists'. A parochial name was even more of a hindrance than ever. Newton's blanket condemnation of the post-war shows – he refused to single out specific works – had a more damaging accumulative effect in that the term 'New English' in time took on a pejorative meaning, and this made the task of attracting new talent increasingly difficult by the late 1950s. However, the club had not stagnated during the war and the work of such new exhibitors as Jean Clark, Bernard Dunstan, Harry Eccleston, Ann R. Le Bas, Robin Mackertich, Charles McCall, Mary Remington and Margaret Thomas began to achieve recognition.[36] In 1946, Dunstan's Oxford and Richmond canvases were particularly admired (see fig. 154). The critic of *The Scotsman* remarked that in the 'comfortable drowsiness' of a Richmond summer, 'Renoir must have been looking over his shoulder'.[37]

Yet, despite the efforts to extend its range, there was a preponderance of London-based canvases during the late 1940s, reflecting the scarcity of materials and the expense of transport systems. To one out-of-town critic there were so many depictions of the metropolis that he expected to encounter a painter on every corner and was surprised when he did not.[38] What London did these painters represent? It ranged from Robert Buhler's *Tow Path, Hammersmith* and Middleditch's *Tea Garden* (both 1948) to John Cole's Kensington and Mayfair shopfronts (fig. 155) to Hall's Pimlico interiors (fig. 157) to Margaret Thomas's Chelsea (fig. 156). There were café interiors, park scenes, side streets and thoroughfares.[39] Although Sickert's enjoinder to the London Impressionists

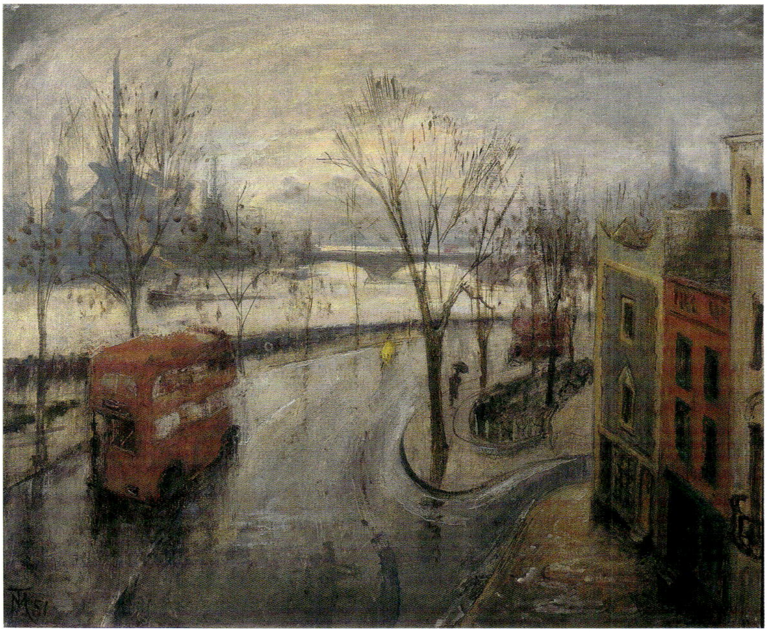

Right
Fig. 156 Margaret Thomas
Chelsea Embankment, 1951
Oil on canvas, 61 x 73.5 cm
Private collection

was part of the legacy, the cockney costers of his pre-First World War canvases had become the clichés of Ealing Cinema, and survived only in the paintings of bargees by Cosmo Clark.

A few London landscapes noted the devastated East End, the post-war reconstruction and the dour optimism of the Festival of Britain, and more than one reviewer commented upon the rebirth of Euston Road academicism in club exhibitions around 1951.[40] For Dunlop, its 'love of low tones' was ubiquitous.[41] There was a sobriety about New English London, but this did not stop its manifestations being regarded as 'companionable'.[42] Stephen Bone, for instance, took this tack, commenting upon the work of John Ward, which was given pride of place in the spring exhibition of 1952. Ward (see fig. 158) was exhibiting an ambitious portrait, bashfully entitled *Study*, and a large *Street Scene, Cheltenham*. The former contained the characteristic selective focus of Euston Road figure painting, and the street corner pub of the latter was regarded as a Cheltenham that visitors would stumble upon 'only by accident'. Yet, for all this, the young Ward through 'personal vision' had the capacity to 'transmute' the commonplace.

His work was accompanied by that of another up-and-coming sub-Euston Road painter, Elinor Bellingham-Smith (fig. 159), whose 'sensitive scumbled landscape' in *The Sandwich Road* (1952) was hailed as the appropriate New English compromise between the Impressionism of its youth and late 1930s realism. Bellingham-Smith had come to prominence recently, having been

Fig. 157 Edward Hall
Interior, Pimlico, 1967
Oil on canvas, 91.44 x 121.92 cm
Collection of the artist's family

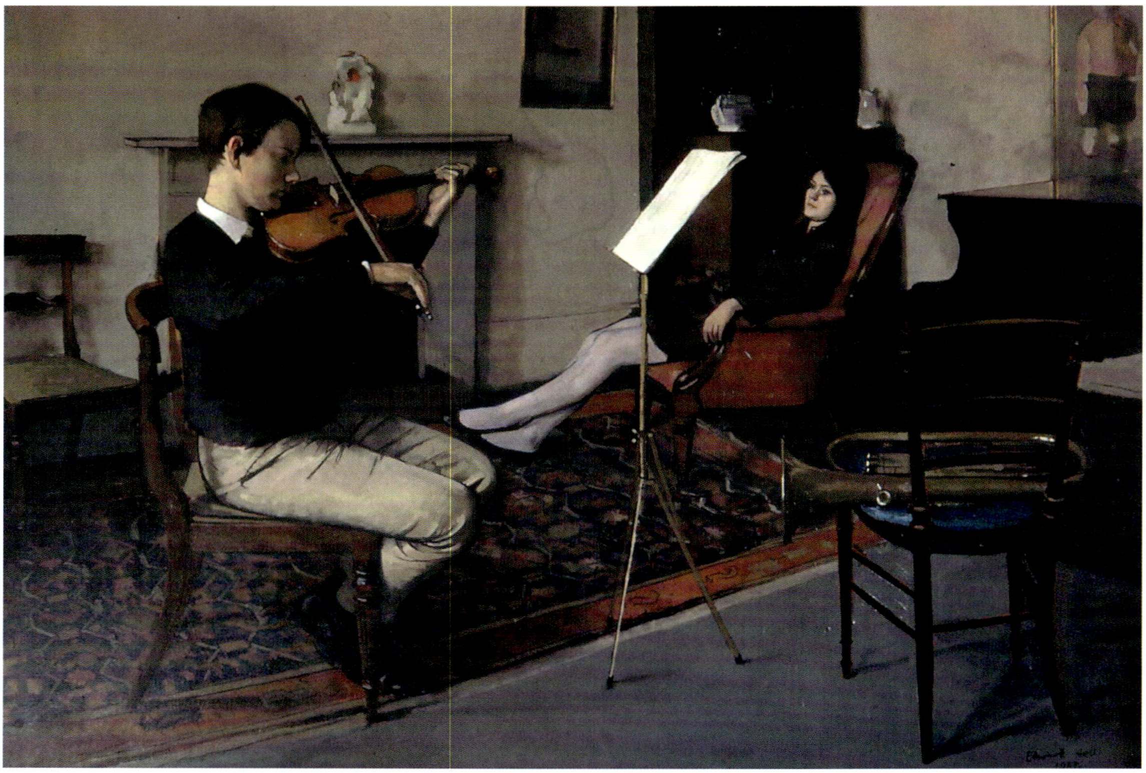

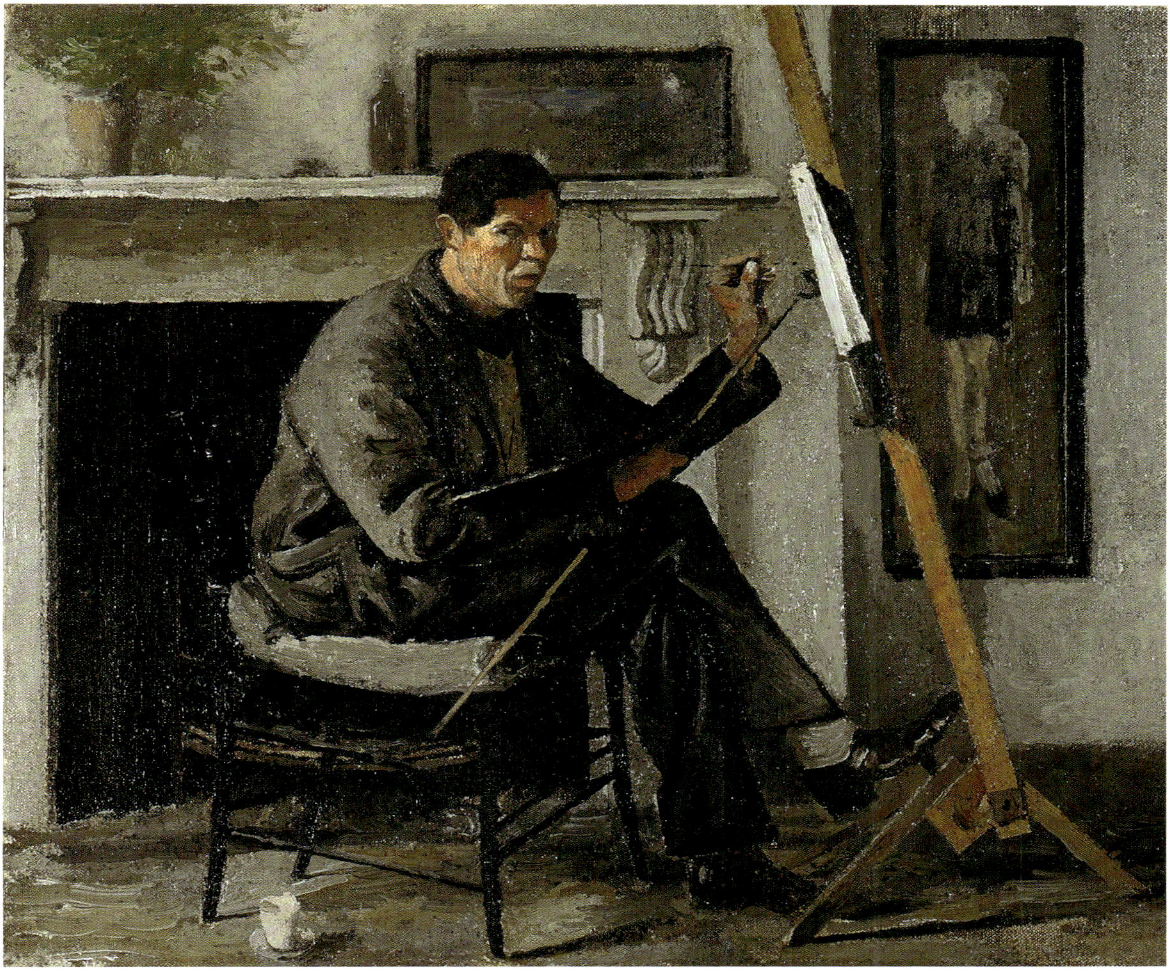

Fig. 158 John Ward
Self-portrait Seated at an Easel, 1947
Oil on canvas, 30 x 36 cm
The Royal Museum and Art Gallery, Canterbury

selected for '60 for '51', an Arts Council show of new works painted to order, to a standard size, as part of its Festival of Britain celebration.[43] Its main effort was, however, concentrated in two 'anthologies' of 'British Painting, 1925–1950', staged in collaboration with Manchester City Art Gallery.[44] While indicating the importance of former New English exhibitors, these shows also demonstrated that of the few internationally recognised British artists, not one was currently associated with the club.[45] This fact was essentially confirmed in two rival accounts of the last hundred years of British painting published to coincide with the Festival.[46]

Despite its continued allegiance to realistic representation, younger painters such as Bellingham-Smith and Charles Oakley (fig. 160) exhibited only once or twice at the club. For their work, John Bratby, Jack Smith, Derrick Greaves, Peter Coker, Peter De Francia and other emergent 'Kitchen Sink' painters sought a more expressive context for working-class Britain than the New English as a

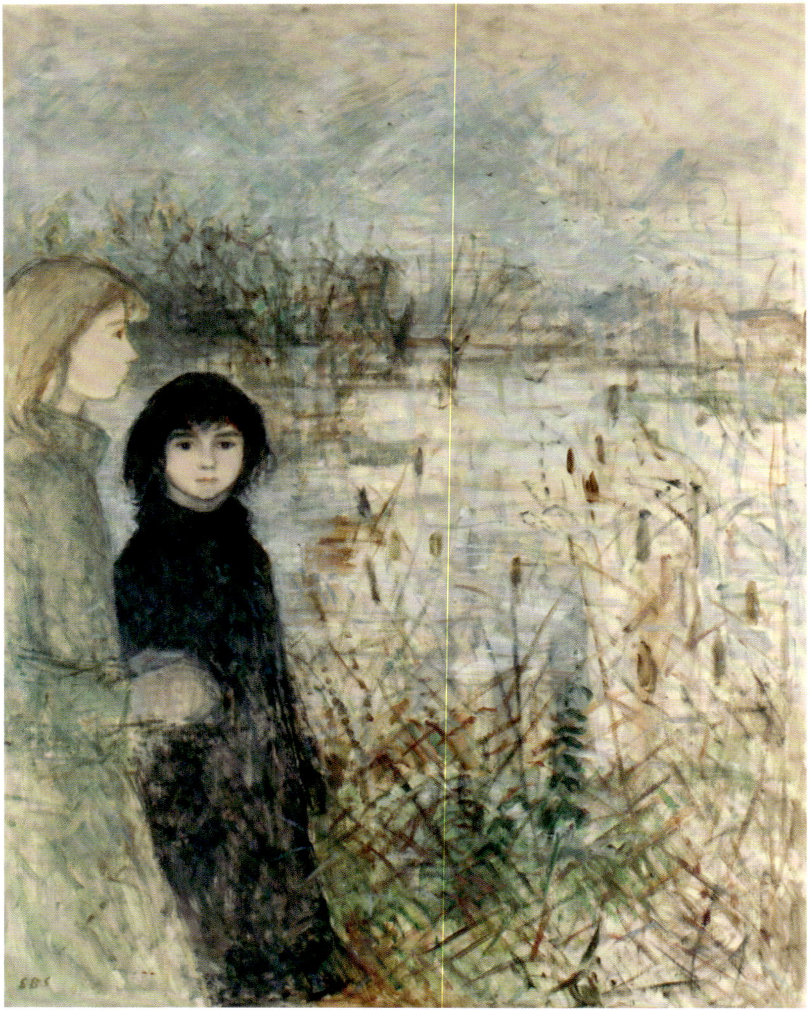

Fig. 159 Elinor Bellingham-Smith
Girls by the Water, *c.* 1951
Oil on canvas, 91.5 x 71 cm
Private collection

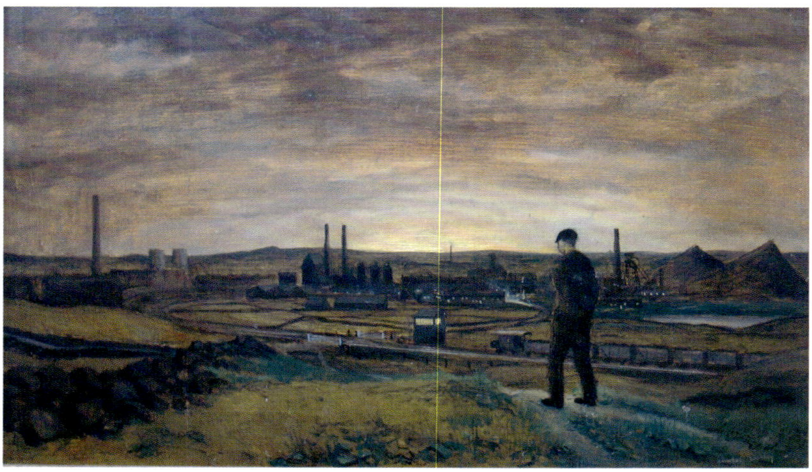

Fig. 160 Charles Oakley
Miner's Evening, 1951
Oil on board, 35 x 58.5 cm
Private collection

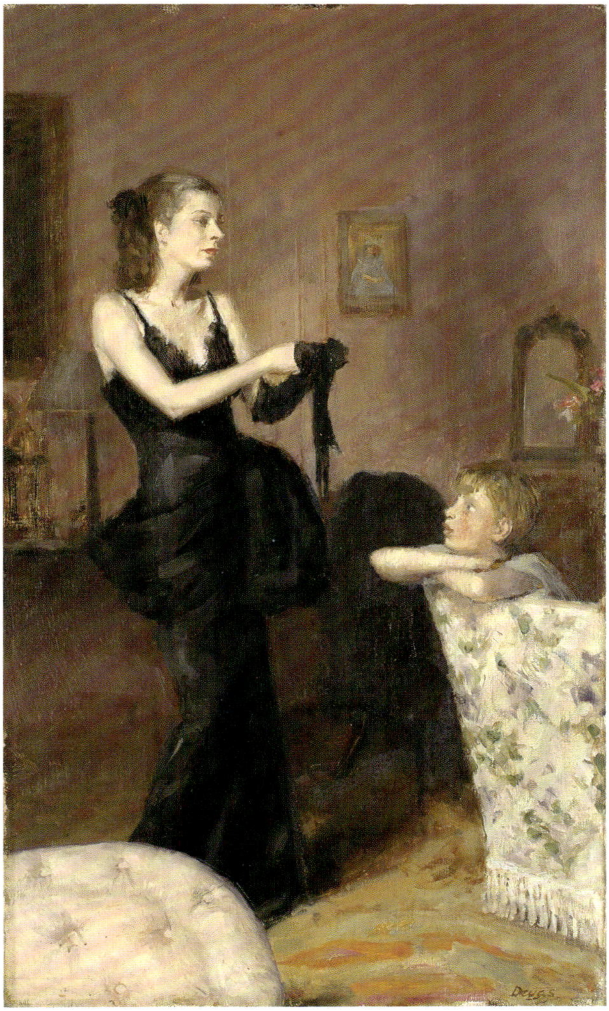

Fig. 161 Anthony Devas
Camilla Sykes and Mark, 1947
Oil on canvas, 56.5 x 51 cm
Bradford Museum and Art Gallery

whole could supply, and they found an outlet in John Berger's 'Looking Forward' exhibitions, which began in 1952 at the Whitechapel Art Gallery, London.[47] The club, to all intents and purposes the natural home for their work, was seen to be carrying too much baggage and in the early 1950s this fault was brutally exposed in the influential but rather recherché publication of Douglas Cooper's catalogue of the Courtauld Collection. By way of background for this distinguished group of Impressionist works amassed for the most part after the Great War, Cooper used the opportunity to provide a scholarly 'put down' of British responses to Impressionism and, with it, the early history of the club.[48] This specialist publication would not matter much, save for the fact that it dictated the approach to the history of British painting in the period between 1880 and 1910 for the next thirty years – to such an extent that, with the revival of interest in Victorian painting in the late 1960s, writers fought shy of Steer's generation, more or less neglecting Newlyn and Glasgow painting. However, even in the early 1950s, the foundations were not totally undermined. Mary Woodall's survey of the early years of the club at the City Art Gallery, Birmingham, in July 1952, attracted good publicity, plus at least one lengthy and balanced critique from the young Denys Sutton.[49] The challenge lay in taking up, re-inventing and arguing for that body of tradition that the club represented.

After 1943, painters such as Devas (see fig. 161), Methuen (see fig. 162) and Eurich (see fig. 163), who had shown occasionally in the 1930s, threw their weight behind the club, emerging as its leading lights at the end of the 1940s. Far from being exponents of outmoded styles, Methuen, for instance, was seen to be moving away from his mentor, Walter Sickert. Writing about his work in 1951, Mary Sorrell cast Methuen in the tradition of Claude, Richard Wilson and Constable in his affection for 'wide expanses of sky', which bring ephemeral effects to the sturdy Georgian façades he frequently painted.[50] Devas, always an independent, had been associated with the Euston Road School but had never been a member.[51] To some extent he represented the broad base of modern realist painting in the club. Like Allan Gwynne-Jones, he insisted upon craftsmanship and the careful recording of tone, evident in his portraits shown at the club and elsewhere in the 1950s. While Methuen and Devas were in a sense 'academic', Eurich was visionary. Having made his début at the club in 1927, he remained a regular exhibitor, being noted for brooding allegorical landscapes that were taken up by Shell Guides.[52]

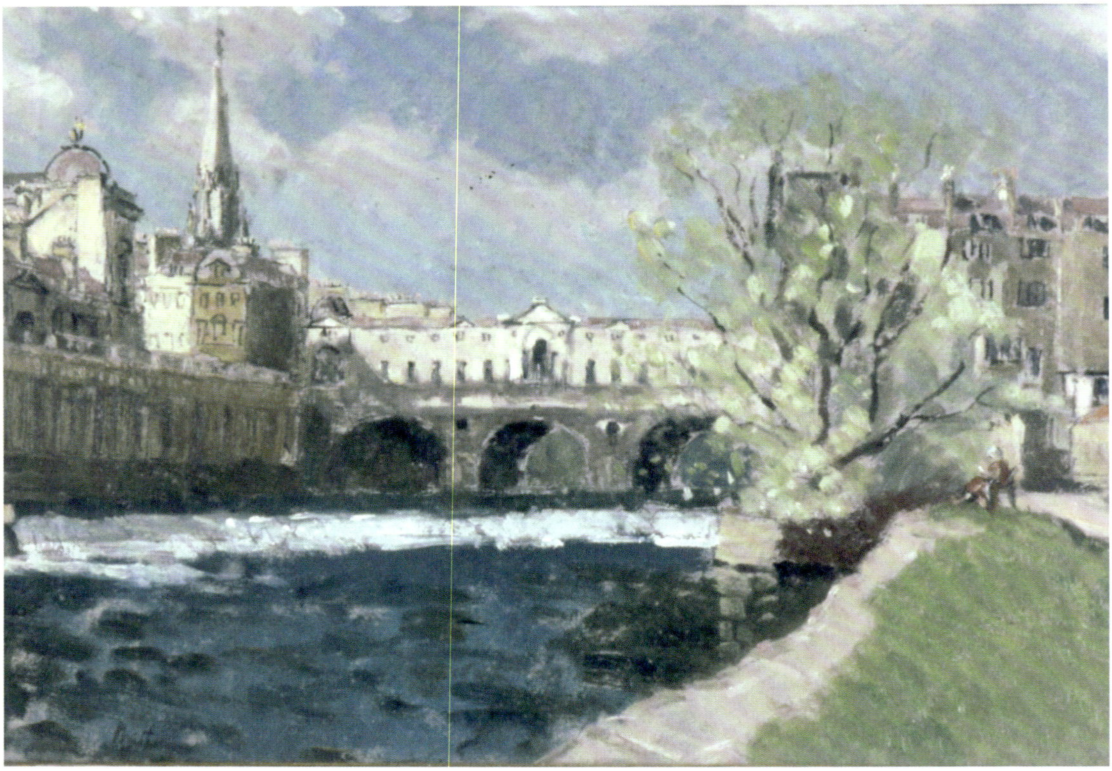

Fig. 162 Paul Ayshford (Lord Methuen)
Pulteney Bridge, Bath, during Restoration, 1951
Oil on board, 33 x 49.5 cm
Purchased 1952. Brighton Museum & Art Gallery

In October 1952, the members-only exhibition at Tooth's in Cork Street confirmed the solidity of the central New English caucus of Methuen, Fisher Prout, Cundall, Dunlop, Connard, Devas, Todd and Alfred Hayward. Methuen's *The Drum and Dome of St Paul's* and Todd's *Nude* were illustrated in the catalogue. Of the younger members, Dunstan showed *The Art Student*, Norman Hepple, *The Tenby Window*, and Margaret Thomas's *Portrait Study of Ruth Anderson*. 'Nothing freakish or experimental breaks their orderly way,' *The Daily Telegraph* critic wryly observed.[53] Despite the generally favourable reviews, only two works sold, and the enterprise returned a loss of £130 to the club. The belief that the club's salvation lay in 'members-only' exhibitions was clearly misplaced. The short steps from caution to conservatism, and from conservatism to reaction, were easily taken, and Stephen Bone's dyspeptic review of the 1953 exhibition, set the style of future annual criticisms:

> It contains no 'modern painting' of any kind, so conservative is the taste shown that one really wonders whether an artist like Stanley Spencer ... would stand any chance before a New English Art Club jury of the present day.

Bone had made his début at the club in 1920 and was one of its most consistent exhibitors, never missing a show until his death in 1958. While always an insider – he showed two works in Tooth's – at arm's length from the jury, he could see that the club was performing 'a useful service by becoming a centre of reaction with higher and stricter standards than the huge Royal Academy can permit itself'.[54] There was, nevertheless, a point in making special provision for young painters who might be deemed too eccentric for the club. After some debate it was decided to institute an associate membership category, similar to that at the Academy, and a draft scheme was debated, amended and agreed.[55]

Yet, despite the fact that critics damned the exhibitions as a whole, they were quick to note new trends and singled out particular pictures for praise. John Berger is typical in this regard. Writing a short piece for the *New Statesman and Nation* in 1954, he observed that the club was 'full of all sorts of replicas', implying that its younger painters were measuring themselves by external standards, while some older members were reproducing earlier well-tested formulae.[56] Though very different from Whistler, Rodney Burn and John Cole in the mid-1950s produced paintings of Chelsea shopfronts, chosen for their picturesque appeal and not as social reference points. Cosmo Clark, who had

Fig. 163 Richard Eurich
The Mariner's Return, 1953
Oil on canvas, 63.5 x 76 cm
Royal Academy of Arts, London

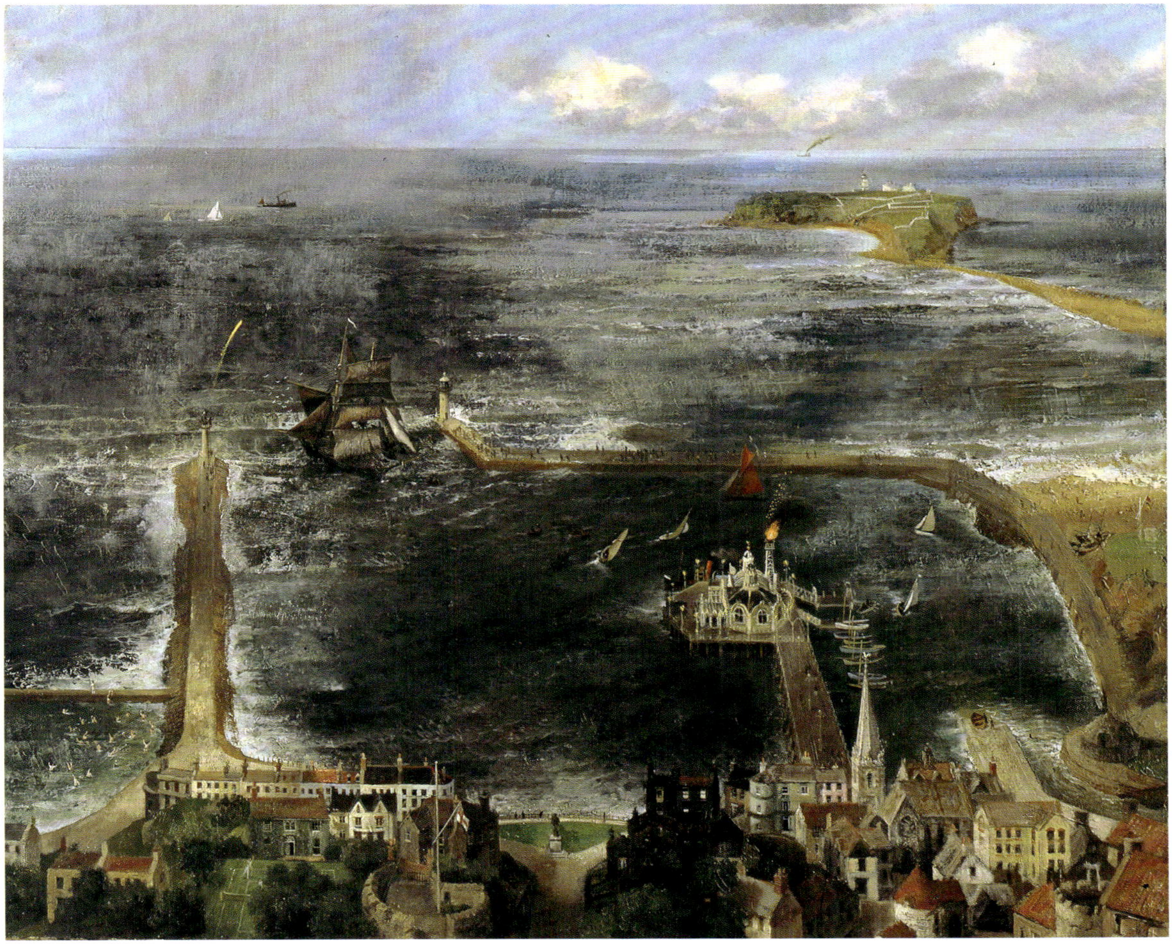

painted Brentford bargees and Kentish fruit-pickers, was not averse to producing nocturnes of the Thames and café scenes in Dieppe – classic New English subjects, but devoid of Whistlerian mystification (fig. 164). With James Fitton, Robin Guthrie and Ruskin Spear, there was a strong element of the 'painting of modern life' about 1950s club and Academy exhibitions.[57]

Younger painters such as Ward, Bellingham-Smith, Margaret Green (see fig. 165) and Lionel Bulmer (see fig. 166) shifted the paradigm even further.[58] As artists who were forging reputations with scenes of everyday life in London and its adjacent coastal resorts, they embraced post-war modernity.[59] Both were producing park landscapes similar to those of Bellingham-Smith, but more highly coloured. They eschewed the fashionable parades and trysting places for municipal spaces where young mothers in 'New Look' coats would congregate with 'kids', 'prams' and 'trikes' – the products and by-products of the post-war 'baby boom'. The 'confidence and warmth' of this social recording was noted by Frederick Laws, who wrote:

> It may seem odd to say that nobody has been catching the different look of girls in their teens today, but it is true. Mr Bulmer has put down their lack of heels, the eyes in the air and something about the way they wear their clothes that is not in the fashion drawings.[60]

Green, 'the most impressive of the New English set of park painters', was passionately committed to the passing spectacle and in her park trilogy of 1955

Opposite top
Fig. 165 Margaret Green
Cycling in the Park, c. 1955
Oil on canvas board, 71 x 91 cm
Private collection

Opposite bottom
Fig. 166 Lionel Bulmer
Winter in the Park, c. 1955
Oil on canvas board, 68 x 99 cm
Private collection

Below
Fig. 164 Cosmo Clark
French People Talking and Drinking, 1953
Oil on canvas, 77.5 x 127.5 cm
Royal Academy of Arts, London

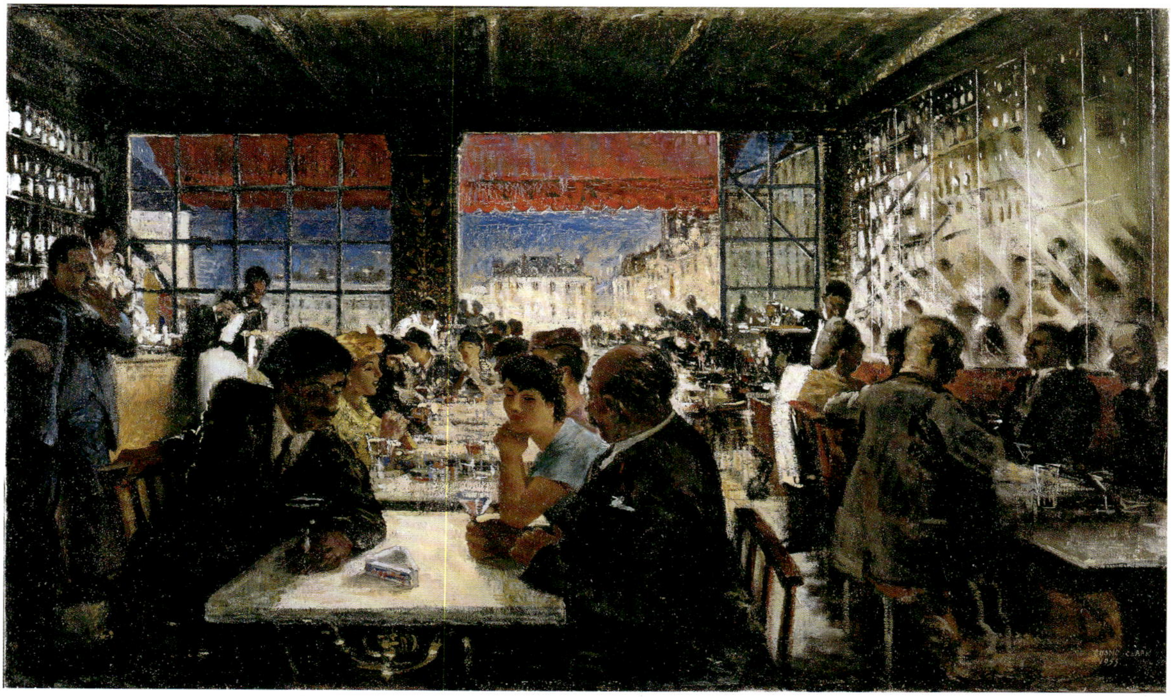

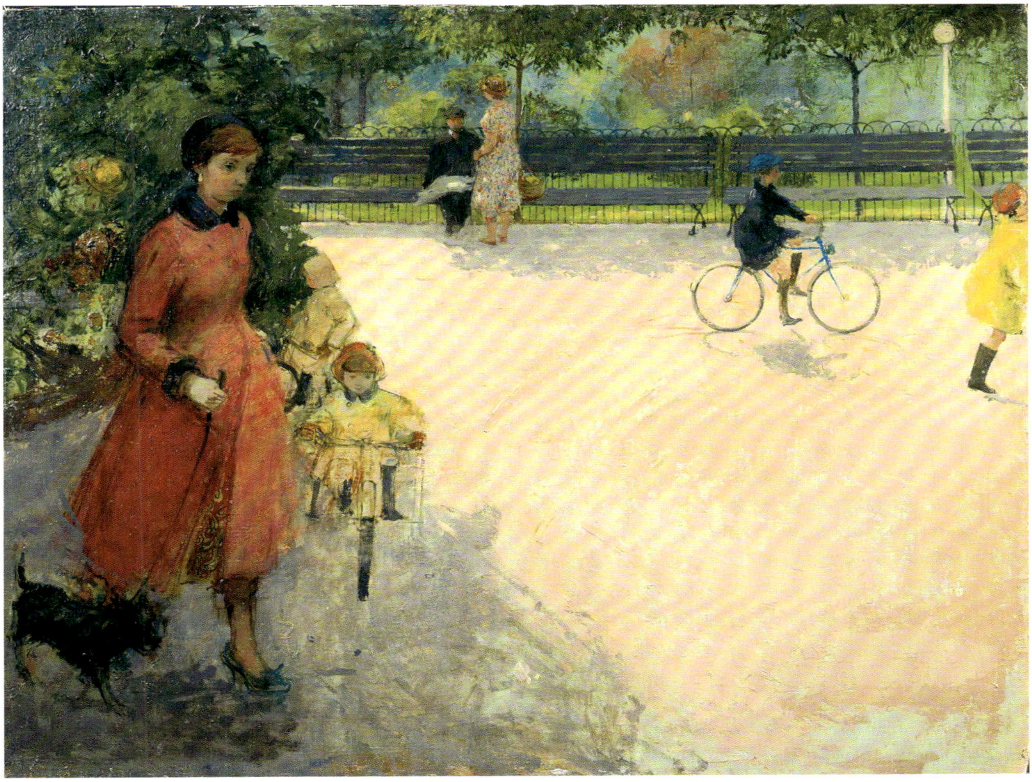

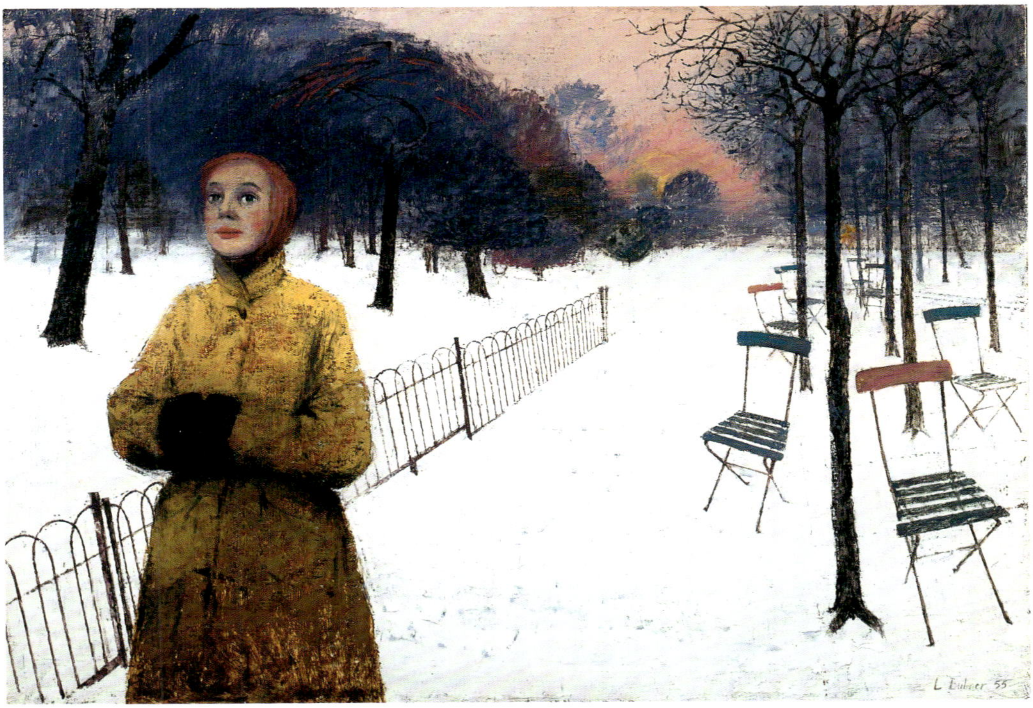
L Bulmer 55

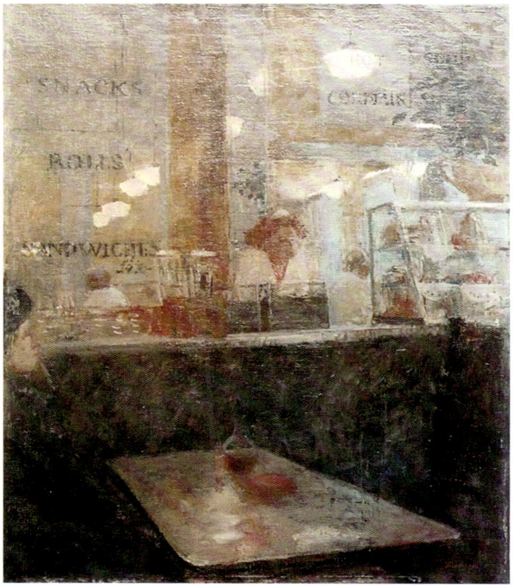

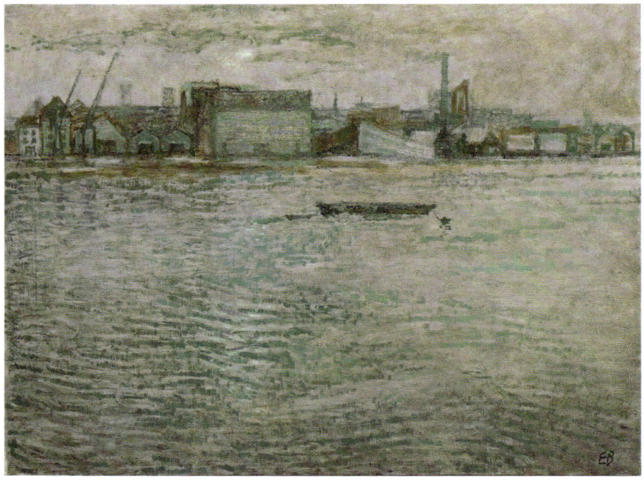

remakes from the mundanities of post-war Britain the themes of the masters – Jean-Antoine Watteau, Thomas Gainsborough and Edouard Manet.

The New English tradition of social recording fanned out from them, into works by Edward Bishop in scenes of Camden Town, Fred Dubery (see, for example, fig. 167), in paintings like *Milk Bar, Melon Stall* and *Spring in Brixton*, all shown in 1956, William Bowyer's *Market Porters* (1957) and *The Salisbury* (1958) and Edward Bishop's Putney, Camden Town and later London river scenes (see fig. 168). John Napper (see fig. 169) was working in a similar vein, and John Melville, whose *Joining a Trade Union* (1955) was regarded as 'sinister', was possibly producing a veiled protest at Tory imperialism manifest in the Suez Crisis.[61] It may be castigated as a 'junior Academy' or 'an aesthetic Neville Chamberlain', but the New English had a sense of itself and its 'brand' in the mid-1950s and its exhibitions were strong.

There are fascinating deviations from the standard simplified view of the period portrayed in 'Kitchen Sink' realism. One example is provided by Richard Eurich, a painter whose wayward narratives in both the Academy and the club render him unclassifiable. Another is Hans Schwartz, a Viennese refugee who fled the Nazis and worked as a labourer while attending Birmingham School of Arts and Crafts. Schwartz started exhibiting at the club in 1956, producing bright Expressionist canvases that in the later phases of his career embraced the late work of Bonnard.[62]

Having returned to the Royal Society of British Artists (RBA) galleries at the end of 1953, club members were increasingly dismayed at the lack of press coverage of its exhibitions. By 1957 Maurice de Saumarez, a still-life and landscape painter on the staff of Leeds University, was asked to convene a small group to review policy and draft a manifesto calling for the rejection of 'esoteric

Fig. 167 Fred Dubery
Café Scene, *c.* 1955–60
Oil on canvas, 76 x 63.5 cm
Collection the artist

Fig. 168 Edward Bishop
The Thames at the Temple, undated
Oil on canvas, 63.5 x 78.8 cm
Private collection

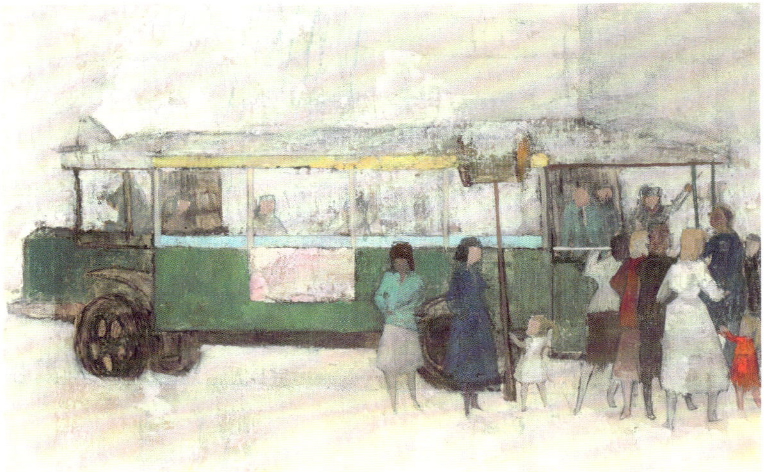

Fig. 169 John Napper
Autobus, 1956
Oil on canvas, 42 × 61 cm
Private collection

and trivial' experiments that have 'divorced' the painter 'from his public' (see Appendices).[63]

> It is time the contemporary painter attempted a more profound interpretation of life and adopted a new attitude, a positive life-enhancing interest in man and his surroundings, in the conviction that regard for life is a more fruitful foundation for Art.[64]

Although it is carefully worded and is not explicit, this Sickertian statement could easily have been read as a belated rejection of European modernism. The word 'esoteric' might still, in the mid-1950s, be applied to Picasso, and 'trivial', to the graphic style of Bernard Buffet that was popular at the time. The call for the re-connection between painter and public, which had been the primary objective of Euston Road realism, needed to be restated in the light of the recent London landscapes. Although some interpreted it as a call for social realism, it came after the emergence of the 'Kitchen Sink' School and coincided with the arrival of 'Angry Young Men', John Osborne and John Braine.[65] The northern male conquering the decadent south was a persistent theme in contemporary writing and, in its space given to L. S. Lowry, Green and the Gateshead amateur painter, Marshall F. Atkinson (see fig. 170), the club was more central to these social, aesthetic and intellectual currents than is generally appreciated. The starting place for the 'more profound interpretation of life' was, in the words of *The Times* critic, 'subjects ... drawn freely from life at the point where town and country merge in the suburban back garden, where people mingle at pleasure resorts or in shopping centres, or sit alone in plain rooms', all of which were found in the club.[66] However, in its conclusion, the 1957 statement – 'The New

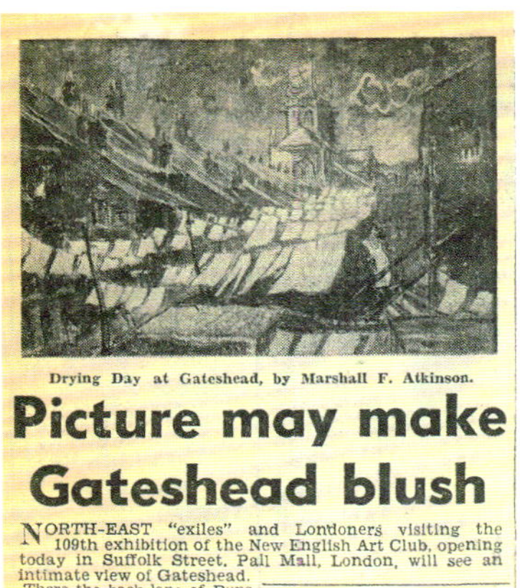

Drying Day at Gateshead, by Marshall F. Atkinson.

Picture may make Gateshead blush

NORTH-EAST "exiles" and Londoners visiting the 109th exhibition of the New English Art Club, opening today in Suffolk Street, Pall Mall, London, will see an intimate view of Gateshead.

There the back lane of Duns-

Fig. 170 Marshall F. Atkinson
Drying Day at Gateshead
Press cutting, *Newcastle Evening Chronicle*, 27 October 1956

English Art Club came into existence as a protest against a false concept of tradition. It stands today against an equally false rejection of tradition' – contains a recognition of what had happened in Western art. The club could never embrace Kitchen Sink painters any more than it could accept the imitators of the momentarily fashionable Europeans, such as Buffet and Nicholas de Stael.[67]

Yet, despite, and perhaps because of its stated position, the critical onslaught continued from Mervyn Levy and Barbara Wright in the *Art News and Review*. The latter delighted in informing readers in 1959 that the club did not know what it was doing, as its grudging admission of abstraction had led to W. C. Wyatt's *Free Orbit* (*c*. 1959) being hung upside down. Its new exhibitors must have felt disheartened by the persistent critical sneer. Eric Newton would, for instance, praise Eurich in a solo exhibition at the Redfern Gallery, but fail to recognise him at the club.[68] He would typically hail the 'new kind of newness' emerging in these exhibitions and then portray young painters as providing no more than the '1957 model in painting', as though picture-making could be likened to the production of clothes and consumer durables. 'They resemble', he declared, 'well-cut and well-tailored suits of clothes which one can admire wholeheartedly as specimens of honest manufacture without being able to distinguish one tailor from another.'[69]

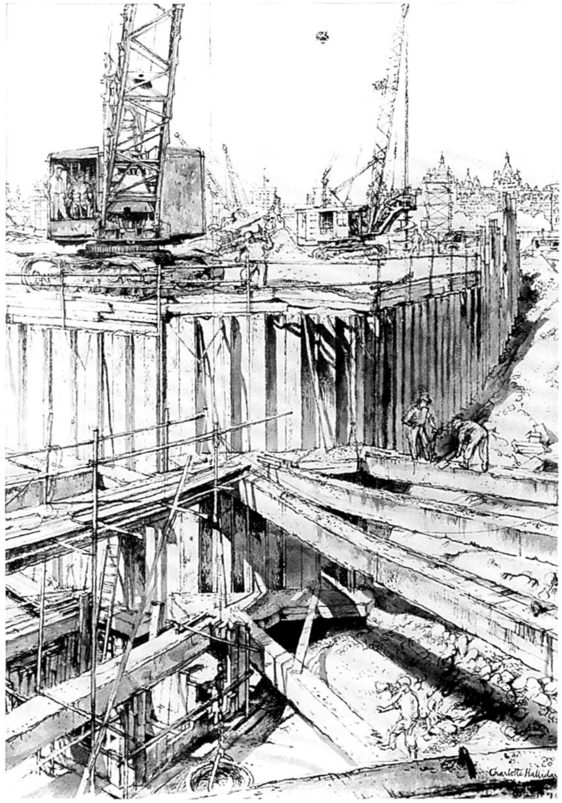

Fig. 171 Charlotte Halliday
The Construction of Shell Headquarters, 1959
Pen and ink on paper, 76 x 46 cm
Collection Scott Wilson, Basingstoke

By 1960, a further reaffirmation of principles was necessary, only this time there was a more realistic assessment of the club's position. There was no use in pretending that the Sickertian message was enough in itself, or that it would mean anything to the public. Indeed, as with the Royal Academy, the club had no 'obvious market'.[70] On the threshold of a new decade there were new social and artistic configurations to acknowledge that were more to do with the growing fascination with art emanating from New York and from American culture generally. London had already seen the emergence of the Independent Group at the Institute of Contemporary Arts, some of whose members' enthusiasm for Hollywood movies, American industrial design and pulp comics was finding fertile ground in the art schools. The statement of 1960 was aimed specifically at consolidating those young painters who shied away from these interests, and for whom the 'Young Contemporaries' exhibition was 'so avant-garde that it fails to represent them'.[71] In essence this revised manifesto was engineered to retain talented 'unknowns' such as Charlotte Halliday, Bob Brown, Ken Howard and Fred Cuming, who had just started to show at the club, as well as more mature exhibitors such as Michael Brockway and Peter J. Garrard, who had joined in the early 1950s.[72] At this juncture Halliday (see fig. 171) received a prestigious commission to produce a series of drawings on the construction of the new Shell Headquarters on the South Bank – Dunstan was also working on a similar subject matter (see fig. 172), while Howard celebrated daily life in Hampstead and Cuming (see fig. 173) the reaches of the Medway at Chatham.[73]

The strategy of inferring that the newer group shows were 'so avant-garde' as to be unrepresentative was deeply problematic. The tide that started to flow with Eduardo Paolozzi and Richard Hamilton at the Independent Group was gathering momentum with Peter Blake, R. B. Kitaj and David Hockney and it proved too strong. By the late 1960s Pop Art had solidified into a kind of orthodoxy. The case is demonstrated by Derek Boshier, who exhibited at the club on only one occasion – as he graduated from Hammersmith School of Art and passed into the Royal College of Art.[74] If the club became sidelined by these painters, its attempt to attract other disenchanted Young Contemporaries was also attacked from within. Ethelbert White, now a veteran exhibitor of watercolour landscapes, declared in the *Hampstead Express* that it was 'losing its character and there seems to be no definite policy about it'. Young artists were being 'forced', before they had 'proved themselves', and most of them 'simply dry up'.[75] In retrospect White's spleen was directed at the emerging conditions in the London art world as a whole. His younger colleagues in the club were not resolutely looking backwards, but they were perceived through a lens that was reactive if not reactionary. For the implacable Newton, the New English was simply 'not up to date' and in 1961 he went on to give more column inches to a show of Victor Vasarely's work.[76] Without strong leadership, the exhibitions of the early 1960s became more crushed and confusing. A few years earlier, in one of the less distinctive exhibitions, it had been wryly remarked that, without their frames, New English paintings might form a seamless patchwork. What struck the spectator in this *mélange* was entirely fortuitous, to the point where, in 1964, a 'Sunday painter atmosphere' prevailed in the exhibition'.[77] There was new talent, but it failed to rise above the prevailing tide of competent craftsmanship.

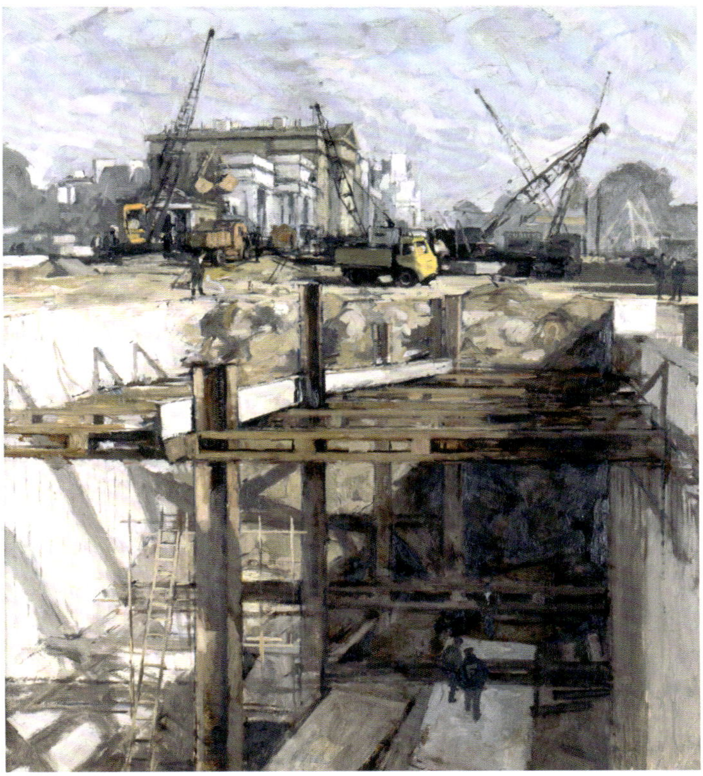

Fig. 172 Bernard Dunstan
Hyde Park Corner, 1961
Oil on board, 105.5 x 86.7 cm
Museum of London

The problems faced by the club at this time were by no means unique. Other societies such as the Royal Institute of Painters in Oil Colours, the Royal Society of British Artists and the portrait and watercolour societies were having difficulty retaining their audiences. By 1960, because all societies were faced with similar problems, discussions were held concerning the formation of an over-arching organisation. Since 1939, with a short break between 1949 and 1952, the club had staged its exhibitions in the Royal Society of British Artists' galleries in Suffolk

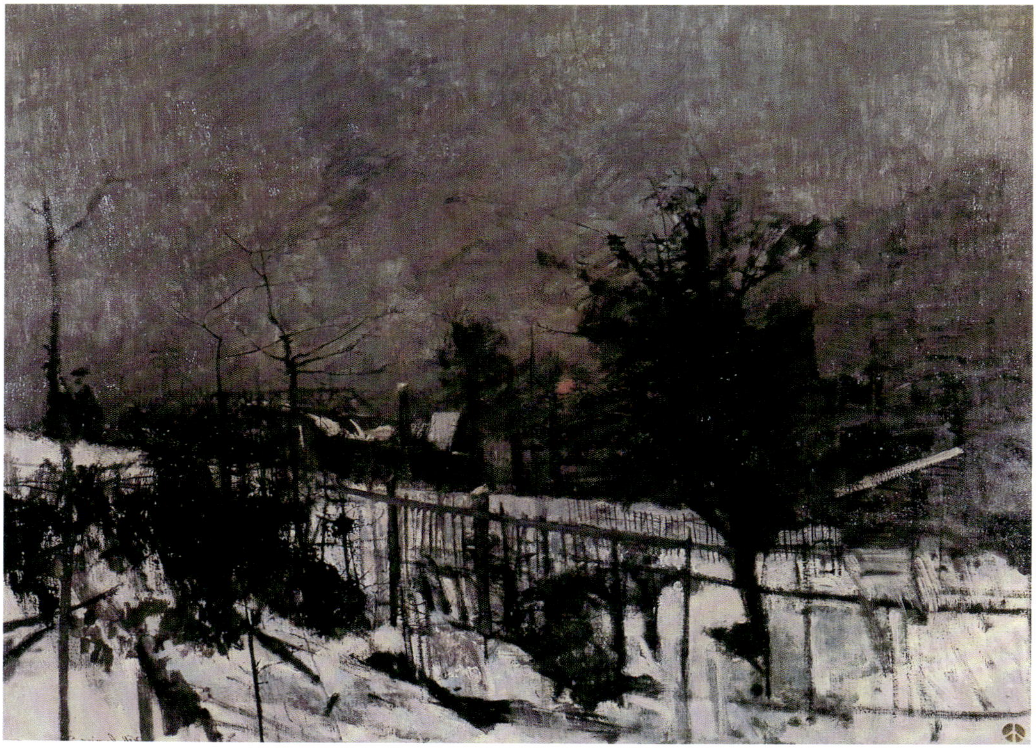

Fig. 173 Frederick Cuming
Snowcape, 1964
Oil on canvas
Private collection

Street. By the late 1950s the RBA leased its office and gallery space to the Royal Society of Portrait Painters (RP) and the Art Exhibitions Bureau, in addition to the club. Costs of central London shows nevertheless continued to rise and all attempts to secure revenue funding from the Arts Council, or from other sources, had failed. In January 1959, Mark Batten, President of the Royal Society of British Sculptors, wrote to *The Times*, appealing to the Treasury and to charitable trusts on behalf of his, the New English and the other societies, in the hope of financial support for annual exhibitions.[78] His plea fell on deaf ears. The RBA, whose galleries looked increasingly shabby, now considered banding together with its tenants to form a federation that would essentially administer and maintain the space, support the societies from a central secretariat and programme exhibitions, concerts, lectures and fund-raising events.[79] The club's executive committee approved these proposals and raised them at a special general meeting on 21 May 1960, when they were ratified.[80] Not all the ambitious plans to refurbish the gallery interiors and provide a new entrance could be implemented, but each of the societies agreed to contribute £500 to the initial capital of the Federation of British Artists (FBA). Yet, for the first time, the club had a secure sense of ownership in the British Artists' galleries in Suffolk Street and, henceforth, all London New English open exhibitions would be held there until the new FBA moved lock, stock and barrel to the Mall Galleries in 1971.

NOTES

1 Herbert Read, 'Art and the People' in *A Coat of Many Colours*, George Routledge and Sons, London (3rd ed.), 1945, pp. 27–30; see also Alex Comfort, *Art and Social Responsibility*, Falcon Press, London, 1946. Comfort's book was dedicated to Read. Keynes and others involved in the formation of the Arts Council inveighed against American culture and Hollywood in particular, as French intellectuals did. There was a growing consciousness of Existentialism – see Gino Severini, *The Artist and Society*, trans. Bernard Wall, Harvill Press, London, 1946.

2 John Rothenstein, 'A Visit to Picasso', *Compass, Current Reading*, December 1945, pp. 48–51. See also John Rothenstein, *Brave Day, Hideous Night*, Hamish Hamilton, London, 1967, pp. 139–144. There had been great curiosity in London during the war concerning Picasso's well-being. An exhibition of reproductions of some of his recent work at Jack Bilbo's Modern Art Gallery in November 1944 went some way towards satisfying this concern; see Cora Gordon, 'London Commentary', *The Studio*, vol. 128, November 1944, p. 153.

3 See Geoff Hassall, *Camberwell School of Arts and Crafts: Its Students and Teachers, 1943–1960*, Antique Collectors' Club, Woodbridge, 1995; Christopher Frayling, *The Royal College of Art: One Hundred and Fifty Years of Art and Design*, Barrie and Jenkins, London, 1987.

4 I am grateful to Fred Dubery and Carl Lazarri for their recollections of Burn and others at the Royal College in the 1950s. Under Robin Darwin the college was expanding its curriculum to include new disciplines such as fashion. See Christopher Frayling, *The Royal College of Art: One Hundred and Fifty Years of Art and Design*, Barrie and Jenkins, London, 1987.

5 Greenham began showing with the club in 1945. *In the Studio*, a work that may be related to *The Art School* (fig. 150), was exhibited at the New English in the winter of 1948. I am grateful to Charlotte Halliday for her recollections of Henry Rushbury and the Royal Academy Schools in the 1950s.

6 William Townsend, 'Introduction' in *The Euston Road School*, exh. cat., Arts Council, 1948, p. 5, confirms what was evident to readers of Denvir, Russell, Newton and Ironside, namely that the term 'Euston Road School' was now being applied to 'any painter producing more or less realistic pictures or a kind of refined impressionism'.

7 Robin Ironside, *Painting since 1939*, Longmans, Green and Co, London, for the British Council 1947; see also John Russell, *From Sickert to 1948: The Achievement of the Contemporary Art Society*, Lund Humphries, London, 1948, and John Piper, 'British Romantic Artists' in W. J. Turner (ed.), *Aspects of British Art*, Collins, London, 1947, pp. 202–10.

8 There were notable exceptions to this rule, such as Margaret Thomas (see figs 156 and 185).

9 *The Arts Enquiry, The Visual Arts: A Report Sponsored by Dartington Hall Trustees*, Oxford University Press, Oxford, 1946, p. 55, describes the New English as 'now the principal recruiting ground for RA Associates'.

10 Eric Newton, 'Painting in Plenty But –', *The Sunday Times*, 20 October 1946. The exhibiting members in the winter of 1946 were Mary Adshead, Clare Atwood, Thomas T. Baxter, Eleanor Best, Muirhead Bone, Stephen Bone, Rodney Burn, Charles Cheston, Philip Connard, Charles Cundall, Robin Darwin, Anthony Devas, R. O. Dunlop, Richard Eurich, Ronald Gray, James Guthrie, P. H. Jowett, Lord Methuen, Margaret Fisher Prout, Lady Patricia Ramsay, Randolph Schwabe, Rupert Shepherd, F. H. S. Shepherd, Ursula Tyrwhitt, Ethel Walker, Ethelbert White and James Wilkie.

11 Roger Fry, *Reflections on British Painting*, Faber and Faber, London, 1934, p. 23.

12 Eric Newton, *Time and Tide*, 3 November 1956.

13 Cora J. Gordon, 'London Commentary', *The Studio*, vol. 136, August 1948, p. 53. Gordon lists Edward Le Bas, Steven Spurrier, Ruskin Spear, Charles Cundall, Charles Ginner, Kathleen Tyson, Dame Ethel Walker, Robert Buhler, Marcella Smith, Carel Weight and the newly elected Margaret Fisher Prout as exemplifying this core of 'Post-New-English' exhibitors. As it contains the names of painters associated with the tendency, who did not actually show in club exhibitions, it amply illustrates the extent to which the authors of the Dartington report (see note 9) were accurate in their observations.

14 This is clear from the photograph included in *The Times* 'Picture Gallery' – see 23 October 1939, p. 12; 31 October 1940, p. 6; 22 October 1943, p. 6.

15 Cora J. Gordan, 'London Commentary', *The Studio*, vol. 135, February 1948, p. 61. Gordon refers to the 'eclectic coldness' of a 'thin grey line of small pictures' which 'grace the enormous height of the RBA walls'. The exhibition was 'an experiment which has been tried several times before with little success.... Considering the outstanding talent of so many members, this show is, in many ways, not one of its best efforts'. A more radical hanging strategy thus could not atone for the fact that key members were saving their best work for the Academy. The practice of double hanging was resumed in 1949 – see *The Times*, 10 May 1949, p. 10.

16 *The Studio*, vol. 136, August 1948, p. 53. In contrast to the Royal Academy Summer Exhibition, club exhibitions only attracted 'picture lovers'.

17 Munnings's speech is quoted in full in *Munnings v. The Moderns*, Tim Wilcox, exh. cat., Manchester City Art Gallery, 1988, pp. 11–15. The context for his outburst was provided by the Tate Gallery's purchase that same year of two early Cubist works by Picasso, *Seated Nude* (1909–10) and *Bust of a Woman* (1909). Munnings had given early notice of his distaste for modern art by co-signing a letter to the Editor of *The Times*, aligning himself with criticism of the 'poor quality' of exhibitions organised by the Council for the Encouragement of Music and the Arts, to coincide with the announcement of his election to the presidency of the Royal Academy in 1944.

18 Rodney Burn, Hon. Sec., 1947–1963, wrote to *The Times*, 9 August 1951, with the signatures of the presidents of nine other artists' societies, having failed to secure better representation for artists on the Arts Council's art panel. He also wrote, with others, on 28 June 1955 regarding a new gallery space in central London.

19 Anon., 'From a Painter's Notebook – 1', in John Lehmann (ed.), *The Penguin New Writing*, Penguin, Harmondsworth, 1945, no. 24, p. 171.

20 Clive Bell, *Victor Pasmore*, Penguin, Harmondsworth, 1945, plates 18, 21, 24 and 31. The effect of these works reverberated on painters like John Napper and Elinor Bellingham-Smith in the 1950s and arguably continued for thirty years in the late work of Lionel Bulmer and Derek Mynott.

21 Lawrence Gowing, 'French Painters and English' in John Lehmann (ed.), *The Penguin New Writing*, Penguin, Harmondsworth, 1947, no. 29, pp. 154–6.

22 After Shepherd, W. L. Clause held the post from 1943 to 1946, relinquishing it for a very brief spell to Lord Methuen.

23 Bernard Dunstan, 'A Direct and Affectionate Response', *Art and Artists*, October 1986, p. 17.

24 I am grateful to Margaret Thomas for her recollections of her 'two-person' exhibition at the Leicester Galleries, in 1950, when she shared with Lord Methuen.

25 This was clear in 1932, for instance, when Gilbert Spencer's *A Cotswold Farm* was shown at the Goupil Gallery, before going to the Academy. It was subsequently purchased by the Tate Gallery. The Academy and the club were not in a strong position in these changing practices of reputation building.

26 Both Nevinson's death in 1946 and that of its secretary throughout the war, William L. Clause, were regarded as a great loss to the club, see

The Times, 11 September 1946, p. 7; 8 October 1946, p. 7. Walker and Bland both died in the early months of 1951.

27 Obituaries: *The Times*, 22 December 1948; *Manchester Guardian*, 22 December 1948; *The Scotsman*, 22 December 1948. MacColl's extensive correspondence reveals that he remained active in the club's affairs up until his death. Rodney Burn, for instance, shortly after his election as honorary secretary, and a few months before MacColl's death, wrote to him seeking to renew their friendship. See Glasgow University Library Special Collections, MacColl Papers, B716, 28 September 1948.

28 *The Listener*, 20 January 1949.

29 Bernard Dunstan, 'A Direct and Affectionate Response', *Art and Artists*, October 1986, p. 17.

30 AGM Minutes, 12 May 1947, and Private Memorandum. Anthony Devas was the prime mover of this idea. The proposed colleges were the Slade, the RA Schools, the Royal College, Central, Chelsea, Goldsmiths, St Martins, Camberwell, Hammersmith and City and Guilds. Hammersmith was dropped in favour of Regent Street Polytechnic.

31 *The Scotsman*, 31 October 1947. In addition to the jury problem, there was an issue in the amount of wall space to be reserved for students and a size restriction – 24 x 20 in. (61 x 51 cm) – was placed upon their submissions.

32 On Philip Connard's proposal, the scheme was abandoned (AGM Minutes, 28 April 1948).

33 Burn, Robin Guthrie and Chisman went to Bristol to see the exhibition and Methuen, Jowett, Schwabe and Gilbert Spencer attended the opening. There were very few sales at any of these shows, although Bristol City Art Gallery acquired a Burn and a Tom Carr as a result.

34 The club was producing a year-on-year loss, which rose to £622 in 1949 (AGM Minutes, 22 October 1949). There was also considerable debate at this point concerning the display and, in some cases, rejection of members' work, in the light of Mary Adshead's resignation. Adshead believed that, as in the Royal Academy, members' works should not be submitted to the jury. This had been a recurring theme at meetings since the club's inception. Executive committees consistently supported the elected selectors and hangers. Members were not permitted to show as a right, and proposals for regular members-only London exhibitions were always regarded as problematic.

35 Bernard Dunstan, 'A Direct and Affectionate Response', *Art and Artists*, October 1986, pp. 17–21. Burn showed consistently from the winter of 1923 to 1979. In addition to street scenes, he painted Thames views at Chiswick and Richmond, and, during the war, paintings of Hampstead Heath. In the 1950s he showed beach scenes at Bembridge that often contain gentle humour, reminiscent of Edward Ardizzone.

36 See, for instance, Philip Mathews, 'The New English Art Club', *Art News and Review*, 1949.

37 'Our London Art Critic', 'Art in London – Season at High Water Mark – "New English" Show', *The Scotsman*, 14 May 1949. Within this group, McCall, who had trained in Edinburgh under Peploe and in Paris under Freisz, brought more liberal attitudes to colour, see Mitzi McCall, *Interior with Figure: The Life and Work of Charles McCall*, The Book Guild, Lewes, 1987. The range of Dunstan's preferences became clear by the time of his second solo exhibition at Roland, Browse and Delbanco in 1954. A review in *The Studio* (G. S. Whittet, 'London Commentary', vol. 148, December 1954, p. 185) refers to Sickert, Bonnard and Vuillard as inspirations for the 'lovely matière' of Dunstan's 'most refreshing and sensitive synthesis'.

38 *The Glasgow Herald*, 16 October 1946.

39 Cole exhibited intermittently from 1924 to 1975, with London shopfront paintings in the early 1950s and street scenes of Brighton and Hastings in the 1960s. A work entitled *Hertford Street, Shepherd Market* (*c.* 1952), for instance, was shown in the spring of 1952. For Cole, see *The Cole Family, Painters of the English Landscape, 1838–1975*, T. J. Barringer, exh. cat., Portsmouth City Museums, 1988. Edward Hall exhibited from 1948 to 1963, showing street scenes of Pimlico in the early 1950s. Buhler began in 1945 and exhibited pictures of Chelsea and Hammersmith.

40 For a general account, see William Feaver, 'Festival Star' in Mary Banham and Bevis Hillier (eds), *A Tonic to the Nation: The Festival of Britain, 1951*, Thames and Hudson, London, 1976, pp. 40–55.

41 R. O. Dunlop, *Landscape Painting: Ma Yüan to Picasso*, David and Charles, Newton Abbot, 1954, pp. 158–9.

42 Neville Wallis, 'New English Tradition', *Art News and Review*, 19 April 1952.

43 For further reference, see *25 From 51: Paintings from the Festival of Britain*, James Hamilton, exh. cat., Sheffield City Art Galleries, 1978. From the New English ranks, L. S. Lowry, Charles Mahoney, R. O. Dunlop, Henry Lamb and John Nash were also selected.

44 In the first 'Anthology', see Foreword, *British Painting, 1925–1950*, Philip James, exh. cat., Manchester City Art Gallery, 1951, Lowry, Nash, Roberts, Spencer, Sutherland and Wadsworth were shown in the Arts Council's own New Burlington Galleries in London. The second 'Anthology' at the Whitechapel Art Gallery, London, contained work by Buhler, Coldstream, Gertler, Ginner, Augustus John, Gwen John, Lamb, John Napper, William Nicholson, Sickert and Walker. Pasmore, a favoured Arts Council painter, appeared in both anthologies. Steer and Tonks were not included.

45 Around 1950 they would have been Alfred Munnings, Ben Nicholson, Henry Moore, Barbara Hepworth, Graham Sutherland and, possibly, Francis Bacon or Stanley Spencer.

46 Hesketh Hubbard, *A Hundred Years of British Painting, 1851–1951*, Longmans, Green and Co, London, 1951; and Anthony Bertram, *A Century of British Painting, 1851–1951*, Studio Publications, London, 1952. Bertram took the opportunity, in concluding his survey, to reflect upon the English tradition. Its strength, he declared, lay in its ability to 'absorb foreign influences'. Whistler and, by extension, the first generation of club members had led English painters back to the use of 'foreign sources for our own purposes'. Bertram finally deferred to Paul Nash on the spirit of the land – the *genius loci* – and bowed out of the argument, leaving it open for Pevsner's Reith Lectures (1956).

47 Berger later characterised these exhibitions as 'refusing current forms of academicism', while foreseeing 'the dead-end of modernism'. See *The Forgotten Fifties*, Julian Spalding, exh. cat., Graves Art Gallery, Sheffield, 1984, p. 46; see also Jonathan Jones, 'John Berger and Looking Forward' in *The Whitechapel Art Gallery Centenary Review*, Catherine Lampert and Andrea Tarsea, exh. cat., Whitechapel Art Gallery, London, 2001 (published in conjunction with the 'Whitechapel Art Gallery Centenary Exhibition'), pp. 64–6; also *Transition: The London Art Scenes in the Fifties*, Martin Harrison, exh. cat., Barbican Art Gallery, London, 2002.

48 Douglas Cooper, *The Courtauld Collection*, Athlone Press, London, 1954. While Cooper's account cannot be dismissed any more than his unfocused attack on British painting in his article on 'The Problem of Wilson Steer' (see Chapter 6, note 76), his portrayal of the early members' battle with the Academy establishment 'for their own benefit' (p. 36), infers more dubious motives than were the case. A similar cast covers his consideration of British responses to Impressionism on the part of both artists and collectors.

49 Mary Woodall Introduction in *The Early Years of the New English Art Club, 1886–1918*, exh. cat., City Museum and Art Gallery, Birmingham, 1952. This exhibition contained 215 items by the club's major exhibitors; see Denys Sutton, 'A Revolutionary Era in English Art', *Country Life*, 25 July 1952, pp. 264–5. Sutton concludes that, with Vorticism, 'a new era had dawned and with it the necessity for the New English Art Club had disappeared'.

50 Mary Sorrell, 'Lord Methuen ARA', *The Studio*, vol. 142, December 1951, pp. 180–3.

51 *Anthony Devas, 1911–1958*, Anne Goodchild, exh. cat., Sheffield City Art Galleries, 1991, unpaginated.

52 *Richard Eurich RA: A Retrospective Exhibition*, Caroline Krzesinska, exh. cat., Bradford Art Galleries and Museums, 1980. For Eurich's earlier work, see 'Artists of Note, no. 18: Richard Eurich', *The Artist*, vol. 11, no. 6, August 1936, pp. 182–5.

53 T. W. Earp, 'Variety in Style in Art Show – Fine Craftsmanship', *The Daily Telegraph*, 17 October 1952.

54 Stephen Bone, 'Cautious Show in Suffolk Street – New English Art Club', *The Manchester Guardian*, 19 October 1953.

55 AGM Minutes, 12 May 1954. Club members were never entirely clear about the purpose of associates, not wishing to regard them as members-in-waiting, and unable to guarantee exhibition space for their work.

56 John Berger, *New Statesman and Nation*, 12 November 1954; he continues, 'but [the club] includes some fine garden watercolours by Lionel Bulmer, a good life drawing by Jane Hurrie, a well-constructed painting of the inside of a tube train by Peter Lowe and a lively beach scene called *Bus Trip from the Pits* by Margaret Green'.

57 Although Ruskin Spear was elected a member of the club in 1944, he did not actually show his work. James and Margaret Fitton exhibited from 1930 to 1934. Like Burn, Fitton's social observation also contained wry humour. Cosmo Clark exhibited regularly from 1927 to 1966, taking in and reworking the full gamut of London subject matter, but looking particularly at its white working classes before the arrival of the West Indian workforce in the mid-1950s. His treatment of bargees and gypsies should be seen in the context of the later work of Laura Knight.

58 At this point Ward and Bellingham-Smith were exhibiting public park scenes at the Academy. Ward's busy Academy piece, *The Playground* (1957), with its swings, roundabouts and climbing frames, is a typical example. Devas also occasionally turned to this subject matter – as in *The Kite Flyer* (1956).

59 For further reference, see *From City to Sea – Lionel Bulmer and Margaret Green*, Ian Collins, exh. cat., Messum's, Cork Street, London, 2002; *Partners in Paint – Lionel Bulmer and Margaret Green*, Ian Collins, exh. cat., Messum's, Cork Street, London, 2005.

60 Frederick Laws, 'Alive and Gently Kicking, New English Art Club', *The Manchester Guardian*, 22 October 1955, p. 5.

61 Mervyn Levy, 'The Devil and the Deep', *Art News and Review*, 29 October 1955.

62 During the 1960s, when he was not showing at the club, Schwartz experimented with bold figurative canvases using photographic source material. He won the Hunting Prize for watercolour in 1981.

63 AGM Minutes, 4 May 1957. De Saumarez was given a wide brief to reconsider the place of student work, the re-introduction of sculpture, invitations to honorary foreign exhibitors, hanging space for students and 'the election of ten young painters who might have views contrary to those of the majority of young members'.

64 *New English Art Club, 110 Exhibition*, 1957, exh. cat., p. 5.

65 The 'Kitchen Sink' painters, John Bratby, Derrick Greaves, Edward Middleditch and Jack Smith, were named by David Sylvester in an article in *Encounter* in 1954. Others, such as Peter Coker and Claude Rogers, are often associated with the group. Middleditch was the only member of the group who was a current exhibitor at the club; see *The Forgotten Fifties*, Julian Spalding, exh. cat., Graves Art Gallery, Sheffield, 1984; *Transition: The London Art Scenes in the Fifties*, Martin Harrison, exh. cat., Barbican Art Gallery, London, 2002. For contextual reference, see Robert Hewison, *In Anger, Culture in the Cold War*, Weidenfeld and Nicholson, London, 1981 (rev. ed., Methuen, London, 1988), pp. 123–33 and 187–94; see also Gene Feldman and Max Gartenberg (eds), *Protest: The Beat Generation and the Angry Young Men*, 1959 (rev. ed., Hamilton and Co., London, 1960).

66 Anon., 'The Middle Course in Art', *The Times*, 21 October 1957.

67 *Transition: The London Art Scenes in the Fifties*, Martin Harrison, exh. cat., Barbican Art Gallery, London, 2002, p. 86, considers the 1956 Venice Biennale as marking the 'demise' of social realism.

68 *Richard Eurich RA: A Retrospective Exhibition*, Caroline Krzesinska, exh. cat., Bradford Art Galleries and Museums, 1980, p. 12.

69 Eric Newton, 'Unrevolutionary Youth – New English Art Club', *The Manchester Guardian*, 15 October 1957.

70 Unidentified source, quoted from Cuttings Book, New English Art Club Archive.

71 Ibid.

72 Halliday began to exhibit in 1958, Cuming and Howard in 1959. Halliday was originally an associate – one of those who were soon accorded membership in 1962. Brown was elected associate in 1964 and given full membership two years later. There was an understanding among some members that the waiting period would be three years. Some associates, however, drifted away and were never confirmed as full members. Garrard and Brockway had begun exhibiting in 1952. Harry Eccleston, John Linfield, Derek Mynott, Hans Schwartz, Elizabeth Scott-Moore, Kathleen Wrigglesworth and Jean Young were all also exhibiting by this time. Of these, Eccleston and Schwartz showed once only, not returning to regular exhibiting until the 1980s.

73 For reference to Halliday's, Howard's and Cuming's work, see, for instance, P. G., 'City Full of Exhibitions – Stand Taken by New English', *The Scotsman*, 10 October 1960.

74 Boshier showed a landscape and still-life at the 1958 exhibition.

75 *Hampstead Express*, 21 October 1960.

76 Eric Newton, 'New in Name', *The Manchester Guardian*, 26 October 1961. Newton wrote: 'It is, in fact, an enjoyable show ... but it is not up to date. If this were an exhibition of automobiles the charge would be damning. But it is an exhibition of paintings and the laws of obsolescence do not apply.'

77 Anon., 'New English Art Club', *The Times*, 27 May 1964.

78 Letters, *The Times*, 6 January 1959, p. 9.

79 In its application for charitable status, only the RBA, the RP and the NEAC were named as initiating bodies – see Executive Committee Minutes, 18 May 1960. The Art Exhibitions Bureau was an agency, not a principal. It represented other societies, such as the Royal British Colonial Society of Artists, the Royal Society of Miniature Painters, Sculptors and Gravers, the Society of Marine Artists, the Society of Aviation Artists, the United Society of Artists and the Artists of Chelsea. The Bureau occasionally circulated 'selections' from New English exhibitions.

80 AGM Minutes, 21 May 1960 and 28 July 1961.

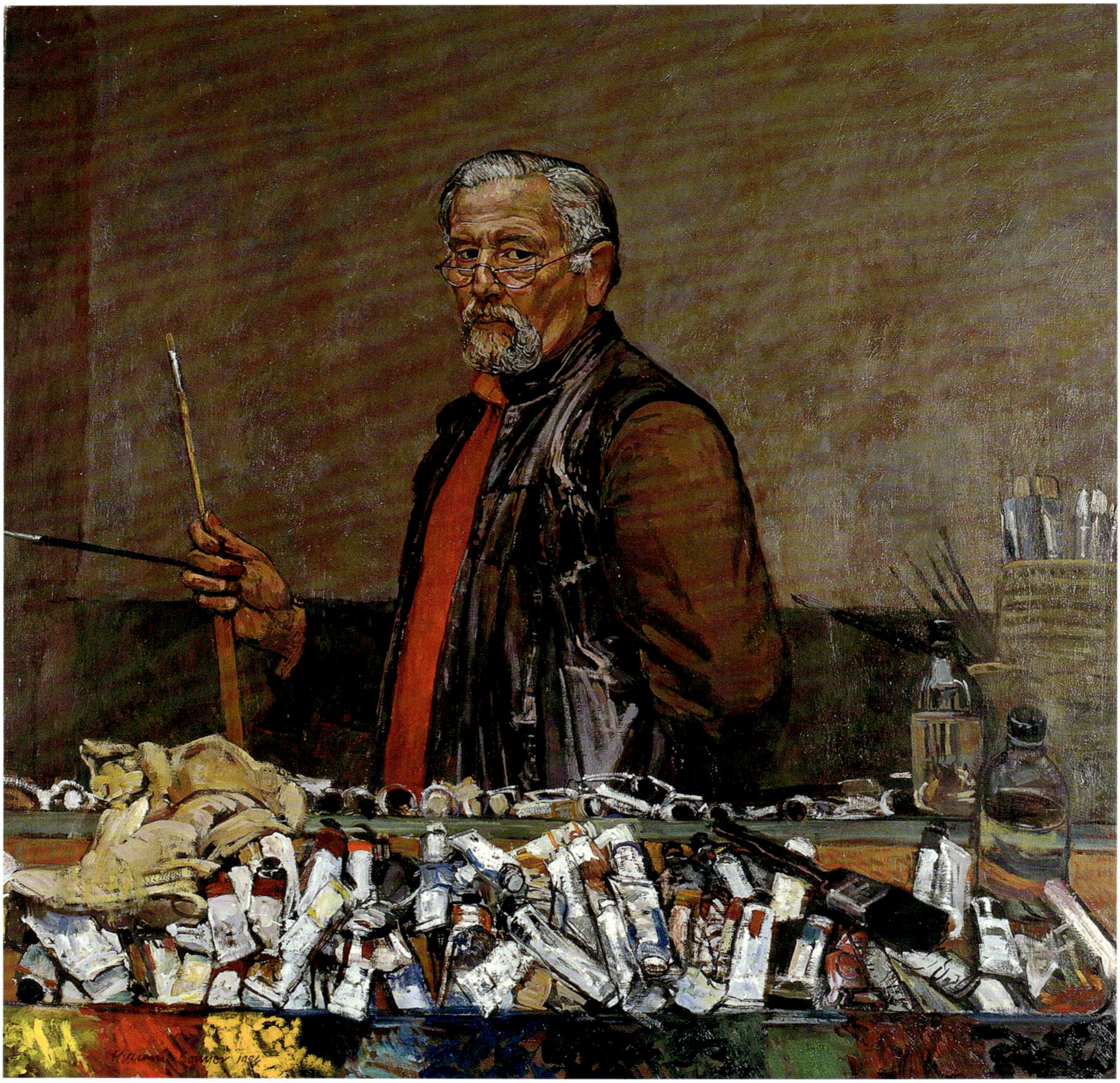

Fig. 174 William Bowyer
Self-portrait, *c*. 1980
Oil on canvas, 101 x 76 cm
Private collection

CHAPTER 8

'Direct and affectionate responses' 1966–1990

In 1961 *The London Magazine* published a special issue on the current state of British painting in which articles written by eminent critics and historians were accompanied by a series of short texts by leading artists. Rodrigo Moynihan, for instance, commented that British painters no longer found it appealing to cross the English Channel and that 'the time-honoured peephole to Paris has been replaced by a window looking out over the Atlantic'. In a longer essay, John Russell confirmed that Paris was no longer 'the capital of art', while a reprint of Harold Rosenberg's essay on 'The American Action Painters' described the distant view from Moynihan's window overlooking the ocean. There were more fundamental points to be made about abstraction. Conceding that, occasionally, it was necessary to return to empirical observation, Alan Bowness challenged the moral authority of 'what is usually called realist painting'. Uncomfortable with Francis Bacon, he hailed Ben Nicholson as 'the most outstanding British painter since Turner', and looked favourably on the young abstractionists, William Scott, Terry Frost, Prunella Clough, Peter Lanyon and Victor Pasmore. Portraiture, the only remaining niche for representation, was, according to Robin Ironside, more about social prestige than art – a point already made by Fry and later taken up and elaborated by John Berger with a Marxist spin.[1]

None of this polemic directly impinged upon the New English and none of its younger contributors was invited to supply quotes about their practice. The more radical 'objective' Coldstream followers of the period, such as Patrick George and Euan Uglow, were loath to become involved with a club that increasingly carried the stigma of the 'Sunday painter'. With the death of Augustus John in 1961, another link with the distinguished past was severed and, even though John had long been regarded as a spent force, his departure left the club metaphorically drifting beyond the safe confines of the English Channel into hostile Atlantic waters. Britain sought finally to shake off post-war austerity and embrace new attitudes. In his Reith Lectures Edgar Wind sensed at this moment that art 'touches us lightly' and has 'lost its sting'.[2] He too was grappling with a world in which everything was increasingly available to everyone, a world in which appreciation knew no limits – when, for instance, advertising graphics, cinema, television and photographic images were no longer confined to a hoarding in a street scene, observed through the grimy naturalistic filter of Euston Road. They coexisted in the mind and could be as potent, expressive and memorable as a Poussin or a Picasso ... *perhaps*.[3] The sagacious Richard Hamilton defined these contemporary conditions as 'the media landscape', pre-dating and, to some extent, predicting

John Berger's polemic in the book and television series, *Ways of Seeing* (1972).[4] The Pop artists of the 1960s, launched in 'Young Contemporaries' exhibitions, consolidated their position in 'New Generation' shows at the Whitechapel Art Gallery, London, and in exhibitions mounted by dealers such as Robert Fraser and John Kasmin.[5] Russell, Bryan Robertson and Lord Snowdon's *Private View*, when it was published in 1965, did not contain any New English exhibitors, with the single exception of L. S. Lowry – although the 'photographic essay' began with text superimposed on an atmospheric image of the old heartland of Cheyne Walk.[6] It goes without saying that the three survey exhibitions, held at the close of the decade to celebrate Pop, abstract and conceptual art, passed without allusion to what had become an anachronism – as an artists' club, a jury-selected annual Salon and as the bastion of traditional methods.[7]

Having encouraged student submissions at winter exhibitions, Cosmo Clark argued against altering the character of the club in order to promote particularly a student membership category. In the event, the first Coldstream Report of 1960 had recommended a new qualification, the Diploma in Art and Design, administered by a short-lived National Council, whose chief officer, Edward Pullée, joined the club as a regular exhibitor in 1963 (see fig. 175).[8] The dramatic changes in British art education in the 1960s and 1970s meant that the skills of perspective and the notation of three-dimensional form in still-life were less systematically taught than before.[9] The disciplines of the life room, the head room, the cast room and the plant room, formerly so important at art schools like the Slade and Camberwell, had been falling into neglect from the late 1950s.[10] Only in a few more traditional establishments such as the Byam Shaw School of Art and Walthamstow Art School was the New English still held in high regard.[11]

Like Pullée, William Bowyer (see fig. 183), who followed Vincent Lines as honorary secretary in 1968, had a distinguished career in art education and both witnessed the gradual downgrading of traditional craft skills, following the emergence of student radicalism in the late 1960s. Critical friends who might speak out for artists' societies were increasingly hard to find, and when the club was remembered at all during the decade of 'Swinging London', it was for its illustrious past. Press coverage shrank to paragraphs in gossip columns. The Fine Art Society's show devoted to 'The Early Years of the New English Art Club' in 1968 collected more notices than the average annual exhibition. But this was no more than a faint fanfare in the year of the Tet Offensive in Vietnam, the Prague Spring, riots at the Sorbonne and student sit-ins in the Hornsey and Guildford art schools.[12]

With the arrival of cool, 'hard-edge' painters, oil paints were replaced with acrylics, and palette and brushes were discarded for spray-guns and masking tape. Frank Stella was venerated. At that moment sinister ministerial monsters were waiting

Fig. 175 Edward Pullée
Toledo, 1991
Oil on board, 50.8 x 60.9 cm
Private collection

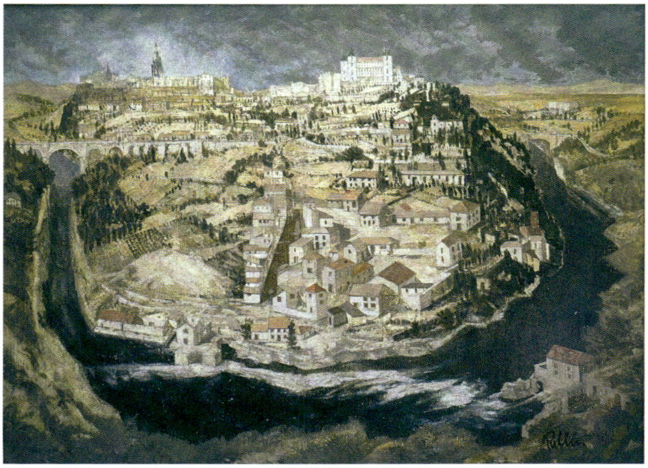

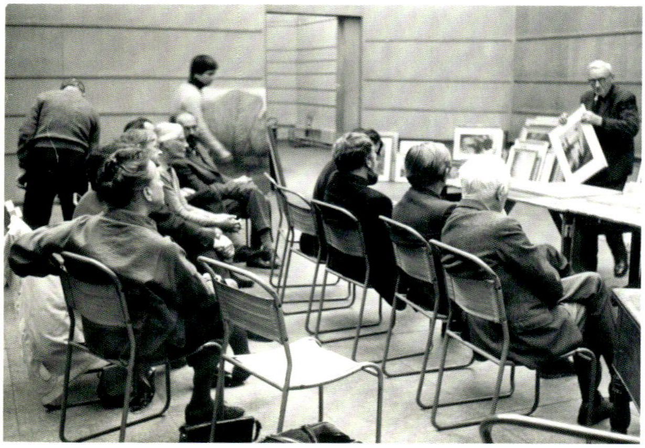

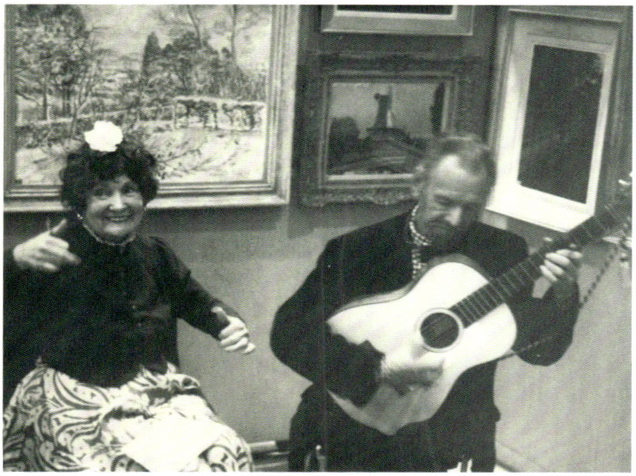

Top
Fig. 176 The last selection jury at Suffolk Street
Photograph, October 1970.
Unknown photographer
NEAC Archive

Above
Fig. 177 Mr and Mrs Ethelbert White serenading a private view
Photograph, *c.* 1960.
Unknown photographer
NEAC Archive

in the wings, and with the subsequent restructuring of higher education and the creation of polytechnics in which art sat alongside commerce, technology and teacher training, the days of the independent art school were numbered. In the mid-1970s Pullée's council was dissolved and its functions transferred into the grander Council for National Academic Awards as the validating body for polytechnic degrees.[13] Although the old ethos persisted for a time, by the early 1980s there were few independent art colleges left.

Club business carried on as usual. Selection continued as before (see fig. 176) and private views were quaintly old-fashioned affairs at which members and guests were treated to spontaneous guitar recitals by Ethelbert White (fig. 177). Associate members were incorporated into full membership in 1964 and those former associates who remained loyal to the club, such as Bob Brown and Charlotte Halliday, were now absorbed. From 1964, however, the number of submissions had started to decrease and this pattern continued with minor fluctuations through to the mid-1970s. The only way to increase revenue was through fee and subscription increases. On average throughout the decade, half of the exhibits were from members, academicians or members of FBA-affiliated societies.[14] While, for some, integration with other FBA societies meant a dilution and a loss of identity, it provided, for the most part, a genial two-way traffic, the benefits of which outweighed any disadvantages. Reflecting on the shows of the 1950s and 1960s, Dunstan recalled that landscape paintings probably 'made up the majority of exhibits at those NEAC exhibitions', continuing the tradition of Steer. Landscape painters of Vincent Lines's generation:

> suffered very little from the rigour now fashionable. They frequented pleasant places, trusted their eyes, and set down their observations in a refined and flexible convention derived from Impressionism and the great English landscapists ... the landscape artists of that period seem to me the most well-balanced. They gave an impression of cheerfulness and serenity ... they did not appear competitive at all. They put me in mind of Degas' remark to an over-ambitious youth, 'In my day we did not *get on*'.[15]

Women painters played a large part in producing 'unshowy' work that contained 'a direct and affectionate response to subject matter'.[16] A life-affirming serenity filled the canvases of Margaret Thomas, Ann R. Le Bas and Jean Clark.[17]

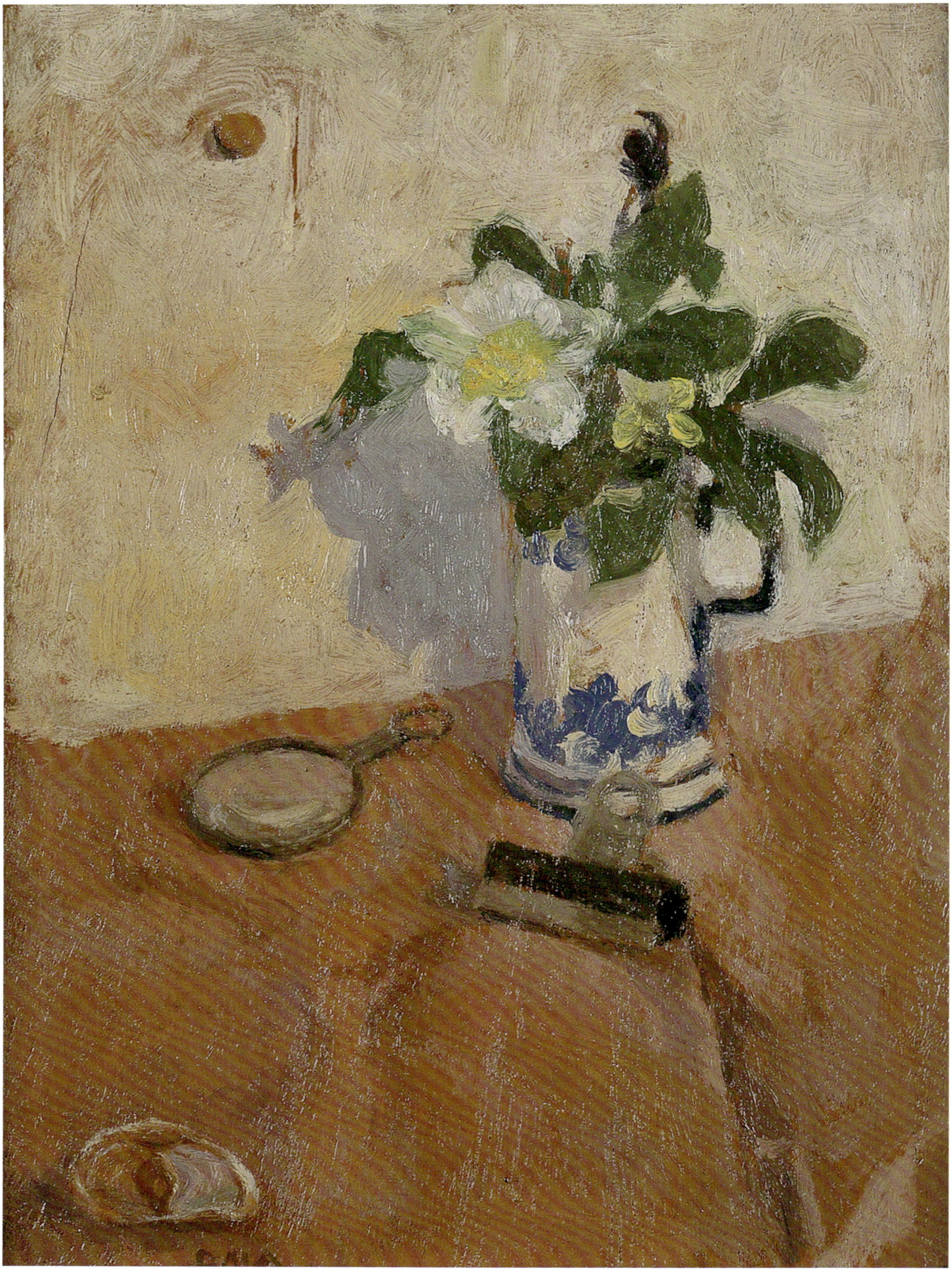

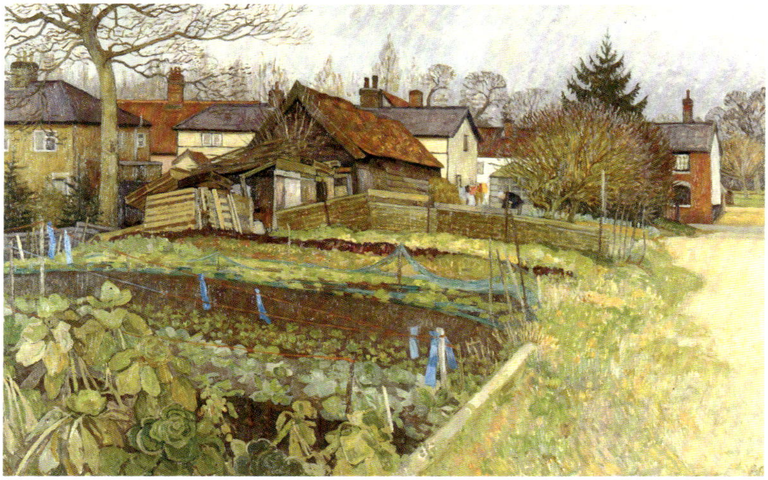

Right
Fig. 178 Diana Calvert
Archie Hubbard's Vegetable Garden, 1984
Oil on board, 76 x 107 cm
Private collection

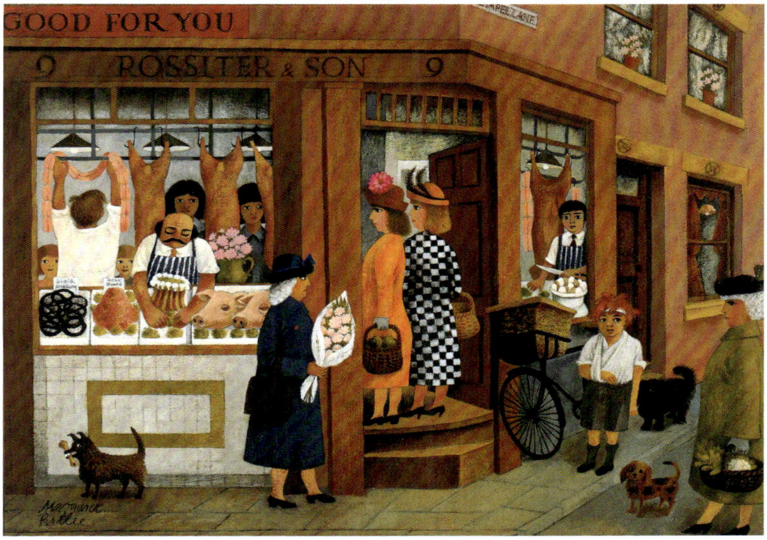

Right
Fig. 179 Margaret Pullée
Butcher's Shop, Leeds, 1969
Oil on canvas, 45.72 x 50.8 cm
Private collection

It characterised the work of Diana Armfield (fig. 180), Diana Calvert (fig. 178), Jane Corsellis (fig. 203), Josephine Harris, Anna Hornby and Susan Ryder.[18] Yet, even with the extraordinary street scenes of Margaret Pullée (fig. 179) bringing a new dimension to the genre of Burn, Guthrie and Cole, the club was not strong enough to regain its former standing.[19] Influential associates such as Ian Simpson and Audrey Melville left and other recent recruits abandoned the club, only to return fifteen years later when its fortunes revived. While it sought to sustain its traditions, the club lost visibility.

By the time the FBA moved to the Mall Galleries in 1971, it had grown to twenty societies, none of which, according to Michael Shepherd in *The Sunday Telegraph*, could be considered avant-garde. Despite the feeling that these groups were a haven for the 'Sunday painter' and the 'evening sketcher', there

Opposite
Fig. 180 Diana Armfield
Christmas Rose on the Studio Table, 1971
Oil on board, 20.3 x 14.6 cm
Private collection

were 'considerable surprises in store for the sharp-eyed'.[20] Among the FBA societies, the New English was the least tolerant of amateurs, but the reservoir of dedicated 'professional' figurative painters was drying up, as art schools converted to conceptual or 'hard-edged' abstraction. It is, as a result, more difficult to stop the clock around 1970 to ask questions about the character and content of club exhibitions than at any other time in its history because its leading painters were not conspicuous builders of public careers demanding frequent critical attention. Peter Fuller, for instance, regarded the work of Peter Greenham and Richard Eurich as 'among the most considerable of the decade', yet he found himself wondering 'how many art students have ever heard their names, let alone seen their pictures'.[21] The values embedded in such artists as Cosmo Clark, Vincent Lines and Charles Mahoney had gone but had not been replaced, and the attendant group of enthusiasts and collectors was dwindling. Dealers like David Wolfers of the New Grafton Gallery would maintain this modest market in mixed exhibitions centred upon the work of New English Associates of the Royal Academy, but the early years at the Mall Galleries were plagued with worries that the club had lost its way and was being swamped by the other art societies affiliated to the FBA (fig. 181). Bowyer remained honorary secretary throughout the 1970s and, in 1975, Edward Pullée succeeded Dubery as honorary treasurer.

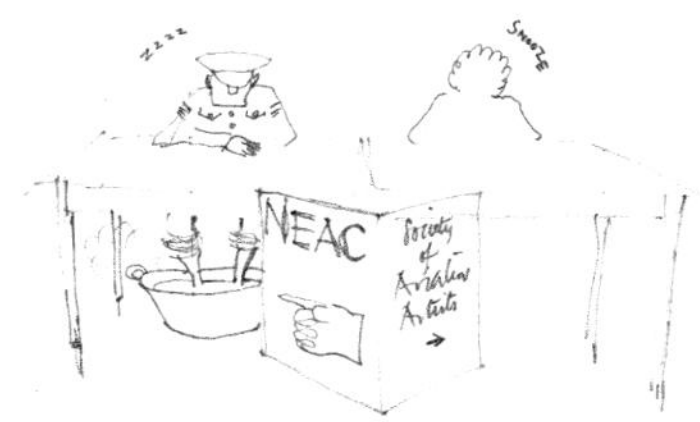

Fig. 181 Charlotte Halliday
Agenda Paper Doodle, 1974
Pen, 7 x 6 cm
NEAC Archive

In an attempt to become as self-sufficient as possible, the executive committee began to meet in each other's homes, away from the Mall Galleries, and to take back a large part of the running of the club. Members-only exhibitions in London – at the Alpine Club, South Audley Street, and at Leighton House, and at Aldeburgh in Suffolk and King's Lynn and Norwich in Norfolk – were organised in addition to the open Salons at the Mall Galleries. All these extra shows entailed a great deal of work and it was realised that more officers were needed on the committee. The post of keeper and assistant keeper were created in 1980, with Edward Bishop being the club's first keeper. Charlotte Halliday, the club's first assistant keeper, assumed the role of keeper in 1989. Ten years earlier, other members were rallying in an attempt to lift the club's profile. Thomas became the club's self-appointed archivist and energetically wrote to supporters and potential sponsors, while Howard, a war artist with the Army at the time (see fig. 182), set up a successful exhibition for members at the Octagon Galley in Belfast – re-establishing the continuing tradition of provincial dealer's shows.[22]

The club's fortunes began to revive, and sales that had plummeted to a mere 17 in 1975 rose to 49 by 1979. Simultaneously, important – though isolated – voices began to emerge from the critical wilderness calling for a much wider understanding of the visual field and for serious discussion about the place of traditional skills. Although the naïve adoption of mass-produced imagery had been one of the liberating aspects of Pop Art, the 'mega-visual' of the late 1970s demanded a critical understanding of meaning and technical filtering.[23] It is no accident that the exploitation of new visual sources in press photographs and cinema stills produced a reassessment of the late work of Sickert at this time.[24] However, there was still general disapproval of simply recording appearances. Painting what you see as you see it was somehow no longer adequate. In polemical articles in the ailing *Studio International*, Andrew Brighton spotlighted what he referred to as 'consensus' painting.[25] It addressed the subject of 'popular', as distinct from 'Pop' painting, and could range from night-class still-lifes to the work of the wild-life and 'big-game' painter, David Shepherd. When he returned to the topic at the beginning of the 1980s, Brighton referred specifically to the Slade craft tradition that was forced into the 'byways and backwaters' by 'art historicist ... state institutions'.[26] He makes clear that:

> This scholarly culture of contemporary art occludes the dumb materiality of painting and has ceased to value the way understandings are made of it, that is through skill, through tacit knowledge.[27]

The achievements of New English stalwarts such as Allan Gwynne-Jones and Peter Greenham were unjustly neglected, as was the unsung mainstream of British painting they represented. They were thoughtful, retiring individuals who, when they talked about 'ideas', meant 'ideas for new paintings' or, specifically, visual motifs – things in life that caught the eye and provoked the desire to paint. It was, of course, a private dialogue, out of kilter with an art world in which 'ideas' signified the explicitly non-visual in a Marcel Duchamp 'readymade'. Only *The Artist* magazine, for which Dunstan had been contributing editor in the 1960s, seemed interested in work that delighted in the record of appearances – albeit in a 'how to' style publication in which discussion of representational issues was often reduced to the merits of particular methods and tools of the trade.[28]

Fig. 182 Ken Howard
Roden Street, Belfast, c. 1979
Oil on canvas, 153 x 183 cm
Private collection

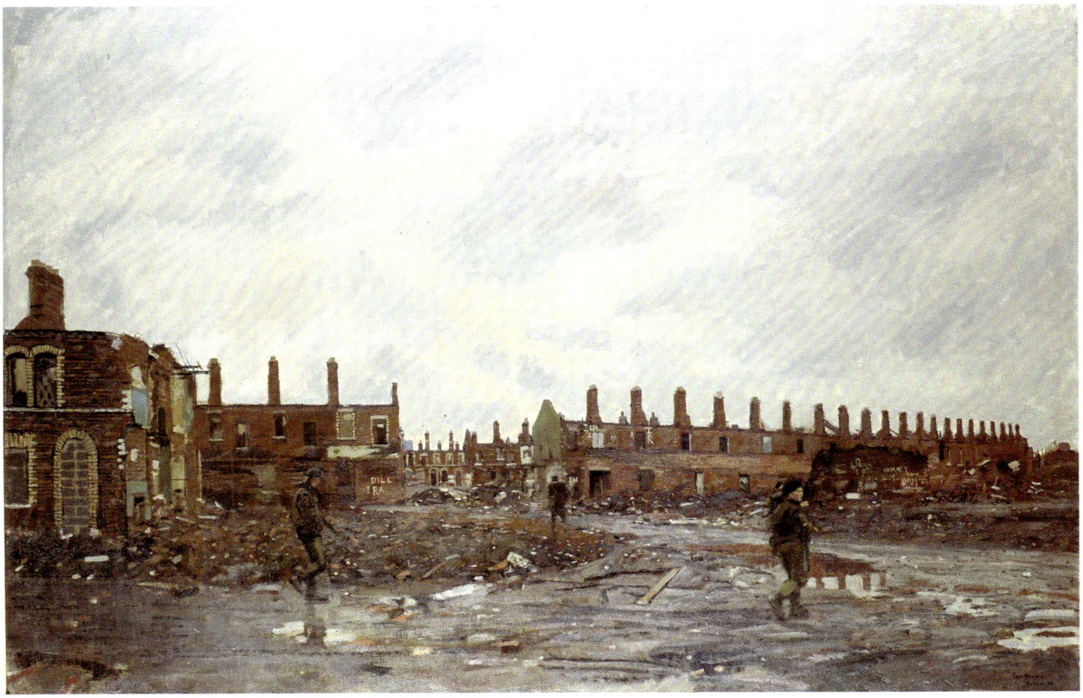

Brighton's position required no mediation, although Peter Fuller, the most coherent iconoclast of modernism of his generation, stood beside him. Berger's obsessions – in *Ways of Seeing* – with advertising and the 'objectification' of women, as by-products of Western materialism, were sharply criticised, but the damage was done and critics like Richard Cork began to talk about the death of painting.[29] Art was more manifestly concerned with the quality of thought than the quality of handwork, a fact confirmed in further arid Arts Council-inspired 'conceptual' shows such as *The New Art* staged at the Hayward Gallery in 1972. The Arts Council, now the principal public patron, had its own academy. The municipalities were only able to add to their collections with its financial assistance and the help of charities, public donations and government-supported quangos – in a bureaucratic paper chase seemingly designed to realise the political objective of local disempowerment.[30] Fuller attacked the outlets of state patronage that, through the Tate/Arts Council nexus, had led to a 'squalid decadence, characterised by a growing dissociation between the artist and *any* public, except the art world public'.[31] In 1937 Coldstream's plea for greater understanding between the artist and the public at large, reiterated in the Sickertian New English 1957 manifesto, was once more in need of restatement.

It remains the case that during much of this period only those New English painters who had become Academicians received national recognition, and then only in shows not supported by the Arts Council. Frederick Gore's exhibition 'British Painting, 1952–1977' at the Royal Academy included New English regulars such as Bowyer, Burn, Cuming, Dunstan, Eurich, Greenham and Gwynne-Jones, as well as those like John Nash, Gilbert Spencer and Claude Rogers, who had once been club members. The exhibition, like Baxandall and James's anthology for the Festival of Britain or Duveen's survey in 1930, afforded the opportunity to analyse the current New English effect. These half-dozen stalwarts were surrounded by 'untitled' abstracts – both gestural and 'cool'; late examples of Pop Art; expressive figuration from Francis Bacon to John Bratby; the impenetrable paint surfaces of Frank Auerbach; the quirky suburban 'visions' of Carel Weight, and much else besides. The selection of quotations that accompanied Gore's catalogue introduction demonstrated the lack of overall coherence and consensus.[32] Recent debates about the viability of the medium were replayed and Cork's belief that painting was less interesting than the 'new media', Installation and Performance art, was destined to reverberate through the next generation.

Where the club's pedigree dictated Duveen's show, it was marginal for Gore's. Its seven representatives had already been absorbed by the Academy as either Associates or full Academicians. They formed an élite within the club, seeking an opportunity to create a dedicated space for representational painting that the Academy, now belatedly courting Pop artists, could not provide. This new relationship with the Academy was first noted by William Packer, who considered that the club's revival in the 1980s had, 'oddly enough', been achieved 'under the encouragement of a number of active members of the present Academy'.[33] Members were often senior figures in other FBA societies – especially the Royal Society of British Artists, the Royal Institute of Painters in Oil Colours and the Royal Watercolour Society – and while FBA politics sometimes usurped the discussion at club meetings, the club undoubtedly felt secure in the regular winter shows at the Mall Galleries. Growing confidence provoked ambition, but there were no critical champions. Even if writers such as Fuller were broadly sympathetic, they did not line up in the manner of Moore and MacColl.

Bowyer and painters of his generation relentlessly promoted the 'New English tradition'.[34] In his case the initial influences of Ruskin Spear and Carel Weight provided the basis for vigorous handling and bold colour, rooted in the familiar tracks of Chiswick Mall and Richmond Terrace.[35] He spoke for most of the members when in 1988 he declared that he really needed 'to be in contact with the subject that [he was] painting'. Paraphrasing Cézanne, he felt that he could stand on one spot and, simply by turning a few degrees, face new and desirable motifs.[36] Art production was hermetic and contemplative; it was attached to familiar places, people and objects; it was about seeing the same old things. He does not mean that there was no variety in it or that the painter could not step outside him or herself, but Chiswick Mall and the estuary at Walberswick (see fig. 183) were Bowyer's patrol.

Bowyer's loyalty to the club, matched that of Tonks and Steer, but, where they witnessed its decline, he presided over its revival. In 1980 the Annual General Meeting reported that submissions had increased to 1,024 and, with fees up from 50p to £1, the historic deficit had been reducing. Sales had also

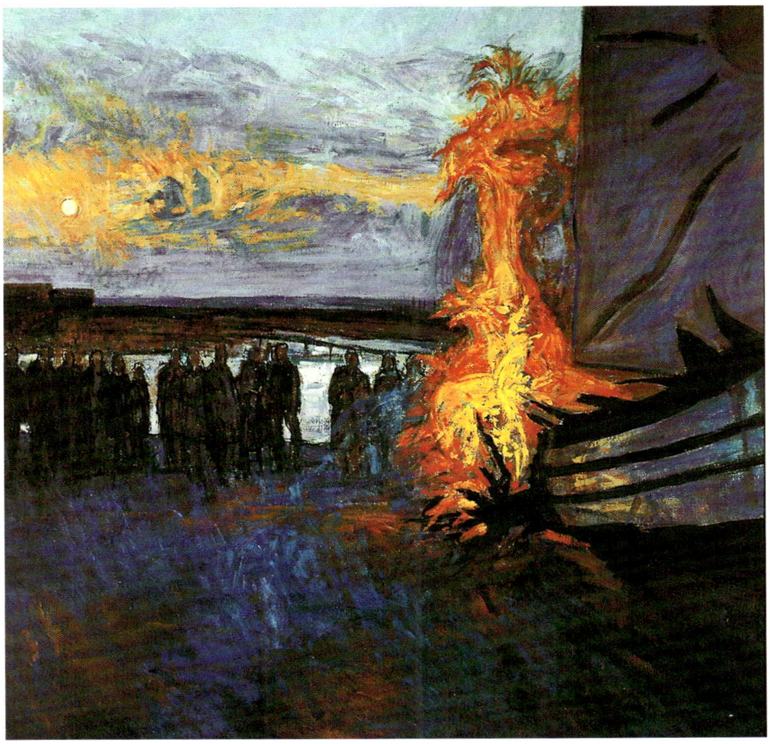

Fig. 183 William Bowyer
Burning Boat, Walberswick, c. 1990
Oil on canvas, 50 x 50 cm
Private collection

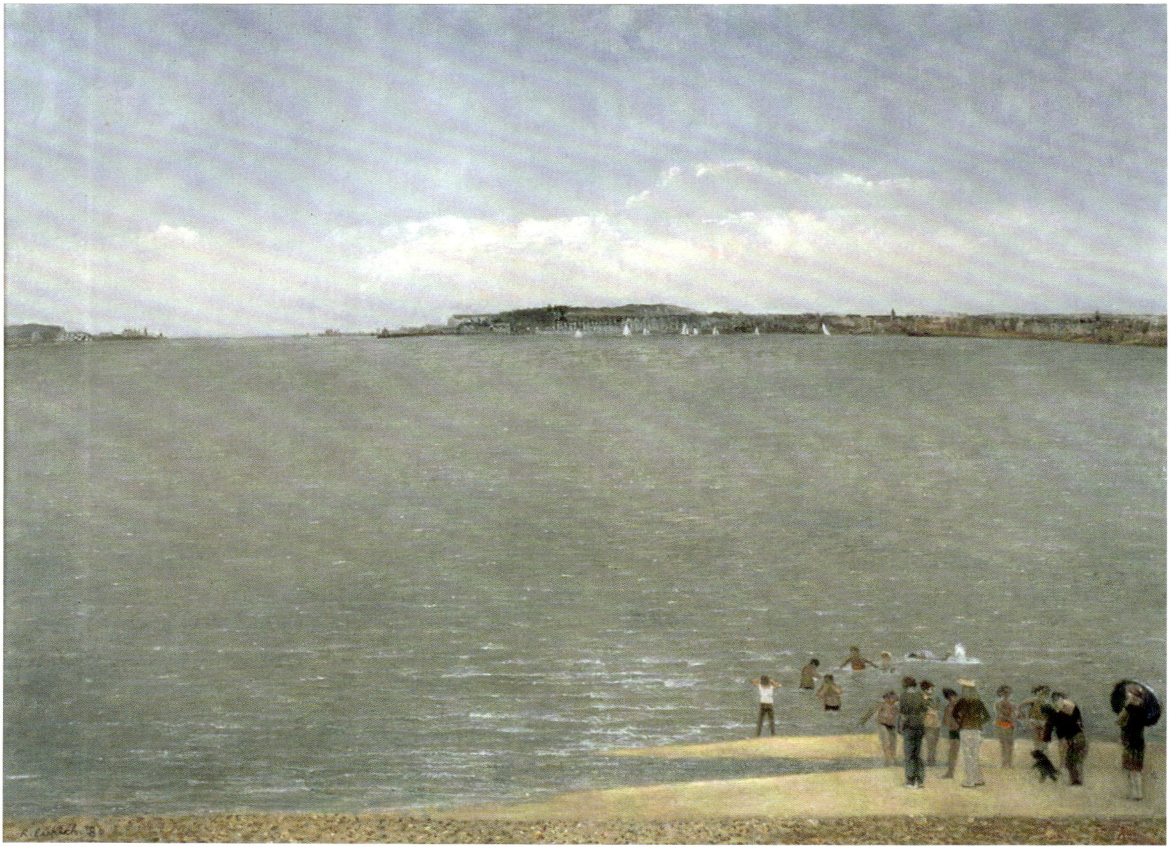

Fig. 184 Richard Eurich
Weymouth Bay, 1980
Oil on canvas, 46 x 76 cm
Private collection

increased by the end of the 1970s.[37] The successful members-only exhibition at Aldeburgh led to more regular 'out-of-town' summer exhibitions and, thereafter, similar shows were held around the country.[38] During the early 1980s, the Hunting Prize was won by stalwart New English painters, Eurich (see fig. 184), Thomas and Howard consecutively. Eurich was aged seventy-seven when he won the prize and it coincided with a major touring retrospective containing 112 works organised by the municipal gallery of his native Bradford. It was impossible not to link the two events, and his 'individuality of vision that insists on subtle distortions and emphases here and there' was greatly admired.[39] Thomas's prize-winning entry in 1982, *The Rembrandt Drawing* (fig. 185), was equally the product of a sustained investigation. Simple, classic studio props are placed on a table and analysed in the presence of Rembrandt, looking down from a postcard self-portrait. It affirmed the continuing importance of still-life painting in Britain in the twentieth century. Having spent years painting in a studio in Edinburgh, Thomas declared influences from both Anne Redpath and Ethel Walker, in work that expressed a hermetic attachment to a particular subject range.[40] Roses placed in an empty bottle, left on a dusty table or favourite chair, beside old postcards pinned to the wall, hint at a story or function as mementoes of a life lived in other places, but brought back to the studio and re-created with affection. Flowers are not 'arranged', as they once were in the era of Adshead, Manson and Benois. Isolated, austere, they come to rest in a manner that expresses their moment, like blossoming twigs in a Shinto shrine.

Its evident joy in everyday experience brought painters such as Bob Brown, Cuming, Harry Eccleston, Hans Schwartz and Rupert Shephard back to the club in the early 1980s, recognising the new strength of its exhibitions and the more vibrant market.[41] Anthony Eyton, a post-war pupil of Rogers and Coldstream and a natural sympathiser with New English Associates at the Academy, found his way into club in 1985, two years before he was elected Academician. In the same year Ken Howard penned the introduction to *Royal Academy Illustrated*, in which he drew attention to some of the New English coterie.[42] Two years earlier, his Hunting Prize-winning entry (fig. 186) had been a formidable upright self-portrait demonstrating a continuing fascination with mirrors and reflections that bring daylight into the darker spaces in which the artist assumes a shadowy presence.

Below left
Fig. 185 Margaret Thomas
The Rembrandt Drawing, 1981
Oil on canvas, 107 x 91 cm
Private collection

Below right
Fig. 186 Ken Howard
Self-portrait at South Bolton Gardens, 1983
Oil on canvas, 183 x 91 cm
Private collection

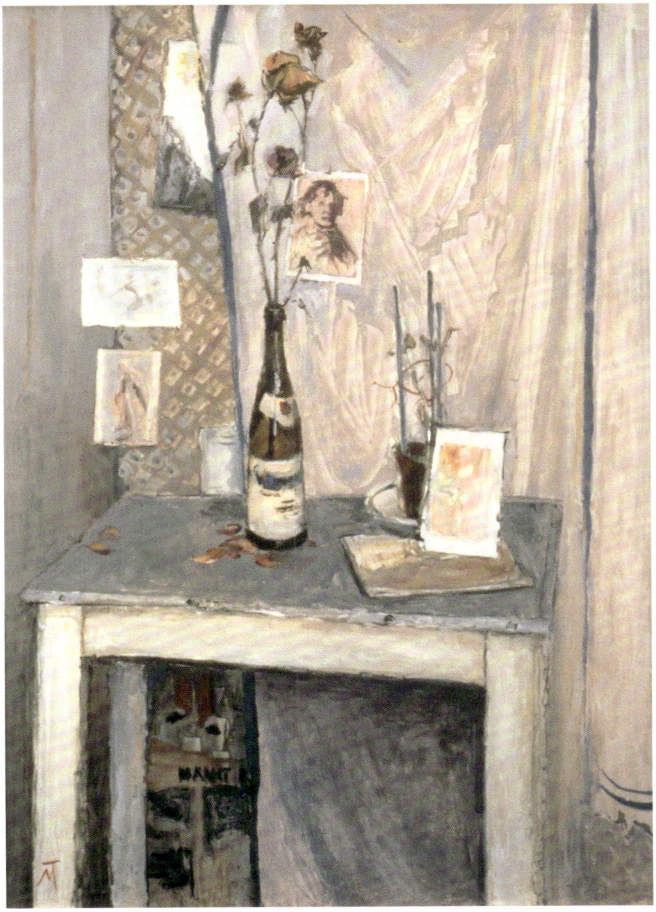

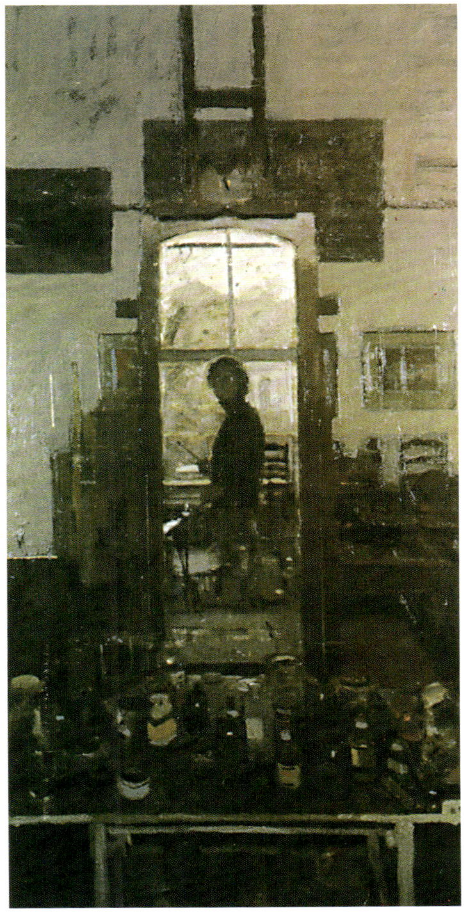

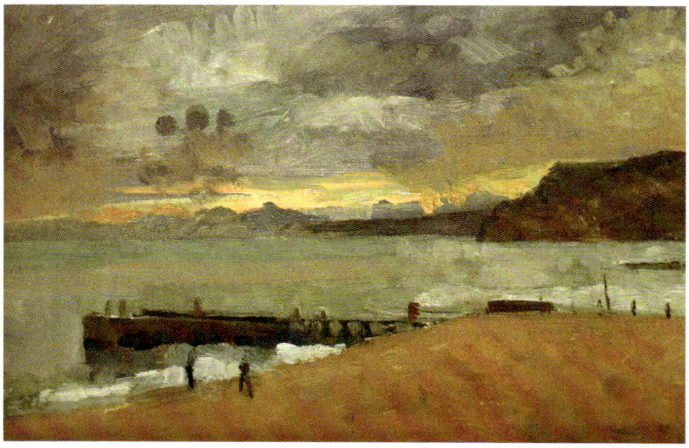

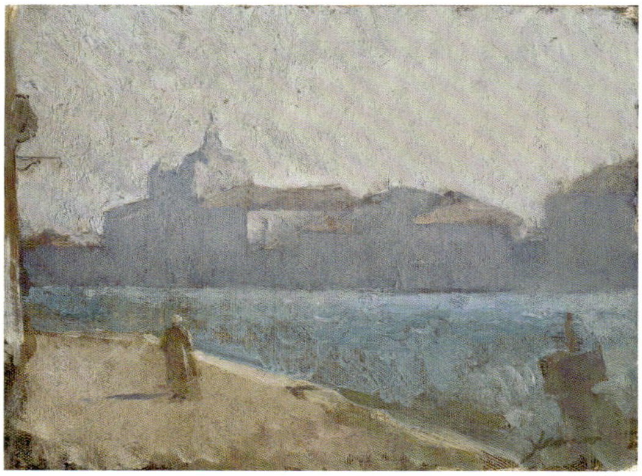

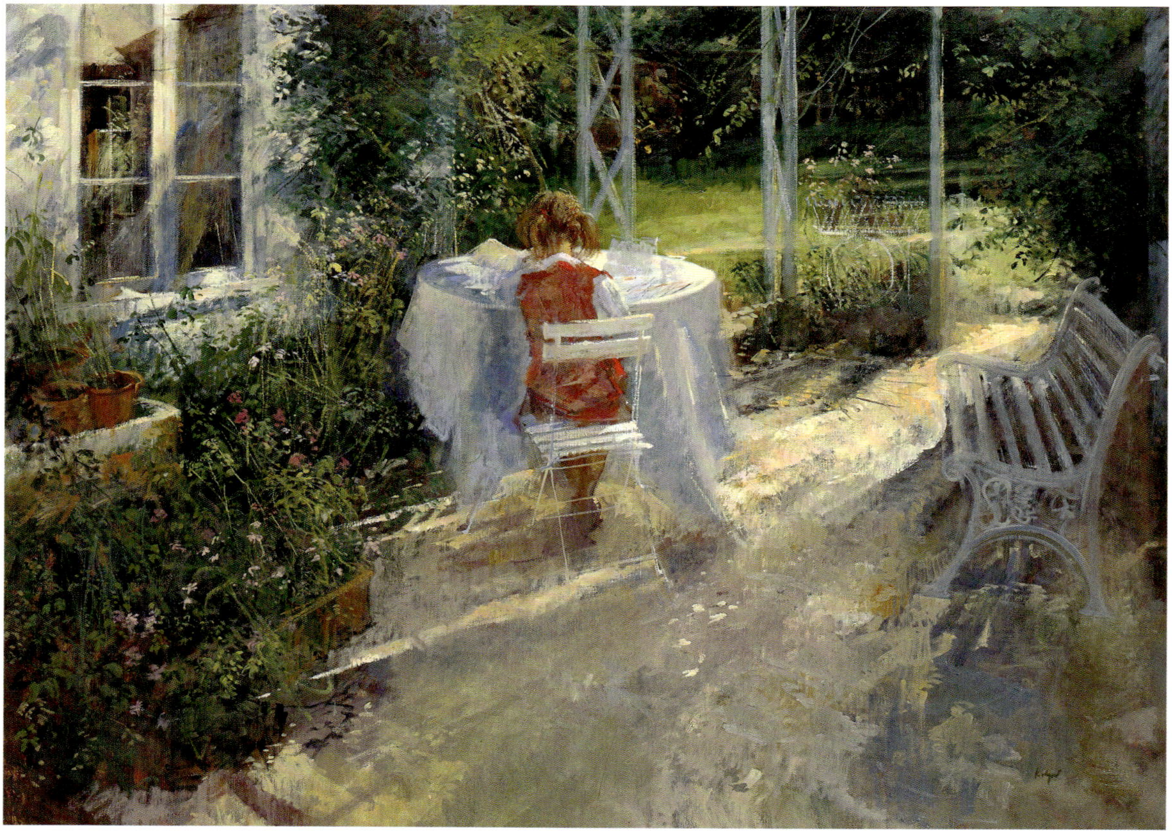

Top left
Fig. 187 Richard Pikesley
Evening Sky, West Bay, 1985
Oil on canvas, 15.2 x 22.8 cm
Private collection

Top right
Fig. 188 Martin Yeoman
Returning from the Shops, 1989
Oil on canvas, 14.6 x 18.4 cm
Private collection

Above
Fig. 189 Peter Kuhfeld
Florence in the Courtyard, 1989
Oil on canvas, 50.8 x 76.2 cm
Private collection

A young cadre, including Peter Kuhfeld (see fig. 189), Tom Coates, Richard Pikesley (see fig. 187), Martin Yeoman (see fig. 188) and Mary Jackson (see fig. 190), were submitting their work from the mid-1970s onwards.[43]

This cluster of painterly *plein-airistes* ensured the furtherance of New English impressionism. All, like Dunstan, Ward, Armfield, Howard, Corsellis, Michael Pullée and Bob Brown, became habitués of Venice – a city that, as is frequently observed, 'was made for painters'.[44] Indeed, in the last thirty years of the twentieth century, there is scarcely a New English exhibition in which Venetian scenes do not appear. In St Mark's or on the Grand Canal there is an air of expectation as famous angles and viewpoints are rediscovered. The gaunt crumbling façades, deserted piazzas and *calli* that exerted a fascination for Whistler's and Sargent's generations are now fronted with friezes of tourists dressed in motley modern colours. Like the teaming figures in a Canaletto they await a pageant, little realising that, for the painter, they are the pageant.

At the same time Tuscany, the Dordogne and Provence replaced the Home Counties landscape. Artists profited from the boom in European travel, in some cases establishing second studios. While this was not a new phenomenon, the shifting emphasis demands explanation. Back in 1965, Bryan Robertson had observed that the younger generation had 'turned its back on the English landscape tradition', feeling that it evoked 'a dated nostalgia, a digression from the basic problems of modern art'.[45] By the mid-1980s this view had begun to change,

Fig. 190 Mary Jackson
Academia Shadow, c. 1990
Oil on board, 24.7 x 24.7 cm
Private collection

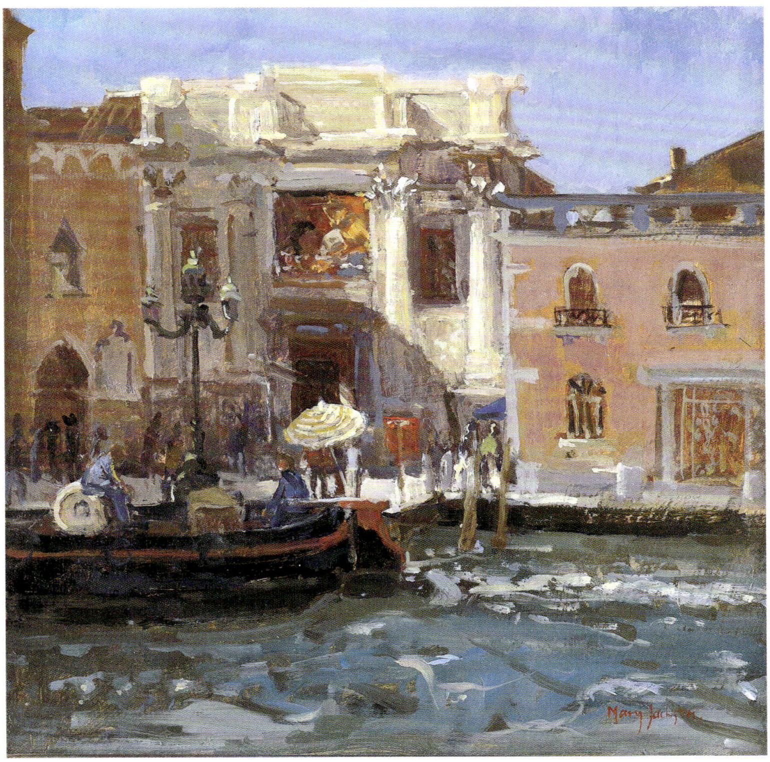

but the balance had tipped in favour of Italy and France. Sargent's *dolce far niente* was revisited for the era of the package holiday and the 'time-share' apartment. Abiding images of alfresco lunches under the trellised vines, by Jackson and Kuhfeld, belie the serious skills that go into their making. They claim the warm south for English art. They substitute a rich palette for the neglected seasides that Cuming and Pikesley observed in the pallor of evening. The Channel Packet boat, once frequented by New English regulars, had become a Hovercraft.

One glowing English exception that did not suffer neglect was the Suffolk village of Walberswick and the neighbouring seaside resort of Southwold. For New English artists these were places with a Steer provenance. In the 1950s they were rediscovered by Margaret Green and Lionel Bulmer, Dubery and Dunstan had painted there and, by the late 1970s, Bowyer was taking his family there for holiday retreats. The little towns at the mouth of the Blyth were to the New English what St Ives had been for Peter Lanyon's generation.[46] However, where the pyrotechnics of the New York School came to Lanyon in sudden Atlantic squalls, Walberswick, in the eyes of Bulmer and Bowyer, presented a seemingly endless succession of calm Post-Impressionist days.

Thomas envied Bowyer's capacity to work out of doors, with the distraction of passers-by.[47] She needed indoor seclusion to commune with her objects. She and Armfield, the leading New English still-life painters in the late twentieth century, were, however, no less heroic. In Armfield's case there is a painterly *intimisme* that recalls the work of Vuillard (fig. 192). Soft, subtle colour application is deployed to celebrate domesticated nature and 'the good things in life that people make and do'.[48] By the mid-1980s they had a formidable group of sympathetic friends in the club, who, like Charlotte Ardizzone, Pamela Kay,

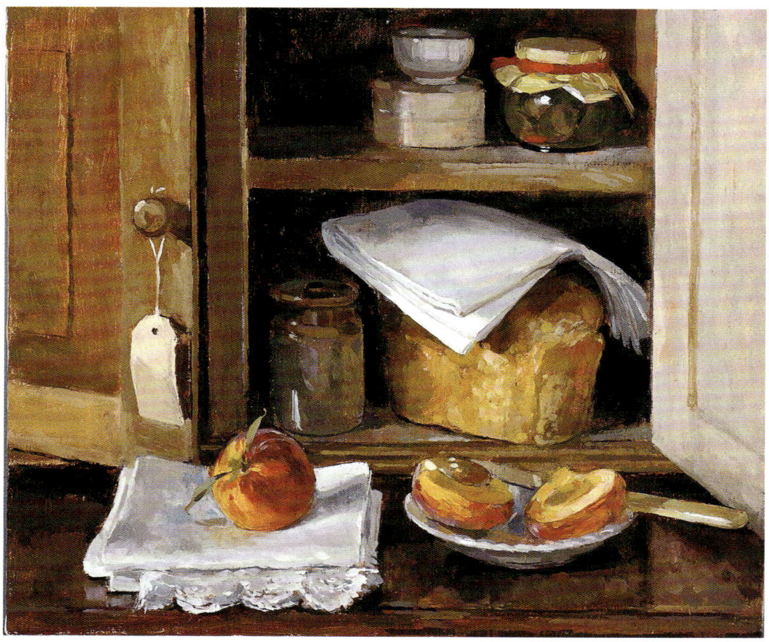

Fig. 191 Pamela Kay
Peaches and Cupboard with Bread, 1989
Oil on canvas, 30.4 x 35.5 cm
Private collection

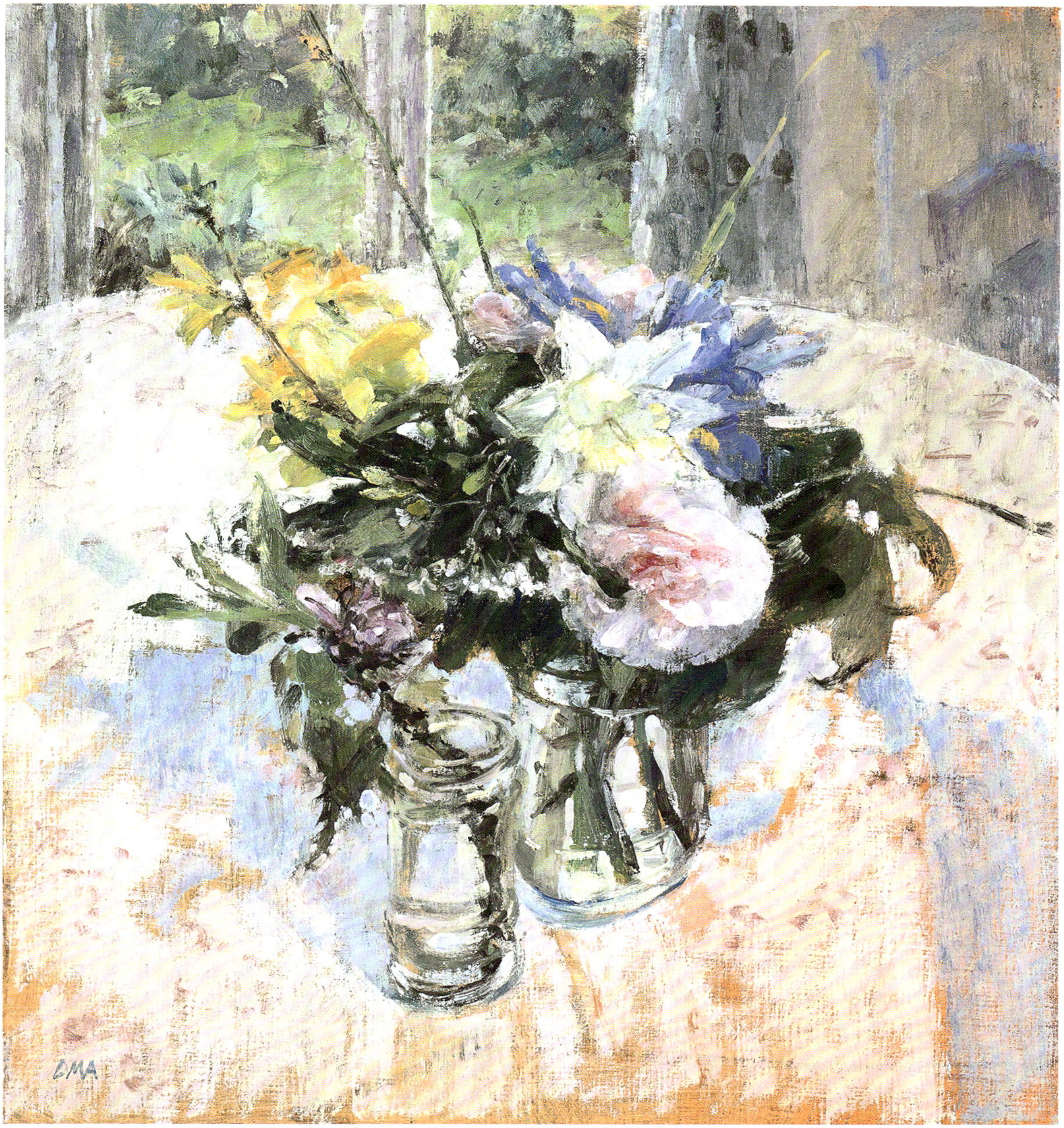

Fig. 192 Diana Armfield
Spring Flowers with Camellia, 1988
Oil on board, 36.9 x 32.4 cm
Private collection

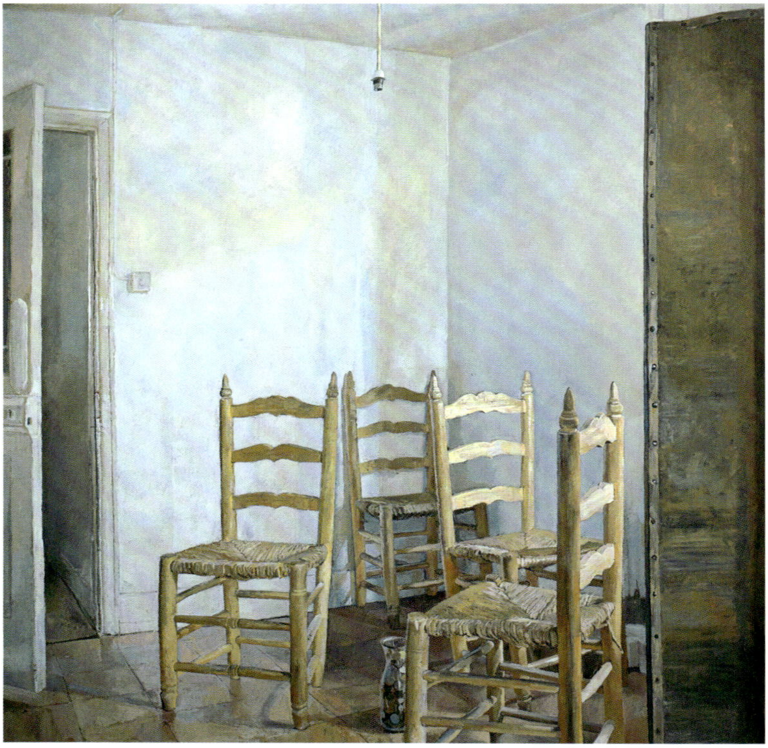

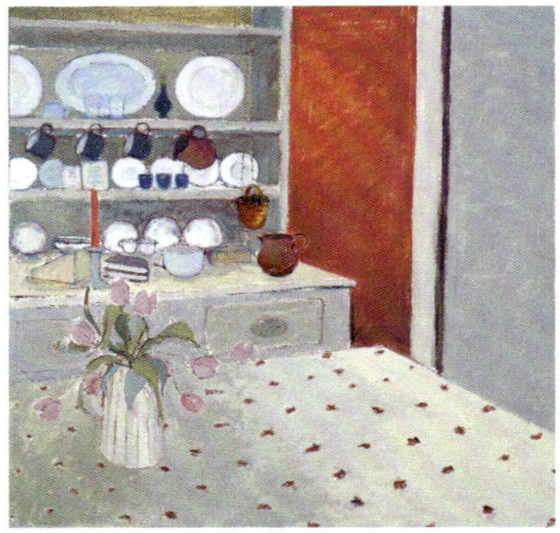

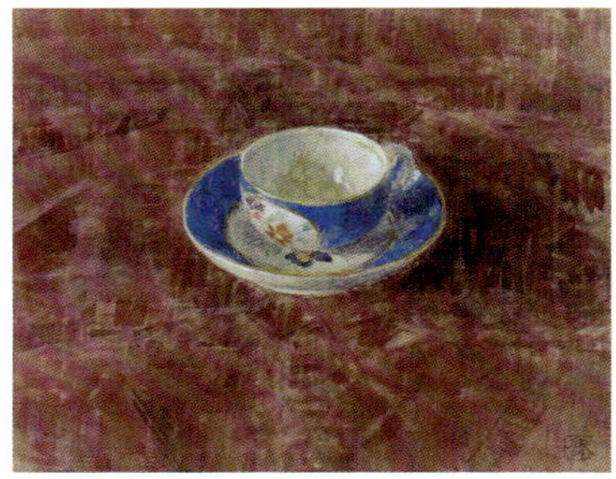

Jacqueline Rizvi and Daphne Todd, focused upon everyday objects. Kay (see fig. 191), for instance, portrays tabletops draped with white cloths on which bowls of flowers or fruit are placed, while Rizvi reduces the objects to a single empty cup or vase (fig. 195). Cézanne's abundance is ranged against the shrill simplicity of a Fantin-Latour. This contrast is mirrored in the work of Ardizzone and Todd – artists whose objects frequently relate to the wider spaces of a room, a courtyard or a landscape. Ardizzone (see fig. 194) talks of Morandi and objects that dominate their surroundings as vivid notes of colour, while Todd is more preoccupied with space. Her *Four Spanish Chairs* (1985; fig. 193) the Hunting Prize winner of 1985, maps the austere white-washed space of a rustic villa.[49]

Similar classifications can be found in the paintings of interiors. After 1985 a typical winter show might take the viewer from the sumptuous drawing rooms of Susan Ryder (fig. 196) and the Spartan attics and workshops of Jason Bowyer and his brother Francis (figs 197 and 198).[50] The decade spawned a fascination for such spaces. It coincides with the emergence of such publications as *The World of Interiors*, and what social commentators referred to as the pornography of possessions. As in 'cabinet' paintings of the nineteenth century, there was a consistent need to reflect upon middle-class aspiration by exposing the spaces of intimate display. Private affluence was seen amid public squalor – to quote the famous phrase of J. K. Galbraith. Ryder's painting celebrated the former, leaving the latter to the painters of the new Glasgow School.[51]

Above left
Fig. 193 Daphne Todd
Four Spanish Chairs, 1985
Oil on panel, 122 x 122 cm
Private collection

Top
Fig. 194 Charlotte Ardizzone
The Dresser, 2001
Oil on canvas, 76.3 x 76.3 cm
Private collection

Above
Fig. 195 Jacqueline Rizvi
Still-life: The Russian Cup and Saucer, 2004
Watercolour, 23 x 32 cm
Collection the artist

Right
Fig. 196 Susan Ryder
The Staircase at Duninald, c. 1990
Oil on canvas, 71 x 45.7 cm
Private collection

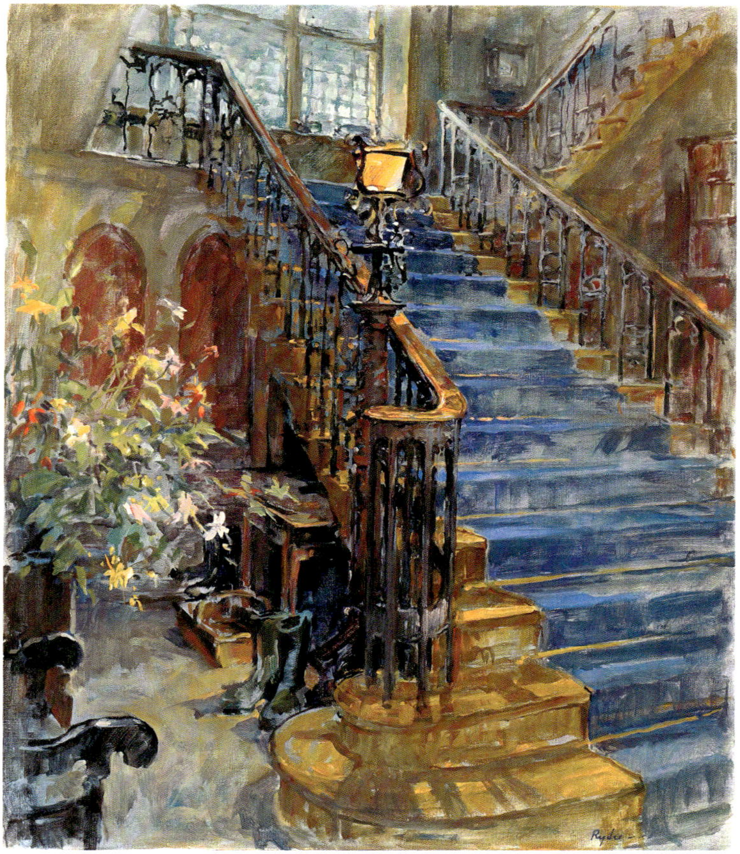

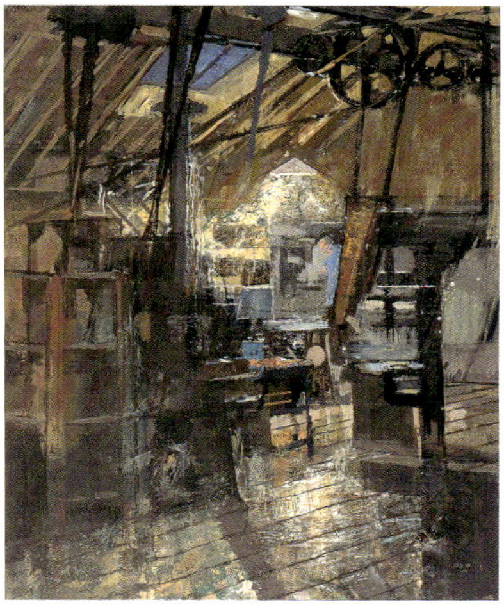

Above
Fig. 197 Jason Bowyer
Belt-driven Workshop, c. 1989
Mixed media on canvas,
152.4 x 121.9 cm
Collection Kew Bridge Steam Museum

Right
Fig. 198 Francis Bowyer
The Studio at 4 o'clock, 2003
Oil on canvas, 100 x 100 cm
Private collection

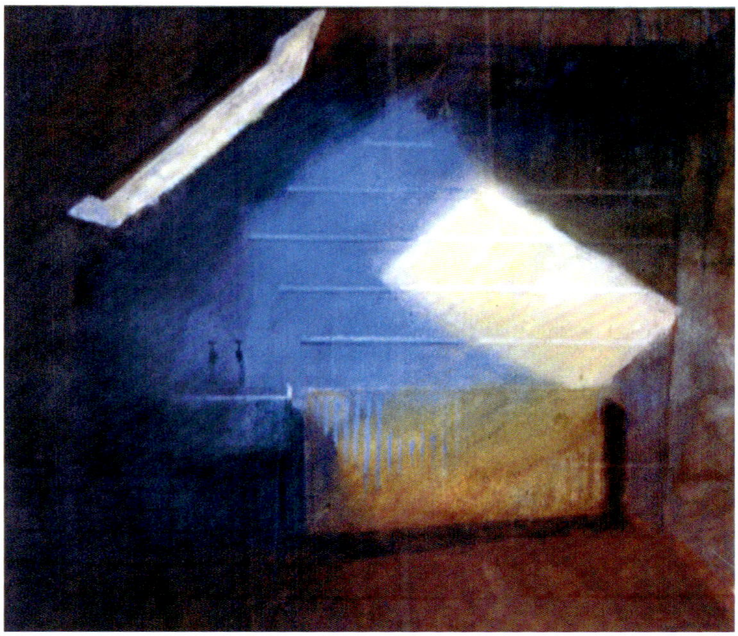

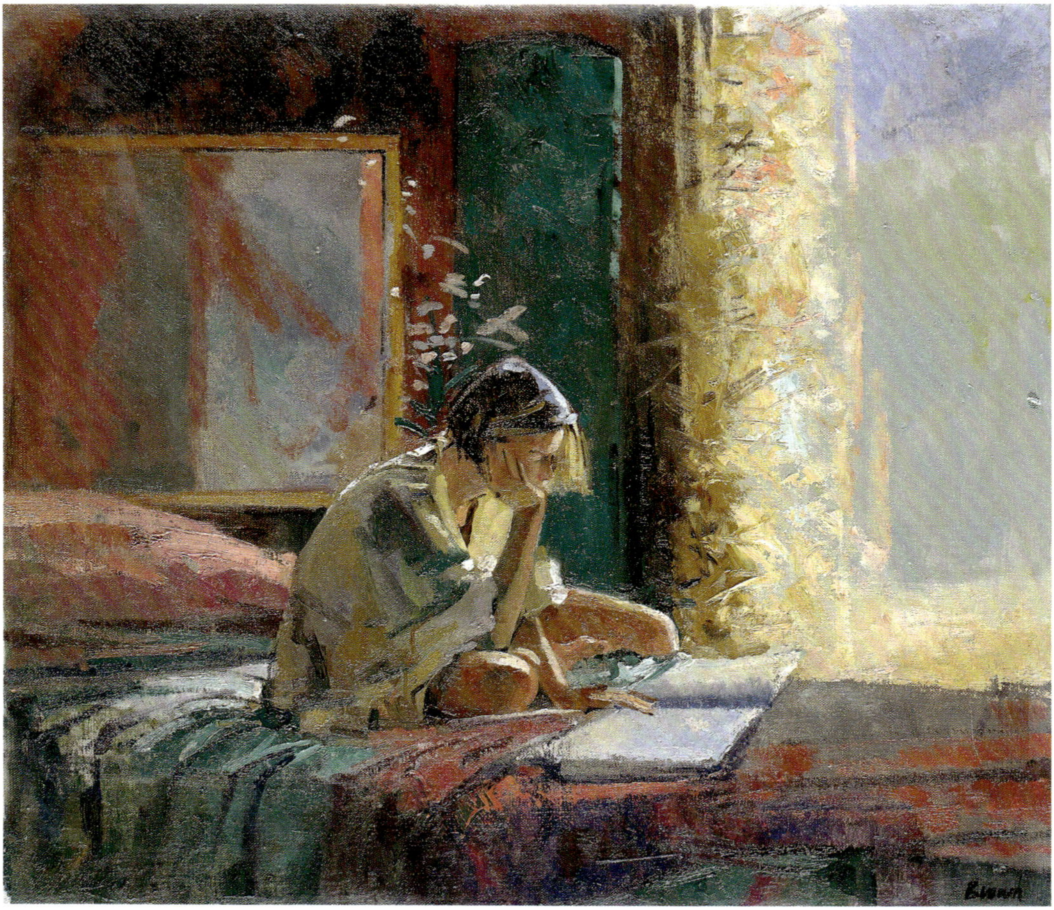

Fig. 199 Robert Brown
Following the Libretto, *c.* 1990
Oil on canvas, 40.6 x 50.8 cm
Private collection

A wide range of approaches is evident in figure painting – in the portraits of Barry Atherton, Jane Bond and James Rushton and in the nudes of Bob Brown (fig. 199), Coates and Howard. Bond's precision contrasts with Rushton's painterliness, while all three 'life' painters delight in the formal arrangement of figure and setting. Not all New English painting around 1990 was confined to the studio. The authority for this genre lay in an earlier generation, in Charles McCall's interiors (fig. 200) and in Dunstan's *intimisme* (fig. 202). Fuller, in the teeth of mega-visual outpourings, admired *Bathroom, Spoleto* (1983) for the artist's genuine perceptions and authentic sentiments – 'through the impressionist play of light, Dunstan's love of world, flesh and woman is self-evident'. He was a better painter than Ewan Uglow.[52] His personal formula of 'pleasant places' matched with a 'refined and flexible convention derived from Impressionism and the great English landscapists' held true for Coates, Howard, Jackson, Pikesley and Cuming.

At the same time painters such as June Berry, Diana Calvert, Jane Corsellis, William Selby and Dawn Sidoli were more eclectic. Corsellis's rich palette, for

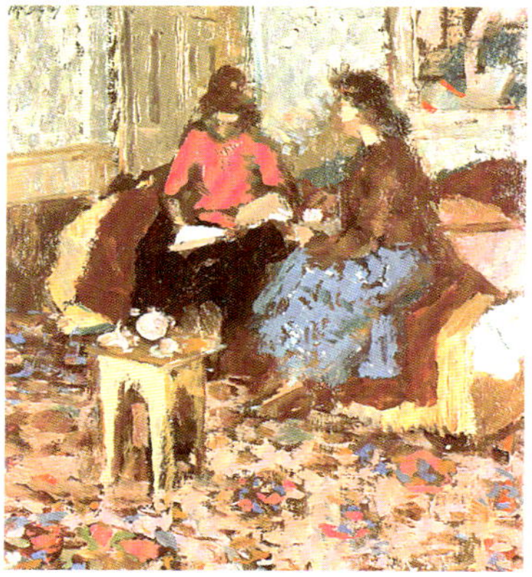

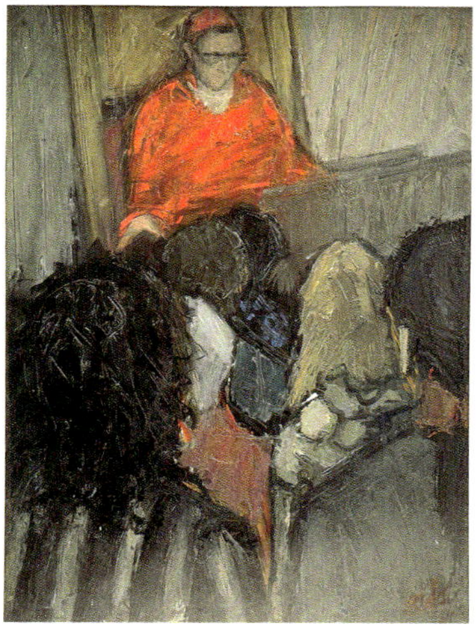

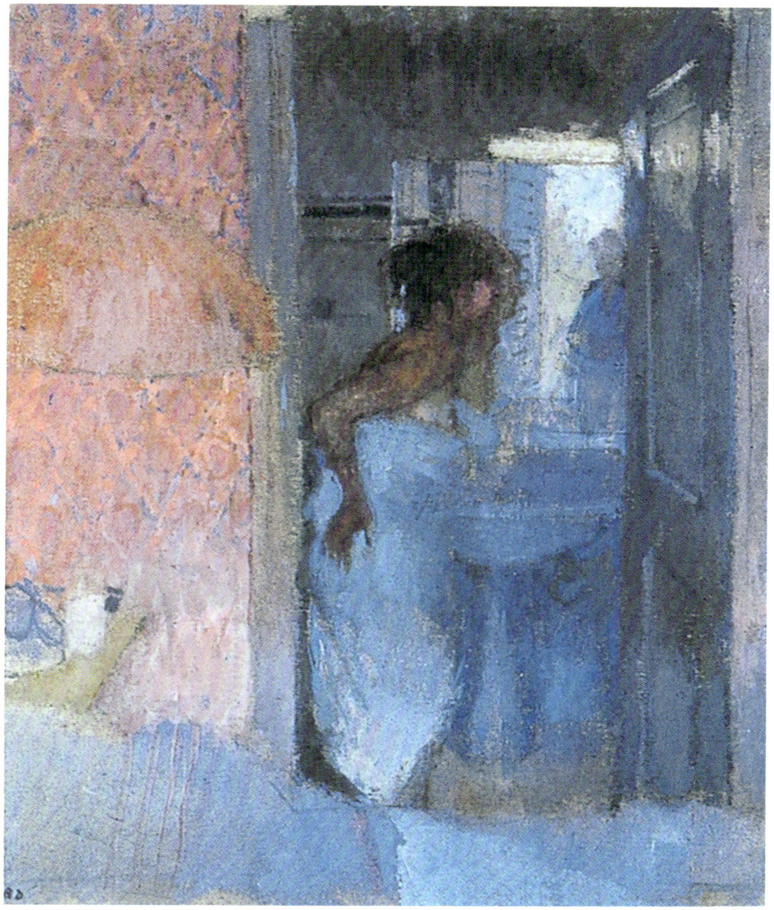

Top
Fig. 200 Charles McCall
The Tea Party, c. 1950
Oil on canvas, 34.3 x 30.5 cm
Location unknown

Above
Fig. 201 Dawn Sidoli
The Bishop's Visit, 1991
Oil on canvas, 35.5 x 27.9 cm
Private collection

Above right
Fig. 202 Bernard Dunstan
Bathroom, Spoleto, 1983
Distemper on canvas, 91.4 x 76.2 cm
Private collection

instance (fig. 203), is accumulated from the experiences of a wide range of exotic locations in Italy, the Far East and North America, while the bold *facture* of a Sidoli (fig. 201) occasionally recalls the painterly patchwork of Joan Eardley.

How significant was this painting at the time of the emergence of BritArt? The New English, despite the obvious truth that the older generation of Bowyer and Pullée spent much of their lives managing art schools, had little impact upon the practice in art education at the time.[53] During ten years of Tory government, 'theory-driven' post-modernist fine-art practice prophetically described by Brighton as an 'attitude' or ideology, 'rather than the practice of particular media', steered education. With the neglect of traditional skills, a National Advisory Body report, delivered in 1987, advocated the teaching of what were termed 'transferable skills', in more general art courses. Fine art practised 'for its own sake' was beginning to be 'edged out in favour of market-directed courses in design'.[54] The young artist's ambition was to win a major prize and be taken up by an influential dealer – rather than patiently build success in group shows or with the New English.[55]

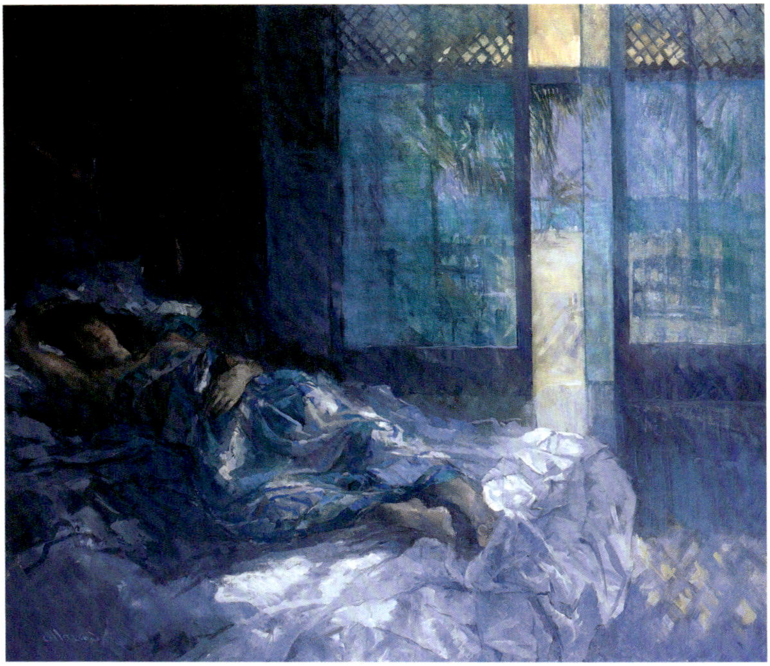

Fig. 203 Jane Corsellis
Resting in the Shade, 1989
Oil on canvas, 114 x 127 cm
Collection the artist

It might seem that a strange time warp brought a group of men and women to the basement rooms of Carlton House Terrace in the 1980s and '90s to select the annual winter show, were it not for the fact that the number of annual submissions remained buoyant. There were plenty of active figurative painters hard at work. Tom Coates's *The Selection Jury of the New English Art Club* (1987; fig. 204), one of a select group of such portraits stretching back to Orpen and beyond, depicts a ritual that enshrines the compromise involved in all self-help artists' societies. David Mills described the 'noisy affair ... occasionally called to order by Bill Bowyer', which in this year took place at Howard's Oriel studio in South Bolton Gardens. If there was no consensus, following democratic practice and governed by the club's rules, a vote was taken.[56] Bowyer was keen to point out that the New English was 'not a clique', implying that all the pitfalls of this consensus selection were recognised. The New English terms of reference were clear. In Armfield's words, painters were upholding 'the value of direct observation coupled with inventiveness, painterliness and imagination'.[57]

But did they reflect middle-class, middle-aged values? Does Coates's picture of jurors seated with their backs to the window facing a canvas – one of 800 that year – portray an anachronism? And what consensus emerges from their deliberations? Despite the vagaries of the art world, the New English had, in the year following its successful centenary exhibition at Christie's, reminded everyone of its presence – and its importance.[58] This exhibition, hastily organised by Anna Robins and Francis Farmar, assisted by Brian Sewell, was an extraordinary capturing of the principal actors in the club's affairs, up to Bowyer's generation.

A discussion on the Radio 4 arts magazine *Kaleidoscope* confirmed the club's central role in the history of British art.[59] The reviewer, Fraser Harrison, made the point, reiterated elsewhere in the press, that such a large survey should have been organised by the Tate Gallery and shown over a longer period. While Christie's concentrated upon a historical exhibition, Sotheby's opened its doors to the current club members for a second exhibition in which the work of Buhler, Cuming and Dunstan was hailed by John Russell Taylor as 'lively and painterly'. However, his headline, 'Contemporary Rebels without a Cause', suggested that the old divisions between the club and the Royal Academy had now been healed and that this painting, filtered by peer group juries, was no longer looking for a critical edge.[60] The well-felt afternoon light and *contre-jour* effects of Coates's *Selection Jury* did not seem revolutionary enough. Robin Stemp commented:

> Say what one will about the Slade influenced post Camden Town/Euston Road school of painting, as exemplified by the New English Art Club, some will criticize it for being unadventurous and low-key. But at least there is no *angst;* no tortured searching for some meaning other than the most important and elusive – that one is alive and aware of the small everyday things that make up one's life.[61]

Armfield was quoted again. Her painting and that of the New English should produce 'some equivalent for the richness of life', and with this comment the whole spectre of Englishness was raised once more. Her world is one in which flowers are brought in from the garden, and placed in a familiar old jug on a table, where the sunlight falls on them. Everyday objects sing.

Following the club's centenary, the Royal Academy staged its survey of 'British Art in the Twentieth Century' in 1987. Intended to be a distillation of the 'modern movement', the selection was restricted to just over seventy artists and echoes of the club's role were confined to the earliest sections devoted to Camden Town. Cork admitted that, as painters such as 'John, Munnings and

Fig. 204 Thomas J. Coates
The Selection Jury of the New English Art Club, 1987
Oil on canvas, 76 x 122 cm
Collection the artist

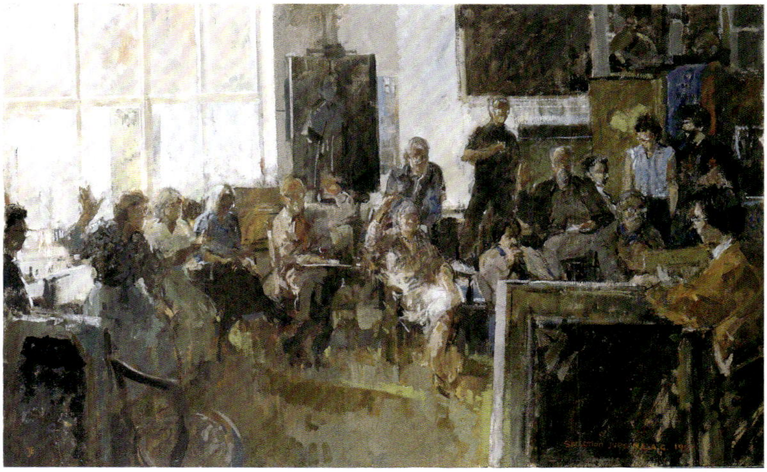

Lowry' were not 'innovators', they, and many others, were left out.[62] Even in its own terms, and by Cork's admission, the enterprise was dubious because it was obliged to include Sickert, an artist never neatly pigeon-holed, and Spencer, a painter 'rooted in earlier traditions'.[63] One could not begin to understand British art by taking one's directions from the Ecole de Paris or the New York School, and avoiding 'the small everyday things'.

However, by 1990, televised, Tate-approved Turner Prize cleverness, outgunning the Hunting in its command of publicity, had invaded the living room. New English painting was forced to wait for the connoisseur of the future, for the discriminating eye that would recognise the qualities in a Cuming or a Corsellis and be prepared to champion them, as Charles Saatchi was doing for the BritArt generation.[64] The collectors were there, supported by such dealers as W. H. Patterson and Manya Igel, but, like Brinsley Ford, they were understated and unsung.[65] In 1988, in an attack on the bombastic abstractions of Gillian Ayres in the Royal Academy summer exhibition, Brian Sewell, art critic of the *Evening Standard*, was prepared to say: 'What quality there is resides less in Academicians than in members of the New English Art Club – Armfield, Howard, Bowyer, Dunstan, Corsellis and their ilk work with measured competence, and within their chosen limits do not disappoint.'[66] This comment might dismiss latter-day Abstract Expressionism, but it was not enough to stem the tide of media publicity and state approval that greeted BritArt in the 1990s. Alternative arguments needed to be marshalled. Peter Fuller, writing in 1988 on 'The Art of England', looked the 'nostalgic myth' in the face, and attacked Fry's and Bell's put-down of English painting and the 'Pevsnerian modernism' that followed it. For him, those who had 'achieved something' worked with a 'sense of continuity with a *British* tradition'.[67] The eccentric and amateur character of this tradition – Fuller liked evening-class students – historically did not find favour with state-managed art production.[68] The scene was set for the culture clashes of the 1990s that, sadly, the writer did not live to see.[69]

NOTES

1 Alan Ross (ed.), *The London Magazine*, vol. 1, no. 4, July 1961, p. 80 (Rodrigo Moynihan); pp. 37–45 (John Russell, 'Paris 1961: the Rearground'); pp. 45–56 (Harold Rosenberg, 'The American Action Painters'); pp. 31–7 (Alan Bowness, 'The Content of Contemporary British Painting'); pp. 57–64 (Robin Ironside, 'Portrait Painting: An Art in Decline'). Ironside's line, that portrait painting was the last bastion of outmoded realism, significant only for its celebration of the social role of the sitter, reiterates Fry's statement in *Reflections on British Painting*, Faber and Faber, London, 1934, that the English patron saw the painter 'merely in his capacity of ministering to the desire for prestige, by painting images of himself and his family'. Fry, it could be argued, accepted this uncritically from Julius Meier-Graefe. The argument was later expanded in aspects of John Berger's essay, 'The Changing View of Man in the Portrait' (1969), reprinted in *Selected Essays and Articles, The Look of Things*, Penguin, Harmondsworth, 1972, pp. 35–41.

2 Edgar Wind, *Art and Anarchy*, Faber and Faber, London, 1963, p. 9.

3 Wind was much preoccupied with the thought that, in 1960, one could travel between London and Paris in a day and visit exhibitions of Picasso and Poussin, appreciating both in equal measure.

4 For Hamilton at this period, see Richard Morphet Introduction in *Richard Hamilton*, exh. cat., Tate Gallery, London, 1970; see also R. C. Kenedy, 'Richard Hamilton Visited', *Art and Artists*, vol. 4, no. 12, 1970, pp. 20–3. For a later commentary of the 'media landscape', see Peter Fuller, *Theoria, Art and the Absence of Grace*, Chatto & Windus, London, 1988, p. 223.

5 For an excellent survey, see *The Sixties Art Scene in London*, David Mellor, exh. cat., Barbican Art Gallery, London, 1993.

6 Bryan Robertson, John Russell and Lord Snowdon, *Private View, The Lively World of British Art*, Nelson, London, 1965, pp. 4–5. It is worth noting that, at this point, when there was a real interest in northern industrial and mining communities in contemporary writing and the theatre, the sole representatives of this phenomenon in London-centred British painting were Lowry and Josef Herman.

7 They were 'Pop Art Redefined', 1969 (Hayward Gallery, London), 'The Art of the Real, An Aspect of American Painting and Sculpture, 1948–1968', 1969 (Arts Council and Tate Gallery, London) and 'When Attitudes become Form', 1969 (Institute of Contemporary Arts, London).

8 Pullée showed landscapes of Yorkshire, Devon, Spain and Italy until 2001.

9 The syntax of still-life had been explored by Dunstan and space mapping by Dubery – see Bernard Dunstan, *Starting to Paint Still Life*, Studio Vista, London, 1969; Fred Dubery and John Willats, *Drawing Systems*, Studio Vista, London, 1972. Although both are written for the general reader, with a 'how to do it' ethos, these two publications demonstrate a profound understanding of medium and genre.

10 The Minister for Education appointed Coldstream as chairman of the National Advisory Council on Art Education in 1959. He reported in October 1960. See *First Report of the National Council for Diplomas in Art and Design* (published by the Council), 1964. It lists the art schools that had been approved to deliver the new curriculum. As a 'degree-equivalent' qualification, the Diploma in Art and Design (Dip. A. D.) was considered more desirable than the National Diploma of Design or the old college diplomas. The pressure of competition obliged most colleges to convert.

11 Camberwell College of Arts continued the practice of calling for a member of its governing body from the club. At Walthamstow, where Green, Cuming and Howard taught under the headship of a New English stalwart, Stuart Ray, membership of the club was an important qualification for new fine-art staff – as well as, according to Howard, a love of old roses. See also Michael Spender, *The Paintings of Ken Howard: Drawn by Light*, David and Charles, Newton Abbot, 1992, pp. 12–14.

12 Bevis Hillier Introduction in *The Early Years of the New English Art Club*, exh. cat., The Fine Art Society, London, 1968. This show contained 137 items by members and exhibitors active in the period from 1886 to 1914. See William Gaunt, 'Early New English', *The Times*, 11 March 1968, p. 6. This period nevertheless saw the emergence of serious art historians – principally Bruce Laughton and Wendy Baron – whose impact on the standing of the club should not be underestimated. Aside from his work on Steer, Laughton organised the Slade centenary exhibition at the Royal Academy in 1972, a project that could not fail to elucidate the old partnership – as well as demonstrate the degree to which Slade/NEAC members formed the bedrock of the national twentieth-century British collection. In his review of the exhibition (*Studio International*, vol. 183, 1972, p. 33), Andrew Forge commented upon the Slade's recent loss of integrity in the face of 'Dip. A.D. art'. Aside from her work on Sickert, Baron curated an important exhibition recalling the Camden Town Group for the Fine Art Society in 1978. Where formerly there had been Arts Council anthologies, this show transformed a field of connoisseur enthusiasm into one of serious scholarship.

13 David Warren Piper (ed.), *Readings in Art and Design Education, 1 After Hornsey*, and *2 After Coldstream*, Davis-Poynter, London, 1973. See also 'The Art Game', *The Observer Magazine*, 21 May 1967, pp. 16–17; also Barrie Sturt-Penrose, *The Art Scene*, 1969, Paul Hamlyn, London, pp. 104–8. In 1968 a celebrated 'sit-in' occurred at the radical Hornsey College of Art in north London. With the creation of polytechnics in 1969, many formerly independent regional art schools were incorporated into the new establishments, with subsequent loss of identity.

14 In 1964, for instance, 154 out of 308 paintings in the exhibition were by club members and those of affiliated societies and the Academy.

15 Bernard Dunstan, 'A Direct and Affectionate Response', *Art and Artists*, October 1986, pp. 17–21. See also Bernard Dunstan, *The Paintings of Bernard Dunstan*, David and Charles, Newton Abbot, 1993, pp. 16–18.

16 Bernard Dunstan, 'A Direct and Affectionate Response', *Art and Artists*, October 1986, pp. 17–21. He sees in this a 'poetic quality, put down in solid painterly terms', but concedes that: 'This description may seem tame to those brought up in the art of the last 40 years; but intensity can exist in apparently quiet forms, and it is a great mistake to assume that it only shows itself in extreme, revolutionary or innovative activities'.

17 Thomas's *Old Coal Tips, Cardiff* (*c.* 1968), shown in the winter of 1968, following the Aberfan disaster two years earlier, took on a contemporary resonance.

18 Armfield started showing in the winter of 1965, Calvert in the spring of 1964, Corsellis in the winter of 1969, Harris in the winter of 1961, Hornby in the winter of 1960 and Ryder in the spring of 1963.

19 Margaret Pullée's highly idiosyncratic watercolours were shown at the club from the winter of 1963. Her son, Michael Pullée, joined his parents as a regular New English exhibitor in the winter of 1966.

20 Michael Shepherd, '6 ? Discovery, Art', *The Sunday Telegraph*, 8 November 1970. By the mid-1960s the idea of the Sunday painter had acquired its current pejorative meaning. It had not always been so. Back in the 1940s, at the time of the publication of Winston Churchill's *Painting as a Pastime* (1948), there had been a greater receptivity to naïve or 'unprofessional' works – see Cora J. Gordon, 'London Commentary', *The Studio*, vol. 136, August 1948, p. 54.

21 Peter Fuller, *Beyond the Crisis in Art*, Writers' and Readers' Publishing Cooperative, London, 1980, p. 42.

22 Howard recalls that he purchased a Reliant Scimitar with a trailer at this point, and took the entire exhibition to Belfast. En route to the Liverpool steamer, he was stopped for speeding.

23 The phrase 'mega-visual', used to describe the post-war proliferation of film, television, printed materials and mass-produced consumer products, first emerged in the writings of Richard Hamilton and owes its origins to the discussions of the Independent Group at the Institute of Contemporary Arts in the 1950s.

24 Richard Morphet's highly influential exhibition, 'Late Sickert', was staged at the Hayward Gallery, London, in 1981.

25 Andrew Brighton, 'Consensus Painting and the Royal Academy', *Studio International*, November 1974, pp. 174–6.

26 Andrew Brighton, 'Where are the Boys of the Old Brigade? The Post-war Decline of British Traditionalist Painting', *The Oxford Art Journal*, vol. 4, no. 1, July 1981, pp. 35–43.

27 Ibid, p. 42.

28 Although in the 1880s *The Artist* carried more news items, the preoccupation with method took a firm hold in the inter-war period.

29 Cork wrote in the *Evening Standard*, 10 August 1972: 'Although I never expect to attend the death of the easel picture as a viable means for the artist, it is becoming increasingly apparent that an enormous amount of the best contemporary art has left the easel picture behind.'

30 This process continued into the 1980s with the rate-capping of local councils under the Thatcher government.

31 Peter Fuller, 'The Crisis within the Fine Art Tradition', *The London Magazine*, vol. 19, nos 1 and 2, April/May 1979, pp. 40–7.

32 T. M. and A. S., 'Remarks on Art, 1952–1977' in Frederick Gore RA, Introduction, *British Painting, 1952–1977*, exh. cat., Royal Academy of Arts, London, 1977, pp. 12–22.

33 William Packer, 'When British Art is at its Best', *Financial Times*, undated cutting, 1989.

34 Bernard Dunstan, *The New English Art Club – A Continuing Tradition*, n.d. [*c.* 1995], a privately printed pamphlet, in attempting to define the club's standpoint, questions the current belief – 'a cliché of art criticism' – that painting should disturb and shock.

35 *A Life in Pictures: Works from the Studio of William Bowyer RA*, Ian Collins, exh. cat., Messum's, London, 2003.

36 Quoted in David Mills, 'William Bowyer: Reflections by the Riverside', *The Artist's and Illustrator's Magazine*, April 1983, pp. 11–13.

37 AGM Minutes, 23 November 1978 and 18 December 1980.

38 Margaret Thomas, one of the prime movers behind these exhibitions, had a studio in the lookout tower at Aldeburgh at this time.

39 Edward Cage, quoted in *Richard Eurich RA: A Retrospective Exhibition*, Caroline Krzesinska, exh. cat., Bradford Art Galleries and Museums, 1980. p. 13; the exhibition toured Bradford, Glasgow, London and Southampton.

40 Ian Collins, 'Homage to Light and Colour', *Eastern Daily Press*, 11 November 1991, reviewing Thomas's exhibition at Sally Hunter Fine Art, London, in her seventy-fifth year.

41 Charlotte Ardizonne, Nancy Carline, Patrick Cullen, Edward Dawson, John Denahy, Roy Durrant, Dorothy Franks-Cowan, Judith Gardiner, Rita Greig, Emille Gwynne-Jones, Joyce Haddon and Ernest Trowell all started showing at the club in the 1970s.

42 Howard notes that the Academy, like the club, was also experiencing a resurgence and he comments specifically on the work of Burn, who had died the previous year, as well as Dunstan, Buhler, Bulmer, Jason Bowyer, Cuming, Anthony Eyton, Edmund Fairfax-Lucy, Green and Jacqueline Rizvi.

43 During the 1980s the club attracted new members and exhibitors, including June Berry, David Carpanini, Ian Cryer, Deirdre Daines, Pauline Fazakerley, David Gluck, Karn Holly, Pamela Kay, David Parfitt, Salliann Putman, William Selby, Jenny Wheatley, Michael Whittlesea and Charles Williams.

44 Julian Halsby, *Venice, The Artist's Vision: A Guide to British and American Painters*, Batsford, London, 1990, pp. 157–70.

45 Bryan Robertson, John Russell and Lord Snowdon, *Private View, The Lively World of British Art*, Nelson, London, 1965, quoted in T. M. and A. S., 'Remarks on Art, 1952–1977' in Frederick Gore RA, Introduction, *British Painting, 1952–1977*, exh. cat., Royal Academy of Arts, London, 1977, p. 12.

46 For further reference, see *The Walberswick Enigma: Artists Inspired by the Blyth Estuary*, Richard Scott, exh. cat., Ipswich Borough Council, 1994; see also Richard Scott, *Artists at Walberswick: East Anglian Interludes, 1880–2000*, Art Dictionaries, Bristol, 2002; see also Ian Collins, *A Broad Canvas: Artists in East Anglia Since 1880*, Parke Sutton Publishing, Norwich, 1990, pp. 64–73; also *The Walberswick Influence: Selected Works from the Studio Estate of Lionel Bulmer, 1919–1992*, Ian Collins, exh. cat., Messum's, London, 2002.

47 Quoted from *A Life in Pictures: Works from the Studio of William Bowyer RA*, Ian Collins, exh. cat., Messum's, London, 2003, opposite plate 37.

48 Quoted from the winter 1992 catalogue profile.

49 Ardizzone stresses the inconsequential and reductive nature of her subject matter: 'To create a work which appears negligible to the viewer ... perhaps a small lemon on a huge colour ground ... feeling and doing so much out of so little ... like Morandi.' See Bruce Wilson and Edward Bishop, 'The New English Art Club', *The Art Magazine*, vol. 10, no. 3, autumn 1981, unpaginated. By contrast, Todd stresses truth to visual appearances – see Jenny Pery, 'Foreword' in *Daphne Todd*, exh. cat., Messum's, London, 2004.

50 William Bowyer's sons, Jason and Francis, began exhibiting at the club in the winters of 1978 and 1991 respectively – both also painted at Walberswick.

51 The contrast between this painting and that of the Glasgow painters Ken Currie, Stephen Conroy and Peter Howson is worth making in that it replays the social divisions in British society that deepened in the Thatcher years. Around 1990, artists and intellectuals often adopted the terminology of French cultural theory in discussion of bourgeois patterns of consumption as they related to private spaces. Art students of the period sought out then-obscure texts, such as Gaston Bachelard's *The Poetics of Space*, trans. Maria Jolas, Orion Press, New York, 1964 (rev. ed., Beacon Press, Boston, 1994).

52 Peter Fuller, *Images of God: The Consolations of Lost Illusions*, Chatto & Windus, London, 1985 (rev. ed., Hogarth, London, 1990), pp. 109–10. Originally published in *Artscribe* in 1983, Fuller describes *Bathroom, Spoleto* and declares it a 'good painting', even though its conventions, which Dunstan had done much to popularise, were 'commonplace'. 'Nonetheless', he continues, 'if I try to tell anyone in the "art world" that I have enjoyed some of Dunstan's pictures, this produces an amused titter; it is assumed to be one of my "perverse" or "provocative" judgements. These days, however, the titter tends to be increasingly uncertain and uneasy'.

53 Brian Sewell, 'The New English Art Club', *Christie's International*, October 1992, p. 26: 'Its present senior members may not be the pride of the Arts Council' but it appealed to 'a broader band of patronage'. It had 'recognized its responsibilities to the modest domestic patron' ... and has 'no recent influence on teaching in our major art schools'.

54 Anthony O'Hear, 'A Crisis in Fine Art Education', *Modern Painters: A Quarterly Journal of the Fine Arts*, vol. 2, no. 3, autumn 1989, p. 78.

55 See Alan Bowness, *The Conditions of Success: How the Modern Artist Rises to Fame*, Thames and Hudson, London, 1989.

56 David Mills, 'The NEAC: Open for Passionate Painters', *Artists and Illustrators Magazine*, December 1987, pp. 30–2. This impression is confirmed by Diana Armfield, who recorded in interview with Julian Halsby, 'for a great many years I attended all selection and hanging days, and there were no occasions more animated, more outspoken to the point of shouting, and more fun to be part of. How often do we think that the figures of the past were somehow larger in character than our

contemporaries. For once I think the NEAC can boast its share of larger-than-life characters.' See Julian Halsby, *The Art of Diana Armfield*, David and Charles, Newton Abbot, 1995, p. 121.

57 Quoted in Julian Halsby, *The Art of Diana Armfield*, David and Charles, Newton Abbot, 1995, p. 31.

58 Although it lacks the caricatural elements of Orpen's *Selecting Jury of the New English Art Club* (1909; frontispiece), used as the cover illustration for the Christie's *Centenary Exhibition* catalogue, Coates's *Selection Jury* was to some extent inspired by it. The exhibition contained 238 items.

59 Broadcast on 12 September 1986.

60 John Russell Taylor, 'Contemporary Rebels with a Cause', *The Times*, 9 September 1986, p. 11.

61 Robin Stemp, 'Typically English', *The Artist*, November 1986, pp. 8–9. Stemp continues: 'Despite the fact that ... most figurative painters of note have at one time shown at the club ... it is generally ignored by the fashionable seers of recent art history with the result that it has become, depending on your attitude, either an oasis of sanity in an increasingly crazy art world or, as its detractors would have it, passionless, bland, and an excuse for a nostalgic wallow ... one could say that blandness creeps in ... perhaps as the RA tries to be ever more radical, up-to-date, terrified of being old hat, the job of the NEAC is to show all the solid, painterly, figurative painters – many of whom do get chucked out by the RA now. It's a funny *volte face* from its original origins, I know.' Despite the fact that he had assisted with the Christie's show, Brian Sewell delivered his verdict in 'The New Wave that Never Was', *Evening Standard*, 28 August 1986 that 'the 1914–18 war exhausted it and it has been in dormition ever since ... The last 70 years have been a doldrums, and the 240 odd pictures in Christie's reflect this'.

62 Richard Cork, 'Reassessing British Art at the RA', *The Listener*, 15 January 1987, quoted from Richard Cork, *New Spirit, New Sculpture, New Money, Art in the 1980s*, Yale University Press, London and New Haven, 2003, pp. 283–7.

63 Robert Hughes, 'English Art in Twentieth Century' in *Nothing if not Critical*, Collins, London, 1990 (rev. ed., Harvill Press, 2001), p. 179. Hughes's review of the exhibition plays up the national, as opposed to international, characteristics of British art, singling out painters Lucian Freud, Leon Kossoff and Frank Auerbach, artists who 'have no equivalents' in American painting.

64 William Packer, 'The Private Sector Celebrates an English Tradition', *Financial Times*, 11 September 1986, recounts the early years and, moving on to the small show of contemporary club members at Sotheby's, notes: 'We can hardly look to it, of course, for any winners of the Turner Prize.' The club makes 'its own wry comment on our official attitudes and expectations. Yet it is noticeable and encouraging that, though these painters may not even hope for such patronage, there is now a more generous acknowledgement of the intrinsic quality of their work,' and he mentions Greenham, Armfield, Howard and Buhler. The Turner Prize was first offered in 1984. Always controversial, it attracted censure in 1989 for its failure to recognise Lucian Freud. The competition was not held in 1990 and was re-launched in 1991 with financial support from Channel 4.

65 Luke Herrmann, *The Ford Collection – II, The Walpole Society*, 60th volume, Walpole Society, London, 1998 (privately printed).

66 Brian Sewell, 'Hung, Drawn and Slaughtered', *Evening Standard*, 12 May 1988, p. 31.

67 Peter Fuller, *Theoria, Art and the Absence of Grace*, Chatto & Windus, London, 1988, pp. 184–215.

68 Amateurism briefly became an issue when, in 1988, HRH The Prince of Wales had a watercolour accepted. The redoubtable Margaret Thomas cast a withering eye on the Prince's efforts and, in an unguarded moment, expressed her disapproval to a reporter – causing a minor ripple in the press. She now concedes that the club's patron has improved over the years.

69 Fuller was killed in a motorway accident in April 1990; see Edward Lucie-Smith, 'Obituaries – Peter Fuller', *The Independent*, 30 April 1990; also Karen Wright et al., 'Peter Fuller, 1947–1990', *Modern Painters*, vol. 3, no. 2, summer 1990, pp. 7–15.

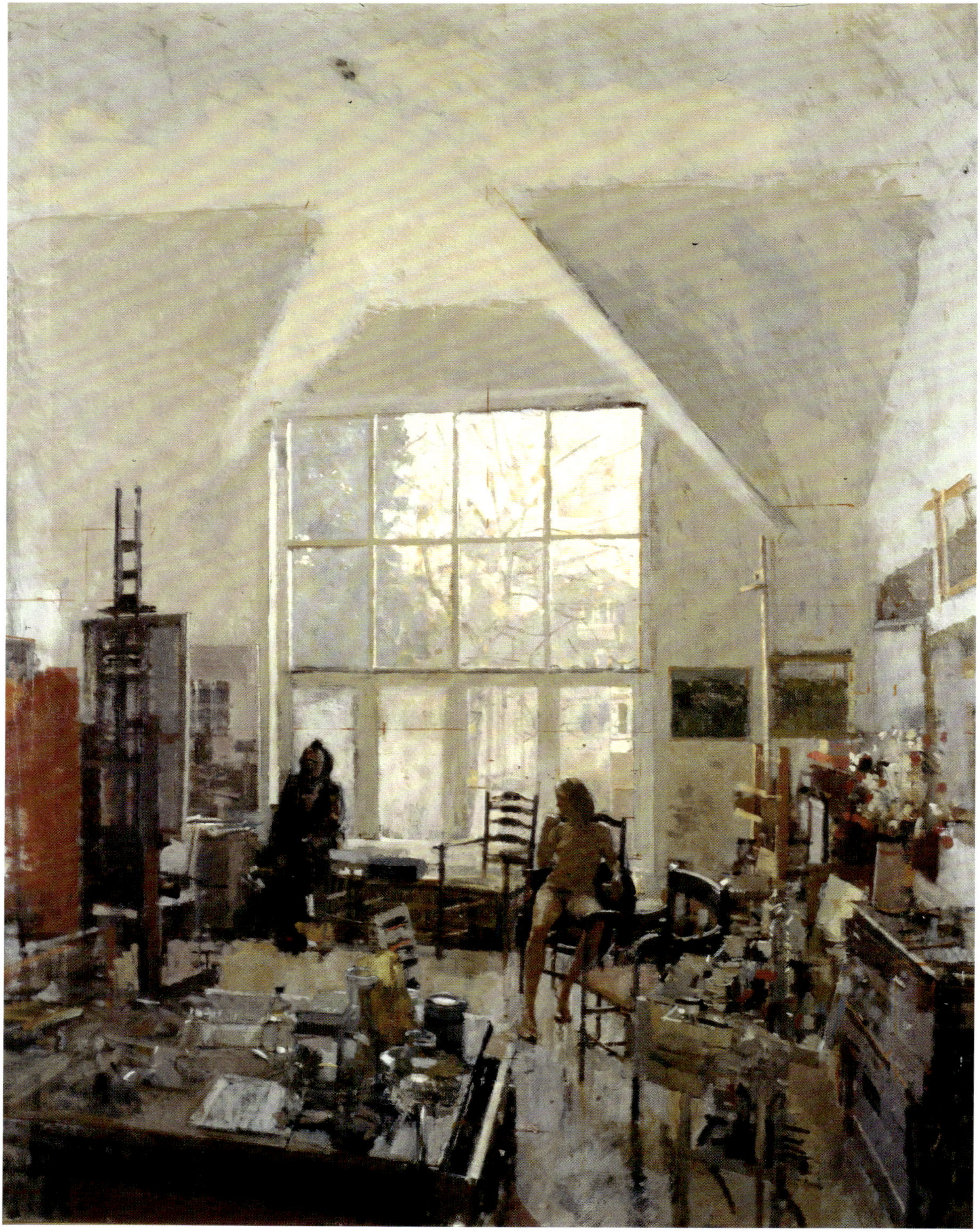

CHAPTER 9 'On with the job' 1990–2000

Opposite
Fig. 205 Ken Howard
The Picture, 1983–4
Oil on canvas, 183 x 152 cm
Private collection

In 1991, a controversial critic stated that the New English Art Club had 'put its head down and got on with the job'.[1] Its members in essence escaped into familiar spaces and surrounded themselves with those things that fed the creative impulse – Halliday in the London streets, Cuming stalking the Romney Marshes, Pikesley observing the low tide at Lyme Regis, Andrew Macara in Royan and St-Jean-de-Luz in France, Howard and Coates with a familiar model, surrounded by the clutter of the studio (fig. 205) and vying occasionally with Kuhfeld and Corsellis for the Grand Canal at dawn.[2] There were important new initiatives – away from the din of the media – in the inauguration of the annual lecture series and, in the later 1990s, the small displays of past members' work (see fig. 206). In 1989 William Bowyer proposed 'companions' of the club – influential individuals who might bring sponsorship and other benefits, such as the Marks and Spencer Young Artists' Prize. But, having remarked that the club exerted 'no recent influence on teaching in our major art schools', Brian Sewell went on to stir up artist-academics.[3] His remarks, for instance, led to articles in *Modern Painters* in which the role and purpose of a degree-level 'national curriculum' for Fine Art education was debated. Sewell was not averse to calling upon the Secretary of State to 'revise and control' its teaching.[4] There were, however, dissenting voices and a series of conferences was held by Wimbledon School of Art and the Tate Gallery on the condition of art education.[5]

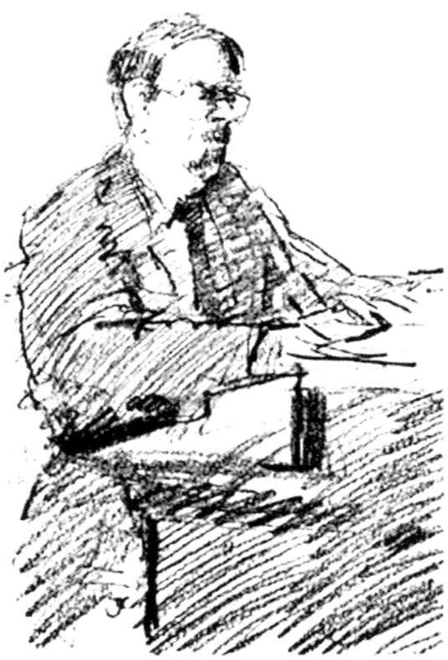

Fig. 206 Thomas J. Coates
Peyton Skipwith Delivering the First New English Art Club Lecture, 1990
Graphite on paper
Collection Peyton Skipwith

The debates had already permeated the club and Jason Bowyer took up the challenge in 1993 to establish the New English Drawing School, a peripatetic academy that would be devoted to an activity that was in danger of becoming a lost art.[6] In this venture he was assisted by Duncan Wood, Karn Holly and Stuart Denyer (see fig. 207). Subsequent AGMs gave positive reports on the drawing school, and its success exposed some of the deficiencies in current art education. At the same time Dunstan produced a pamphlet, circulated to members, entitled *The New English Art Club – A Continuing Tradition*, celebrating both 'mainstay' observational painting and the 'expressionism', 'invention' and 'satiric' work that the club had accepted. Drawing had its 'rightful place' in teaching; indeed, it was the reason why the school had been started.[7] However, the walls of the state-financed arts faculty Jericho did not fall before the trumpets of the New English School of Drawing, and, by 1995, William Bowyer was calling for tougher controls on membership in the club, and the return of associates as 'members-in-waiting'.[8] Successful school sessions in London and elsewhere had raised the club's profile. The following year, after useful behind-the-scenes work by Diana Armfield and Karen Armitage, a companion fund-raiser, it was announced that His Royal Highness the Prince of Wales, an advocate of representational drawing, had agreed to become Exhibiting Patron.[9]

William Bowyer's long service to the club ended in 1997. He was succeeded by Howard, who, although a reluctant conscript, took office with a reforming zeal and the backing of a group of new members.[10] A time of change inevitably led to renewed debates about 'newness', 'Englishness' and whether the club was really a club. While annual open exhibitions continued (see fig. 208), Howard realised that, if the New English wanted to gain patronage but would not change its name, it needed to be led by a president. Its principal office bearer, a de facto president, could no longer be described as an 'honorary secretary', a role that always implied a higher authority. The club also needed 'friends', who were, by definition, a group of loyal supporters and collectors.[11] It was decided that, unlike museum groups and Friends of the Royal Academy, their number and function should be limited. The historic reasons for preserving the status quo – going back to the club's democratic origins – were no longer relevant if new private and corporate collectors were to be courted and the allegiance of young painters retained. Around 2000, the club had attracted new members in Peter Brown, David Cobley, Tom Espley, Tom Fairs, Roy Freer, Jennifer McRae, Ruth Stage, Benjamin Sullivan and Neale Worley, artists who brought new approaches to figure and landscape painting. This range of talent

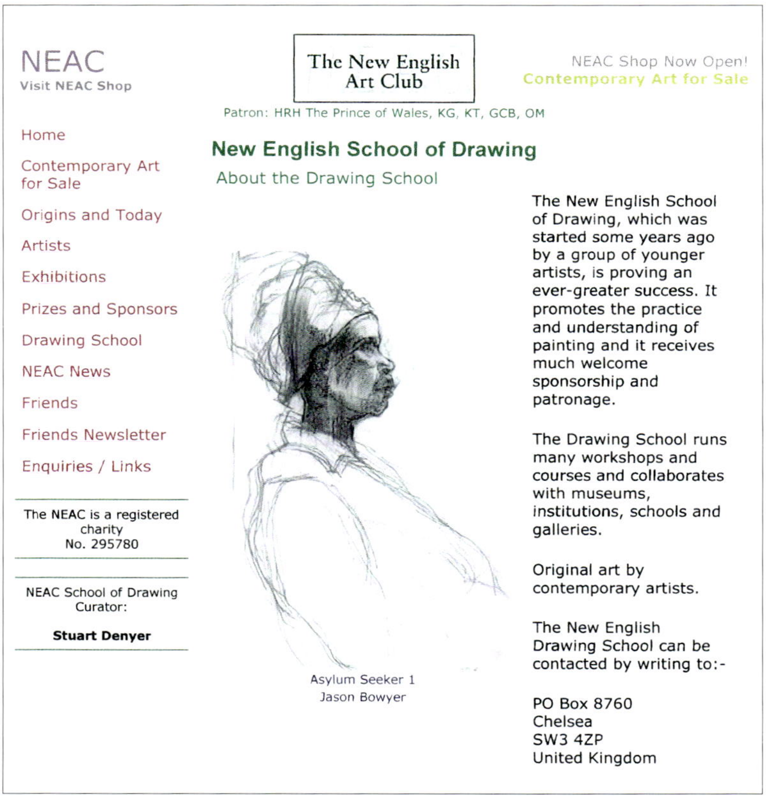

Fig. 207 Website publicity material (containing Jason Bowyer *Asylum Seeker 1*, 1999) for the New English School of Drawing, *c*. 2001–04

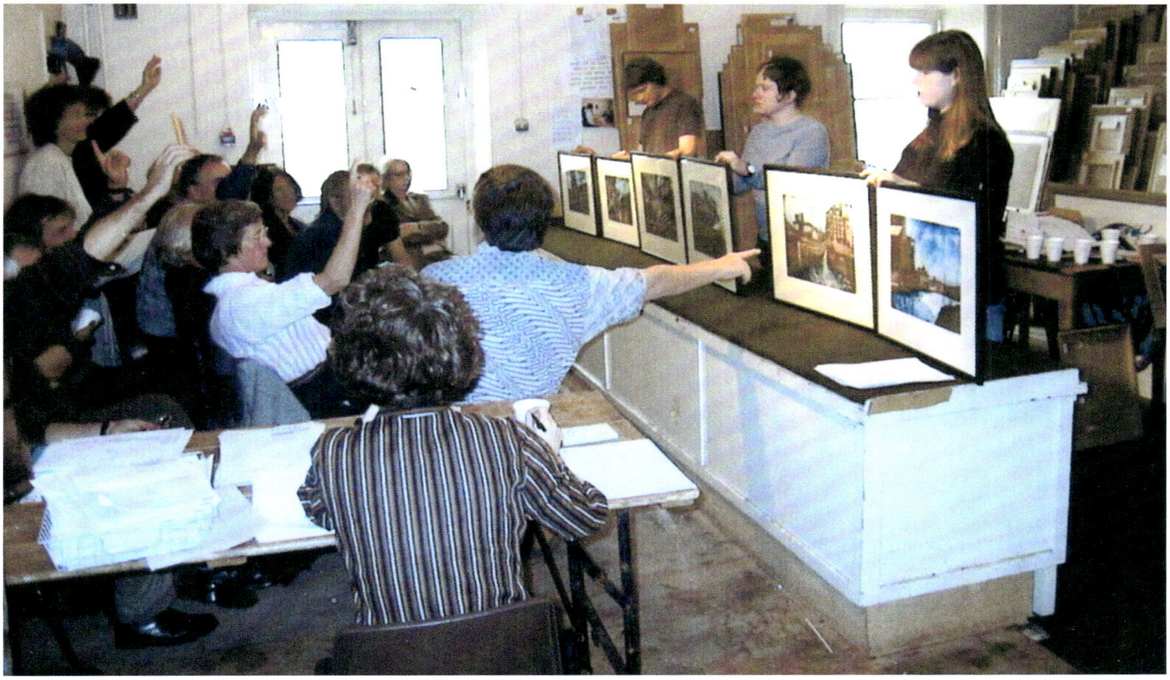

Fig. 208 The selecting jury of the New English Art Club
Photograph, 1999.
Unknown photographer
NEAC Archive

nonetheless maintained the New English reputation for using the medium to record what was directly observed.

Howard stood down in 2003 and the president's role was taken by Coates, a painter with a strong reputation and a profound allegiance to the club. The twenty-first-century Executive Committee was much preoccupied with the future direction of the club – as its predecessors had been. Old issues that have haunted the New English since its foundation re-emerge as identity is refashioned. The steady stream of new members confirm that there is a role for an artist-led Salon committed to traditional ways and means without being reactionary. Having experienced half a century of art essentially selected by dealers and Arts Council officials – variously described as 'gatekeepers', 'brokers' and 'arbiters' – the club provides space for the makers of images to regain control. Self-absorbed behaviour patterns, orientated to marketing, celebrity and self-promotion, need to change. Dunstan quietly intoning Degas – 'In my day we did not *get on*' – gathers the momentum of a roar. The undertow is an enduring fascination with an old medium and all the sophisticated skills involved in its deployment. The New English was never only concerned about a tradition that developed from Impressionism; it always looked for a mood of seeing, a fascination with something in life – in a medium that talks back to its handler. There are few accolades today for those who, simply and without fanfare, follow their practice, and there is less sense of community in the world of art than there was, even a generation ago. In this sense, the club runs counter to prevailing trends and there is still a need to bring artists together in order to reinforce their importance to society through professionalisation.

For those interested in British art, the New English is a remarkable survival. Built upon procedures invented in the eighteenth century, overhauled in the nineteenth and defended in the twentieth, it lives on in the present. There can be no intrinsic rightness in the idea of a group of peers judging fellow artists' work and awarding special privilege – and exhibition space – on this basis. Yet, since the Renaissance, they have been the fundamental practices of guilds and professions. First formed in opposition to corrupt Academy cabals, the club achieved much more than was ever intended. In giving exhibitors the right to vote for their own selecting juries, in providing a home for those who would otherwise have experienced rejection either by the Academy or the avant-garde, and in supporting educational reform, its members infiltrated the art world at all levels. However, with the death of Steer, it was increasingly forced into reacting to events and, like many great British institutions, it seemed simply to continue with no real purpose – that is, if we only believe the rhetoric of critics and the orthodox accounts of British art since the Second World War.

More research in the thirty years after the war, for instance, will completely alter the way we think of those years. Even in what Coates calls 'the doldrums' of the late 1960s, the club was quietly renewing itself. The catalogue statements may have done nothing to alter the opinions of Arts Council mandarins, but they have little to say about the splendid light, subtle colour or intriguing composition of the exciting, but now neglected, painting for which the club was formed. Change, in organisations like the New English, occurs incrementally, its pace speeding up and slowing down in line with external factors and the passing of generations. There could be no master plan. New strategies have been discussed in depth, voted on and implemented to a greater or lesser degree since its formation. At times the past is a drag, at others it is the tail wind. One generation rejects its fathers and mothers, another finds good in them.

Coates's new selecting jury in the early years of the twenty-first century clearly accept that their time is not wasted. They are liberated from the feeling that one exhibition must be remade in the image of the last. But can they only ever choose those whose values replicate theirs? Are they always trapped? If Sickert arrived today with a risky painting of an 'exotic' dancer, the modern equivalent of his music-hall performers, would it be accepted? Does the club stand for something in painting that only it can achieve? Newness and Englishness may be less debated, but they are still there, still part of the turf, and, if never completely reconciled, they remain essential to the club's distinctiveness.

Overleaf
Detail of fig. 204

NOTES

1 Brian Sewell, 'The New English Art Club', *Christie's International*, October 1991, p. 26.

2 For Halliday, see *Illustrated London News*, January 1991; for Howard, see Michael Spender, *The Paintings of Ken Howard, Drawn by Light*, David and Charles, Newton Abbot, 1992, and Anon., 'The Life and Work of Ken Howard', *The Cornishman*, October 1992; for Corsellis, see Julian Halsby, 'Jane Corsellis, in Conversation', *The Artist*, March 1993, pp. 12–14; also Jane Corsellis, *Atelier Series: A Personal View*, David and Charles, Newton Abbot, 2000; for Cuming, see Christian Tyler (ed.), *Fred Cuming, A Figure in the Landscape*, Unicorn Press, London, 2000.

3 Brian Sewell, 'The New English Art Club', *Christie's International*, October 1991, p. 26.

4 Brian Sewell, 'Dear Peter Brooke', *Modern Painters*, vol. 5, no. 4, winter 1992, pp. 62–4. See also Anthony O'Hear, 'Naturally Creative?', *Modern Painters*, vol. 6, no. 1, spring 1993, pp. 52–5, and Andrew Vincent (moderator), 'Colonel Blimp and Rousseau Debate Modernity', *Modern Painters*, vol. 6, no. 2, summer 1993, pp. 66–8.

5 Paul Hetherington (ed.), *Artists in the 1990s, The Education and Values*, Tate Publications, London, 1994. They were mildly anarchic and incoherent events.

6 Minutes, Executive Committee, 18 February 1993; Jason Bowyer, 'New English Drawing School', *The Artist*, October 1993, pp. 20–1.

7 Bernard Dunstan, *The New English Art Club – A Continuing Tradition*, 1995 (privately printed).

8 From 1993, AGM Minutes document successful drawing schools run by Karn Holly, Stuart Denyer, Duncan Wood and Francis Bowyer. Fund-raising for these activities was in the hands of Karen Armitage. There was, nevertheless, concern that trends in art education had led to a general de-skilling. William Bowyer brought forward new proposals in 1995 for the re-introduction of the associate membership category, which involved the artist presenting a drawing portfolio to the Executive.

9 AGM Minutes, 18 November 1996.

10 Between 1990 and 1995, John G. Blockley, Stuart Denyer, Michael Fairclough, Bo Hilton, Anthony Morris, Arthur Neal, Richard Sorrell, Jaqueline Williams and Duncan Wood had joined the New English.

11 Howard, for instance, presided over a dramatic increase in the income of the club, underwriting its financial stability.

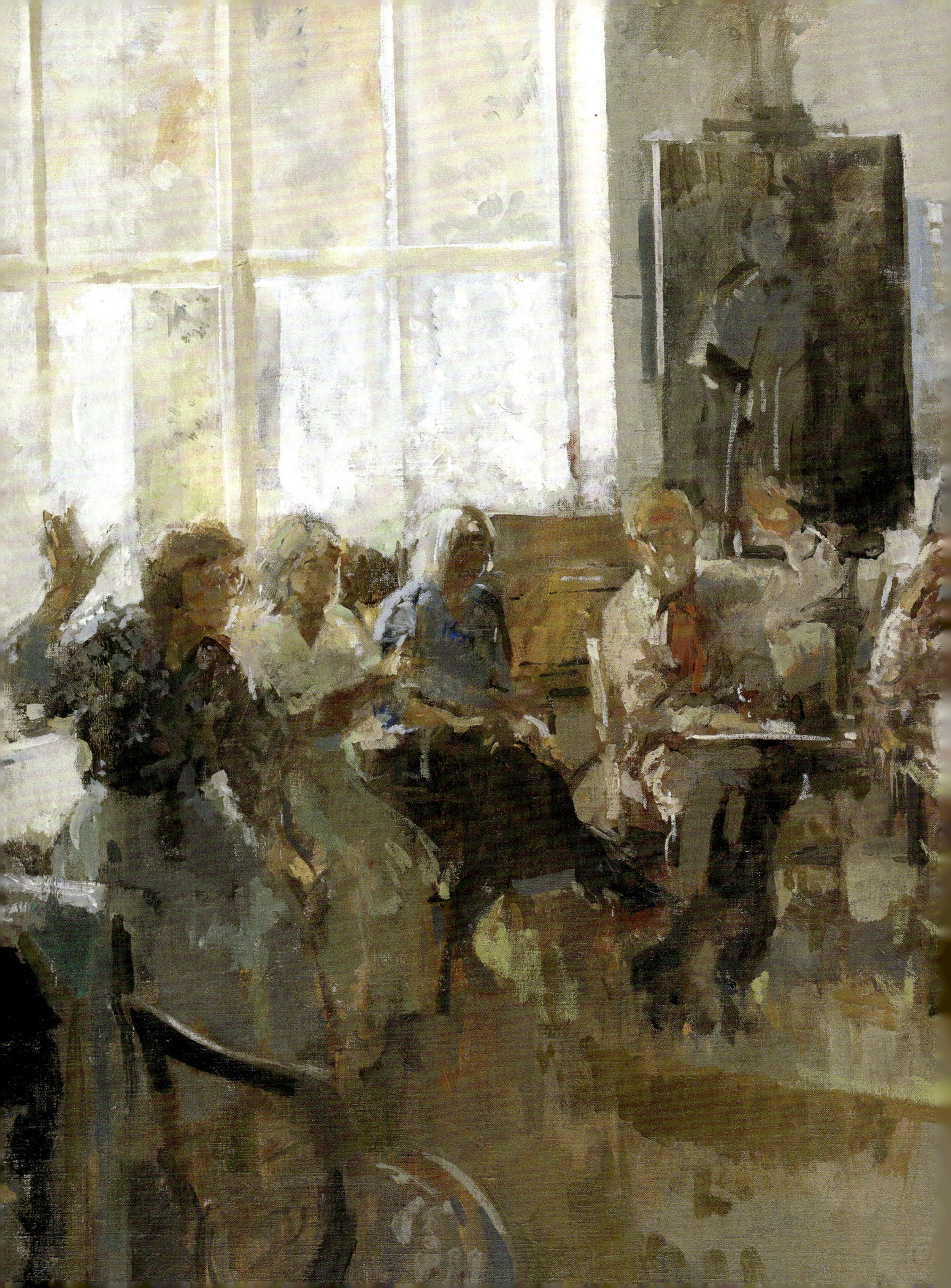

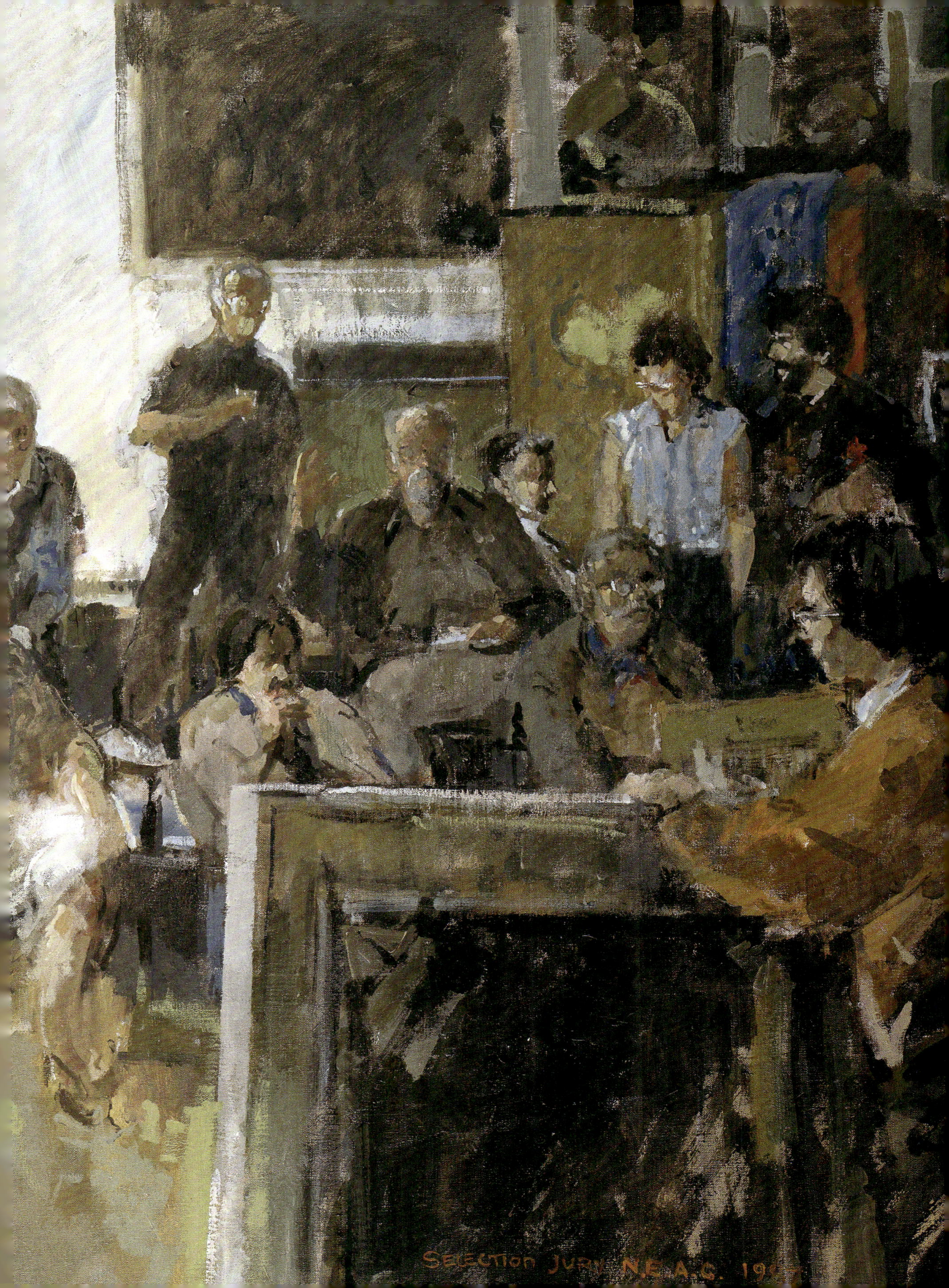
SELECTION JURY N.E.A.C.

NEW ENGLISH ART CLUB

FOR the last seven centuries there has been a continuous tradition in European painting. Today we are fast losing touch with it. The feverish experiments of the twentieth century have resulted in painting becoming increasingly esoteric and trivial. Recently we have had paintings dealing only with the application of paint. Many of these experiments have been important but the pursuit of experiment *for its own sake* has led the artist into a cul-de-sac, limited the contents of his pictures so that they have become meaningless, and divorced him from his public.

We can only judge painting by the standards achieved in the past, standards of the European tradition of which we are a part. At its best, painting made a vital, profound, and personal comment on man, his environment and his beliefs.

It is time the contemporary painter attempted a more profound interpretation of life and adopted a new attitude, a positive life-enhancing interest in man and his surroundings, in the conviction that regard for life is the most fruitful foundation for Art. We are living in a new age, but the fullest interpretation of this age still necessitates the use of the great visual discoveries of space, light, design and colour.

The New English Art Club came into existence as a protest against a false concept of tradition. It stands today against an equally false rejection of tradition.

5

New English Art Club Members Sale at Sotheby's, September 2002

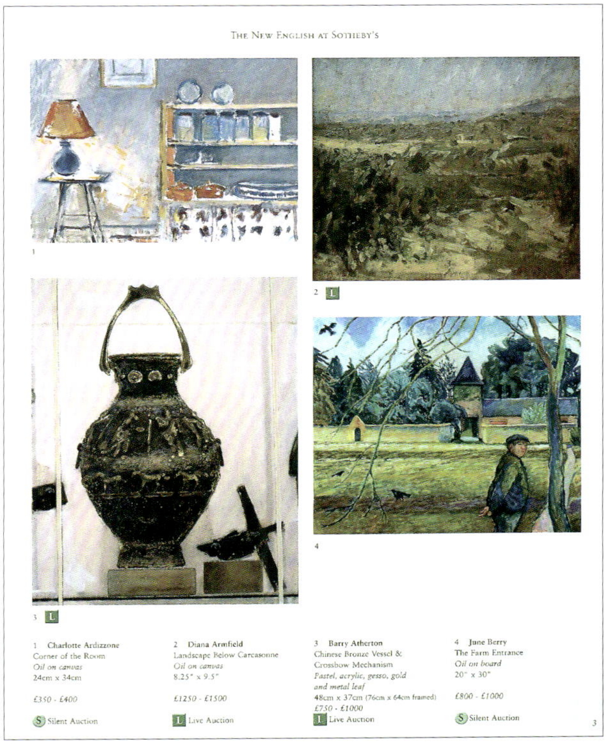

THE NEW ENGLISH AT SOTHEBY'S

1

2 L

3 L

4

1 **Charlotte Ardizzone**
Corner of the Room
Oil on canvas
24cm x 34cm

£350 - £400

S Silent Auction

2 **Diana Armfield**
Landscape Below Carcasonne
Oil on canvas
8.25" x 9.5"

£1250 - £1500

L Live Auction

3 **Barry Atherton**
Chinese Bronze Vessel & Crossbow Mechanism
Pastel, acrylic, gesso, gold and metal leaf
48cm x 37cm (76cm x 64cm framed)
£750 - £1000

L Live Auction

4 **June Berry**
The Farm Entrance
Oil on board
20" x 30"

£800 - £1000

S Silent Auction

3

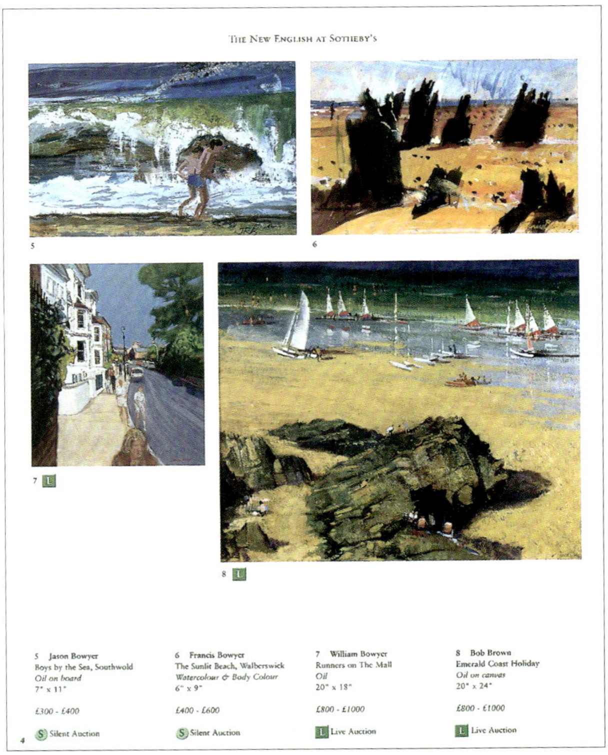

THE NEW ENGLISH AT SOTHEBY'S

5

6

7 L

8 L

5 **Jason Bowyer**
Boys by the Sea, Southwold
Oil on board
7" x 11"

£300 - £400

S Silent Auction

6 **Francis Bowyer**
The Sunlit Beach, Walberswick
Watercolour & Body Colour
6" x 9"

£400 - £600

S Silent Auction

7 **William Bowyer**
Runners on The Mall
Oil
20" x 18"

£800 - £1000

L Live Auction

8 **Bob Brown**
Emerald Coast Holiday
Oil on canvas
20" x 24"

£800 - £1000

L Live Auction

4

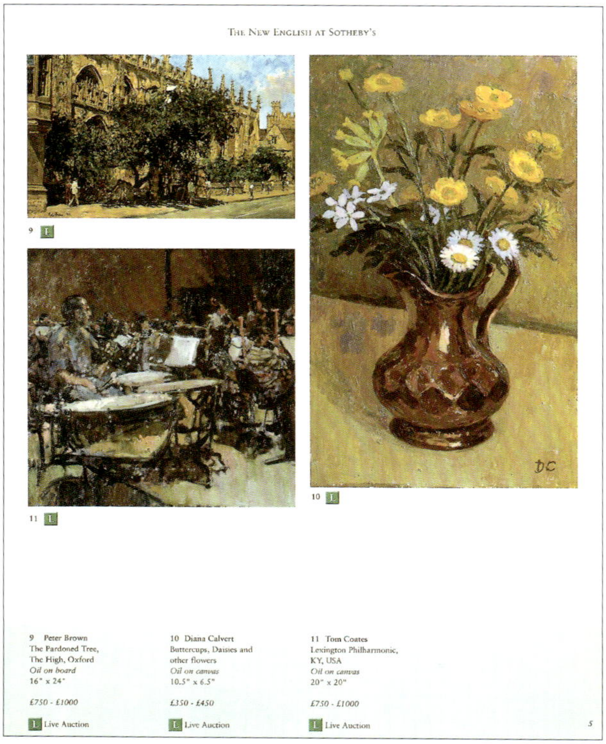
THE NEW ENGLISH AT SOTHEBY'S

9 L

11 L

10 L

9 Peter Brown
The Pardoned Tree,
The High, Oxford
Oil on board
16" x 24"

£750 - £1000

L Live Auction

10 Diana Calvert
Buttercups, Daisies and
other flowers
Oil on canvas
10.5" x 6.5"

£350 - £450

L Live Auction

11 Tom Coates
Lexington Philharmonic,
KY, USA
Oil on canvas
20" x 20"

£750 - £1000

L Live Auction

5

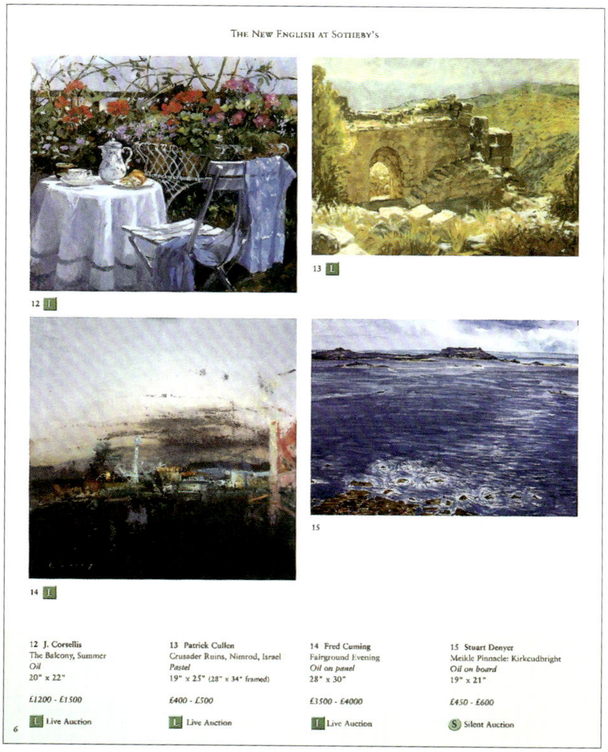
THE NEW ENGLISH AT SOTHEBY'S

12 L

13 L

14 L

15

12 J. Corsellis
The Balcony, Summer
Oil
20" x 22"

£1200 - £1500

L Live Auction

13 Patrick Cullen
Crusader Ruins, Nimrod, Israel
Pastel
19" x 25" (28" x 34" framed)

£400 - £500

L Live Auction

14 Fred Cuming
Fairground Evening
Oil on panel
28" x 30"

£3500 - £4000

L Live Auction

15 Stuart Denyer
Meikle Pinnacle: Kirkcudbright
Oil on board
19" x 21"

£450 - £600

S Silent Auction

6

In the Sotheby's catalogue of paintings by the New English Art Club, the captions for cats 15 and 23 are incorrect and should be transposed.

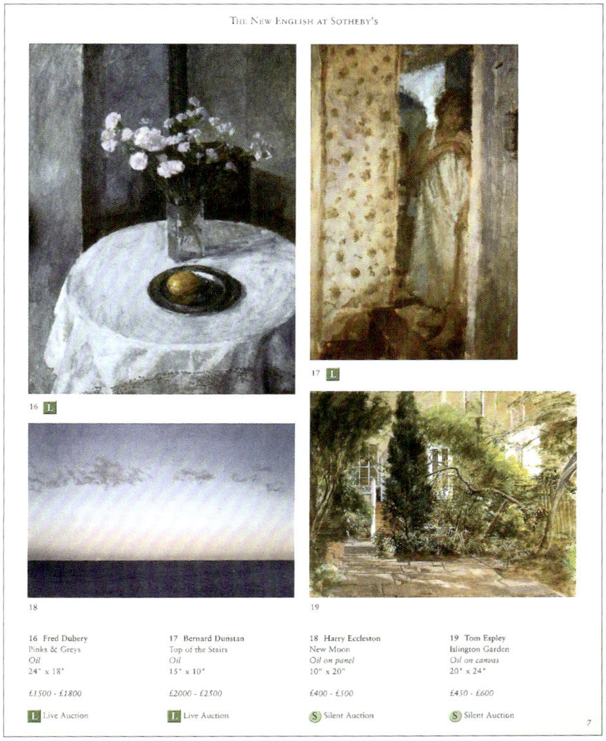
THE NEW ENGLISH AT SOTHEBY'S

16 L

17 L

18

19

16 Fred Dubery
Pinks & Greys
Oil
24" x 18"

£1500 - £1800

L Live Auction

17 Bernard Dunstan
Top of the Stairs
Oil
15" x 10"

£2000 - £2500

L Live Auction

18 Harry Eccleston
New Moon
Oil on panel
10" x 20"

£400 - £500

S Silent Auction

19 Tom Espley
Islington Garden
Oil on canvas
20" x 24"

£450 - £600

S Silent Auction

7

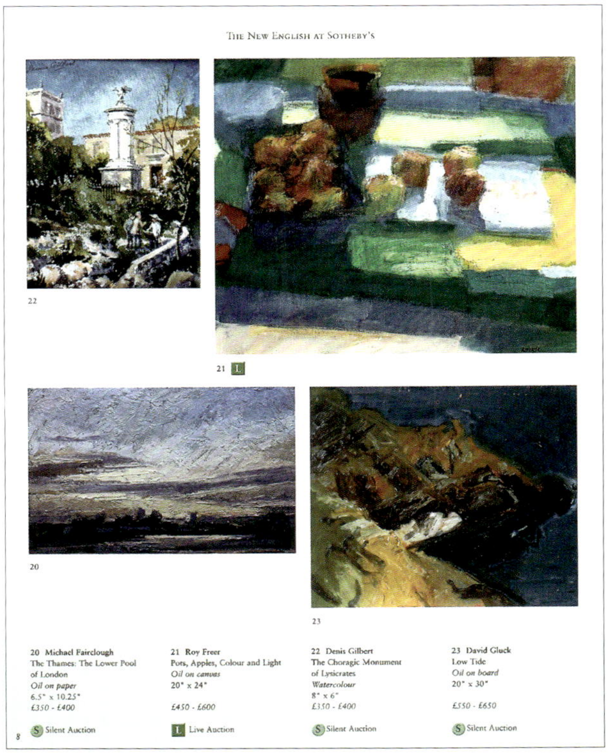
THE NEW ENGLISH AT SOTHEBY'S

22

21 L

20

23

20 Michael Fairclough
The Thames: The Lower Pool of London
Oil on paper
6.5" x 10.25"
£350 - £400

S Silent Auction

21 Roy Freer
Pots, Apples, Colour and Light
Oil on canvas
20" x 24"

£450 - £600

L Live Auction

22 Denis Gilbert
The Choragic Monument of Lysicrates
Watercolour
8" x 6"
£350 - £400

S Silent Auction

23 David Gluck
Low Tide
Oil on board
20" x 30"

£550 - £650

S Silent Auction

8

The New English at Sotheby's

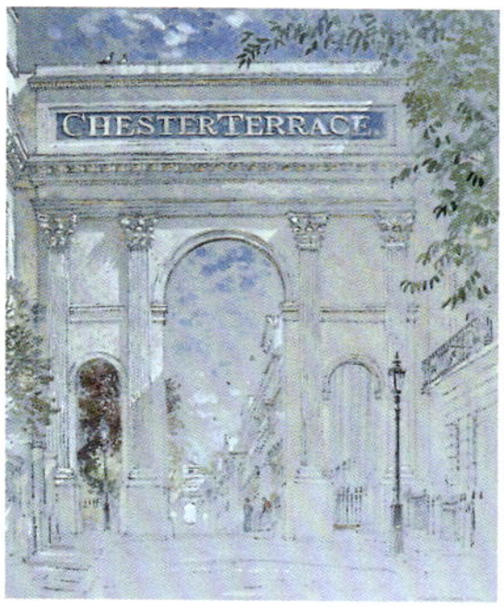

24 L

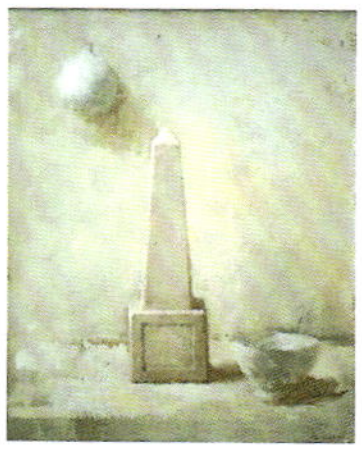

25

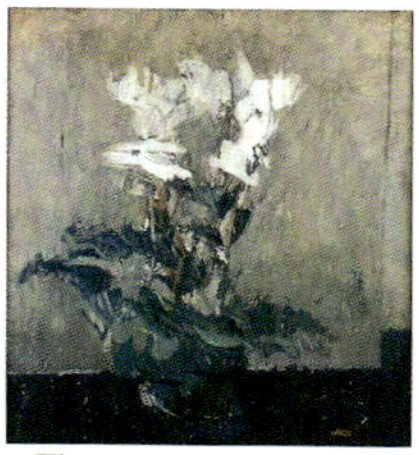

26 L

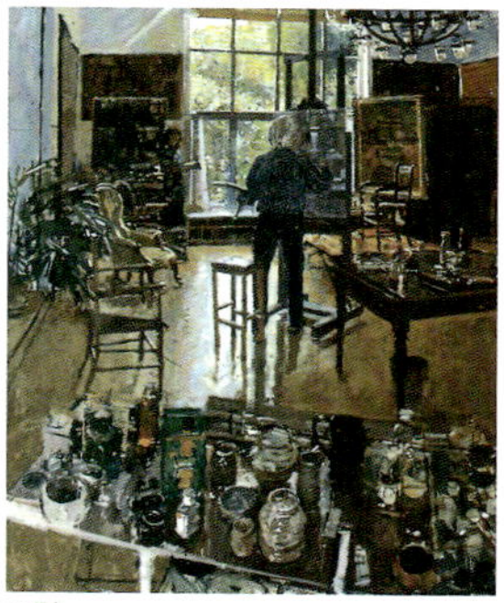

27 L

24 Charlotte Halliday
Chester Terrace
Watercolour
15" x 12"

£450 - £600

L Live Auction

25 Charles Hardaker
Still Life with Obelisk
Oil on canvas
20" x 16"(25" x 21" framed)

£750 - £1000

S Silent Auction

26 Karn Holly
Cyclamen
Oil on board
19" x 18"

£750 - £1000

L Live Auction

27 Ken Howard
Oriel 2002
Oil on canvas
48" x 40"

£4000 - £5000

L Live Auction

9

The New English at Sotheby's

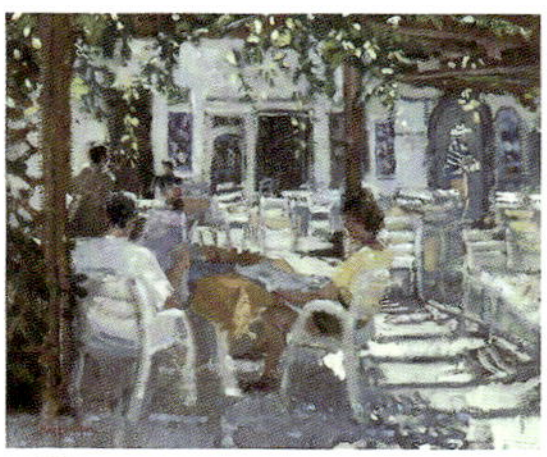

28 L

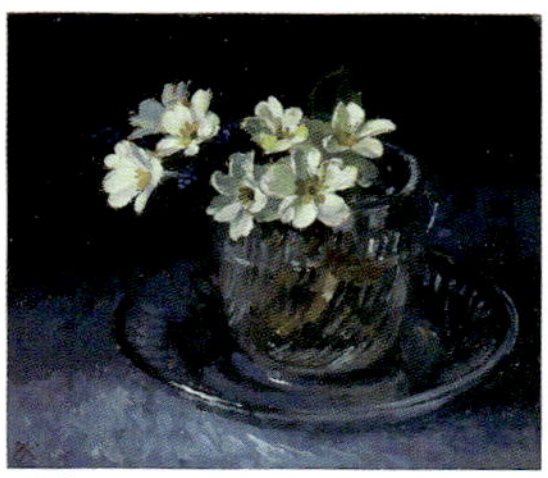

29 L

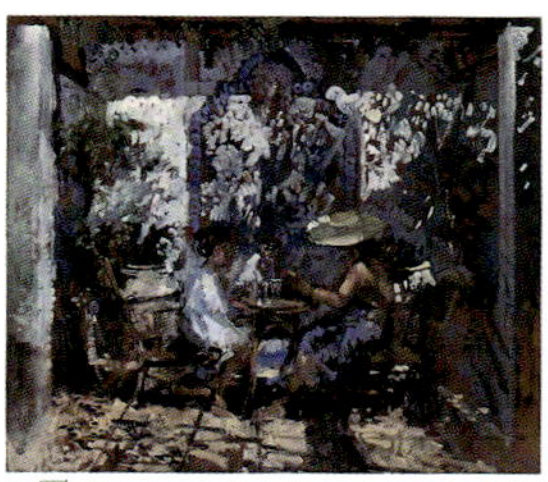

30 L

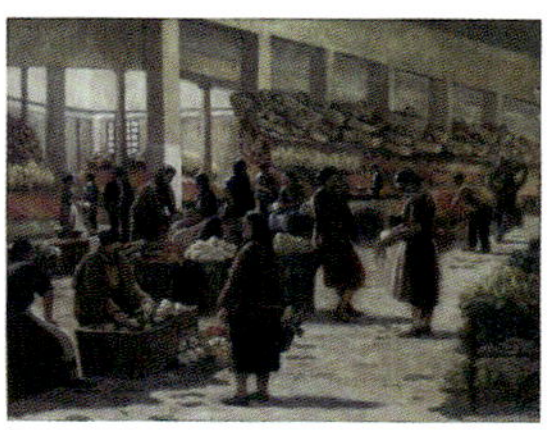

31

28 Mary Jackson
Morning Coffee,
Giglio, Italy
Oil on canvas
10" x 12"
£500 - £750

L Live Auction

29 Pamela Kay
Primroses in Turkish Cup
Oil on board
7" x 8"

£650 - £750

L Live Auction

30 Peter Kuhfeld
A Courtyard in Spain
Oil on Panel
14" x 16"

£1500 - £2000

L Live Auction

31 Ann Le Bas
Funchal Fruit Market, Madeira
Oil
18.5" x 22.5"

£400 - £500

S Silent Auction

10

THE NEW ENGLISH AT SOTHEBY'S

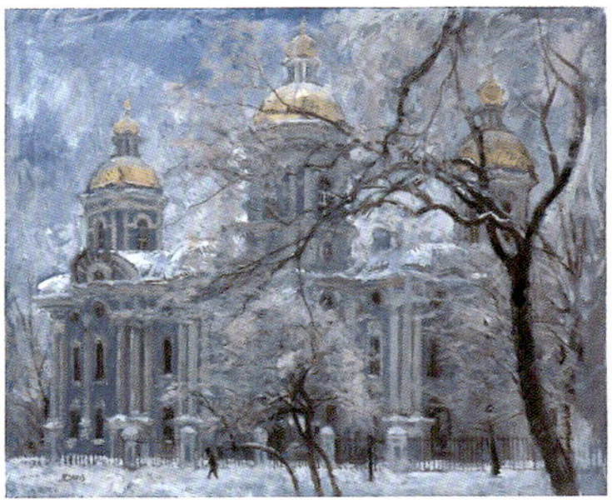

32 L

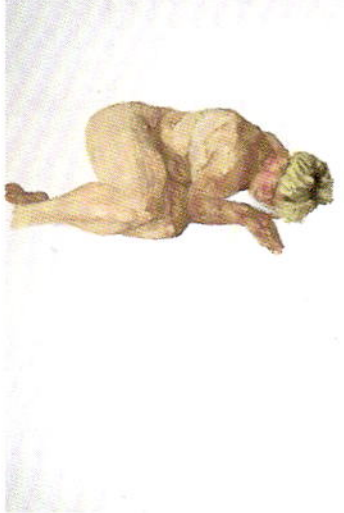

33

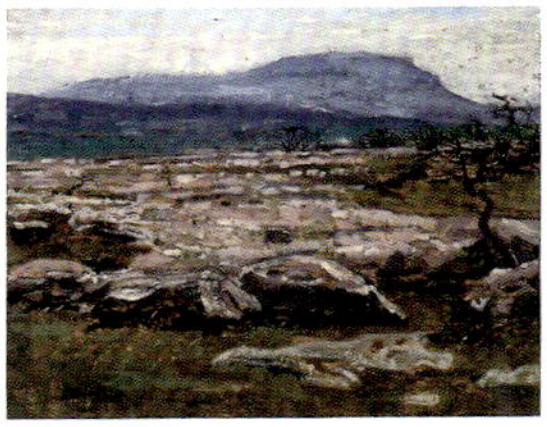

34

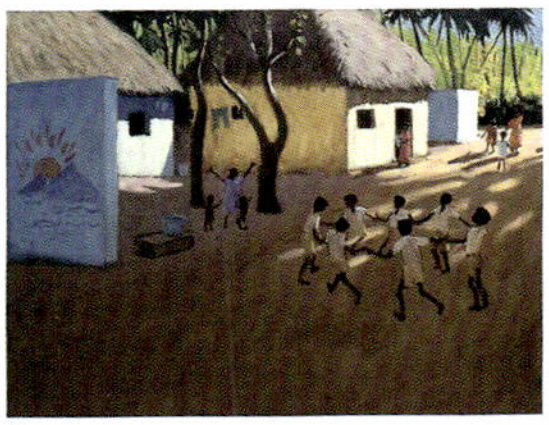

35

32 Anthony Morris
St. Nicholas Cathedral,
St. Petersberg
Oil
20" x 24"
£1500 - £2000

L Live Auction

33 Jennifer McRae
Nude Asleep
Oil on paper
20" x 16"

£350 - £400

S Silent Auction

34 Jack Millar
Evening Pen-y-Ghent
Oil
16" x 20"

£1100 - £1500

S Silent Auction

35 Andrew MacAra
Children Playing: Southern India
Oil
25" x 30"

£1500 - £2000

S Silent Auction

11

THE NEW ENGLISH AT SOTHEBY'S

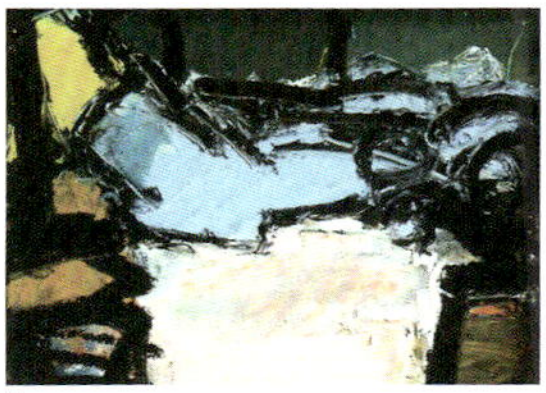

36

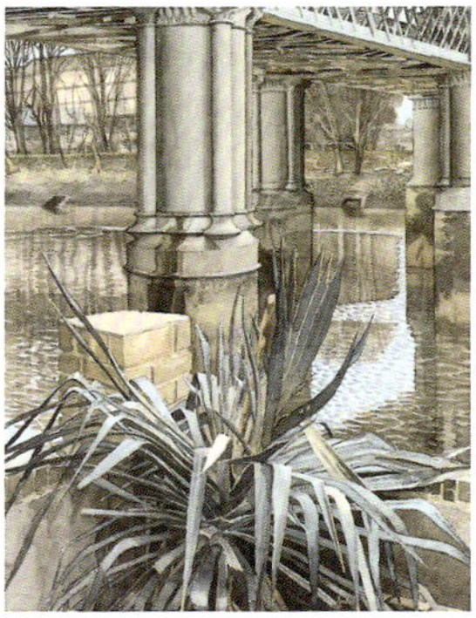

37

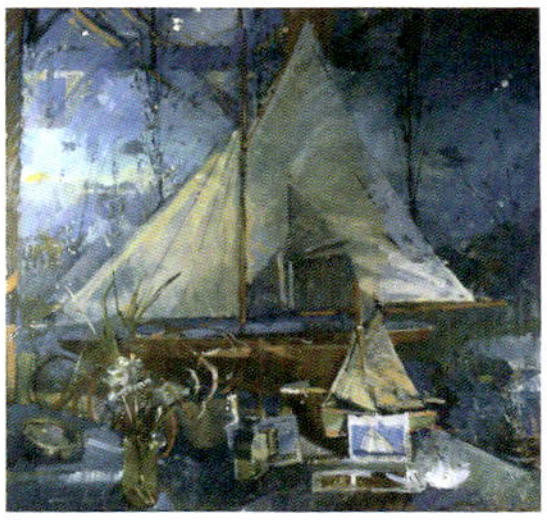

38

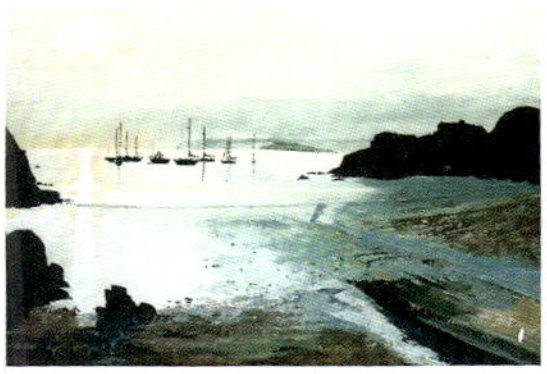

39

36 Aurthur Neal
Blue Nude
Oil Pastel
8" x 11"

£400 - £600

S Silent Auction

37 David Parfitt
Bridge and Yucca
Watercolour
24" x 18"

£550 - £750

S Silent Auction

38 Richard Pikesley
Pond Yachts: Evening
Oil
24" x 32"

£1000 - £1500

S Silent Auction

39 Michael Pullee
Hope Cove: South Devon
Oil
18" x 24"

£700 - £900

S Silent Auction

12

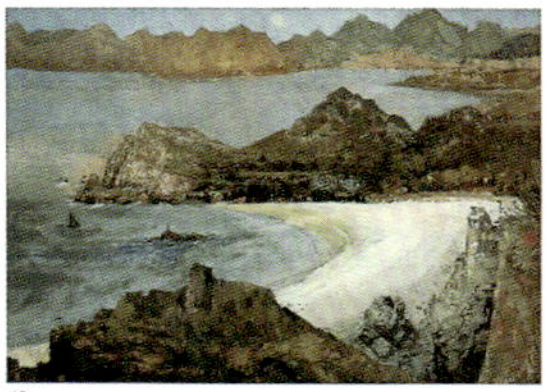

40

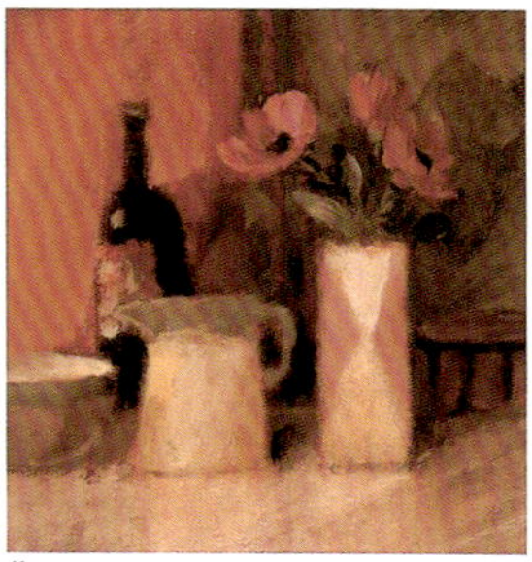

41

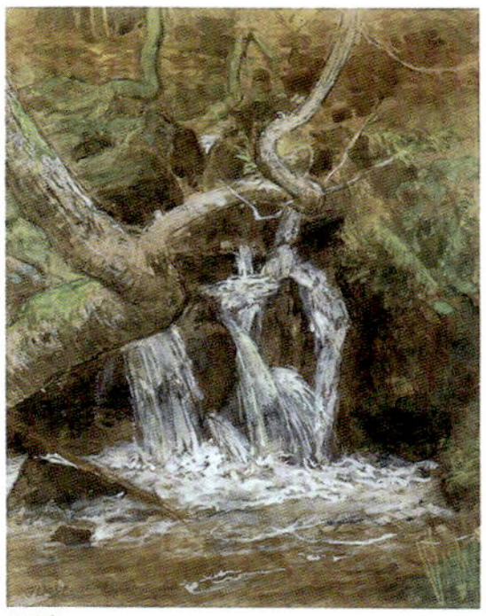

42 L

40 Edward Pullee
Bay of Antalya: Southern Turkey
Oil
12" x 18"

£700 - £900

S Silent Auction

41 Salliann Putman
Red Still Life
Oil
13" x 12"

£400 - £500

S Silent Auction

42 Jaqueline Rizvi
Waterfall below Cader
Watercolour on buff paper
16" x 12"

£600 - £800

L Live Auction

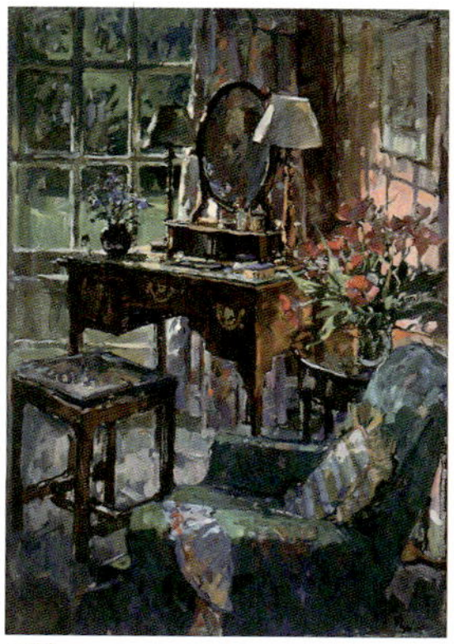

43 L

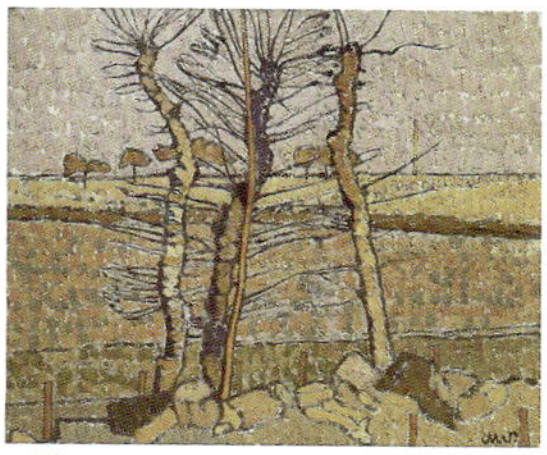

44 L

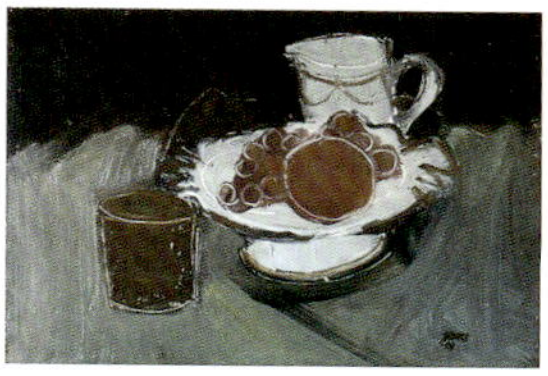

45

43 Sue Ryder
Bedroom Flowers
Oil
28" x 20"

£2000 - £2500

L Live Auction

44 Maurice Sheppard
Small Breton Landscape
Oil on canvas
8" x 10"

£450 - £550

L Live Auction

45 Dawn Sidoli
Still Life with Patterned Jug
Oil
12" x 16.5"

£400 - £500

S Silent Auction

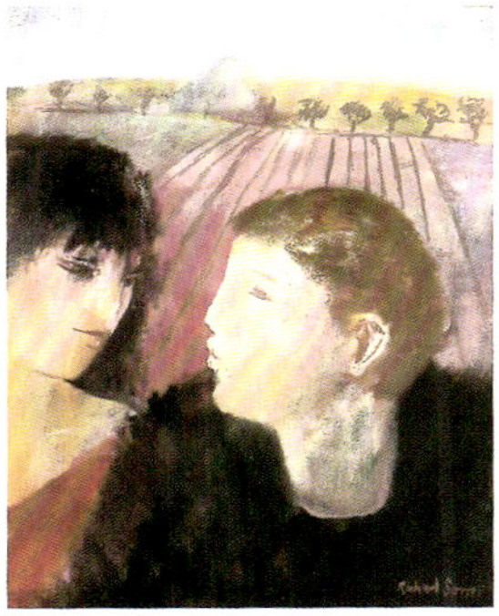

46

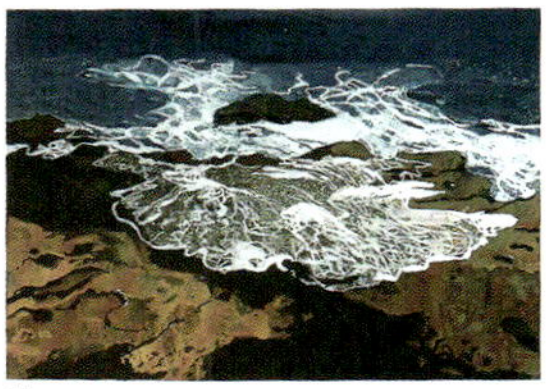

47

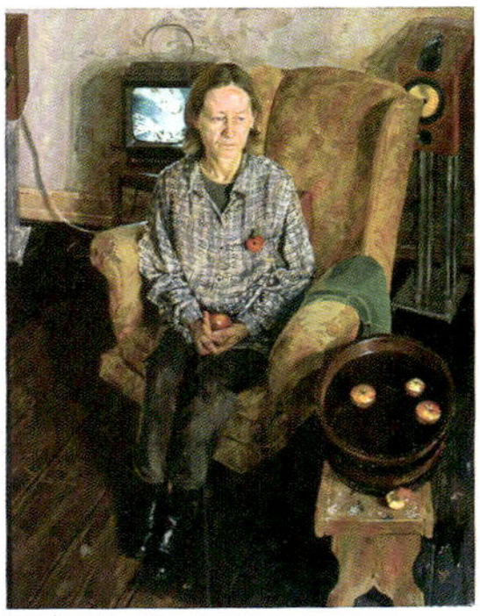

48 L

46 Richard Sorrell
October
Oil on canvas
18" x 15"

£650 - £850

S Silent Auction

47 Ruth Stage
Ocean Wave, Australia
Egg Tempera
28" x 20"

£500 - £700

S Silent Auction

48 Benjamin Sullivan
Apple Bobbing
Oil on canvas
30" x 24"

£1200 - £1500

L Live Auction

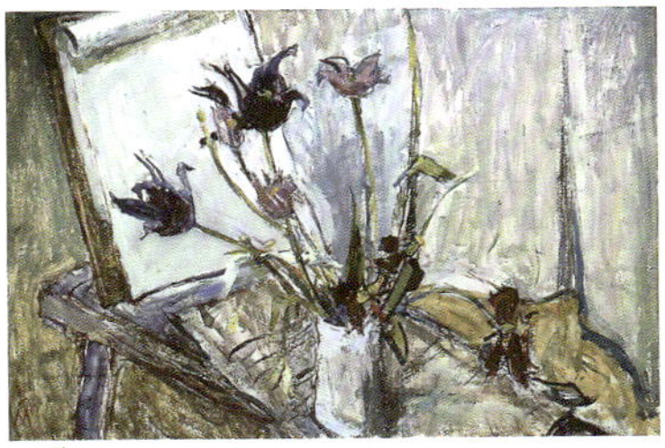

49 L

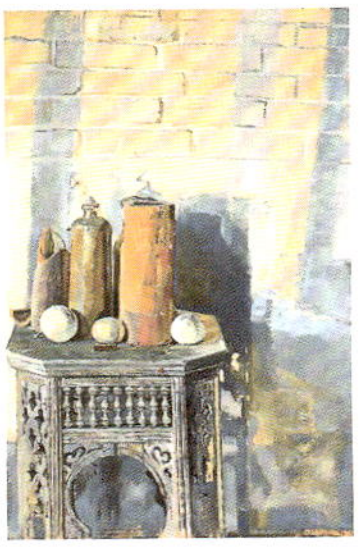

50

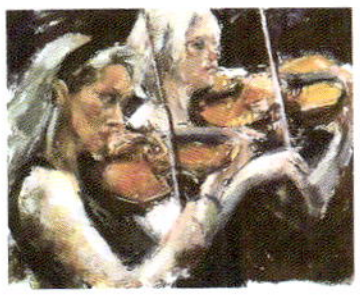

51

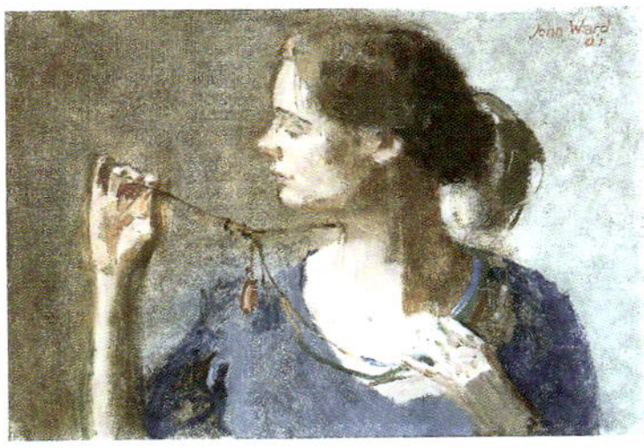

52 L

49 Margaret Thomas
Donkey with Tulips
Oil
20" x 30"

£1500 - £2000

L Live Auction

50 Daphne Todd
Still Life in Winter Sunlight
Oil on Panel
30" x 20"

£2500 - £3000

S Silent Auction

51 Jonathan Trowell
Violins
Oil
8" x 10"

£350 - £400

S Silent Auction

52 John Ward
Girl with Necklace
Oil on canvas
14.5" x 21"

£1000 - £1500

L Live Auction

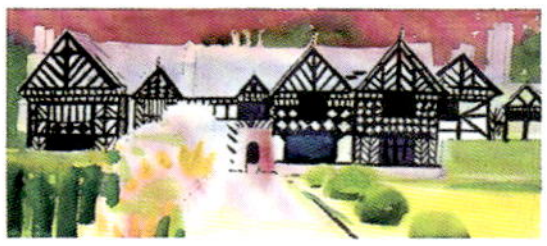

53

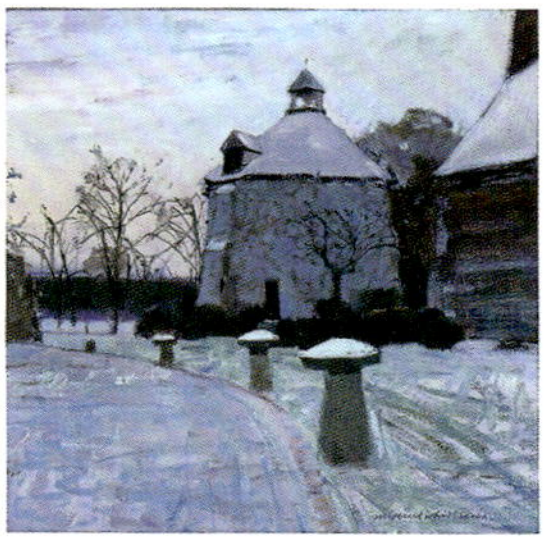

54 L

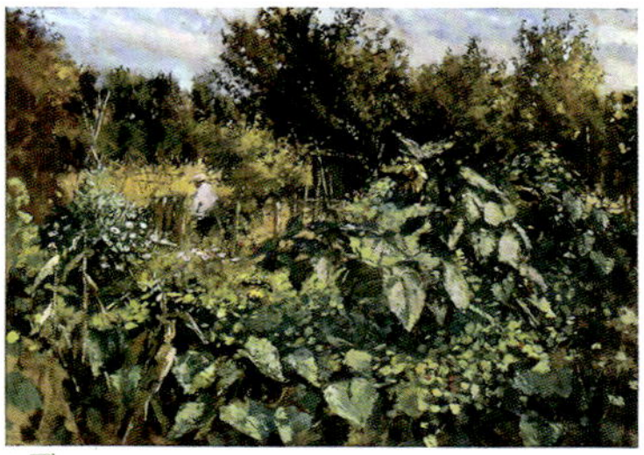

55 L

53 Jenny Wheatley
Speke Hall
Watercolour
5" x 11.5"

£350 - £400

S Silent Auction

54 Michael Whittlesea
The Dovecote in Winter
Oil on canvas
15" x 15"

£750 - £950

L Live Auction

55 Jacqueline Williams
Kim's Allotment
Oil on board
27.5" x 37"

£1250 - £1500

L Live Auction

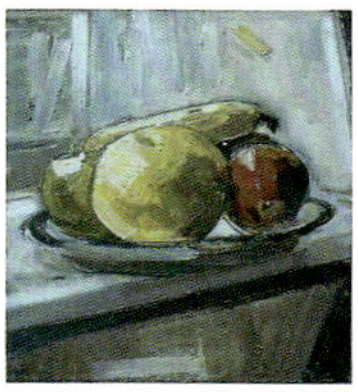

56

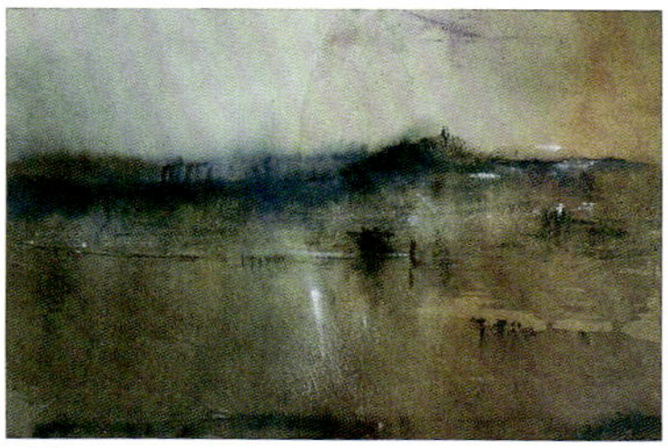

57 L

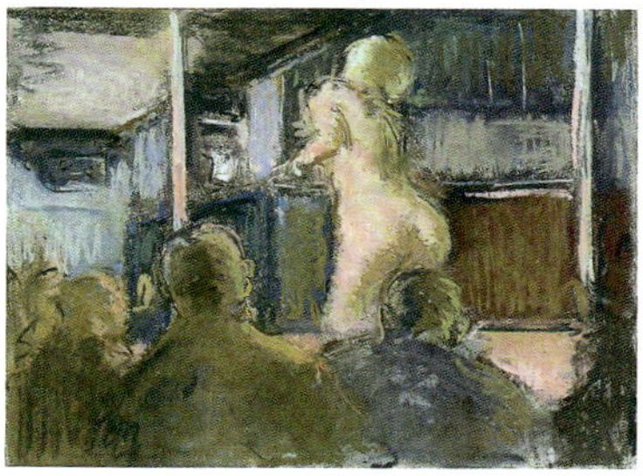

58 L

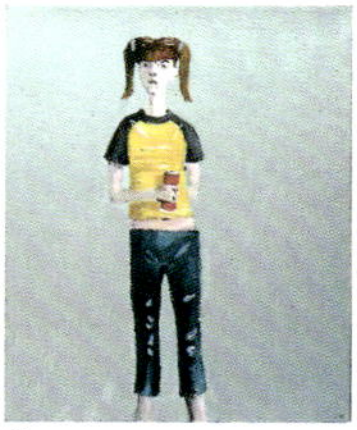

59

56 Duncan Wood
Still life with Grapefruit
Oil
20" x 18"

£700 - £900

S Silent Auction

57 Leslie Worth
Evening on the Northern Coast
Watercolour
10" x 14.25"

£700 - £900

L Live Auction

58 Martin Yeoman
Strip Bar
Pastel over monotype
15.75" x 19.75"

£1200 - £1500

L Live Auction

59 Charles Williams
Girl with can
Oil on canvas
12" x 10"

£350 - £400

S Silent Auction

Select Bibliography

Books

Allen, Brian (ed.), *Towards a Modern Art World: Studies in British Art 1*, Yale University Press, London and New Haven, 1995

Anderson, Ronald, and Anne Koval, *James McNeill Whistler, Beyond the Myth*, John Murray, London, 1994

Arnold, Bruce, *Orpen: Mirror to an Age*, Jonathan Cape, London, 1981

The Arts Enquiry, The Visual Arts, A Report sponsored by Dartington Hall Trustees, Oxford University Press, Oxford, 1946

Baile de Laperriere, Charles, *The New English Art Club Exhibitors, 1886–2001*, 4 vols, with a Foreword by HRH The Prince of Wales, KG, KT, GCB, OM, Hilmartin Manor Press, Calne, 2002

Baldry, A. L., Introduction, *Contemporary Figure Painters*, Studio Publications, London, 1925

Baldry, A. L., *Modern Mural Decoration*, George Newnes, London, 1902

Baldwin, Stanley, *On England and other Addresses*, Philip Allan, London, 1926 (rev. ed., Penguin, London, 1937)

Baron, Wendy, *Perfect Moderns: A History of the Camden Town Group*, Ashgate, Aldershot, 2000

Baron, Wendy, *Sickert*, Phaidon Press, London, 1973

Bate, Francis, *The Naturalistic School of Painting, Offices of The Artist*, 1887

Bell, Clive, *Since Cézanne*, Chatto and Windus, London, 1929

Bell, Clive, *Victor Pasmore*, Penguin, Harmondsworth, 1945

Bendix, Deanna Marhon, *Diabolical Designs: Paintings, Interiors and Exhibitions of James McNeill Whistler*, Smithsonian Institution, Washington DC, 1995

Berger, John, *Selected Essays and Articles: The Look of Things*, Penguin, Harmondsworth, 1972

Bertram, Anthony, *A Century of British Painting, 1851–1951*, Studio Publications, London, 1951

Blythe, Ronald, *The Age of Illusion: England in the Twenties and Thirties, 1919–1940*, Hamish Hamilton, London, 1963 (Penguin Books ed., 1964)

Borland, Maureen, *D. S. MacColl: Painter, Poet, Art Critic*, Lennard Publishing, Harpenden, 1995

Bowness, Alan, *The Conditions of Success: How the Modern Artist Rises to Fame*, Thames and Hudson, London, 1989

Browse, Lillian, *William Nicholson*, Rupert Hart-Davis, London, 1956

Carter, Miranda, *Anthony Blunt: His Lives*, Macmillan, London, 2001

Causey, Andrew, Introduction, *Poet and Painter: Letters between Gordon Bottomley and Paul Nash, 1910–1946*, Oxford University Press, Oxford, 1955 (rev. ed., Redcliffe, Bristol, 1990)

Chamot, Mary, *Modern Painting in England*, Country Life, London, 1937

Chesneau, Ernest, *The Education of the Artist*, Cassell, London, 1886

Chesneau, Ernest, *The English School of Painting*, Cassell, London, 1885

Clements, Keith, *Henry Lamb: The Artist and his Friends*, Redcliffe, Bristol, 1985

Collingwood, R. G., *Outlines of a Philosophy of Art*, Clarendon Press, Oxford, 1924

Collingwood, R. G., *Principles of Art, Clarendon Press, Oxford*, 1938 (rev. ed., Oxford University Press, Oxford, 1978)

Collins, Ian, *A Broad Canvas: Artists in East Anglia since 1880*, Parke Sutton Publishing, Norwich, 1990

Comfort, Alex, *Art and Social Responsibility*, Falcon Press, London, 1946

Cooper, Douglas, *The Courtauld Collection*, Athlone Press, London, 1954

Cork, Richard, *New Spirit, New Sculpture, New Money: Art in the 1980s*, Yale University Press, London and New Haven, 2003

Cork, Richard, *Vorticism and Abstract Art in the First Machine Age*, Gordon Fraser, London, 1976

Dubery, Fred, and John Willats, *Drawing Systems*, Studio Vista, London, 1972

Dunlop, R. O. RA, *Landscape Painting: Ma Yüan to Picasso*, Seeley Service, London, 1954

Dunstan, Bernard, *The Paintings of Bernard Dunstan*, David and Charles, Newton Abbot, 1993

Dunstan, Bernard, *Starting to Paint Still Life*, Studio Vista, London, 1969

E. B. G., *Charles Shannon*, Ernest Benn, London, 1924

Eliot, T. S., *Selected Prose*, Penguin Books, Harmondsworth, 1953

Emmons, Robert, *The Life and Opinions of Walter Richard Sickert*, Faber and Faber, London, 1941

Feldman, Gene, and Max Gartenberg (eds), *Protest: The Beat Generation and the Angry Young Men*, Souvenir Press, London, 1959 (rev. ed., Panther, London, 1960)

Flint, Kate (ed.), *Impressionists in England: The Critical Reception*, Routledge and Kegan Paul, London, 1984

Flower, Newman (ed.), *The Journals of Arnold Bennett, 1896–1910*, Cassell, London, 1932

Ford, Boris (ed.), *The Cambridge Guide to the Arts in Britain, vol. 8, The Edwardian Age and the Inter-War Years*, Cambridge University Press, Cambridge, 1989

Fothergill, John, *James Dickson Innes*, Faber and Faber, London, 1946

Fox, Shirley, *An Art Student's Reminiscences of Paris in the Eighties*, Mills and Boon, London, 1909

Frayling, Christopher, *The Royal College of Art: One Hundred and Fifty Years of Art and Design*, Barrie and Jenkins, London, 1987

Frazier, Adrian, *George Moore, 1852–1933*, Yale University Press, London and New Haven, 2000

Fry, Roger, *Reflections on British Painting*, Faber and Faber, London, 1934

Fry, Roger, *Vision and Design*, Penguin, Harmondsworth, 1920

Fuller, Peter, *Beyond the Crisis in Art*, Writers' and Readers' Publishing Cooperative, London, 1980

Fuller, Peter, *Images of God: The Consolations of Lost Illusions*, Chatto and Windus, London, 1985 (rev. ed., Hogarth Press, London, 1990)

Fuller, Peter, *Theoria, Art and the Absence of Grace*, Chatto and Windus, London, 1988,

Galbally, Ann, *Charles Conder: The Last Bohemian*, The Meigunyah Press, Melbourne University Publishing, 2002

Gleadowe, R. M. Y., *Albert Rutherston*, Ernest Benn, London, 1925

Goodwin, Michael (ed.), *Nineteenth-Century Opinion*, Penguin, Harmondsworth, 1951

Graves, Robert, and Alan Hodge, *The Long Weekend: A Social History of Great Britain*, Faber and Faber, London, 1941

Gruetzner Robins, Anna, *Walter Sickert: The Complete Writings on Art*, Oxford University Press, Oxford, 2000

Halsby, Julian, *The Art of Diana Armfield*, David and Charles, Newton Abbot, 1995

Halsby, Julian, *Venice, The Artist's Vision: A Guide to British and American Painters*, Batsford, London, 1990

Harries, Meirion and Susie, *The War Artists*, Michael Joseph, London, 1983

Hartrick, A. S., *A Painter's Pilgrimage through Fifty Years*, Cambridge University Press, Cambridge, 1939

Hassall, Geoff, *Camberwell School of Arts and Crafts: Its Students and Teachers, 1943–1960*, Antique Collectors' Club, Woodbridge, 1995

Henley, W. E., *Views and Reviews: Essays in Appreciation, II Art*, David Nutt, London, 1902

Herrmann, Luke (ed.), *The Ford Collection – II, The Walpole Society, 60th Volume, 1998*, The Walpole Society, London, 1998

Hewison, Robert, *In Anger: Culture in the Cold War*, Weidenfeld and Nicolson, London, 1981 (rev. ed., Methuen, London, 1988)

Hewison, Robert, *Under Siege: Literary Life in London, 1939–1945*, Weidenfeld and Nicolson, 1977

Hind, C. Lewis, *Hercules Brabazon Brabazon, 1821–1906: His Art and Life*, George Allen, London, 1912

Hind, C. Lewis, *The Post-Impressionists*, Methuen, London, 1911

Holme, Geoffrey (ed.), T. W. Earp Introduction, *Flower and Still-Life Painting*, Studio, London, 1928

Holmes, Charles, *Notes on the Post-Impressionist Painters, Grafton Galleries, 1910–11*, Philip Lee Warner, London, 1910

Holmes, Charles, *Self and Partners (Mostly Self), being the Reminiscences of C. L. Holmes*, Constable, London, 1936

Holroyd, Michael (ed.), *The Genius of Shaw*, Hodder and Stoughton, London, 1979

Holt, Ysanne, *British Artists and the Modernist Landscape*, Ashgate, Aldershot, 2003

Hone, Joseph, *The Life of Henry Tonks*, Heinemann, London, 1939
Hubbard, Hesketh, *A Hundred Years of British Painting, 1851–1951*, Longmans, Green, London, 1951
Hughes, Robert, *Nothing if not Critical*, Collins, London, 1990 (rev. ed., Harvill Press, London, 2001)
Hulme, T. E., *Speculations: Essays on Humanism and the Philosophy of Art*, ed. Herbert Read, Kegan Paul, London, 1924
Hunt, Diana Holman, *Latin among Lions: Alvaro Guevara*, Michael Joseph, London, 1974
Ironside, Robin, *Painting since 1939*, Longmans, Green, London, 1947
Ironside, Robin, *Wilson Steer*, Phaidon Press, London, 1943
Jeffrey, Ian, *The British Landscape, 1920–1950*, Thames and Hudson, London, 1984
John, Augustus, *Chiaroscuro: Fragments of an Autobiography*, Jonathan Cape, London, 1954
Kains Smith, S. C., *Painters of England*, The Medici Society, London, 1934
Kay, Arthur, *Treasure Trove in Art*, Oliver and Boyd, London, 1939
Konody, P. G., and S. Dark, *Sir William Orpen, Artist and Man*, Seeley Service, London, 1932
Lago, Mary, *Christiana Herringham and the Edwardian Art Scene*, Lund Humphries, Aldershot, 1996
Laidlay, William James, *The Origin and First Two Years of the New English Art Club*, John Lane, London, 1907
Laidlay, William James, *The Royal Academy: Its Uses and Abuses*, Simpkin, Marshall, London, 1898
Lambert, R. S. (ed.), *Art in England*, Penguin, Harmondsworth, 1938
Laughton, Bruce, *The Euston Road School: A Study in Objective Painting*, Scolar Press, 1986
Laughton, Bruce, *Philip Wilson Steer*, Clarendon Press, Oxford, 1971
Laughton, Bruce, *William Coldstream*, Yale University Press, London and New Haven, 2004
Laver, James, *Between the Wars*, Vista Books, London, 1961
Lehmann, John (ed.), *Penguin New Writing*, no. 24, Penguin Books, Harmondsworth, 1945
Lew, Henry R., *In Search of Derwent Lees*, published privately, Victoria, Australia, 1996
Lines, Vincent, VPRWS, *Mark Fisher and Margaret Fisher Prout, Father and Daughter: A Record of a Hundred Years of Painting*, published privately, London, 1966
Lloyd-Morgan, Ceridwen (ed.), *Gwen John Letters and Notebooks*, Tate Publishing, London, 2004
[MacColl, D. S.], *Illustrated Memoir of Charles Wellington Furse ARA*, Burlington Fine Arts Club, London, 1908
MacColl, D. S., *The Life, Work and Setting of Philip Wilson Steer*, Faber and Faber, London, 1945
McConkey, Kenneth, *Edwardian Portraits: Images of an Age of Opulence*, Antique Collectors' Club, Woodbridge, 1987
McConkey, Kenneth, *Memory and Desire: Painting in Britain and Ireland at the Turn of the Twentieth Century*, Ashgate, Aldershot, 2002
MacDougall, Sarah, *Mark Gertler*, John Murray, London, 2002
Manson, J. B., *Hours in the Tate Gallery*, Duckworth, London, 1926
Mariott, Charles, *Modern Movements in Painting*, Chapman and Hall, London, 1920
Masterman, C. F., *The Condition of England*, Methuen, London, 1909, (rev. ed., with J. T. Boulton, 1960)
Meadmore, W. S., *Lucien Pissarro*, Alfred A. Knopf, New York, 1962
Meynell, Wilfrid (ed.), *The Modern School of Art*, 4 vols, Cassell, London, n.d. [c. 1887]
Moore, George, *Confessions of a Young Man*, Heinemann, London, 1886
Moore, George, *Impressions and Opinions*, David Nutt, London, 1891
Moore, George, *Modern Painting*, Walter Scott, London, 1893
Morris, Edward, *French Art in the Nineteenth Century*, Yale University Press, London and New Haven, 2005
O'Byrne, Robert, *Hugh Lane, 1875–1915*, The Lilliput Press, Dublin, 2000
Orpen, William, *The Outline of Art*, George Newnes, London, n.d. [c. 1925]
Pery, Jenny, *The Affectionate Eye: The Life of Claude Rogers*, Sansom, London, 1995
Peters Corbett, David, Ysanne Holt and Fiona Russell (eds), *The Geographies of Englishness, Landscape and the National Past, 1880–1940*, Yale University Press, London and New Haven, 2002
Prettejohn, Elizabeth (ed.), *After the Pre-Raphaelites: Art and Aestheticism in Victorian England*, Manchester University Press, Manchester, 1999
Price, Julius M., *My Bohemian Days in Paris*, T. Werner Laurie, London, 1913
Quilter, Harry, *Sententiae Artis*, William Isbister, London, 1886
Read, Herbert, *A Coat of Many Colours*, George Routledge and Sons, London, 1945
Reitlinger, G., *The Economics of Taste: The Rise and Fall of Picture Prices, 1760–1960*, Barrie and Rockliff, London, 1961
Robertson, Bryan, John Russell and Lord Snowdon, *Private View: The Lively World of British Art*, Nelson, London, 1965
Rothenstein, John, *Autobiography. 3. Time's Thievish Progress*, Cassell, London, 1970
Rothenstein, John, *Brave Day, Hideous Night*, Hamish Hamilton, London, 1967
Rothenstein, John, *Modern English Painters*, vol. 1, Eyre and Spottiswoode, London, 1952
Rothenstein, William, *Men and Memories*, vol. 1, Faber and Faber, London, 1931
Russell, John, *From Sickert to 1948: The Achievement of the Contemporary Art Society*, Lund Humphries, Aldershot, 1948
Rutter, Frank, *Art in My Time*, Rich and Cowan, London, 1933
Rutter, Frank, *Evolution in Modern Art*, George G. Harrap, London, 1926
Rutter, Frank, *Since I was Twenty-five*, Constable, London, 1927
Rutter, Frank, *Some Contemporary Artists*, Leonard Parsons, London, 1922
Rutter, Frank, *Théodore Roussel*, The Connoisseur, London and New York, 1926
Schiff, Sidney, Preface, *John Nash*, The Fleuron, London, 1925
Scott, Richard, *Artists at Walberswick: East Anglian Interludes, 1880–2000*, Art Dictionaries, Bristol, 2002
Sitwell, Osbert (ed.), *A Free House, or the Artist as Craftsman, Being the Writings of Walter Richard Sickert*, Macmillan, London, 1947
Spalding, Frances, *Roger Fry: Art and Life*, Granada, London, and University of California Press, Berkeley and Los Angeles, 1980
Spalding, Frances, *Twentieth Century Painters and Sculptors, Dictionary of British Art, vol. 6*, Antique Collectors' Club, Woodbridge, 1990
Spender, Michael, *The Paintings of Ken Howard: Drawn by Light*, David and Charles, Newton Abbot, 1992
Spender, Stephen, *The Thirties and After: Poetry, Politics, People, 1933–1975*, Fontana/Collins, London, 1978
Stevenson, R. A. M., *Velasquez*, ed. D. Sutton and T. Crombie, G. Bell and Sons, London, 1962
Sturgis, Matthew, *Walter Sickert: A Life*, HarperCollins, London, 2005
Sturt-Penrose, Barrie, *The Art Scene*, Paul Hamlyn, London, 1969
Taylor, John Russell, *Bernard Meninsky*, Redcliffe Press, Bristol, 1990
Thackeray, W. M., *The Paris Sketch Book*, John Macrone, London, 1840 (rev. ed., George Routledge and Sons, London, 1885)
Thornton, Alfred, *Diary of an Art Student of the Nineties*, Sir Isaac Pitman and Sons, London, 1938
Thornton, Alfred, *Fifty Years of the New English Art Club, 1886–1935*, Curwen Press, London, 1935
Thorold, Anne (ed.), *The Letters of Lucien to Camille Pissarro, 1893–1903*, Cambridge University Press, Cambridge, 1993
'Tis', *Masters of Modern Art, Charles Shannon ARA*, Colour, London, n.d., [c. 1920]
Trevelyan O. M., and G. M. Trevelyan Foreword, *Fifty Years, Memories and Contrasts: A Composite Picture of the Period, 1882–1932, by 27 Contributors to 'The Times'*, Thornton Butterworth, London, 1932
Turner, W. J. (ed.), *Aspects of British Art*, Collins, London, 1947
Warren Piper David (ed.), *Readings in Art and Design Education, 1, After Hornsey*, and *2 After Coldstream*, Davis-Poynter, London, 1973
Weinberg, Barbara H., *The Lure of Paris, Nineteenth-Century American Painters and Their French Teachers*, Abbeville Press, New York, 1991
Weiner, Martin J., *English Culture and the Decline of the Industrial Spirit 1850–1980*, Cambridge University Press, Cambridge, 1981
Weintraub, Stanley (ed.), *Bernard Shaw and the London Art Scene, 1885–1950*, Pennsylvania State University Press, University Park, 1989
Weisberg, G. P., *Beyond Impressionism: The Naturalist Impulse*, Harry N. Abrams, New York, 1992
Wilcox, Denys J., *The London Group, 1913–1939: The Artists and their Works*, Scolar Press, London, 1995
Wilenski, R. H., *The Modern Movement in Art*, Faber and Faber, London, 1928 (8th ed., Faber and Faber, London, 1946)
Wilenski, R. H., *An Outline of English Painting*, Faber and Faber, London, 1946

Willesdon, Clare, *Mural Painting in Britain, 1840–1940: Image and Meaning*, Oxford University Press, Oxford, 2000
Wind, Edgar, *Art and Anarchy*, Faber and Faber, London, 1963
Windsor, Alan (ed.), *Handbook of Modern British Painting, 1900–1980*, Scolar Press, London, 1992
Woolf, Leonard, *After the Deluge: A Study in Communal Psychology*, Hogarth Press, London, 1931 (rev. ed., Pelican Books, London, 1937)

Exhibition Catalogues

Abstraction: Towards a New Art, Painting 1910–1920, Peter Vergo Introduction, Tate Gallery, London, 1980
AIA: The Story of the Artists International Association, Lynda Morris and Robert Radford (eds), Museum of Modern Art, Oxford, 1983
Albert Rutherston, 1881–1953, Max Rutherston, 180 New Bond Street, London, 1988
Allan Gwynne-Jones, David Brown, National Museum of Wales, Cardiff, 1982
Alvaro Guevara, 1894–1951, John Rothenstein Introduction, P. & D. Colnaghi, London, 1974
The Ambrose McEvoy Exhibition, Christian Brinton, Duveen Brothers, New York, 1920
Anthony Devas, 1911–1958, Anne Goodchild, Sheffield City Art Galleries, 1991
Art in Britain 1890–1940: An Exhibition of Paintings, Sculpture, Drawings and Documents from the Collection of the University of Hull, Malcolm Easton, University of Hull, 1967
The Artist as Evacuee: The Royal College of Art in the Lake District, 1940–1945, Robert Woof, The Wordsworth Trust, Grasemere, 1987
The Art of Gerald Leslie Brockhurst, Thomas B. Brumbaugh, Andrew Ladis and Patricia Phagan, Georgia Museum of Art, University of Georgia, 1993
British Artists and the Second World War, Sir Colin Coote Introduction, Arts Council Gallery, Cambridge, 1965
British Painting, 1925–1950, Philip James Foreword, Manchester City Art Gallery, 1951
British Painting, 1952–1977, Frederick Gore RA Introduction, Royal Academy of Arts, London, 1977
The Cole Family, Painters of the English Landscape, 1838–1975, T. J. Barringer, Portsmouth City Museums, 1988
C. R. W. Nevinson, The Twentieth Century, Richard Ingleby et al., Imperial War Museum, London, 1999
Degas, Jean Sutherland Boggs et al., Metropolitan Museum of Art, New York, 1988
A Dream of Fair Women: Gerald Leslie Brockhurst, RA, 1890–1978, Anne Goodchild, Graves Art Gallery, Sheffield, 1987
The Early Years of the New English Art Club, Bevis Hillier Introduction, The Fine Art Society, London, 1968
The Early Years of the New English Art Club, 1886–1918, Mary Woodall Introduction, City Museum and Art Gallery, Birmingham, 1952
The Earthly Paradise, F. Cayley Robinson and the Painters of the Birmingham Group, Charlotte Gere Introduction, Fine Art Society, London, 1975
The Edwardians: Secrets and Desires, Anna Gray, National Gallery of Australia, 2004
The Euston Road School, William Townsend Introduction, Arts Council, London, 1948
Ethel Walker, Frances Hodgkins, Gwen John, T. W. Earp, Tate Gallery, London, 1952
The Flower Show: An Exhibition on the Theme of Flowers in Twentieth-Century British Art, Norbert Lynton, Stoke-on-Trent City Art Gallery and Museum, 1986
The Forgotten Fifties, Julian Spalding, Graves Art Gallery, Sheffield, 1984
From City to Sea – Lionel Bulmer and Margaret Green, Ian Collins, Messum's, London, 2002
The Grosvenor Gallery: A Palace for Victorian Art, Susan Casteras and Colleen Denney (eds), Yale Centre for British Art, New Haven, Laing Art Gallery, Newcastle upon Tyne, 1996
Gwen John and Augustus John, David Fraser Jenkins and Chris Stephens (eds), Tate Britain, London, 2004
Hard Times, Social Realism in Victorian Art, Julian Treuherz, Manchester City Art Gallery, 1987
Henry Tonks and the 'Art of Pure Drawing', Linda Morris (ed.), Norwich School of Art Gallery, 1985
Impressionism in Britain, Kenneth McConkey, Barbican Art Gallery, London, 1995
James Bolivar Manson, 1879–1945: An English Impressionist, David Buckman, Maltzahn Gallery, London, 1973
J. D. Innes, Augustus John Preface, Graves Art Gallery, Sheffield, 1961
J. D. Innes, David Fraser Jenkins, National Museum of Wales, Cardiff, 1975
John Currie, Paintings and Drawings, 1905–1914, Sarah Griffiths, Stoke-on-Trent Museum and Art Gallery, 1980
John Singer Sargent, Elaine Kilmurray and Richard Ormond (eds), Tate Gallery, London, 1998
Joseph Southall, 1861–1944, Artist-Craftsman, Charlotte Gere, Birmingham City Art Gallery, 1980
Landscape in Britain, 1850–1950, Frances Spalding and Ian Jeffrey, Hayward Gallery, London, 1983
A Life in Pictures: Works from the Studio of William Bowyer RA, Ian Collins, Messum's, London, 2003
London Group 1914–1964, Jubilee Exhibition, Fifty Years of British Art, Dennis Farr and Alan Bowness, Tate Gallery, London, 1964
Modern Art in Britain, 1910–1914, Anna Gruetzner Robins, Barbican Art Gallery, London, 1997
Mr Whistler's Gallery, Pictures at an 1884 Exhibition, Kenneth John Myers, Freer Gallery of Art, Smithsonian Institution, Washington DC, 2003
Munnings v. The Moderns, Tim Wilcox, Manchester City Art Gallery, 1987
The New English Art Club Centenary Exhibition, Anna Gruetzner Robins and Francis Farmar, Christie's, London, 1986
The Old Matsukata Collection, Shoichi Ijiri et al., Kobe Shimbun, Kobe, 1989
Overcoming All Obstacles: The Women of the Académie Julian, Gabriel P. Weisberg and Jane R. Becker, Dahesh Museum, New York, 2000
The Painters in Grez-sur-Loing, Toru Arayashiki (ed.), Japan Association of Art Museums, Tokyo, 2000
Painting in Newlyn, 1880–1930, Caroline Fox and Francis Greenacre, Barbican Art Gallery, London, 1985
Paintings and Drawings from the Sir Edward Marsh Collection, Harold Nicholson Introduction, Arts Council, London, 1953
Paris 1889: American Artists at the Universal Exposition, Annette Blaugrund (ed.), Pennsylvania Academy of the Fine Arts, Philadelphia, 1989
Partners in Paint – Lionel Bulmer and Margaret Green, Ian Collins, Messum's, London, 2005
Percy Horton, 1897–1970: Artist and Absolutist, Janet Barnes, Sheffield City Art Galleries, 1982
Pound's Artists, Ezra Pound and the Visual Arts in London, Paris and Italy, Richard Humphreys et al., Tate Gallery, London, 1985
Richard Eurich RA: A Retrospective Exhibition, Caroline Krzesinska, Bradford Art Galleries and Museums, 1980
Rodrigo Moynihan: A Retrospective Exhibition, Lawrence Gowing, Royal Academy of Arts, London, 1978
Sargent's Women, Warren Adelson et al., Adelson Galleries, New York, 2003
A Selection of Paintings and Drawings from the Rutherston Collection, S. D. Cleveland Foreword, Arts Council, London, 1955
Sickert, Wendy Baron and Richard Shone (eds), Royal Academy of Arts, London, 1992
Sir George Clausen RA, 1852–1944, Kenneth McConkey, Cartwright Hall, Bradford, 1980
The Sixties Art Scene in London, David Mellor, Barbican Art Gallery, London, 1993
Sixty Works by Joseph Southall 1864–1944, from the Fortunoff Collection, George Breeze, Peyton Skipwith and Abbie N. Sprague, Cheltenham Art Gallery and Museum, 2005
Spencer Frederick Gore, 1878–1914, Frederick Gore and Richard Shone, Anthony d'Offay Gallery, London, 1983
Spencer Gore in Richmond, Frederick Gore Foreword, Museum of Richmond, 1996
Stanley Spencer, Richard Carline, Andrew Causey and Keith Bell, Royal Academy of Arts, London, 1980
Stanley Spencer, Timothy Hyman and Wright, Patrick (eds), Tate Britain, London, 2001
The Thirties, A. J. P. Taylor and Ian Jeffrey Introductions, Hayward Gallery, London, 1979
Thomas Lowinsky, Monica Bohm-Duchin, Tate Gallery, London, 1990
Three on Holiday at Rye, 1913, A Group of Post-Impressionists, Lucien Pissarro, James Bolivar Manson, James Brown, Malcolm Easton and Michael Parkin, Parkin Gallery, London, 1980

Tom Carr: A Retrospective, T. P. Flanagan Introduction, Ulster Museum, Belfast, and Douglas Hyde Gallery, Trinity College, Dublin, 1983

A Tonic to the Nation, The Festival of Britain, 1951, Mary Banham and Bevis Hillier (eds), Thames and Hudson, London, 1976

Transition, The London Art Scene in the Fifties, Martin Harrison, Barbican Art Gallery, London, 2002

25 From 51: Paintings from the Festival of Britain, James Hamilton, Sheffield City Art Galleries, 1978

Vorticism and its Allies, Richard Cork, Hayward Gallery, London, 1974

The Walberswick Enigma: Artists Inspired by the Blyth Estuary, Richard Scott, Ipswich Borough Council, 1994

War Artists, Anon., Tyne and Wear Museums, Newcastle upon Tyne, n.d. [*c.* 1985]

The Whitechapel Art Gallery Centenary Review, Catherine Lampert and Andrea Tarsea, Whitechapel Art Gallery, London, 2001

While *The New English* has been in press, pre-1960 material cited herein as 'New English Art Club Archive' has been donated to the Hyman Kreitman Research Centre at Tate Britain, London.

Photographic Acknowledgements

All works of art are reproduced by kind permission of the owners. Specific additional acknowledgements are as follows:

Brighton, © The Royal Pavilion, Libraries & Museums, Brighton & Hove: figs 40, 162
Canterbury, © The Royal Museum and Art Gallery: fig. 158
Hull, © Hull City Museums and Art Galleries: fig. 120
Liverpool, © National Museums on Merseyside: figs 12, 16, 67, 76, 111
London, © AKG Images/Erich Lessing: figs 21, 36
London, © Bridgeman Art Library: figs 20, 22, 28, 38, 58, 62, 84, 95, 97, 113, 118, 125, 132, 140, 143, 161
London, © Christie's Images: figs 2, 10, 13, 39, 117, 138
London, courtesy the Fine Art Society: figs 45, 90, 91, 116
London, courtesy of Hunting PLC: figs 184, 185, 186 and 193
London, © Imperial War Museum: fig. 104
London, courtesy of Messum's: figs 8, 59, 157, 165, 166
London, © Museum of London: figs 47, 131, 172
London, © National Portrait Gallery: frontispiece
London, courtesy of the New English Art Club Archive: figs 1, 149, 176, 177, 181, 207, 208 and p. 244
London, courtesy of Pyms Gallery: back cover, figs 5, 35, 41, 51, 53, 57, 61, 66, 82, 124, 130
London, © Royal Academy of Arts: figs 142, 163, 164
London, courtesy of Sotheby's: figs 17, 23, 72, 122, 127, 139, 159 and pp. 245–52
London, © Tate, 2006: figs 19, 32, 54, 56, 60, 71, 74, 79, 88, 92, 98, 100, 106, 108, 114, 123, 136
London, © V&A Images: figs 102, 147
Manchester, © Manchester City Galleries: figs 118, 145
New York, © The Metropolitan Museum of Art: fig. 80
Newcastle, © Tyne and Wear Museums: figs 14, 137
North Aston (Oxfordshire), © Elizabeth Harvey-Lee: fig. 144
Nottingham: courtesy Nottingham City Museums and Galleries: figs 63, 101
Paris, © Photo RMN: fig. 18
Philadelphia, © Philadelphia Museum of Art: fig. 7
Portsmouth, © Portsmouth City Museums and Records Service: fig. 126
Somerset, courtesy of the Court Gallery, Nether Stowey: fig. 34

Works by living artists are reproduced with their kind permission and are copyright © the artist. For all other works in copyright specific acknowledgements are as follows. (All reasonable effort has been made to trace the copyright holders of all works shown. This has not been possible in some cases and the publishers regret any unwitting infringement of copyright.)

Mary Adshead, Muirhead Bone and Stephen Bone © estate of Mary Adshead: figs 70, 117, 136
Clare Atwood © the Artist's Estate: fig. 47
© the estate of Elinor Bellingham-Smith: fig. 159
© the estate of Edward Bishop: fig. 168
© the estate of David Bomberg: fig. 102
© Bridgeman Art Library: © courtesy of Charles Cundall RA, RWS: fig. 113; Anthony Devas © estate of the artist: fig. 161; Richard Eurich © estate of the artist: fig. 184; Allan Gwynne-Jones © the artist's estate: fig. 125; Augustus John © courtesy of the artist's estate: fig. 77, 78, 79, 85, 141; C. R. W. Nevinson © the artist's estate: figs 103, 131; Sir William Rothenstein © courtesy of the artist's estate: figs 46, 53, 55; Gilbert Spencer © courtesy of the artist's estate: fig. 112
© the estate of Thomas Carr: fig. 146
J. D. Cast © by permission of the artist's estate: fig. 128
© the estate of George Clausen: figs 7, 14
© Thomas J. Coates: fig. 204
© DACS, London, 2006: © estate of Gwen John. All Rights Reserved: fig. 62; © estate of John Napper. All Rights Reserved: fig. 169; © estate of Walter R. Sickert. All Rights Reserved: figs 22, 32, 63, 97; © Estate of Stanley Spencer. All Rights Reserved: figs 106, 137; © Estate of Edward Wadsworth. All Rights Reserved: fig. 126
© the estate of Francis Dodd: fig. 83
© Luke Gertler: front cover, figs 93, 95
© the estate of Margaret Green and Lionel Bulmer: figs 165, 166
© the estate of Alvaro Guevara: fig. 110
© the estate of Robin Guthrie: fig. 123
© the estate of Edward Hall: fig. 157
Clara Klinghoffer © Michael J. Laurence: fig. 135
John Lavery © By courtesy of Felix Rosenstiel's Widow & Son Ltd, London, on behalf of the Estate of Sir John Lavery: fig. 5
© the estate of D. S. MacColl: fig. 71
Lord Methuen © trustees of the Corsham Estate: figs 147, 162
© estate of A. R. Middleton Todd: fig. 152
© Winifred Nicholson Trust: fig. 140
© the estate of Lucien Pissarro: fig. 75
Edward Pullée, Margaret Pullée © estate of the artist: figs 175, 179
© The Estate of John David Roberts: fig. 101
© Royal Academy of Arts: figs 142, 163, 164
© Estate of Henry Rushbury: fig. 143
© the estate of C. H. Shannon: fig. 52
J. E. Southall © reproduced with permission of the Barrow Family: fig. 90
Henry Tonks © Family of the artist: figs 54, 124
© Tate, London, 2006: figs 92, 100, 108, 114
© the Ethelbert White Estate: fig. 116
© the artists: pp. 245–52

Index

Numerals in *italic* type indicate pages with illustrations